History of Interior Design and Furniture

From Ancient Egypt to Nineteenth-Century Europe

Robbie G. Blakemore

Line Drawings by Julie L. Rabun

WILEY

Publishers Since 1807

New York • Chichester • Weinheim • Brisbane • Singapore • Toronto

Cover design: Mike Suh

This text is printed on acid-free paper. ☺

Copyright © 1997 by John Wiley & Sons, Inc. All rights reserved.

Published simultaneously in Canada.

This publication is designed to provide accurate and authoritative information in regard to the subject matter covered. It is sold with the understanding that the publisher is not engaged in rendering legal, accounting, or other professional services. If legal advice or other expert assistance is required, the services of a competent professional person should be sought.

6   7   8   9   10   01   00   99

Library of Congress Cataloging-in-Publication Data

Blakemore, Robbie.
    History of interior design and furniture: from ancient Egypt to nineteenth-century Europe / Robbie Blakemore; line drawings by Julie L. Rabun.
       p. cm.
    Includes bibliographical references and index.
    ISBN 0-471-28676-1
      1. Interior decoration—History.   2. Interior architecture—History.
   3. Furniture design—History. I. Title.
NK1710.B57   1996
747.2—dc20

96-36414
CIP

To
my sister, Lorena, and my brother, Glenn
and
in memory of my mother, Glenn A. Blakemore,
and my sister, Nelle B. Marrs
Through their love, support, and ultimate good humor,
they have been my preeminent advocates!

Contents

Preface .... *vii*

1 Egypt, c. 3200–341 B.C. *1*

2 Greece, 500–30 B.C. *23*

3 Rome, 509 B.C.–A.D. 476 .... *39*

4 Middle Ages, 1150–1550 .... *59*

5 Italian Renaissance, 1460–1600 .... *81*

6 French Renaissance, 1450–1600 .... *103*

7 English Renaissance, 1500–1660 .... *117*

8 Italian Baroque, 1600–1700 .... *139*

9 French Baroque, 1600–1715 .... *155*

10 English Baroque, 1660–1702 .... *175*

11 French Rococo, 1700–1760 .... *205*

12 Early Georgian, England, 1715–1760 .... *227*

13 Early French Neoclassic, 1760–1789 .... *263*

14 Early English Neoclassic, 1770–1810 .... *281*

15 Late French Neoclassic, 1789–1820 .... *307*

16 Late English Neoclassic, 1810–1830 .... *325*

17 Nineteenth-Century French Revival Styles, 1815–1870 .... *343*

18 Nineteenth-Century English Revival Styles, 1830–1901 .... *357*

Selected Bibliography *377*

Index *381*

Preface

This historical survey of interior design and furniture is for readers interested in the evolution of space planning, interior architecture, decorative detail, and furniture design, and in the interrelationships between these aspects of residential design. Changes in style and taste are analyzed in terms of the cultural milieu of each prevailing mode. The period covered moves from ancient Egypt through European developments, including 19th-century revival styles.

The historical setting of each design period provides the foundation for the most pertinent factors influencing design. It outlines briefly such facets as climate, defense, technology (materials and construction techniques), politics, pattern books, the transfer of design ideas through influential individuals, social ambience, and economic conditions.

Space planning is presented in terms of the floor plan as well as three-dimensional characteristics. Interior arrangements sometimes reflected the unsettled conditions of a period. At other times in the evolution of the plan, change in manners culminated in formal arrangements or social habits resulted in informal sequences of spaces.

Interior architecture is outlined in terms of each element: floors, walls, chimneypieces, windows, doors, ceilings, and stairways. These components also reflect prevailing directions of a specific period; a case in point is the design and position of windows to take advantage of the surrounding landscape, a tenet significant in the Picturesque movement.

In some periods in the history of interior design, decoration was emphasized. For example, Robert Adam, although an architect, was a prominent decorator. The segment on ornament is intended as a summary of the decorative motifs important in each stylistic period.

Furniture design is treated in a succinct manner. Examples of specific types of furniture are described and illustrated. The reader can take the information from these descriptions and apply it to other pieces so as to define and identify particular styles.

Design moves on a continuum. In the progression of one style to another, stylistic features of the previous style were combined with characteristics of the forthcoming style. For this reason dates are particularly difficult to define precisely. It is rare that form and ornament within a given stylistic period are static. Therefore, it is more important for the reader to develop the ability to analyze features of design within the context of commonly defined attributes of each style.

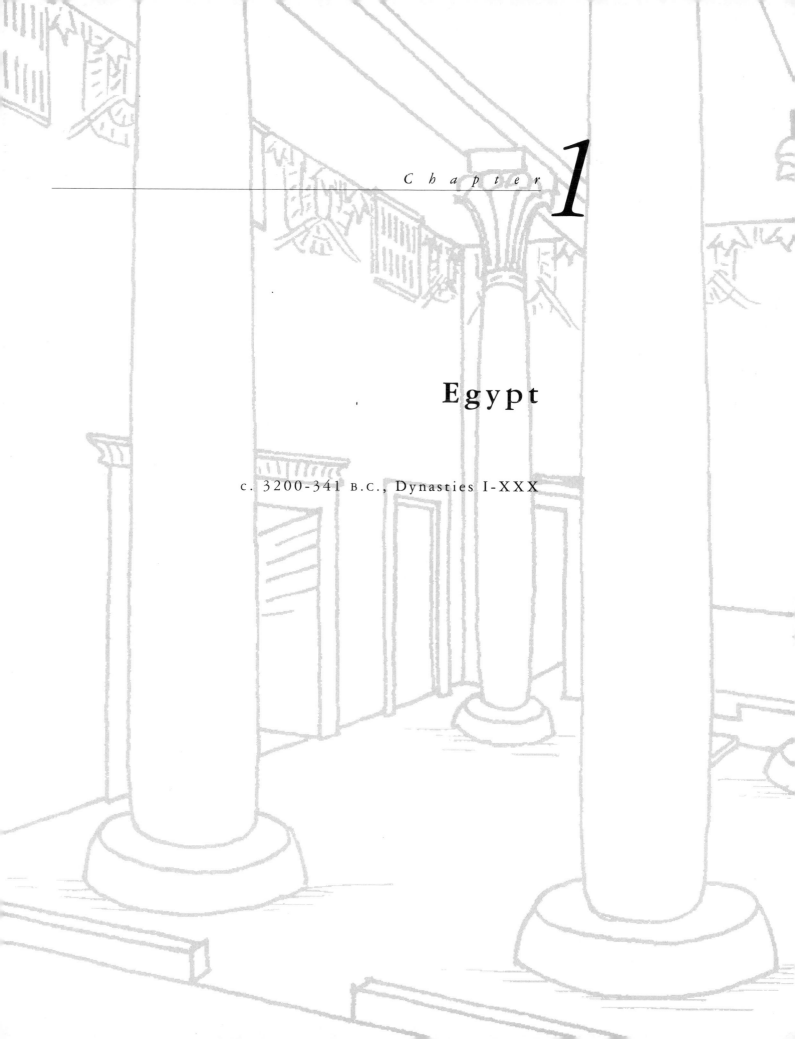

Chapter

1

Egypt

c. 3200-341 B.C., Dynasties I-XXX

HISTORICAL SETTING

The Nile River was the life-giving geographic feature that allowed ancient Egypt to attain its height of artistic development in the dynastic periods from around 3200 B.C. to 341 B.C.; the river flows north about 900 kilometers from Upper Egypt to Lower Egypt, where it empties into the Mediterranean Sea.

This artery of fertile land in the Nile River Valley is bounded on the east by the Arabian Desert and the Red Sea and on the west by the Libyan Desert. Although it is an arid country with little rainfall, the fertility of the land is replenished regularly each year by silt deposits resulting from annual summer floods (July to September) due to the spring rains in the uplands of Ethiopia. In addition to the benefits for agricultural production, the river was critical in ancient times for transportation of indigenous building materials, communication, and trade with other regions.

Timber suitable for furniture production and building construction was not widely available in ancient Egypt; what was available was small and importation was essential. Due to the limited local supply Egyptians became proficient in using short lengths of wood as extensions. Imported timbers used in building construction included cedar, pine, fir, and cypress. Information on the Palermo Stone of around 2613 B.C. reveals that in the reign of Sneferu, 60 ships were constructed and sent to the Syrian coast for cedar. Structurally, the Egyptians needed large timbers to construct their large-scale buildings; consequently, they cut trees in Lebanon and transported the logs to Egypt.[1] Imported woods that figured prominently in furniture construction or decoration included ash, yew, ebony, elm, boxwood, and linden. Although small in dimension, acacia, palm, and sycamore were available locally and were used for house construction; when a palm tree was past fruit-bearing age it was used for beams of houses. Local vegetation served as a source of inspiration for decorative schemes for both architecture and furniture design, often with symbolic connotations.

The most prevalent building material for small-scale structures (as houses and palaces) was the mud of the Nile, since it was economical and easy to use without advanced tools. Frequently mud was the covering for the pliable reeds and rushes that were interwoven and plastered to form wattle-and-daub construction. Other uses of the mud were to form solid mud walls or bricks. Brick made from the clay was sun-dried, although the Egyptians had the technical knowledge to produce glazed tile as early as the First Dynasty (3200-2980 B.C.). Monumental architecture (temples, funerary structures, military installations) was the product of stone, which was abundant.

The enormous scale of monuments was due to the nature of the material and the methods of excavating the stone blocks, transporting them, and lifting the blocks into position. The quantity and variety of stone available in Egypt meant that granite, sandstone, limestone, and alabaster were preferred over basalt, quartzite, and schist. Both wood and stone were used in trabeated construction (synonymously termed *post-and-beam* or *post-and-lintel* construction), in which uprights (posts) support horizontal members (beams or lintels). The proximity of the posts is related to the tensile and compressive strength of the spanning material. For example, stone is high in compressive strength but limited in tensile strength; and to span great distances without intermediate vertical support a material must have high tensile strength; therefore, to compensate for the limited tensile strength of this spanning material, stone posts need to be placed close together, although some authorities believe that the Egyptians overcompensated in this regard. The forest of columns that characterizes the interiors of monumental architecture is a function of the strengths and limitations of the building material. The same interruptions of interior space by columns also characterized wood structures, although this depended on the size of the spaces to be spanned.

1. Geoffrey Killen, *Ancient Egyptian Furniture* (Warminster, Wilts, England: Aris & Phillips Ltd, 1980), 2.

The character of ancient Egyptian exterior and interior architecture was also influenced by a climate in which there was minimal rainfall, intense sunlight, and little variation in temperature. These conditions led to architectural features that fostered indoor-outdoor relationships, including flat roofs, porticoes and loggias, windows placed high in the wall and roof ventilators to direct air to the innermost rooms, and open interior courts. The Egyptians of the period believed in life after death and placed objects of daily use in tombs for use in the hereafter. This aspect of culture, together with the arid climate, is largely responsible for our knowledge about and the preservation of ancient Egyptian art and architecture.

Motivation for most architectural monuments (as tombs and temples) was rooted in religious belief. Religion was, however, highly complex, since the system of belief was not uniform. In practice, Egyptian religion was polytheistic. Gods were associated with specific towns or regions. When one town perceived the greater power of another town's deity, its residents sometimes combined its attributes with those of one of their own gods. Thus a single religious tenet could be embodied in several deities with disparate external appearance. New deities emerged when the attributes of existing ones were combined. Gods might represent celestial bodies, depict human or animal forms, or portray a combination of human and animal features. Gods were the focus of specific temples, represented through reliefs and paintings in all types of architecture, and delineated in furniture design and other decorative arts.

Badawy draws a parallel between the tripartite spatial arrangement of the cult temple with that of domestic architecture. Sequentially, from the entrance, the temple characteristically was comprised of the following spaces: (1) the pylon and courtyard, often with a portico, (2) a hall in which the ceiling or roof was supported by columns, termed *hypostyle*, (3) the *naos*, or sanctuary, which contained the statue of the god. Correspondingly, the house spaces included: (1) the reception vestibule, (2) a columned central living hall, (3) bedroom. From the entrance to the rear, spaces became accessible to fewer people, and more private. In the case of the temple, only the priest responsible for the cult ritual could enter the naos.[2] For commemorative purposes, household stelae were often erected in honor of the popular household god Bes, who was depicted as a dwarf with features that are part human and part animal (tail, mane, and ears of a lion).

Egyptian society was highly stratified. At the top of the hierarchal scale was the pharaoh, or king, whose powers were divine and who represented god on earth. Along with the king, princes and those who could trace their origins to the royal family wielded political power at this level. From his position of wealth and power the pharaoh was committed to such undertakings as promoting trade, protecting his country, and supporting crafts and encouraging the arts. Judging by the depictions of crafts activities in wall paintings and sculptures, handicrafts were highly esteemed by the ancient Egyptians, who were skilled in many media including metal, fiber, glass, and clay. However, these craftsmen, along with the peasants, were at the lower echelon of society. The middle class was comprised of priests, mayors, provincial governors, administrators, and high executive officials. These class distinctions were reflected in the decor and the size of a house, its number of rooms, the materials used, and the density of structures in cities. The residences of richer citizens were at times in walled enclosures with specialized outbuildings.

It is evident that a number of factors influenced design in this ancient setting. These included the Nile river and its vegetation, technology (materials and construction techniques), climate, religion, and social hierarchy. During the dynastic periods of ancient Egypt one or a combination of the foregoing factors affected spatial relationships, interior architecture, and furniture design.

---

2. Alexander Badawy, *Architecture in Ancient Egypt and the Near East* (Cambridge: MIT Press, 1966), 35.

SPATIAL RELATIONSHIPS

From pictorial evidence, excavations, and models of houses placed in tombs it is possible to ascertain the evolution of typical space configurations of the dynastic periods. Pictorial documentation (as paintings on tomb walls) gives information as to the number of stories in structures, the functional use of spaces, and interior architectural features, while excavations attest to the size of spaces, room relationships, and illustrate the differences among various classes of citizens. The pottery models furnish more information about exterior architectural features; their significance is especially important in illustrating those characteristics that influenced the interior. Termed *soul houses,* the clay models were placed in tombs as receptacles for food offerings. From these it is possible to discern details about ventilation, porticoes, columns, loggias, windows, and doors.

Spatial Features of the Floor Plan and Three-Dimensional Spatial Characteristics

These documentary sources largely confirm that stylistic features characterizing domestic architecture throughout the dynastic periods were established during the Old Kingdom (c. 3200-2270 B.C.). Variations occurred according to the economic and social status of the owner but there seem to be underlying principles of organization resulting from the influence of climate, religion, and the functional uses and adjacencies of spaces. The similarities and differences can be observed in: (1) a craftsman's house (Figure 1-1) at Deir el Medina built during the Eighteenth Dynasty (1580-1314 B.C.) for the men working on the Necropolis, (2) a country villa (Figure 1-2) at Tell el-Amarna constructed in the New Kingdom (1580-1085 B.C.), and (3) a large urban mansion for a high official (Figure 1-3) in El Lahun (or Kahun), a temporary town for workmen and officials who were building the pyramid for a pharaoh of the Middle Kingdom (2131-1785 B.C.).

Bright sunshine, intense heat, little rainfall, and prevailing breezes were climatic factors responsible for features in each of the aforementioned residences. These factors are reflected in stylistic characteristics that were conducive to indoor-outdoor activities—the flat roof, portico, loggia, and open forecourt, and the fact that there were few windows. Since a pitched roof was unnecessary to repel rain and, therefore, not essential for the arid climate of Egypt, flat roofs were appropriately used for cooking, storage, and relaxation;

FIGURE 1-1 Plan and Elevation, Craftsman's Residence, Deir el Medina. Tripartite division. A street; B reception; C hall with clerestory window between two roof levels; D bedroom with corridor shown below; E kitchen with stairs ascending to the roof.

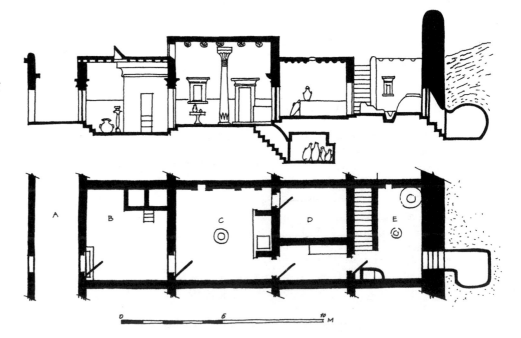

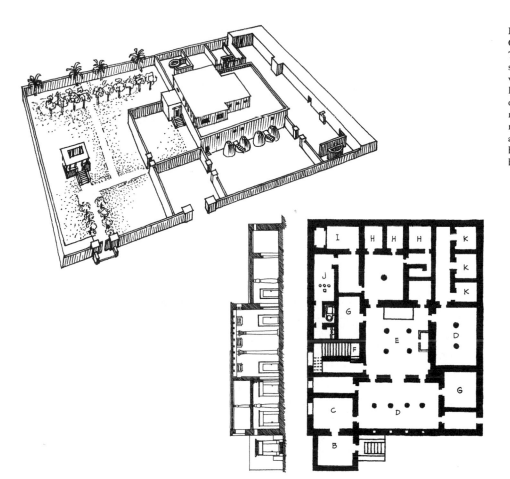

FIGURE 1-2 Plan, Plot Plan, Cross Section of Country Villa, Tel el-Amarna. Tripartite division. A court; B porch; C vestibule; D reception; E hall or living room; F stair to the loggia overlooking the court; G store room; H bedroom; I master bed room within harem area; J anointing room with adjacent bathroom and closet; K Guest bedrooms.

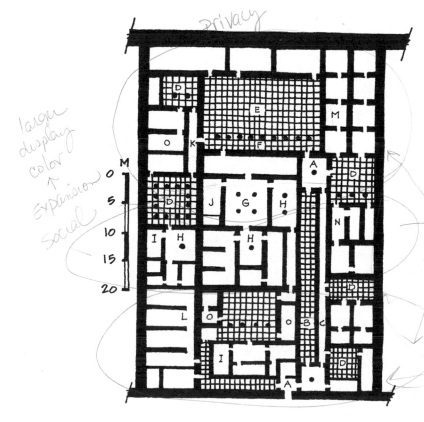

Compressed space - lower darker smaller

Privacy

large display color ↑ expansion social

FIGURE 1-3 Plan, Urban Mansion, El-Lahun (or Kahun). Tripartite division. A vestibule; B west corridor; C east corridor; D court; E main court; F columned portico; G reception; H hall or living room; I bedroom; J master bedroom; K harem; L stables; M granaries; N offices; O storage.

Entry
Public
Sacred
Tripartite

FIGURE 1-4 Portico. Columned
portico with a northern orientation.

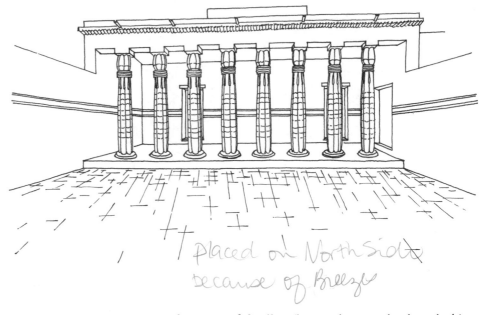

*placed on North side
because of Breeze*

the country villa incorporates a *loggia,* a roofed gallery (here at the upper level overlooking an open court) which functioned as another space for relaxation (see Figure 1-2). Originating near the central hall of the villa, a stair with landings ascends to the roof, while a single flight from the kitchen is used in the craftsman's house. Not only were the portico and its associated court conducive to indoor-outdoor endeavors but also the orientation toward the north or northwest took advantage of the prevailing breeze. A *portico,* a roofed porch upheld by columns, became a widespread, distinctive feature of affluent, middle-class houses by the Middle Kingdom, having been a royal symbol during the Old Kingdom (Figure 1-4).[3]

A commonality among houses of all classes was the use of the tripartite plan, which included reception room(s), a central hall or living room, and the private area. Of these functional areas, the ceiling of the central hall was typically higher than that of adjacent rooms. This allowed the incorporation of windows placed high in the wall, termed *clerestory* windows; since the roof level of this central hall rose above contiguous roof surfaces, the relative position of a clerestory window was between two roof levels (see Figures 1-1 and 1-2). This allowed light to penetrate the innermost spaces and provided ventilation to counter the intensity of heat from the very brilliant sun. Directed to capture the prevailing breeze, ventilators placed on the roof were another means by which light and air could enter the house.

The *craftsman's residence,* a one-story structure of 75 square meters, was organized on a longitudinal axis wherein each room opened directly from the preceding space. The bedroom was flanked by one small corridor leading from the central hall to the kitchen (see Figure 1-1). Beginning with the reception room, which was below street level, each rectangular space was ascended by one or two steps; therefore, the rooms with the lowest ceilings were the bedroom and kitchen. Based on an analysis of ruins, as well as other documentary evidence, it has been concluded that changes in both floor and ceiling levels were typical. The ceiling of the central hall rose above adjacent rooms. In this plan, starting with the reception room, each room is raised by one or two steps.

Rooms of small dwellings had more functional demands than larger residences and typically were more economical in terms of space and materials. While the craftsman's residence may be representative of spatial arrangements for this type of house, the activities

3. Earl Baldwin Smith, *Egyptian Architecture as Cultural Expression* (Watkins Glen, NY: American Life Foundation & Study Institute, 1968), 199.

which took place in each space would have varied from house to house. The reception room sometimes housed animals, served as a work room for craft activities, or functioned as a food preparation area. This room also at times contained a platform used as an altar to the god Bes. In the adjacent central or main hall, primary living activities of the household took place. This main hall was usually the loftiest space in a dwelling and, depending on its size, had one or more columns. A built-in dais was often used as a divan on which mats or rugs were placed. The part religion played in the lives of Egyptians in this period is attested to by the fact that, here too, a stela served as a commemorative shrine in the false door. The kitchen at the rear of the house was provided with an oven and other food preparation equipment. Leading from here were stairways giving access to a cellar for storage and to the roof for outdoor activities and/or for storage; in some small residences the stairway originated in the reception room.

Outside of the towns, where land was not at a premium, more space could be devoted to the *country villa,* with its walled enclosure and dependencies; chapel, granaries, kitchens, storerooms, chariot house, servants' quarters, and stables are examples of typical dependencies within the walled enclosure but which were not necessarily under the roof of the residence (see Figure 1-2). The wealth and social position of the owner are reflected in the spatial arrangement of the villa with its ancillary units. Compared to residences of owners lower on the socioeconomic scale, greater complexity is evident not only in the floor plan but also in three-dimensional spatial features.

The sequencing of rooms followed the norm in which a tripartite arrangement begins with the reception spaces and is followed by the great hall or living room and private section. Two reception rooms served as a transition to the living room from the porch; however, as was often the case, another reception room was included on the west side of the house. The central hall, square in plan, was a large space of approximately 169 square meters, with four columns to support the ceiling structure; the usual built-in furnishings were included in the form of a lustration slab, low dais, and a sunken brazier. It is surmised that the dais was used for family meals and for sitting during the day.

The master's private suite consisted of its own reception area accompanied by the master bedroom, other bedrooms (some used for the harem), a bathroom (equipped with a closestool), and an anointing room. At one end of the master bedroom the room narrowed to form an alcove for the bed, set on a dais. Comparatively isolated, other bedrooms for guests were accessed from the two-columned reception room.

Adjacent to the central hall the stairway ascended in three flights and two landings to the loggia at the main roof level of the residence; this gave a two-story configuration encompassing the stairway, the first reception room (vestibule), and the columned reception area on the first floor (see Figure 1-2). Placed on the north to capture the prevailing breeze, the loggia was a gallery at an upper story overlooking the open court. Recreational activities took place here.

Three-dimensional space delineation was enhanced in a number of ways. The spatial continuum of the Egyptian interior focused on the central hall. From the first reception room, largely a static space, one entered a space more dynamic due to the positioning of the columns and the stronger light. Two factors accentuated the progress from this point to the central hall. First, although there were three doors, the viewer could not fully comprehend the adjoining space and its greater volume and, second, anticipation of movement into this central space was dramatized by the move from dimness to brightness. Having entered the central hall, the greater volume is emphasized in a number of ways: greater ceiling height; ceilings with high textural interest due to the structural system or that were painted in a pattern of brilliant colors; the use of clerestory windows placed high in the wall with the consequent use of window gratings of wood or stone by which strong light and shadow were cast. All of the foregoing were used to define space and facilitate movement through the space. The crescendo of three-dimensional experiences as one moved from the entrance to the focus on this centralized space was experienced in reverse by movement into the private area.

The *city mansion* represents a typical house for a prosperous official (see Figure 1-3). The mansion, like buildings in the craftsmen's section of the town, had common walls with neighboring mansions and, typical of planning concepts for residences of any size, a tripartite arrangement in functional relationships. Similarities in the plan of the country villa are obvious but greater complexity is evident. Parallel corridors originated from the vestibule. The eastern corridor led past three courts that serviced offices and terminated in a series of spaces used for granaries. Premier access to the family quarters in the central section of the plan, on the other hand, was from the western corridor, leading as it did to the main court, which had a columned portico on the south side in order to take full advantage of the prevailing northern breeze. Through a series of reception rooms one approached the one-columned main hall, then the private area with bedrooms and bathroom.

The western portion of the residence was relegated to women. A new feature in the plan of the Middle Kingdom was the provision of a harem, appropriately associated with the master's apartment. Located near the harem the master's bedroom, again, was recognized by the narrowing of the room to provide an alcove and dais on which the bed was placed. Access to this section was only from the main court. With its own tripartite arrangement, the harem was serviced by two courts. Courts could be fully roofed or partially roofed. In the range of rooms on the southwest, the stables were approached only from the main vestibule.

INTERIOR ARCHITECTURE AND DECORATION

Documentary evidence of interior architecture and decoration of the Egyptian domestic residence comes from a variety of valid sources—texts, representations (drawings, paintings, reliefs, models), excavations. Textual evidence is limited in information for domestic building for ordinary citizens, but written documentation discloses many details about palaces.

From the tombs of private citizens as well as those of the pharaohs, paintings and drawings on the walls disclose invaluable information about residential building. Based on the sections of houses depicted it is known that houses were sometimes more than one story high; these representations disclose such features as spatial relationships, functional uses of spaces, interior architectural details, and decorative elements. Since domestic architecture was not constructed with permanence as a goal, no fully developed artifact for study is available. Therefore, to reconstruct the typical interior it is essential to rely on fragmentary evidence from a variety of sources, among which are those found in excavations of building sites.

A number of excavation sites are significant in this regard. El Lahun was a planned town built for workmen employed to construct the pyramid for Pharaoh Senusert II in the Twelfth Dynasty (1887-1850 B.C.). It included residential structures for the artisans and workmen as well as for the high officials; the latter would have been furnished with a class of house designated as a mansion. Archaeological evidence, by revealing the structural outline, yields information about actual sizes and space relationships; fragments of painted plaster and wall paintings, window gratings, column features, and so on give details essential for reconstructing the representative interior.

Materials and Decorative Techniques

The annual deposits of alluvial soil in the Nile Valley provided substantial amounts of raw material for plaster, which had widespread use as a base for decorative painting used in residences at all socioeconomic levels. Clay plaster (coarse or fine), gypsum plaster, and whiting plaster (gesso) each had a function in the preparatory technique for decorative or mural painting. Straw was the binder for coarse clay plaster (some sand was inherent in the soil); this type was usually the first coat applied to mud or brick walls. Upon the coarse layer a coat of finer clay plaster was often applied, or it could be applied directly to the walls. While straw was not an essential ingredient, it could be added to fine clay plaster. Regardless of which procedure was employed, the final coat of plaster, the primary base for mural painting, was usually gypsum.[4]

Gypsum plaster was utilized in three different ways. First, it was used as a coating when walls had been clay-plastered; with the application of whitewash to fill the pores it became an appropriate foundation for mural painting. Second, defects in the foundation material were leveled, making it a suitable surface for mural painting. Third, surface irregularities intended for relief designs were reconditioned.[5]

Beyond plaster, wood and stone each served as a ground for painting. Stone was abundant in Egypt and limestone was the most prevalent; following its period of ascendancy sandstone became the preferred stone. Whitewash was applied before painting or before a color wash could be applied. Although paint was sometimes applied directly to wood, especially for furniture, it was customary to coat the wood with whiting plaster composed of whiting and glue (termed *gesso*). The surfaces of columns or stelae are examples of wood bases needing a coating of whiting plaster.[6]

The technique used for mural painting by the Egyptians is frequently referred to as *fresco,* a process whereby painting is accomplished by applying pigment to wet lime plaster. Although the term *lime plaster* is used, the evidence suggests that lime was not used by the Egyptians until the Ptolemaic period (305-30 B.C.);[7] rather, gypsum plaster was employed. Experiments have revealed that brush marks are left on the surface when painting is undertaken on the wet Egyptian gypsum plaster and, therefore, they did not use the true fresco process.[8] In true fresco the paints are integral with the plaster and do not, therefore, peel.

The protective coating for mural painting was either varnish or beeswax. The use of colorless varnish to cover the murals seems to have begun in the Eighteenth Dynasty. Beeswax, on the other hand, was used both as a coating and as a binder in which pigment was mixed with the wax.

Interior Architecture and Decorative Elements

Interior architectural detail and treatment of surfaces on the interior were regulated, in part, by the hierarchical status of the resident. Differences in material, construction technique, and decorative processes are evident. Reflected in material and construction technique, a craftsman's residence employed lighter materials for ceiling and roof in the use of poles spanning partition walls, above which were placed sticks and twigs plastered with mud. The more expensive method would have been to cover the undersides of the poles with plaster as a surface on which to paint. Expressed in decorative processes, faience inlay used for mansions would have been replaced by color applications for a workman's house. However, Badawy suggests that economy was also an issue in the palaces as "columns and uraei cornices were inlaid on the side most likely to be seen, while they were just painted on the reverse."[9] Despite these differences, similarities existed among the residences representing various socioeconomic levels.

---

4. A. Lucas and J. R. Harris, *Ancient Egyptian Materials and Industries* (London: Edward Arnold, 1962), 76-77.
5. Ibid., 77.
6. Ibid., 354-355.
7. Ibid., 76.
8. Ibid., 356.
9. Alexander Badawy, *A History of Egyptian Architecture: The Empire (the New Kingdom), From the Eighteenth Dynasty to the End of the Twentieth Dynasty, 1580-1085 B.C.* (Berkeley: University of California Press, 1968), 152.

Floors

Floors were covered with a variety of materials. Probably the most widely used paving was mud plaster or brick made from the mud prevalent in the Nile River basin. Sometimes a liquefied mixture of gypsum concrete was poured, providing a uniform sheet for the floor surface. Less frequently used was stone, which was employed as a lining where moisture was a problem; stone slabs have been found in bathrooms. Found in a natural state in ancient Egypt, electrum, an alloy of gold and silver, was used as a partial facing on some pavements; the color depended on the relative proportion of gold to silver. In palaces, glazed tile was sometimes utilized.

Whitewash was the finish for many paved floors, a good background for painted floor surfaces. Decorative themes were often based on the plant and animal life of the environment. For example, in successive rectangular frames painters might depict a pond with fish, lotus, and other aquatic plants, ducks, geese, bouquets of flowers, and greenery thickets. A recurring theme was the portrayal of traditional enemies of Egypt in paintings or inlay for interiors as well as furniture; underfoot was an appropriate place for their portrayal. Colors progressively increased in intensity from floor to ceiling so that the most subdued hues were used at floor level while the most brilliant were reserved for the ceiling. In this manner vertical movement was encouraged.

Walls

The primary surfacing material for walls was plaster applied to a base of brick or mud. Other materials and decorative techniques were contingent on the economic means of the resident. For the affluent, stone and glazed tile were used to line walls. Glazed tile had been used in the Third Dynasty (2778-2723 B.C.) to line walls, but in the New Kingdom (1580-1085 B.C.) it became more widely utilized in palaces.

Ornamental treatment for wall surfaces included designs accomplished in techniques integral with the wall, such as painting, inlay, and relief. In addition, mats and rugs were actually hung on walls, or designs representing rugs and mats were painted on the walls as a decorative treatment. Paintings included geometric arrangements, religious subjects, plant patterns, and animal life. Faience tiles were frequently used as architectural inlay but a wide repertoire of variations in surface treatment was possible. These included application of relief through a buildup of glaze, painted designs applied on the glaze before the final glaze firing, or contrasting colors applied to incised designs in the glaze before the final glaze firing. Common colors were green, blue, and blue-green.

Relief from low to high was attained by the use of other materials. Plaster was fashioned into relief patterns and wood carvings have been observed in palaces. Low relief was painted as gold or metal, or electrum was fashioned in relief for architectural ornament. The sheet metal was attached with rivets or an adhesive, depending on the thickness of the overlay. If wood was the base, it was first covered with gesso and gold attached with an adhesive.

Often a wall was divided into areas between floor and ceiling—the dado, the main field, a frieze and cornice; on the other hand the wall was sometimes without division (Figure 1-5). The aforementioned materials and decorative techniques were alternatives in the treatment of each of these wall surfaces. The *dado,* described as the lower part of the wall distinguished in some manner from that above, could be simple or complex. In a craftsman's house the dado was whitewashed and bordered above with a painted gray stripe, but more complex ornamental arrangements were possible. For example, one dado was comprised of a floor-level narrow band decorated with an undulating line; above this were large amuletic signs, one representing life (Ankh) and one symbolizing protection (Sa). Each of these was separated by a superimposed rectangular arrangement suggesting paneling. The dado was surmounted by a succession of figures depicting the god Bes dancing.

In the main field, Egyptian figures were distinctively represented as flat and two-dimensional. Perspective was not understood and there was no attempt to suggest depth

Cornice

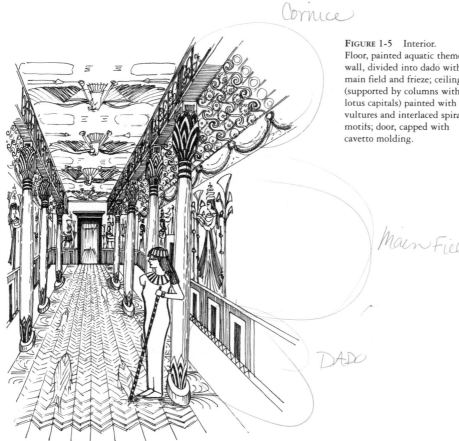

FIGURE 1-5 Interior. Floor, painted aquatic theme; wall, divided into dado with main field and frieze; ceiling (supported by columns with lotus capitals) painted with vultures and interlaced spiral motifs; door, capped with cavetto molding.

Main Field

DADO

Capital

Shaft

Base

FIGURE 1-6 Interior. Columns (incurved at the base) support major beams with finish spaces between; palm capital with abacus above. Upper wall with painted frieze integrated with grated clerestory windows.

and volume. Typically the human form was depicted in both profile and frontal view; head and legs were in profile while eyes and upper torso were frontal. Artistic canon required that men be portrayed with brown-red skin, women with yellow.

The frieze lying close to the ceiling was treated in a variety of ways. Painting was widely used, but painted low to high relief was incorporated also. Fragments from excavations reveal that in one modeled and painted frieze clerestory windows were simulated to coincide with the level and grating design of the actual windows (Figure 1-6). Cavetto molding was often used near the ceiling level. This was also the crowning molding used above door and windows.

Windows and Doors

The jambs of a typical door or window supported a lintel above which was a torus molding or a crowning cavetto cornice (see Figure 1-5). Jambs supporting only a lintel formed a simpler treatment; the opening was usually square-headed. Ornamental techniques to enhance the jambs and lintels included inlay, pigment, and carved relief. The relief designs were often covered with thin sheets of gold or electrum, or paint was applied thickly. Faience and gold were used as inlay materials; although inlaid, the inserted glazed tiles could be in relief also. Symbolically, an addition of gold bequeathed life to figures of gods and the pharaoh. Sheet copper was sometimes applied with bronze or copper nails to cedar wooden doors. Pigment contributed to the colorful Egyptian interior—for example, a series of bright horizontal stripes in different hues with prominent use of red, blue, and yellow. Bright red was a hue frequently used for jambs, lintels, and shafts of columns. The rectangular windows were covered in openwork screens composed of vertical or horizontal bars, patterns of circle tracery, or lattice; grating materials could be stone or wood.

Ceilings

Serving as structural support for the ceiling, stone or wood columns interrupted some interior spaces such as reception rooms and the main hall. Columns provided upward visual thrust closely related to the structural and decorative detail of the ceiling. Each column consisted of a *base, shaft,* and *capital.* Wooden shafts set in limestone bases were common; however, shafts were sometimes stone, particularly in monumental structures. The capital, the uppermost part of the column, was superimposed by an *abacus* (a plain block), which served as the transition to the horizontal structure above.

Design inspiration for the column originated with the plant life of the Nile River Valley. Prominent among the local vegetation were the palm, lotus, and papyrus, of which the palm was preferred for domestic architecture. The cross section of the shaft could represent earlier structural arrangements or the stem of a plant. First, in early structural methods, bundles of reeds had been bound at intervals by flexible bands of a plant material; thus, the cross section of the shaft imitated a cluster of reeds resulting in a parallel series of narrow convex semicircular moldings (termed reeding) or, conversely, a series of parallel channels or flutes (termed fluting). Second, the stem of the papyrus plant was triangular in cross section, which was the inspiration for the shaft of this form of cross section. Third, there were circular sections typical of many single stem plants. Typically, the column shaft was curved inward near the base, although the palmiform shaft was essentially cylindrical in form.[10] Five bands at the top of the shaft were characteristic. The surmounting capital was a conventionalized design based on the lotus bud or flower (symbol of Upper Egypt), the palm and palm fronds, the papyrus bud or flower (symbol of Lower Egypt), or by combinations of these (Figure 1-7). With the penchant of the Egyptians for applications of strong color it is not surprising that decorative schemes for capital details were often painted; sculptural techniques were also employed.

Structural methods were largely responsible for the extent and character of ornamental decoration used on ceilings. Used for more humble residences, roughly cut and closely spaced beams were exposed. Covering the beams above was a perpendicular layer of small twigs or reeds; on top of this tier was a covering of matting, above which was the roofing material. When the underside of the matting was plastered, beams and plaster surfaces were often whitewashed or painted. A more refined result was attained when the beams were concealed, resulting in a flat ceiling free of structural evidence above it. With this technique small poles were set perpendicular to and underneath the beams; mats were then fastened beneath the poles. A plaster layer applied to the mats provided a smooth foundation for painting. Alternative to the two foregoing methods was a system of exposed beams comprised of a beam of larger size perpendicular to which were placed beams of more

10. Badawy, *Architecture in Ancient Egypt and the Near East,* 69.

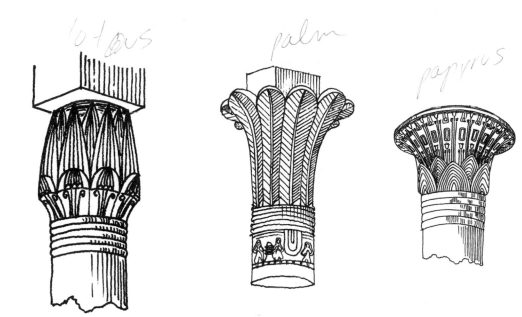
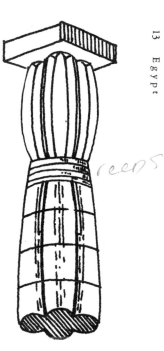

FIGURE 1-7 Capitals and Column Section. Capitals and shaft of column, left to right: lotus; palm; open papyrus flower with base representing the lotus (a composite capital), shaft section influenced by the original method of tying reeds together to form a single column, five bands at the top of shaft, capital representing the papyrus bud.

diminutive size. Plaster covered the beams; the resulting compartments and beams could be painted in flat color or patterns.

Countless examples of ceiling patterns are known to have included geometric and religious themes, scenes from nature, or some combination of these (Figure 1-8). Examples of overall patterns include diaper arrangements, linked spirals and rosettes, and linked spirals wherein the interstices featured bulls' heads. The central position of religion was attested to in many ways. Design motifs depicted on ceilings encompassed symbolic features such as a series of painted vultures, representing protection, some of which had wing spans of sixteen feet. Also signifying protection was the winged solar disk which, when combined with the cobra (uraei), denoted royalty. Scenes from nature were revealed in the depiction of flying ducks with nests for young birds; a grape arbor pattern, and figures shown in clumps of papyrus.

FURNITURE

Furniture design reveals the same influences reflected in other arts of the dynastic periods: religion, inspiration from familiar objects, technology (materials and construction tech-

FIGURE 1-8 Ceiling Patterns. Linked spirals with rosettes in the interstices or arranged in bands; frequent use of plant life.

niques), and social hierarchy. In particular, the size and stature of the people affected chair design. Their belief in life after death dictated that worldly goods were placed in the tombs for use in the afterlife; the decorative objects also placed there were those suited to the status in life of the deceased. Sealed in tombs and preserved due to climatic conditions, the most prevalent extant examples of ancient Egyptian furniture represent those of royalty or upper-class citizens.

Materials and Construction Techniques

Timber suitable for use in furniture construction was not widely available in Egypt; therefore, builders relied on imported woods. Due to unsuitably short lengths of local woods, by the Middle Kingdom (2131-1785 B.C.) the Egyptians began to use the scarf joint to extend lengths; dimensions of furniture changed perceptibly. The scarf joint was used to join two pieces of wood at the end grain by using a double dovetail-shaped piece about half the depth of the two pieces to be joined (Figure 1-9).

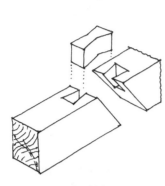

FIGURE 1-9   Scarf Joint. Utilized to extend the length of timbers due to short lengths of local woods. With permission of Aris & Phillips Ltd.

Although wood was the primary material used in the production of furniture, other materials were used for structural and decorative purposes. Wet strips of leather wrapped around structural members, for example, shrank on drying to tighten mortise and tenon joints (Figure 1-10). Beyond its use as a binding material, leather was used in sheets to form the seats of stools and chairs. While ivory was not used extensively in the structure of furniture, examples of ivory furniture legs are in the Metropolitan Museum of Art, New York. Faience, colored glass, lapis lazuli, amethyst, onyx, turquoise, gold, silver, ivory, carnelian, and ebony were among materials that had widespread decorative use.

The decorative process by which these materials were used was inlay, whereby the pieces were let into a common ground with the surface level. Compared to contemporary standards these materials were thick (2 mm to 4 mm). The resulting designs can be classed as either *marquetry* (representational) or *parquetry* (geometric); however, both representational and geometric designs could be found on the same piece of Egyptian furniture. Gold and silver were not only used as materials for inlay but also as the covering for a wooden core; for example, for decorative results gilding or thicker sheets of gold would be applied. The application of very thin sheets of gold foil over an object is termed *gilding*. Gesso was sometimes used as an adhesive; alternatively, it was fashioned into a relief design to which gold foil was applied. Thicker sheets of gold or sliver were first beaten into a design after which the sheet was applied with gold or silver nails to the wooden core of an identical relief design.

Painting for decorative effect was accomplished in a number of ways. The wooden piece was first covered with gesso, which served not only as a base on which to paint but also covered defects inherent in the wood. Subject matter of the paintings followed those

FIGURE 1-10   Method of Securing Joints. Wet leather thongs wrapped around structural parts and threaded through drilled holes of the adjoining part tightened the joint on drying.

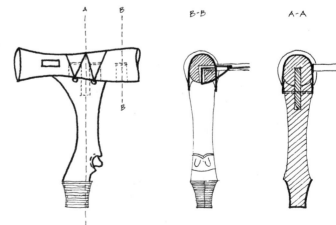

of interiors, but pieces were also painted in single flat colors—white, red, and brownish-yellow were popular.

Veneer, plywood, and *bending* were techniques of woodworking. Veneer was used frequently by the Egyptians. A sheet of more expensive wood or other material covered the surface of a wood of lower quality; the veneer was not let into the core as inlay pieces are. Lucas and Harris cite caskets from the tomb of Tutankhamen in which the veneer was comprised of strips of ivory framing marquetry panels.[11] Plywood is known to have been utilized. As is typical today, it was composed of layers of wood in which the grain direction of each layer was perpendicular to the preceding layer; by this means warping was prevented and strength was increased. Small wooden pegs were used to join the different layers. Ash, an important wood, had qualities which made it suitable for steam bending, but it has not, as yet, been proved definitively that this technique was used.

Egyptian furniture makers used a wide variety of joints. The dowel and the mortise and tenon were widely employed. The dowel is a cylindrical piece of wood fitting into holes of corresponding size in the two pieces to be joined. It was used by itself or in conjunction with another jointing method; for example, a dowel was sometimes inserted into the mortise and tenon joint to make it more secure. If the dowels came to the surface they were sometimes capped with another material, as gold or ivory or ebony. With the mortise and tenon joint as a means of joining two pieces of wood, the rectangular projection of one piece *(tenon)* fitted into a hole *(mortise)* of corresponding shape and size; frequently the tenon was visible, since it extended through the adjoining piece; through dowels and/or tenons are a reference to their visibility as they penetrate the structural member (Figure 1-11). Other joints included the butt, the half joint, and the miter, with its many variations.

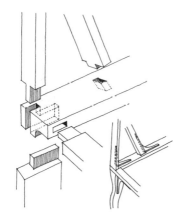

FIGURE 1-11 Chair Jointing Methods. Mortise and tenon joint used to attach the back above the seat rail, the legs below the seat rail, and to join the seat rails. Bracket used to brace the juncture of the seat rail and stiles. Drawing of the Louvre prepared by College Technique Boulle, Paris.

Typical Pieces and Stylistic Features

Seat Furniture

One of the earliest types of seating was the stool, used by all levels of society, royalty and ordinary citizen alike. Stylistic variations were numerous. Lattice stools represented one of the most popular types (Figure 1-12). These were rectangular in form, with some combination of the following features: square section legs (with no splay) connected by a perimeter stretcher; both vertical and diagonal struts joining the stretcher with the seat rail; a flat or single-cove or double-cove seat surface; seat surface materials of interwoven rushes, reeds, or wooden slats. Holes drilled in the seat rails were used to integrally attach the interwoven reeds or rushes by passing the strands through the holes as they were woven to form the string seat.

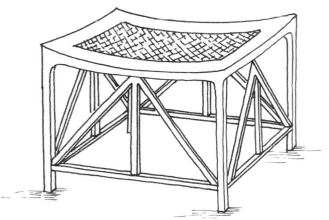

FIGURE 1-12 Lattice Stool. Perimeter stretcher connect square section legs; struts between the stretcher and the seat rail; single cove seat; interwoven seat surface. Drawing from a photograph taken at the Turin Museum. Printed by permission of the Egyptian Museum, Cairo.

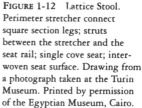

11. Lucas and Harris, 454.

FIGURE 1-13 Folding Stool (c. 1400 B.C.). Duck's head connects to the floor level stretcher (round in section); single cove seat. Copyright British Museum.

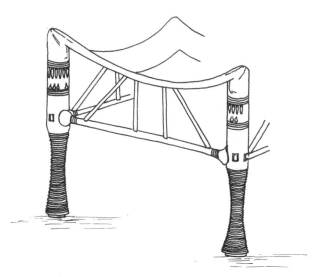

FIGURE 1-14 Stool, Round Section Legs. Probably shaped by hand rather than turned by lathe. Double coved seat rails. Struts connect stretcher to seat rail. Drawing from a photograph taken at the British Museum. By permission of the Egyptian Museum, Cairo.

FIGURE 1-15 Stool with Animal Legs. Legs directionally positioned. Motif symbolizing the union of Upper and Lower Egypt used between the stretcher and seat rail. Double coved seat using board surface. Drawing from a photograph. By permission of the Egyptian Museum, Cairo.

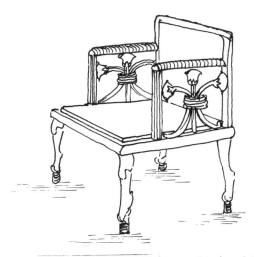

FIGURE 1-16 Chair of Hetepheres (c. 2600 B.C.). Wood overlaid with gold. Early chair with straight back. Directional animal legs; arm support rises from side seat rail, armrests parallel with the floor, open treatment of the underarm with papyrus flowers bound together. Drawing from a photograph. By permission of the Egyptian Museum, Cairo.

The preponderance of other stools varied widely in design. Among the most interesting is the folding stool (Figure 1-13). Each of the diagonal pieces terminated with a duck's head, the beak of which connected with the floor-level stretcher of round section. Seat rails were rectangular in section and coved. The mechanism for pivoting was a bronze rivet. The seating surface was frequently leather.

Many round-legged stools were characteristic during the Eighteenth Dynasty (Figure 1-14). Basically cylindrical in shape, the top portion of the leg and the foot were essentially the same diameter, but just below the stretcher the leg began to narrow and then swelled again at floor level. Incised lines characterized the narrowing neck. Although these gave the impression of having been turned, there is no technological evidence to support this theory. The space between the perimeter stretcher and the seat rail was sometimes filled with a lattice arrangement. Sometimes no intermediate treatment was utilized; the inclusion of a filling was not essential to make the stool structurally sound.

Animal-leg stools had the distinction of realistically carved feline or canine legs which were placed directionally; that is, it was possible to distinguish back from front legs. A

FIGURE 1-17 Chair with Inclined Back, c. 1400-1295 B.C. Incline accomplished by moving lower back toward front of chair with three struts connecting back seat rail with crest of the back. Courtesy of the Brooklyn Museum, 37.40E, Charles Edwin Wilbour Fund.

reeded, truncated conical base was used below the carved animal foot, usually sheathed with a metal (Figure 1-15). The only consistent commonalities among this group were the latter features. Otherwise there were variations in the seat surface, which was coved or flat; materials were woven rush or board. Perimeter stretchers were used on some while, alternatively, one stretcher united the rear legs and another stretcher joined the front legs. One especially fine example from the tomb of Tutankhamen had a design motif representing the union of Upper and Lower Egypt in the space between the stretcher and seat rail.

At first chairs were status symbols and, consequently, were used by nobility and high officials. By the Eighteenth Dynasty (1580-1314 B.C.) they were probably used in ordinary households. In the developmental sequence the chair emerged by adding a back to the stool (Figure 1-16). At first, the back was straight and without incline and then, when the slant back was added, a profile view of the chair revealed a triangular opening formed by the addition of three struts in the back connecting the seat rail with the crest of the back (Figure 1-17). In placing the lower part of the back slightly toward the front of the seat, the inclined back support was formed.

The class of chairs (with square section straight legs, straight or inclined back, and without arms) would have some combination of the following characteristics: There were two stretchers, one to connect the front legs and one to join the back legs. Seats were square with a flat surface and most had through tenons. Attached to the seat rail and the stile of the back was a wooden bracket of the same angle. The inclined back was comprised of wooden slats, either spaced regularly or abutting. Variations to the above might be in the addition of directional animal legs and in the curved form of the cresting rail of the back. If arms were added they had armrests that were parallel with the floor and arm supports that were placed on the side rail, but short of the front seat rail. The space under the armrest was often filled with symbolic motifs and could be open or solid.

Directional animal legs were joined with perimeter stretchers; the space between the stretcher and the seat rail was variously treated with symbolic motifs, lattice, etc. Seats were flat or coved (single or double). Finials were used sometimes to head the legs at seat level. Arms, when employed, were either solid or featured open-work designs. Arm supports were essentially parallel with the floor and the arm rest originated from the side seat rail, short of the front seat rail. Inlay and applications of precious sheet metal were frequently utilized.

(a)

(b)

FIGURE 1-18   Chair of Princess Sitamun (XVIII Dynasty, c. 1400 B.C.). Replica. Gilding for carved decorative detail; structural change in the curved back rest. Replica, Property of Baker Furniture Research Museum.

FIGURE 1-19   Table (XVII-XVIII Dynasty, c. 1530 B.C.); Thebes. Wood. Splayed legs with perimeter stretcher. Torus molding under the tabletop surface. All rights reserved The Metropolitan Museum of Art, New York, Gift of Lord Carnavon, 1914. (14.10.5)

More elaborate chairs used more expensive materials and methods, especially for royalty (Figure 1-18). Found in the tomb of the parents of the wife of Amenophis III, who ruled 1417-1379 B.C., this chair illustrates a number of ornamental and structural techniques: carving, gilding, and veneering. The reeded, truncated cylindrical base for the foot was covered with silver, carved ornament was covered in gold leaf, and gilding was used for the finials of a woman's head-crest and the front legs. The veneer for the seat frame and back was attached by glue and wooden pins. A concave backrest was new in the New

Kingdom, as was the rounded stretcher. The backrest portrays dual images of the princess Sitamun, daughter of Amenophis III. She is depicted as receiving an ornate collar; a band of lotus flowers and buds is shown above this scene. On the cresting rail of the back symbolic carved motifs were incorporated: the disk signifying the sun with wings, and serpents *(uraei)*, which denoted royalty.

Tables

Tables are known to have been used extensively during the dynastic periods; proof of this lies in the fact that so many were represented in paintings and in sculptural reliefs. That so few have survived is perhaps due to the fact that a very common use was to place them outside burial chambers to receive food offerings. Aside from their religious use, functional uses for the household included the practice of using tables as workbenches, stands for vases, individual tables for dining, and perhaps for display of valuable objects.

A popular type of table seems to have been rectangular in shape, with splayed legs and a perimeter stretcher (Figure 1-19). In this example a small torus molding was used above the rail with a cavetto molding serving as a transition to the tabletop. Similar tables were constructed where the square sectioned legs rose straight and where the cavetto molding was eliminated. Hieroglyphs sometimes were used to decorate the edges of these pieces.

Storage Pieces

Chests were used variously as containers for jewelry, clothing, cosmetics, and linens, as well as for an assortment of other household articles (Figure 1-20). Many chests had square sectioned legs, short or tall, which continued up to form the stiles of the storage compartment. Those with tall legs most often employed the stretcher, with infill designs that included such arrangements as lattice and hieroglyphs; the latter had magical signif-

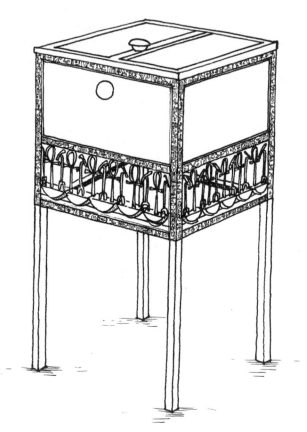

FIGURE 1-20 Chest. Wood partially gilded. Square section legs continue as stiles of the body of the piece. Hieroglyphs used symbolically and decoratively above the stretcher. Drawing from a photograph. By permission of the Egyptian Museum, Cairo.

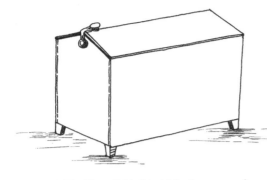

FIGURE 1-21 Chest. Gable lid with knobs on top and body around which a cord was wrapped for closure. Drawing from a photograph. By permission of the Egyptian Museum, Cairo.

FIGURE 1-22 Hieroglyphs. Magical significance attributed to symbols, left to right: *ankh* (life); *neb* (all); *djeb* (stability or endurance); *sa* (protection); *was* (dominion); *sma* (union).

icance in assisting the deceased in their journey in the afterlife (Figures 1-21 and 1-22). Lids for chests had a range of configurations including flat, single- or double-pitched gable, and domed. Closure for the lids was typically accomplished by wrapping a cord around two knobs, one placed on the body and one on the lid. The insides of chests were often divided to systematize storage. Judging by the extant examples, it is evident that Egyptian cabinetmakers were cognizant of panel construction.

Decorative techniques ran the gamut from simple to highly complex. Methods included veneer, inlay, painting, and carving; gesso covering the wood frames served as a base for painting as well as for gilding.

Beds

While there were variations in the style of beds over the dynastic periods, there were also basic similarities (Figure 1-23). Overall the frames of beds were comprised of side rails which were rounded, often elliptical, but occasionally rectangular in section. Reinforcing members were used to connect the two side rails; of wood or leather, at first these were flat and later curved, and their function was to support the surface of the bed. When the side rails extended beyond the bounds of the frame the ends often were in the shape of an open papyrus flower; alternatively, the ends of the rails flared within the bounds of the frame where the perpendicular cross rail intersected. These side rails could be straight, but many times they dipped in the center, which in effect accentuated the higher part of the bed where the head rested; a footboard was typical at the other end. The bed surface was attached to the rails in either of two ways: (1) slots cut through the frame through which webbing of leather was interlaced, or (2) woven techniques that entailed wrapping the rail with linen cord, reed, or rush which was then woven into a matting.

FIGURE 1-23 Bed. Curved side rails with rectangular cross section functioned to raise the head; footboard divided into three decorative panels. Bed surface of interwoven material. Brackets reinforce the side rails and the stiles of the back. The Egyptian Museum in Cairo.

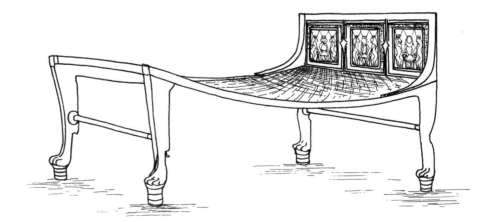

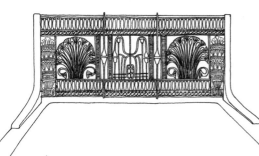

Figure 1-24 Bed Footboard. Gold-covered footboard. Symbol of the union of Upper and Lower Egypt decorates the center panel. The Egyptian Museum in Cairo.

The footboard was the most decorated part of the bed and featured typical decorative techniques (Figure 1-24). While a single panel was sometimes used it was common to divide the footboard into three panels, each visually separated by the use of a papyrus molding. A repertoire of decorative motifs typical of the period was utilized in standard materials and techniques; however, plain slats were used also. Dowels were used to attach braces to the side rails and the stiles of the footboard; gold or other capping materials were used to cover the dowels.

Supporting the frame of the bed were animal legs placed in a directional position; one stretcher at each end connected the legs. Baker suggests that over the period of the Old Kingdom (3200-2270 B.C.) there is a sequence in the use of specific animal legs from early to late, as follows: (1) bull's legs; (2) thinner legs with hoofs resembling the gazelle; (3) feline with paw foot and claw; (4) lion's leg. The latter was the most generally used.[12] Under the paw or hoof there was a reeded and truncated cone-shaped base or drum which was often sheathed with metal, as gold, silver, bronze, or copper.

The Egyptians slept with their feet toward the footboard panel. Their heads rested on rigid headrests which were constructed of wood or of stone; occasionally these were slightly padded. Usually the headrests had a curved upper section on which the head rested and a column that separated it from a base. The designs ranged from simple to ornate.

ORNAMENT

Ornamental detail was often associated with symbolism. Among the more important motifs, listed here with the symbol of each, were winged sun (royal dignity); *ankh* (life); *djed* (endurance); *was* (dominion); *sa* (protection); sma (union); *neb* (all); scarab (eternal life or resurrection); serpent (royalty); vulture (protection). Animal life and plant material of the Nile River Valley figured prominently in both architecture and furniture design; the palm, papyrus, lotus, and palmette were frequent design elements. In addition, motifs originating with the Egyptians and used in subsequent stylistic periods included the sphinx, spiral, guilloche, and wave pattern. The scarab, sun disk, serpent, human figures, and gods and goddesses (often with combined features of both human and animal forms) were also significant.

12. Hollis S. Baker, *Furniture in the Ancient World* (New York: Macmillan, 1965), 144.

Chapter 2

Greece

c. 500-c. 30 B.C.:
Classical or Hellenic (c. 500-c. 330 B.C.)
and Hellenistic (c. 330-c. 30 B.C.)

HISTORICAL SETTING

Although there are no precise dates for the periods of Greek culture, the Bronze Age extended from c. 3000–c. 1100 B.C. In this era different forms of architecture developed based on geographic region, which may have had implications for types of secular and residential planning in later periods. Centered on mainland Greece, Crete, and an Aegean island group (the Cyclades), the cultures of these territories are respectively termed *Helladic* (also designated *Mycenaean*), *Minoan,* and *Cycladic;* the latter, however, showed significant Minoan influence beginning c. 2000 B.C. After the Bronze Age, the Dark Ages were a period of disarray and impoverishment (c. 1100–c. 800 B.C.) followed by an interval of progressively greater prosperity and advancements (c. 800–c. 500 B.C.). Greek culture reached its ascendancy in c. 500–c. 330 B.C., an era termed *classical* or *Hellenic.* It was the practice of the Greeks, having developed a form type, to refine it rather than create a multitude of new forms. This period was succeeded by the *Hellenistic* period (c. 330–c. 30 B.C.), during which the emphasis was on elaboration of basic forms, the characteristics of which the Romans later copied or adapted. Hellenic or classical and Hellenistic are the ancient Greek periods treated in this discussion; however, although direct derivation of plan types from the pre-Hellenic period cannot be determined with certainty, there are obvious similarities. Some minimal reference to this will be included in the ensuing discussion.

Major contributors to the development of Greek arts were the Dorians, Ionians, and Aeolians. The Dorians and Aeolians began migration to Greece in the late Bronze Age; the Ionian settlements began in the late Dark Ages. These groups were at the forefront of Greek culture in the Hellenic period. The extraordinarily creative Ionians occupied the coast of Asia Minor, the islands east of the Greek peninsula, and the territory around Athens; the Dorians settled primarily in the Peloponnesus (the southernmost region of the peninsula), the southwestern coastal strip of Asia Minor, and the neighboring Aegean islands; the Aeolians were located on the northwestern coast of Asia Minor and in the northern section of the peninsula.

Geographically, Greece was a mountainous country surrounded by three seas— Aegean, Mediterranean, and Ionian. There were essentially two implications related to these geographic features, one to competition among city-states, the other to trade. The unity which characterized many other cultures was hindered in Greece because of the difficulty of communication between areas of settlement, since the landscape was dominated by mountains, small valleys, and islands. This isolation fostered great independence both on the part of the small communities and of individuals. Arable land was at a premium, unable to support a growing population. Thus the seas and colonization provided an outlet that led to advances in architecture, a major contribution of the ancient Greeks for succeeding artistic developments in other countries and in later centuries.

Economic stability in the eighth century B.C. led to expansion in several ways. Emigration intensified and colonies were established in southern Italy and in Sicily. Here the colonists were liberated from the traditionalism of their homeland and greater impetus was given to architecture. Also, the ability of the colonists to trade agricultural products for a limited number of man-made products led to industrial expansion in Greece. In addition, mercantile interests in the East began to exert themselves, but while some decorative elements were accepted, the Greeks, independent as was their character, tended to adapt rather than duplicate designs of foreign products. Architecture seems to have been little affected by the interaction with the East. One area of Greek interest, unshared by Eastern artists, was in the accurate rendition of the human figure, of substantial importance for architectural reliefs as well as for freestanding sculpture.

Areas of settlement were organized into independent city-states whose governments were oligarchical, tyrannical, or democratic. The impetus to democracy was hastened by the cooperation among city-states that banded together to defeat invasions by the Persians. Central to the democratic achievement was Athens under the leadership of Pericles (443–429 B.C.) during the classical period; under his rule the affluence of Athens reached its zenith, leading to unprecedented building activity and the highest achievement in Hellenic art and architecture of this period.

The Peloponnesian War (431-404 B.C.), primarily between Athens and Sparta, led to the domination of Sparta. Subsequently, other city-states attempted to attain political supremacy. Following a period during which Macedonia imposed a federation, Philip of Macedonia (reigned 359-336 B.C.) unified Greece. His son, Alexander the Great (reigned 336-323 B.C.), conquered the Persian Empire and extended the territories under Greek control to Egypt, Syria, and Pergamum (an ancient city of Asia Minor). As a result, art and architecture of the Hellenistic period were in greater demand and the direction of influence was extended eastward.

Ideally suited to the public architecture of prime importance to the Greeks, marble was a building material in abundant supply in Greece. Builders resorted to the use of powdered marble to coat coarser materials to accomplish the precise outlines and smoothness they desired. Since early building had relied on rock, sun-dried brick, and timber, it is possible that early plan types and structural methods may have influenced early marble structures.

The climate was suited to outdoor activities. It was the practice of Greek men to place great attention on outdoor public ceremony. In the interpretation of documentary evidence, probably too much emphasis has been given to an apparent lack of focus to residential building. While it was not customary for gentlemen to have jobs, they would have had business dealings and probably did not have the fortitude to stay outside all day. Within the household the dining room was a male domain in which decorative enhancement was emphasized. Civic rituals and debate were extremely important to men, but they did spend time in their homes. Offices and workrooms undoubtedly would have been provided in the household, particularly for foreign residents who had commercial interests and who inhabited the type of house represented in this discussion. The influence of climate on residential design is observed also in the provision of a courtyard and the location of interior rooms around the court to take advantage of the southern sun. As a response to unexpected showers and hot sun, porticoes and colonnades were prominent architectural features.

To the climate and the materials used may also be attributed the fact that there are so few material remains available for the study of residences. Materials like sun-dried brick vanished despite exterior structural features designed to protect the walls from deterioration from rains. However, due to the fact that the bases to these walls were constructed of stone, it has been possible, in a limited manner, to reconstruct the evolution of the typical floor plan through systematic archaeological excavations, but precise knowledge is scant.

SPATIAL RELATIONSHIPS

While archaeological excavations give information about the spatial relationships of the plan, reconstruction of three-dimensional features is more difficult. Postulations can be made based on the material remains of the lowest levels of buildings. Archaeological evidence provides limited details since only fragmentary remains are available for investigation. Better archaeological evidence is available from the time of Alexander the Great, who ruled Greece from 336 to 323 B.C.

Other details about space relations can be found in the works of literary figures. Information about earlier classical characteristics is found in such writers as the playwright Aristophanes, the historian and essayist Xenophon, and the writer and philosopher Plato. Pollio Marcus Vitruvius, active from 46 to 30 B.C., was a Roman architect, writer, and theorist whose work, *De architectura,* in ten volumes, is the only complete discourse on architecture from this period; it was primarily Hellenistic in approach. Not widely used in the author's own time, the manuscript had extensive influence beginning with the Renaissance.

Classical Greek and Roman architecture has had astounding influence both structurally and decoratively in subsequent periods, especially beginning with Renaissance Italy. Interpretations of classical architecture have been both literal translations and adaptations. Subsequently, derivations from ancient Greece and Rome in different periods of interior architecture have included such features as axial planning, natural light as a prominent design element, the atrium plan, the role of the colonnade as a factor in space delineation, and structural use of the column, among others. Also emanating from classic architecture is the wide range of architectural decoration used for the enhancement of interior structural features as well as for the decorative arts, especially in furniture design. The latter have included a wide range of moldings, the vocabulary of design ornament which the classical designers used to decorate structure, and the decorative use of structural elements such as the orders, pediments, and so on.

The role of the orders was significant in defining spaces of the Greek interior; not only did they divide spaces horizontally but they were also instrumental in creating visual interest by the attention drawn to them vertically through decorative detail in the capitals and in the entablature. The classical orders consist of the column with its base (generally), shaft, capital, and entablature (each with its constituent parts), and are classified by the capital as Doric, Ionic, Corinthian, or Composite. The simplest of the orders was the Doric. Doric columns, in Greek versions, had no base and stood directly on the stylobate (the Romans incorporated a base); however, differing in the treatment of the base, a Greek denticular Doric order is illustrated (Figure 2-1). The shaft of the column was slightly curved (termed *entasis*) and fluted; each flute was separated by sharp edges *(arrises)*. Heading the column was the capital consisting of *annulets* (horizontal fillets), an *echinus* (in profile, a quarter-round molding), and an *abacus* (a flat square element serving as a transition from the capital to the entablature). Horizontally disposed above the capital was the entablature, comprised of the *architrave,* the *frieze,* and the *cornice.* The lowest member of the entablature was the architrave, which corresponds to a lintel; typically it had one vertical plane. The frieze, the middle member, was comprised of alternating *triglyphs* and *metopes;* metopes were the spaces between the fluted triglyphs. Comprised of a series of moldings, the cornice was the horizontal, crowning, and projecting member of the entablature. Gabled buildings had a raking cornice which followed the pitch of the triangular gable or pediment; the *tympanum* was the center space formed by the boundaries of the horizontal cornice and the two raking cornices. Sometimes this space was plain and sometimes filled with sculptural relief.

Offering greater diversity, the Ionic order was typically more slender than the Doric (Figure 2-2). The column, resting on a base of any of several moldings, had a fluted shaft, each channel of which was separated by a fillet. Dividing the shaft from the capital was a

FIGURE 2-1   Greek Doric Denticular Order. Saylor, Henry. *Dictionary of Architecture,* New York: John Wiley & Sons, Inc., 1952.

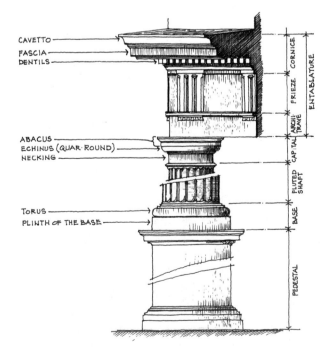

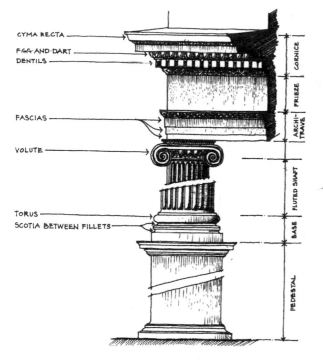

CYMA RECTA
EGG·AND·DART
DENTILS
FASCIAS
VOLUTE
TORUS
SCOTIA BETWEEN FILLETS

CORNICE
FRIEZE
ARCHI-TRAVE
FLUTED SHAFT
BASE
PEDESTAL

FIGURE 2-2 Greek Ionic Order. Saylor, Henry. *Dictionary of Architecture*, New York: John Wiley & Sons, Inc., 1952.

FILLET

CAVETTO

SCOTIA

OVOLO

CYMA RECTA

CYMA REVERSA

TORUS

row of bead-and-reel molding. Opposite sides of the capital had pairs of volutes which were deeply furrowed and ribbed; between each volute was an echinus molding carved with an egg and dart and a smaller band of bead molding comprised of a series of small half-round sections. The architrave of the entablature was comprised of three vertical planes while above it the frieze was either plain or served as a space for a band of sculpture. A dentil molding was used frequently at the base of the cornice; diversity characterized the combination of moldings. Commonly used moldings were fillet, cavetto, scotia, ovolo, cyma recta, cyma reversa, and torus (Figure 2-3).

The most ornate and slender of the orders was the Corinthian (Figure 2-4). Contrary to the Ionic, this order had the advantage of an arrangement of design elements for the capital with effective viewing from all sides. At the same time, the capital was deeper (simi-

FIGURE 2-3 Classical Moldings fillet (flat band separating other moldings); cavetto (concave approximating a quarter-round); scotia (strongly concave, casts a strong shadow); ovolo (convex, lower portion deviates from the vertical plane); cyma recta (ogee curve, convex portion nearer the wall); cyma reversa (reverse ogee, concave portion nearer the wall, convex above and concave below); torus (strong convex of semicircular outline).

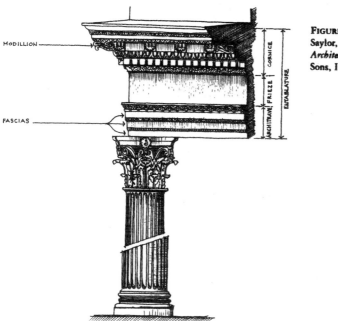

MODILLION
FASCIAS

CORNICE
FRIEZE
ARCHITRAVE
ENTABLATURE

FIGURE 2-4 Corinthian Order. Saylor, Henry. *Dictionary of Architecture*, New York: John Wiley & Sons, Inc., 1952.

lar to an inverted bell in overall shape). The base and shaft of the Corinthian and Ionic columns were similar. The Corinthian capital had two rows of carved acanthus leaves at the base. Above this were larger acanthus leaves, from which stemmed the volutes positioned at the corners of the abacus; two smaller volutes curved toward the center just under the abacus. The sides of the abacus could be concave, resulting in points at the corners visually supported by the volutes; the abacus could also be square or chamfered at the corners. The architrave of the Corinthian entablature was developed in three planes, each of which might have been separated by a carved molding. The frieze was normally decorated with a band of sculptural relief while the cornice was often dentiled. The soffit of the cornice was often highly ornamental, sometimes with coffered sections divided by brackets. This order was invented in Athens around the fifth century B.C., but it was not favored by the Greeks. Extensively used by the Romans, their version was the prototype used in the Renaissance.

Proportion and correcting optical illusions were major considerations of the Greek architects. Proportions of columns, entablatures, moldings, and ornament varied among the orders and in their rendition as practiced by the Greeks and Romans. The module for heights of the parts was determined by the diameter of the column. Refinements related to correcting optical illusions involved horizontal and vertical alterations. Long horizontal features that would appear to sag were curved upward in the center; vertical elements that would appear to fall forward were inclined inward at the top.

Future periods of design were influenced by the characteristics observed in classical Greek and Roman architecture. These are reflected in space planning, interior architecture, and furniture design.

Spatial Features of the Floor Plan and Three-Dimensional Spatial Characteristics

By the mid-Bronze Age a type of simple plan developed that impacted space planning into the Hellenistic period. Called a *megaron,* it was comprised of three components: (1) a hall, (2) a storeroom at the back, and, later, (3) a porch. The walls of these first structures were not strictly rectangular. In the late Bronze Age this Mycenaean plan became predominant in Crete and the Cycladic islands, after which its influence spread to the coastal regions of Asia Minor. In palace settings megaron structures were sometimes constructed as independent units serving as apartments; these often opened from a great court, a feature continuing into later residential architecture. Still based on three compartments, the long rectangular form included, in sequence, a porch, an optional anteroom, and a hall (the largest space) (Figure 2-5). In the center of the hall of this late 13th-century B.C. megaron was a circular hearth set with a raised edge to form a basin for the fire; in some cases a lantern was placed on a flat roof above to draw off the smoke. The number and arrangement of columns surrounding the hearth varied.

A residence at Priene of the late 4th or 3rd century B.C. illustrates how elements of this modified megaron plan were adapted to later functional need (Figure 2-6). Here the porch opened from a court and provided access directly into the hall, the large room immediately behind it; the plan is expanded by the addition of rooms on each side. A pediment may have surmounted the porch supported by columns *in antis* (when columns are placed between a pier or pilaster at the thickened end of a projecting wall they are said to be *in antis*). While the height of the porch is surmised to be as tall as 20 feet, surrounding rooms probably were not given equal height.

Wherever they settled, the Greeks preferred a plan in which the emphasis was on the distribution of rooms around a court, as revealed in a 2nd century B.C. plan. Since the emphasis was on inward orientation and privacy, the entrance was through a passage between two rooms (Figure 2-7). Columns encompassed the atrium, forming a peristyle court. In order to allow the winter sun to penetrate more deeply into the residence, a Rhodian peristyle was utilized in which the columns on the north were taller. Construction for the latter entailed the placement of a bracket on the taller columns to receive the lin-

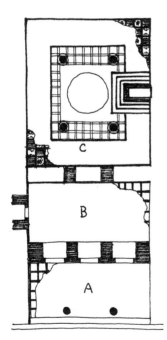

FIGURE 2-5 Megaron, Portion of Tiryns Palace (late 13th century B.C.). Space sequence: A porch; B anteroom; C hall or living room; D door leading to smaller adjacent rooms. Lawrence, A.W. *Greek Architecture*, Yale University Press: 1983, p. 96.

(a)

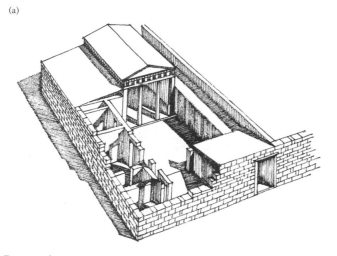

FIGURE 2-6 Plan and Conjectural Exterior Reconstruction (late 4th or 3rd century B.C.). Plan sequence: A court; B porch (prodomus); C living room or hall (oecus); D servants or storage; E exedra. Cook, R.M., *Greek Art, Its Development, Character, and Influence.* Weldenfeld and Nicholson Publishers. Plate 92a and 92b.

(b)

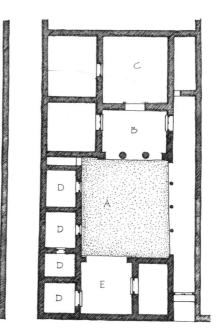

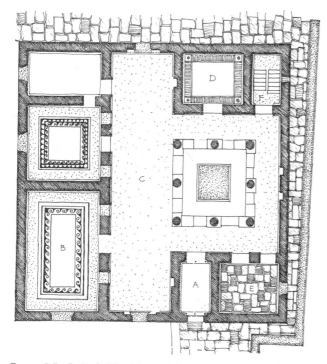

FIGURE 2-7 Peristyle Plan, Maison de la Collene, Delos (2nd century B.C.). Inwardly oriented. Spaces: A main entrance; B main living room (oecus); C courtyard with square peristyle; D dining room (andron); E kitchen; F stairs to upper stories. Cook, R.M., *Greek Art, Its Development, Character, and Influence.* Weldenfeld and Nicholson Publishers. Plate 93b.

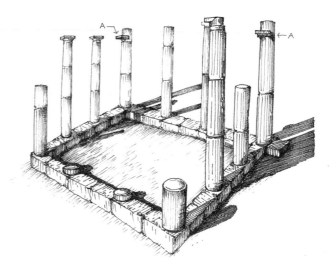

FIGURE 2-8 Rhodian Peristyle, Maison des Masques, Delos (2nd century B.C.). Construction allowing winter sun to penetrate the courtyard; A brackets of taller columns to receive lintels from the lower columns. From a photograph by Lawrence, A.W., *Greek Architecture.* Yale University Press, 1983, p. 329, Fig. 324.

tels of the lower columns (Figure 2-8). A cistern was occasionally placed under the court to collect rain water entering the *compluvium*, an opening in the roof. For household worship an altar for a cult statue was sometimes provided in the court. The exterior door sometimes led directly into the court, often the largest space. In the inner court, one or more colonnades were occasionally used instead of the peristyle arrangement.

When a free space in the court area extended unimpeded to the exterior walls, the residence may be referred to as a *pastas house* (See Figure 2-7). Main and ancillary rooms located on the north, facing south, took best advantage of the Rhodian peristyle with the com-

FIGURE 2-9 Conjectural Section, Maison de la Collene, (See Figure 2-7). Wall divides into dado, main field, cornice, and attic. Doric peristyle columns at ground level with colonnaded gallery above. Cook, R.M., *Greek Art, Its Development, Character, and Influence*. Weldenfeld and Nicholson Publishers. Plate 93c.

pluvium above. Situated around the court were such spaces as a living room *(oecus)*, storerooms, kitchen, bathroom, and dining room; the largest room was usually richer in decoration than other rooms around the court. The dining room *(andron)* was usually located in a corner of the house. Male members of the household gave dinner parties there. Couches were arranged around the perimeter of the room and it was the practice to recline on these to eat. Sometimes the couches were placed on platforms, at other times directly on the floor. The bathroom and latrine usually drained into an open or closed drain behind the house; latrines were occasionally placed on the second floor also.

The number of stories varied from one to four floors, but the most common arrangement was the one- or two-story residence. In this example a wooden stair in two runs led to the bedrooms on the second floor, a location often relegated to women of the household. At this level a colonnaded gallery was not uncommon (Figure 2-9). From this conjectural section it is evident that the vertical and horizontal relationships of the space plan anticipate Roman houses in the alternation of light levels, the changes in ceiling heights, the provision of the compluvium and associated impluvium (a basin in which water was collected from the opening in the roof).

INTERIOR ARCHITECTURE AND DECORATION

An incomplete picture emerges from the evidence available in attempts to reconstruct the definitive Greek residential interior. Remains are isolated, with little information about relative proportion; on the other hand, more detail is available for public buildings primarily due to building materials that were more durable than those used for residential construction, but here, too, much has been lost, since few buildings are in prime condition near the roofs. However fragmentary, archaeological excavations have allowed researchers to develop a picture of a range of characteristics for interior architecture and decoration. Other documentary evidence comes from tombs, wall paintings and reliefs, and vase paintings.

Materials and Decorative Techniques

Construction techniques and indigenous materials such as stone (marble and limestone), wood, clay, and thatch were the determinants responsible for interior structural features. Trabeated construction, used by the Egyptians, continued to be employed by the Greeks. Stone was used for civic architecture except for the frame of the roof and the ceiling. Depending on the internal span of wooden structures, columns were essential to support

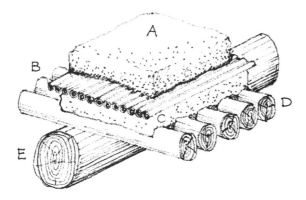

FIGURE 2-10 Construction between Upper Story Floor and Ceiling Below. Construction layers: A clay floor for upper level; B reeds or rushes; C clay layer; D smaller ceiling beams; E large main beam. From a photograph by Lawrence, A.W., *Greek Architecture*. Yale University Press, 1983, p. 20, Fig. 1.

the superstructure. It was common, therefore, for spaces to be interrupted by these internal supports through the use of a peristyle arrangement or colonnades; walls functioned as intermediate support also. Although marble columns were sometimes used in residential construction, wooden posts were probably more common, in some instances the capitals being of stone.

Walls for private houses were typically constructed of sun-dried mud brick over a foundation of rubble (fired brick came into general use in the Roman period). Due to the low compressive strength of unfired brick, walls tended to be quite thick. Brick size varied—for example 1' x 2' and 4" deep, 18" x 27" x 4 3/4" deep. On the interior a plaster coat covered the brick as a base for decorative wall treatment.

Treatment of floors ranged from the simply utilitarian to decorative. Compacted earth floors were used by families of all economic levels, but wealthier homeowners of the classical period often used plaster, painting, or mosaic. Upper stories had either earthen or wooden floors. One technique for constructing the clay floor for upper levels included layers of materials that from the upper floor level to the ceiling beams of the floor below, included clay over reeds or rushes pressed into another layer of clay laid on an arrangement of ceiling beams of the lower floor (Figure 2-10).

Techniques for decorative floor treatment included three categories of mosaic utilizing such materials as pebbles, glass, and stone set in a mortar. Introduced first, the pebble mosaics were primarily black and white with supplementary use of other colors; the pebbles were uncut. It was principally a linear art form; strips of lead or terracotta were sometimes used to sharpen the outline of figures. A later development was the technique of tessellated mosaic, in which small, squarish pieces (*tessera*) of such materials as stone, glass, and gilded tesserae were set in mortar and ground to a smooth surface; the size of the individual tessera ranged from 1/8" to 1/16" or smaller. A specialist was often employed to lay up the figure panel designs on trays which were then inserted into the floor. Simpler abstract ornament was then laid by other craftsmen. This technique was ideally suited to pictorial and painterly effects due to the infinite shading potential of such small tesserae. Used more rarely than tessellated mosaics, a still later technique was *opus sectile,* in which the individual pieces were larger and cut to fit a predetermined abstract arrangement; some authorities refer to this technique as inlay rather than mosaic. It was not suited to pictorial approaches nor were the Greeks particularly interested in this approach.

Interior Architecture and Decorative Elements

Floors

The specific mosaic technique generated distinctive decorative or pictorial effects. Pebble mosaics most typically were rendered with white figures on a black background, alternatively black on white; there was sporadic use of colors including red, blue, yellow.

Design characteristics included abstraction, symmetry, concentric arrangements, and frames of lozenges or squares; accompanying design motifs were mythological figures, fantastic animals, and floral ornaments.

Lending themselves to pictorial outcomes, tessellated mosaics were ideally suited to subtle use of light and shadow under the influence of painting. *Trompe l'oeil* (French for 'deceives the eye') techniques were not totally embraced by the Greeks. However, through various illusionistic devices the viewer was persuaded to believe that he was looking at three-dimensional objects; knowledge of perspective and depth perception through skillful use of modeling with light and shadow were important here.

Pictorial effects were not easily attained with the *opus sectile* technique, since subtle gradations were not practical due to the larger size of the individual pieces. The resulting designs tended to abstraction and symmetry. The Romans used this technique to a greater degree than the Greeks.

In Greek residences mosaics were used only in the most important rooms. The dining room and its anteroom were such spaces, as well as, occasionally, the basin of the court. Besides an overall floor design, mosaics were sometimes used to mark the position of furniture, as dining couches. The latter was employed especially in the Hellenistic period and later by the Romans. Nonmosaic floors were plastered and painted.

Walls

Related to economic level, the simplest treatment of walls was unplastered mud brick; for wealthier citizens plastering and painting were common but, depending on the importance of the room, more elaborate enhancement was favored. Tomb paintings reveal that the wall was often divided into three zones: dado, main field, and cornice; portions above the cornice are termed *attics* (see Figure 2-9). Examples of paint applications include an entire wall painted an intense solid red (a favorite hue), a white dado capped with yellow and a red field, and white walls with a red dado of approximately one meter. In addition to the foregoing, materials and structural elements were simulated in the main field in a number of ways. Courses of stone were represented by paint, incised lines, or molded plaster. In the Hellenistic period more elaborate means were employed in which: (1) stone was imitated through painting (termed *incrustation*) or through modeling and painting to imitate marble, (2) architectural elements were represented by illusionistic painting, (3) the main field was treated with modeled plaster to depict pilasters and entablatures, and (4) pictorial painting was introduced in the main field. The latter two means were not widely favored by the Greeks but were broadly used by the Romans. It must be noted, however, that the use of murals is difficult to ascertain, since only fragmentary evidence is available.

Lighting was accounted for by the use of lamps. Small niches on the floor plan represent spaces used for holding lamps.

Windows and Doors

Fenestration was not a significant factor in wall design, particularly on the first floor, where the emphasis was on inward orientation. When windows were installed they were placed high in the wall, while those of upper floors were more numerous and showed variation in both shape and size. Windows had plain frames of either wood or stone; some extant material evidence indicates that sometimes they were ornately conceived in the later Hellenistic period. Pilasters occasionally marked the boundary of windows and, alternatively, were used to separate windows. A wide door leading from the main living room to the courtyard was placed between two windows (see Figure 2-7).

Either wood or stone was employed for door frames also; marble was particularly appropriate for prominent doorways, where moldings were used to highlight this definition. The elaboration of frames is well known for its use in Greek secular and religious architecture but less extant evidence is available for residential structures. Both single- and two-leafed doors of wood were hung with rods extending from the sill to the lintel, which allowed them to pivot. While attention was not lavished on decorating the door leaves it is known that in public architecture they were occasionally paneled. Another treatment was to cover the door with a sheet of bronze; studding was sometimes used decoratively. Instead of doors, passageways were sometimes partitioned by fabrics hung in the doorway.

Chimneypieces

The Greeks did not have chimneypieces as we know them today but they did provide for the escape of smoke from the interior environment. Some authorities believe that smoke was diverted through the gable ends, although earlier, if the roof was flat, a lantern on the roof placed above the hearth provided for the dispersion. In addition, the upper part of large clay storage jars formed elementary chimneys.

Ceilings

A great deal of information about ceilings is lost, but some valuable knowledge comes from tombs and wall paintings. Coffering, composed of recessed panels in the ceiling, was either genuine or simulated; also, flat painted ceilings were employed. Vitruvius, in his writings, observed that cedar was ideally suited for ceiling coffers. Ceiling design would have been particularly important in the dining room in view of the fact that it was the Greek custom to eat reclining. Greek influence in ceiling design is observed in stucco ornamental relief of the Romans in the 1st century A.D. Designers of the Renaissance and subsequent periods paid remarkable attention to this decorative embellishment.

Ceiling height varied depending on the story; first floor ceiling heights were in the vicinity of 13 feet, those of the second floor lower. With the emphasis on the court, the impluvium, and the associated compluvium at roof level, it was not uncommon to have one ceiling height extend through more than one floor level (see Figure 2-9). Attention to the alternate intensities of light as implied by the foregoing was particularly evident in the space planning of the later Romans.

FURNITURE

Sculptural reliefs and vase paintings are the best documentary sources of information about Greek furniture. Significantly, furniture is also depicted in terracotta and bronze statuettes. To these sources must be added the contribution that literature has made to our knowledge of furniture; for example, in a satyr play, a deity reclines on a couch while frolicking satyrs encompass a flute player who sits on a klismos. The latter are characterized by a back concave cresting rail and legs which, from the side view, are concave in outline.

Literary evidence of mythological scenes or events contemporary to the period, when added to visual evidence, give mutual confirmation of these decorative art forms. Chronological developments can be determined through the study of Greek vase painting, where faithful details are delineated.

Materials and Construction Techniques

Some of the few pieces of furniture or parts of furniture that have survived are constructed of metal (copper, bronze, iron) or marble. Bronze fragments housed in museums reveal tangible evidence of its use as a furniture material. A bronze leg in the form of a reeded pilaster which terminates in a lion's paw is housed in the Palermo Museum, Sicily. The prototypes for these materials, judging from the details, were of wood—thus, information about wood construction techniques can be ascertained. Wood was used extensively by the Greeks in the construction of furniture; oak, maple, cedar, boxwood, olive, citron, and beech are thought to have been important. Among imported woods were maple, ebony, and citron. The more precious woods, such as maple and ebony, were used as veneers to cover less expensive woods.

FIGURE 2-11 Klismos Chair. Detail,
Vase Painting (5th century B.C.).
Lightly scaled example. Legs: concave,
rectangular section, flared at seat rail,
through tenon. Stiles of back continuation of leg. Back: horizontally curved.
Ashmolean Museum, Oxford.

FIGURE 2-12
Klismos and Diphros,
Vase Painting (5th
century B.C.). Stool
(diphros) with turned
legs. Copyright British
Museum.

Illustrated on vase paintings and in sculptural reliefs, wood joinery entailed the use of
both dowels (round in section) and tenons (rectangular in section) to connect structural
members, as seat rails to legs. Therefore, a prominent construction detail is revealed to be
the through dowel or tenon—that is, the dowel or tenon attached to the seat rail extends
through the leg in an aperture of like shape to become a visible design and structural element (Figure 2-11).

Leather thongs or cords were interlaced for the surfaces of seat and reclining furniture.
Two means are illustrated in vase paintings; in one, the thongs or cords are wrapped around
the rails (Figure 2-12). Another technique was containing the weaving within the frame
bounded by the rails.

Decorative enhancement was attained through the use of inlay, carving, and painting.
Costly woods, gold, ivory, and gems were all used by the Greeks in inlay work. Painting

to cover blemishes or to simulate more expensive woods was practiced; also, brilliant poly-chrome effects were attained by painting favorite design motifs on furniture surfaces.

In addition to hand shaping the Greeks employed other implements and techniques for shaping wooden parts. When the lathe was introduced in Greece after the 7th century B.C., the legs of furniture became round in section, sometimes varying in diameter, and other curvilinear elements were initiated. Later in the period turnings became complex, and it is evident that wood turning was influential in the manner in which metal furniture was fashioned. These sculptural forms were often introduced at the juncture of the leg and the seat rail. Although the theory is unproved, some authorities speculate that bending may have been instrumental in forming structural parts.

Typical Pieces and Stylistic Features

Interiors were sparsely furnished with such pieces as couches or beds, stools, chairs, chests, tables, and shelves. Many of these forms were derived from Egypt and the Near East; however, the Greeks added new features. Typical differences stem from the Egyptian tendency to naturalism in their renditions compared to the Greek emphasis on stylization. Tracing the developmental stages of furniture forms is made easier by the fact that vase paintings and sculptural reliefs can be categorized by chronological period. This provides significant documentary evidence for an assessment of evolutionary changes in furniture design.

Seat Furniture

Individual seat forms included the throne, klismos, and stool. Of these, the throne (thronos) was specialized for use by deities and by persons of prominence. Thrones intended for outdoor use were constructed of marble and used in such places as theaters; thus, many of these have survived. Over time thrones changed from heavy with less ornament to slender with more decorative detail. Characteristically, there is tremendous diversity in structural elements as well as in the ornamental detail. Thrones were made in both backed and backless versions, and their height varied; both paneled and open designs were employed. Finials were sometimes in the form of the lotus bud or palmette, motifs derived from Egypt. The thronos often had armrests, but there were also armless versions. At times terminating in a ram's head, the armrest was apparently placed low on the stiles of the back. The sphinx was occasionally used for the arm support. Legs were primarily of three types: rectangular, turned, or animal; these often ended in animal hoofs or paws, but some were simple and undecorated. Apparently the straight leg with a rectangular cross section was a Greek innovation. Frequently this leg was symmetrically incut, below or near the center, and framed with a molded volute (C-scroll); often incorporated above and below the volute was a carved or painted palmette with a rosette. The space between the stretcher and the seat rail was decoratively ornamented with fantastic creatures, lions, sphinxes, and so on. Also, thrones with solid bases and rectangular or curved backs were depicted. This type of leg is seen on a vase painting of a couch.

Widely used in households, the *klismos* was a type of chair which was developed and perfected by Greek craftsmen. At first it was a lightly scaled form that, in the Hellenistic period, became heavier, a characteristic retained by the Romans. About at shoulder height the horizontally curved back was supported by three uprights, two stiles and an intermediate splat; narrow at first, the back became deeper with a more pronounced curve (see Figure 2-11). The seats were essentially square with the seat surface of interwoven leather thongs or cord. From the side view the legs were incurved (concave) with a rectangular cross section, plain and narrow at floor level, wider at seat level. The top of the front legs are either flush with the seat rail, or extend slightly above. Unlike in Egyptian methods of construction, it was typical of the klismos for the rear legs to continue in one piece as stiles of the back.

The stool (*diphros*) was a commonly used piece intended for use by both deities and human beings. Although Egyptian antecedents are evident in the design of the stool, a

FIGURE 2-13 Table, Limestone Statuette (6th century B.C.). Trapezoidal tabletop. Copyright British Museum.

lightly scaled piece, there was no attempt by the Greeks to place animal legs in a directional position. Stools were of several types, each of which is illustrated in vase paintings or in sculptural reliefs: (1) turned legs, (2) legs that were rectangular in cross section, and (3) folding X-stool with legs and hoofs of a deer—a pin allowed the stool to pivot. Within this repertoire of stools there were countless design details that coincided with the leg shape. For example, on those with turned legs, at the juncture of the leg with the seat rail a spherical enlargement produced a sculptural effect (see Figure 2-12). Likewise, on those with rectangular cross section legs (some taper as the klismos, apparently rare, and some are untapered) the swelled part is appropriately a tapering block with a tenon of like shape. Alternative leg endings include plain, hoofs that turned outward, or lions' paws that turned inward.

Tables

Small, portable, and light, tables *(trapezai)* were more commonly used by the Greeks than by the Egyptians. Tables were used primarily at mealtime, when individual tables were brought to the dining room loaded with food for the diners, who reclined on the couch to eat. When not in use the table was pushed under the couch, so its height was regulated by that of the couch; the three-legged version was more stable on uneven floors, although there were some with four legs. In some vase paintings dogs were depicted under tables and couches, presumably to eat food disposed of by the diners.

Tabletops were of three shapes: rectangular, trapezoid, or round. Rectangular, sectioned legs tapered downward with no terminal unit or terminated in an animal paw; they are also shown on vase paintings as having the concave curve of the klismos. For the table with a trapezoid top and three legs, the single leg is centered and flush at the narrow end while the two legs at the wider end are inset; the legs are usually joined by a T-shaped stretcher (Figure 2-13). The wider end was placed nearer the head of the couch. Introduced by the 4th century B.C., the round-topped table was supported by plain legs or by three carved animal legs, sometimes deer legs with terminating hoofs (Figure 2-14). The round table was used in the andron also. Two other tables were of significance: (1) a round-topped

FIGURE 2-14 Table (Hellenistic Period). Wood. Animal legs. Royal Museums of Art and History, Brussels, A1857 (photo A.C.L.).

FIGURE 2-15 Chest, Terra-cotta Relief (c. 460 B.C.). Panel construction. Fret decoration on stiles and rails. Lion paw ending to legs.

table with a single pedestal support, and (2) a rectangular-topped table with two transverse supports—this type may have been designed for outdoor use.

Storage Pieces

Chests were used for the storage of clothing, jewelry, and other household items. Like their Egyptian prototypes, Greek chests were primarily rectangular and often paneled (Figure 2-15). Lids were hinged, usually flat, and extended beyond the storage compartment; gabled or arched lids attained popularity later in the period. A Locrian terracotta relief (c. 460 B.C.) illustrates a richly ornamented chest where the stiles, rails, and legs were enhanced by the use of the Greek key (sometimes referred to as fret); this chest has one patterned panel. The low legs were often extensions of the stiles, either tapered or untapered; paws sometimes formed the terminating motif for the legs, or else the legs might be plain.

Beds

The couch (kline) had multiple functions, since it was used as a sofa and bed as well as for reclining at meals. Unlike the Egyptian bed, the Greek couch was designed with a headboard; the separate head rest was dispensed with. Head- and footboards (fulcra) were occasionally extravagantly decorated, some with depictions of gods and goddesses, the head of a mule, and so on. A few headboards were similar to the klismos and when that was the case, concave legs were employed. One type of leg, with a rectangular cross section, was like that described for the throne, in which symmetrical incisions were cut near the center or below and framed with a molded volute (C-scroll). Near the headboard the leg sometimes extended above the rail in a volute. Or, like the turned leg of a stool, the juncture of the leg with the seat rail was rendered as a spherical enlargement with sculptural overtones. The head of the bed was sometimes higher than the foot.

The bed surface on which the mattress was placed was constructed of interwoven vegetable fibers or leather thongs. In literary accounts rugs and blankets were mentioned, although sheets were rarely noted.

ORNAMENT

The ornamental vocabulary of the Greeks had a far-reaching influence on subsequent stylistic periods, either copied or adapted. Used extensively by the Greeks, these patterns have included the following: zigzags, concentric circles, lotus, spirals, leaf patterns (laurel, ivy), guilloche, scrolls, volutes, meanders (frets), wave patterns, palmettes (anthemion, honeysuckle), rosettes, bead-and-reel designs, leaf-and-dart designs, etc.

Rome

Republic, 509 B.C.-27 B.C.;
Early Empire, 27 B.C.-A.D. 192;
Later Empire to A.D. 476

HISTORICAL SETTING

Layers of overlapping factors were instrumental in the formation of Roman arts during the later Republic and in the Early Empire periods of Rome. Foremost among these influences were geographic position, conquests, technology, priorities in social life, and religion.

While several races were prominent among the settling peoples of the Italian peninsula, two, in particular, were instrumental in shaping the arts of the Romans—the Etruscans and the Greeks. The Etruscans had come from Asia Minor and brought with them cultural influences from the Orient and Greece; before the rise of Rome they represented the preeminent civilization in Italy. However, through external colonization between 750 and 500 B.C., the Greeks, a seafaring people, settled in Sicily and along the coastal areas of southern Italy.

The geographic area ruled by the Etruscans ultimately extended from the southern region of Campania to the Plain of the Po in the north. Within this territory was the young city of Rome, which suggests that it probably was under Etruscan rule until around 500 B.C. Since the Etruscans were outstanding builders, the Romans would have observed technical achievements in architecture based on arcuated construction. The Etruscans attained their zenith in the 7th and 6th centuries B.C.; the disintegration of this forceful empire was a combined effort of the Romans and the invading Gauls from the north in the 5th and early 4th centuries B.C. The Romans established hegemony over central southern Italy through the defeats of the Etruscans and other groups posing threats to their advances. Then they looked further south to the prosperity engendered by the Greek cities.

Among the most affluent and influential cities established by the Greeks were Syracuse and Taranto, the former on the island of Sicily and the latter on the southern coast of Italy. Of the two areas, Sicily reached greater heights of development than the settlements of the southern peninsula. Roman jurisdiction of Taranto and southern Italy was established in 272 B.C. With their domination of the peninsula and later the addition of Sicily as a Roman province, the Romans could examine the temples, theaters, and walls of their new territory as outstanding examples of architecture from which they could draw inspiration. Thus began the assimilation by the Romans through their conquests of the more refined civilization of the Greek colonies in southern Italy.

With Rome achieving supremacy over the Italic peoples and consolidating its pivotal and commanding position in the Mediterranean, Italy was now in a position to extend its influence through other conquests; thus Rome served as a catalyst in spreading art and civilization throughout its vast empire. Three Punic Wars between 264 B.C. and 146 B.C. led to the acquisition of the islands of Sicily and Sardinia and the addition of Carthage as a province. Rome was the greatest power west of China and controlled commerce in the western Mediterranean. Ultimately, Roman territorial holdings extended from the Persian Gulf in the east to Spain in the west, southern boundaries included the coastal region of North Africa and spread northward to the Rhine River and Britain. Geographical boundaries of the Roman Empire were the largest during the 200-year period beginning with the rule of Augustus in 27 B.C.; this period is generally referred to as the *Pax Romana*.

While Greece was under Roman domination (200 B.C.-A.D. 330) the Romans assimilated Greek culture; Hellenistic artistic traditions were accepted and perpetuated by bringing artisans and art to Rome. (The Greeks, on the other hand, avoided the cultural innovations of the Romans.) Not only did the Romans have the purchasing power to acquire works of art but also they had developed a system of transportation through road building that allowed them to bring to Rome the artisans whom they so greatly admired.

These conquests and contacts, particularly among the Etruscans and Greeks, had far-reaching implications for Western architecture and the decorative arts. In building, the Romans continued to use the post-and-lintel construction system (trabeation) of the Greeks. Differences existed in the use of the column: The Greeks used it structurally only; however, the Romans employed it both as a structural and as a decorative element for both the exterior and interior. Then, in terms of furniture design, while the Greeks were concerned with refining types where form and proportion were of major import, the Romans focused on ostentatious display, often through extravagant ornamentation. But in the use of the arch with the associated vault and dome they were also influenced by the Etruscans with whom they had earlier contact. By combining trabeated and arcuated systems of construction the Romans were able to dispense with the emphasis on the straight line inherent in the post-and-lintel method to attain free-flowing interior space and to introduce curved forms economically.

This technological breakthrough was feasible due the the discovery of concrete in the 2nd century B.C. *Concrete,* a compound of cement with proportionate amounts of water and coarse and fine aggregates such as sand, pebbles, crushed stone, and brick, altered the form of exterior and interior architecture as well as the manner of conceptualizing interior space. This new material could be easily manipulated and accounts, in part, for the similarities that exist in the architectural character of structures over the vast Roman territory; further, the Romans typically sheathed the concrete with stone or brick, materials widely available in all parts of the empire. To marble, used by the Greeks almost exclusively for major structures, the Romans in Italy added terra-cotta, brick, and other stones including travertine, alabaster, and porphyry.

The primary examples of Roman architecture date from the period between 100 B.C. and A.D. 300. An analysis of major structures gives some indication of the social values held by the Romans. These were utilitarian facilities that met their needs for religion (tombs, temples), commerce and law (basilicas), recreation (thermæ or public baths, theaters, circuses) and celebrating victories (memorial columns). In addition, the type of residence was, to some degree, a reflection of the social position of the resident. The *domus* or private dwelling probably developed from the Greek plan; in Italy it was designed to meet the privacy needs of the family, to give protection from the heat, and to provide light and ventilation by means of the atrium. Wealthier citizens might have had a town house in addition to a country villa; in fact, Cicero is reported to have had eight homes, of which seven were villas in the country. A range of social and economic classes were inhabitants of Pompeii; its houses represented largely middle- to upper-class residents. In the cities there were both luxurious town houses for those higher on the social scale as well as tenements for lower-class citizens. In tenements entire families might have inhabited one small room. While society was stratified by boundaries between classes it was possible to be upwardly mobile and to cross boundaries.

The rights of women were directly related to class. As members of the upper and middle class women could own property, make their own wills, take advantage of educational opportunities, attend public functions, and influence politics. Family life was highly prized by the Romans and women were highly respected. The family hearth was sacrosanct. In fact, in Roman religion, Vesta was goddess of hearth and home. Publicly, the Temple of Vesta was provided with an eternal flame tended by six vestal virgins; vows of celibacy were imposed for 30 years, after which they were free to marry. It was the responsibility of the virgins, representing the best families, to see that the flame was never extinguished. Should their vows be broken, they were given a public funeral and buried alive. In each household, regardless of social station, an altar for a household god was provided.

The interrelatedness of the influencing factors illustrates the dependence of Roman arts on the cultures of other races. At the same time advances in technology (materials and construction techniques) allowed the Romans to attain innovations in spatial features which exceeded those cultures represented in their conquests.

SPATIAL RELATIONSHIPS

Roman admiration of Hellenistic Greek arts, importation of Greek scholars and craftsmen, and introduction of concrete, along with arcuated construction, were largely responsible for the spatial characteristics, interior architecture, and decoration of buildings. Whereas the Greeks used the column for its structural properties, the Romans often used it in a nonstructural and decorative sense; however, they excelled at freeing up interior space, particu-

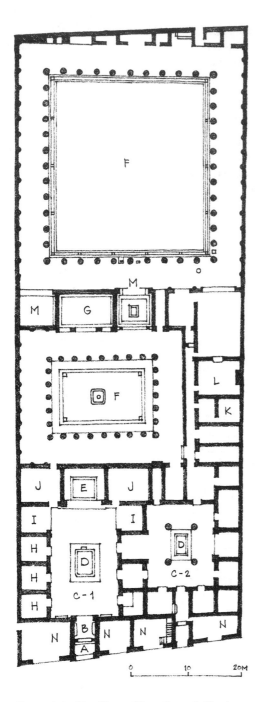

FIGURE 3-1   Plan, House of Faun, Pompeii. Visual axis A through G. A vestibulum; B fauces; C atrium (C-1 tuscanicum, C-2 tetrastylum); D impluvium; E tablinum; F peristylum; G exedra; H cubicula; I alae; J triclinia; K bath; L kitchen; M summer triclinia; N tabernae. Gemeinnützige, Leonard von Matt, CH-6374 Buochs, Switzerland.

larly in secular and utilitarian architecture. Their great architectural achievements were to be a recurring prototype for centuries to come.

Spatial Features of the Floor Plan and Three-Dimensional Spatial Characteristics

Preserved by ash from the eruption of Vesuvius in A.D. 79, the cities of Pompeii and Herculaneum near the Bay of Naples in Italy give material evidence of a way of life for the upper-class Roman citizens for whom it was a favorite resort. Pompeii came under the domination of the Romans in the 1st century B.C., but Greek influence before that was due to the colonization of Cumae, the oldest and most powerful coastal colony near Pompeii. Archaeological excavations of the Greek floor plan provide information about spatial relationships of the Roman floor plan, although very limited information is available with regard to the three-dimensional characteristics of Greek interiors; these comparisons are therefore more tenuous. Floor plans employed by the two cultures, however, illustrate obvious similarities such as inward orientation, axial planning stemming from the megaron, use of the atrium, and use of light as a prominent design element.

Although floor plans were varied, an axial arrangement (including the fauces, atrium, tablinum, and peristyle) represents a prevalent type known to have been used by the Romans in Pompeii; deviations were sometimes imposed by the size and shape of the site or by later additions (Figure 3-1). The domus was typically flush with the street. Usually a room was located on each side of the rather long, narrow entryway. Rooms belonging to the residence opened to the interior of the house while shops opened onto the street.

Beginning at the street level and moving through the house, the following were spaces traversed by the visitor. The long, narrow entryway was comprised of two spaces. The *vestibulum* was the inset, covered area immediately off the street. This led to a door, which opened into the *fauces,* where the ceiling was low. Furnishing ventilation and defined by natural light, the *atrium* (the main reception area) characteristically had an aperture in the roof (termed *compluvium*) through which rainwater could enter for storage in a cistern located under the *impluvium* (a basin of the same size as the compluvium). The *tablinum,* a space between the atrium and the peristyle with the most commanding view of the house, could be shut off or serve as passage to the peristyle; alternatively, an adjacent corridor provided access to the garden at the rear. Providing the optimal long view of the axial organization was the *peristyle,* a columned courtyard often featuring fountains and gardens with an infinite variety of designs. Finally, on the same axis was the *exedra,* one layout of which was a room with a full view of the garden through a full-width opening.

Additional rooms surrounded the atrium. Each *cubiculum* or bedroom had one door opening into the atrium. Other spaces were the *alae,* recesses with one wall completely open to the atrium, often located to the right and left of the axis. Around the peristyle were private apartments, dining rooms *(triclinia),* bedrooms, bathing facilities, toilets, and other specialized spaces to which visitors were admitted by invitation only. The *triclinia,* so called because of the practice of arranging three couches *(kline)* in a U-shape formation for dining, were set up in various locations such as under the peristyle roof or in the open air; there are instances of rooms provided on each side of the tablinum, one for summer (open to the portico) and one for winter (an enclosed space).

Functionally, the atrium and tablinum figured prominently in the ceremonial duties of the male head of the household. Clarke indicates that "the tablinum was the seat of power in the domus, controlling the axis of entry that formed its link with the business of the outside world."[1] As clients entered the atrium the visual axis directed attention to the head of household in the tablinum; he was either seated or standing, dressed in his toga, to conduct business including political and economic interests. Clients were employees, family members, slaves, freedmen, and so on.[2]

Rituals pertaining to family rites or ceremonies were conducted in the atrium. Since only one permanent shrine has been located, Clarke suggests that in oblations to ancestors the family may have used portable altars. More important, he indicates, was the worship of the penates, the lares, and the genius, and for these there were permanent shrines (paintings, statues, altars). *Penates* were deities whose function was to safeguard the household; the *lares* (household gods) were depicted as pairs of young men donning country clothes and holding drinking horns. The *genius,* on the other hand, was the fertility spirit that assured the life of the family. The many shrines to the lares uncovered in Pompeii and Herculaneum suggest that they were of greatest consequence.[3]

The presence of many lararia points to the rituals localized in specific spaces in the domus. Usually located in a corner of the atrium or in the kitchen area, these shrines included, in addition to statues or paintings of the two lares and the genius, other symbols of good fortune, such as the serpent. The lares received a variety of offerings, including incense, spelt, grapes, garlands of grain, honey cakes, honeycombs, first fruits, wine, and even blood sacrifices. At the lararium, the paterfamilias regularly prayed and offered sacrifice to the family lares.[4]

Since privacy was important, the orientation of the domus was inward; few windows were incorporated on the first floor. Most of the houses in Pompeii were single-story residences, although occasionally there were second-floor rooms above the shops as well as over other selected spaces. The second floor above shops was sometimes rented; when upper-level rooms were incorporated in the private section of the residence near the peristyle, the spaces are thought to have been used for slaves or for family bedrooms.

The Romans were expert in the manipulation of three-dimensional space. This is noted particularly in public architecture but is also observed, on a smaller scale, in residential design (Figure 3-2). The dimensions of the interior were enhanced by the spatial progression of the series of spaces along the axial arrangement, in which there was alternation of size of space, of light level, and of ceiling height. Within the architectural enclosure cues to movement through space were enhanced by the use of light along the central axial path. From the fauces, a low-light-level space, one entered the atrium, which was illuminated by natural light filtering through the compluvium; this light source optimized three-dimensional spatial perception vertically (Figure 3-3). Then the more dimly lit tablinum led into the brilliantly lit peristyle, open to the sky, and the terminal point of the axis (Figure 3-4). The same compression and release along the axial sequence occurred with regard to ceiling height and size of space beginning with the fauces (low ceiling and small scale), and the atrium (tall ceiling and larger scale), and progressing through the tablinum (lower ceiling and smaller scale) to the peristyle (total release) (Figure 3-5).

Two other means used by the Romans to modulate interior space deserve mention. One employed the use of a subsidiary structure within the atrium, the other illusionistic devices. While columnar support for the roof opening was not always used, occasionally columns positioned at the corners of the impluvium were used to support the architrave of the compluvium (one column height has been measured at 22 1/2'); once in a while more

1. John R. Clarke, *The Houses of Roman Italy. 100 B.C.-A.D. 250: Ritual, Space, and Decoration* (Berkeley: University of California Press, 1991), 6.

2. Ibid., 4.

3. Ibid., 7-8.

4. Ibid., 9.

FIGURE 3-2 View of Pompeian House from Vestibulum to Peristyle. Visual axis. Foreground: atrium with impluvium below and compluvium above, higher ceiling level. Tablinum beyond with lower ceiling and light level. Peristyle beyond.

FIGURE 3-3 View from Atrium to Fauces and Vestibulum. Atrium with higher ceiling level shown in relation to the lower ceiling and light level and of the fauces.

FIGURE 3-4 View of Ceiling Height of Tablinum in Relation to Atrium. Compression and release of ceiling heights and light level as occupants move through the spaces. After original photograph by Michael Larvey, Austin, Texas.

FIGURE 3-5   Peristyle. Open to the sky with residential spaces surrounding the open area.

45   Rome

than four columns surrounded the impluvium. This ancillary configuration encouraged vertical exploration of space made more dynamic by the filtered light; depth perception was also fostered here by the impluvium, with its raised frame for capturing the rainwater entering the residence. This framework provided a focal point but allowed the visitor to look through it for exploration of the emphatic axial arrangement. The difference between Greek and Roman axial planning lies in the fact that the Greek axis ended with a wall, while with the Romans, spatial perception became the most unimpeded at the terminus.

Other means were utilized to emphasize volumetric space. For example, at the second story level of the atrium in the Samnite House painters depicted simulated architectural elements consisting of columns separated by lattice fencing, which gave powerful emphasis to the third dimension (See Figure 3-3). In addition, cross axes were incorporated to extend spatial experiences, as with the *ala* (an open front room) on each side of the atrium.

Decorative painting on the walls of ancient Pompeii are well preserved. Among the four styles of painting were those which effectively modified space and the way in which the viewer perceived it. The Romans were competent in the use of perspective and in this way they rendered space through trompe l'oeil painting. For example, the walls of the interior architectural enclosure were obscured by using perspective to portray illusionistic architectural vistas, open gardens, and so on. Psychologically, therefore, the viewer experienced extended space.

INTERIOR ARCHITECTURE AND DECORATION

The Romans gave far more attention to the interior than did the Greeks, whose architectural focus was the exterior, viewed as sculpture. Ornamental and decorative exuberance characterized Roman interiors as they drew upon the repertoire of Hellenistic design elements. Among changes they introduced that related to the orders were the elimination of fluting, the introduction of the modillion in the cornice, the addition of the Composite and

Tuscan orders, and greater reliance on the Corinthian capital. The Composite order combined elements of both the Ionic and Corinthian orders. The Tuscan order, on the other hand, resembled the Doric, but was simpler. Typically the Greeks used the orders for their structural qualities; in fact all architectural elements were used to reinforce structural integrity. The Romans, on the other hand, used orders and other architectural features for their decorative qualities—for example, pilasters, broken pediments, freestanding columns located in front of load-bearing walls, etc. A variety of media and techniques was responsible for accomplishing these ostentatious environments.

Materials and Decorative Techniques

The primary examples of Roman architecture date from the period between 100 B.C. and A.D. 300. One might expect with the empire's vast territory that local building materials would determine architectural character; however, similarities can be accounted for by the use of concrete. To marble, used almost exclusively by the Greeks for major structures, the Romans in Italy were able to add terra-cotta, brick, and stone. The range of materials included quality sand and gravel, lava, travertine, alabaster, and porphyry. A material independent of locale, concrete was inexpensive and could be manipulated easily; it was made of an amalgam of aggregate and mortar and was laid in courses, contrary to 20th-century practice. Facing materials often applied to interior surfaces were marble, mosaic, and plaster.

Concrete was also responsible for the alteration of interior spaces. The designer progressed from the arch to the vault and dome with the potential to economically cover vast interior spaces without intermediate support. Thus this material contributed to the molding of interior spaces with the consequent variety of room shapes, domes, apses, vaults, interior colonnades, niches, and so on. In view of the facts that walls were constructed of cement and stone covered with plaster and that there were few windows, the walls of the interior were essentially uninterrupted.

Stuccowork figured prominently in the enrichment of Roman interiors in the form of painting and relief designs. It formed the base for (1) simulated architectural features such as coffered ceilings, columns with fluting, moldings, and cornices; (2) architectural enrichment typical of the period, including lyres, egg and dart motifs, cupids, caryatids, swans, etc.; (3) decorative relief applied to walls and ceilings in allover designs; and (4) the foundation for wall painting prevalently used to decorate all types of buildings.

The material used most extensively by the Romans was lime plaster. Lime, not found naturally, was calcined calcium carbonate processed from such materials as marble, limestone, and chalk. A second ingredient for purposes of giving body was sand combined with another component such as marble dust, volcanic earth, crushed tile, or alabaster dust; inclusion of the latter components was a function of their availability in a particular geographic region. Vitruvius recommended that preparation of the plaster foundation consist of six layers: three rough undercoats with three top layers of finer plaster composed of lime, sand, and marble dust (or similar material). Archaeological evidence, however, reveals that this recommendation was not always followed.

Techniques for forming damp plaster relief designs varied. One or more of the following methods could be employed: (1) premolded elements applied to the wet plaster base, (2) a mold to press a relief design into the wet plaster, (3) design elements modeled by hand in situ. The higher the relief, the greater the need to have an armature for holding the plaster units in place, such as nails or pegs driven into the undersurface or projecting brick. While wooden tools have largely disappeared, bronze and bone tools provide documentary evidence of how these were used for shaping. To construct a convex molding, for example, the trowel (concave in contour) would be run along the wet plaster to form a continuous molding.

The fresco technique of painting on wet plaster and the use of perspective rendering did much to visually extend enclosed spaces. A smooth, polished plaster surface was essential as a base for fresco painting of fine quality. In addition to the fresco technique, tempera was employed to add details to dry plaster; tempera is an emulsion in which pigment is combined with a binding medium, such as egg, and water. By examining the seams resulting from this technique it is possible to reconstruct not only the order in which work was undertaken but also the amount of work accomplished in a day. For example, wall zones were painted from top to bottom. In one style of wall painting (see later section on walls), seams surrounding small separate pictures in the center of an aedicula suggest that these were painted last. Some styles of painting called for two types of craftsmen to be employed: one a wall painter and the other a more highly skilled and trained picture painter.

Both mosaic and painting lent themselves well to the limitations imposed by the variety of curved shapes that could result from the use of concrete and that demanded flexible techniques. The mosaic technique utilized small pieces (termed *tesserae*) of various materials set in mortar to form a design; materials included, but were not limited to, one or a combination of the following: terra-cotta, marble, glass (including some with gold leaf, twisted glass rods, or cut glass), shells, pebbles, limestone, and mica. Polychrome mosaic could result from either the color of the mortar or that of the tesserae, which tended to be very small. Brilliant indicates that "depending on the fineness of the mosaic, the tesserae range in size from small cubes, about 1 cm. on each edge, to stones with almost nine times the area and six or seven times as deep."[5]

Mosaics were used for floors, walls, and ceilings. The Romans distinguished between floor and wall mosaics; for floors the technique was termed *tesselatum,* while the wall technique was called *opus musivum.* Differences could be in the materials, texture, and shapes of the tesserae. Floors, for example, were more often of stone or terra-cotta with a flat smooth texture, due to functional need. On the other hand, materials for walls and vaults were more often of glass and shells; in light of the materials used wall mosaics were often brighter in color and the tesserae, often of glass, were sometimes set at an angle to capture light and sparkle. However, when color was a factor stone was used for walls and glass was employed for floor tesserae. Shell was inappropriate for floors.

In preparation for laying the mosaic, a cartoon of the design was drawn on the next to last layer of plaster. Then a small portion of the final layer of wet plaster was applied to receive the tesserae, taking into account the space that could be covered before the plaster dried. Occasionally, when complex designs were to be worked, the cartoon was sketched on the final layer of wet plaster before the tesserae were implanted. Another means of setting tesserae was to implant the individual pieces in sand in the final design form, after which a piece of cloth or paper was glued to the arrangement and the tesserae lifted from the sand; sections were then laid in the wet mortar. Finally, after the bedding mortar had set, the paper was removed by soaking it with water to dissolve the glue.

Interior Architecture and Decorative Elements

Interior surfaces—floors, walls, ceiling—can be described broadly as revealing an obsession with ornament and ornamental pattern, a passion for luxurious materials and techniques, a preoccupation with illusionistic devices which treated solid surfaces as transparent or otherwise optimized the dimensionality of the plane, and a predilection to elaborate any surface. These interests were responsible for the animated effects the Romans attained in interior ensembles.

---

5. Richard Brilliant, *Roman Art from the Republic to Constantine* (London: Phaidon Press, 1974), 138.

Floors

Floor design figured prominently in the decorative schemes of the Roman interior. Patterns created by the materials and techniques varied with time. Among the possibilities were terra-cotta laid in a herringbone pattern or in *opus signinum*, where crushed terra-cotta embedded in cement produced a red floor; slabs of polished marble or limestone cut in rectangular shapes, which was expensive; *opus sectile*, in which large pieces of colored stone cut in polygonal shapes were inlaid in abstract and figured patterns; and mosaic, which differed from *opus sectile* in that very small tesserae were used.

The Romans produced simple to highly complex mosaics in intricate detail. While floor mosaics were sometimes laid uniformly in one color without adornment, others were characterized by varied borders and panel shapes framing subjects such as masks, deities, portraits of poets or philosophers, animals, astrological signs, landscapes, and rural scenes. Panel shapes for these were rectangular, octagonal, hexagonal, square, lozenge-shaped, or circular; although a design could be composed of a single panel shape (each laid side by side), complicated arrangements of several shapes were sometimes interwoven in one surface pattern.

Border design for the panels and for the overall composition was often comprised of ornament derived from architecture and textiles, such as the meander, fret, and guilloche. The decorative center of a room was often organized to take into account its architectural frame as well as the position of the openings into spaces. Further, mosaics were sometimes laid to form a border designating the position of the couch.

Chronologically, the early emphasis was on illusionism, where painterly effects were achieved through the use of very small tesserae in minute changes in hue, shade, and tint for modeling. Over the Roman periods of stylistic development changes meant that illusionism was reduced, color was less used for modeling, and the tesserae were enlarged.

In the early period from c. 200-80 B.C. a great deal of attention was given to the use of the illusionistic *emblema* which was a pictorial mosaic set into the decorative scheme of the floor. This unit of design was executed by a specialist who arranged the tesserae in a tray that was then transported to the site; less skilled craftsmen were then responsible for laying the surrounding mosaic. Walls of this period were treated as solid, with little attention to any illusionism that would direct attention beyond the plane.

Geometric arrangements received greater emphasis from c. 60-40 B.C. Less emphasis was given to the use of the illusionistic emblemata for floors; generally, more uniform geometric patterns were preferred. These competed less with walls treated illusionistically during this period. Three-dimensional effects were attained, however, through the use of shaded meanders and other geometric motifs. Polychrome effects were attained using bold, brightly colored marble inserts.

Beginning around the end of the first century B.C. flatness of mosaic design was emphasized for both the floor and the wall, replacing the illusionism and polychrome effects of the previous period. Still geometric and using a great deal of black and white, thin bands were used to define interior architecture; two-dimensional representations of plant forms were sometimes incorporated into the scheme. Mosaic floors were also executed in one color.

Walls

The Romans used painting as the predominant means of treating walls; however, mosaic and stone revetments, along with painted and molded plaster, were also employed. While there was sequential development of the widely recognized painting styles, precise dates cannot be assigned and style characteristics for each period are not discrete, since characteristics of one style began to appear before it became a prominent feature of the next style. Studying the paintings of Pompeii, August Mau first articulated these differences in the late 19th century by assigning them to four groups, according to stylistic features. In chronological order, these were designated as *Incrustation, Architectural, Ornate,* and *Intricate;*

in this discussion, however, the terms first, second, third, and fourth styles will be used. The period covered is from c. 200 B.C. to the end of the 1st century A.D.

In the first style (sometimes referred to as *incrustation,* 200-60 B.C.) walls were treated as solid, with an emphasis on stucco relief to imitate the texture of stone and paint to simulate a wall faced with marble; the effect was plastic and architectonic (see Figure C-1). Colors such as red and yellow were applied as marbling to simulate stones laid as stone masonry. Walls were divided into three zones: dado, middle, and upper; stucco was the medium used to render moldings between zones and for pilasters and capitals. Prominent passageways were given special attention through the use of pilasters to suggest the support of the lintel in trabeated construction.

While the first style relied on stucco for its illusions, the second style (at its height in the mid-1st century B.C.) accomplished illusionism primarily through the use of paint and perspective rendering (see Figure C-2). In fact, the viewer was projected beyond the plane of the wall through the use of architectonic representations that could be interpreted as real three-dimensional construction; trompe l'oeil architecture was all-important. Feigned architectural elements were depicted in such a manner as to make the viewer believe columns were actually supporting a ceiling, for example. Large-scale human figures began to be used. White stucco moldings were employed as for a dentiled cornice at the juncture of the wall and ceiling. Continuing from the first style was the use of simulated stone masonry, but the blocks were depicted as longer and less high. Looking forward to the third style in the late second period was the alteration of painted architectural elements to a less architectonic appearance; for example, proportions of columns were altered to become extremely slender and ornamentation began to be applied to architectural elements. This second phase is sometimes referred to as *architectural,* 60-20 B.C.

The height of popularity for the third style appears to have been from the end of the 1st century B.C. to around the mid-1st century (c. 20 B.C.-A.D.60); this style is sometimes termed *ornate* (see Figure C-3). A stylistic feature having its origin in the late second period was the tendency to deviate significantly from architectural form to primary emphasis on ornamental representation based in architecture, such as columns and pilasters. Architectural elements were extremely attenuated. The inclination was to emphasize the flat plane of the wall and to use brilliant red, black, or white for continuing fields of color. Thin columns, pilasters, and friezes were employed to bound such fields. In these aedicular arrangements[6] illusionistic landscape pictures without great depth were depicted in which the human figure was not the center of interest but of subsidiary interest. Early figurative painting at this time was characterized by delicate color, no strong accents, and clearly drawn figures, isolated and small, with open space around them. Late in the period spaces were filled with action. The wall was still divided into three zones but at the top of the dado an additional horizontal band was inserted on which stylized Egyptian motifs were often portrayed; the impetus for the latter was the fact that Octavius defeated Anthony and Cleopatra in 31 B.C., and in the following year Egypt became a Roman province. In the early part of the third period perspectives that pierced the walls were generally avoided; however, later in the period the wall began to open up again. Painted architectural elements were generally decorated with a pervasive use of delicate ornamentals.

Architectural representations continued in the fourth style (termed *intricate*) with no attempt to copy real architecture; in fact, depth was emphasized with spatial illusionism as the aim (see Figure C-4). Compositions reveal the emphasis to be on space, light (backlight being important), and airy renditions. These fictional units of architecture are reminiscent of stage-building of the Roman theater *(scaenae frons);* a wall was sometimes composed of a stacked series of these. But to emphasize the opaqueness of the wall, panel fields of one color were alternated with illusionistic panels. In addition, textiles provided a source of inspiration for panel design. These were presented in conjunction with painted archi-

---

6 Aedicular arrangements in this situation consisted of fields framed by columns or pilasters and crowned by a pediment.

FIGURE 3-6 Wall Painting, Fourth Style, Bands of Dado. Bands divided into segments with illusionistic perspective drawings. After Original photograph by Michael Larvey, Austin, Texas.

tectural structures and were sometimes centered with figures. Compared to the third style, figurative painting was more forceful, with greater attention to three-dimensional rendering of the human body; the same interest is noted in sculpture of the same period. Parallel with the theatrical architectural renditions and those representing textiles was a third type of panel treatment in which there were side-by-side colored panels in which red, white, and black figured prominently.

In the fourth style the dado was divided into three horizontal bands, as it had been in the third style, but now more extensively (Figure 3-6). It became customary for these bands to be divided into segments for illusionistic perspective drawings.

Stucco moldings, sometimes projecting strongly, were extensively used in the fourth style and often in conjunction with painted detail. For example, a frieze might be decorated with figures, beasts, palmettes, and so on. Also, walls were sometimes plastically conceived through the integral combination of paint and stucco, with architectural elements rendered in plaster and in perspective, along with painted detail.

Although painting was of paramount significance in the Roman decorative scheme, there were other treatments as well. Stone for wall revetments was used, especially for public buildings but in some instances for residential structures; wealthier citizens used this treatment late in the Empire. Porphyry was widely used, characterized by its dark red color in which crystals of white or red feldspar are embedded. Granite, limestone, and marble were also used as veneers. Rarer marbles were sometimes imported from Egypt or the Aegean.

Mosaics that decorated walls were laid in large expanses as well as in small sections. Both columns and pilasters were surfaces to which mosaics were applied. Glass tesserae combined with gold were employed in areas where light could produce animated surfaces and became important in spatial variety. Since these were wall surfaces the tesserae could be angled to enhance contrasts of light and shadow. Vivid, bright surfaces could be attained because of the use of glass as the principal material; both material and technique could produce the same types of pattern and flexibility as painting for use in curved forms resulting from the use of concrete as a structural material.

The Romans introduced the screen wall, composed of columns arranged in front of a load-bearing wall. An entablature was used to unite the two. Columns were the source for other prominent features related to wall design. Wall surfaces were sometimes articulated by the regular placement of pilasters or engaged columns, thus becoming ornamental; decorative use was also made of such architectural features as pediments, capitals, and entablatures. Walls were also penetrated by niches and aediculae.

Windows and Doors

Walls were largely uninterrupted with windows in the Roman interior. When windows were used they were set high in the wall and varied in size. Apertures were covered by sliding wooden shutters, glass, or iron grille gratings; in archaeological examinations of Pompeii glass and lead strips were discovered. In addition, translucent sheets of mica, termed *lapis specularis,* were sometimes used.

Doors, often tall and narrow, were constructed of wood (painted or paneled) or bronze. Cylinders attached to the lintel and the doorsill allowed the doors to pivot; in the Casa del Tramezzo di Legno (House of the Wooden Partition) is an example of three-paneled double doors separating the tablinum from the atrium. The use of a folding gate-like partition that slid into position on bronze pins, as revealed in House of the Bicentenary at Herculaneum, is also indicated. Doors were single- or double-leafed. Frequently the lintel of the door frame extended beyond the jambs of the doorway. As revealed in a painting in the cubiculum of the Villa Boscoreale, near Pompeii, classical orders may have ornamented the frames of doors although they were frequently unadorned. In the Boscoreale painting pilasters with full entablature were indicated in intricate detail; however, full entablatures were not always used for door frames or cased openings. To mark a principal passageway from one space to another (as from the fauces to the atrium or atrium to tablinum or atrium to alae), cased openings were sometimes marked by squared piers (feigned and not essential for structural support); other fictive architectural supports were employed also (see Figure 3-4).

Ceilings

Ceilings were either flat or vaulted; the introduction of concrete contributed to the latter. Curved surfaces lent themselves to the decorative techniques of painting, mosaic, and stucco relief. In addition, coffering, comprised of recessed panels (termed *lacunae*), was used in an allover pattern for both flat and curved ceiling surfaces; frames were made of wood or stucco. The lacunar contours varied—octagonal, square, circular, diamond-shaped—and the centers were embellished with such decorative devices as terra-cotta plaques, painting, mosaic, and flat paint (Figure 3-7).

FIGURE 3-7 Coffered Ceiling. Stucco. Round medallions connected by s-shaped bands. Gemeinnützige, Leonard von Matt, CH-6374 Buochs, Switzerland.

Stucco relief was either modeled in situ or stamped by patterned molds in low relief while the plaster was damp. Here, too, an allover pattern was attained with infinite variation including but not limited to rounder patterns, geometric arrangements of interlocked squares and circles, concentric organizations, interwoven bands encircling rosettes, designs based on textiles, and borders based on carpet. Painted designs such as abstract foliage and flowers, mythological scenes, landscapes, grotesques, sacred scenes, representations of the planetary system, and animals were often rendered within the framework of the foregoing. Stucco framework was sometimes white or white rendered against a colored background, and gold leaf was occasionally employed.

A clearly defined division between the ceiling and wall was often articulated by a stucco cornice molding crowning the wall. Ultimately, however, the division between the two was blurred, possibly in the interest of a more harmonious approach to the design of the interior.

FURNITURE

Although there is a paucity of actual pieces of furniture available for study, documentary evidence from literary sources, reliefs, wall paintings, sarcophagi, and marble and bronze parts extend our knowledge about characteristics of Roman furniture. From these sources it is clear that the Romans relied on Greek prototypes of the Hellenistic period for their inspiration. Generally, Roman furniture displayed an intense interest in opulence and revealed a costly and exuberant taste; it was often more ornate than the Greek. With Roman ascendancy and after Greece became a Roman province in 146 B.C., Rome became the clear disseminator of Greek furniture. It is often difficult to ascertain whether a piece is of Greek or Roman origin; nonetheless, Romans did make original contributions.

Materials and Construction Techniques

The materials used by the Romans in the construction of furniture were wood, metal, and stone. Of the woods that appear to have been most highly valued were maple and citron; however, in addition, beech, oak, holly, willow, fir, cedar, and lime were used. Among the rarer woods, primarily used for decorative purposes, were ebony and satinwood (imported from Africa). Especially useful for outdoor purposes were marble and limestone; in fact, the substantial marble trestle tables were the inspiration for craftsmen of the Italian Renaissance.

Although few examples of wood furniture are extant, metal pieces give a good indication of the characteristic features of Roman furniture. Bronze was the metal most widely used; it was the material for the fulcra (head- or footrests) of couches on an otherwise wooden framework as well as for such pieces as tables and folding stools. The metals, including iron and copper, had the advantage of being sturdy and longer lasting than wood.

Tenons, dowels, nails, and glue were the means used to join parts of furniture, as had been common with Greek craftsmen. For decorative techniques such as veneering and inlay, glue was particularly important.

With their interest in ostentatious display, elaborate methods of ornamentation are noteworthy, including carving, inlay, veneer, painting, plating, and turning. Using the motifs typical of the Romans and the Greeks before them, inlay materials included gold, silver, ivory, tortoiseshell, ebony, and bronze. Although Pliny objected to using a more expensive wood to cover another wood, veneering was common. Painting was employed to simulate the graining of more expensive woods. Plating, in which gold, silver, ivory, and bronze were customary, was used by wealthier citizens. Records reveal that solid gold or silver was occasionally used to construct furniture. The lathe was responsible for the extraordinary diversity of turned members, which provided a decorative note for the most typical furniture forms of the Roman period.

Typical Pieces and Stylistic Features

Seat Furniture

Typical pieces of seat furniture included the throne, chair, couch, and stool. Thrones were depicted as seats for the gods. The base of the throne had either turned legs, rectangular legs with incisions, or solid sides. An infinite variety of complex turnings typified the thrones with turned legs; when there were arms the arm support seems to have been a continuation of the legs. Backs were sometimes paneled. Thrones with rectangular cross-sectioned legs and cut-out incisions followed Greek models closely, while those with solid sides were more substantial and more imposing than Greek prototypes (Figure 3-8). Solid-sided thrones were used for official functions. Backs for these were rounded or rectangular; bases were solid with carved relief designs such as the sphinx, griffins, and winged monsters (Figure 3-9).

A chair, the *cathedra*, drew heavily on the Greek klismos. It was often heavier than its prototype. For example, the curved crest board of the back was sometimes deeper and more strongly curved. A miniature lead chair with straight legs rather than the characteristic curved legs is in the holdings of the British Museum (Figure 3-10).

FIGURE 3-8   Leg of Rectangular Cross Section. Rectangular cross section legs with cut-out incisions based on Greek models. Used on seat furniture and couches.

FIGURE 3-9   Throne. Red marble. Solid supports. Stepped arm. Rounded solid back. Large paw feet.

FIGURE 3-10   Cathedra, Miniature Lead Chair. Based on the Greek klismos but with straight legs. Copyright British Museum.

Stools

Stools form another group of seating furniture, of which the *sella curulis* was of greatest significance. As a seat of honor and symbol of legal authority, it was used by high magistrates or by the emperor; in representations of these it is revealed that the person seated has a higher status than the person standing beside him. Bronze was the material most common for this stool. The major stylistic feature of many of these stools is the double reversed curve (or curved X-form). A sella curulis in the National Museum, Naples, has as a leg ending the head of a fowl (Figure 3-11). An adaptation of the sella curulis is revealed on a coin in the Hunterian Museum, Glasgow, in which the legs are composed of series of straight interlaced staves forming the X-form with a runner foot; the Savonarola chair of the Italian Renaissance is similar (Figure 3-12).

Tables

The Greeks used tables primarily for dining but the Romans had greater use for them, so this type of furniture multiplied. Some tables were collapsible and transportable. Roman tables of great consequence were those with trestle supports, tripods, and those with a single central support. Although the trestle table was used by the Greeks, it was more popular with the Romans (Figure 3-13). The trestle was a substantial piece of furniture with

FIGURE 3-11 Stool of Curule Form. Bronze. Double reversed curve. Legs end in head of fowl. Museo Archeologico Nazionale, Naples.

FIGURE 3-12 Roman coin illustrationg Interlaced Staves for Seat Furniture. Seat form depicted with a series of interlaced staves. Prototype for the Italian Renaissance Savonarola chair.

FIGURE 3-14 Table. Bronze. Three animal legs with terminal paw feet on triangular base with incurved sides. Winged sphinx above animal legs. Museo Archeologico Nazionale, Naples.

either a wooden or a marble top; the solid stone trestles (upright slabs of marble) often had profiles of griffins, satyrs, or other winged animals and monsters the center of which was carved with leaves and flowers. This table was the prototype for the Renaissance refectory table. A particular preference of the Romans appears to have been the tripod table with a round top; some of the tops were in the form of a basin and some in the form of a flat surface. Three handles were attached to the side of the basin. Supports for tripod tables were legs derived from a quadruped; for example, parts of the lion were represented in combination with the head just under the tabletop, followed by the chest, leg, and paw, which rested on the platform. Another example is a table in which the platform is triangular, with concave sides above which legs are designed in two stages: the lower section of quadruped origin, the upper winged sphinxes that form the immediate support for the table top (Figure 3-14). The material was important in terms of the scale of the pieces, since the

FIGURE 3-16 Fulcrum of Couch. Swan's head terminal to fulcrum. Turned legs mounted on floor level stretcher.

bronze tables were more lightly scaled while heaviness characterized those constructed of marble. In the early 19th century these pieces served as inspiration for the English Regency and the French Empire. Other table types included those with the single support and those used for candelabra.

Storage Pieces

Information about storage pieces comes from representations on sarcophagi. Cupboards are depicted as rectangular in form on low legs that continue as stiles for the body of the piece. Closure for these included paneled double doors or curtains, while others revealed open shelves. Functionally, this piece was used for storing household articles, scrolls, and so on.

Beds

Used for dining and reclining, the couch was a common furniture form. The arrangement of couches for dining was to set three at right angles. The position of the fulcra was significant: The upper couch had a headrest; the lower, a footrest; the middle, neither head- nor footrest. Great attention was lavished on the fulcra. Among the forms employed were swans' heads, horses' heads, and the heads and busts of satyrs, lions, ducks, and elephants. The lower end of the fulcra often had a medallion with a head (Figure 3-15). Railings were ornamented with flowers, leaves, mythological scenes, acanthus, palmettes, and rosettes; both inlay (copper, glass, silver) and relief designs were executed on the railings. Turned legs, some with runner feet and others without, appear to have been most prevalent (Figure 3-16). However, some legs were of rectangular section. An innovation of the Romans was the addition of the back to the couch.

ORNAMENT

Both in form and in ornament Roman design was based on Greek prototypes. Floral and leaf arrangements included festoons, wreaths, rinceaux, and arabesques. Human figures were used in wall paintings as well as in three-dimensional support positions. From the animal world, lion, ram, dog, serpent, swan, and eagle motifs were employed. Attention was given to fanciful figures such as the sphinx, grotesques, and griffins. Among the repertoire of other decorative elements the following were used: fret, honeysuckle, anthemion, swastika, and egg and dart.

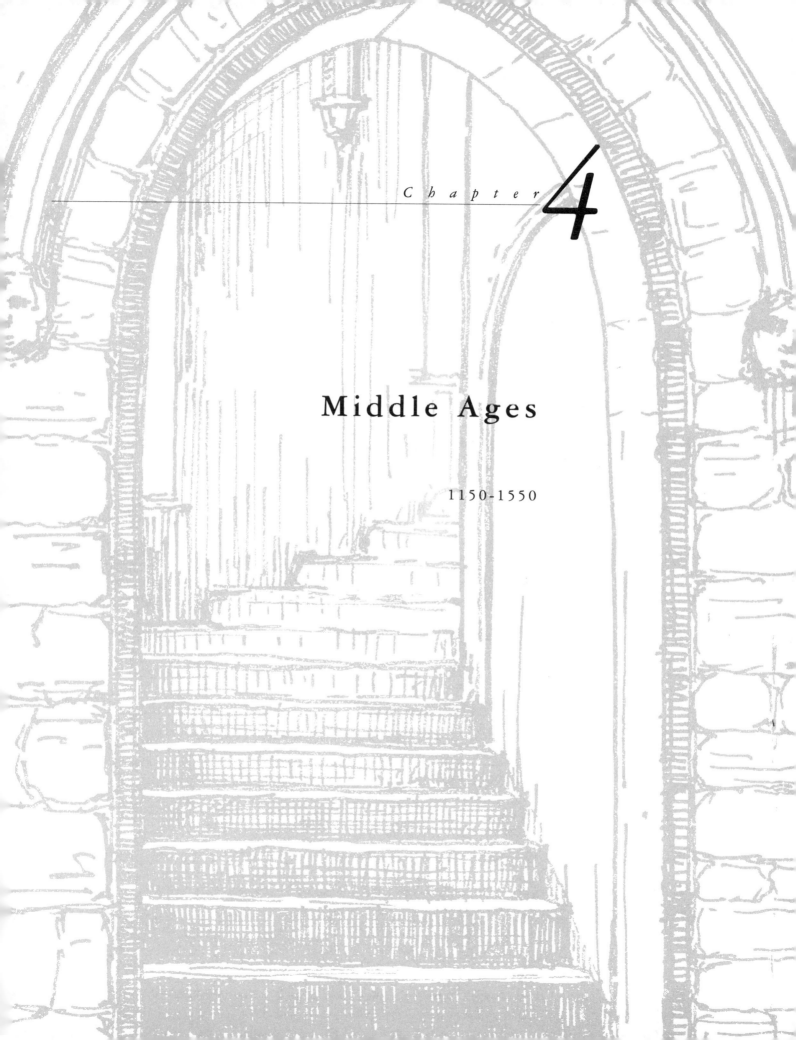

Chapter 4

Middle Ages

1150–1550

HISTORICAL SETTING

From the collapse of the Roman Empire to the end of the Middle Ages two international styles of art had the greatest import for medieval western Europe: Romanesque (mid-11th through the end of the 12th centuries) and Gothic. Romanesque received its impetus from the wealth of the Church, notably from the monasteries. The Gothic style was important for cathedral building throughout the period from the 12th through the 15th centuries; however, as the 13th century progressed greater attention was given to secular architecture, including colleges, castles, fortifications, town halls, and domestic architecture. Ecclesiastical architecture has received extensive analysis; therefore, the thrust of this section will be on domestic interior architecture and the decorative arts of England and France, with emphasis on England.

The feudal system and prevailing unsettled conditions were the major integrally related factors influencing domestic building of the Middle Ages. Feudalism was a social order based on an agricultural economy in which protection was given to the serf, villein, or peasant by the lord of the manor (*seigneur*) in return for use of the land and for services (often military). To maintain such an operation a great man might have as many as 500 serfs in his household, while lower on the social scale the gentry might have an average of 70. Since the Church had extensive land holdings it had great leverage in structuring feudalism; its hierarchical system was somewhat comparable to that of the feudal system.

In the early Middle Ages castles were one response to unsettled conditions under which precedence was given to fortification. This precluded great attention to comfort and luxuries for living quarters. Although the castle served as the military stronghold for the feudal lord, the multistoried keep served as the residential unit; it was centered in a bailey (open ground space) and a concentric arrangement of a walled enclosure with towers and moat(s). The need for fortification influenced interior design through the inclusion of such features as small windows, very thick walls, and the remote location of stairs relative to the main entrance. As castles adapted to more settled conditions in the later Middle Ages they became more like manor houses in their level of comfort. This focus was the result of outdated military tactics requiring less stringent measures for defense and of strengthened monarchical power, with a concomitant decline in conflict among the nobles.

Communal living characterized early medieval living arrangements and this social need was met by the hall, which provided space for yeomen and freeholders as well as for the family of the lord; it was used for sleeping, dining, amusement, and for executive purposes. In the castle setting, when more space was needed for communal living arrangements, a separate building to serve as the hall was sometimes constructed within the walled enclosure; in fact, building expansion in the early period often resulted in a series of loosely connected buildings. Emulation of the living quarters of the feudal lord was subsequently revealed in the smaller houses of those who received protection from and lived in such close proximity to him. The inclusion of the hall ultimately became an integral part of residential planning, as noted in manor houses of the nobility and gentry.

The manor house, like the castle, changed over the course of the Middle Ages. At first defensive in nature, fortification became less vital as the times grew more peaceful. The response to unsettled times is noted in the fact that these structures were built around a courtyard, sometimes fortified by moat and wall.

The monasteries and church officials wielded great power for they were wealthy, had extensive land holdings, and could build profusely. Monasteries also provided protection for their dependents and housed them in various buildings. As well, these dependents constructed houses in towns that grew up around the monasteries; both in material and environment these structures reflected the region in which they were built. Within the community surrounding the monastery, craftsmen practiced their trade in shops within their residences. Through the support of the bishops and abbots for the designers of cathedrals, artists, and craftsmen, their influence on architecture was remarkable. The clergy upheld exceedingly high standards of craftsmanship; as a consequence of the the dissolution of the

English monasteries by Henry VIII in the 16th century, standards of craftsmanship declined, lacking the supervision of the clerics. The religious zeal of the period is reflected in the emphasis given to the construction of splendid cathedrals. This fervor is attested to by the fact that the inclusion of a chapel within houses of the nobles was imperative.

A transient lifestyle typified the Middle Ages in part due to volatile conditions and, in the case of the nobility, widely scattered land holdings that needed supervision. In view of this, lords and their retainers relocated frequently, which might require one to two moves a month. Permanence in furnishings was precluded; therefore, valuable furnishings needed to be transportable to be installed in the new environment. Tapestries, an important part of the interior decoration, were easily portable; the vacant rooms in the new setting could be quickly transformed into more comfortable spaces with pictorial appeal. Another example of the influence of transience and unsettled conditions is reflected in instances where the rare glazed windows were removed and stored in a secure location while the lord made his circuit of visits.

Geographically, England was in an insular position, which led to different directions in architecture (both exterior and interior) and furniture design. However, historical events led to intercourse with other countries, allowing the English to assimilate international ideas. Two in particular should be mentioned: contact with France and the Crusades undertaken by European Christians. In part, the influence from France was a result of the marriage of Henry II to Eleanor of Aquitaine (whose marriage to Louis VII of France was annulled); thus the French and English began the struggle over the duchy of Aquataine, culminating ultimately in the Hundred Years War (1337-1453). Eleanor established her own court at Poitiers, which became the center of great artistic activity. English forces occupied more than half of France during the conflict; a manifestation of this influence resulted in the unification of traditionally diverse buildings into a quadrangular arrangement around a court. Interchange of artistic ideas also resulted from the Crusades, undertaken between the 11th and 14th centuries in an attempt to regain the Holy Land, which was under Muslim rule. Eastern influence was felt particularly from the Fourth Crusade, which was diverted to Constantinople, where the Europeans were exposed to the arts of the Byzantine Empire.

Trade arrangments both at home and with other countries also led to international influences on the arts of England. In the early 15th century the need of the Netherlands for English wool promoted sheep-growing in certain districts of England. Thus, increased industrial activity brought increased wealth and prosperity, which in turn stimulated domestic building activity on the part of prosperous yeomen and traders.

Climate had a part to play in the design of domestic architecture. Steep pitches for the roof to dispense with snow and rain yielded elaborate and complex structural details, since the hall was frequently two stories tall and the roof timbers were exposed.

France was subject to the same influences as the English. Fortification was essential for monasteries, castles (châteaux), town houses (hôtels), and palaces; towns were also reinforced against marauders by town walls. Castles were placed on high ground above rivers and featured some of the same defensive measures as their English counterparts, but as times became more peaceful they were converted into residences; typically, they had a domestic courtyard with a medieval spiral staircase. Town houses, largely built by wealthy merchants and church dignitaries, were arranged around a courtyard with a medieval staircase in the center.

SPATIAL RELATIONSHIPS

Modifications to the space plan that occurred over the Middle Ages were a response to changed functional demands on the part of the household as well as to adjusted needs regarding fortification. At first, assorted separate structures formed the medieval compound, but as the demand for safety measures became paramount these were consolidated into more compact buildings. Two types of plans emerged, one based on a walled enclosure and the second based on a central court. The first, often a castle, was a concentric arrangement of one or two moats and walled enclosures in the center of which was the keep; not only was it a stronghold but also a residential unit. In the second arrangement the court was encompassed by accommodations for communal living, private spaces, and service quarters; it should be noted, however, that even manor houses were sometimes surrounded by a moat and walled enclosure. Purposes of spaces important at the beginning of the medieval period were modified; more specialized rooms were added to meet new functional demands and provisions for greater privacy were incorporated. These reflected greater attention to domestic comfort within the framework of diminished need for massive fortified structures and accrued wealth from commercial activities. The primary public spaces affected by modifications were the hall, great chamber, and chapel. However, at the beginning of the period the space of greatest significance was the hall.

Spatial Features of the Floor Plan and Three-Dimensional Spatial Characteristics

Communal living was organized around the hall in early medieval houses. The lord with his retainers and tenants used it for sleeping, dining, recreation, administration of justice, calls to arms, ritual, reception of guests, and living room. As functional and social needs shifted over the course of the Middle Ages, this space finally became an entrance hall in the late Tudor period in England, during the reign of Elizabeth I, 1558-1603. At first the hall might have been a separate building, but later it had standard relationships to the kitchen, buttery, and pantry, the screens passage, and private spaces as they emerged.

Early in the Middle Ages the disposition of space within the hall was based on an ecclesiastical model of an aisled arrangement in which a row of columns separated the nave from the aisles. However, new structural techniques for roofing were initiated, leading to the concomitant ability to span greater distances without intermediate support. The hall was usually two stories in height and was located at ground level or on the first floor above ground level. These uninterrupted open spaces could be expansive in influential households; for example, at Penshurst, Kent, the hall was 2615 square feet, while the Bishop's Palace at Wells was 6842 square feet; Poundisford Park, Taunton, is representative of many smaller halls with a square footage of 448. Until the wall fireplace became standard, the central open stone hearth was common in houses where the hall was at ground level; a louver in the roof allowed for the dispersion of smoke.

The entrance to the hall was from the screens passage at the lower end of the hall (Figure 4-1). The screen separated the hall from this cross passage, which led to courts on either side of this nucleus of the medieval house. Normally there were two doorways in the screen; above the screen, forming the ceiling of the screens passage, was the musicians' gallery opening to the hall (Figure 4-2). Leading to this prominent (and often decorative) feature was first a *spere* (a short screen set perpendicular to the long wall of the hall), then a movable screen, and, finally, the screen that was incorporated into the structure of the building. The purpose of each of these was to divert drafts from the central hearth. The extension of the screen to its full width gave the best protection from drafts and wind.

At the upper end of the hall (opposite the screen) was the dais, a raised platform reserved for the lord to oversee his subjects; with the lord seated in the center of the great high table, family and important guests were seated on each side of him. The dais was the focal point of the hall both because of its elevated position and the accompanying decorative enhancement at this end of the hall; these proclaimed the hierarchial status of the lord. Embellishments behind the great high table might include such elements as a bay window, tapestries, or a cloth of estate. Flexibility in the hall was paramount to meet the many functional demands on this space. Therefore, tables for dining were arranged longitudinally, perpendicular to the great high table and dais, and since these consisted of boards placed on trestles they could easily be dismantled to meet other purposes of this space.

FIGURE 4-1 Plan of Haddon Hall, Derbyshire (built in stages from c. 1375). Earliest structure with darkened walls. A porch; B Screen passage; C hall; D parlor; E wine cellar; F passage to kitchen; G buttery, H court; I chapel. Lodgings around court. Architectual Book Publishing Co. Stamford, CT.

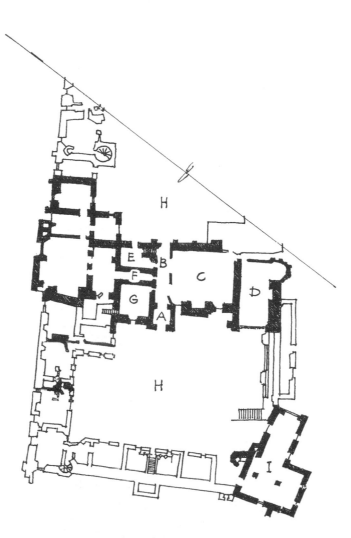

FIGURE 4-2 Hall Screen of Haddon Hall, Derbyshire (1475). Screen with two of three doors beyond leading to service area. Minstrel gallery above. Courtesy of Country Life Picture Library

From the dais the lord could retreat to the privacy of the chamber (first termed *solar*), located either at the ground level or on the first floor. The withdrawal of the lord from communal living in the hall to the chamber led to alterations in the stair, the chamber itself, and the size of the hall. At first access to the first floor chamber was by a narrow spiral stairway, but as the chamber began to be used for official functions as a room of state, the stair gradually received greater prominence through increasing breadth and magnificent treatment.

Earlier the chamber fulfilled the need of the lord for greater privacy, comfort, and solitude; occasionally, private meals were taken there, although dining was primarily in the hall. Alterations probably originated in royal households based on the following: (1) the decision of the king to move the great high table to the chamber; (2) the removal of the bed from the great chamber to a room beyond; (3) allocation of the chamber to the status of a room of state for more public ceremonial occasions, which in turn necessitated new spaces to which the family could withdraw for meals and other spaces for privacy beyond. Beginning with the chamber the sequence of spaces was chamber, withdrawing room, bedchamber, dressing, closet. A sequence of spaces ranged from more public and ceremonial spaces (the great chamber) to those which were most private (closet). Since corridors were not yet a commonly accepted feature of the floor plan, these were thoroughfare rooms whereby a person must travel through each space to access the next room in sequence.

The chamber gradually became a splendid backdrop in its function as a room of state, instead of a room in which routine activities of daily life took place. Its function changed over the medieval period. Finally, it was both architecturally and decoratively significant in concept and formality. It became typical to locate it on the first floor and sometimes make it open to the roof.

The most private space was the closet. It was used by the lord for meditation and most personal devotions as well as for business matters. Sometimes the closet (oratory) was merged with the chapel whereby the closet was placed to look down onto the chapel; the lord could hear mass from his most private space.

While they did not replace the parish church, chapels were often incorporated within the residence of the houses of great men and more wealthy landowners. The celebration of mass was an everyday occasion, and marriage ceremonies and christenings were held there sometimes as well. To oversee these functions in households of means, both clergy and choir were sometimes in the employ of the lord. One frequent location of the chapel was near the dais end of the hall at ground level, just beyond the parlor. Occasionally it was placed on the first floor near the lodgings.

The origin of the parlor is uncertain, but it is known that early in the Middle Ages these spaces were part of the monastic dwelling; documentary evidence points to secular use of the parlor by the latter part of the 14th century. At Haddon Hall it was placed adjacent to the hall as an informal space (see Figure 4-1). It appears to have been used as a sitting room and as a dining room; it was not part of the ceremonial system. By the early 16th century it was used exclusively as a dining and reception room.

Lodgings could be either suites of rooms or single spaces, the extent of which depending on the wealth and social position of the landowner. Those rooms reserved for important guests might have two or three chambers and a privy (garderobe). These spaces were used by whomever the lord of the manor designated—important visitors, retainers, servants (more substantial lodgings were deemed appropriate for higher echelons of servants). Regardless of who inhabited a designated room, was considered his/her private space. While no one location within the floor plan was typical, at Haddon Hall these spaces were arranged around the court (see Figure 4-1).

Privies were important ancillary spaces variously termed garderobe, latrine, privy, privy chamber, and so on. Girouard suggests that the term " 'privy chamber' seems to have been used both for the room through which a privy was reached and for the privy itself." [1] Frequently the privy was placed over a shaft for the disposal of waste.

While architecturally insignificant, service rooms were highly important in the operation of the household. These included such spaces as kitchen, buttery, pantry, bakehouses, slaughterhouses, brewery, etc. The most important of these—kitchen, buttery, and pantry—were located beyond the screens passage near the lower end of the hall (see Figure 4-2). Opposite the screen were three doors that provided access to these spaces: one door to the pantry, one to the buttery, and between these, a door to a corridor that led to the kitchen. To oversee certain designated spaces, servants were highly specialized; for example, the yeoman of the pantry dispensed bread while the yeoman of the buttery distributed beer.

The principle spaces of the medieval household were incorporated in most houses of any size at the end of the period; these included the kitchen, great chamber, chapel, lodgings, and hall. Architecturally, the timber framing of the open trusses of the hall was the most significant in terms of the articulation of interior space. A *truss* (a rigid frame, normally a triangular arrangement) was composed of a variety of members. Briefly described in terms of a rectangular hall, the longitudinal walls served as the upright supports on which a beam (sometimes referred to as a *wall plate*) was laid longitudinally. Connecting the wall plates across the shorter span of the space was a *tie beam;* this structural member was the base of the truss. At the apex of the roof or ceiling was the *ridgepole,* a horizontal member of the sloping ceiling. From each longitudinal wall the rafters connected the wall plate and the ridgepole; thus, the juxtaposition of the rafters (connected to the ridgepole and wall plate) and the tie beam formed the triangular frame of the truss. *Purlins* were horizontal structural members that connected the roof rafters. *Collar beams* were sometimes employed to join opposite rafters. Some of the more common open trusses used in the medieval hall were aisled, crown-post, cruck, and hammer beam.

Each of the foregoing had a primary influence on the distinct character of the spaces defined. The ceiling plane in the hall was the most prominent focal point of this space and when it was, in addition, the most decorative of the open trusses, the amount of attention it commanded was intensified. Distances of span were governed by materials and construction technique, as noted in earlier discussions; therefore, if the distance was too great it was essential that intermediate support be included. In *aisle construction* the space was divided into a central nave and aisles, as in ecclesiastical architecture (Figure 4-3). To support the truss, then, *arcade posts* were set in from the wall to serve as support for arcade plates (beams, placed longitudinally, that were equivalent to the wall plate described in the description of the truss without aisles). This system allowed for more floor space but, on the other hand, space was obstructed with the arcade posts defining the aisles. In *crown-post* construction, within the framework of the truss pairs of opposed rafters were joined by collars, underneath which was the *crown plate* (beam), which ran parallel with and below the

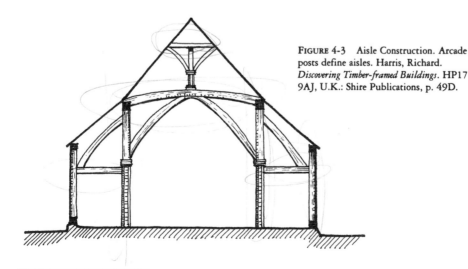

FIGURE 4-3 Aisle Construction. Arcade posts define aisles. Harris, Richard. *Discovering Timber-framed Buildings.* HP17 9AJ, U.K.: Shire Publications, p. 49D.

1. Mark Girouard, *Life in the English Country House: A Social and Architectural History* (Harmondsworth, Middlesex, England: Penguin Books Ltd., 1980), 57.

FIGURE 4-4   Crown Post Construction. Crown posts of varying cross section connect tie beam to crown plate. Harris, Richard. *Discovering Timber-framed Buildings*. HP17 9AJ, U.K.: Shire Publications, p. 49A and p. 62, Fig. 32.

ridgepole (proportionate relationships varied). A *crown post* originating in the center of the tie beam connected the tie beam to the crown plate. The decorative potential lay in the use of moldings and in the pattern of bracing that originated from the connection of the crown post to the tie beam, collar, and crown plate. The cross section of the crown post could be cruciform, octagonal, chamfered, rebated, etc. Evidence suggests that this type of decorative treatment was associated with dwellings of families of high status.

Cruck buildings appear to have been first used by the upper strata of society (Figure 4-5). In this type of construction pairs of curved structural members (termed *crucks*) originated at the sill and extended to the ridgepole. In the ceiling the crucks were connected to the tie beam or collar. They braced the roof purlins; the latter supported the rafters and were placed longitudinally between the wall plate and ridgepole. In *hammer beam* construction a short beam projected at wall plate level and was perpendicular to it (Figure 4-6). From below it was supported by a curved brace alone or, additionally, it was sometimes used with a corbel and wall post. The hammer beam then carried an arched brace above. The effect was to allow greater spans of uninterrupted floor space. With the potential for greatest elaboration, carving or paint was used to embellish the structural parts.

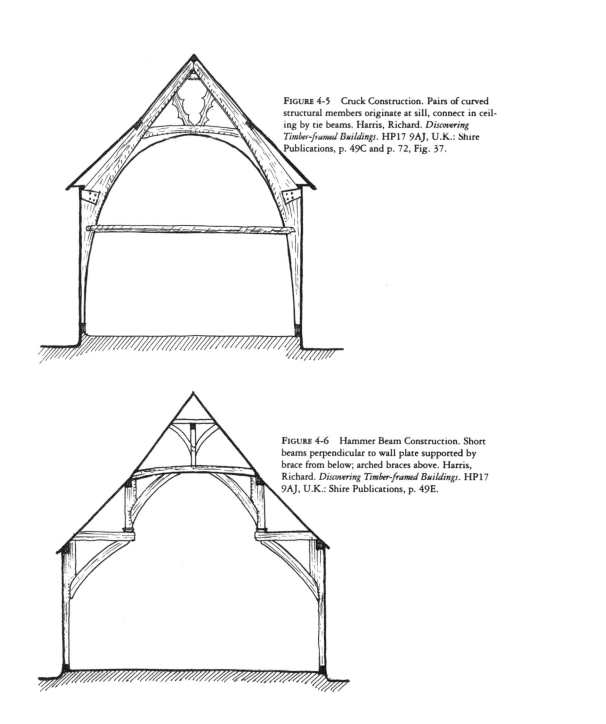

FIGURE 4-5 Cruck Construction. Pairs of curved structural members originate at sill, connect in ceiling by tie beams. Harris, Richard. *Discovering Timber-framed Buildings.* HP17 9AJ, U.K.: Shire Publications, p. 49C and p. 72, Fig. 37.

FIGURE 4-6 Hammer Beam Construction. Short beams perpendicular to wall plate supported by brace from below; arched braces above. Harris, Richard. *Discovering Timber-framed Buildings.* HP17 9AJ, U.K.: Shire Publications, p. 49E.

INTERIOR ARCHITECTURE AND DECORATION

Both secular and religious ritual were played out in the public areas and the lord displayed wealth and power through prominent decorative and architectural features. Each of these elements was important in articulating interior spaces.

Materials and Decorative Techniques

Wood, ceramics, stone, and plaster were the materials that provided the base for the decorative techniques employed in the medieval period. These correlated with the status of the household. Prominent decorative techniques included painting and carving.

Carving was used on paneling and on structural parts; painting was sometimes used in conjunction with it. Enhancement with paint was through flat color application as well as decorative treatments, among which were simulations of masonry by using colored lines on plaster washes, ornamental detail applied to friezes, and figurative events on such areas as friezes or murals on walls.

Interior Architecture and Decorative Elements

Floors

Materials used for the floor of the medieval period included flagstone, brick, tile, wood, and plaster. When compacted earth was not used for the ground floor, the favored material was stone slab, which varied by region of the country; slate, granite, marble, and sandstone would have been in the better residences. Earthenware tiles varied in color, size, and shape. Checkerboard arrangements were sometimes employed with insertions of figurative representations including those of the animal world, heraldic devices, and faces. It was the practice to scatter rushes over floors (especially in the hall), as revealed by a letter written by Erasmus (before 1530) to a physician of Cardinal Wolsey: "The floors are commonly of clay, strewed with rushes, under which lies unmolested an ancient collection of beer, grease, fragments, bones, spittle, excrements of dogs and cats, and everything that is nasty."[2] Wide oak planks were common for upper floors. Although carpets were not normally used, woven rush matting was widely employed by all classes.

Walls

Interior wall surfaces were primarily of wood and plaster. Textiles and the integral use of paint, murals, and carved relief provided the chief decorative applications.

At first the wainscot consisted of plain boards with chamfered edges that were laid vertically between either upright planks or studs; it was often painted a flat green color. Additionally, wooden wall surfaces were applied by the clapboard technique where, on the room side, the surface could be flush or reveal an overlap of the boards (Figure 4-7).

> The workman grooved one edge of a board and then cut one side of the groove to a knife-edge. One edge of the adjoining board was then planed to a feather edge so as to fit tightly into the groove of its neighbour and fade away just at the knife-edge of the groove. Where used for a partition or where the boarding was to be visible on both sides, the flush side presented a beautifully even surface broken only by the fine lines of the vertical joints; so fine were these that they could easily be stopped with paint or plaster, and were admirably adapted as a ground upon which to apply painted decoration in colors.[3]

Although wood paneling was introduced in the medieval period for screens, it was more prominently employed in the 16th century (Figure 4-8). At this time it may have been used only on the lower part of the wall. Paneling was framed by *stiles* (vertical wood pieces) and *rails* (horizontal), with the panel being thinned on the edges to fit into these framing members. Carving on the panel surfaces featured such motifs as linenfold, grapevines, and ogive.

For plaster walls whitewash was often employed, but color applications were also used; for example, simulation of masonry was attained through the use of colored lines on whitewash. Additionally, painted friezes or murals were utilized. Subjects for the murals included religious themes (nativity scenes, the lives of saints, etc.), lives of great men, wars, hunting, court life. While murals were employed for decorative purposes in Great Britain and

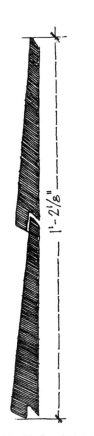

1'- 2⅛"

Figure 4-7 Clapboard Technique. Wall construction allowing flush wall surface on one side and overlap of boards on the other. Architectural Book Publishing Co.

2. A translation as quoted in Nathaniel Lloyd, *A History of the English House from Primitive Times to the Victorian Period* (Northam, Sussex: Great Dixter, 1931; reprint, London: The Architectural Press, 1975), 80. page citations are to the reprint edition.
3. Ibid, 73–74.

on the Continent, they were more widely used in the Mediterranean area in the permanent residences of nobles or monarchs. If castles were visited only rarely, walls were often undecorated.

Woolen cloths, painted canvas, and tapestries were other forms of decorative treatment for walls. These textile hangings were typically located on the upper part of the wall and hung on pegs. To bring attention to the dominant part of the hall textiles were hung at the dais end. The advantage of using textiles was the fact that they were easily transportable and installed as families moved from residence to residence. Subjects for figurative tapestries included those of mural paintings: religious themes, epic deeds of legendary or historic heroes, hunting scenes, and heraldic (genealogical) motifs. The lower part of the wall was often treated with wainscot in the great houses.

Windows and Doors

The size and shape of windows varied as the need for defensive measures decreased and as wealth increased through the medieval period. Early in the period very small windows were typical, while later the area devoted to windows was larger and lighter. Within any one residence it would have been typical to have windows of different configurations; for example, at 13th-century Little Wenham Hall, Suffolk, the façades consisted of lancet windows at ground level while at other levels there were rectangular openings; lights were triple, double, or single, with an embracing (or containing) pointed arch.

These same differences would have been reflected on the interior in terms of the number of lights but, while on the exterior the window was set near the surface of the façade, on the interior the deep embrasure was widely splayed, reflecting the thickness of the wall. A window seat was often constructed within the splayed depth. The contour of the embrasure for the whole may have been similar to or different from that of the

---

4. A dripstone or hood-mold was a molding that projects from the surface of the building; its purpose was to deflect rain. The contour varied from rectangular to round to pointed. Similar moldings used on doorways and window openings of the interior were decorative.

exterior. A case in point is the Manor House, Martock, Somerset, in which, on the exterior, cinquefoil lights outlined with a pointed arch were set within a dripstone or hood-mold[4] (in this case rectangular to encompass the two-light windows) (Figure 4-9). However, on the interior, the rectangular encompassing dripstone molding was omitted but the transom cinquefoil lights (popular in the 15th century) outlined with the lancet arch were retained. The aperture of the deeply splayed embrasure reflects the profile of the five-lobed cinquefoil lights.

Throughout the medieval period both square and pointed window heads were used. When glass was not available to small householders of the 13th, 14th, and 15th centuries, vertical wooden bars set diagonally were regularly spaced across the openings. Wooden shutters on the inside provided protection against the elements. One means of operation of the shutters was the provision of grooves in the sill and the wall plate along which the shutters slid. Other means of attachment included hook and strap hinges; iron bands, to secure the boards, that slid into the reveals of the wall; and hinges at the sill that required a prop when pushed up. Examples of transomed windows with glazed upper lights and wooden shutters for the lower portion exist. Shutters were occasionally fretted, painted, and pierced.

Before glass became generally available late in the medieval period, the covering material for windows could have been thin horn, waxed paper, or oiled linen, each of which was secured with wooden lattice. During the reign of Henry VII windows, instead of being considered part of the structure of the house, were deemed to be part of the furnishings. The value attached to these glazed windows can be discerned in the practice of removing and storing them in a secure place when the owners traveled away from home for extended periods of time. When glass was used panes were diamond-shaped and set in lead; then, through the use of wires, the panes were attached to holes in wrought-iron frames. At first windows were stationary; later, casements were mounted on hooks with decorative latches.

The configuration for windows varied. Although square-headed windows were used, arched frames were very common. The trend in arch configuration was that in the 15th century they became flattened and were common in the 16th century. Common curves for the arches included lancet, ogee, and the four-centered arch. In the 13th century the two-light lancet window was predominant, the proportions of which were slender; plate tracery, in the form of a quatrefoil or other decoration, was cut into the stone of the spandrel above the two lights. Bar tracery was introduced into England from France in the 13th century; in this type of tracery the geometrical spandrel decoration consisted of

FIGURE 4-10 Door. Rectangular hood mold ending in decorative bosses. Successive rectangular frames surround three sides of the arch with ornamental spandrels. Drawing after a photograph by Hugh Braun, taken from *An Introduction to English Mediaeval Architecture*, p. 256 © 1967.

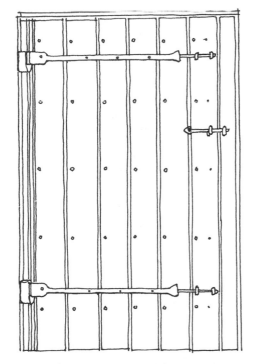

FIGURE 4-11 Door. Board and batten with strap hinges. From Calloway, Steven. *The Elements of Style*. © 1991. Michael Beazley Publishers, a division of Reed Books.

FIGURE 4-12 Door. Linenfold carved door panels. From Calloway, Steven. *The Elements of Style*. © 1991. Michael Beazley Publishers, a division of Reed Books.

lines continuing from the mullions to converge in the spandrel, forming a network of intersecting ribs.

Examples of doors from the medieval period reveal them to be sometimes ornamental and sometimes simple. The openings for doors usually had arched heads set within either arched or rectangular moldings; rectangular heads were also set within rectangular moldings. Typical arches included four-centered, two-centered, and ogee. The decorative development of doors is similar to that of windows and fireplaces. The following comments successively relate to the outer moldings (hood-mold) and work toward the door opening (door head). When the arch was a prominent design feature the hood-mold capped the overall design and duplicated the curves of the adjacent arch; the hood-mold often ended with decorative bosses at the springline for the next arch in sequence. A rectangular frame combined with the arch at the door head could also begin with a rectangular hood-mold followed by a rectangular frame enclosing a four-centered arch; the spandrels in such cases were often sunken and ornamentally treated with tracery (Figure 4-10). Decorative detail of the period included such motifs as crenellated moldings, crockets, quatrefoils (and variants), and ball-flowers.

Door leaves were primarily of the board and batten variety, comprised of vertical boards on one side secured with horizontal battens on the reverse; the number of battens could be discerned by the position of the nail heads (Figure 4-11). Strap hinges were attached to the door jamb by hooks or piv-

FIGURE 4-13 Hooded Chimneypiece (c.1180). Joggled lintel supported by corbels. Based on a photograph. Architectural Book Publishing Co., Inc.

FIGURE 4-14 Chimneypiece. Firebox opening of four-centered arch set in rectangular frame with ornamental spandrels; decorative frieze and cornice above. From the Keep at Tattasall Castle, Lincolnshire, England.

oted on a plate set within the jamb. Late in the period paneling was sometimes employed, with carved designs on the panel, as linenfold (Figure 4-12). The linenfold motif was so called because it resembled loosely folded linen; some historians see symbolic significance in the depiction of linen folded over the chalice.

Chimneypieces

Having met the most rudimentary functional needs with the central hearth, chimneypieces became significant sculptural renditions for interior architecture over the medieval period. The location of the hearth was first moved in front of and on a long stone wall where a hood dispelled the smoke through a hole in the wall. Later the hearth was recessed into the wall. When full height flues were introduced the flue was often framed in timber and coated with plaster of lime and horsehair on the outside and with dung and horsehair on the inside.

A pyramidal hood began to be used in the 12th century. The lowest of the structural sequence of supports for a hooded fireplace were corbels and the joggled lintel. Of stone or wood, a *corbel* extended from the surface of the wall as a support for the lintel; the corbel ends were frequently carved and often graduated into narrower shafts or jambs below. A *joggled lintel* was composed of pieces in which the projection of one piece fitted into a corresponding indentation in an adjacent part; the purpose of the joggled lintel was to prevent slippage (Figure 4-13). Following this construction approach it became common to have a long central lintel in which only the ends were joggled. A molded string course was frequently placed between the lintel and the initial slope of the hood. Usually there was no mantel shelf. Sometimes lamp brackets were located at the lintel level and at the juncture of the wall and projecting hood. The pyramidal hood was used longer in France than in England.

Although sometimes the design of the chimneypiece was reminiscent of the hood when the hearth became recessed into the wall, one form introduced in the late 14th century became very typical of the 15th century (Figure 4-14). The configuration consisted of

5. Margaret Wood, *The English Mediaeval House* (London: Phoenix House, 1965), 266-267.

the four-centered arch heading the firebox opening and set within a rectangular frame in which ornamental spandrels were important; above this were a decorative frieze and cornice. This structure was sometimes bordered on the outside by engaged columns, the capitals of which typically continued the moldings of the cornice. Often executed in brick, a discharging (relieving) arch of segmented form surmounted the whole.[5]

Another form used in the 14th century and which continued in the 15th century was one with a molded surround for the rectangular firebox opening. A decorative frieze or a frieze combined with a cornice was the surmounting treatment. Frequent use was made of a series of square panels centered with ornament typical of the period for the adornment of the frieze. Although many of this type were flush with the wall sometimes a mantel shelf was incorporated.

A number of decorative motifs were used on the frieze, cornice, and spandrels; these were carved and sometimes both carved and painted. Examples of embellishment for the frieze included side-by-side placement of panels of cinquefoil arches; a series of quatrefoils combined variously with such motifs as the shield, patera, merchant's marks, and flowers; and a running vine ornament. Adornment for the cornice could include such motifs as shields, heraldic ornaments, fruit, and running ornaments; the cornice was sometimes crenellated and spires with crockets were also occasionally incorporated in the design. Spandrels were carved with foliation, quatrefoils, shields with tracery, and other designs.

Ceilings

The most commanding ceiling of the medieval period was that of the hall, which extended two stories in height and featured the structural detail of open beams supporting the pitched roof. Prevalent ceiling constructions were defined in the section on spatial features of the floor plan and three-dimensional spatial characteristics. Carved ornament was sometimes added at structural points. Two examples: (1) the rose with the rays of Edward IV where the tie beams joined the curved braces underneath at Stokesay, Shropshire, and (2) alternating representations of the heads of kings or bishops at the ends of hammer beams at Pilgrim's Hall, Winchester. The surfaces of hammer beams as well as spandrels within the structural system were also sculpted with ornament of the period.

Exposed beams were employed for flat ceilings also and in the late 15th century the soffits were carved. When the beams were not square in cross section they were laid flat, in which case it was common for the spacing between them to be about the width of the beam, an indicator of the medieval period. Another treatment for flat ceilings was to use thin boards (joined by tongue and groove) to which were applied molded strips of wood to simulate paneling. At the juncture of the molded ribs were carved bosses; materials used for these were wood or sometimes wood combined with lead. Occasionally, molded ribs also divided papier-mâché panels executed in relief designs. For ceilings in residences of the upper classes painting sometimes filled the spaces between beams, liernes, and ribs of vaulted ceilings. Sometimes molded strips of wood were applied to a flat boarded ceiling dividing it into panels. Paintings were similar to those of stained-glass windows. At Haddon Hall a painted checkerboard design is interspersed with heraldic devices (see Figure 4-8).

In ecclesiastical architecture heraldic motifs were used symbolically to be understood by an uneducated populace. To denote position and/or identity they were used by guilds, trade associations, and city governments, as well as by royal and noble families. Unicorns, flowers, crowns, chains, keys, and other emblems were carved on wood and stone and painted on glass.

Stairways

Both circular and straight flights of stairs were constructed during the medieval period. The most typical interior stair was circular and of the newel type. This class of staircase, having been an architectural feature of the preceding Norman period, was primarily utilitarian in that it served a defensive purpose when placed in turrets, and although it

FIGURE 4-15   Stairs. Circular stairs framed with lancet hood molding ending in decorative bosses. Architectural Book Publishing Co. Stamford, CT.

continued to be used over the period under discussion, its protective function was to become inconsequential. Starting at the ground and rising to the roof, the newel staircase had a central post to support the curved narrow ends of the steps (Figure 4-15). Treads were of wood, stone, or brick. Outside stairs to the residence were straight and often included one turn.

FURNITURE

Like interior design, English and French furniture styles were governed by some of the same influencing factors: unsettled conditions, the role of monastic communities and guilds in maintaining standards of workmanship, and the correlation between architecture and furniture design. However, the outcome in terms of artistic quality differed. While there is a dearth of furniture extant representing the medieval period, information to supplement the few surviving pieces of furniture comes from such contemporary primary sources as wills, descriptions in inventories, representations in works of art, and illuminated manuscripts.

Often nomadic due to the constant upheaval of the period, upper-class families and medieval kings traveled from residence to residence with a few pieces of furniture that were constructed to meet the need for transportability. Typically the articles taken with them were simple and often crudely built chests, tables, and chairs; left behind in the castles was the heaviest furniture, such as dining tables, beds, and built-in pieces. Along with the portable furniture were textiles, which had the advantages of being particularly lightweight and of providing quick decorative enhancement in the new abode.

Both guilds and monastic communities were influential in supporting crafts. Monastic groups emerged as a force in crafts in the 12th and 13th centuries. They were instrumental in maintaining high standards of workmanship; when their influence was absent the criterion of workmanship was often crude.

In the 12th century craft guilds grew quickly and continued in importance until the 17th century in England, while in France their influence continued until the late 18th century. When the craft guilds set standards of workmanship and price, their role was extensive. Further, they were influential in (1) establishing and protecting the status of their members in society; (2) preventing intrusion from other localities; and (3) specifying an orderly training system based on levels of competence in craftsmanship, designated by the titles of apprentice, journeyman, and master.

English and French furniture was similar in its simplicity of form—rectangular, vertical, bulky, and sturdy. Significant differences lay in the fact that French pieces were more highly finished and showed greater skill in the arrangement of design elements with more impressive aesthetic character.

In both England and France, analogies can be drawn to illustrate a relationship between architecture and furniture design. It was a period of high religious devotion and both structural and decorative elements from architecture influenced the form and ornament of medieval furniture. For example, spires of the Gothic cathedral were the model for furniture finials on which crockets (bud-like protrusions) were carved. Circular tracery on furniture resembled the rose windows of architecture. Reflecting trends in 15th century architecture, English furniture became simpler, while at the same time French forms grew more complex.

Materials and Construction Techniques

Wood was the primary material for furniture of the medieval period. Most early English furniture of this era was of oak, which was indigenous to England; valuable but rare were deal and chestnut. Walnut was a favored wood in France.

Techniques of construction became more refined over the period. However, early chests, heavy and crudely constructed, were sometimes fashioned from hollowed logs bound by iron straps. Board or plank construction was an advance and lighter in weight. In the latter it was possible for a chest to be constructed of six boards (lid, bottom, front and back, two end pieces extended to form the support of the piece). The front and back pieces were rabbeted to receive the end pieces and secured by oak dowels or iron nails; the lid was attached by wrought iron strap hinges. A cross batten on the lid (placed near the end and on bottom of it) lay parallel to the outside of the end pieces when the lid was closed; the purpose of this piece was to prevent warpage of the lid.

Refinement in construction came with the introduction of panelling to England from the Continent in the second half of the 15th century. The panel system was based on (1) a framework of stiles and rails joined with mortise and tenon joints secured with dowels, and (2) panels with thin edges that fitted into grooves cut into the stiles and rails. The joiner, a highly skilled craftsman, replaced the carpenter, who had been previously responsible for constructing furniture.

Carving, painting, and the application of textiles to furniture were the primary means of adornment. Carving of both blind and pierced tracery was frequently used to ornament furniture of the medieval period. In blind tracery the carving was cut into but not through the piece, while in pierced tracery the carving penetrated and cut through the pieces. The latter was important for furniture designed for food storage, where air circulation was significant. While extant painted pieces are not widely available, ample primary evidence reveals that this decorative technique was in abundant use. Using tempera or wax, articles were sometimes painted in overall flat colors (scarlet, azure, gold), or a pattern was rendered on free surfaces. The ornamental qualities of painting and carving were sometimes combined to produce scintillating surface embellishment. Textiles also played a substantial part in the decoration of rooms and furniture; illuminated manuscripts give ample evidence of their role. Examples include their use as valances, brilliant and luxurious cushions, bed hangings, cloths of estate for ceremonial chairs, canvas covers for uncarved surfaces on which figurative subjects were painted, and surface seating for the folding X-stool.

Typical Pieces and Stylistic Features

Furniture served two purposes in the medieval period: utility and to denote hierarchal position. First of all, some pieces were constructed strictly for practical reasons. Such was the case for one of the most common pieces of furniture fabricated in the medieval period, the chest. Used for both the storage and transport of articles in a nomadic society, it could, depending on its structural detail, also serve as a seat, bed, or table. The chair, representing a second purpose for which furniture was constructed, was used symbolically to express status in society—authority, rank, and power.

FIGURE 4-16 Chair, French or Flemish (15th century). Carved oak. Vertical emphasis, rectangular, paneled. Hinged seat for access to storage underneath. Back panel carved with Tree of Jesse; linenfold carved panels below seat. All rights reserved, The Metropolitan Museum of Art, The Cloisters Collection Purchase, 1947. (47.101.67)

Seat Furniture

Seat furniture—chairs, stools, and benches—reflected the hierarchal nature of medieval society. A chair was a seat of authority and the most important person in the household sat in a chair; consequently few are extant from this period. Symbolizing their lower status, other members of the household sat on stools or benches. Stylistically, the chair was characterized by the following: a rectilinear and box-like shape with an emphasis on verticality; paneling on its back and arms and underneath the seat; a full enclosure under the seat that served as storage, with access through a hinged seat (Figure 4-16). Panels were carved with ornaments relating to Gothic architecture. Luxurious textiles were sometimes thrown over this type of chair and cushions may have been used.

A limited number of curule chairs influenced by classic Roman prototypes were made in this period but the curule continued to be a form fabricated in succeeding stylistic periods. Upholstery is known to have been used for these. One example consisted of embroidered velvet attached to leather and slung between the uprights for the back; traces of the fabric that covered the wooden frame remain. French curule chairs were typically more lightly scaled than comparable English models.

Stools

In the hall benches placed at the table were used by members of the household. These pieces symbolized their lower status, for it was the lord of the manor who sat in the chair on the dais. The bench and the stool were stylistically very similar; the bench was simply a longer version of the stool (Figure 4-17). A stool often served multiple functions: seat, table, and, on occasion, storage. The seat was made of a board supported by two solid and splayed trestles, the bases of which were notched in the form of an inverted V or an ogee arch. The apron was often deep, and although the form and construction were typically medieval, the carved decoration sometimes revealed the early introduction of the Renaissance ornament of Romayne work (a human head carved in a medallion) in an otherwise Gothic piece. A related piece was the *dossier,* a wooden bench with a high paneled back that was an integral part of the wainscot of the room.

FIGURE 4-17 Stool, English. Carved oak. Trestle supports with ogee arch cut into the base. Romayne medallions carved on apron. All rights reserved, The Metropolitan Museum of Art, Rogers Fund, 1921. (21.95.3)

Tables

Since the hall was used for many different functions it was important that the furniture also contribute to varied need. The dining tables were constructed in two parts so that they were easily dismantled by servants and placed to the side. The top (referred to as the table, from the Latin *tabula,* meaning board) was separate from the base; supporting legs and rails were termed *frame.* In contemporary literature the two pieces were called *table with frame.* Some authors ascribe the derivation of the term *chairman of the board* to the medieval practice of designating the status of the person of honor by seating him in a chair at the board.

Storage Pieces

Lack of consistency in the designated names for storage pieces in contemporary documents precludes strict reliance on terms used in the literature of the period. Reliance must be placed instead on bits and pieces of information on function and on consistency in the use of today's terms. As a group, storage pieces of both England and France were sometimes freestanding and sometimes integral with built-in wall paneling. The dresser *(dressoir)* in England was an open shelf piece used for display in the medieval hall. It was sometimes canopied. In France comparable pieces attained great height and were sometimes dismantled following meals.

French carving as well as iron mounts for hasps and lock cases can be described as exceedingly detailed and of the highest artistic quality; the openwork backed with red velvet vividly highlighted the detail. Figuring prominently in ornamental detail were such

FIGURE 4-18 Credence, French (late 15th century). Carved oak. Traceried panels. Linenfold panels of lower section. All rights reserved, The Metropolitan Museum of Art, Rogers Fund, 1907. (07.40)

motifs as the trefoil, quatrefoil, fleur-de-lis, and grotesque animals. The human figure was not widely used in France.

Of the cupboards, the English *aumbry* and the French *armoire* appear to have been comparable pieces. Doors enclosed shelves or hanging space for clothes. A variety of storage uses for these pieces included food, dishes, all manner of other household goods, and arms.

The French *buffet* and *crédence* deserve mention. The design of the buffet, a dining room piece, varied. Buffets were partially closed. Open shelves were for the display of silver; the closed storage was placed on an open stand with paneled back.

The term *crédence* originated from a custom *(credentarius)* in Italy whereby foods for the nobility were tested for poison (Figure 4-18). It was used both for a table placed near the dining table and for storage concealed by doors. Like the buffet, the crédence was placed on a stand with a paneled back and a shelf near the floor.

Chests, however, were perhaps the most versatile pieces of furniture (Figure 4-19). Many extant chests had been the property of the Church and were used as receptacles for valuable contributions. In a nomadic society chests were constructed also because of the need to transport goods from residence to residence. Other functions served by the chest were seat, table, and occasionally bed.

At first the chest was probably constructed of a hollowed-out log bound by iron bands. Some extant joined types date from the 13th century. In the 14th century ornament assumed a more important role; much of this decoration was based on details of Gothic church architecture. Carved tracery consisted of such details as arcades of cusped arches and roundels arranged within embracing pointed arches. While some of the ornament was carved directly into the surface of solid wood, it was also sometimes applied. At the beginning of the 16th century Renaissance detail was sometimes introduced—for example, heads within medallions—but it was combined with Gothic motifs such as the linenfold. Front panels on the chest were also decorated with carved depictions from legends or Scripture.

Beds

Beds of the early medieval period sometimes had a post at each corner rising approximately 15 inches above the mattress. If a canopy was used, it was not an integral part of the design. However, late in the period the bed had become a magnificent display of sumptuous and costly textiles as revealed in 15th-century manuscripts. Such significance was attached to these beds that they were often specifically enumerated in wills.

Canopies were of several configurations; some covered the length of the bed, some half, while others were conical in arrangement. If, in the household, there was more than one person of estate, the full-length canopy *(tester)* was for the one of highest rank. The draped bed consisted of the canopy (often hung from the ceiling), the headboard (termed *dossier* in France), and curtains. Curtains were hung from the canopy and could be fully drawn to counter drafts. In France, fabric was often the material used for the dossier and the canopy. Curtains were attached to the ceiling with cords, and in conjunction with this a frame was constructed. Textiles used by the wealthy classes consisted of tapestries, brocatelles, and damasks.

ORNAMENT

As noted previously, ornament was borrowed from architecture in the form of tracery, linenfold, crockets, bunches of grapes with vine leaves, maple leaves, curled cabbage, quatrefoil, trefoil, and heraldic motifs. Checker carving, stylized flowers, and the ball-flower (a carved ball in the raised center of three or four grouped leaves) were also used prominently for decorative detail in furniture. In addition, around 1530 a motif important during the Italian Renaissance was introduced. Called in England Romayne work, it consists of a medallion within which is carved a head in profile.

Chapter 5

Italian Renaissance

1460-1600

HISTORICAL SETTING

Italy was the springboard for the Renaissance in architecture and the visual arts, beginning in 15th-century Florence. In other western countries stylistic progression was from Roman to Early Christian, thence to the Romanesque and Gothic of the Middle Ages. However, Italy (except for Venice) had not adopted the Gothic style. Thus the rich heritage of ancient Roman arts provided fertile ground for a return to the classical style based on the use of Roman orders of architecture. Like the Romans, Renaissance architects used the orders structurally as well as decoratively. The typical architect of the Renaissance in Italy was exceptionally versatile in that he not only performed services as an architect but as painter, sculptor, furniture designer, etc.

Among the factors responsible for the fascination with classical antiquity during the Italian Renaissance, two were especially consequential. First, the rediscovery of the treatise on architecture by Vitruvius (Marcus Vitruvius Pollio), Roman architect and theorist; although he was not influential in his own time his works did provide some impetus for classicism in later periods. Second, there were readily available Roman models from classical antiquity in Italy, which had been the center of an empire in the classical period. The domains of Rome had spread from Great Britain to present day Iran and lands surrounding the Mediterranean Sea.

The treatise by Vitruvius inspired Leon Battista Alberti (1404-1472) to write the first architectural treatise of the Renaissance. Of utmost importance to him was the convenience of the interior layout. He began writing the treatise around 1452 but it was first fully published in 1485. In turn this prompted a series of influential treatises to be written and published by such prominent architects as Filarete (Antonio Averlino), Francesco di Giorgio, Sebastiano Serlio, and Andrea Palladio, each of whom expressed intense interest in classicism.

Alberti recommended the use of architectural elements such as the column, pilaster, and architrave, which he often employed decoratively, not structurally. As an advocate of classical antiquity his interest was reinforced on a visit to Florence in 1428, where he met such forward-looking artists as the architect Brunelleschi (1377-1446), an originator of the Renaissance style who meticulously studied, measured, and drew models of classic antiquity; Luca della Robbia (1400-1482), a leader in the modern movement and a sculptor whose works were based on classical antiquity in the media of marble and glazed terracotta to enhance architectural design; and Lorenzo Ghiberti (1378-1455), a medievalist at first but subsequently a prominent proponent of the classical revival of the Renaissance, a collector of classical sculptures keeping abreast of the latest developments in the current realm, and a sculptor whose metal relief ornament embellishes the doors of the Baptistery of Florence.

The works of Filarete (Antonio Averlino) (c. 1400-c. 1469) were based on Alberti. Of the 21 books of his treatise, all but three were devoted to architecture, and his manuscripts were widely distributed. He attempted to introduce to northern Italy classicism based on that of Brunelleschi, who had studied Roman architectural forms and construction. Of major interest to Filarete was the treatment of architecture as a unified whole.

Francesco di Giorgio (1439-1501 or 1502) was influenced by the works of Vitruvius and the treatise by Alberti. He was, however, more practical in his method. Leonardo da Vinci (among the greatest artists of the Renaissance) was personally acquainted with him and possessed one of his architectural manuscripts. He was committed to classicism and on his visits to Naples he drew antique artifacts.

Directed to the layman rather than to the professional, the pattern book of Sebastiano Serlio (1475-1564) was widely used throughout Europe. His goal in producing this book was to provide practical information rather than a purely theoretical work. It was the first well-illustrated book on architecture. The treatise was published in six parts between 1537 and 1551, and a seventh was published posthumously in 1575. Francis I of France appointed him painter and architect to the court in 1541 as the result of the publication of his third and fourth books.

Devoting his career exclusively to architecture, Andrea Palladio (1508-1580) was the foremost professional architect of the later 16th century. Based on a two-year study of the architectural ruins in Rome, Palladio's approach to planning was archaeological; however, his use of classical motifs in ways contrary to the original context or meaning was mannerist. "But the rules which he derived from a study of the ancients, and which he frequently broke in his own work, came to be accepted almost blindly as the classical canon, at any rate for domestic architecture."[1] While he showed little concern for function or practicality he revealed an extraordinary interest in the conceptualization of the interior as pure architecture in terms of spatial effects. The style of Inigo Jones, English architect of the early 17th century, and the English Palladian movement of around 1715 were influenced by the works of Palladio.

Engraved wood blocks and copper plates were new printing techniques that stimulated the dissemination of information from these treatises and spread new designs to other areas of Italy and Europe. Published treatises by prestigious architects ranged in subject from theory to practical applications. Decorative artists and artisans used designs by these and other designers for components of interior architecture—ceilings, doors, woodwork, and window treatments. The influence of the treatises gradually intensified from the last decades of the 15th century to the late 16th century as designers felt the need to unify decorative schemes.

Interest in classical antiquity during this period was significantly reflected in education, the use of architectural and decorative elements, and a penchant for collecting ancient Roman models. First of all, it became incumbent on gentlemen to be knowledgeable about classical arts as well as to study ancient philosophers, mythology, etc. Patronage of the arts significantly advanced under the tutelage of powerful families, many members of which were well versed in classical architecture and theory. To such patrician families as the Medici, the Strozzi, and the Rucellai, the magnificent surroundings of their impressive residences represented to them how the ancient Romans must have lived.

Individual artists, architects, and artisans had either a patron or client association with the persons who employed them. Patron relationships, typical of northern Italy, implied that individuals were hired on a long-term basis through which they might provide a variety of design services. Princes, cardinals, popes, and others of high status often competed for the services of talented artists. To their families, promotion of the arts was not only a civic virtue and social obligation but also represented power. A client relationship, on the other hand, entailed temporarily hiring a freelance specialist for a single work. The latter arrangement suggested a lower status.

While classical antiquity was an overriding influence, designers responded within the context of other influencing factors. Geographically, Italy was organized into small states, independent cities, and some republics. Florence, Rome, and Venice, with their surrounding territories, were three important centers. Design in these regions was affected by available building materials and climate. In Florence and Rome small windows helped to avoid the intensity and heat of the sun; extensive use of the *cortile* (courtyard) with the colonnade was a response to this. In Venice, however, large traceried windows (inherited from the Gothic period) and balconies moderated the reflection of summer heat by capturing breezes from the sea.

Stone and marble were readily available to Florence and Rome, while Venice, because of its location on the Adriatic Sea, could import by water any material it wanted. The architectural character of Venice was strongly influenced by its commerce with, and its unique position relative to the East. Humid conditions of Venice precluded the use of fresco popular in other regions of Italy.

Excavations of Roman sites yielded marble for reuse, stone calcined for lime, and artifacts for collectors. From these, designers either copied or were inspired to adapt Roman

---

1. Nikolaus Pevsner, John Fleming, and Hugh Honour, *A Dictionary of Architecture* (Woodstock, N. Y.: The Overlook Press, 1976), 380.

decorative detail such as the candelabrum, grotesque images, the compartmentalization based on Pompeian organization for such areas as the ceiling, and the decorative use of classical orders.

Humanism permeated the Renaissance; in contrast to the medieval concept of world order, the importance of man as the highest form of creation was stressed. The value of the human in his own right and the exploration of classical civilization became parallel concerns, and yet elements of the Christian heritage were maintained. Italy had been the center of the Roman Empire and the rich remains of this ancient period became the basis for the predominant thread running through the arts of this period of rebirth. Whereas the medieval period had emphasized verticality and the ephemeral nature of man, it seemed important to designers of the Renaissance that emphasis should be given to symmetry and horizontality. Fundamental to the Renaissance theory of beauty was the theory that spatial movement within spaces was enhanced by calculating mathematical ratios. Part of the equation was based on a measure of the human body, the module, and multiples of it thus determining the system of proportional relationships. Within this system both real and fictive architectural space were dealt with in defined scaled proportions of rooms. In addition, convenience and durability received greater consideration in design than heretofore.

SPATIAL RELATIONSHIPS

In the Renaissance it became evident that the altered needs of ruling families required different types of houses than those of the medieval period. Not only were city palaces (*palazzi*) constructed to express the power and affluence of influential families but now they could also build country villas for relaxation without the need for fortification and without the need to conform to the restricted spaces of the city.

The perceived need for greater privacy influenced the arrangement of interior spaces. The response lay in the sequencing of rooms and greater attention to protocol. With more public spaces nearer the vestibule, a linear arrangement met these demands: Rooms for greater privacy were set farther from the main entrance, as were rooms that could be accessed only by persons of high privilege.

Spatial Features of the Floor Plan and Three-Dimensional Spatial Characteristics

The plan of the Renaissance palazzo was often rectangular in an axial arrangement; in this sense there is a commonality with the Pompeian plan, often characterized by alternating intensity of light along an axis (Figure 5-1). Rooms were usually square or rectangular, with interior walls perpendicular to or parallel to the façade. Exceptions to this were the occasional oval rooms in the second half of the 16th century; some other rooms were octagonal. The disposition of spaces within the plan was often symmetrical except when restricted by such conditions as an irregular building plot.

On entering a palazzo a gate or front door at which a guard was stationed was followed by a standard progression of spaces. The main entrance opened onto the vestibule, from which one entered the cortile, surrounded by an arcaded colonnade; behind this were summer apartments, shops, kitchen, bathrooms, storage areas, and so on. From the cortile a grand staircase led to the *piano nobile,* the main story above ground level usually containing the main apartments. Since corridors were not typically included in the plan the innermost rooms were accessed by going through other rooms in the sequential arrangement; sometimes the *loggia* could also be used to gain access to rooms.

The concept of the apartment was introduced by the Italians in the latter part of the 15th century and became common in the 16th century in France as well as in Italy. By the 17th century the French had refined this idea in an *enfilade* arrangement, which England subsequently adopted. Although arrangements varied, principles for a typical distribution

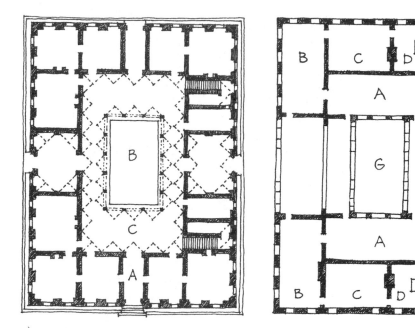

FIGURE 5-1 Palazzo Strozzi, Florence (1489). Left. Ground Plan: A vestibule; B cortile, arcaded on each of the three stories of the Palazzo Strozzi; C stairway to the piano nobile. Right. Piano nobile with two ceremonial apartments: A loggia, passageway to the ceremonial apartment; B sala; C antechamber; D bedchamber, position of the bed noted; E rooms of undetermined use; F circular stairway for private exit and access to the ceremonial apartments. G cortile below.

of spaces within the apartment were outlined by leading architects with regard to the specified disposition of rooms, the decrease in room size as one went further into the sequence, the progression (often linear) through the spaces from public to private (architect Francesco di Giorgio recommended the position of rooms be related to the order of privacy), and the provision of stairs for a private exit or entrance at the end of the sequence. The main apartment was at the piano nobile level, usually the first floor above ground level; more than one apartment per residence was common. While the main apartments were at the piano nobile level in the palazzo, some duplication was provided on the ground floor to take advantage of its cooler atmosphere during the summer.

At the piano nobile level the most important rooms were the *sala*, the bedchamber (or *camera*), and antechamber. As the first room in the sequence, the sala was used for such functions as banquets, entertainment, and dining. The sala was the most public room, situated between the bedchamber and the entry, the largest space in the progression of rooms and the one with the highest ceiling. Sometimes incorporated in the plan was an adjacent smaller room called the *saletta,* a diminutive dining room for the inhabitant of the primary bedchamber. Dining also sometimes took place in a loggia, an openair space on the piano nobile. The loggia was also used as a *galleria* for the display of sculpture, paintings, etc.

Next in the sequence of spaces was either the bedchamber or an interceding room termed the antechamber. Several bedchambers were provided for members of large families. While husbands and wives might have separate apartments, each with its own progression of spaces, sometimes they were provided with adjacent bedchambers. The bedchamber was the central space in the apartment. Private at night, it could have other uses in the daytime—as a reception room on the occasion of a wedding or on the presentation of a new baby, or as a drawing room. For great families of considerable wealth the demands on such a space could mean that bedchambers of more restricted access were provided farther on in the disposition of rooms.

If the antechamber preceded the bedchamber in the succession, the bedchamber automatically became more private, since the principle of organization was for spaces to become more private on progression from the entry to the innermost reaches of the apartment. Introduced in the 15th century and becoming common in the 16th century, the antechamber was a multifunctional space that accommodated various activities such as dining, the reception of friends, private audiences, and that provided a sleeping space for servants.

At the piano nobile level beyond the sala, antechamber, and bedchamber were, sometimes, more private spaces: a studio, a lavatory (WC or *necessari*), a personal chapel, a gallery, and a storage space termed a *guardaroba*. The studio or *scrittoio* (termed *closet* in England and *cabinet* in France) housed valuable documents, books, and costly objects requiring a secluded space for security reasons. This room also served for scholarly pursuits—writing, reading, contemplating, etc. Considered a highly private room, to gain access to this space a person had to be a cherished friend of the owner or to have the qualifications deemed appropriate for recommended admission to the collection.

A personal chapel was included in the private residence only by special papal indulgence. To be granted the privilege of a chapel required considerable wealth and a superior position of influence. This space was usually characterized by luxuriant decorative effects. It could be used as an audience chamber and for private devotions.

Lavatories were placed in various locations. One recommended position was near the spiral staircase, which often provided a secluded space whereby special visitors could escape secretly. It should be noted that a closestool was frequently placed in the bedrooms.

The guardaroba was a storage area for such items as furnishings, clothes, armor, jewelry; it was often supervised by a guard. Architects suggested that this space be located near a wide stairs for ease in transporting goods from one floor to another.

The exploration of three-dimensional space was enhanced in a number of ways. The vestibule, often arched, was not only the link to the street but through it vision was extended along the main axial sequence. From this vantage point the individual viewed the spaces, the characteristics of which optimized visual extension. Three-dimensional perspectives were aided by the sequence of architectural spatial features through which vistas within and beyond the confines of the residential structure were gradually viewed. Directional cues were given by the alternation of light level, beginning with the subdued light of the vestibule. The intense illumination of the arcaded cortile, open to the sky, was shielded by the upper floors. Across the cortile on an axis with the vestibule, lower light levels were again attained; at this point vistas were sometimes incorporated by an opening to a garden beyond, or a grand staircase might be included at this point.

The arcaded cortile, square or rectangular, was the most important organizing element of the palazzo. From this private, sunlit space access to all parts of the residence was attained. Through the rhythmic arrangement of the surrounding columns a foundation and implied enclosure provided access to ground-floor spaces such as shops, guest rooms, summer apartments, service rooms, and offices. But the illumination of the space encouraged visual extension of vertical space. Within this open air volume, horizontal strata were formed by each of the two to three stories; tiers were articulated in various ways such as with different orders of pilasters, glazed passages, open loggias, etc. The focal points formed by the contrasting decorative and architectural details of each stratum prompted vertical visual extension by the viewer.

A monumental grand staircase of two straight flights of stairs linked the cortile with the piano nobile (Figure 5-2). The main apartments at this level were rectangular or square and graduated in scale and size as the individual progressed through the spaces. The linear progression of the rooms making up the apartment (along with diminishing sizes) enhanced third-dimensional interest and development along this main axis. Since the sala was normally the first and largest in the sequence of rooms, another means often used to enhance vertical three-dimensional development was the interest created by the ceiling; patterns were created by treatments such as multiple layers of beams, coffering, and various structural means to attain vaulting. The tiers of wall decoration (often three) with their detail also encouraged vertical exploration.

Renaissance artists often showed intense interest in employing principles of exact perspective to create optical illusions of three-dimensional spaces. Through the use of fresco techniques painters played a highly significant role in trompe l'oeil painting of walls and ceilings by depicting the illusion of depth and distance within Italian Renaissance buildings. By these means painters dissolved the opaqueness of the walls by illustrating distant landscapes and cities as well as figurative motifs; fictive architectural elements such as log-

FIGURE 5-2 Palazzo Doria Tursi, Genoa (1568). Momumental stairway leads to the piano nobile. Climatic interior spatial treatment often relegated to majestic stairs conveying light and spaciousness.

gias, niches, doors, and vaults were also depicted. On occasion tiers of perspective renditions in painting were combined with those of marquetry, also represented in perspective.

INTERIOR ARCHITECTURE AND DECORATION

Materials and Decorative Techniques

Both woodworking techniques and painting were used to extend space. Of the decorative techniques used for both walls and furniture, intarsia (and later marquetry) was a central phenomenon of the period, used to represent perspective schemes of architecture, landscape, and figurative motifs. *Intarsia* was a technique whereby shaped pieces of inlay material were set into ground material; the hollowed-out space was of like shape to the inlay piece. *Marquetry,* representational in nature, was comprised of pieces of wood (and other materials such as shell and ivory) fitted together as a continuous surface on a core of less expensive material; in other words, it was a veneer technique. Pieces for intarsia were as thick as four millimeters; it was not practical to produce marquetry until machinery was developed which would allow wood to be cut into uniformly thin pieces. To attain shading variations in the pictorial renderings, different woods were used. In addition, color differentiation was attained by scorching the woods.

As noted above, fresco was used to paint the perspectives that gave the illusion of spatial extension to many Renaissance walls and ceilings. The technique involved the application of pigment mixed with water to damp plaster made of slaked lime. However, since some color change ensued due to the chemical interaction with some pigments with water, an additional process called *fresco secco* was utilized. With the latter application, the plaster ground was allowed to harden, after which pigments were mixed with lime water and applied to the dry plaster.

For interior architectural features a variety of materials were employed including wood, marble, metal, stone, stucco, and terra-cotta.

Interior Architecture and Decorative Elements

In Italian Renaissance interiors more attention was given to ceremony than to comfort. Forms were forceful and precise. Nothing was ambiguous; cubic forms predominated. Lines were clear and decisive.

Floors

Two ceramic materials were often used during the Italian Renaissance: terra-cotta and majolica *(maiolica)*. Terra-cotta tile was used by all levels of society. These tiles (square, rectangular, hexagonal) were laid in a variety of geometric patterns capitalizing on differences in color. Examples include tile laid in a herringbone pattern, laid in parallel lines, or set in overall circular patterns within rectangular frames repeated over the surface of the floor. *Majolica* tiles (low-fired pottery with a tin glaze) were used on floors to notably outstanding effect. These tiles were decorated in several colors. Designs impressed into the damp clay were filled with glaze; ridges formed by the impression separated the glazed areas.

Brick was frequently employed in more humble dwellings. Available in a variety of textures and shapes, bricks were ribbed or rough in surface and sometimes glazed. They were typically square or hexagonal.

Although stone was used for floors of public buildings it had more limited use in residences; the primary stones included marble, granite, serpentine, and porphyry. Parquet of stone was used only for the most prominent floors and when the understructure was strong enough to support the heavy weight. Early in the 15th century when stone was used, small pieces in patterns of circles, triangles, and squares were employed; the size of these increased up to the year 1600. Marble was particularly important for ceremonial apartments; often laid in checkered patterns, these apartments were often divided by strips placed longitudinally and laterally. Marble was employed in yet another way through the use of *terrazzo,* in which chips of marble were embedded in cement.

While wood was not widely used for floors during this period, it was probably used for upper floors. The use of wide planks was characteristic. According to evidence from paintings of the period, wooden floors appear to have been used in private spaces as platforms for desks and seats.

Stylistic coordination of the entire interior scheme governed the relationship of interior architectural surfaces. This meant that floor design echoed that of the ceiling, employing the same divisions.

Walls

An unprecedented variety of decorative wall treatments characterized Italian interiors of the 15th and 16th centuries. It was not uncommon to have more than one medium used in the design of walls within one room, including some combination of the following: painting, plaster, stucco, wood paneling (sometimes enhanced with marquetry), and movable wall hangings. Venetian interiors of the later Renaissance often included within one room a combination of media—oil and fresco painting, carved marble, and stucco reliefs.

While no one formula was used for wall divisions, a generalization can be made about the prevalent separation of horizontal strata, of which there were often three: (1) a dado on the lower part of the wall represented by either paint or paneling; (2) the main field; and (3) a decorative frieze with a complete entablature or a cornice above the decorative frieze. It would be impossible to enumerate all variations, but two prominent ones should be noted, one related to the use of wall hangings and the other associated with the use of illusionistic painting sometimes encompassing an entire wall.

Movable hangings such as tapestry, velvets, damasks, painted and gilt leather, and linen painted with scenes extended decorative enhancements of the interiors. The position of these was frequently below a painted frieze. Hooks embedded in the wall provided one means of hanging these materials. Tapestries were associated with wealthy upper-class clientele since they were very expensive, not only because they were imported from such centers as Brussels, Tournai, and Arras, but also because of the time-consuming weaving process. Used singly at first, sets of tapestries in the 16th century covered entire rooms; some hung from ceiling to floor. The design of these was two-dimensional at first but then perspective representations in the 16th century conveyed the illusionism and space-extending qualities typical of fresco painting. Textile hangings were associated with their appropriateness for summer or winter; heavier textiles such as velvets and tapestries were more suitable as winter hangings, while linens and silken fabrics were more fitting for summer installations.

Most walls were plastered and then whitewashed or painted with a color, or the plaster served as the base for a mural or for repeat patterns in fresco; however, simple whitewashed walls continued to be used far into the Renaissance period. Among the painting techniques fresco predominated, but oil painting on canvas installed on both walls and ceilings was also significant. Venice and Florence were particularly important in the use of oil painting. Following the stylistic trends of the period in which they were made, oil paintings were produced on canvas and then hung on walls or ceilings. Of the pictorial scenes favorite motifs involved the use of perspective, which extended the spatial confines of the room; these trompe l'oeil effects made the viewer uncertain about what was real and what was imaginary.

Simulations of architectural elements such as columns, entablatures, pediments, and niches with statues are nowhere better illustrated than in the Villa Barbaro at Maser, designed by Palladio with paintings by Veronese (see Figure C-5). Illusionistic devices were rendered in compartmentalized arrangements, in continuous friezes, and on entire walls. A wide variety of subjects was illustrated: astrology, the seasons, the ages of man, the hunt. The depiction of contemporary figures, sometimes five times life size, represented the influence of humanism on fresco painting; these idealized human figures were also a reflection of the mannerism typical of the last three quarters of the 16th century. Frescoes frequently required two painters with different specialties: one proficient in perspective and the orders, the other expert in figure painting.

Overall repeat patterns such as checks, lozenges, and stripes were executed in fresco also. In addition, damasks, velvets, and figured silk were painted in fresco. Simulations extended to depictions of leather, tapestries, and doors fronted by textile portieres. Painting was also used to simulate other materials such as marble.

The decorative repertoire was extended through the use of stuccowork in relief and wood surface treatments. Stucco relief was sometimes combined with fresco. Following the decorative vocabulary of the Romans, stucco reliefs were often set within framed panels. Stucco was also used as the medium for the portrait busts, painted or gilded, that enhanced architectural elements of rooms as chimneypieces, the cornices of wood paneling, doors, and windows. As the Renaissance style approached that of the baroque period molded stucco figures became important. Marble and terra-cotta, more expensive materials, were also used in the production of portrait busts.

Rectangular panels of wood surrounded by moldings of various profiles were either plain or decoratively enhanced with marquetry, but they were also occasionally painted with oil-bound pigments. Applications of large and architectonic wood paneling extended to various heights:[2] (1) the dado, approximately waist high, located on the lower portion

---

2. In this work the term *dado* is used to describe wood paneling extending to approximately waist height *or* when a molding is used to mark this position independently or as part of this designated position on a wainscot *or* when this portion of the wall is treated differently from that above. The wainscot, on the other hand, is the term used to describe wood paneling extending above the dado.

FIGURE 5-3   Ducal Palace, the Hall of Paradise, Mantua (15th and 16th centuries). Wall divided into three areas. Architectural classic elements introduced. Coved transition from wall to ceiling. Typical compartmentalization of composition.

of the wall; (2) the wainscot sheathing the full height of a room; and (3) wainscot placed at or above eye level with the portion above treated with fresco or some other means of decoration (Figure 5-3). When a wainscot was the wall application, a molding sometimes designated the dado level within the composition. Details of the wainscot also provided the opportunity to display decorative objects when the cornice was deep enough to serve as a shelf. Usually the upper part of the wall was more richly adorned.

Wall treatments using antique classical ornament recurred frequently throughout the Renaissance, regardless of the medium used. Two of the most significant were the grotesque and the candelabrum (Figures 5-4 and 5-5). The candelabrum was organized symmetrically along a central stem and vertically disposed. Its use was primarily as border decoration such as the surrounds of windows; sometimes, however, motifs were picked out from the candelabrum to use as repeat units for a frieze. Becoming popular at the end of the 15th century, the grotesque required a larger plane and resembled the arabesque. Motifs such as the sphinx, representations of portions of human and animal figures, monsters, and medallions were interwoven with foliage and flowers in flowing lines. While it was rendered symmetrically, liberties were taken since the details of pairs of motifs were not identical. Grotesques sometimes covered an entire wall and were depicted in fresco and stucco and on textiles and majolica; this unit was frequently set within a frame. Vertically arranged, the arabesque was a combination of plant and animal forms arranged in an intertwining manner.

Windows and Doors

By the first half of the 15th century most important houses had glazed windows; larger expanses of glass characterized the Renaissance compared to the medieval period. Window openings were first round-headed; these were replaced by rectangular frames. In the beginning windows had no frame except for the finish provided by the wall material of stone or plaster. As the Renaissance progressed architectural elements such as pilasters,

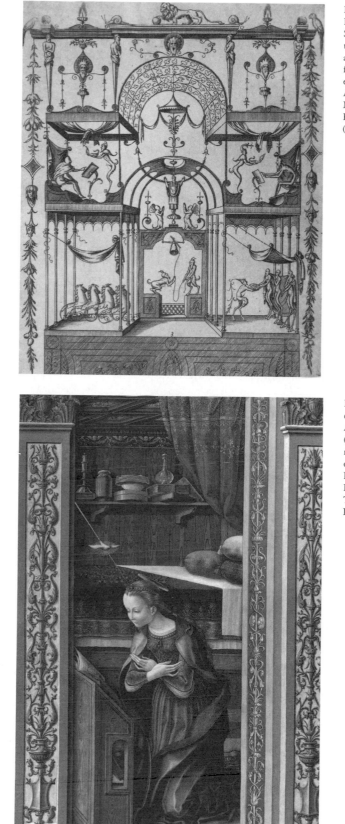

FIGURE 5-4 Engraved Grotesque Design (first published, 1530). Symmetrical. Comprised of fantastic motifs. Used for small or large areas of any proportion. Designers faithfully copied or adapted engraved designs. From *Levoires.* All rights reserved, The Metropolitan Museum of Art, Harris Brisbane Dick Fund, 1928. (28.98.4)

FIGURE 5-5 Candelabra depicted in Carlo Crivelli's, *Altarpiece: Annunciation, with Saint Emidius* (1486). Symmetrical. Fantastic motifs of great variety organized on each side of a vertical stem. Primarily a border design. Reproduced by courtesy of the Trustees, The National Gallery, London.

moldings, and entablatures were added. In the 15th century architects dealt with roundels of glass manufactured in Venice but, while this glass let in light, it was not transparent. Roundels of glass are depicted in a painting by Vittore Carpaccio, *The Dream of Saint Ursula* (early 1490s); lead cames secured these roundels as they were fitted in wooden frames. The resulting interstices from setting adjacent roundels were often fitted with glass of a different color. Rectangular panes of crystalline glass known for its clarity became available by the beginning of the 16th century; Vasari[3] noted that better panes of glass were imported and stated that English, Flemish, and French glass was superior.

Rectangular windows were common by the third quarter of the 15th century. The glazed panes were framed in wood and set within deep reveals. Casement windows that opened inward were common; this was the case even when the operable part was set within a larger enframement. Before glazed windows became common wooden shutters were prominent; these were hung singly or in pairs. When they were divided horizontally, each half worked independently and opened inward.

Some of the most extravagant detail was lavished on doorways. The degree of opulence was regulated by the importance of the room in the sequential arrangement of the apartment system; the most lavish treatment was relegated to the doorway by which one entered an important room. Carved wood and marble were utilized for door surrounds. It was not uncommon for different materials and colors to be employed in the design of a single door surround. More modest doors were undecorated. Intarsia decoration, important in the latter part of the 15th century, was often employed on paneled doors. At first geometric, later designs were figurative at the close of the century; for example, the impression of niches or open cupboards was rendered in perspective. Many doors were left plain, with interest created through the use of carved moldings. In the 16th century decorative detail depended almost exclusively on carved moldings. Doors were either single- or double-leafed. False doors were often painted in frescoed rooms since symmetry was significant to Renaissance architects. Although plain surrounds were used for doorways, some doors were encompassed additionally by a tabernacle frame consisting of columns or pilasters supporting an entablature and capped with a pediment (Figure 5-6). If the doorway was finished with only an entablature, the cornice was sometimes sufficiently deep to display decorative objects (Figure 5-7). These impressive superstructures signified social position.

Chimneypieces

Among the architectural and sculptural focal points of a Renaissance room were the chimneypieces. These were often imposing wall features, in scale with the size of rooms; the firebox was sometimes as much as eight feet in height. But some architects, including Vincenzo Scamozzi, a follower of Palladio, established guidelines for size, indicating that in a small room the opening should not be above chest level.

At first the conical-hooded medieval type which projected strongly into the room was retained. This was replaced with a pyramidal form of hood with which architects experimented from the mid-15th to the mid-16th century. As the firebox was set farther into the wall, the amount of projection of the hood into the room was reduced. Alterations in the detail of the overmantel hood involved its curved shaping as well as the addition of decorative relief; the arms of the owner were often added to the face of the hood. Sebastiano Serlio was instrumental in that he illustrated ten designs for chimneypieces in Volume IV of his treatise, first published in 1537; his camouflage pattern utilized a waisted pyramid form with sphinxes added to soften the effect. Patterns for the use of classical orders were also included in Serlio's treatise. Thus, below the hoods of many chimneypieces was the frequent use of a complete entablature utilizing elements borrowed and adapted from classical architecture and ornamental detail; the part most highly decorated was the frieze, on which relief designs were frequently carved. Support for the entablature was diverse and

---

3. Giorgio Vasari was a painter and author. Through his work of 1550 (revised in 1568), *Vite de' più eccellenti architetti, pittori e scultori italiani,* he significantly influenced architectural taste.

FIGURE 5-6 Door. Ornately treated door enframement to important rooms. Tabernacle frame: pilasters support an entablature capped with a segmental pediment.

included pilasters, brackets, columns, and caryatid figures. Although a firebox surround was not always used within this frame, the architrave trim was molded and was characterized by having ear pieces (termed *crossettes* or *ancon*). A design appearing in a treatise by Vignola was influential in chimneypiece design in 18th-century England and America (Figure 5-8).

Ceilings

Flat, vaulted, and coved ceilings were prevalent forms; the surfaces of these were of every description. For the flat ceilings the simplest treatment was the open-beamed ceiling in which the smaller beams were closely and regularly spaced along one dimension of the room. Supporting the smaller beams from below and perpendicular to them were heavy beams; these were more widely spaced and rested on corbels embedded in the masonry of supporting walls.

Although more than one type of vault was used in the Italian Renaissance, a common type was the barrel (or tunnel) vault. At the terminus a lunette was formed on the wall framed by the vault. An intermediate type of ceiling was the cove, which offered a concave transition from the wall to the ceiling; as the coves intersected at the corners, verti-

FIGURE 5-8 Engraving, Chimneypiece (executed for the Palazzo Farnese, Rome, in 1560 and published in 1563 in the treatise *Regoladelle cinque ordini,* by Vignola). A source of inspiration for English and American architects in later centuries. By courtesy of the Trustees of the Sir John Soane Museum, London.

FIGURE 5-9 Coffered Ceiling, Villa Cambiaso in Albaro. Classic Roman influence in the Italian Renaissance. Octagonal coffers surrounded by the guilloche.

cal diagonal planes were created (see Figure 5-3). The horizontal plane of coved ceilings was often flat.

Any of the foregoing were decorated with an incalculable variety of subdivisions. Compartmentalization into squares, octagons, lozenges, and circles often resulted from the arrangement of beams. The design of coffered ceilings relied on Roman designs (Figure 5-9). Around the middle of the 15th century coffering was generally deep, with emphasis given to rectangular panels. After mid-century octagonal coffers of equal size were placed adjacent to each other with square panels formed by the interstices; elaborate carved decoration enhanced the frames of the coffers. Sizes and shapes of coffering changed in the 16th century. While at first shapes were angular, they later became varied and characteristically irregular and fanciful in shape.

Wood was the material used in the best 15th-century rooms; the decoration of wood consisted primarily of painting, gilding, and carving. In the 16th century stucco and paintings became important means of ornamenting ceilings. Elaborate sculptural stucco frames surrounded fresco paintings and oil paintings on canvas; such mannerist details antedated the 17th century baroque period of which they were typical. Sixteenth century Venetian ceiling design surpassed that of other centers in the extravagance and intricacy of its renditions. Ceiling painting in important rooms became a dominant feature in the second half of the 16th century.

Strong separation of the wall and ceiling was accomplished through the use of the cornice, which when deep provided an opportunity to use more classical motifs such as the egg and dart. Beginning in the 16th century the continuity of wall and ceiling decoration was emphasized in that no architectural elements defined these as separate zones; stucco relief, for example, was carried from the vaulting to the wall.

Stairways

Staircases were of two primary types: one for private needs, the other a major formal approach to the main apartment(s). A small spiraling staircase was sometimes used to service the more private areas of the apartment, allowing persons to enter or escape discreetly. Constructed in straight flights, major staircases rose from the courtyard to a point nearest the sala. When two major staircases served the piano nobile, one accessed each apartment in cases when a married couple needed two apartments. The location of the main staircase leading to the piano nobile, often providing dramatic access, was often fairly near the the vestibule (see Figure 5-2).

FURNITURE

Rooms of the Italian Renaissance were sparsely furnished. The furniture was characteristically imposing, dignified, and often massive; ornamentation ranged from restrained to the highly decorative. Although the pieces were essentially rectilinear with horizontal emphasis, the Savonarola and Dante chairs with strong structural curves are exceptions. Fabrication techniques remained essentially the same as in the medieval period; however, the decorative techniques required exceptional skill on the part of the furniture craftsman. These included the processes of inlay, veneer applications, and carving. Some relief designs were achieved by the application of gesso to furniture pieces.

Materials and Construction Techniques

The primary wood for the finest furniture of the 15th and 16th centuries was walnut; other woods included pine, cypress, chestnut, elm, and poplar. Decorative enhancement often required a variety of woods to attain gradations of hue and shading. The mortise and tenon joint continued from the medieval period as the predominant type of joint. The dovetail joint, introduced in the 13th century, became standard in the 15th.

Of the inlay processes intarsia and certosina were preeminent. Each required the gouging out of the base material in the shape of the rather thick piece to be inserted. Intarsia involved the inlay of multicolored woods, the color of which was sometimes altered by scorching with hot sand; as a technique, it was particularly important from 1475 to 1525. *Certosina,* on the other hand, was popular in the 15th century and used bone or ivory as the inlay materials. While marquetry was not an inlay technique, similar designs were attained by this veneer technique in which the entire surface of the article was covered with thin pieces woods of varying colors; three-dimensional effects were achieved through the use of perspective depicting figurative ornaments, landscapes, townscapes, creative arabesques, etc. Continuity of surface was important when these techniques were employed.

Relief ornament using carving became the preferred means of embellishing furniture in the 16th century. Both incised and chip carving were usually executed in low relief. In *incised carving* the resulting design was flush with the surrounding wood, since wood was cut from around the figures which appeared in silhouette from the sunken ground. *Chip carving* was accomplished by a succession of small, unconnected gouges using conventional motifs and geometric patterns. High relief was an attribute of much 16th century carving.

Popular in the 15th and early 16th centuries, *pastiglia* was another means of attaining relief ornament. With this process the furniture piece was first covered with coarse linen or fine canvas, after which thick, creamy *gesso* (composed of gypsum plaster, glue, and whiting) was either painted on in successive layers until the desired relief depth was attained or the ornament was cast in molds and then applied to the surface. Sharpening the ornament was accomplished by working around the designs while the gesso was still damp. Color embellishments were rendered by gilding both the relief and ground, or the white gesso was retained against a colored ground.

Turning became of higher decorative value in the 16th century, although it had been used in the 15th century as well. Finials, bedposts, and furniture legs were frequently turned. The art of the turner was considerably expanded during the baroque period in the 17th century.

Typical Pieces and Stylistic Features

Seat Furniture

Chairs in the medieval period were rare, since they served as status symbols. Still relatively scarce until the 16th century, the folding Savonarola and Dante chairs (based on the curule form of Roman prototype) were the principal types constructed in the 15th century. Both were of the X-type, usually with strong, structurally curved supports of curule form.

The material for the seat and back of the Dante chair was of tooled leather or velvet slung from the side rails (Figure 5-10). Two sets of curule forms (X-shaped legs) were used, one for the front and one for the back. The curule in the front continued to form the arm support while behind it extended as uprights of the back. Armrests, usually ending in a whorl and extending beyond the arm supports, were parallel to the floor. Stretchers (runner feet) connected the front and back legs; these were sometimes undercut but at other times were flush with the floor. The extension of the stretcher beyond the legs was carved in different contours—lions' feet, for example.

Also a folding chair, the Savonarola was constructed of a series of interlaced wooden strips of curule form; there are examples, however, of straight interlaced staves (Figure 5-11). The crest of the back was usually of shaped outline and enhanced with carving or inlay decoration. Armrests and stretchers were treated in a manner typical of the Dante chair. A cushion was often used for the seat.

In the 16th century, while these chairs continued to be fabricated, a rectilinear chair with a tall back became more prevalent (Figure 5-12). Upholstered seats and backs were often used, but this rectangular chair was also constructed with a wooden seat and irregularly shaped crosspieces in the back. Square sectioned legs, typical of these chairs, continued to form the arm supports in the front and the stiles of the back; armrests were parallel with the floor and extended beyond the arm supports. Carved finials often finished the stiles of the back. The position of the stretchers varied: in the back, one higher; on the sides, placed near the floor or, alternatively, a runner stretcher connected front and back legs; in the front, no stretcher, or a deep upright stretcher of ornamental outline.

FIGURE 5-10 Dante Folding Chair, Lombardy (16th century). Walnut. Based on the Roman curule prototype with two sets of X-forms. Certosina inlay. All rights reserved, The Metropolitan Museum of Art, Fletcher Fund, 1945. (45.60.41a, b)

FIGURE 5-11 Savonarola Chair, Lombardy (c. 1500). Walnut. Influenced by the Roman curule form. Characterized by a series of interlaced staves. Intarsia of ivory and metal.

FIGURE 5-12 Sedia (late 16th century). Walnut armchair from the Borghese Palace, Rome. Leather upholstery attached with decorative nail heads. Stretchers at different heights; upright decorative front stretcher.

FIGURE 5-13   Sgabello, Venice (16th century). Octagonal seat. Trestle support. Fan-shaped back.

FIGURE 5-14   Panchetto, Upper Italy (16th century). Octagonal seat. Three legs. Back often fan-shaped.

A comparatively small chair originating in the 15th century was the *sgabello,* an armless back stool (Figure 5-13). It usually had an octagonal seat that rested on solid trestle supports, one in the front and one in the back. The fan-shaped back was narrow at seat level but strongly flared at the crest of the back. This form of chair became more ornate in the late Renaissance, often with elaborately outlined trestles and ornately carved embellishments. Similar to the sgabello was the *panchetto,* which differed in that it had three splayed legs instead the two trestle supports (Figure 5-14).

The *cassapanca,* a multiple-seat unit, served as a chest as well as a seat. Solid, massive, and rectangular, this piece was usually mounted on a dais (Figure 5-15). A hinged lid for the chest portion served as the seat. Early in the period the cassapanca was often decorated in intarsia but later it was ornamented with high-relief carving in the stylistic character of the period. Paneling was used in a variety of configurations. Located above the rectangular back was sometimes an elaborately carved cresting.

Storage Pieces

Throughout the Renaissance the *cassone,* a storage chest, was one of the most common articles of furniture (Figure 5-16). The hinged lid had either a flat or a shaped lid. A succession of carved moldings sometimes led to the flattened portion of the lid. The shapes of the body of the cassone were primarily of three types: simple rectangular forms, convex (boat-shaped) forms, or shapes contoured like a sarcophagus. If the cassone did not rest directly on the floor, it was mounted on four legs, often in the shape of carved lions' paws, or on a molded dais. Typically, the earlier cassone was ornamented with inlay techniques while later ones were decorated with high-relief carving. In addition to these methods of decoration, outstanding painters were employed to enhance the surfaces of panels.

The *credenza,* a cupboard, was a significant piece of furniture (Figure 5-17). There was great variety in the design of these; the following is a description of one type, which often

FIGURE 5-15 Cassapanca. Florence (mid-16th century). Walnut. Hinged seat for storage below. Carved cartouche and masks in panels. All rights reserved, The Metropolitan Museum of Art, Rogers Fund, 1912. (12.135.8)

FIGURE 5-16 Cassone, Northern Italy (mid-16th century). Walnut. Carved in high relief typical of the Late Renaissance. Mounted on animal feet. Band of *gadrooning* carved at the base of the cabinet. Copyright The Frick Collection, New York.

FIGURE 5-17 Cupboard, Tuscany (c. 1490-1500). Carved cupboard. Stop-fluted pilasters with Ionic capitals support frieze and cornice, reflecting classical influence. All rights reserved, The Metropolitan Museum of Art, Rogers Fund, 1916. (16.154.12)

incorporated architectural elements. Under a rectangular top surface that extended beyond the storage compartment below, three drawers were placed in the frieze; at the end and between the drawers enframed carved masks were used for ornamentation. The molding under the drawers changed direction by projecting forward below each mask. Doors below corresponded both in width and number to the drawers in the frieze. Vertically disposed framed panels and sometimes pilasters were used as separating units for the doors; these were of equivalent width to the framed masks in the frieze. Their decoration was sometimes in the form of caryatids or arabesques, or represented fluted pilasters. The deeply formed base of the credenza was composed of a series of moldings supported below by four carved animal feet, often lions' paws; bracket feet had been characteristic of those constructed earlier in the Italian Renaissance.

Tables

Dining tables (rectangular, long, and narrow) were introduced (Figure 5-18). One type, constructed of trestle supports, was complex in outline, and, at the end of the 15th century was often highly ornamented with carving. If the trestle did not rest directly on the floor the terminal support was sometimes that of a boldly carved lion's paw. Stretchers connecting the solid supports were placed at different levels. As the design of these became more advanced, tabletop surfaces, often of wood or marble, became thicker with additional moldings carved with motifs typical of the period; when an apron was added, drawers were sometimes included. The trestle support was followed by one with substantial legs connected with stretchers placed near the floor. Many smaller tables were designed to be used in the center of the room or for occasional purposes. Tabletops were octagonal, hexagonal, square, or round. The bases were columnar, baluster, or pedestal.

Beds

The medieval bed (or *letto*), often raised on a dais, continued to be constructed. These beds often had paneled headboards, footboards, and platforms; tall headboards often had a projecting cornice, the horizontal surface of which could be used for display. Evidence from paintings of the Italian Renaissance suggests that sometimes chests or benches were installed parallel to three sides of the bed. Based on a painting by Carpaccio's, *The Dream*

FIGURE 5-18 Refectory Table, Florence (1500-1550). Carved walnut dining table. Trestle support terminating in lion feet. Copyright The Frick Collection, New York.

FIGURE 5-19 Bed, Adapted from Sodoma, *Alexander Visiting Roxana,* Farnesina, Rome (c. 1511). Probably an architect designed bed depicted by Sodoma. Classical elements: stop-fluted columns resting on plinths and massively scaled entablature.

of Saint Ursula, the bed with posts had been introduced by the early 1490s; the posts upheld a tester with a valance. Some posts were continuations of turned legs, while others originated from a dais. In the early 16th century beds became more architectural in concept and some were in fact designed by architects; such a bed, illustrated in a c. 1511 painting by Sodoma, *Alexander Visiting Roxana,* showed classic influence in that the tester is in the form of an entablature supported by fluted columns resting on a plinth base (Figure 5-19). In some instances pictorial evidence reveals that a massive tester in the form of an entablature was suspended from the ceiling independent of structural support.

Textiles were highly significant in the treatment of beds. These served to guard against insects or to insulate the occupants against cold weather; these functions suggest the use of different textiles suitable for summer and winter. The curtain was often mounted inside the tester on iron rods. Another use of textiles was to suspend the material from a single hook in the ceiling; the fabric could be pulled to surround the bed.

ORNAMENT

Ornamental detail for interiors and furniture largely revolved around the the design vocabulary of the classical Roman period. Executed in painting, intarsia, certosina, marquetry, and carving the following motifs or design configurations were prevalent: arabesques, acanthus leaves, cartouches, grotesques, gadroons, guilloches, rinceaux, classical figures, egg and dart designs, bead and leaf motifs, anthemia, caryatids, candelabra, patera, masks, and classic molding outlines.

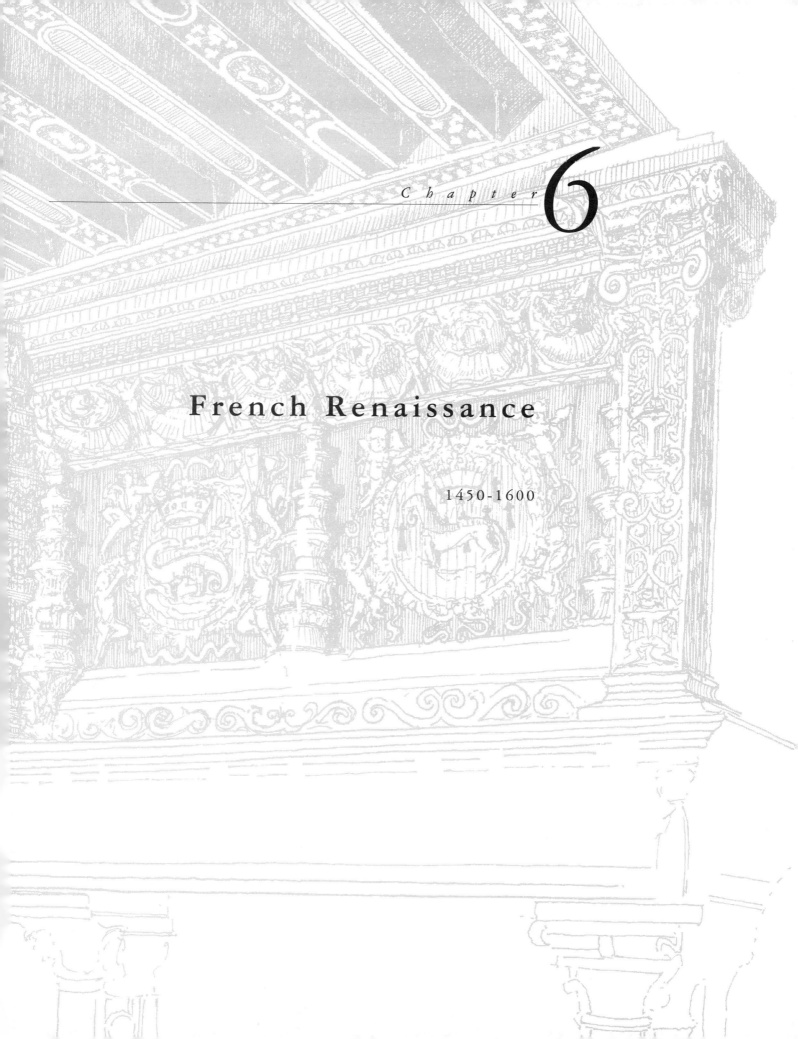

Chapter 6

French Renaissance

1450–1600

HISTORICAL SETTING

The military expedition into Italy in 1495 by Charles VIII to reclaim the Angevin possessions marked the beginning of a period of Italian Renaissance influence on the arts of France. Descending the peninsula as far as Naples, the French noblemen had ample opportunity to observe architecture and decorative arts and the role of prominent Italian families in supporting artistic endeavors; this engendered a new attitude on the part of French aristocracy as to what they could do to champion the arts. Further contacts with Italy continued through other military campaigns by Louis XII and Francis I, which reinforced the influence of the Renaissance movement. With Francis I's enthusiasm for the arts, his eagerness to employ Italian artisans, and Frenchmen traveling to Italy to study at the height of the Renaissance, the time was ripe for the widespread adoption of the classical in France.

This classicizing influence was facilitated by Italian artists being brought to France in the employ of the crown. Francis I, the ardent patron, went to great lengths to bring foreign artists to France as well as to allow French artists to study in Italy. Among the influential Italian artists were Leonardo da Vinci, who arrived at the court of Francis I in 1516; Francesco Primaticcio, who came to Fontainebleau in 1531; Benvenuto Cellini, primarily a goldsmith and metalworker, who was in the employ of Francis I from 1540 to 1545; and Sebastiano Serlio, who came to the attention of Francis I through the publication of the third book of his treatise on architecture and who became painter and architect to the French court in 1541. The Italian Renaissance influence was first reflected in the residences of French nobles and ministers.

Since the Gothic style was thoroughly entrenched in France, the full influence of this new classical vocabulary was slow to emerge. At first, in a transitional period, new decorative motifs were applied to medieval forms. In architecture it was the aim of promoters to modify medieval structures to embrace the classicism they observed in Italy; for example, when Charles VIII returned to France, it was his intent to alter the fortified Château d'Amboise to be more in line with attributes of the Italian style. Châteaux built in the first half of the 16th century continued to incorporate both medieval and Renaissance features in varying proportions until finally classical concepts as well as details were integrally related in design. By the end of the reign of Francis I in 1547 the Renaissance was in full flower in France, with the highest development represented in the period to 1575.

When Henry II died in 1559 a thirty-year period of civil strife began. The period can be characterized as one of anarchy and profligacy. Religious wars involved the Huguenots (French Protestants) and their role in the predominately Catholic country. A general massacre of the Huguenots was planned for Saint Bartholomew's Day in 1572. Many Huguenots were architects and craftsmen who contributed considerably to the arts of France. Consequently, many of these artists fled the country to England and the Netherlands; the impact of this on the arts of other countries is noteworthy, since they engaged in their art in their adopted countries. In 1598 Henry IV, the first Bourbon king, issued the Edict of Nantes, ending the Wars of Religion and defining the rights of Protestants to private worship; this prompted some of the exiled artisans to return to France.

Building activity was curtailed during this thirty-year period of anarchy. Since many Protestant architects suffered from religious persecution and were in exile, a paucity of architectural talent was available; in fact Charles IX, in 1569, dismissed all Protestants in royal employ. It cannot be said that decadence pervaded all the arts of this period of civil strife, for some pure classical design was undertaken. Reacting to a period of relatively straightforward and simple forms, there was a growing tendency toward exaggerated forms and greater elaboration. The Valois kings were naturally disposed to extravagance.

SPATIAL RELATIONSHIPS

At the beginning of the French Renaissance residential structures were primarily of three types: manor houses, town houses, and châteaux. Manor houses were distinguished from castles in their lack of fortification, although they did sometimes incorporate a wall or moat for protection. Town houses, on the other hand, were designated according to the socioeconomic level of the inhabitants: (1) *hôtels* for wealthy merchants and professional men (town mansions if owned by the nobility), and (2) *maisons* for middle- and lower-class occupants. The overall plan of the town house included a court around which buildings were constructed on more than one side. A screen wall in which the entrance was placed usually separated the house from the street.

Castles or châteaux were country palaces of the aristocracy; they were often irregular in outline and fortified by a surrounding wall. Defensive measures included moats, drawbridges, and circular towers. As the interest in alterations to these medieval structures peaked, Renaissance features were incorporated. Modifications to the châteaux buildings was usually undertaken in one of two ways: (1) alteration of the existing Gothic structure, or (2) construction of a new main building *(corps de logis)* on the original foundation.

Spatial Features of the Floor Plan and Three-Dimensional Spatial Characteristics

In the transitional phases modifications to the floor plan were least affected by the advent of the Renaissance. Gradually emphasis was given to symmetry, rectangular plans, and uniform spacing.

In the first phase of the French Renaissance, town house plans revealed little change and were like those of the 15th century. For small châteaux and manor houses attention was usually given to symmetry in renovations; however, if the structure was new the court was always rectangular (Figure 6-1). The greatest changes were noted in the châteaux; here, too, attention was devoted to greater regularity and expanded accommodations.

Spaces typical of castle keeps at the beginning of the French Renaissance included the following: hall, gallery, and apartments; the latter were composed of a chamber, antechamber, and wardrobe. The nucleus of castle life was the hall, located on an upper floor with an equivalent space below for cooler summer use or for the kitchen. A gallery incorporated in the later medieval period was used for exercise. Apartments were ser-

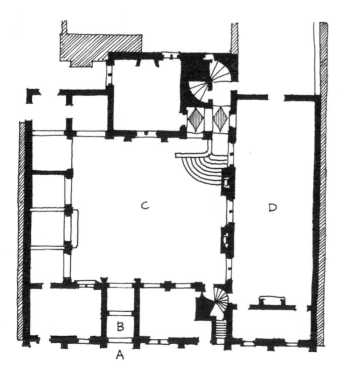

FIGURE 6-1   Plan of Town Mansion, Hôtel d'Ecoville, Caen (1535-38). Four sides of rectangular court surrounded by building: A street, B entrance, C court, D hall. Linear arrangement of rooms. Courtesy of Hacker Art Books, Inc. New York.

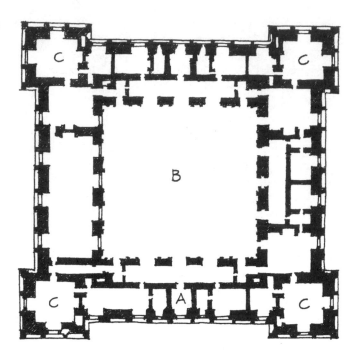

FIGURE 6-2   Plan of Château of Ancy-le-Franc (1539-1546). Mature Renaissance style. Emphasis to symmetry. Arcaded court. Square pavilions at corners, often with apartments: A entrance, B court, C pavilions. Courtesy of Hacker Art Books, Inc., New York.

viced by spiral stairs placed in the turrets. The only straight flight of stairs gave to access to the hall.

In the initial stages of the French Renaissance some patrons and architects favored the medieval château type but with greater regularity of plan, as observed at Château Chambord, built between 1526 and 1544. Medieval features included a moat, a walled enclosure, and four circular towers for the keep. There were eight self-contained apartments on each story, four in the corners and four in the towers. The famous dual stairway centers the hall of Greek cross plan. This remarkable staircase, with its twin spiral flights, allows those ascending and those descending to be unaware of each other.

Resembling the Italian Renaissance cortile the mature French Renaissance plan had a rectangular arcaded court with buildings of equivalent height on four sides; the internal court was retained, although it was no longer needed for defensive purposes. It was typical to have a basement with two main stories above, while a corner pavilion extended one story above the top floor; square pavilions as terminal features projecting at each corner of the structure; main apartments often located in these pavilions or in the main blocks. Typically the court entrance was in line with the principal apartment. The gallery normally had one principal story. The château of Ancy-le-Franc, built between 1538 and 1546, embodies these characteristic features of the mature French Renaissance style (Figure 6-2).

INTERIOR ARCHITECTURE AND DECORATION

Like the evolution of the floor plan in the French Renaissance period, there was no systematic approach to the manner in which Italian interior architectural and decorative detail were employed. The French designers were more inclined than the Italians to retain Gothic elements; in addition, they were not as knowledgeable about classical design. To their credit, however, the French artisans were more cognizant of the impact of construction as an element influencing design.

To the medieval castle of Fontainebleau the addition of the Francis I Gallery represented a merger of Italian ideas carried out by two Italians but with characteristics which were indisputably French. It represents the full flowering of the French Renaissance in the later years of the reign of Francis I and its continuation through the reign of Henry II, after which it declined. To undertake the interior decor of this gallery Francis I brought to France two Italians, Giambattista di Jacopo (Il Rosso) and Francesco Primaticcio. The School of Fontainebleau originated with this group.

Material and Decorative Techniques

The range of materials and decorative techniques were present in the Francis I Gallery at Fontainebleau. Among these were carved and inlaid panels, figurative subjects executed in fresco, and stucco to enframe paintings and for independent sculptural reliefs. The integration of media, as the combination of stucco relief elements to frame paintings, gave impetus to its decorative potential.

Interior Architecture and Decorative Elements

In the residences of the wealthy were spaces that typically were more luxuriously treated than others; these included entrances, staircases, halls of state, and chambers. In decorating these interiors the French learned from the Italians who worked at Fontainebleau that the totality of the interior scheme was more important than the individual parts; for example, paintings and sculpture, as parts, had to be perfected within the context of the whole.

Floors

Through the period a variety of materials was employed, including stone, marble, tile, brick, and wood. Italian Renaissance influence was in the use of majolica tile, which could be arranged in a pattern. In the Francis I gallery at Fontainebleau wood parquet was arranged in a herringbone pattern. Bands of tile, often blue, of running patterns were sometimes utilized to surround panel subdivisions.

Walls

Paneling was used to cover entire walls or to cover them only partially; intarsia was often used as a decorative technique. Sometimes stone or plaster was employed, but these were rarely painted. Fresco was also used early in the period; stone was arranged in a high dado. Evidence of Renaissance influence is noted in the use of medallions. Painted cloths or tapestries were frequently hung on walls. The latter were particularly important since it was still the practice for families to travel from residence to residence, and these served as an expedient means to make rooms quickly inhabitable.

As Renaissance influence began to be mixed with the design vocabulary of the earlier period, the proportion and arrangement of the orders did not adhere to classical practice. Designs for capitals were varied and included the use of plant and animal forms, cornucopias, human forms, and volutes, while the shafts were decorated with arabesques, interlacing patterns, circles, and lozenges.

The Francis I gallery had a high wainscot with inlaid walnut rectangular panels of various sizes carved in classical motifs (see Figure C-6). The *cartouche* (an oval frame with decorative detail centering it as well as surrounding it) was frequently used and with it motifs such as urns, swags of fruit, masks, and figures; these elements were sometimes divided by engaged columns. Italian motifs used by the team of Italian designers included putti, chimeras, garlands, and masks. In addition they introduced strapwork, a new motif, which was subsequently adopted in Italy as well as other European countries. Above the wainscot high-relief stucco decoration surrounded the cartouche, in the center of which was a fresco painting representing a change of subject matter from a religious orientation to classical subjects. Stucco was treated in a variety of ways: painted in colors, gilded, or left white.

Beginning around the mid-16th century an inclination to focus on one centralized design unit within panels as the preeminent feature developed, along with a predilection for larger and bolder models. Decorative detail for walnut paneling included carving, gild-

Figure 6-3 Door, Château of Blois. Tall, narrow door panels. Pilaster with classic detail. Set in deep reveal. Courtesy of The Château of Blois.

ing, marquetry, and inlays of ivory, ebony, and precious metals. High-relief stucco frames continued to be used when fresco, tapestry, or dyed leather were utilized.

Windows and Doors

The number and size of windows increased in the early years of the French Renaissance. Square-headed windows were usual. For glazing roundels were often used, as had been the case in Renaissance Italy; lead glazed windows were utilized in only the best rooms while oiled linen and paper were the norm in others. Shutters were also used.

In the first half of the 16th century the most prevalent type of window was two lights wide with one transom; the mullion and transom divisions formed the Latin cross. Often in the second half of the century windows were composed of six lights and a mullion with two transom divisions. Window heads were square, but some had rounded shoulders. Gradually, classical influence was introduced through the incorporation of pilasters and entablatures as enframements.

Doors were set in deep reveals. They were built in a variety of shapes and in small panels; classical architectural features may have been used in the surrounds (Figure 6-3). Carving and sculpture were used for ornamental decoration.

Chimneypieces

Initially the hood for the fireplace was placed over a firebox that was open on three sides. The hood was often supported by corbels. By the beginning of the 16th century the chimney breast projected strongly into the room and often was carried to the ceiling; supports for the overmantel included columns, caryatids, satyrs, and pilasters (Figure 6-4). Columns and entablatures were employed without regard for classic proportions. These monumental structures often appeared in tiers, heavily ornamented with a variety of decorated panels, carved relief designs, niches, and so on.

Figure 6-4 Chimneypiece, Château of Blois. Panels with salamander (crest of Francis I) and ermine (crest of Claude of France). Heavy, clustered columns support hood. Classical and architectural in concept. Pilasters flank the overmantel. Courtesy of The Château of Blois.

In the second half of the 16th century the design was essentially unchanged. Chimneypieces continued to be very strong focal points in the room, highly ornamented, often with sculptural reliefs and freestanding statues, divided into tiers, the firebox enclosed on three sides and often extending to the ceiling. On the other hand, they became more classical in detail and architectural in concept. In very large spaces it was not uncommon to have two monumental stone chimneypieces in the same room.

Ceilings

Stone, wood, and plaster were the materials used for ceilings of the French Renaissance. Flat ceilings of exposed wooden beams were used early in the period and into the 17th century. Characteristically, large girders (horizontal beams) were perpendicular to and supported smaller beams (or joists); the girders were placed far apart while the small beams were many and placed close to each other. The beams were sometimes painted with small patterns (Figure 6-5, see also Figure 6-4).

Vaults, which ranged from simple to complex, consisted of barrel, dome, and rib. Arrangements for both flat and vaulted ceilings included extensive use of coffering (recessed panels) of various shapes (Figure 6-6). Decorative elements for relief designs in the centers of the coffers were those typical of the period in which it was constructed. A coved transition from the wall to the ceiling was sometimes used.

Stairways

Three types of stairs were used during the French Renaissance—spiral, straight flights parallel to the wall, and dogleg flights that were parallel, without a central stairwell (see Figure C-7). Straight flights in the early period were used only for access to the hall. At the beginning of the period, when the castle plan was prevalent, it was common to place spiral stairs in the turrets to service the apartments; the spiral continued to be used but became less frequently employed as the 16th century progressed; at this time it was not always placed in the turrets.

FIGURE 6-5　Ceiling, Exposed Beams. Flat ceiling with girders and perpendicular small beams painted with patterns.

FIGURE 6-6　Ceiling, Vaulted and Coffered, Chambord. Lacunae with symbolic motifs including the salamander and cipher of Francis I. © Jean Feuillie/CNMHS, Paris.

FURNITURE

Furniture design followed that of both exterior and interior architecture in the proportionate relationship between form and decorative detail. At first motifs borrowed from the Italian Renaissance were added to basically medieval forms, while later both forms and ornamental detail showed the influence of classical ideals.

Political instability meant that in the beginning of this period families still moved from household to household, which prompted the continued construction of folding chairs and beds and the frequent use of textiles; all of these were easily transportable. Later, interest centered on comfort, a more elegant lifestyle, and new artistic endeavors prompted by the influence of the crown.

Materials and Construction Techniques

Throughout the French Renaissance medieval construction techniques were still in use, including the mortise and tenon, dovetail, and tongue and groove. Advances included the mitered joint and an overall ability to make less obtrusive joints; the advantage of the latter was to make it easier for the craftsman to carve continuous surface decoration.

Oak continued to be used in the French Renaissance, but it was gradually superseded by walnut, a softer wood that lent itself more easily to the carver's chisel. Other woods included lime, ash, and cedar.

Decorative processes included marquetry, inlay, carving, and polychrome enhancement. Italian influence was instrumental in introducing marquetry, in which materials were adhered to a carcass of wood. Among the inlay materials were marble, gold, ivory, soft colored paste, and expensive woods (such as ebony). Any of these could produce polychrome enhancement. High relief and other projecting parts had applications of silver and gold.

Typical Pieces and Stylistic Features

Furniture of the French Renaissance can be divided into two phases: Francis I and Henry II. The Francis I style, the first period, encompassed the reigns of Charles VIII (1483-1498), Louis XII (1498-1515), and Francis I (1515-1547). In this period of transition, Italian Renaissance and Gothic motifs were applied to essentially medieval forms. For example, on the same piece of furniture such popular Renaissance motifs as the arabesque or the rounded arch were used with Gothic features such as the linenfold, crockets, and pinnacles. Important classical elements were introduced including columns in the round, the pilaster (more popular than the column), often decorated with grotesques and culminating with a capital, and moldings carved with classic details such as the egg and dart. Symmetrical arrangements were based on organization around a central motif, perhaps a bow of ribbon or a candelabrum. Early use of the realistically portrayed human as a design element was often in the form of a head enclosed within a medallion or a laurel wreath; in the later Renaissance the nude was exquisitely portrayed, first in high relief and then in low relief.

Designated the Henry II style, the second period covers the reigns of Henry II (1547-1559), Francis II (1559-1560), Charles IX (1560-1574), and Henry III (1574-1589). While decoration of furniture was primarily affected in the first period, with the Henry II style structural form and decorative detail were those of the fully developed French Renaissance. But while the new forms were clearly based on and influenced by foreign models, the French designers creatively modified them to produce a style of their own. The influence of architectural features applied to furniture was of paramount importance; such elements included use of the entablature (or parts of it used independently), pilasters, pediments, classic moldings, carved decorative detail, and caryatids. Sometimes these were used in correct classical proportions.

Seat Furniture

Francis I. The retention of the rectilinear high panel back chair, with or without storage under the seat, represents a medieval form which continued to be constructed throughout the 16th century (Figure 6-7). Known as a throne chair, one form had the following characteristics: a paneled base enclosed for storage, access to which was through a hinged seat; a square seat surface; armrests parallel with the floor and enclosed underneath; a tall paneled back in two stages separated by classic moldings, the lower panel of which was taller. The introduction of classic elements included the use of the pilaster for the stiles of the back and, in the larger back panel, the symmetrical arabesque in a complicated intertwining arrangement of plant and animal forms.

Henry II. By the middle of the 16th century chairs became lighter in scale. Minimally decorated, they tended to be simple and rectangular. Backs were comprised of either a simple horizontal rectangle unconnected to the seat and upheld by the stiles, or a thin splat was used to connect a rail at seat level with the cresting of the back (Figure 6-8 and 6-9). Armrests sometimes had a downward curve, often extending beyond the uprights and ending in scrolls or rams' heads; the arm supports (sometimes in cyma profile) rose

FIGURE 6-8 Armchair (c. 1590). Carved walnut. Arms: cyma curve arm supports, ram's head ending to shaped armrests. Legs: united by H-shaped stretcher, columnar legs in front with rectangular section in back. Copyright The Frick Collection, New York.

FIGURE 6-9 Side Chair (c. 1610-1643). Walnut. Upholstered back panel and seat. Columnar legs joined by perimeter stretcher.

above the legs. Connected by a perimeter or H-shaped stretcher close to the floor, legs were column-like, baluster, or square in section and unturned; small bun feet were often used at the end of the legs under the stretcher. A shaped and ornamented apron was placed below, often curving downward, and perpendicular to the seat. This type of chair was either all wood or a combination of wood and upholstery.

The *caquetoire* (from the French word meaning gossip) was introduced about the mid-16th century (Figure 6-10). Characteristically it was a lightly scaled wooden chair with a tall, narrow paneled back attached to the trapezoid seat (wide at the front, narrow at the back), and shaped armrests (an aerial view would reveal outward-curving shapes for each). Legs at each angle of the seat were closely spaced at the back and wider at the front; a perimeter stretcher, mounted on small bun feet, joined the legs.

Tables

Francis I. A massive medieval table of the trestle type continued to be used into the Francis I period. The tabletop was often removable. Dining took place in any room, since no space was designated for this function in the plan. Typically, a carpet was placed on the table; this might have coordinated with other textiles in the room in which the table was placed.

FIGURE 6-10   Caquetoire (c. 1575). Carved walnut. Tall, narrow back. Trapezoidal seat. Columnar legs joined by perimeter stretcher. Copyright The Frick Collection, New York

Henry II. Tables fabricated after mid-century relied strongly on Italian models. From rather simple beginnings the table became a highly ornamented form. A massive rectangular tabletop was supported by four or more legs or, alternatively, on two fan-shaped trestles (wider at the top and narrower where attached to the stretcher) (Figure 6-11). The frieze was richly carved with ornaments such as palmettes, gadroons, acanthus, and strapwork; drawers were sometimes inserted in the frieze. Among the design elements on the highly ornamented trestles were satyrs, terms, caryatids, griffins, rams, and a variety of fantastic animals. The floor level bases the trestles were mounted on were perpendicular to the connecting stretcher, which was placed on or near the floor; sometimes arcading was placed between the tabletop and the stretcher. Pedestal tables with round or square tops also originated in this period, as did the draw table. The draw table was constructed as a means of extending a table's length; of two levels, the lower was divided in half so that when it was pulled out at each end the size of the table expanded twice its original length (Figure 6-12).

FIGURE 6-12   Draw Table (second half 16th century). Carved walnut. Arcade ends. Copyright The Frick Collection, New York.

Storage Pieces

Francis I. A storage piece of this period represents the continuation of a medieval form in which the enclosed rectangular upper section rested on an open base with a pan-

FIGURE 6-13   Dressoir (16th century). Medieval form with Renaissance classical detail. Band of gadroon carving decorates the plinth base and frieze of center section. Bun feet. Adapted with permission of Sterling Publishing Co. Inc., NY, NY from *Classical European Furniture Design* by Jose Claret Rubira, published by Gramercy Publishing Company, English translation © 1989 by Sterling Publishing Co., Inc., Originally published in Spain as *Meubles de Estilo Frances*, © 1974 by Editorial Gustave Gili, S.A.

FIGURE 6-14   Armoire è Deux Corps (second half 16th century). Walnut cupboard in two parts. Triangular pediment supported by double columns. Lower section wider than upper. Bun feet. Inlaid plaques of marble. The Metropolitan Museum of Art, Rogers Fund, 1906. (06.147)

eled back; often the piece was mounted on a plinth base. The number and arrangement of the doors varied (Figure 6-13). The carved decoration was primarily a repertoire of Gothic motifs with the introduction of Renaissance detail such as the round arch, fleur-de-lis, and carved head within a medallion borrowed from Italy.

Henry II. Beginning with the reign of Henry II (1547), the storage piece became more architectural, which was reflected in the use of such features as the entablature (or its independent parts) and columns or pilasters carved with reeding or fluting (See Figure C-8). Above the plinth base, open in the front, the supports could be columns or the fantastic figures characteristic of the period, while the solid back was most frequently paneled.

Distinction in terminology among storage pieces was arbitrary and consistency was nonexistent. Thus, the storage piece described in the following might be called a buffet, armoire, dressoir, or cupboard. Assuming importance in the latter half of the 16th century was a tall piece designed in two stages, the upper stage recessed on three sides. Two doors were incorporated in each section; in the lower section, doors were wider than those in the upper stage (Figure 6-14). Carvings on the doors within oval or rectangular frames some-

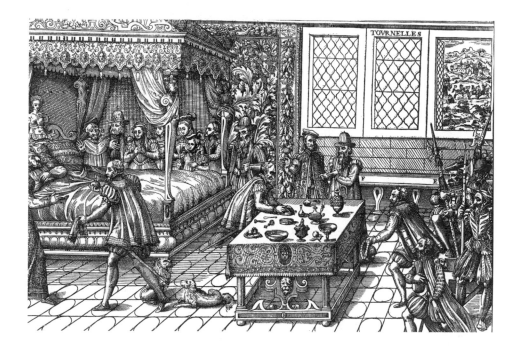

FIGURE 6-15 Bed Depicted in Woodcut, *The Death of Henri II* (1519-59), Jacques Perrisin. Terminal figures support the tester of sumptuous textiles. Philadelphia Museum of Art: Gift of Mrs. William M. Elkins, in memory of William M. Elkins.

times featured mythological figures or other subjects. Pilasters, columns, and decorated panels were frequently used to separate the doors. The crest of the piece varied—a complete entablature, a triangular or segmental pediment (often broken and centered with finials varying in contour), or a complex arrangement of elements. The piece was surmounted on bun feet, a plinth base, or block feet.

Beds

Henry II. Few beds are extant from this period. Based on evidence from contemporary engravings and paintings it appears that the most common bed was the four-poster that upheld a tester. The bed was richly ornamented with carving on the cornice and frieze; finials were mounted above the tester in line with the posts or columns. Instead of columns, sometimes *terms* (pedestals that tapered toward the base on which a bust was sometimes mounted) or *caryatids* (female figures used to support an entablature) were employed. The headboard was extravagantly carved; there was no footboard (Figure 6-15).

ORNAMENT

Francis I. The ornamental details of this period continued to draw upon a repertoire of Gothic motifs but with the introduction of elements from the Italian Renaissance. The latter included such decorative motifs as grotesques, sphinxes, dolphins, griffins, medallions, human heads in profile within medallions, columns, and pilasters.

Henry II. With the late French Renaissance and an essentially architectural style, designers tended to follow rather strict rules of classical art. Furniture often gave the impression of architecture in miniature, including the orders and pediments. Thus, carved ornament derived from the classical entablatures included the individual use of guttae, triglyphs, friezes, cornices, and combinations of these. Structural supports from architecture were heavily used in furniture design: columns (engaged or freestanding), along with capitals, pilasters that simulated the column, and caryatids. In addition, other figures from classical antiquity used as supports were griffins, tritons, and sphinxes. Palmettes, fluting, gadrooning, egg and dart motifs, grotesques, acanthus leaves, plumes, and mythological figures were also common decorative designs.

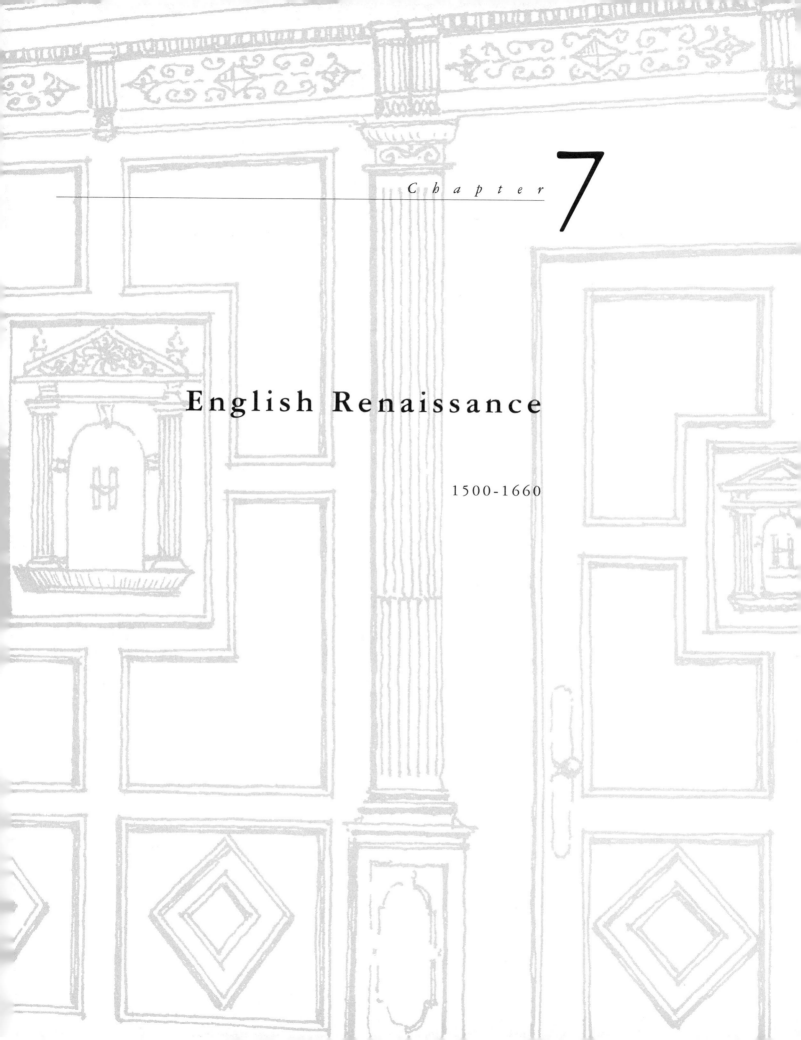

Chapter 7

English Renaissance

1500-1660

HISTORICAL SETTING

The English Renaissance took place while two lines of English monarchs, Tudor and Stuart, occupied the throne. The Tudor monarchs were Henry VII (1485-1509), Henry VIII (1509-1547), Edward VI (1547-1453), Mary (1553-1558), and Elizabeth I (1558-1603). In the Stuart line were James I (1603-1625) and Charles I (1625-1649). The period of the Commonwealth during which Oliver Cromwell was the Lord Protector ensued. While design during the reign of Henry VII was medieval, the reign of Henry VIII can be considered a period of transition in which there is evidence of Italian Renaissance influence on design but it was not yet fully absorbed. Highly influential in the progression of the English Renaissance during Elizabeth's reign was the construction of Somerset House (1547-1552). Surrounding Edward Seymour (Duke of Somerset who became Protector in 1547) were men who had an active interest in, and promotion of, the classical approach. In the early 17th century changes in stylistic development began to occur. First, Inigo Jones (1573-1652) showed a tendency to the baroque; at the same time, however, he demonstrated a predilection for High Renaissance models. Second, the outbreak of the Civil War in 1642 led to the appointment of the Puritan Oliver Cromwell as Lord Protector. The implications for design were that little building activity was undertaken during the civil disturbance and that the religious tenet of the Puritans stressing simplicity was reflected in furniture design. The succeeding Baroque period gained momentum in 1660.

Henry VIII, a benefactor of the arts, provided the stimulus for the adoption of the Renaissance style. In his employ were two Italian sculptors, Pietro Torrigiano and Giovanni da Maiano. The Florentine Torrigiano introduced Renaissance design to England when he was commissioned by Henry VIII in 1512 to design the tomb of Henry VII and his wife, Elizabeth. Da Maiano, a Tuscan known primarily for his role in the dissemination of the Italian Renaissance, was employed in the 1520s at Hampton Court; the decorative sculpture of Roman emperors in roundels was undertaken in terra-cotta. Other minor Italian artists in the service of the court contributed to the spread of Italian Renaissance design; for example, Toto del Nunziata was retained to work on Nonesuch, a palace built by Henry VIII. However, in the first half of the 16th century Italian Renaissance ideas were assimilated only gradually and primarily through the application of motifs to basically medieval forms.

Other acts of Henry VIII were to have far-reaching implications in terms of the influence on the arts in the succeeding Elizabethan period. The antiecclesiastical policy of Henry VIII was, in part, the result of the denial by the pope to grant an annulment of his marriage to Catherine of Aragon, the widow of his brother. Then, because of his marriage to Anne Boleyn Henry was excommunicated; he subsequently transferred papal powers to himself as head of the Church of England, which he divested from Rome. The ramification of this move for the arts was the dissolution of the monasteries.

First of all Henry appropriated the monastic lands and sold them to private families. A spate of building activity followed, either in the form of new structures or of the renovation of monasteries into palatial residences. Secular interests also meant that wealthy men who had previously put their money into the Church now felt free not only to build but to furnish their residences more luxuriously. In addition, the dissolution of monasteries had consequences for standards of craftsmanship and for education. Craftsmen in the medieval period had been under the supervision of the Church, which had high standards of workmanship, and without this supervision standards of craftsmanship declined. "For a generation or more after 1540, many of the pieces produced by native joiners were of comparatively poor construction and ornament."[1] Due to the emancipation of the laity, education became a priority, whereas it formerly had been the purview of the clergy; the Tudor

---

1. Ralph Fastnedge, *English Furniture Styles, 1500-1830* (Middlesex, England: Penguin Books Ltd., 1955), 13.

monarchs were firm believers in education. One result was that libraries were added to buildings as a matter of course by the end of the 16th century.

Two problems which Elizabeth I encountered during her reign were the debt her father had incurred and the religious difficulties that continued to surface. Complications of the alienation from Rome recurred during this period. Catholics were not allowed to worship freely but, determined to do so, Catholic families sometimes incorporated "priest's holes" into chimneypieces to hide the cleric if officials of the state should arrive unexpectedly.

During Elizabeth's reign, however, there was overall prosperity. Due in part to trade with the Low Countries and to the acquired wealth of merchants, building activity increased. Preeminent among residences constructed or enlarged during the reign of Queen Elizabeth I were those termed prodigy houses, a term coined by Sir John Summerson, noted authority on English architecture. Among these exceptional houses were Longleat, Hardwick, Burghley, Montacute, Wollaton, and others. These houses were built specifically for visits from the Queen and her extensive entourage, as she made four annual tours into the countryside to visit her subjects. On these visits she was apprised of the problems encountered by her subjects. The consequences were that her popularity increased and that she saved money, since her hosts paid all her expenses. Prodigy houses continued to be constructed almost to the start of the Civil War in 1642 with slight modification. While there was continuity, there was also change in the Jacobean period in the early years of the 17th century.

Pattern books and the migration of craftsmen to England were foreign influences at work during the Elizabethan and Jacobean periods. Generally the greatest impact was from the Low Countries, with whom the English enjoyed strong commercial connections. With advances in foreign trade and industry a new propertied class arose whose wealth and affluence led to an appreciation for higher standards of luxury. The engraved designs from German and Flemish pattern books provided the basis for the English interpretation of the Italian Renaissance in both architecture and furniture design. The 1577 Flemish pattern book *Architectura* by Johannes da Vries was especially influential; the illustrations were architectural in concept but overelaborate. Also instrumental in the development of Italian design in England was a translation of a work by Sebastiano Serlio. Robert Peake of Holborne published, in 1611, *The First Book of Architecture made by Sebastian Serly, translated out of Italian into Dutch and out of Dutch into English.* But to Inigo Jones goes the credit for bringing to England the pure Italian style instead of a Jacobean hybrid.

Inigo Jones visited Italy around 1600 and again in 1613-1614. During the latter visit he probably purchased a number of Palladio's original drawings; he also represented the Earl of Arundel in the acquisition of Italian antiques while at the same time extended his own knowledge of ancient architecture. A great admirer of Palladio, Jones embraced the Italian's system of proportion and borrowed many motifs from him. Jones's knowledge of Italian stage design is illustrated in his drawings for the court masques; through these activities he was probably able to incorporate architectural elements that influenced the direction of architecture in England. In 1611 Jones was appointed surveyor to Prince Henry, whom he advised on architecture; after his second visit to Italy he was appointed Surveyor to the Crown. Documentary evidence suggests that he was not responsible for the many buildings which have been attributed to him. However, two highly significant ones were the Queen's House (based on an Italian villa, 1618-1635), and the Banqueting House (based on an Italian palace, 1619-1622).

Approaches to the planning and design of Gothic and Renaissance buildings differed, the newer trend led by Inigo Jones. Architecture of the Gothic period was the outgrowth of ideas of many persons and alterations were made as work progressed; in addition, the nature of material was the governing factor for form. The Renaissance approach, in contrast, was one in which the product was the work of a single person. The designer worked to strict principles regardless of the nature of the material; the precise tenets revolved around order and proportion.[2]

SPATIAL RELATIONSHIPS

Since planning for defense with accompanying fortification was no longer essential as had been the case in the medieval period, E- and H-shaped plans were introduced. There was a growing desire for increased specialization of rooms and greater interest in comprehensive planning. The premier arrangement of spaces en suite in the late 16th and early 17th century plan related to the adjacency of the great chamber, withdrawing chamber, best bedchamber, and gallery. Although these rooms were often on the second floor, sometimes the chamber was on the first floor with the other rooms on the second. Spatial relationships remained essentially the same from the late 16th century to the third decade of the 17th century.

Having observed the disadvantages of the typical arrangement, Sir Henry Wotton espoused his ideas in a publication of 1624 entitled *Elements of Architecture.* This was not a pattern book but a down-to-earth building guide. Among his suggestions he advocated elimination of excessive ornamentation; orientation of rooms according to points of the compass; adjacencies of rooms of related function, as kitchen to dining room; changes to correct the weakness of the room arrangement whereby the innermost room could be accessed only by going through all the other rooms. Regarding the latter Sir Wotton commented on the disadvantage of this sequential arrangement since "they [designers] do cast their *partitions* as when all *Doors* are open a man may see through the whole *House,* which doth necessariely put an intollerable servitude upon all the *Chambers* save the Inmost, where none can arrive, but through the rest."[3] Wotton was widely traveled in France, Switzerland, Germany, and Italy; in these countries he was able to study some of the best examples of their architecture. He greatly admired Leon Battista Alberti, architect of the first Renaissance building in Florence, whom he acknowledged as the greatest architect "beyond the Alps." Like Alberti, whose treatise had been based on Vitruvius, Wotton felt that the early Roman architect was the authoritative base for the Italian Renaissance.

Spatial Features of the Floor Plan and Three-Dimensional Spatial Characteristics

The hierarchical arrangement of spaces in the manor houses could be deduced from the exterior. The significance of the level or floor could be determined by the height of its windows, which were taller on stories devoted to ceremony. The main façades of houses were almost invariably symmetrical but the apartments within were not. Many practices that impinged on spatial arrangements typical of the medieval period continued in the late 16th and early 17th centuries; hierarchical sequence of spaces within state apartments was retained.

Communal life was still important in the manor houses; therefore the hall continued to be used for servants' dining as well as for entertainment. However, as communal living became less important due to the removal of the family to more private spaces, the approach to the great high chamber by way of an impressive stairway became essential. For example, at Hardwick, Derbyshire, the grand staircase leads from the ground floor (devoted primarily to servant's activities) to the first landing from which the private spaces emanate on the first floor above ground level[4] and on to the second floor landing from

2. Nathaniel Lloyd, *A History of the English House from Primitive Times to the Victorian Period* (Northam, Sussex: Great Dixter, 1931; reprint, London: Architectural Press, 1975), 95. Page citations are to the reprint edition.

3. *Elements of Architecture,* by Sir Henry Wotton, printed by John Bill, London, 1624, p. 72 as quoted in Nathaniel Lloyd, *A History of the English House from Primitive Times to the Victorian Period* (Northam, Sussex: Great Dixter, 1931; reprint, London: Architectural Press, 1975), 89. Page citations are to reprint edition.

4. Hereafter first floor will refer to the first floor above ground level.

First Floor

Second Floor

FIGURE 7-1 Hardwick Hall, Derbyshire. Family Apartments, First Floor: A Upper part of hall; B Gallery; C Low Great Chamber; D Withdrawing Room; E Stairway to Great High Chamber; F Bed Chamber. State Apartments, Second Floor: A Great High Chamber; B Withdrawing Chamber; C Green Velvet Room; D Long Gallery; E Staircase and Upper Landing.

which rooms dedicated to affairs of state were arranged (Figure 7-1; see also discussion of stairways and Figure 7-9).

Gradually the hall became a room used almost exclusively as an entry. Since it was the introductory space for visitors to the household, it was usually a lavishly decorated space. Both one- and two-story ceiling heights were employed; at Hardwick the upper portion of the hall extends through the first floor. In the medieval period the position of the ground level hall was parallel to the façade, while in the Elizabethan era it was usually perpendicular. Although the lord of the manor had moved to more private rooms for family dining, the hall still had a dais at one end and a screen at the other.

By the 17th century, in the sequence of rooms in a typical state apartment, access to the great high chamber was by way of an impressive stair from the hall. The chamber was often comparable in size to that of the hall. As the ceremonial center of the household, the high chamber was richly decorated and served a variety of functions such as dining, entertainment, lying in state, dancing, receiving distinguished visitors, and masques. The masque was a dramatic entertainment performed by members of the household; it was usually mythological or allegorical in subject and generally ended with dancing.

Adjacent to the chamber was the withdrawing room. Although it had diverse uses, a major purpose was as a space for members of the family and visitors to retire to while the chamber was being set up for another function, as a banquet. *Banquet* was a term used for a way of passing time while the hall or great chamber was being set up for after-dinner activities, although separate banqueting houses were sometimes set up on the lawns.[5] The withdrawing room was thus a private sitting and reception room. In addition, servants slept here, since the private bedchamber was in the room beyond.

The gallery, located on the first or second floor, was either fully enclosed or open on one side to provide a covered passage. It was used as a space for exercise as well as a portrait gallery.

Important for the family, but not part of the state apartments, was the parlor, more common than in the medieval period. It was used primarily for family dining and for an informal sitting room; in larger houses more than one parlor was sometimes incor-

5. Mark Girouard, *Life in the English Country House: A Social and Architectural History* (Harmondsworth, Middlesex, England: Penguin Books, 1980), 104-105.

porated. The most common position was under the great chamber and often on the ground floor.

In the second half of the 16th century the staircase became an important ornamental feature. Frequently a distinguishing feature between the Elizabethan and the Jacobean arrangements for staircases was that the dogleg was more typical in the 16th century while in the 17th century the stair was built around an open stairwell. The flights of dogleg stairs are parallel and zigzag without the benefit of a stairwell.

Chapels were normally incorporated in houses of wealthy and influential landowners. The chapel was frequently closely associated with the most private room in the house, the closet. The chapel was often two stories high and the closet immediately above it; an occupant could look down from the closet into the chapel. Women, and sometimes the lord, watched the progress of the service below from this vantage point. The closet was used for private prayers and occasionally for christenings and marriages. The private chapel did not replace the parish church, which was often located near the major household.

INTERIOR ARCHITECTURE AND DECORATION

Renaissance detail began to be incorporated in interiors in the first half of the 16th century, although the medieval lingered throughout the century. When Pietro Torrigiano came to England he brought with him other Italian artists to work on Hampton Court, and while Renaissance detail was incorporated, the hall was essentially medieval in concept, but with classical detail added to old forms. In this great hall of medieval hammer beam construction, the influence of the Italian Renaissance was revealed in only a small way in the luxuriantly embellished lanterns used as pendant drops, carved by a London craftsman. This hall was built by King Henry VIII between 1532 and 1536 to replace the earlier one of Cardinal Thomas Wolsey. In his eagerness to have the reconstruction completed the king ordered work to be undertaken both by day and at night by candlelight.[6]

Materials and Decorative Techniques

Carved wood, plaster, and iron encased in plaster were the materials of significance especially for ceiling design in the 16th and early 17th centuries. Beginning in the early 16th century the suspended ceiling came into use. At first these treatments continued to reveal the heavy, massive beams while the smaller joists of the floor above were covered, a structural arrangement that continued late into the Elizabethan period. The major beams were molded and, in addition, the soffits of the solid oak timbers were ornamented with carving. Alternatively, a separate carved wood strip was applied to the soffit of the beam. Another means of attaining relief was to encompass the beam in plaster so that carved designs could be rendered in situ while the plaster was wet. Then, when all structural members were concealed, an overall elaborate plasterwork ornamental facing called *pargework* was used to decorate ceilings and sometimes walls; this treatment was introduced during Elizabeth's reign and continued in use into the Jacobean period. Plaster was worked in situ or molded and then applied. For very deep relief, as in pendant drops, iron forms were used to serve as the backing around which the plaster was molded.

Interior Architecture and Decorative Elements

Mention has been made of the impact of pattern and architecture books on the spread of the Renaissance style. Of great import was the work by Vredeman de Vriese of Antwerp; his pattern book, entitled *Architecture,* was published in 1577. Craftsmen from the Low Countries were also at work in England because of close trade relations. The engraved

6. G. H. Chettle, John Charlton, and Juliet Allan, *Hampton Court Palace, Greater London,* revised with additions by Juliet Allan (London: Her Majesty's Stationery Office, 1982), 25.

designs for such elements as chimneypieces, decorative details, and columns were adapted by English craftsmen.

The earliest book on architecture to be printed in England was by John Shute and entitled *Chief Groundes of Architecture*, published in 1563. An employee of the Duke of Northumberland, Shute had personal knowledge of Italian Renaissance design, having visited Italy in 1550. He was familiar with the designs of Palladio and Michelangelo and had knowledge of Vitruvius and Serlio. His views on the proportions of the orders coincide with these authorities; in England their use was mostly limited to carved wood or molded plaster detail.

Floors

The material most commonly used for interiors of the 16th and early 17th centuries was brick. Tile (glazed, patterned, and plain), wood, and flagstone were used by all classes. Types of stone varied by geographic region; slate, granite, marble, and sandstone were available. While stone was confined to the ground level, wood was the preferred material for the upper floors, where oak and elm boards were sometimes as much as 24 inches wide. Plastered floors, occasionally painted, were sometimes employed. Carpet was not common, but rush matting laid on the finished floor was. Occasionally the matting was installed on wet plaster so that it was literally bonded to the floor.

Walls

Wall treatments of the 16th and early 17th centuries were basically of three types: paneling, plaster, and textile hangings. Installations were sometimes combinations of these. In the early 16th century wall treatments were primarily medieval, although ornamentation revealed the use of decorative detail based on Renaissance design. For example, Romayne work was used in which heads, often in profile, were carved in medallions on architectural elements (Figure 7-2). The embellishment of panels also included the linen-

FIGURE 7-2 Oak Panel of Renaissance Design (early 16th century). Romayne work with the head carved in the roundel. Architectural Book Publishing Co. Based on a photograph.

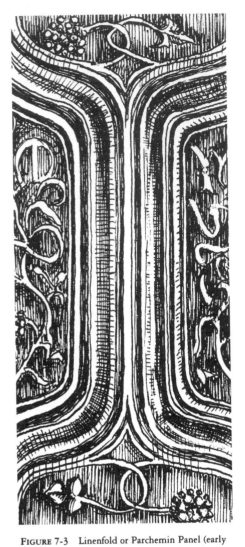

Figure 7-3 Linenfold or Parchemin Panel (early 16th century). Ogival splayed ending from the central spine of the carved ornament with the addition of vine ornament in the interstices. Architectural Book Publishing Co. Based on a photograph.

Figure 7-4 Great High Chamber, Hardwick Hall, Derbyshire. Walls decorated with tapestries, paneling, and plaster frieze. Tapestries: Brussels portray the story of Ulysses. Paneling: engravings of classical authors, philosophers, and Roman emperors decorate the panels. Frieze: modeled plaster with subjects related to the forest. Chimneypiece: alabaster and blackstone; frieze of strapwork and cabochon units supported by engaged columns. © National Trust Photographic Library.

fold (sometimes referred to as *parchemin*), a Gothic motif, which was used in parallel with Renaissance details (Figure 7-3).

Plaster was in widespread use throughout the period. Applied to a foundation of brick, stone, or lath, it was often painted with whitewash. More decorative uses included its application with other materials. At Hardwick Hall, in the high great chamber, a very deep plaster frieze worked in high relief and painted was placed above a set of eight Brussels tapestries illustrating the story of Ulysses (Latin for Odysseus) who, in Greek mythology, was a leader in the Trojan War (Figure 7-4). Since the house was constructed as a hunting lodge, the frieze suitably depicts Diana (a Roman goddess of the forest and animals) with her maidens commencing a quest through the forest in pursuit of boar and stag. The sets of tapestries which Elizabeth Shrewsbury purchased for Hardwick determined the size of both the high great chamber and the gallery. For example, 13 Flemish tapestries depicting the story of Gideon were purchased for her gallery, which measured an impressive 166 feet long, 22 to 40 feet wide, and 26 feet high; hanging in front of the tapestries were paintings, a popular fashion in the 17th century (see Figure C-8).

FIGURE 7-5 Barham's Manor House, Higham, Suffolk (16th century). Wall: painted design over studs and plaster; intertwined octagons with foliage in black; floral and pomegranate motifs center the squares. Architectural Book Publishing Co. Based on a photograph.

Sixteenth-century examples illustrate the use of plaster between studs over which textile designs were painted (Figure 7-5). The painting covers both the structural oak members and the plaster (clay daub) inserts. Painting on plaster also simulated paneling, which included representations of the stiles and rails, strapwork decoration on the panels, and even the pegs used to secure mortise and tenon joints in actual wood construction, as at St. Helen's Lodge Ipswich (c. 1600).

Wood paneling was applied to the structural frame, stone, or brick. It was primarily of three heights: dado, ceiling, or the frieze placed just below the ceiling. If the paneling was not full height tapestries often were hung above the dado; alternatively, when the paneling stopped short of the ceiling a plaster frieze might be used above, or a wooden frieze might be installed above the main order below. In the last quarter of the 16th century panel arrangements began to be more architectural in concept and in the Jacobean period treatments tended to become more classically correct.

Although no great changes in design took place from the Elizabethan to the Jacobean period of the early 17th century, some variation in wood paneling can be observed. Before Elizabeth's reign, tall rectangular panels with heavy moldings were the norm. Then, in the second half of the 16th century, while large-scale framing continued, moldings became more slight and the shape of the panel became square. Some variation in the shape of the panels did occur. For instance, a rectangle in the center of the panel was surrounded by four L-shapes, all of which were formed by applied moldings; this arrangement was also employed on furniture (Figure 7-6). Elaborate patterns for paneling were also introduced, as in the high great chamber at Hardwick (see Figure 7-4). Larger square panels with slight moldings were common, but at the same time variations in shape occurred; geometrically applied moldings provided some decorative enhancement.

Ornamental treatment of the panels included the use of carving, inlay, strips of applied moldings, some painting, and applied split spindles (a favorite Jacobean element). Embellishment included some of the following motifs: Romayne work, linenfold, florals, arabesques, foliate forms, fruit, flowers, cartouches, cabochons, and family arms. Arcading began to be used in the last quarter of the 16th century but became more prevalent in the

FIGURE 7-6   Holland House (early 17th century). Paneling: architectural in concept; larger panels of early 17th century; pilasters separate the paneled sections

FIGURE 7-7   Paneling from Exeter (early 17th century). Panels: sections divided by carved pilasters; inconsistent level of panels. Plinth of pilaster: centered with cabochon characteristic of fully developed Jacobean style. Architectural Book Publishing Co. Based on a photograph.

Jacobean period. A distinctively Jacobean ornamental device consisted of a pyramidal form mounted on four balls with an additional ball at the apex. Renaissance detail increased during the Jacobean period.

Sections of paneling were constructed in widths of four to six panels. These were then mounted on the wall and butted together. At first no attempt to cover the juncture was undertaken and the stiles were double wide at this point; sometimes, however, the outer stiles were trimmed to half width so that the juncture was the width of a single stile. As greater classical influence prevailed, pilasters were applied as separate pieces to the double-wide juncture. At first the divisions of the pilaster and the panel did not coincide; these parts were united when, for example, the molding terminus for the pedestal continued as the dado cap around the room; this indicated that they were designed together

(Figure 7-7). Sometimes engaged columns instead of pilasters were used to separate the panel sections into bays.

Windows and Doors

The value attached to English Renaissance windows was indicated by the fact that until the last quarter of the 16th century windows were considered furniture and could be designated in wills as separate pieces of property; a legal decision in 1579 considered them fixtures.[7] The use of glass for windows increased throughout the century, although great houses had glazed windows for most of the period. Toward the end of the century England had at least 15 glass manufacturers. For most of the 16th century diamond-shaped glass panes were most prevalent but sometimes roundels were used and sometimes heraldic patterns of glass were inserted. In the 17th century rectangular panes predominated but, here too, many patterned arrangements were introduced. The panes of glass were held in position by grooved bars of lead (cames) which in turn were attached to iron surrounds within the window frame. In the absence of glass other materials such as horn or paper were used.

Windows were set in frames of stone, brick, or wood; mullions and jambs were deeply molded and transomed windows began to be used in the late 16th century. While some windows were stationary others were of the casement type, designed to open outward and restrained by iron fixtures.

Materials for the door surrounds included wood, stone, and brick. The doorway opening was often flat-headed, but the four-centered arch was still in use through the 16th century. In fact medieval detail merged with the classical detail introduced around the middle of the century. A manifestation of this is revealed in a door surround composed of plinths supporting pilasters headed with Corinthian capitals and an entablature; the door paneling, however, is more traditional in the use of applied battens forming a large lozenge in the center.

The importance of a door, and thus a room, could be measured by its treatment. More prominent rooms were introduced by more decorative and often paneled doorways; less important doors were characterized by the simpler batten treatment. By the 17th century, with the growing influence of the classical, impressive pedimented doorways were more frequent.

Chimneypieces

A major architectural feature in rooms of the late 16th and early 17th centuries was the chimneypiece; it was often the most conspicuous and ornate decorative feature of the room. Medieval and classical elements were mixed throughout the period; the four-centered arch continued in use from the medieval era to the early 17th century. However, the firebox was usually rectangular.

Emphasizing its importance was the extension of the chimneypiece into the room and its design, enhanced in stages with elaborate decoration. Sometimes it rose to the ceiling, where its cornice continued around the room. Materials were often wood, marble, plaster or combinations of these; carving and painting were techniques associated with the foregoing materials to attain the flamboyant embellishment that the Elizabethans admired.

The lower stage of the chimneypiece was frequently made up of an entablature (or part of it) supported by columns on plinth bases, pilasters, or caryatids (see Figures 7-4 and C-8). Examples of surface treatments for columns or pilasters included fluting, stop-fluting, strapwork, and foliage; the capitals were Doric, Ionic, or Corinthian. The decorative overmantel was often developed in stages and frequently capped with an entablature. The combinations in the arrangements are quite varied: panels (often divided by columns or pilasters supporting a frieze or cornice), niches, rounded arches. The decorative vocabulary was also diverse: coats of arms, strapwork, foliage, human figures, allegorical and scriptural scenes, applied split spindles, and cabochons.

---

7. Lloyd, 71.

Figure 7-8 Ceiling, Long Gallery, Blicking Hall, Norfolk (1616-1627). Ceiling: wide interlaced plasterwork ribs cast in plaster of Paris; other detail executed by hand including the strapwork filling the spaces between the broad plaster bands.

Ceilings

Primary ceiling configurations were flat, coved, or vaulted. Italian Renaissance elements began to appear early in the 16th century as applications to a basically medieval interior, but some diminishing echoes of medieval treatments continued into the late century. The early 17th century represents a continuation of the late 16th, although there were some relatively minor variations.

Ranging from simple to elaborate ornamental surface designs, the most prominent decoration for the ceiling was pargework, a means of creating relatively low-relief designs using plaster (Figure 7-8). Configurations of endless variety were accomplished. Molded plastic ribs were arranged in complex geometric designs forming compartments; in the panels formed by the ribs were lower-relief designs in the field. At first the ribs projected deeply, but as the Jacobean period approached they became flatter and broader. Decorative detail included: (1) molded embellishments such as fruits and flowers, on the soffits of the ribs, (2) the use of pendant drops or bosses at the convergence of ribs, and (3) ornamental relief in the fields. In the latter, strapwork (most favored in the early 1600s) was widely employed but, in addition, these designs were supplemented by motifs such as floral and other organic motifs, heraldic devices, rosettes, representations of animals, cabochons, and pyramids.

Stairways

The medieval spiral stairway continued in use throughout the English Renaissance. New to this period was the use of the stairway as a processional route to the high great chamber (Figure 7-9). Arrangements of increasing use were (1) straight flights with no

turns or landings, (2) dogleg, and (3) flights built around an open stairwell. The latter was more typical of the early 17th century, while the dogleg was more common in the Elizabethan period. The stairs were closed string, the characteristic of which was a diagonal member covering the ends of the risers and treads.

The balustrade became an important interior architectural feature and grew even more decorative in the baroque period of the late 17th century. Balusters were of great variety; both turned and flat carved pilaster-like members were used. The latter, sometimes pierced, were introduced in the early 17th century. Turnings were occasionally columnar, but many other versions were undertaken by the turner; for instance, the upper and lower sections were mirror images of each other. Another treatment, this time of Dutch influence, was a carved panel that, instead of separately mounted balusters, was inserted between the handrail and the diagonal brace. This was an introduction of the early 17th century and the panel resembled strapwork. Handrails were at first strongly molded but later in the period became flatter.

The stair was introduced by a square newel that was highly decorated with carving or inlay, and as one ascended carved pendant drops emanating from the floor above yielded further decorative interest. The newel became a very important decorative device; some newels were turned, some were solid square newels, and some were paneled. Average houses had simply treated newels. Strapwork was sometimes used as the decoration for newels executed on solid wood as well as on paneled versions. Finials of assorted design ranged from simple turned variations to elaborate heraldic versions of the owner's coat of arms; the pierced obelisk was a favorite decorative motif of the Jacobean period.

At Knole in Kent, a staircase of the early 17th century is a superior example of trompe l'oeil painting. On the wall opposite the balustrade is a painted mirror image of the balustrade including the newel and its leopard finial from the owner's coat of arms (see Figure C-9 and C-10).

FURNITURE

Furniture exhibited the same direction in design development. Foreign sources were of considerable influence, designers being motivated by publications. Particular decorative features were based on Flemish and German pattern books, from which the English derived such elements as floral and checkered inlays, strapwork, and low-relief carved arabesques. Italian artists and craftsmen came at the invitation of Henry VIII, introducing the Renaissance in England. Classical motifs were applied to medieval models. Also, Dutch and Flemish immigrants constructed furniture; high-quality furniture was imported as well.

Many design features were retained in the Jacobean period. Minor changes were made in furniture design, but generally there was continued emphasis on display and comfort. The court cupboard, for example, was a significant furniture form used specifically to display some of a family's most valuable objects. In the interest of comfort some upholstery was introduced in the Elizabethan period, with somewhat greater attention given to comfort in the early 17th century. In the Cromwellian period, due to the religious orientation of the Puritans, furniture forms were produced where the emphasis was on simplicity rather than extravagance or comfort. Further, since the money supply was short, extravagance could not be supported because of the labor-intensive techniques needed for elaborate ornamentation.

Materials and Construction Techniques

For the structure of furniture oak was the most favored wood, but ash, elm, and walnut were also employed. Craftsmen used native woods for inlay, whereby the surface wood was cut away and thin pieces were inserted for the design composition. Woods included bog oak for darker values, holly and poplar for lighter values, and stained woods. A widely used design that capitalized on the contrast of light and dark woods was the checker ornament.

In addition to inlay, prominent decorative processes were carving, turning, and painting. Carving in the Elizabethan period was executed in an extravagant and unruly manner so that the grotesques, masks, and strapwork (more significant in the early 17th century) were not highly finished. In the Jacobean period, on the other hand, carving was in such low relief that it projected little beyond the surface of the wood. It thus lacked the greater three-dimensionality that characterized Elizabethan carvings.

The use of turning was evident in the period of the Tudors, but it was more important as a decorative device during the reign of James I. Applied split spindles were common; paper was glued between two blocks of wood that were then turned on a lathe as if they were one piece. After turning the blocks were separated and applied, often with glue, as separate pieces to such surfaces as stiles. Frequently the spindles were stained black to simulate ebony. Early in the 17th century these applications were frequently shaped like balusters, which were short, circular in cross section, curved in outline, and swollen in outline near the base. Distinctions were made between the responsibility of the turner on the one hand and of the joiner on the other. A joiner's guild was first granted a charter in 1570.

Early in the Tudor period painting was prominently used, but the practice declined during Elizabeth's reign. However, some paneling and furniture was still painted during the 17th century. Painting was sometimes used in conjunction with carved detail; remnants of green and red have been revealed in extant pieces.

Wax or oil was used to finish pieces of furniture. A preference for rubbing linseed oil into the surface was typical by the mid-16th century, while beeswax was the choice finish during the 17th century.

Construction did not change drastically from the medieval period. Although paneled chests were introduced in the early 16th century, paneling became of great consequence later in the century and into the 17th century. In this system, regardless of its use on chests or other pieces, a panel (thinned on the edges) was fitted into stiles and rails that were channeled to receive them. The stiles and rails were fitted together with the mortise and tenon, held in position with dowels and without benefit of glue.

Typical Pieces and Stylistic Features

Houses, even among the wealthy, were sparsely furnished during these periods. Pieces were often multifunctional, either designed specifically for more than one purpose or designed specifically for one purpose, but with use expanding as needed for other functions. Of the former, the chair-table should be mentioned; the back served as a tabletop which, when folded down, rested on arms parallel with the floor. Designed specifically for storage of valuables, linens, and clothing, the chest was occasionally used as a table and sometimes as a bed.

Seat Furniture

Chairs, benches, stools, and settles were the primary types of seat furniture constructed in the Elizabethan and Jacobean styles. Changes in stylistic orientation occurred during the period of the Commonwealth.

Similar in form to the medieval chair but lacking storage space under the seat, the wainscot chair was primarily for the lord of the manor as he presided over the activities in the hall. Sometimes another one was available for the lady of the household; other persons sat on stools or benches. Although the wainscot was more lightly scaled than earlier chairs, it still was heavy and rectangular (Figure 7-10). In the Elizabethan period the back rose straight or was slightly raked; it was customarily paneled with carved or inlaid decoration. If there was a decorative cresting of the back it was located on the top rail between the stiles. The wainscot was an open arm chair in which the armrests (essentially parallel with

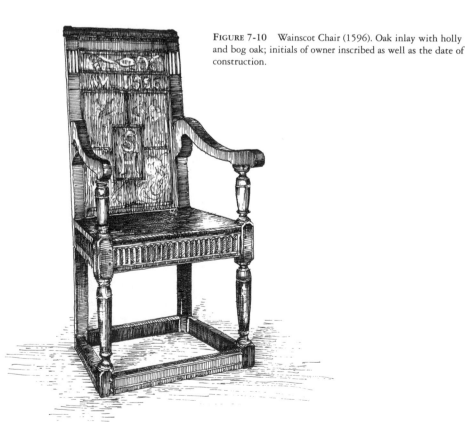

FIGURE 7-10 Wainscot Chair (1596). Oak inlay with holly and bog oak; initials of owner inscribed as well as the date of construction.

FIGURE 7-11   Hackets, Wainscot Chair. Hackets (roughly triangular in form and attached to stiles) fill the space below the crest extending beyond the stiles. Crest of Flemish S-scrolls. Courtesy of John T. Kirk.

FIGURE 7-12   Farthingale Chair (1620-1640). Upholstered oak. Designed to accommodate the extreme width of women's dress. Columnar front legs with rectangular cross section of the rear legs. Perimeter stretcher. By Courtesy of the Board of Trustees of the Victoria and Albert Museum, London.

the floor) extended beyond the arm supports, often ending in a whorl. The arm supports were continuations of the legs. Under the square seat the front legs were turned, while the back legs were usually rectangular in cross section and continued to form the stiles of the back. A perimeter stretcher connected the legs; it was placed close to the floor or at floor level. The aprons of these pieces were sometimes shaped.

Changes in the design of the wainscot in the Jacobean period were that the cresting of the back often extended beyond the stiles with the addition of hackets (Figure C-11). *Hackets* were tapering elements, wider just under the crest and narrower as they ended near arm level (Figure 7-11). The cresting was often very decorative; frequently the ornament was composed of symmetrically disposed Flemish S-scrolls with carved acanthus leaves. Armrests in this style tended to drop in the front rather than remaining parallel with the floor, as in the Elizabethan period.

The farthingale chair was prominent in the early 17th century (Figure 7-12). This was an upholstered, armless chair designed to accommodate the fashion for extreme width in women's dress. Upholstery was sometimes velvet- or turkey-work; the latter was an imitation of an oriental fabric in which yarns were pulled through a coarse fabric, knotted, and cut. The upholstered square seat was high while the back, also upholstered, was rectangular, unusually low, and disposed horizontally with a space between it and the seat. Front legs were often turned in columnar form, ending in a square section at floor level. The perimeter stretcher was inserted into these blocked sections. The four legs were connected with a perimeter stretcher. A chair of similar form was constructed during the Commonwealth, except that the upholstery was less decorative, consisting of leather fastened with brass studs (Figure 7-13). The Puritans felt that decorative upholstery was inappropriate and indecorous. The turning of the front legs of these Cromwellian chairs was often of a knob-turned type consistent with the period.

FIGURE 7-13 Cromwellian chair (1640-1680). Oak. Simple form typical of the period. Leather upholstery attached with brass nails. Ball turning for front legs and stretcher; U-shaped stretchers at two levels. By Courtesy of the Board Trustees of the Victoria and Albert Museum, London.

FIGURE 7-14 Yorkshire-Derbyshire Chair (mid-17th century). Back consists of two crescent-shaped rails with elaborate carving. Intermittent turned and blocked sections for front legs joined by a turned stretcher. Applied split spindles decorate the stiles. By Courtesy of the Board of Trustees of the Victoria and Albert Museum, London.

During the Commonwealth a chair designed with some frequency was the Yorkshire and Derbyshire type, a lightly scaled chair introduced around the mid-17th century; it continued to be constructed during the succeeding period of the Restoration. Two types of backs were fashionable. One was comprised of two crescent-shaped cross rails mounted between the stiles of the back (Figure 7-14). The other was characterized by arcading between a cross rail above seat level and the cresting of the back; each arcaded section was divided by turned members. The stiles were embellished with applied split spindles; the finials of the stiles were frequently scrolled toward the center of the back. Stretchers for these chairs were commonly at two levels, but variations occurred. One example had stretchers placed near the floor connecting the front and back legs as well as the back legs themselves; on the other hand, the upper stretchers on the same chair connected the front legs as well as the front and back legs. The connecting stretcher for the front legs was often turned; the front legs had alternate turned and blocked sections where intersecting structural members were inserted. Popular turning configurations at this time included the knob, bobbin, baluster, and, just before the Restoration, the twist turn.

During the reign of Charles I fully upholstered pieces of furniture were introduced based on French models (Figure 7-15). However, the English did not like the French wife of Charles I and were in no mood to accept the frivolities represented in this approach, since approximately 40,000 of his subjects died of the plague in the year in which he was crowned. There is evidence that comfort was important to some subjects, since they complained of uncomfortable seating. Sir John Harrington, for example, noted that it might be appropriate for "the state of the chamber to have easye quilted and lyned formes and stooles for the lords and ladies to sit on, which fashion is now taken up in every merchant's

FIGURE 7-15 Sofa (1610). Upholstered sofa with fringe decoration. Turned front legs. Perimeter stretcher placed near the floor. Attention to comfort noted in use of upholstery and in the use of the hinged upright above the armrest which let down for limited reclining. © National Trust Photographic Library/Horst Kolo.

hall, as great plank forms . . . and waynscot stooles so hard that since great breeches were layd aside, men can scant endewr to sitt upon."[8]

Tables

Board and trestle dining tables, which were easily demountable, continued to be fabricated after the draw table was introduced in the late 16th century (Figure 7-16). When fully extended the tabletop of the draw table was almost double its original length. This was accomplished was by pulling out the two under-leaves, to each of which were attached a pair of extended "arms." These armed runners were constructed in a manner that allowed the top portion to be level with the two leaves when lengthened and at the same time prevented the leaves from being drawn too far. The bases of these tables were highly ornamented. The heavy and exaggerated legs were called *bulbous,* synonymously termed *melon* or *cup and cover;* above and below this protrusion the diameter of the turning was significantly less. The lower portion of the cup and cover was often carved with an acanthus leaf, while the top portion was often ornamented with gadrooning; atop this was often a capital, sometimes Ionic. The legs supported a decorative apron (or frieze) enhanced by carving or inlay. Motifs included the lunette, guilloche, checker design, and gadrooning. Below, the legs were united by a perimeter stretcher placed at or near floor level. Changes that occurred in the Jacobean period included lower relief carving, more slender cup and cover legs, and greater use of strapwork designs, but the form remained essentially the same. Tops of dining tables were thinner during the Commonwealth.

A variety of side tables was introduced during the reign of James I and were constructed throughout the remainder of the 17th century. A gateleg table was introduced,

---

8. Sir J. H. and others, *Nugae Antiqual: being a collection of original papers in prose and verse* (1804 edition) 1: 202, quoted in Ralph Fastnedge, *English Furniture Styles from 1500 to 1830* (1955; reprint, Baltimore: Penguin, 1964), 31. Page citation refers to reprint edition.

FIGURE 7-16 Draw Table (16th century). Checker inlay on the frieze. Cup and cover legs support the whole; acanthus leaf carved on the cup section with gadrooning on the cover, Ionic capital. By Courtesy of the Board Trustees of the Victoria and Albert Museum, London.

FIGURE 7-17 Nonesuch Chest. Chest inlaid with architectural representation of the palace built by Henry VIII. Type popular between 1560 and 1600. By Courtesy of the Board of Trustees of the Victoria and Albert Museum, London.

which allowed the drop leaf of the table to be raised, thereby enlarging the tabletop surface. The type of turning is a guide to the stylistic period in which these were fabricated.

Storage Pieces

The medieval boarded chest was made until the 17th century, but the paneled chest made its appearance at the beginning of the 16th, with ornament typical of the period such as Romayne work, derived from the Italian Renaissance. In the Elizabethan period the paneled chest sometimes was highly architectural in concept, which yielded exemplary architectural models; these were often termed *Nonesuch* chests (Figure 7-17). Sometimes the fronts of the chests were arcaded, the sections separated by stiles or pilasters. Early use of the floral arabesque is noted in the Jacobean period. The chest of drawers evolved from the

FIGURE 7-18 Court Cupboard (late 16th century). Oak and walnut, carved and inlaid. Upper section with three storage compartments separated by acanthus brackets; surmounted by frieze and cornice. Lower part open with bulbous legs in the front and plain rear legs which support a frieze carved with the guilloche motif. Inlaid checkered design on heavy lower shelf. Based on a photograph.

FIGURE 7-19 Press Cupboard (c. 1600). Storage on two levels. Upper section: divided into three parts with sides canted; bulbous legs support the frieze carved in a lunette design. Lower section: fitted with two doors carved with round arches; frieze of midsection repeats the lunette design of the upper portion.

chest, beginning before the 17th century with one drawer under the chest portion; it was referred to as a *mule chest*. More drawers were gradually added and the true chest of drawers came into being by the middle of the 17th century.

Two types of cupboards predominated for storage and for display, the court cupboard and the press cupboard. The *court cupboard* (primarily for display) had either three open shelves or, alternatively, one level of enclosed storage (Figure 7-18). The storage section was often divided into thirds, the center section of which was slightly recessed and parallel with the front, while the sides were canted. The cup and cover leg was often used on two levels but in one example fantastic animals were used on one level while the bulbous form was used on the other. The friezes of these pieces were carved or inlaid with ornament appropriate to the period in which it was constructed; drawers were sometimes camouflaged behind the friezes.

Press cupboards had fully enclosed storage on two or three tiers (Figure 7-19). The upper storage section was sometimes arranged in thirds, as was the court cupboard, and turned members supported the frieze at each end. When the bulbous support was removed it was replaced with pendant drops. Sometimes this storage tier was fully parallel with the front of the piece. Doors on the lowest tier concealed either drawers or shelves.

Beds

Beds were large and elaborately decorated after mid-16th century; by this time the canopy or tester that had been suspended from the ceiling in the medieval period was supported by posts at the foot and by the headboard (Figure 7-20). The columns at the foot rested on low or tall pedestals that were paneled, provided with molded caps and bases, and enhanced with carved or inlaid detailing. The bulbous form was part of the column and the shaft above was ornamented with treatments such as fluting and strapwork designs; the column was capped with a capital such as the Ionic or Doric. The tester was supported by the columns and the headboard, which were often architecturally conceived. An entablature was elaborately embellished with carved or inlay designs. The woodwork of the roof of the tester was a surface for rich display also; bold moldings were arranged to imitate coffering and the recessed areas were decorated with motifs typical of the period; the disposition of the bed ceiling could also resemble the panels of walls and furniture. Painting was

FIGURE 7-20 Great Bed of Ware (late 16th century) Carved and painted. Architecturally conceived. Tester supported by heavy columns resting on an elaborate pedestal base. Intricate compartmentalization. By Courtesy of the Board of Trustees of the Victoria and Albert Museum, London.

FIGURE 7-21 Detail, Great Bed of Ware (late 16th century). Carved, painted, inlaid. Ceiling of tester coffered in manner similar to wall and furniture treatments of the period. Headboard composed of realistically painted figures in high relief and columns to separate panels. By Courtesy of the Board of Trustees of the Victoria and Albert Museum, London.

sometimes used in conjunction with carving, as on the Great Bed of Ware, constructed in the late Elizabethan era. On this bed realistically painted decorations included baskets of fruit supported by the term, lion masks, and, on the ceiling, roses were painted red with green leaves.

The often costly and extravagant textile hangings were hung from a metal rod on the inside of the canopy; these hangings were referred to as *furniture*. The headboard was also compartmentalized through the use of paneling formed into squares, rectangles, or arcades (Figure 7-21). To divide the tiered arrangement such elements as pilasters, engaged

FIGURE 7-22   Bed Frame. Tester supported by the headboard and columns at the foot of the bed. Mattress frame attached to the headboard but free of the columns.

columns, and terminal figures were used; horizontally, strong moldings separated units. A frame supporting the mattress was attached to the headboard but stood free of the columns at the foot, resting on its own legs (Figure 7-22).

ORNAMENT

Slight differences between styles existed in the balance and significance given specific motifs; distinctions in the execution of structural parts and in characteristics of carving were greater. Carving was more sculptural in the Elizabethan style than in the Jacobean, where carved detail was in lower relief and more highly finished. In addition, greater stylization characterized the ornament and it was developed with less extravagance. Decorative structural elements illustrating changes in the Jacobean style from the Elizabethan include the thinning of the bulbous form and the increased use of turnings for decorative purposes. The Puritans accepted the decorative use of turnings.

Prominent motifs used in the Elizabethan style included the following: guilloche, gadroon, bands of geometric inlay, wreathed heads, Romayne work, masks, human figures, strapwork, arabesques, acanthus leaves, caryatids, grotesques, terminus figures, figurative subjects, and fruit and flower motifs such as grapes and leaves. Ornamental use of architectural elements included the entablature (or its parts used separately along with classical details such as dentils, modillions, and moldings), columns, pilasters, and arcading.

In the Jacobean period classical detail continued. Ornaments of Flemish derivation, including arabesques and grotesques with strapwork, were extensively used as well. Strapwork was often carved on friezes and panels; repeated motifs were also carved on the strapwork. Early 17th-century designers made less frequent use of the following motifs: masks, terminus figures, caryatids, and figurative subjects. Frequently used motifs included the guilloche, lunette, lozenge, fluting, and arcading. Split spindles, sometimes baluster in contour, were often applied to surfaces such as the stiles of chairs and to case pieces. Simplicity characterized the Cromwellian style.

Italian Baroque

1600-1700

HISTORICAL SETTING

The term *Baroque* was first used as a derogatory description of a style that originated in Italy and flourished in the 17th century. According to some authors the word, in its disparaging sense, derived from the Portuguese *barraco,* an irregularly shaped pearl. It became an accepted term in art history and criticism by Burckhardt's use of it in the 19th century.

The style of the Baroque, occurring between Mannerism and the Rococo, was an outgrowth of concerns about the reforms needed within the Roman Catholic Church. The criticism of Protestants centered on administrative and doctrinal issues. Among specific concerns were the practice of purchasing and selling church offices and the involvement of the papacy in corrupt Roman politics. On doctrinal matters, however, the church stood firm on its prerogative to interpret the Bible. In contrast to the Renaissance emphasis on humanism, the idea that new attention should be directed to spiritual values of greater import than man himself gained momentum.

With the intent to reestablish discipline and spiritual life, reform measures emanated from the Council of Trent (1545-63). This resulted in guidelines established by the Church for the use of artists and patrons; artistic works for the Church had to communicate biblical truths and, among other stipulations, to strictly follow specified propriety in the treatment of nudes. Following a period when the emphasis was on strict instructional approaches, a new religious mood evolved characterized by its emotional, ebullient impact. Stylistic consequences yielded renditions that emphasized drama, contrast of light and dark, movement, and the use of vigorous diagonals and curves.

The undisputed leader in the arts in the first half of the 17th century was Italy; the Baroque movement originated in Rome under the auspices of the ecclesiastical leaders. Particularly instrumental as arbiters of taste were Urban VIII (Barberini), who reigned from 1623 to 1644, and Innocent X (Pamphili), whose term as pope was from 1644 to 1655. While the style originated in Rome, it must be remembered that Italy was a conglomeration of independent city-states; having both secular and ecclesiastical rulers was divisive. There were, therefore, regional stylistic variations. For example, in southern Italy the style manifested strong Spanish overtones in that ornamentation was more extravagant compared to that of the northern Italian Baroque.

Despite the decline of the economy and the intervention of foreign powers there was a great deal of building activity. Evidence of great poverty in various centers abounds but there were many exceedingly wealthy families as well; in fact, the number of new wealthy families increased in the 17th century. Families associated with the papacy, including the Barberini, Borghese, Chigi, and Pamphili, were extremely well off. Some of the richest and grandest palaces and villas were constructed for them. Trading families and bankers were among those whose fortunes increased during this period. Competition among the ruling families meant that they rivaled each other in ostentatious display in their palaces as well as in the churches they supported.

The construction of country villas as well as city palaces for the ruling families required the services of many artisans. These artists often played more than one role in the design and decoration of domestic interiors; they were in many cases proficient in architecture and/or sculpture and painting. The goal of the Baroque was harmony or unity of parts in the overall composition of the interior.

Considerable talent and facility in more than one art form contributed to this overall goal of consonance. As a result, architecture, painting, and sculpture were merged in a way that did not capitalize on the unique properties of each medium; rather, architecture assumed the pliable properties of sculpture, or architecture and sculpture took on the properties most characteristic of painting. Noteworthy among this multitalented group with were Pietro da Cortona, Carlo Maderno, Gianlorenzo Bernini, and Francesco Borromini.

Pietro da Cortona (1596-1669), primarily a painter, practiced the art of architecture also and began his career in Rome. Among his most important commissions were frescoes for the highly influential Barberini family. For their palace he painted the *Allegory of Divine*

Providence and Barberini Power. "This, his most famous painting, is a triumph of ILLUSION-ISM for the centre of the ceiling appears open to the sky and the figures seen from below (di SOTTO IN SU) appear to come down into the room as well as soar out of it."[1] In Florence he was commissioned by the Grand Duke of Tuscany to execute paintings for the Palazzo Pitti. His innovation there was to combine stucco and fresco in a new fashion that became influential, as when Le Brun, in France, formulated for Louis XIV the style of decoration for the Galerie d'Apollon at the Louvre.

Having been given the responsibility for the additions to St. Peter's (begun by Bramante with later modifications by Michelangelo), Carlo Maderno (1596-1629) was the most important architect in the period just prior to the Baroque. His design for the Palazzo Barberini for the family of Urban VIII was original in that instead of locating parts of the building around a cortile he started with one block of the building and added wings. Maderno's innovation for the Palazzo Mattei di Giove (on a corner lot) lay in the provision of two entrances. From the secondary entrance a visitor viewed the stairway, configured in a manner "so that on the first floor it leaves the visitor on the axis of the upper loggia, from which the rooms of the *piano nobile* open. This is an early hint of the vistas which Baroque architects were to use to such effect in the creation of their staircases."[2] His later work was accomplished in conjunction with Bernini and Boromini.

Among the preeminent artists (architects, painters, sculptors) of the 17th century was Gianlorenzo Bernini (1598-1680). The palaces he designed have been altered to the extent that his original intent cannot be fully interpreted. For the Palazzo Barberini (1629) his efforts were confined to modifications of Maderno's design. However, his ecclesiastical works fully express the Baroque ambience in his ability to merge into a decorative whole architecture, sculpture, and painting. His art was characterized by the contrast of light and dark, dramatic movement, bold scale, and the use of luxurious materials. While there are differences in works produced for ecclesiastical and secular building, some of the basic stylistic characteristics are common to each.

Francesco Borromini (1599-1667) was also a prominent architect of the Italian Baroque. Borromini felt his training as an architect was appropriate for his commissions while Bernini (with no training in architecture) considered his knowledge of sculpture and painting equally fitting for architectural work. Although he was minimally involved in domestic building, Borromini's innovations for ecclesiastical structures were a creative force. For example, his originality in the treatment of the dome deviated from common practice. The coffering for S. Carlo alle Quattro Fontane (1638-41) was based on a design by Serlio, the Renaissance architect. The design of cross, hexagon, and lozenge shapes was applied in full three dimension to the oval dome rather than to flat or vault ceilings; movement and illusion were created in the fact that the coffers were gradually reduced in size in the direction of the lantern. At the Palazzo Barberini, where he worked with Maderno, it was probably Borromini who introduced the spiral staircase, an exceptional structural accomplishment. Other secular works for which he was responsible were the Spada Palaces and a palace and villa for the Falconieri. His mental problems and his inability to work well with his colleagues finally led him to commit suicide.

SPATIAL RELATIONSHIPS

The overall configuration of the residence during the Baroque period represents a change from the Renaissance. During the Renaissance, blocks of the structure surrounded a cortile. With the 17th century it was common to have more open planning, which resulted in wings attached to the square or rectangular block of the primary section. A case in point

1. Harold Osborne, ed., *The Oxford Companion to Art* (Oxford: Clarendon Press, 1970; reprint, 1986), 283. Page number from the reprint edition. By permission of Oxford University Press.
2. Anthony Blunt, ed., *Baroque & Rococo, Architecture & Decoration* (New York: Harper & Row, 1978), 28.

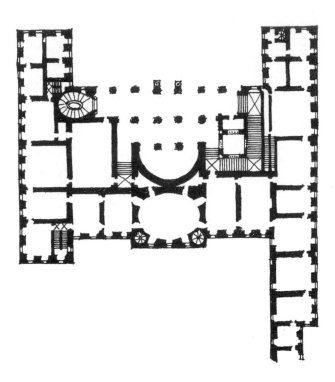

FIGURE 8-1   Plan, Palazzo
Barberini, Rome (1628-1633).
Enfilade arrangement.
Introduction of oval spaces. *Art
and Architecture in Italy, 1600 to
1750*, by Rudolf Wittkower,
Yale University Press Pelican
History of Art: 1969.

is the Palazzo Barberini, under construction from 1628 to 1633, to which Maderno, Bernini, and Borromini each probably contributed some part in the design, although documentary evidence is uncertain (Figure 8-1). This palace is of modified H-form with a deep forecourt. The main façade is comprised of seven bays in three stories. The surrounds of the third floor windows are in feigned perspective. They give the impression of the same size opening as those below them; this treatment was probably essential for internal arrangement. Here, as in both villa and palace design, internal and external relationships were considered in planning.

Three innovations to the internal arrangement of the palace were related to the stairs, the shapes of spaces, and the position of spaces in relation to the façade. The stairway was organized in four flights around a square, open well. One of the primary characteristics of the Baroque period was a sense of movement and one way to achieve this was to use oval spaces rather than round (see Figure 8-1). Thus the interconnecting oval hall as well as the oval stairway were unprecedented, this dynamic shape was used by a number of architects in the design of ecclesiastical structures. On piano nobile level it was new to have the hall perpendicular to the façade rather than parallel with it.

Axial planning was central to the Baroque interior; rooms were distributed symmetrically. The Palazzo Barberini plan illustrates this in the disposition of groups of rooms in each wing; no connecting corridor was used with either group. The enfilade is an ordered, axial arrangement of a succession of doors through a series of rooms. The doors lie close to the outer wall. This type of arrangement was commented on in a contemporary document.

It is the custom here in winter to invite the chief ladies of the town (married women only) to come to play at cards on winter evenings for three or four hours' space; and this one night in one palace, another night in another palace. In every chamber the doors are set open and for the most part you shall see eight or ten chambers on a floor, going out of one another, with a square table holding eight persons, as many chairs, two silver candle sticks with wax lights in them and a store of lights round about the room. At the hour appointed, company being come, they sit down to play, a cavalier sitting between every lady and all the women looking as fine in cloths and

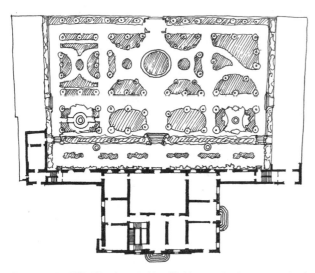

FIGURE 8-2 Villa Plan, Poggio Torselli, Tuscany (17th century). Axial arrangement encompassing the approach to and through the residence to the garden beyond.

FIGURE 8-3 Salone, Poggio Torselli. Scale, size, and grand proportions of Baroque interiors.

jewels as if they were going to a ball. The doors of all these rooms being open, the lights great, the women glittering and all glorious, you would take these palaces to be the enchanted palaces of the Old King of the Mountain.[3]

Poggio Torselli, a 17th-century villa in the Tuscan countryside, illustrates similar space planning concepts; projecting wings are attached to the single central block of the villa (Figure 8-2). Axial planning encompassed not only the tree-lined approach to the villa, through the residence, but to the garden beyond. First of all, a cypress-lined avenue led to the main entrance. From the main door through the entry hall and the salone the occupant not only had a clear view of but also access to the garden beyond. The interior arrangement exemplified axial planning also. In the central block of the villa the symmetrical distribution of the rooms was in enfilade arrangement, three rooms each with a succession of doors in alignment.

Grand proportions of rooms were typical of Baroque interiors. The salone, for example, was given high priority. At the Poggio Torselli the salone measured 50 feet long, 30 feet wide, and 25 feet tall, the height encompassing both the ground and mezzanine levels. Investigation of the totality of the space was encouraged by centers of interest at different levels such as niches embracing statuary, decorative and elaborate entablatures, pediments, cartouche wall reliefs framed with stucco drapery, and the strong relief of the coved transition to the ceiling. From the balconies an occupant could overlook the vast dimensions of this salone (Figure 8-3).

Pietro da Cortona was inspired by antique statues, reliefs, the architecture of Michelangelo, paintings by Caravaggio and Raphael, and antique Roman architecture.

---

3. As quoted in William M. Odom, *A History of Italian Furniture from the Fourteenth to the Early Nineteenth Centuries,* 2 vols. (Garden City, New York: Doubleday, 1918/1919), II, 20-21.

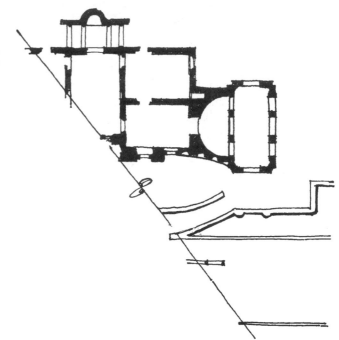

FIGURE 8-4   Plan, Villa del Pigneto, Rome (prior to 1630). Spatial modulation using semicircular apses set off by columns. Influence of solari of Roman baths. *Art and Architecture in Italy, 1600 to 1750*, by Rudolf Wittkower, Yale University Press Pelican History of Art: 1969.

Regarding the latter, in the space planning for the Villa Sacchetti del Pigneto, now destroyed, he incorporated two semicircular apses set off by columns, a feature that originated with the solaria incorporated in Roman baths (Figure 8-4). This created spatial interest but allowed visual extension. Columns to divide spaces can also be observed in the organization of the gallery in the Palazzo Colonna, in which Antonio Dei Grande (active 1647-71) used freestanding columns in the openings between the gallery and square anterooms at each end. Spatial organization using columns was also typical in the late 18th century in England.

Another innovation of this period was in the size of the vestibule. By increasing the size it was possible for coaches to drive in for protection from the elements.

INTERIOR ARCHITECTURE AND DECORATION

Materials and Decorative Techniques

Contributing to the splendid backgrounds that characterized Baroque interiors were the materials and techniques. These represent a continuation of those employed in the late 16th century and carried over into the 17th. Among the most important were fresco, molded stucco, and carved woodwork.

The greatest emphasis in the 17th century was on fresco painting; in fact, the standard by which a painter was judged competent was his proficiency in fresco painting. Using this technique Annibale Carracci (1560-1609) was a transitional figure between High Renaissance and Baroque illusionism. For the gallery at the Palazzo Farnese he used a system of fictive architecture that was not yet fully quadratura. Although quadratura painting had existed in the 16th century Annibale modified his approach in that he painted scenes and set them in frames as if they were easel paintings. "Illusionistic architectural painting *(quadratura)* . . . [was] aimed at extending real architecture into an imaginary space."[4] His representations were vital, animated, dramatic, and monumental. Imitations of other materials were painted as well—for example, figures represented in simulated stucco and roundels in simulated bronze.

4. Rudolf Wittkower, *Art and Architecture in Italy, 1600-1750,* 3rd ed., rev. (Harmondsworth, Middlesex: Penguin, 1973), 36.

FIGURE 8-5 Painted Ceiling, Grand Salone, Palazzo Barberini by Pietro da Cortona. Simulation of stucco shells, masks, etc. Alinari/Art Resource, NY.

The dominant painter of the High Baroque was Pietro da Cortona, whose freedom of execution shows him to have been influenced by the Venetians. For the Grand Salone of the Palazzo Barberini he created (through paint) an illusion of architectural framework on which he depicted simulated stucco shells, masks, etc., and rendered within it a maximum number of figures in crowded compositions; in this fresco he depicted the *Glorification of Urban VIII's Reign* (1633-39). Figures appear in front of fictive architecture (Figure 8-5). In later renditions he used real stucco and, characteristic of the Baroque, his forms were pliant and exuberant.

Cortona . . . followed basically the North Italian tradition descending from Mantegna through Veronese, but he changed and amplified it by making use of the local stucco tradition, by applying to the framework *quadratura* foreshortening, and by employing and transforming Mannerist conventions of figure projection in front of architecture. At the same time, he showed awareness of the Correggiesque space continuum. Moreover, he devised the middle field in the typically Venetian mode of *sotto in su.*[5]

Sotto in su (an Italian term meaning "up from under") refers to the use of perspective to represent figures in extreme foreshortening; the figures are often depicted as flying.

Andrea Sacchi (1599-1661), a contemporary rival of Cortona, represents the classic tradition of the middle 17th century. Unlike Cortona, he used a minimum number of figures in order to illustrate individualized meaning through countenance, action, and animation. In light values he employed rich and warm color schemes.

While stucco was simulated in paint it was also exceedingly important as an actual material. It was used for a multiplicity of interior elements such as chimneypieces, pediments, busts, a variety of emblems, and cartouches.

Interior Architecture and Decorative Elements

Italian Baroque interiors were monumental settings that provided a background for social events; intimacy was not a consideration. This represents continuity with the Renaissance, in which the procession through rooms provided the setting for such activities as banquets, balls, and receptions. Ornamentally, fresco, stucco, carved wood, and other materials and techniques were the vehicles that provided the imposing and magnificent stage settings of this period. The trend in fresco in the 17th century was from deep tones with crowded compositions to high-key and less compact compositions. Real stuccos, simulated stuccos, and carved wood were used to frame the frescoes or painted canvases. As noted, fresco was the most extensively used painting technique in which illusionism played a considerable part.

Some interiors were relatively simple; many of these have not survived. On the other hand, palaces of the wealthy were lavishly decorated; these represent the work of style leaders and many have been preserved.

Floors

Disparate colors and patterns were used. Materials included tile, marble, stone, and brick. Wood arranged in parquet patterns was also employed. Chips of marble were embedded in cement and ground smooth to form a flooring termed *terrazzo.*

Walls

While paneling continued in use during the Italian Baroque, stucco and paint were more common; the Italians excelled in plasterwork. Painting and fresco paintings were sometimes enframed with plaster. Among the subjects were hunting scenes, landscapes featuring villas, and gardens distinctively laid out to coordinate with the interior layout of the residences; the frescoes often appeared to be pictures hung on the walls. Niches capped with shells were inset into plastered walls, as were niches of other shapes, which contained busts or full-length figures (see Figure 8-3).

Textiles were used on walls also. These included velvets, damasks, and tapestries. Velvets, for example, were used in the reception rooms of the Palazzo Pitti, where the planets were the painted subjects. A tapestry works was, in fact, set up by Cardinal Francesco Barberini, nephew of Urban VIII. Tapestries, paintings, and sculpture in the same room were sometimes symbolically related.

Marble was occasionally used for walls. However, since it was so expensive it was employed primarily in residences of the very wealthy. As the craftsmen used paint to simulate stucco and other materials, they imitated marbling on wood.

---

5. Wittkower, 165-166.

FIGURE 8-6 Door Entablature, Salone, Poggio Torselli. Concave entablature with vertically canted architrave frame.

FIGURE 8-7 Door with Two Leaves. Alternating vertical and horizontal panels, scenes painted within. Reverse side unpaneled, painted scene encompassing two leaves.

Windows and Doors

Classical elements often surrounded windows and doors—for example, pediments (both arched and triangular), pilasters, entablatures, and round arches. With the Baroque emphasis on plasticity, the stucco craftsman shaped the frames to be consistent with stylistic trends. Borromini's compositional approach emphasized a continuous line between the pediment and the opening; the sides of the surround were sometimes projected forward

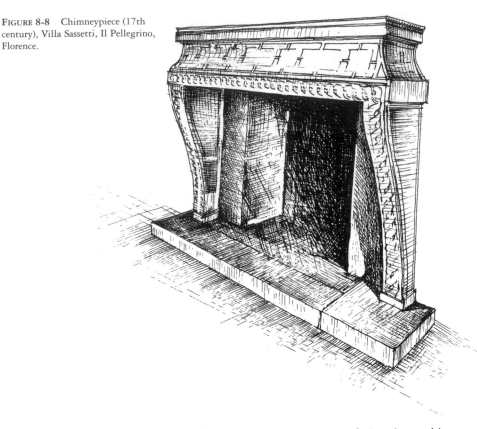

FIGURE 8-8 Chimneypiece (17th century), Villa Sassetti, Il Pellegrino, Florence.

from the wall plane. Another means of attaining movement was to design the entablature in a concave curve (Figure 8-6). When rectangular enframements were employed, the architrave was sometimes projected laterally at the level of the lintel; this is referred to as an earpiece or crossette. Still another treatment was to divide the door leaves into panels, the centers of which had painted scenes; the reverse was handled as continuous painted surfaces uniting the two leaves (Figure 8-7).

Chimneypieces

During the Renaissance the chimneypiece was a prominent feature of the interior; it was often hooded and projected strongly into the room. However, in the Baroque period the projection was less evident. Some chimneypieces were very simply treated with a carved surround; occasionally figures framed the opening on each side. Large brackets sometimes supported the mantel (Figure 8-8). Stuccowork of modeled figures sometimes covered the Baroque architectural features of the mantelpiece.

Ceilings

Ceiling treatments ranged from the highly complex to the simple; the ceilings themselves were either flat or vaulted. Materials (stucco, paint, and fresco) and/or illusionistic techniques based on in-depth knowledge of perspective through the use of quadratura or *sotto in su* often contributed to the dominance of the ceiling as a prominent focal point in rooms, particularly in the homes of wealthy and ruling families. These quadratura frescoes, through their illusionism, dramatically extended the vertical dimensional qualities of interior spaces.

Italy was dominant in fresco decoration during the Baroque period, especially in ceiling embellishment. They were imitated throughout European design centers but no one attained the magnificent and sensational quadratura of the Italians. While Cortona at first executed his ceilings in fresco, he later introduced a new decorative approach by combining fresco with stucco. In the Palazzo Pitti he used these techniques for a series of rooms

FIGURE 8-9 Ceiling, Sala di Apollo, Palazzo Pitti, Florence (1647). Stucco. Alinari/Art Resource, NY.

named for the planets. Wittkower described the ceiling of one of these rooms by Pietro da Cotrona, the Sala di Apollo, in which he used fresco and real stucco (Figure 8-9).

The wealth of these decorations baffles accurate description. One meets the entire repertory: figures and caryatids, white stuccoes on gilt ground or gilded ones on white ground; wreaths, trophies, cornucopias, shells, and hangings; duplication, triplication, and superimpositions of architectural and decorative elements; cartouches with sprawling borders incongruously linked with lions' heads, and palmettes, cornucopias and inverted shells . . . a seemingly illogical joining, interlocking, associating of motif with motif. Unrivalled is the agglomeration of plastic forms and their ebullient energy.[6]

A simpler treatment is illustrated in the stucco relief on the coved ceiling of the Poggio Torselli; in bold relief the design exemplifies the characteristics of the Baroque by which movement is attained in a free and florid method of adornment (see Figure 8-3). When the coved ceiling was used, the cornice served as a precise boundary between the wall and ceiling; an entablature was also the base from which the cove was initiated. The coved ceiling gave the *stuccatore* (stuccoworker) an opportunity for unrestrained freedom in design.

Stairways

The stairway generated a great deal of architectural interest in this period (Figure 8-10). The staircase hall exemplifies the breadth and dignity characteristic of the times. Stairways of the Italian

FIGURE 8-10 Staircase Hall, Palazzo di Giustizia, Bologna (1695) by Giambattista Piacentini. Monumental space representing a fusion of architecture and sculpture. *Art and Architecture in Italy, 1600 to 1750,* by Rudolf Wittkower, Yale University Press Pelican History of Art: 1969.

6. Wittkower, 167.

Baroque period were often characterized by their gradual ascent. The balustrade was composed of boldly conceived balusters separated at intervals by paneled sections, the whole united by a broad handrail. Statuary was placed on the newel and above each panel of the balustrade surrounding the stairwell at the landing of the upper hall (wealthier citizens collected and displayed antique sculptures as well as modern examples). Drama was heightened in this space not only by the use of sculptures but by the treatment of the walls of the upper hall, which were articulated by paired pilasters supporting an impressive entablature; masks in relief were used on the capitals of the pilasters. Roundels on the wall enclosed busts or full-length figures above which were deeply modeled shells. The vastness of space was enhanced by the position of both architectural and decorative elements.

FURNITURE

Rome was the birthplace of the Baroque. The middle fifty years of the 17th century saw the most exaggerated phase of the style. After this time France became the undisputed leader in the arts throughout Europe; Italian furniture then reflected the influence of the Louis XIV style.

Toward the evolution of the Baroque, however, there were major influences from Spanish noblemen and the papal aristocracy. The Roman Church realized the power that art could have to inspire and, therefore, to fend off the Counter-Reformation they became preoccupied with extravagance and ostentatious display; these were means to overwhelm viewers. The Baroque style was ideal for this purpose since the emphasis was on exaggerated movement and stimulating contrasts. The Jesuits were highly instrumental in spreading the style; they had the financial resources to plan and ornament religious structures in a manner conducive to influencing their group through stimulation of the senses. The same characteristics permeated all arts of the period, secular as well as ecclesiastical.

In the 16th century Italy had been invaded by armies of major European powers and was influenced by an array of foreign influences. In the 17th century both Italian Renaissance and Spanish influences impinged the Italian Baroque style. The Renaissance affected the early years while the Spanish influence was felt during the first half of the century. Spanish domination was at its apex in the initial stages of the 17th century but Italy did not adopt the excesses that characterized the arts of the Spaniards. Italian Baroque thrust was given to the use of rich materials, to the theatrical, and to pretentiousness.

The role of furniture in the decorative scheme was to emphasize social status and it showed some of the ornamental excesses typical of the interior. Suites of furniture became closely coordinated with the entire decorative scheme, including interior decorative elements and architectural features. There was a significant difference in furniture designed for state apartments and furniture designed for private spaces or for ordinary houses for those on the lower strata of society. The latter were normally purely utilitarian pieces.

Materials and Construction Techniques

In the 17th century construction techniques and materials were not radically different from those of the Renaissance. Carving was the preferred method of decorating furniture; it was executed in a plastic and often flamboyant manner. Walnut was a principal furniture wood. Configurations for turning were diverse.

Pietra dura was a type of mosaic using colored stones for cabinet panels, tabletops, and so on; it was introduced in Italy in the late 16th century. The center of this art was Florence where a factory was established in 1588. Known by the Ancient Egyptians but rediscovered in northern Italy, *scagliola* replaced pietra dura as decorative enhancement in the late 17th century; it was an imitation marble composed of gypsum, marble chips, coloring material, and glue. Elaborate polychrome inlay work was characteristic.

Lacquer was widely used in Venice for two reasons: First, due to its geographic position Venice was strongly oriented toward the East and, second, high-quality wood was expensive. The technique was, for the most part, raised gilt with chinoiserie subjects.

FIGURE 8-11   Armchair, Tuscany.

FIGURE 8-12   Walnut Armchair, Lombardy.

FIGURE 8-13   Carved Wood Armchair, Venetian (second half of 17th century). By Courtesy of the Board of Trustees of the Victoria and Albert Museum, London.

Imitation lacquer of one color was also employed.

Italian textiles were in demand not only in Italy but in other European centers as well. These were popular for walls as well as for upholstery. Lucca was particularly known for its silks, Genoa for its cut velvets.

Typical Pieces and Stylistic Features

Seat Furniture

Armchairs *(sedia)* with high backs, primarily rectangular, were constructed through the 17th century. The example illustrated has upholstery attached with exposed nail heads (Figure 8-11). Although the back is not attached to the seat there are examples in which

this is the case. The emphasis is on carved and turned members for stretchers, arm supports, and finials. Armrests that have deeply carved endings with downward curves extend beyond the arm supports, which rise directly above the legs. Spiral turnings for the stretchers and the arm supports are interrupted by blocked sections at intersecting structural points. Stretchers are at two levels: an H-shaped one on the lower level and two transverse ones placed higher, just under the seat rail in the front; at the higher level an unturned stretcher connects the rear legs.

The next change to occur in chair design was to lower the back (Figure 8-12). Among the most exaggerated forms of the Italian Baroque is an example in the Victoria and Albert Museum; foliated scrolls are used as structural supports in an exceedingly flamboyant manner (Figure 8-13). These boldly treated curves culminate in an upright front stretcher of carved acanthus leaves centered with a cartouche.

A side chair in the Wallace Collection is of carved walnut (Figure 8-14). Two shaped wood panels of the back are plastically carved; the upper one has an inlaid oval with a spray of foliage. The trapezoid seat has its narrower dimension in the front. Replications are evident in details below the seat and the back: (1) carving on the legs matches that of the stiles of the back, and (2) upright stretchers have duplicate outline configurations like the panels of the back.

FIGURE 8-14 Carved Walnut Side Chair (17th century). Replication of elements below and above seat level. Reproduced by permission of the Trustees of the Wallace Collection.

Tables

Table forms were diverse. The Italian royal palaces featured those of marble mosaic. The tops were often inlaid with geometric designs in the pietra dura technique and were, therefore, very costly; tables constructed and decorated in this manner were valued and used in princely palaces all over Europe. The ministers Richelieu and Mazarin, who served the French queens acting as regents in the 17th century, imported this highly prized type to France.

The most common type of table for the upper classes was made of walnut. Variety characterized tables in terms of sizes and shapes, silhouettes of turned members, and configura-

FIGURE 8-15 Walnut Table. Type used in monasteries and domestic interiors for dining.

FIGURE 8-16 Diversity of Turnings for Tables. A Early seventeenth century. B and C Mid-17th century.

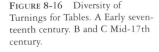

FIGURE 8-17 Carved and Gilt Lime Wood Center Table (early 17th century). Reproduced by permission of the Trustees of the Wallace Collection.

tions of stretchers. The rectangular and octagonal tops were supported by turned members of diverse form. Supports of carved lyre shapes illustrate the influence of the Spanish on the design of Italian Baroque furniture. Among the conformations for the stretchers that braced the legs were perimeter, H-shape, and X-shape; many stretchers were square or rectangular in cross section, while others were turned.

The most common form of table, typically used for dining in the monasteries and some domestic residences, was one with single turned supports mounted on a base; sometimes these were connected by a longitudinal stretcher (Figure 8-15). The number of single supports varied with the length of the table, which was sometimes eight to twelve feet long. Turning configurations were abundant. The contour for stretchers connecting these legs also varied: some were perimeter placed near the floor, some joined the legs in an H-shape, some were rectangular or square in section, and some were turned (Figure 8-16).

A center table of limewood has a red Egyptian porphyry top; the edging of gilt

FIGURE 8-18 Carved Wood Armoire, Parma (second half 17th century). The Baroque style at its height.

bronze beading is a later addition. The heavy trestle supports have caryatid mermaids under which are heavy paw feet. Double scrolls are united by a foliated spray (Figure 8-17).

Storage Pieces

Storage pieces included the cassone, the credenza, the armoire, the cabinet, and the chest of drawers. The cassone was the least important in the 17th century, although some continued to be constructed. Tops were raised by a series of moldings, many of which were concave. Mounted on molded bases the form tended to curve in at the base. Regardless of the type of storage piece, raised panels were preferred.

An *armoire* is a veritable display of the decorative detail that characterized the Italian Baroque style at its height (Figure 8-18). The exaggerated treatment of the cresting is comprised of plastically conceived scrolls, vases of flowers, and shell. Between the boldly conceived entablature and molded base the tapering console originates above with a deeply formed scroll and ends with an acanthus leaf and smaller scroll. The double doors are intricately paneled and carved.

Beds

According to contemporary accounts of foreign travelers and Italian writers, some beds were lavishly treated and inlaid with precious and semiprecious stones. John Evelyn, the English diarist, commented on silver furniture and elaborate iron beds. Although few beds are extant to represent the Baroque period, it is known that some were from the hand of the upholsterer; the wooden parts of these were of little ornamental value. The fashion for heavily draped beds was a reflection of French influence in the second half of the 17th century. One type of bed in general use was of carved walnut constructed with or without a canopy. Some beds had intricate carving on the headboard as well as on the turned posts; gilding was sometimes used to enhance such elements. These beds stood on their four legs directly on the floor, but some were placed on a *predella* (platform). Designers drew upon the repertoire of motifs typical of this period for decorative detail.

A Venetian bed of the mid-17th century has an elaborately carved crest comprised of foliated scrolls centered with a cartouche. Below the intricately carved finials the posts are spirally turned. Fluted pilasters divide the arched spaces of the headboard (Figure 8-19).

ORNAMENT

Regardless of the motifs employed, the prevailing characteristic was one of plasticity in which theatrical display was a prime consideration. Among the most common ornamental details were putti, banderoles (motifs configured as ribbons), volutes, S- and C-scrolls, large foliated scrolls, grotesques, human figures, heraldic devices, arabesques, vases of flowers, cornucopias, elements derived from architecture, palmettes, cartouches, caryatids, and shells.

FIGURE 8-19 Carved Walnut Bed, Venice (mid-17th century).

Chapter 9

French Baroque

1600-1715

HISTORICAL SETTING

The Louis XIII style, transitional period that helped form the French Baroque, began with the accession to the French throne of the first Bourbon monarch, Henry IV, in 1589; it continued to the time when Louis XIV took personal control in 1661. The fully developed French Baroque style, Louis XIV, reached its culmination around 1700. Through the period of transition a number of factors were instrumental in the direction of the arts: acts of royalty with regard to the establishment of workshops, support for industries and, through this, the centralization of the arts under the protection of the crown; foreign influences through the nationalities of artists and craftsmen under the umbrella of the Louvre workshops; the influence of foreign queens who, with their chief ministers, acted as regents during the minorities of Louis XIII and Louis XIV; and deterrents to the progress toward the French Baroque.

The institution of royalty was popular at the death of Henry IV in 1610. France was prosperous and respected abroad. Even though Henry IV signed the Edict of Nantes, allowing religious freedom to the French Protestants, the act failed to establish a climate in which the arts flourished. However, the fruits of his labors toward artistic endeavors were to be felt later in the century.

There were far-reaching implications to Henry IV's establishment of free workshops in the Louvre that gave royal patronage to artisans—sculptors, painters, cabinetmakers, etc. These artists and craftsmen were also provided apartments. In addition to economic support, artisans were provided with an environment in which art could thrive. When Henry IV first established the workshops, many of the craftsmen were from other countries (Flanders, Italy, Spain). French artisans completed their apprenticeships in the Low Countries. With this plethora of influences a national style was not forthcoming until the genuine French Baroque was fully developed in 1660.

Henry IV also supported industries such as the Gobelins tapestryworks and the Savonnerie carpet manufacturers. The culmination of this initial support came to fruition during the reign of Louis XIV, when the arts were centralized under the control of the crown and government. This had two advantages. First, the Bourbon monarchs perceived art as one of the fundamental components contributing to the stature and distinction of the state. Second, they felt that glorification of the crown was expressed through the arts they patronized.

Two queen regents were instrumental in bringing foreign influence to France in the 17th century before 1661: Marie de Medici (mother of Louis XIII) and Anne of Austria (mother of Louis XIV). The former was Florentine but favored Flemish art; however, Flemish art was strongly influenced by the Italian Baroque. During her regency there was a spate of building activity by the new nobility and the bourgeois; consequently, the demand for luxurious furnishings escalated. Anne of Austria was Spanish; however, she was strongly influenced by her Italian minister of state.

The policies of the chief ministers of state, Cardinal Richelieu (1624-1643) and Cardinal Mazarin (1643-1661), had a compelling influence on the direction of the arts. Richelieu, for example, was intent on using the arts to aggrandize the monarchy. His goal was to establish absolute royal power in France. Mazarin, chief minister during the regency of Anne of Austria, followed many of the same policies as Richelieu. Each of these cardinals was predisposed to attract to France outstanding Italian artisans, since both men were from Italy. Among the architects, sculptors, painters, and stuccoists who brought the Italian Baroque style to France in the formative stages of the French Baroque were Romanelli, Guercino, Gramaldi, Cortona, Algardi, and Bernini.

The development of the French Baroque was interrupted by the outbreak of civil disturbances known as the Fronde, from 1648 to 1653. These outbreaks were aggravated by the tyrannical manner of Cardinal Mazarin, who promoted royal authority over the Parliament of Paris. His policies resulted in heavy fiscal burden for citizens. In addition, his policies aggravated ongoing religious tensions in their political repression of the Protestants.

Assuming power when he was only 23, it was the ambition of Louis XIV to use the arts to express the brilliance and splendor of the court. Contrary to previous efforts, the policies of Louis XIV provided a coordinated effort to raise royal distinction and stature in the eyes other countries. The king appointed Jean-Baptiste Colbert (1619-1683) as Surintendent des Bâtiments, a minister responsible for buildings of the crown as well as other artistic endeavors. This office was paramount in the organization of the arts that led to the imposition of unified standards. Colbert was the virtual dictator in the direction the arts took during the reign of Louis XIV. The King aspired to present a visual image of the majesty and prestige of the French crown; thus, the expansion of Versailles, the decoration of its sumptuous interior, and extravagance of the decorative arts, were vivid embodiments of this aim. Toward the king's goal, among the first acts of Colbert was to establish the Academy of Architecture, the function of which was to give the stamp of approval for all official undertakings.

A major appointment by Colbert was Charles Le Brun (1619-1690), who provided the thrust for the magnificent decorative schemes at Versailles; he, as well as Colbert, was instrumental in helping impose a strict criterion of taste and in establishing centralized control of the arts. Not only was he designated as the first painter to the king but he also directed the reorganization of the Gobelins factory. Having been purchased by Colbert in 1662, Gobelins was elevated to the Manufacture Royale des Meubles de la Couronne (Royal Manufactory of Court Furniture) in 1667. Le Brun supplied models and designs for the artists and craftsmen (such as cabinetmakers, sculptors, and weavers) and supervised, both at Gobelins and at the Louvre, the work of the ateliers responsible for the production of the decorations for the royal palaces. The result of these unified efforts was that France replaced Italy as the artistic leader of Europe during the reign of Louis XIV. While there were still foreign influences, French designers were able to assimilate these and develop a national style; for example, the German and Flemish artisans who remained at Gobelins were a positive force, with the French craftsmen attaining competence in tapestry weaving and other arts.

In 1685 Louis XIV revoked the Edict of Nantes, which had allowed religious freedom for French Protestants. Many of these Protestants were artisans; approximately 200,000 fled the country. This seriously affected the decorative arts industry. Holland, England, and Colonial America benefited from the exiles' technical expertise as craftsmen and there was a major dissemination of style characteristics from France to these countries.

In the late 17th century, France dominated the arts in Europe. The Louis XIV style was creative, original, and innovative, yet open to outside influence. France became the source to which other countries looked for artistic inspiration in the late 17th and 18th centuries.

SPATIAL RELATIONSHIPS

Space planning during the 17th century evolved through salient works of key architects. The contributions of each of these progressively impacted design. The changes in space planning in 17th-century France are seen in the major works of the following architects. Salomon de Brosse (1571-1626), representing the first decades of the century, was a transitional figure. He designed the Luxembourg, a palace for Henry IV and his queen, Marie de Medici. A classicist, François Mansart (1598-1667) extended the Château of Blois through his design for the Orléans wing, to which his creative contribution was the dramatic use of light; he was among the first to arrange the stairs around an open square well. In 1648 his space plan for the Hôtel du Jars illustrated a trend in which the main residential block was designed two rooms deep rather than the previous one room. In the latter light came into the spaces from two sides. The Château de Maisons exemplifies a typical town house plan. Louis Le Vau (1612-1670) also showed a flair for the dramatic in his use of light and dark in the design of a staircase and in the early introduction of asymmetrical planning in his design for the Hôtel Lambert (1640). The Château Vaux le

Vicomte (1657) became a plan typical of country houses of the period. Among the most prominent of the architects during the reign of Louis XIV was Jules Hardouin-Mansart (1646-1708). When he was only 28 he was commissioned by the king to design a château for the royal family. Over his career he was elevated to highly responsible appointments, among which were Architect to the King, First Architect to the King, administrator of the third phase of building at Versailles, and Surveyor of the Royal Works. He had the ability to combine classicism with the Baroque in decoration as well as in spatial manipulations.

Many of the architects of the ensuing period were trained in the offices of Jules Hardouin-Mansart as he completed the final phase of building for Versailles. However, the names of prominent individual architects did not surface during this later period of Louis XIV in view of the policy to standardize design and to follow established rules. In addition, from 1690 extensive building could not be undertaken due to the limitation of fiscal resources, since the state was near bankruptcy because of the excesses in building during the reign of Louis XIV.

Gradually, beginning in the Louis XIII period, greater attention was paid to privacy and comfort. This was true for both houses of the wealthy and those of the middle class.

Spatial Features of the Floor Plan and Three-Dimensional Spatial Characteristics

When Salomon de Brosse designed the Luxembourg palace (constructed 1615-1624) there were both differences and similarities to the previous architectural period (Figure 9-1). Rectangular in plan, a pavilion was placed at each angle of the main residential block. A pavilion centered the main residential block and divided the structure into symmetrical units. The main staircase was usually placed in this central pavilion in the early 17th century. Wings perpendicular to the principal building enclosed two sides of the forecourt and extended to pavilions located at the angles of the range of buildings along the front of the

FIGURE 9-1 Luxembourg Palace, Paris (1615-1624) by Salomon de Brosse. Pavilions at each angle of the residential block.

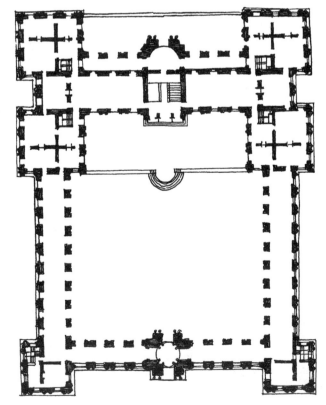

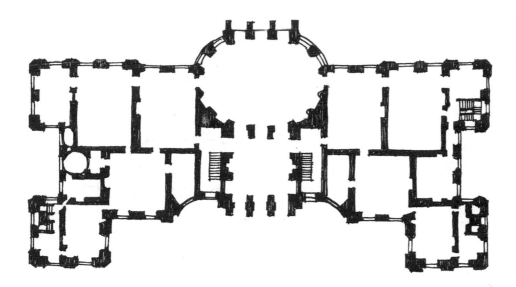

FIGURE 9-2 Château Vaux le Vicomte (1657) by Louis Le Vau. Vestibule and principal staircase separated. Courtesy of Hacker Art Books, Inc., New York.

159

French Baroque

court. Another pavilion centered the entrance wall, which emphasized the main approach to the grounds. At the Luxembourg palace the buildings surrounding the forecourt were high but, later, in the designs of Le Vau and François Mansart, the court was surrounded by low ranges of buildings; in fact, it was often customary for these architects to use a low wall or iron rails for the entrance wall.

The space planning of both François Mansart (Château de Maisons, 1642-1651) and Louis Le Vau (Château Vaux le Vicomte, 1657) owed much to the earlier plan of Luxembourg in the use of the pavilions at the angles of the principal residence and at the angles of the forecourt. However, as noted above, the walls of the court tended to be lower. Another difference was that the principal staircase was no longer placed in the vestibule; rather, it was constructed in an adjacent space to the right or left of the main entrance.

Vaux le Vicomte may be taken as typical of country residences of the period of Louis XIV (Figure 9-2). Nicolas Fouquet (the wealthy Superintendent of Finances) commissioned Le Vau to design his château. (Colbert and the king suspected Fouquet of mishandling state funds and he was subsequently imprisoned for life.) For this magnificent structure Le Vau collaborated with André Le Nôtre, responsible for the garden setting, and Le Brun, the painter and decorator. The prominent central pavilion was significant for a number of reasons: (1) the oval salone projected into the garden and was given emphasis on the exterior by its domed roof; (2) the entrance vestibule no longer contained the grand staircase, since the main apartments were now located on the ground floor—rather, the stairs placed to the right and left of the entrance, and; (3) this section divided the residence into symmetrical apartments, one side for the king on the occasion of his visits and one for Fouquet.

The rooms of the apartments at such châteaux were in an enfilade arrangement. A hierarchal sequence of spaces within an apartment began with the more public and moved progressively to the more private. The salone, introduced during the formative years before 1665, was a public space which was used for banquets, balls, and so on; it served as the introduction to two suites, one on each side of the residential block. The apartment consisted of antechamber, chamber (sometimes more than one), and cabinet (the most private space); access to the latter space was given only to the most favored persons. Within the apartment the state bedchamber was the climax of the principal suite; a royal bed (from which the king greeted guests) was often set behind a proscenium arch in an alcove and separated from the main body of the room by a balustrade beyond which only specified persons could step. A bed was sometimes set off by curtains and columns; spaces on each side of the bed were called *ruelles.*

Besides the main apartments the number of small suites increased throughout the 17th century. For example, at Vaux le Vicomte the antechamber served as the introduction

FIGURE 9-3 Parisian Hôtel de Lionne, Louis Le Vau. Typical town house.

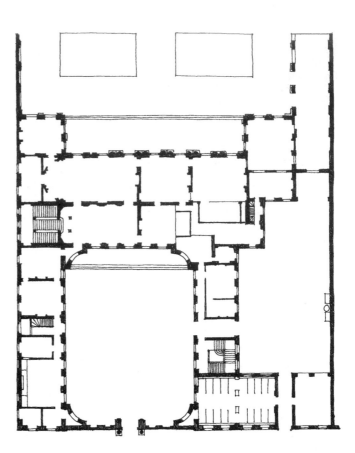

not only to the main suites but also to smaller apartments. Particularly in mansions of the wealthy, a gallery was included as an adjunct to the apartment.

The typical town house (Parisian Hôtel) evolved during the latter period of the ministry of Richelieu largely through the combined efforts of François Mansart and Le Vau. Instead of the one-room depth of the principal residential block, the plan of the main block was usually two rooms deep. The primary rooms were located on the garden side of the residence; although the arrangement varied with the architect, rooms were commonly grouped according to social priority (Figure 9-3). An antechamber preceded the cabinet; sometimes there were intermediate chambers as well. On plans of the 17th century a dining room was sometimes indicated. Since there were usually no corridors, service stairs were incorporated to provide more convenient access to other parts of the house. Wings enclosing one or two courts projected toward the street and were connected by a range parallel with it. In these wings domestic service rooms such as pantry, kitchen, and butler were provided. It was also customary for stables to be placed in proximity to the main residential spaces opening onto the courts. There were obvious disadvantages to this arrangement in view of the distance for food delivery from the kitchen to the main residence; the servant had to traverse many rooms or cross the court or ascend the stairs to upper levels. It must be remembered, however, that the thrust of the Louis XIV style was toward ostentatious display.

While many rooms were rectangular, devices were used that provided drama and encouraged exploration of three-dimensional space. The vehicles employed by François Mansart and Le Vau can be characterized as Baroque features: (1) the variety of interior spaces (round, oval, rectangular with semicircular recesses) and the distinctive variations in ceiling configuration, such as the dome or barrel vaulting; (2) the encouragement of vistas accomplished through the use of the enfilade in the arrangement of apartments, vistas from the main suites to the landscaped garden or natural outdoor scene, and the extraordinary sense of distance created by the use of Baroque painting where figures moved through illu-

FIGURE 9-4 Staircase vault. Château of Blois, Orléans Wing (1635-1638), François Mansart.

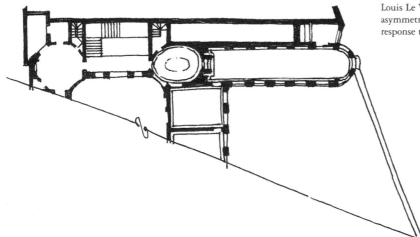

FIGURE 9-5 Hôtel Lambert, Paris (1640), Louis Le Vau. Principal floor. Early use of asymmetrical planning. Interior planning a response to the view of the countryside.

sionistic architectural space; (3) vertical perspectives resulting from the dramatic use of light and dark contrasts in the staircase—such contrasts were generated directly by light sources or by the direction of light from obliquely located light sources; and (4) the height of the salone—usually two stories tall.

For the Orléans wing (1635-1638) at the Château of Blois, Mansart used the Baroque approach in varying the shapes of interior spaces and vistas. However, his most remarkable technique was the extraordinary manner in which the light source, blocked by the first floor gallery and invisible from the main staircase, provided drama in the stairwell (Figure 9-4). In dramatic expression Le Vau showed his indebtedness to Mansart in the design of his first important work, Hôtel Lambert (1640), built for the pretentious financier J. B. Lambert on the Ile-St-Louis in Paris. The plan of the principal floor expresses his interest in the dramatic (Figure 9-5). The staircase, arranged around an open stairwell that doubles back on itself, exploited light and dark contrasts. As the principal floor was approached the occupant encountered two vestibules, one oval and one octagonal. Le Vau capitalized on the view of the river Seine through the linear relationship of the vestibules and long gallery; the overall arrangement is an early use of asymmetrical planning.

INTERIOR ARCHITECTURE AND DECORATION

The Flemish painter Peter Paul Rubens was instrumental in bringing the Baroque influence to France. He was favored by Marie de Medici, who commissioned him in 1622 to paint a series about her life for the Luxembourg palace; with this series the height of Baroque decorative painting was attained. The increased interest in the classical reached its apex in the culminating period of Louis XIV. Interior architecture was strictly conceived.

Materials and Decorative Techniques

Forms and techniques of the later French Renaissance continued to be employed during the transitional period of Louis XIII. Plaster with fresco, exposed beams with small painted patterns, and white and gold stucco were prominent in the rendition of the interiors. Illusionist painting was used at Fontainebleau by the Italians (Primaticcio and Rosso) in the decoration of the ceiling of the Francis I gallery. During the period of Louis XIV stucco, gilding, and painting continued to be the primary decorative materials and techniques; the difference was in the stylistic character of the latter part of the 17th century.

Interior Architecture and Decorative Elements

Floors

Stone and marble were the materials used throughout the 17th century. However, marble was used more frequently in the latter half; wood often replaced marble on the upper floor levels. Parquet patterns (geometric) were employed early in the century at the Luxembourg Palace of Marie de Medici, but the treatment became more widespread as the century progressed. The diagonally positioned lozenge was a frequently used configuration, as were patterns in squares. The term *parquet* (meaning the enclosure or office of the public prosecutor) originated with the practice of a king or other administrative officer in rendering judgments from a raised platform, the floor treatment of which was different from the other floors in the same space.

Though rare, highly complex marquetry (representational) was occasionally used. At Versailles one such floor was installed in the Cabinet Doré for the Dauphin (Figure 9-6). The border was designed with regularly spaced oval motifs. The center was composed of a symmetrical arrangement of strapwork and elaborate scrolls of leafage. This floor was removed in 1688.

Walls

At first carved wood paneling *(boiserie)* was a favored means of covering the lower part of the wall and horizontality was emphasized. Characteristically the field of the panel projected beyond the level of stiles and rails; a bolection molding surrounded the panels (Figure 9-7). The upper part of the wall was ornamented in a variety of ways: textiles were sometimes applied; illusionistic murals were painted within architectural frames; paintings also included portraits and landscape. In the cabinet of the Hôtel Colbert de Villacerf rectangular panels are ornamented with polychrome grotesques (see Figure C-12). In the middle of the 17th century the emphasis began to change from horizontality to verticality, and the dado often became taller. Classical influence was introduced in the use of pilasters to divide the wall vertically. An entablature surrounding the room was a prominent feature heading the wall. An alternative means of treating the entablature was to use *consoles* (curved brackets) spaced regularly within it; Le Brun introduced the use of paired consoles in the frieze (see Figure C-13). Sometimes a convex molding replaced the frieze. In the latter part of the century marble was used as a sheathing in geometric arrangements, especially important for the interiors at Versailles. Wood continued to be employed with either painted arabesques or molded stucco reliefs. When colors were applied they tended to be

FIGURE 9-6 Marquetry Floor, Cabinet Doré, Versailles (removed 1688). Musée des Arts Décoratifs, Paris. Union Centrale des Arts Décoratifs.

FIGURE 9-7 Mural Decoration (c. 1630s). Probable intent to insert paintings in large framed panels. Ashmolean Museum, Oxford.

pale tones. Oak and pine were favored woods for paneling; in France it was more common for wood to be painted rather than left in its natural state. Both graining and marblizing were used in the treatment of wood. In the case of the former painting was used to simulate more expensive woods, while in the latter painting was used to imitate marble.

Since the crown supported tapestry production this wall treatment was significant. Subjects included allegorical, historical, and religious themes but the depiction of royalty in these scenes was often stressed. Tapestries for less wealthy purchasers often had more simple repeat patterns. Damasks and velvets also figured prominently in wall applications. When embossed leather was used it was sometimes ornamented with a metal foil either highlighted with brilliant color, gilded, or silvered with a wide variety of motifs.

Due primarily to technological advances, the use of mirrors gained momentum during the 17th century. Sometimes the mirror was used architecturally and set within an enframement on the wall, but mirrors were also framed independently and hung in front of the wall surface treatment. In the Cabinet aux Miroirs in the Château de Maisons, Mansart set panes of mirror glass within moldings integral with the wall. Some installations had four panes of mirror glass comprising one panel, since larger panes could not be produced at this time. To mount the panes, they were abutted and large-headed fasteners were used at the corners.

Windows and Doors

The area of the wall devoted to windows increased during the 17th century. Windows in the earlier part of the century were tall and narrow but they usually extended only to the dado. However, later they sometimes rose from the floor to almost ceiling level and had double valves (sometimes termed *French windows*), in which the casements pivoted from the jamb. This type of window was introduced in the residence of Madame de Rambouillet.[1] When wood frames replaced the stone transoms and mullions and with rectangular panes it was possible for the casements to open outward. Both flat and round heads were used for windows. Panes of glass at the beginning were small and sometimes lozenge in shape but, as revealed in French engravings of the 17th century, other conformations for smaller panes were also employed. Sometimes paintings were used to ornament the insides of window glass including portraiture, figurative designs, or scenes.

In the earlier part of the century most of the glass used in France was imported from Venice. Glass manufacturing was established in Paris in 1665 and soon thereafter it received royal patronage. The state of technology using the method of blowing precluded the production of large panes of glass. The method of casting was not effectively developed until the last decade of the century; this method allowed larger sheets of glass to be produced.

Doors, like windows, changed during the century. Early they were single valved, while later double-valved doors were typical. Doors were of paneled wood and ornamented with carving and gilding. They were usually flat-headed; above the head a variety of overdoor configurations were combined into one unified composition. The enfilade of the Hôtel Lazun illustrates the doorway treatments typical of the period around 1660 (see Figure C-14). In the foreground the architrave surround is carved with the classical laurel motif, which to the Greeks and Romans was a symbol of glory. Heroes were crowned with laurel wreaths. The laurel leaves are bound periodically with ribbon. In the rectangle immediately above the door opening are festoons of leaves, flowers, and so on that emanate from wavy ribbons.

Chimneypieces

Engravings by leading designers were highly instrumental in the design of this prominent interior feature. The chimneypiece was the focal point of each room as visitors pro-

---

1. Madame de Rambouillet, along with a group of other well-known personalities, including François, duc de La Rochefoucauld, exerted great influence on French literature.

FIGURE 9-8 Chimneypiece, adapted from *Livre d'architecture* (first edition 1632), Jean Barbet. Massive, highly complex, and sculptural features more typical of early 17th century.

FIGURE 9-9 Chimneypiece, adapted from *Cheminées et lambris à la mode* (published 1690s), Pierre Le Pautre. Use of glass for the chimneybreast; bolection molding surround for the firebox.

gressed through the principal apartment; therefore, a great deal of ornamental detail was lavished on this principal architectural feature. A number of publications were influential: Jean Barbet's *Livre d'architecture* (1632 and 1641) and Jean Le Pautre's *Cheminées à la moderne* (1661) and *Cheminées à l'Italienne* (1665), which included recommendations for compact pieces. Through the mid-17th century the chimneybreast was massive, sculptural, and highly complex (Figure 9-8). Paintings had frames of carved wood or stucco relief. The relief might include a variety of motifs among which were figures, broken pediments, swags, scrolls, cartouches, and various classical elements (pilasters, entablatures, pediments). The *cartouche,* used in a variety of positions within the composition, was a sculptural ornamental tablet often framed by a molding enhanced by carving that resembled scrolls (see Figure 9-8). Later in the century the chimneybreast became less massive, with simpler ornamentation of overmantel configurations; in fact, toward the end of the century one characteristically restrained treatment was to install mirror glass on walls (Figure 9-9). The evolution of the firebox was toward lower, wider, and smaller openings often surrounded by a bold bolection molding. A mantel shelf was not always constructed, but when it was the chimneybreast was often at the plane of the wall. Robert de Cotte, nephew of Jules Hardouin-Mansart, is credited with having recommended the reduction in size of the firebox, lowering the composition, and introducing the mantel shelf.

Ceilings

After the chimneypiece the most important focal point of the Baroque interior was the ceiling. Early in the 17th century a continuation of the 16th-century beamed ceiling pre-

FIGURE 9-10 Ceiling Pattern from an Engraving, Possibly by Jean Cotelle (1640s). Classical decorative detail for a geometrically and symmetrically arranged composition. From the volume described in Parker's catalog Volume I, number 395: Folio volume containing a collection of designs, chiefly for the decoration of ceilings. Ashmolean Museum, Oxford.

vailed, featuring small painted patterned designs; this treatment continued for more modest interiors. Ceiling contours were varied: flat, barrel-vaulted, dome-vaulted, and with a coved transition from wall to ceiling.

The techniques of ornamentation for ceilings included painting, fresco, and stucco, but some ceilings were without decoration and painted white. Engraved patterns were available to architects. Among the most important were engravings by Jean Cotelle (1607-1676) whose designs were later incorporated in published works; one edition was available in 1640 (Figure 9-10). In a geometric and symmetrically arranged composition the decorative frames of the various units were of classical derivation such as the guilloche, laurel leaves, raies de cour, beading, etc. Jean Le Pautre, designer and engraver, was also influential.

The use of illusionist painting was employed at Fontainebleau in the previous century when the Italian designers Primaticcio and Niccolo were commissioned to decorate the ceiling of the Gallerie d'Ulysse. Simon Vouet (1590-1649), familiar with the work of the late 16th century in Italy, executed important works in stucco relief and fresco in the 1630s and 1640s; for these he opened illusionistic spaces through the use of *sotto in su.* The next major development was through the work of Le Brun, who worked for the crown at the Louvre and at Versailles. The ceiling of the Apollo Drawing Room, the climax of the State Apartments at Versailles, was the work of Charles de Lafosse, a pupil of Le Brun. At the corners of the ceiling the sky was depicted, giving a sense of great spaciousness. In the alterations to Versailles, begun in 1671 and 1686, the style changed to lower relief, particularly in the figural elements. Illusionistic panels were set within frames. Increasingly, however, direction was toward the use of non-illusionistic panels.

Stairways

Spatial manipulations and drama in the modulation of light were contributions of 17th-century architects. In the period of Henry IV the stairway was located in the center of the main block of the residence; then the location changed and it was placed to either the right or left of the vestibule, the main entrance. In the first half of the 17th century François Mansart introduced the arrangement of the stairs around an open square well; in addition, he capitalized on the dramatic use of light for the stairwell when he designed the Orléans wing of the Château of Blois (see Figure 9-4).

Among the most important works of Le Brun was the Great Staircase of the Ambassadors at Versailles; the stairway was destroyed in 1752 during the reign of Louis XV, but an engraving exists which records design details. It was situated in an oblong hall. A broad flight of stairs ascended to a landing from which two flights emanated, one to the right and one to the left, and led to the gallery of the next floor. Colored marble revetments were applied to the walls and marble was used for the stairs. A skylight lit the stairway. Alterations late in the century included balustrades made of metal, curved sweeps, and steps (in plan) that were curved instead of straight.

FURNITURE

At the beginning of the century a French style had not yet been developed, since the French preferred styles inconsistent with creative expression on the part of native designer craftsmen. Thus furniture needs were handled in a variety of ways. In some cases there was a preference for the taste of the 16th century with very few alterations. However, nobles and people of the court sometimes preferred to send to other countries for their furniture, such as Italy, Netherlands, or Spain. In other instances French craftsmen were commissioned to make replicas of foreign models. With no centralized theme contradictions due to the many influences at play abounded. The French did not adopt the excesses that characterized Flemish designs. With the plethora of influences a national style was not developed during the Louis XIII period.

An identifiable French style became evident around 1660. At this point France became the artistic leader for Europe. The Louis XIV style was accomplished by tightly controlling design, which was endorsed only if it met the standards set forth by the *maîtres ornemanistes* (master ornamentalist). Le Brun was the person who administered this approach to an official art.

Materials and Construction Techniques

Generally, methods of construction used in the previous century continued in the Louis XIII period. At the intersection of structural points a square ending was maintained. Lathe turning (spiral, baluster, vase, etc.) was used both structurally and decoratively; turned parts were often split and glued to the surfaces of furniture as ornament. In addition, moldings were applied to give emphasis to cornices, panels, and so on, but the moldings were generally thicker than those used in the Renaissance.

Both solid wood and veneered pieces were constructed; however, the division of responsibility of the craftsmen was important: A *menuisier* (a joiner) worked in solid wood and did carving while the *ébéniste* was a specialist in veneer. The ébéniste worked primarily for wealthy families and the crown since veneering was time-consuming and therefore an expensive process. The materials used in these decorative processes were expanded to include unusual woods (such as ebony), tortoiseshell, jasper, lapis lazuli, agate, bone, and metals. Woods used for structure were primarily oak, walnut, and pear; because of its ease of carving walnut became more prevalent.

During the period of Louis XIV emphasis was given to the perfection of techniques rather than to radically new processes. For example, in veneering there was greater investigation into extending the range of colors through the use of a wider variety of valuable woods as well as expanded use of other materials (such as brass, pewter, horn painted on the underside, etc.) and how materials were used in combination. André Charles Boulle (1642-1732) perfected a type of marquetry utilizing brass and tortoiseshell which bears his name. His technique involved cutting the two sheets of materials simultaneously; thus, enough material was available for two pieces of furniture, one with tortoise as the background *(en première partie)* and the other with brass as background *(en contre partie)*. The difficulty lay in the fact that the veneer materials in combination, laid on a carcass of wood, had different qualities, which meant that they reacted differently to changing atmospheric conditions; boulle-work was a fragile technique. To protect the corners of such pieces ormolu mounts (gilded bronze) were applied; other uses of these also included handles and escutcheons.

Solid wood furniture continued to be constructed, even though emphasis was given to veneered pieces; typical solid wood pieces included chairs, buffets, and cupboards. These were decorated with carving and highlighted with gold or silver. The reason was that interiors were designed as ensembles and furniture needed to coordinate with the stucco wall detail. Solid gold and silver furniture has not survived, since a state financial crisis in the late 18th century meant that these pieces were melted.

The practice of using lacquer was new to the period of Louis XIV. Oriental lacquer was admired by the French to such an extent that they imported furniture and disassembled it. The panels were then incorporated into French pieces and often enframed with ormolu to protect the edges.

Typical Pieces and Stylistic Features

Seat Furniture

Louis XIII. Chairs were generally more comfortable than before due to the use of upholstery; the forms appeared less formidable and stiff due to the introduction of curves that softened the outline. The introduction of wool upholstery fabrics, termed *moquettes,* were typically designed with small motifs in many colors. Henry IV became so enamored with silk that he planted mulberry trees in the Tuileries Gardens; silkworms feed on mulberry leaves.

Available in both tall-backed and low-backed versions, chairs were usually rectilinear but sometimes the outline was softened with a serpentine cresting of the back; tall-backed versions were customarily reserved for use as state chairs (Figure 9-11). The lower back was normally separated from the seat. Seats were ordinarily trapezoidal or square.

FIGURE 9-11 Louis XIII Armchair. Emphasis on turning. Tall back with serpentine crest.

Armchairs (*fauteuil*) had armrests that were essentially parallel with the floor. Some armrests were straight while others formed a downward curve. The armrests extended beyond the arm supports, where they ended with such decorative ornaments as whorls, lions' heads, and rams' heads although some had a simple turned button ending. Arm supports were continuations of the legs. Stretchers were placed at two levels: The lower-level stretcher was of H-shape and the higher a single transverse stretcher placed in the front. Turned legs were typically in a range of contours such as columnar, knobbed, spiral, baluster, etc. Seats were square or trapezoidal. Stools (*tabourets*) were numerous due to protocol, since the most important person was the only one who sat in an armchair; some of the stools were of folding X-shaped forms.

Louis XIV. Protocol dictated the height of seat furniture. From the highest to lowest rank, here is the hierarchy of chairs: the high-backed upholstered armchair (*fauteuil*); the high-backed armless chair (*chaise*); and the upholstered stool (*tabouret*). There are accounts that as many as 1,300 stools were used at Versailles.

A typical high-backed armchair can be characterized as follows: a tall, fully upholstered rectangular back with a space between the seat rail and the lower rail of the back; a fully upholstered seat, essentially square; arm supports in a cyma curve rising directly above the legs; armrests that in outline have a downward curve originating on the stile of the back and extend in bold whorls beyond the arm supports; four legs of the baluster or pedestal type which are square in cross section beginning with an incut neck below the seat and enlarging and then tapering to a blocked section at the level at which the stretcher attaches to the legs. Stretchers were either H-shaped or X-shaped. The feet were often square in section below the blocked section; bun shapes were also used (Figure 9-12). When the X-shaped stretcher (termed *saltire*) was used it was usually comprised of scrolls, rises in the center with a decorative carved motif at the intersection, and sometimes a clearly defined finial. In the Louis XIV style carving generally replaced turning. Late in the Louis XIV period forms became more relaxed and lightly scaled with more delicately conceived curves. The walnut chair illustrated retains the high rectangular back (Figure 9-13).

FIGURE 9-12 Louis XIV Armchair. Carved and gilt wood. Tapestry upholstery. Pedestal legs united by an H-shaped stretcher made up of S-scrolls; bun feet.

FIGURE 9-13 Louis XIV Armchair. Carved and gilt walnut. Late 17th-century features: relaxed curves, cabriole legs, saltire stretcher, pied de biche.

The armrest and arm support form one continuous curve beginning above the leg. Cabriole legs end in the *pied de biche* (or cloven hoof foot); the saltire stretcher unites the legs.

Other changes over the period of the late 17th century were that arm pads began to be introduced and that the cresting of the back began to be of serpentine outline. Except that it was armless, the chaise had essentially the same characteristics as the armchair, and the base of the tabouret had the same features as the other chairs.

Tables

Louis XIII. Generally, small tables had surfaces supported by turned legs in a variety of configurations with stretchers of H- or X-form. At the center of the stretcher an ornament was introduced, such as a knob or vase. Some of these tables were used for writing. This was not a new type since it appeared in inventories of the 16th century.

One popular table type had a rectangular top with extension underleaves that allowed the length to almost double; turned pendant drops decorated each corner of the tabletop. The apron (or frieze) was supported by seven columnar legs. The heavy molded stretcher of greater length was crossed with two transverse sections. Flattened bun feet were used under each arm of the stretcher (Figure 9-14).

Louis XIV. Great varieties of tables for an equally large number of functions were produced in the Louis XIV period. One was the *bureau plat* (writing table). Three drawers were usually incorporated in the frieze, the center drawer of which was usually recessed. Those fabricated in the latter part of the 17th century often had cabriole legs. Some were decorated with Boulle-work. Sometimes separate storage pieces featuring drawers or open storage accompanied this piece.

Other specialized uses for tables included games, toilet, tea, and candlesticks. Some of these were very large, with intricate detailing. Designed to complement the interior ensemble, they were often placed against the wall. Tops of tables were treated in numerous ways. Materials included wood (sometimes simply painted) and marble. Decorative techniques were mosaics, marquetry of Boulle-work or wood, and so on, sometimes combined with elaborate carving (Figure 9-15). The carved table at the Metropolitan Museum of Art is a case in point. Gilt is used on the carved wood with a marble slab for the tabletop surface. Below the decorative carved frieze is a pierced apron of scrolls and leafage in pendant position. Pedestal legs (sometimes called baluster) are joined by an X-shaped stretcher, each arm of which is in the form of an elaborately carved S-shape.

FIGURE 9-14 Louis XIII Table. Walnut extension table. Columnar legs, stretcher, bun feet. From *Furniture Past and Present* by Louise Ade Boger. Copyright © 1966 by Louise Ade Boger. Used by permission of Doubleday, a division of Bantam Doubleday Dell Publishing Group, Inc.

Storage Pieces

Louis XIII. Cupboards of several types illustrate characteristic features of the Louis XIII period. These often had simple panels with moldings as the sole means of ornament. Strong moldings identified the levels of storage. There was a strong projecting cornice (Figure 9-16). These features are observed in this *armoire à deux corps,* built in two stages in which the top portion is narrower than the base. The decoration on the panels is the widely used faceted diamond point ornament accomplished through the use of molded wood pieces.

FIGURE 9-16 Louis XIII Armoire à Deux Corps. Walnut. Emphasis on moldings. Decoration on doors diamond point, spiral turning on stiles. Strongly projecting cornice. From *Furniture Past and Present* by Louise Ade Boger. Copyright © 1966 by Louise Ade Boger. Used by permission of Doubleday, a division of Bantam Doubleday Dell Publishing Group, Inc.

FIGURE 9-17   Louis XIV Commode en Tambeau. Follower of Boulle, French 19th century. Boulle-work of tortoiseshell and brass. Copyright The Frick Collection, New York.

FIGURE 9-18   Louis XIV Armoire. Perhaps from the hand of André Charles Boulle. Ebony, brass, and tortoiseshell. Classical subjects in larger panels. Reproduced by permission of the Trustees of the Wallace Collection.

Louis XIV. The commode or chest of drawers was introduced in the Louis XIV period. Initially this piece was in the form of a sarcophagus; it resembled the cassone of the Italian Renaissance and the coffers of France. The first two pieces of this type are thought to have originated with Boulle. The top overhangs the two-drawer commode. The piece is ornamented with ebony veneer using marquetry of tortoiseshell and brass. Ormolu is employed for the handles, escutcheons, framing for the drawers, and on the curved legs. The piece is unusual in that it is mounted on eight legs, the short inner ones have spirally contoured outlines while the large outer ones are cabriole in form, end in paw feet, and and are headed with a female bust (Figure 9-17).

Both tall and low cabinets were constructed. Boulle's armoire is typical of the Louis XIV period. Boulle used marquetry of wood as well as his own veneer technique, the resulting design being representational. An armoire thought to be from the hand of Boulle is in the Wallace Collection, London (Figure 9-18). Ebony, brass, and tortoiseshell are the materials. This piece was made in nine parts so that it could be transported easily. *Première partie* (tortoiseshell background) is used on the large rectangular panels and *contre partie* (brass background) is used on the smaller horizontal panels. In addition, decorative ormolu mounts (chased and gilded brass) are applied to the surface. Structurally, the armoire illustrates the rectilinear and architectural character of these large forms. Classical subjects are used within each of the larger panels.

Beds

Louis XIII. Wooden parts for beds do not survive from this period. The emphasis was on upholstery and these textile parts were primarily from the hand of the tapissier (tapestry-worker). Until about 1670 textiles played a major role in the draping of the bed. Kings and queens received their subjects from their beds, as did princes and princesses.

Louis XIV. The resplendent, imposing beds of the Louis XIV period were draped with rich textiles. Those sumptuously treated beds designed specifically for the state bedroom were purely ornamental, for it was here that the monarch received his or her subjects. But the draped bed was also used by ordinary citizens, the degree of elaboration a reflection of the wealth of the owner. The draperies served a purpose in that they kept out drafts and, therefore, kept warmth within the confines of the bed. The four-post bed *(lit à colonnes)* continued to be constructed to the end of the Louis XIV period, after which it lost favor until the Louis XVI period. In the late 17th century the bed was constructed with both a headboard and a footboard; a textile hanging the width of the tester was customarily placed on the wall behind the headboard.

The design for a state bed illustrates the highly decorative drapery treatment of the eminently influential Daniel Marot, the French Huguenot who fled from France to Holland and then to England, where he became a designer to William III. His designs represent a blending of Louis XIV and Dutch styles (Figure 9-19).

ORNAMENT

Louis XIII. Commonly employed ornament of the Louis XIII period included lions' heads, rams' heads, female busts, vases, mascarons (grotesque mask in caricature), lions' paws,

FIGURE 9-19   Influence of Daniel Marot, State Bed (c. 1690). Decorative drapery in the style of Daniel Marot. Based on *lits à la Romaine* treatment. By Courtesy of the Board of Trustees of the Victoria and Albert Museum, London.

diamond point designs, clusters of fruit, foliated scrolls, cornucopias, flowers, cartouches, and geometric patterns.

Louis XIV. Favorite motifs used by Le Brun included lyres, sun disk emblems of the king, crowns, foliage, chimeras, and cornucopias. Decorative details based on animal forms were popular, including lions' heads, lions' paws, rams' heads and horns, griffons, stags' hooves, and dolphins. Some were based on flora such as flowers, waterlily leaves, acanthus leaves, fruit, and oak leaves. Other popular decorative elements were trophies, coats of arms, shells, mascarons, small flowers set within diaper patterns, and interlaced strapwork bounding lozenges or squares.

Chapter 10

English Baroque

1660-1702

HISTORICAL SETTING

With the restoration of Charles II to the throne in England there was great jubilation. Pepys, the diarist, wrote that "The shouting and joy expressed by all is past imagination."[1] This event marked the beginning of unprecedented interaction of political and aesthetic influences contributing to the complex network of factors responsible for the transmission of fashion that swayed English taste at this time. Both foreign and domestic elements impinged on English arts of this period.

Political calm and economic prosperity were essential in order for the arts to flourish after the chaos caused by civil war and the Commonwealth. Charles II was able, during his reign from 1660 to 1685, to avert open hostility among his subjects. Some political dissatisfaction lay in the great landowners wanting power for themselves and limited authority for the crown; they supported neither the divine right of kings nor government by autocracy. Nonetheless the Whig nobility accepted the monarchy and prospered during this period; nobles gained in political stature and significantly increased their land holdings by purchasing the estates of small landowners. The latter had suffered hardship due to the enclosure system, unfair game laws, and, later, taxes imposed to pay for the wars of William III. The enclosure system meant that lands formerly available to common use were closed in, with an adverse effect on the poor. Since large landowners were not negatively impacted by these policies and practices and since affluence was increasing, the result was a gradual increase in building activity during the reign of Charles II with consequent expenditures for interior design and furnishing of country houses influenced by the latest Baroque style.

In addition, a spate of building in the city of London was necessitated because of the devastation caused by the great fire of 1666. The talents of Sir Christopher Wren, along with the architects Roger Pratt and Hugh May, were needed to coordinate the reconstruction of London. Wall thickness, floor height, and the use of brick were stipulated as a result of the recommendations contained in the Rebuilding Act of 1667. This provided stimulus for new styles in architecture, furniture, and decoration as well as for all trades associated with the building and furnishing of new structures.

Country house building was at a virtual standstill from 1685 to 1688 due to political uncertainty and an unsettled state of affairs during the reign of James II. Hostilities, submerged while Charles II ruled, were brought to the fore with the accession of James II. Issues revolved around the rights and privileges of Parliament and the openly professed Catholicism of the king. The conflict culminated in the Glorious Revolution of 1688, which affirmed the permanent sovereignty of Parliament; the result was the transfer of power to the Whig nobility.

The Whigs then accepted William III and Mary II as joint constitutional monarchs. As a consequence of this change in monarchy, influence on the arts emanated from both Holland and France; Daniel Marot, the French protestant, introduced French ideas into Holland and subsequently worked in England. Further influence can be attributed to Charles II's having spent his exile years in both France and Holland; William had been the only son of William II, Prince of Orange of the Netherlands, and Mary was the Protestant daughter of James II. Artistic initiative now passed to the noblemen and the nouveau riche; many monumental country houses were constructed, requiring large amounts to be spent on decorating and furnishings.

The transmission of fashion ideas within the country was the responsibility of English gentlemen and the nobility. Although the group was very small, its members had the education, cultural awareness, and wealth essential to keep abreast of the latest changes in architecture and design. They observed and possibly emulated the influence of decorative arts from France, Holland, and the rest of Europe, and the interior decorative detail accomplished by foreign craftsmen working in England. The gentleman was the key person and

---

1. Robert Latham and William Matthews, eds. *The Diary of Samuel Pepys,* vol. 1 (Berkeley: University of California Press, 1970), 158.

the conduit for the spread of style to those lower on the social scale. Often the gentleman had the one important household in a village; here was embodied the latest in English art and decoration.

Baroque manifestations in the arts which were to evolve came primarily from France and secondarily from Holland. Charles II, a cousin of King Louis XIV, had spent a portion of his exile in Paris. He and the Royalist sympathizers with him were impressed by the luxuries of the court; on their return to England, they promoted these fashions from abroad. Other foreign aesthetic influences were promulgated by commerce, the revocation of the Edict of Nantes, design publications, and travel.

A number of factors were instrumental in bringing Dutch influence to England during the late 17th century: commercial interchange between the countries, Dutch immigrants who worked as craftsmen, the residence of the exiled English court in Holland, and the accession of William and Mary as joint rulers. The Staadholder, William, Prince of Orange, brought with him from Holland craftsmen who were influential in disseminating Dutch taste. However, the House of Orange (as well as the Stuart monarchs) looked to Paris as the center of European culture and was the primary promoter of French artistic ideals in Holland. This interest in French arts was extended by the immigration to Holland of thousands of Huguenots, French Protestants, who were persecuted when Louis XIV, in 1685, revoked the Edict of Nantes, which had allowed religious freedom for this group.

Since many of the Huguenots were skilled craftsmen and highly talented designers, they had profound influence on commercial and artistic life of the countries in which they settled. For example, Daniel Marot, following his departure from France in 1684, became a designer for the Staadholder in Holland. When William of Orange became King William III of England, Marot continued to provide designs, this time for royal residences such as Kensington Palace and Hampton Court.

But the artistic influence of Marot and other French designers was dispersed in other ways also. French engravings were sold individually (an ornament, a candlestand, etc.) or by category in sets (as chimneypieces, specialized pieces of furniture, ornamental details); also, designs were accumulated and sold as books. Highly influential in England were the published works of such designers as Marot (a Parisian who studied under Le Pautre and worked in the studio of André Charles Boulle); Jean Le Pautre (a leading proponent of the the style of Charles Le Brun, French architect and designer); and François Blondel, a designer in his own right, who reissued in 1673 an architectural work by Louis Savot that gave information on such aspects as space planning and the location of specific interior architectural elements. These engravings could be purchased through printsellers in London and well as in Paris.

The travels of influential English citizens who resided in Paris as well as of architects who studied abroad were instrumental in spreading French fashion. For example, ambassadors who spent several years in Paris were witness to the latest fashions through their associations with French aristocracy; not only did they buy French furnishings but they sometimes brought French artists and craftsmen to work on residences built on their return to England. Foreign craftsmen came to the attention of Englishmen who traveled; for instance, the architect Hugh May, who spent time in Holland during the Commonwealth, gave a commission to the eminent sculptor and carver Grinling Gibbons.[2] Painters receiving prominent commissions in England included Antonio Verrio (an Italian who came to England after a period of time in France) and Louis Laguerre (a Frenchman who was taught by Le Brun and worked at Versailles).

In 1665 Sir Christopher Wren (a noted English architect who received a royal appointment as surveyor general in 1668), on a trip to Paris, was witness to the building projects and activities underway for the court of Louis XIV at the Louvre, Versailles, and Fontainebleau. He had the opportunity to make his own drawings of

---

2. Grinling Gibbons was born of English parents in Rotterdam. Having received his early training in workshops in Holland, he came to England around 1667. The influence of the Dutch flower painters is evident in his wood carvings.

details that impressed him and also purchased design books and engravings for reference on his return home. Cumulatively, all of these interacting factors impacted English space planning, interior architecture, furniture design, decorative detail, and social etiquette based on the prevailing Baroque models, primarily from France and Holland.

SPATIAL RELATIONSHIPS

The *formal house* is the term used by Mark Girouard to acknowledge a specific approach to the use and arrangement of interior spaces during the period from 1630 to 1720. Social protocol governed all facets of life; in turn, space planning, interior architecture and decoration, and furnishings all contributed to this central theme. Noblemen and gentry who followed Charles II into exile became aware of the formal planning prevalent in France and Holland; however, Italy had initiated this planned distribution of spaces, which provided the impetus for other countries. Meeting the needs of royalty, this spatial arrangement was subsequently adapted by the aristocracy, after which it was emulated by those of lower rank.

Spatial Features of the Floor Plan and Three-Dimensional Spatial Characteristics

Devised to meet the needs of royalty, a palace would typically have had both state apartments and family quarters. A state apartment was provided for the king for ceremonial use; a comparable suite of rooms was provided for the queen, who represented alliance with another country, thus demanding equivalent attention. Typically, state apartments were located on the first or second floor, but there were also instances in which they were placed on the ground floor. The importance of interior spaces was expressed on the exterior by the architectural emphasis given by a centrally projecting facade capped with a pediment to signify the state center and/or forward-projecting terminal points of the facade to denote the paramount importance of certain spaces in a sequence of rooms.

Family quarters were typically in separate wings or on different floors than the state apartments. The several apartments in one residence were needed not only for the less formal use of the king and queen but for family members who inhabited the palace—sons, daughters, and so on.

Upper-class English citizens who built the grand country houses utilized the concepts of apartments and sequences of spaces they observed in the residences of royalty. Apartments of state would be used by the person of premier influence in the community and would have been devoted to the use of the king, should the influential owner be the recipient of the honor of his visit. Like palace planning, accommodations for private use were also provided.

Within the apartment the preferred order of rooms was termed *en enfilade.* Although there were many variations, rooms in the enfilade were aligned one after the other, with connecting doors close to the exterior wall. Social order was reflected in this architectural arrangement, which indicated that each room in the sequence from the great chamber to the bedchamber and closet was more important and more magnificent in decoration than the preceding. Within this series the following rooms were significant: great dining chamber, antechamber, withdrawing chamber, bedchamber, and closet (Figure 10-1).

The great dining chamber (also called great dining room, great chamber, and later salone, or dining room), as the name implies, was the place where formal dining took place and was the first in the series of rooms; when placed between apartments it functioned as the introductory room for each apartment. Tapestries were often hung as the wall treatment for this space, but contemporary documents suggest that there was concern about the retention of food odors which prompted the recommended use of leather. Again, in the late 18th century, Robert Adam suggested leather for dining spaces.

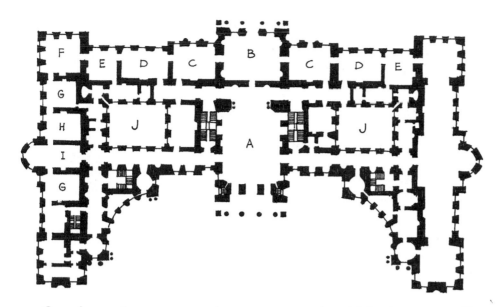

FIGURE 10-1 Blenheim Palace, Oxfordshire. A Great Hall, B Salone, C Antechamber, D Drawing Room, E Great Bedchamber, F Grand Cabinet, G Bedchamber, H Antechamber, I Vestibule, J Little Courts. Architectural Book Publishing Co.

General reception rooms next in sequence were the withdrawing room and/or antechamber. While both of these rooms were included in some plans, the antechamber, used alone, was so called because it preceded the most important room, the bedchamber. These rooms were adorned more elaborately than the preceding space.

The culmination of the enfilade was the bedchamber and, finally, the closet (or cabinet); these rooms had the richest decor. While the bedchamber was public, it was not as public as the comparable space in France. Charles II is said to have used his bedchamber not only for receiving visitors but for dining. In some instances the bed was set off from the rest of the room by a railing. The state bed, highly elaborate, was placed here, but it was not usually slept in; it was so important, however, that it was usually drawn on the plan.

The most private rooms beyond the bedchamber were the closet, the garderobe, and the dressing rooms. The most serious business was undertaken in the closet. Sometimes it was used as the culminating space to which a very important person of rank was taken, in which case it too received magnificent decoration. Further, the closet was used as a private study or for meetings with a group of close advisers. The garderobe was the space for clothing storage or the room in which the close stool was placed.

How far the visitor to the household was allowed to penetrate this sequence was an indication of his standing with the owner. The highest honor was afforded a guest who was escorted by the owner to either the bedchamber or the closet. The visitor, advancing through the directionally arranged apartment, would have observed the chimneypiece, the most prominent feature of the room, on the facing wall or on the wall opposite the windows.

Even modest houses incorporated the concept of formal arrangement. In the apartment at Beningbrough Hall, North Yorkshire, the number of reception rooms are fewer and the closet is not aligned in the same manner as at Blenheim; however, from the state dressing room the enfilade is evident (Figure 10-2; see also Figure 10-6). Greater space limitations could mean that further variations were needed. When space was unavailable for a central hall and salone, the sequential relationship between these and the apartments was altered by placing them on separate floors.

Leading to the apartment and the first space a visitor would enter was a hall, which functioned differently in the 17th century than it had during earlier periods. While formerly it had been a multifunctional room in which all the household members dined and where the servants slept, now it was a room for entry and waiting and sometimes a banquet room. It introduced the state center, sometimes was two stories in height, and, depending on the position of the state apartments, a grand staircase might have emanated or in an adjacent space. This would have been consistent with the ritual of the period.

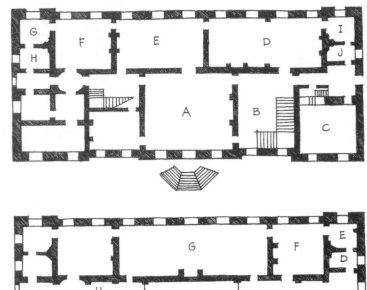

FIGURE 10-2
Beningbrough Hall,
North Yorkshire.
Smaller residence with
number of reception
rooms reduced. Top:
Ground Floor A Great
Hall, B Great Stair, C
Study, D Drawing
Room, E Dining
Room, F State
Bedroom, G State
Dressing Room, H
State Closet, I Dressing
Room, J Closet.
Bottom: *First Floor* A
Upper Part of Great
Hall, B Great Staircase,
C Reading Room, D
Bathroom, E Dressing
Room, F Lady
Chesterfield's Room, G
Saloon, H Back Stairs.

FIGURE 10-3 Sudbury, Derbyshire.
Staircase hall from upper landing.
Plasterwork by James Pettifer, 1675.
Ceiling painting early 1690s by Louis
Laguerre.

FIGURE 10-4 Sudbury, Derbyshire. Salone with shallow central dome with painting, *Four Seasons,* by Louis Laguerre. National Trust Photographic Library, London.

181 English Baroque

Subtle drama was introduced when the stairway was indirectly lighted. The staircase provided a space for spatial experiment; from the base one seemed compelled to ascend by indirectly lighted spaces. In addition to the indirect light, the highly decorative ceiling at Sudbury (viewed both from the upper landing and from the ground level through the open stairwell) is noteworthy in contributing to the vertical accentuation of space (Figure 10-3).

The back stairs assumed greater importance for private exit or entrance for important visitors who wished to avoid the normal entrance to the apartment, the use of servants in the discharge of their duties, some of which were disagreeable, and even clandestine visits. Contrary to earlier practice, when servants used this means of service to increase their social status and when gentlemen servants of rank used the position as a form of education, the social status of servants was generally low during this period. Thus provisions were made to make this class of servants less evident in terms of dining, sleeping, and the discharge of their duties generally.

Emphasis was given to rectangular spaces. One deviation from the strict rectangularity of spaces was the use of plaster coffered false domes which were sometimes employed as at Sudbury where, in the salone, Laguerre's ceiling painting was inserted in the shallow dome (Figure 10-4). However, constructed domes and vaults were occasion-

FIGURE 10-5 Corridor, Beningbrough, North Yorkshire. Variation in compartment space articulation through the use of domes, vaults, and flat ceilings. © National Trust Photographic Library.

ally used to provide variety, as at Beningbrough. Here vistas provided the proximate relationship of rooms. The provision of corridors was an important planning concept of Baroque designers. Along a corridor at Beningbrough a variety of oval, square, and rectangular compartments were created by the use of domes, vaults, and flat ceilings. In addition, the periodic use of trompe l'oeil effects generated by decorative painters such as Laguerre and Verrio significantly altered the way in which spaces were perceived. Examples of such treatments can be observed in such great houses as Reigate Priory and Burghley and at Windsor Castle. Like the Italian Baroque painters who feigned architectural elements, Verrio created unlimited space by causing confusion on the part of the

spectator as to what was real or imagined. Typically, he obliterated the rigid divisions between wall and ceiling. French painters tended to place paintings within the architectural frame so that no delusion was engendered.

The provision of axes to attain spatial distance was an important planning concept. Corridors, enfilade arrangements, and other room adjacencies were employed for visual extension. Longitudinal axes were achieved usually by corridors or the enfilade, but lateral axes were equally significant. Often an interlocking axis was provided through the adjacent relationship of the hall and the great chamber. Through the latter views into outdoor spaces were encouraged (Figures 10-5 and 10-6; see also Figures 10-1 and 10-2).

INTERIOR ARCHITECTURE AND DECORATION, 1660-1715

The English Baroque represents an interlude between two Palladian revivals. One had been prompted by the travels of Inigo Jones in the early 17th century to study the Renaissance architecture of Italy, especially that of Andrea Palladio, while the other was generated through the publication of the first volume in 1715 of *Vitruvius Britannicus,* a work in two volumes by Colen Campbell in which the work of Palladio and Inigo Jones was featured. In the hands of the Italian originators of the Baroque, which replaced the classicism of the Renaissance, characteristics included (1) the preference of curves over straight lines; (2) complex forms; (3) the amalgam of sculpture, painting, and architecture, with the result that painting or sculpture often contributed more to the overall effect than architecture; (4) introduction of elements of surprise, as through the use of light; (5) elaborate ornament and rich materials; and (6) large scale.

While the Baroque style was initiated by the Italians and subsequently adapted by France and northern European countries, France replaced Italy as the arbiter of taste but used it without the religious significance it had in Italy. The English Baroque was primarily a modification of ideas from France and the Netherlands. This was true for a number of reasons. Most of the leading English Baroque architects had not traveled in Italy; premier among these Baroque architects were Sir Christopher Wren, Sir John Vanbrugh, William Talman, Thomas Archer, and Nicholas Hawksmoor. Their knowledge of design trends was gleaned from books and engravings, many of them French, which could be procured in London or obtained on visits to Paris. In addition, Charles II and his court, along with other noblemen, had spent their years of exile in France and Holland and had observed firsthand the Baroque decorative schemes of these countries. These were modified to suit the tastes and conditions of England.

Materials and Decorative Techniques

Rooms of state, representing the formal ritual of life of nobles and gentry, were the most extravagantly decorated spaces. The rooms received the best efforts of architects and craftsmen, who blended the arts of architecture, painting, wood carving, and plasterwork. Premier among materials and decorative techniques was the use of plasterwork; the most superlative English examples date from this period. Great heights of elaboration were attained.

The material to accomplish this virtuoso plasterwork was composed of lime, sand, and water; animal hair added to the mixture gave tensile strength and acted as a binder. Since the job was among the messiest to be performed, the plasterer's work was undertaken before the finish floor was laid and before the paneling was in place. Coves, cornices, soffits of stairways, and ceilings were areas frequently requiring the talents of these craftsmen. The most skilled plasterers working at this time included Edward Goudge, Robert Bradbury, and James Pettifer; some had the ability to provide their own designs also.

The work of the plasterer could be accomplished by modeling in situ or by using molds. Features that were highly complex and deeply undercut (as coats of arms and human figures) were modeled in situ. To accomplish this higher-relief ornament, plaster was mounted on such materials as wire, wood, and leather.

For repetitive work it was faster to use molds; the plaster units were subsequently put in place. Plaster applied over brackets of wood, for example, required that the wood correspond to the proximate outline of the finished component. Frequent need for moldings necessitated the use of a tool with the molding profile which could be run along the damp plaster to refine the shape or outline. Beard, the noted English authority on craftsman techniques, believes the proportion of molding to free modeling to be three to one.

Next in popularity for the decoration of interiors was wood carving. In the sequence of craftsmen who decorated the interior, the wood-carver would have undertaken his installations late, after the paneling was installed. Primarily used by the carvers were such woods as lime and other fruitwoods, oak, and cedar. Sometimes two or three layers glued together were worked as one piece. The carved pieces were fixed into position with glue and metal pins. The productions of wood-carvers included applications to such areas as door frames, ornamental cornices, chimneypieces, balustrades, surrounds for overdoor panels, and paneling. The work of the virtuoso wood-carver Grinling Gibbons was widely imitated.

Decorative painting became increasingly important during the last two decades of the 17th century. Two foreign craftsmen were preeminent in the realm of wall and ceiling painting, the Frenchman Louis Laguerre and the Italian Antonio Verrio. Two techniques were primarily employed: oil on plaster and paint on canvas. With oil on plaster it was first essential to prime the surface of the plaster with size or a thin layer of paint to prevent absorption of the finish paints. Some painters, however, preferred to paint scenes on canvas mounted on the wall. In executing the paintings, painters gave careful consideration to the compass point of natural light in order to produce the most effective shadowing.

Interior Architecture and Decorative Elements

Influenced as they were by the French and Dutch, the English selectively took Continental ideas and modified them to suit their taste. Except for financial restraints, Charles II would have come closer in his own projects to the grandeur he observed in the court architecture and decoration of his cousin, Louis XIV. Artistic initiative in England originated with the monarchy, after which it passed to noblemen and the newly rich commoners. Great Baroque houses were constructed in the last decades of the 17th century and the early years of the 18th century.

Of paramount consideration for the interior was a unified concept. Le Brun had demonstrated its significance in the decoration of French royal palaces and Parisian hôtels. A unifying principle meant that all details in the interior worked together to support the interior architectural scheme; this extended to such components as the designer felt reinforced his composition, including chimneypiece, paneling, shutter paneling, mural schemes, bed hangings, and furniture. Daniel Marot introduced French ideas to Holland and, through his work for William II, to England.

Floors

Parquet floors were used less frequently in England than in France. The origin of the term parquet stems from the more elaborate floor treatment often used in the fenced area that designated the space for the king or other prominent or aristocratic person; this space was often raised to give it further emphasis.

The first known instance of a parquet floor in England was that installed in the apartment of Henrietta Maria, the Queen Mother, in Somerset House on her return from exile in 1660. She would have observed similar floors laid for her mother, Marie de Medici, in the Luxembourg. The Queen's Closet at Ham House retains its parquet floor of strapwork-like design, although it does incorporate a few representational elements (see Figure C-15). An economical means of achieving similar effects were floors painted to represent parquet.

Both marble and oak flooring was used. Rooms paved with marble tended to be installed in more important spaces. Marble was often set in squares of black and white. This material was especially recommended for the ground level, where wooden floors had the disadvantage of being deteriorated by moisture.

Oak was the primary wooden flooring for which wide floorboards were used. In order to keep the wood in its natural color, wax was used for the finish. Another wood occasionally used was deal (pine). The English ambassador imported deal after he observed its use in Sweden; he was particularly impressed with the smooth, white surface attained by rubbing it with cold water and slaked lime.

Walls

A spectrum of wall surfaces was used for English Baroque interiors, including wood paneling, mirrors, tapestries, textiles, leather, paintings, and tile. Wall paneling was the

FIGURE 10-7 State Bedchamber,
Beningbrough Hall, North
Yorkshire. Fielded panels. Bolection
molding for the firebox surround.
© National Trust Photographic
Library.

most common treatment; it was used by all levels of society. The principal woods were oak
and pine, sometimes walnut and fir. While deal was usually painted, oak was either left
untreated or varnished to seal the wood. In France, oak paneling was usually painted.
Carved wood moldings were occasionally gilded.

The practice of treating wood to look more than naturally elegant was typically
Baroque. Several means were used to accomplish this. Graining, a painted simulation of
another wood, was used as an economical means to imitate a more expensive wood.
Replications included oak, walnut, olive wood, and cedar. Closely related to graining was
marbling, whereby a less expensive wood was painted to imitate marble. Celia Fiennes
observed that at Newby "the best roome was painted just like marble, few roomes were
hung."[3]

Wood panels became larger in the Baroque phase, contrary to the early 17th century
practice of using many small panels (Figure 10-7). Although sizes were diverse, fielded
panels framed with bolection moldings were from three to six feet wide. Depending on the

3. Celia Fiennes (1662-1741), through her observations and writings as a traveler, left a remarkable
record of architectural history and social norms.

FIGURE 10-8 State Drawing Room, Chatsworth, Derbyshire. Mortlake tapestries (c. 1635). Ceiling painting by Louis Laguerre. Courtesy of Country Life Picture Library.

187 English Baroque

height of the room, two or three heights of panels might be used. Panels below the dado corresponded in width with those above. Often adjoining the horizontal surface of the ceiling was a complete entablature, not always classically molded, although a coved transition was sometimes utilized above the entablature. Occasionally pilasters were interspersed regularly with the panel system, although this practice became more prevalent in the early 18th century. However, in 1693 fluted ionic pilasters were used to separate the panels at Dryham Park, Gloucestershire; these were placed above the dado with panels of equivalent width below.

Often used along with paneling was a variety of surface materials; among those observed today in extant houses and noted in inventories of the period are tapestries, damasks, brocatelles, velvets, worsteds, painted hangings, and leather. Inventory records of Dyrham Park reveal Flemish tapestries, silk damask hangings, and velvets among its furnishings. An extraordinary example of textile materials used in conjunction with paneling can be observed at Ham House where, in the Queen's Closet, the present series of hangings of brocaded satin with silk borders was installed around 1679 (see Figure C-15).

If a family had the funds, tapestries were ordered to fit exactly into a prescribed space. Otherwise, alterations were made by one of several means including folding the border, cutting the border, or extending the tapestry around a corner of the room. In the Chatsworth state drawing room tapestries were cut to fit the space; the current moldings were installed around 1830 (Figure 10-8). The Mortlake tapestries (c. 1635) depicting biblical scenes by Raphael and entitled *Acts of the Apostles,* are thought to be original to the room. The coves and ceiling were painted by Laguerre.

Surface materials customarily used for the most important rooms included tapestry, silk damask, velvet, and leather; worsted, on the other hand, was used for less important rooms. Since one custom was to have sets of hangings—one for winter and one for summer—it was appropriate to provide some means by which these could be easily exchanged; among the solutions included mounting the textiles on frames that could be attached to walls and using a system of hooks and eyes.

More permanent was the use of leather for walls in the late 17th century. One process resulted in so-called gilt leather; the hide was surfaced with tinfoil, after which it was pressed in a mold to obtain a relief design. Subsequently, the background was textured while the relief pattern was painted.[4] The vestibule at Dyrham Park is covered with stamped and painted Dutch leather, where it is applied above the dado in large squares with motifs of fruit, flowers, and putti. A major production center for stamped leather was the Low Countries, while England produced comparatively little.

Mirrored walls, although not widely used, are known to have been installed. Nell Gwynne and Louise Querouaille, each a mistress of Charles II, had closets faced with paneling of mirror. Since large plates were not in production at this time it was the practice to abut small plates of mirror, holding them in position with studs. Celia Fiennes, observing these on piers at Chippenham, was astonished that the entire figure of a person could be viewed at once.

Windows and Doors

The casement window with transom continued to be used in the late 17th century. With the introduction in 1685 of the the double-hung window (also referred to as sash window), openings became wider. At first, only one sash could be moved while the other was stationary, but later a system of weights and pulleys allowed each sash to work independently. Characteristically, the window extended from the dado to the architrave of the entablature. Sometimes the elaborate carved heading of the window extended onto the entablature, as at Chatsworth (Figure 10-9). The carving of wood above the window head extends onto the entablature; from the associated swags carved drapery is in a pendant arrangement parallel to the window frame. Most of the carvings at Chatsworth are in lime wood. Remodling in the Baroque style took place in the last decade of the 17th century. Exceptional examples of carved overmantels, door frames, window heads, and wall panels are illustrated at Chatsworth. All of these were completed in two years, an extraordinarily brief time, by a team of apprentice carvers.

To control light and provide insulation, shutters were used in most great houses. Shutters were sometimes folded within the deep reveal, paneled to correlate with the wall paneling, or if there were no shutters the jambs were paneled.

Doors were paneled also; most common was the use of six to eight panels which ranged in size. Consistent with the illusionism employed elsewhere in interiors of this period and with the interest in symmetry, doors were sometimes simulated; a contemporary of the period complained that there was so much use of both real and feigned doors that there was no place for pictures or furniture.

Most windows and doors of fine rooms had carved and molded frames (architraves). Carvers sometimes decorated these moldings with naturalistic and delicate motifs; they were first carved, usually in a softer wood, and then applied to the oak frame. There are instances of the use of massive architectural doorcases, as at Sudbury, where engaged columns and pilasters were employed.

Overdoor treatments of important rooms received modest to extravagant treatment (see Figures 10-5 and 10-6). Among these included simply framed overdoor paintings,

---

4. Peter Thornton, *Seventeenth-Century Interior Decoration in England, France, and Holland* (New Haven: Yale University Press, 1978), 118.

FIGURE 10-9 Window, Chatsworth, Derbyshire. Window head carving extends onto the entablature. Limewood. Courtesy of Country Life Picture Library.

189　English Baroque

often used in conjunction with carved details; deeply undercut carvings overlapping surrounding moldings, as the architrave of the entablature that crowned the wall; and segmental pediments (now and then broken).

Chimneypieces

Foreign influence emanating from France and Holland is evident in the design of chimneypieces. Jean Barbet and Pierre Le Pautre, French ornamentalists, each published sets of engravings for chimneypieces. Daniel Marot, entering the service of William of Orange (later William III of England) in 1685, brought the influence of French decorative schemes from Berain[5] and Le Pautre to Holland. Later, Marot provided designs for Hampton Court and Kensington Palace, both royal residences for William and Mary.

Through the influence of Marot the English employed the corner fireplace, with shelves for the display of ceramics such as Delftware and Oriental porcelain, both of which

5. Jean Berain (1636-1711) was a French designer whose style ranged from Louis XIII to Régence. He designed in several media and decorative arts.

had become very fashionable. Although the corner fireplace was not widely accepted, at Beningbrough Hall there are six (see Figure 10-2). John Evelyn, the diarist, was particularly acerbic about this feature when he explained he did not favor the fashion introduced by the king, since it would be particularly ineffective for grand rooms; he did acknowledge, however, that the style could be a respectable solution for small rooms.

Especially in state rooms the position and design of the chimneypiece were given much attention because this was the most prominent feature the visitor saw in each successive room of the enfilade; the position was usually on the far wall as one progressed through the sequence or on the wall opposite the window wall. Compared to the previous period the chimneypiece was closer to the wall, less massive due to the elimination of sculptural ornament, and less architectural in concept. In addition, the firebox was lower and smaller than earlier 17th-century types.

Highly characteristic was the use of a bolection molding of colored marble for the firebox surround. The configuration of the chimneybreast above this was varied. Paneling was sometimes continued in the chimneybreast, where the focus was a painting, a mirror, or applied carvings. Often, no mantel shelf was included; when it was included it was narrow. The state rooms at Chatsworth in Derbyshire are good examples. Here the chimneypieces that are original to the Baroque period project slightly. The fireboxes, surrounded by bolection moldings, are surmounted with panels of shaped frames within which are parquet arrangements of wood; surrounding the panels are highly elaborate carvings of naturalistic flowers, foliage, and amazingly realistic renditions of fish and game (see Figure 10-8). An early use of scagliola as a decorative treatment for the fireplace surround is observed at Ham House (see Figure C-15).

More simple are chimneypieces located in the state bedchamber, Beningbrough. Immediately above the firebox is a horizontally disposed rectangular panel (sometimes a mirror) that is the same width as the framed firebox; between this and the entablature is a large panel corresponding to surrounding panels. Similar arrangements of the chimneybreast are illustrated in Pierre Le Pautre's *Cheminées et Lambris à la mode* (Stylish ways of arranging a chimneypiece).

Ceilings

After the chimneypiece, the most decorated feature of a room was usually the ceiling (see Figures 10-3 and 10-4). Virtuoso plasterwork as a primary means of embellishment typified this period but declined in the late 17th century. Typically, the ceiling was deeply compartmented with an emphasized center—an oval, circle, rectangle or other complex contour; surrounding this centerpiece were ancillary divisions. The soffits of the ribs were decorated with plaster ornamentation including such motifs as naturalistic fruit, foliage, curling flowers, putti, and animals. Similar enrichment was often used on the cornice. Early in this period motifs were tightly packed, while later treatments were free and natural.

Edward Goudge, Robert Bradbury, and James Pettifer were among the most talented plasterers. Edward Goudge was not only a noteworthy craftsman but also could provide his own designs for plasterwork. The architect with whom he worked, William Winde, wrote that he was the best master plasterer in England.[6] He is credited with having executed the chapel and staircase ceilings at Belton; for these Beard reveals that the fruit and foliage were individually molded.[7]

Bradbury and Pettifer were the two craftsmen responsible for the exuberant decoration for six ceilings at Sudbury, Derbyshire, in 1675. The most spectacular of these is plasterwork in the Long Gallery, a room 138 feet long and 23 feet wide (Figure 10-10). The ceiling has such sculptural motifs as shells, curling flowers, foliage, grasshoppers, and acanthus leaves; palm fronds and busts of Roman emperors alternate in the cove. The center of

---

6. Geoffrey Beard, *Decorative Plasterwork in Great Britain* (London: Phaidon Press, 1975), 221.

7. Ibid, 71.

the compartments was left plain; however, 20 years later, in the early 1690s, George Vernon, owner of Sudbury, altered the original scheme by commissioning the painter Louis Laguerre to fill panels in other rooms with figurative painting.

In the last decades of the 17th century decorative painters became the premier ornamentalists for ceilings as well as for walls. Mythological scenes were fashionable, but occasionally a national hero was depicted; the latter is illustrated at Blenheim in the salone, where an apotheosis of the Duke of Marlborough is painted on the ceiling. In devoting emphasis to painting England was following the fashion of the court of Louis XIV, where extravagant paintings were employed in the decoration of the Palace of Versailles.

The Italian painter Verrio came to England in 1671 and decorated the Windsor state rooms. Members of the nobility, seeing his work for Charles II, commissioned him to execute paintings for their country residences. Subsequently he was employed by each of the Stuart monarchs and his work at Hampton Court continued into the reign of Queen Anne. Prominent commissions for the nobility that can be seen today include those for the Duke of Devonshire at Chatsworth, where he painted the ceiling in the state dining room. For the Earl of Exeter at Burghley in 1695-1696 he painted a mythological scene on the walls

FIGURE 10-11 Salone, Burghley, Northamptonshire. Mythological scenes by Antonio Verrio, 1695-1696. Sensational Baroque illusionism. No divisions between walls and ceiling; figures appear to walk into the room. Courtesy of Country Life Picture Library.

and ceiling of the salone (or Heaven Room) (Figure 10-11). Characteristic of Baroque illusionism, the scene depicts a colonnaded court from which figures appear to fly and to walk into the room. Typical of Verrio's style was the energy of the loosely conceived compositions and the omission of rigid divisions between wall and ceiling. He was in demand until his death in 1707.

The French painter Laguerre succeeded Verrio at Burghley. By contrast to his predecessor's compositions, Laguerre's were architectural in concept and academic. A pupil of Le Brun, Laguerre worked at Versailles before coming to England around 1684. Representative works may be seen at Chatsworth, Sudbury, and Blenheim. At Chatsworth he painted all of the state room ceilings, except for the state dining room, with mythological subjects. For Sudbury, George Vernon commissioned Laguerre to fill the blank plasterwork panels with figurative paintings. In the great hall, these were located on the soffit below the landing, the slope of the upper flight of stairs, and on the ceiling; for the salone, the painting in the central shallow dome depicts the four seasons. All of these were painted on plaster rather than canvas (see Figures 10-3 and 10-4).

Stairways

The provision of a grand staircase depended on the position of state rooms; therefore, if these were on an upper level then a correspondingly elegant staircase was essential for the great houses. It could emanate from the great hall or from an adjacent space. Earlier in this period foliated panels formed the balustrade.

At Sudbury is an exceptional example of the pierced panel type in which the strong play of light and shadow is attained by carving. Characterized by very deep undercutting of giant scrolling acanthus leaves, the balustrade is carved in pine and painted white, as was the custom. Carved baskets of fruit atop the newels could be removed at night by replacing them with candelabra or lanterns. The wall side treatment is paneled corresponding to the balustrade (see Figure 10-3). An alternative treatment was the baluster form of balustrade, for which a variety of turnings was employed. Balusters that are spirally turned, three to each tread, are at Reigate Priory, Surrey. Both open and closed string stairways were used.

The stateliest of houses used wrought- or cast-iron balustrades during the last quarter of the 17th century. Of primary influence was the French smith Jean Tijou; he settled in England around 1687 and worked there for about 20 years. Extant staircases show that his book, *A New Book of Drawings,* published in 1693, was used by other smiths. Chatsworth's magnificent staircase approaching the state rooms was executed by Tijou.

FURNITURE: CAROLEAN AND WILLIAM AND MARY

Revolutionary changes took place in furniture design following the return of Charles II and the restoration of the monarchy. Evelyn observed that "the king brought in a politer way of living which soon passed to luxury and intolerable expense." After the somber period of the civil war and the subsequent rule of the Puritans, with their aversion to pretension and their emphasis on simple, austere, functional furniture, the court and Royalists were ready for changes in fashion and the luxuries they had observed in Holland and France.

New decorative processes allowed the designers to attain the opulence that characterized the Baroque period in England. Although the same materials and techniques were used throughout the late Stuart era, three furniture styles are discernable. The *Carolean* (also termed *Restoration* or Charles II) style covers the period following the restoration of Charles II in 1660 and the reign of his brother, James II (1685-1688). The following style, termed *William and Mary,* was prevalent from 1689 to 1702; together with Queen Anne, these styles are sometimes collectively referred to as the Age of Walnut because of the widespread use of this species of wood. Although attributions of style are not always clear-cut, generalizations can be made from identifying features.

Materials and Decorative Techniques, 1660-1702

Transformation was reflected in decorative processes and in the introduction of new furniture forms that were a response to new social demands. Among the new types were daybeds, chests of drawers, and writing pieces with fall fronts.

For these pieces walnut was used extensively; to increase the supply it was necessary to import the wood from France and Virginia. Both solid and veneer forms were common. Oak continued in popularity from the earlier part of the 17th century but was used mainly when furniture forms were traditional. These and other woods were employed for the prominent decorative processes that characterized the late 17th and early 18th centuries.

Curved and carved forms, with the consequent play of light and shadow, were the delight of Baroque designers and craftsmen (Figure 10-12). Embellishment was in the pervasive use of C- and S-scrolls and in the use of Gibbons-inspired ornate renditions such as realistically carved foliage, fruits, vegetables, flowers, amorini, fish, and game. These were

FIGURE 10-12 Evolution of the
Cane Chair, 1660-1702. Forms:
simple to ornate; bands of carving;
lower back to taller and narrower;
crest of back between uprights to
arched crest covering the uprights.

used both structurally and ornamentally; elaborate carvings enriched backs, scrolled legs, and upright stretchers for chairs and stands for case pieces. Carving was at first on a solid ground but later in the Carolean period pierced work became typical.

Turning was an equally important decorative process. A variety of configurations were employed but with the introduction of the Carolean period the dominant form was spiral turning. Narrow and deep hollows were characteristic of English spiral turning, but in Holland the spirals were thick, with closely spaced twists. In the William and Mary style greater variety of turning is evident.

English craftsmen attained lavish effects through veneering; among the most popular styles were quartering, cross banding, burl, marquetry, and parquetry. In the veneer process thin layers of wood, or wood with other materials, were glued to a carcass of less expensive wood. Capitalizing on the figure of wood, complex patterns were formed by the way in which the wood veneer was laid on the carcass. A method known as *quartering* used four successive slices of wood to form a decorative pattern (Figure 10-13). Crossbanding, used on case pieces, consisted of a border often employed on drawer fronts; the grain direction

FIGURE 10-13 Quartering.
Successive layers of veneer arranged
to form unusual patterns. Drawer
front.

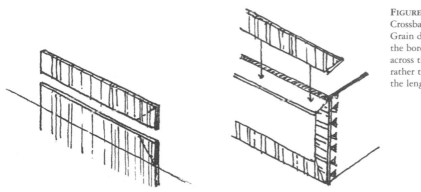

FIGURE 10-14
Crossbanding. Grain direction of the border runs across the width rather than along the length.

of this border was perpendicular to the surface it surrounded (Figure 10-14). As the century progressed banding strips became narrower. A mottled appearance was attained by laying on the carcass slices of burl veneer obtained from a growth on the trunk or root of a tree. The richest and most intricate surface embellishments were attained through marquetry and parquetry.

Marquetry designs are representational; that is, the design source is recognizable—flowers, birds, and foliage. The motifs were executed in woods of different colors; the range of colors available was extended by staining or by scorching wood with hot sand. Floral and larger-scale designs were typical of the Carolean period (Figure 10-15). More typical of the William and Mary style was the use of much finer-scale designs such as seaweed marquetry; unlike floral marquetry, only two different woods were employed (Figure 10-16). The delicate spiky and linear design of seaweed marquetry was introduced around 1690 and required exceptional skill to execute.

FIGURE 10-15 Marquetry. Pine carcass. Floral marquetry of walnut, ebony, and other woods. By Courtesy of the Board of Trustees of the Victoria and Albert Museum, London.

Pieces of a material laid in a geometric pattern on a carcass is termed *parquetry.* Although this technique could assume many forms, one type which became popular was *oysterwork.* Utilizing small branches of trees, a series of thin transverse slices were cut; laid on the carcass, these oval or circular configurations revealed the annual rings (Figure 10-17). Bands of oystering were used in conjunction with marquetry, or oyster pieces were used in an overall design.

The penchant for brilliance and extravagance was satisfied in part by the use of *japanning,* which became popular during the reign of Charles II. This technique was used by English craftsmen to imitate Oriental lacquer (see Figure C-16). The taste for oriental

curiosities was given impetus through the imports of the East India Company. Imported lacquer panels were inserted into pieces of furniture of English manufacture or they were made into entire pieces of furniture. This led to the development of japanning. On black or colored grounds, often red, chinoiserie designs were applied. In 1688 *A Treatise of Japanning and Varnishing* by John Stalker and George Parker was published; it gave instructions on the processes and included engraved designs. This technique was practiced by both amateurs and skilled japanners.

Typical Pieces and Stylistic Features: Carolean, 1660-1689

Seat Furniture

Chairs continued to be seats of honor in the period of Charles II; persons of lesser rank sat on stools. Even in the 18th century, during the reign of George II, on the occasion of the marriage of Frederick (his son), the English princesses, in protest of this practice, refused to sit on stools while their brother and his bride sat in chairs at the dining table. Until their point was made they remained in an antechamber.

FIGURE 10-18 Carolean Chairs. Left: Charles II Arm Chair, 1680-1685. Walnut, carved, spiral turning. All rights reserved, The Metropolitan Museum of Art, Kennedy Fund, 1918 (18.110.39). Center: Walnut, carved, turned. By Courtesy of the Board of Trustees of the Victoria and Albert Museum. Right: Walnut, carved. By Courtesy of the Board of Trustees of the Victoria and Albert Museum, London.

Charles II and his courtiers were responsible for the introduction into England of the Continental type of chair with caning for seats and backs. Early in the period chair backs were lower, with the center between the posts either filled with caning or with a series of spirally turned uprights. Blocked sections alternated with spiral turnings where there were intersecting structural members. Spiral turning was characteristic of legs, arm supports, and uprights of the back. Stretchers were placed at two levels: H-shape, lower; the front and back, higher (Figure 10-18). In the evolution of the chair in the late 17th century the back became taller using the aforementioned features (see Figure 10-12).

A fully developed Carolean chair typically had a tall, rectangular back with posts that were continuations of the legs. Uprights were surmounted by carved finials. Connecting the uprights of the back were two deep bands of pierced carving, one at the crest and one placed several inches above the seat rail; the band of carving at the crest was typically placed between the uprights. Separated from the posts, the center of the back was caned. On either side of the caned area were wide bands of pierced carving. Seats of caning were squarish in shape, with the wood frame carved in a low-relief pattern. The armrests of rounded section were gracefully shaped with a hollow downward curve; carved scrolled ends extended beyond the arm support and curved outward. Originating above the legs, the arm support was often a double-C, S-shape, or a turned continuation of the leg. Below the seat level, the front legs were often of the molded double-C type or characterized by blocked sections separated by spiral turning. The back legs were often spirally turned between blocked sections and most often differed from the front legs. The lower H-shaped stretcher and the higher back stretcher were turned in various configurations, often spiral or baluster. The front stretcher was a flat, carved member placed on end; the carved pattern of this upright stretcher was often the same as the cresting and the lower rail of the back.

Besides the chair, other seating or reclining pieces were created. The upholstered wing chair was introduced during the reign of Charles II (see Figure C-15). In some contemporary documents these were termed *sleeping chayres,* since ratchets allowed the occupant to recline. These chairs were richly upholstered in velvets or needlework. Below the seat, legs and stretchers were in the regular fashion. Prevailing characteristics were also used for such pieces as the stool and daybed.

The daybed was a new form that became very popular during the Restoration period; the back was lower than the chair but its features evolved in a similar manner. The popularity of this form reflected the more relaxed social atmosphere of the day.

Stools corresponded to the stylistic development of the chair; the shape of the seat varied: square or rectangular and, in rare instances, round. They were often part of a set of seating furniture or were sometimes ordered to harmonize with a state bed. Children or persons of lower social standing were frequently relegated to stools.

The settee, or couch, began to appear at the Restoration, one form of which combined two chair backs with a long seat. The settee usually had six legs; its other structural and decorative features followed those typical of the period. Like stools, these were usually part of a set of furniture.

Tables

Smaller round or oval gateleg tables eventually replaced the long draw table. These tables usually had two drop leaves supported with two gatelegs, occasionally with four. Of oak or walnut, a variety of turnings were employed for legs and stretchers: spiral, vase, and sometimes a combination of these. Meals were served at several tables rather than at one long table, which had been customary earlier in the century. Since the center of the room was usually kept free of furniture, there was an obvious advantage in keeping these tables against the wall until they were moved into position for dining.

Tables for other purposes were constructed. Some were designed to stand in the center of the room and consequently were finished on all sides, while other tables, intended to stand against the wall, were ornamented on three sides. Tables had stretchers connecting spirally turned legs. Decorative techniques followed the fashions of the Restoration period; this included marquetry and parquetry or combinations of these. Functionally, these tables were used for writing, cards, or tea service.

Storage Pieces

This group of pieces included the chest of drawers, the chest on stand, the dressing table (drawers for storage), and the small desk on a stand. The finer examples of these pieces were veneered, some featuring large-scale floral marquetry and some parquetry with oyster veneer (see Figure 10-17). Drawer fronts of these case pieces could have bands surrounding them in crossbanding or a herringbone pattern. Typically, a half-round molding applied to the carcass surrounded the drawer. Introduced late in the Charles II reign, the chest on stand consisted of a chest of drawers placed on a stand; five spirally turned legs were joined by a perimeter stretcher, shaped on three sides but a straight one on the back. Bun feet were placed immediately below the stretcher.

Typical Pieces and Stylistic Features: William and Mary, 1689-1702

Seat Furniture

Chairs of the William and Mary style were generally lighter in form than those in the Restoration style. Proportionately, backs were narrower and taller, with uprights that were often baluster turned. While the elaborate pierced and arched crest often rested on the uprights instead of being contained between them, as in the Carolean style, the arched form was sometimes placed between the uprights (Figure 10-19). A carved rail was placed some inches above the seat rail. The center of the back was treated in a variety of ways, among which were caning, which filled the space and joined the uprights; panels, separated from the turned uprights, consisting of bands of carving in the center of which was fine mesh caning; and a filling of highly complex carving (see Figures 10-19, 10-20, and 10-21). Seats tended to be smaller than their Carolean counterparts. Armrests extended beyond the arm supports in volutes with a pronounced outward turn, termed *ram's horn* (see Figure 10-19). Leg shapes for chairs and other furniture forms included an adaptation of the Louis XIV pedestal leg (pillar), trumpet, scroll, and inverted cup (Figure 10-22). The variation of the pedestal leg began just under the seat rail

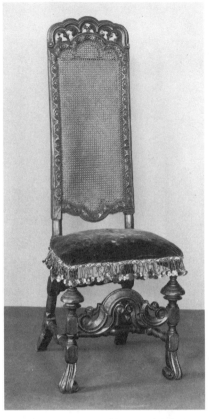

FIGURE 10-19   William and Mary Chair. Walnut. Arched crest, columnar turned posts frame back, ram's horn arms. Dimensions: 54 1/2" x 28 1/2" x 22 1/2". By Courtesy of the Board of Trustees of the Victoria and Albert Museum, London.

FIGURE 10-20   William and Mary Chair, c. 1690. Walnut, carved, use of fringe, inverted cup leg terminates in Spanish foot. By Courtesy of the Board of Trustees of the Victoria and Albert Museum, London.

FIGURE 10-21   William and Mary Chair, c. 1690-1695. Painted beech, carved. By Courtesy of the Board of Trustees of the Victoria and Albert Museum, London.

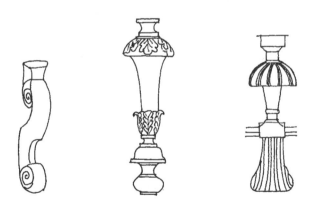

FIGURE 10-22   William and Mary Variation in Leg Type. A S-scroll, B inverted cup with bun foot, C inverted cup with Spanish foot.

with an incut neck; below an enlarged cap the leg, square or octagonal in shape, tapered to a blocked section at stretcher level; below this the foot was molded into square or octagonal forms. Alternately, the most frequently used feet were Spanish and bun. Early, the upright stretcher continued to be used, but it was often set back and when this was the case, the H-shaped stretcher continued to be employed. When the upright stretcher was eliminated an X-shaped stretcher (also termed *saltire*) was used and a finial was placed at the center. Side chairs had similar characteristics.

Upholstered chairs were stylistically similar to cane chairs. Both seats and backs were covered with luxurious fabrics such as damask, velvet, and needlework. Equally important

in giving a sumptuous impression was the use of fringe. Its purpose was twofold: (1) to cover the juncture of upholstery to the frame, and (2) to serve as adornment. Opulent fringes were often made of silk, gold, or silver, but worsted was sometimes utilized.

In form and ornament stools and settees were similar to the chair. Upholstered settees had the overall arched contour of two chair backs placed side by side. The tall back was fashioned with or without wings and the closed arms had outward-scrolling C-shapes. Typically, the six legs were joined with side-by-side saltire stretchers, each of which had a decorative finial at the center.

Tables

Tables were among the most varied of forms of the late 17th century. Some were highly ornamental while others were strictly functional. Legs, stretchers, feet, and ornamental detail followed the prevailing fashion. At the Metropolitan Museum of Art is a lowboy in the William and Mary style that is supported on S-scroll legs terminating in bun feet. A flat stretcher joins the legs. Seaweed marquetry in reserve panels ornaments the table tops, apron, and stretcher. The flattened S-scroll leg lent itself to decorative veneer treatment (Figure 10-23). A richly carved X-shaped stretcher rises in the center; on its apex is a decorative finial. Carved pendants originate from the frieze.

Tea tables figured prominently in meeting the growing demand for this drink.

Storage Pieces

A number of decorative techniques for ornamenting the surfaces of case pieces typified William and Mary furniture. The evolutionary changes in marquetry design are evident by comparing a Carolean example with pieces from around 1690 and later. Seaweed marquetry was highly characteristic, having been used on both curved and flat surfaces; it was used in all over designs as well as set within reserve panels. A premier distinction

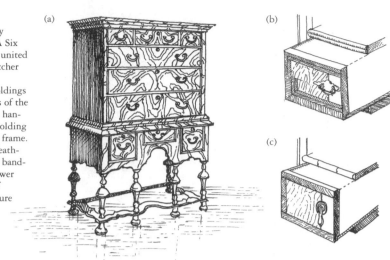

FIGURE 10-24 William and Mary Chest on Stand. A Six inverted cup legs united by perimeter stretcher (echoes the apron shape), strong moldings separate two parts of the piece. B Teardrop handle, half-round molding applied to carcass frame. C Herringbone (feathered) and/or cross banding frame the drawer front. Courtesy of Country Life Picture Library.

FIGURE 10-25   William and Mary Dressing Table, c. 1690. Oak, inverted cup legs with bun feet, saltire stretcher, teardrop drawer pulls.

of case pieces was the remarkable way in which figured walnut veneers were used. Crossbanding continued to be employed; another pattern, herringbone, was created when the band consisted of two pieces laid side by side with the grain of each running diagonally (Figure 10-24). While carving was not as prominent during the reign of William and Mary as it was in the previous two reigns, turnings of great variety were employed.

A wide assortment of storage pieces was designed in the last decade of the 17th century. This included the dressing table, the chest on stand, the chest of drawers, writing furniture, and the cabinet. Regardless of the functional use of the upper section, stands that were the bases for these had similar stylistic characteristics.

Structural features of the base of the chest on stand (or the base itself, standing alone, which was the lowboy) included four to six turned or double-C legs connected with a straight or shaped perimeter stretcher and bun feet (see Figure 10-24). For both the dressing table and the chest on stand, the configuration for the drawers was to have a shallow one in the center flanked on each side by deep drawers; a half-round molding was placed on the carcass surrounding the drawers (Figure 10-25). Shaped aprons were often echoed by the contour of the stretcher. Usually, strong moldings separated the base from the upper section of the highboy. Drawer pulls were distinctively shaped drop handles: teardrops or axedrops of iron or brass, often mounted on round or decorative rosettes.

The dressing table had characteristics similar to the chest on stand. The Metropolitan Museum of Art example has four legs instead of the six that were often used on the base of the chest on stand, the two middle legs are replaced by two pendant drops. A saltire stretcher connects the legs (see Figure 10-25).

Beds

The tester bed was the focal point in important bedchambers; therefore, the design and decoration of this kind of bed was of paramount significance (Figure 10-26). Attention was drawn to the bed for two primary reasons. First, its excessive height made it an imposing piece; some were 14 feet tall. Second, lavish attention was focused on the

FIGURE 10-26 William and Mary Bed, c. 1695. Textiles most significant part in design of beds. By Courtesy of the Board of Trustees of the Victoria and Albert Museum, London.

textiles with which it was treated. In fact, the importance attached to the drapery is evidenced by the proportionate expenditures for the various parts of the bed. One example based on the total cost of the bed reveals that 88% was for upholstery, 9% for feather finials, and 3% for the wood frame. Patterned velvets, silk damask, chintz, and brocade were the materials utilized.

Textiles were used for the cornice, tester, valance, and drapery. Curtains were hung from rods using rings on all four sides. Placed in front of the hanging at the head of the bed was a highly ornate headboard, often of raised embroidery. At times a carved and pierced cornice was covered with the same textiles as the bed hangings. The most prized finial treatments were those utilizing ostrich feathers.

ORNAMENT

Carving, turning, and stucco were major techniques employed to achieve the often elaborate decorative detail of the late 17th century. Grinling Gibbons was a master at wood carving and realistically sculpted ornamental detail; he had many imitators. He and other craftsmen embellished such surfaces as panels, moldings, architraves, and mantels. Characteristically, carving and stucco ornament were in high relief and compositions were deeply undercut.

Regardless of the medium used to accomplish decoration for furniture or interior architectural features, motifs were often arranged in festoon, swag, pendant, or frame configurations. The repertoire of motifs often included some combination of the following: flowers, fruit, foliage, acanthus leaves, game birds, fish, figures (amorini, cherubs' heads, and masks), shells, arabesques, and scrolls (S, C, and Flemish).

Chapter 11

French Rococo

1700-1760

HISTORICAL SETTING

Before the end of the 17th century the formality and flamboyance that had characterized the major portion of Louis XIV's reign began to change. In the 18th century a new social attitude began to assert itself; the direction was toward relaxation and pleasure, and this was followed by subsequent changes in the arts. The modifications gradually were reflected in smaller and more intimate apartments, in a general softening of ornamental style, in the design of furniture more conducive to conversation, and in greater attention to comfort. The Rococo was almost solely a style for the court, aristocracy, and the nouveaux riches. Having attained a new financial position, the bourgeoise began to emulate the newly established manner of life. Later they assumed leadership in matters of taste.

As these alterations began to surface in the early 18th century changes that reflect them continued to be revealed in the progressive development of the Rococo. Styles of the 18th century using Rococo ornament do not coincide with the dates of the reigns of the monarchs. When Louis XIV died in 1715 his great-grandson was only five years of age. Philippe d'Orléans acted as regent for the period from 1715 until his death in 1723, and then Cardinal Fleury directed governmental policies until 1726. Louis XV ruled until his death in 1774. From 1700 to 1775 three stylistic periods can be identified: Régence (1700-1730); Louis XV (1730-1765); and Transitional Louis XV-XVI (1765-1775). The latter was followed by the classical style of Louis XVI (1775-1790).

Government, with the regency of Duc d'Orléans, was established in Paris rather than at Versailles. However, the court returned to Versailles in 1722. The Regent was an ardent supporter of decorative arts and architecture. With this interest it is not surprising that many advances in the arts emanated from his residence, the Palais Royal. Some of the major contributors to the development of the Régence and the Louis XV styles first received their support from the Regent; these included the painter Jean-Antoine Watteau (1684-1721), the architect and decorator Giles-Marie Oppenord (1672-1742), and the wood-carver Jean-Bernard Toro (1672-1731).

During the years of Louis XIV society had been subjected to a centralized government that had sought to control their thoughts as well as the arts, even to the smallest detail. Relieved of this domination, interest became centered on amusement and licentiousness. As was evident in literature and the arts, there was much intrigue with common people, country life, and foreign cultures. Rather than an exploration in depth about these subjects, it was the novelty that was important.

In ornamental style the changes were first noted around 1690 in the designs of Jean I. Bérain (1640-1711). Bérain's designs were instrumental in the initiation of a movement leading to the Rococo of the 18th century. The lighter style was illustrated in his grotesques and arabesques; in addition, he is credited with the introduction of *chinoiserie* (decorative motifs based on Oriental designs) and the fashion for *singeries* (the use of the monkey as ornament). Engravings by Bérain exemplify his use of combinations of arabesques, chinoiserie, and singeries.

Reaction to the formality, pomp, and ceremony of the 17th century meant that the reliance on classical antiquity was subordinated in the early 18th century until, with the full flowering of the Rococo during the reign of Louis XV, virtually no traces were to be found. A further ramification of this reaction was the smaller size of apartments, created either by the renovation of larger apartments into smaller suites or by constructing new residences. Such planning contributed to the felt need for intimacy of this new society. Furniture (stiff and formal in the Louis XIV period and designed to line the wall) reflected a desire for personal comfort and an interest in conversation; chairs, for example, became more lightly scaled, easily moved, and more suited to the smaller boudoirs.

A division of responsibility among furniture craftsmen existed in the 17th century. Guilds were important in establishing stringent requirements in order to attain the master level of competence. But the court reserved the right to hire craftsmen who were not members of guilds; this is not to imply, however, that furniture made for the court was inferior in quality. Statutes passed in 1730 and validated by Parliament in 1751 made it mandatory that the stamp of the master appear on furniture as verification of its having come from the hand of a specific craftsman. Therefore, an unparalleled level of perfection in craftsmanship prevailed for the Louis XV style.[1]

When constructing furniture, the major craftsmen were a *menuisier* (joiner) and an *ébéniste* (specialist in veneering). Although their specialities differed, these craftsmen, working in the same guild, functioned as independent groups. In the ornamentation of furniture further specialists were dictated by the nature of the techniques: carvers, painters and gilders, upholsterers, and lacquerers. In addition, for the ormolu mounts two craftsmen were required: a *fondeur-ciseleur* (who cast and chased the mounts) and a *ciseleur-doreur (who gilded the mounts)*. Beyond this there were the *marchand-merciers,* who were furniture dealers and who, in their contacts with clients, brought business to the craftsmen. There were implications for stylistic trends in the marchand-mercier's intermediary position between customer and craftsman.[2]

One piece of furniture was often the work of several craftsmen. The specialization of crafts is illustrated in an example of a Louis XV commode: (1) an extant drawing is revealed to have been the original source of the design; (2) the *ébéniste,* A. R. Gaudreau, refined the design and constructed the body; and (3) the *fondeur-ciseleur,* J. Caffiéri, cast the bronze mounts (see Figure C-17). The mounts bear the stamp of Caffiéri while the name of Gaudreau, who worked for the Crown, is not imprinted on the piece. Authentication for the role of the ébéniste is based on stylistic analysis as well as on documentary evidence of royal purchases.

A reaction to the extravagances of the Rococo began to assert itself around the mid-18th century. Prompting this were: (1) publications of engraved designs, (2) the examples set by Madame de Pompadour and Madame du Barry, and (3) the excavations from antiquity of two classical cities. First of all, there were publications of engraved designs, pattern books, and reproductions of ancient classical masterpieces. For example, Nicholas Cochin campaigned for the return to the taste of the previous century through his *Supplication aux orfèvres, ciseleurs, sculpteurs en bois pour les appartements* (1754), and the Comte de Caylus' *Recueil des Antiquités Egyptiennes, Etrusques, Greques et Gauloises* (1752) depicted illustrations of ancient models. Madame de Pompadour's brother was chosen to study classical remains in Italy from 1749 to 1751 under the auspices of Cochin and the architect Soufflot. In addition, the court began to show a preference for the new approach, as evidenced by the choices made by two mistresses of Louis XV, Madame de Pompadour and Madame du Barry. The former was immensely influential politically and an avid patron of the arts; the latter was not politically motivated but affected the direction of arts through her choices of furniture and decoration for the Pavillion de Louveciennes, constructed in 1771 in neoclassical style. The excavation of the ancient cities Herculaneum and Pompeii probably aroused the greatest enthusiasm in the trend toward an influence of antiquity; these discoveries prompted an intense interest in the private houses of the ancients, their furniture, murals, and lighting. Thus, in the transition period between the Rococo and the style of Louis XVI, ornament was affected first in the grafting of classical ornament onto basically Louis XV forms and then in the greater restraint of forms by the gradual straightening of curved lines that became typical of Louis XVI furniture.

SPATIAL RELATIONSHIPS

Spatial Features of the Floor Plan and Three-Dimensional Spatial Characteristics

While some changes in interior arrangements occurred during the periods of Régence and Louis XV, major differences in space planning were minimal. At the beginning of the 18th

---

1. Helena Hayward, ed., *World Furniture* (New York: McGraw-Hill, 1965), 110.
2. Ibid., 111-112.

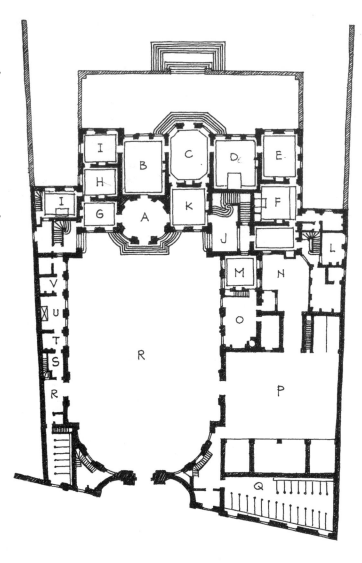

FIGURE 11-1 Plan, Hôtel de Matignon (1722-1724), Jean Courtonne. A Vestibule, B Salle du Dais, C Salone, D Chambre de parade, E Grand Cabinet, F Chambre à coucher, G Antichambre, H Chambre, I Cabinet, J Grand Escalier, K Salle à manger, L Garderobe, M Salle du commun, N Cour des Cuisines, O Cuisine, P Cour des Ecuries, Q Ecuries, R Grande Cour, S Vestibule, T Antichambre, U Chambre en Niche, V Cabinet.

century three theories affecting space planning began to be important considerations for the architect: *convenance, bienséance,* and *commodité. Convenance* dealt with the functional relationships of parts of the plan but it also meant that there should be agreement among such aspects as the position of rooms in the plan, the size of the space, the ornamentation, and general character. In addition, *convenance* dictated an arrangement that differentiated between public and private rooms. Through *bienséance* consideration was given to the form of the structure as it related to the intended function or purpose; for example, the position in society of the owner should be reflected in the type of residence. And, finally, *commodité* governed the fullest utilization of space.

Jean Courtonne (1671-1739), who was thought highly of by Blondel,[3] was the designer of Hôtel de Matignon, constructed between 1722 and 1724 (Figure 11-1). The internal plan is well articulated on the exterior, since the pavilion in one case extends into the garden while in the front the projection emphasizes the main entrance into the vestibule. Contrary to many plans, the typical axial arrangement from the grand court through the vestibule and salon to the garden is offset. The stables are located to interfere minimally

3. Jacques-François Blondel (1705-1774), a minor architect, was a highly influential writer and academic theorist. A French traditionalist who admired the work of the 17th-century architect Mansart, Blondel was instrumental in the promotion of neoclassicism. He was a professor at the Académie royale de l'architecture beginning in 1762. Among his publications was *L'Architecture français* (1752-1756).

with the main residence and kept at a distance from the *cuisine* (kitchen) as well as from the *salle à manger* (dining room). Deviating from the rectilinear spaces of many rooms, the vestibule here is crowned with a flat vault having a rise of only 16 inches. The vestibule and the salone each form the center of a sequence of rooms; the vestibule, in fact, forms the introduction to two sequences of rooms. On the left the route was through an antechamber to a chamber with the cabinet beyond and, on the right, through the *salle du dais* to the cabinet. The salon also served as a prelude to apartments. The enfilade in this latter sequence is typical in that the wall facing visitors as they progressed through the apartment was ornamented with a chimneypiece, a major focal point of most rooms. Positioned away from the vestibule, the main stairway was remarkable in terms of construction; of masonry, the stairs had no supporting wall on the stairwell side.

Architect Jean-Baptiste Alexandre Le Blond (1679-1719) in 1710 recommended the rooms that should comprise the apartment in a Parisian residence *(hôtel)*. According to him the group of rooms termed *appartement de parade,* used for entertainment and the reception of visitors, should include a vestibule, an anteroom, a salon, a bedroom *(chambre de parade),* a study, and, additionally, if desired, cabinets and dressing rooms. At this time a one-story salon was typical, whereas a two-story salon was usual in the previous period. On the other hand the *appartement de commodité* was less formal and consisted of rooms designed for comfort and more easily heated; these rooms were usually on the main or upper floors.

The Hôtel de Janvry (1732-1733) represents affinities with as well as advances in overall relationships and interior space planning in comparison with the early 18th century (Figure 11-2). Similarities in general relationships include the low entrance wall bounding the inner forecourt; the shaped ending of the court toward the street; the one-story service areas bordering the court; the living quarters across the court at the rear; and the two-story main residence. In general, the ground story was often higher; sometimes an entresol was incorporated between the ground and first story, provided for servants.

Consistent with the previous period there was continued reliance on the three theories of planning. From the vestibule two stairways replaced the grand stairs, one to the right and one to the left. The *appartement de parade* was still incorporated, including the enfilade as a unifying arrangement; beyond this was the need to provide private rooms separate from these public spaces. On the first story a considerable advance was the provision of a system of corridors to facilitate entrance to bedrooms and service areas. Other passages and concealed staircases were included to minimize traffic through other rooms. Light and venti-

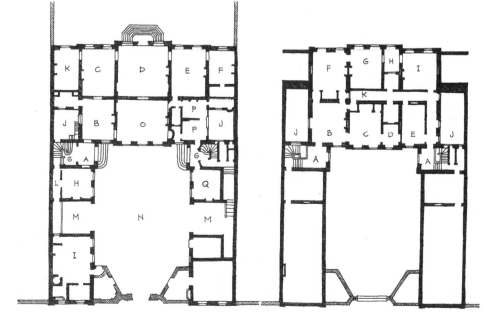

FIGURE 11-2 Hôtel de Janvry (1732-1733). Ground Floor Plan (left): A Vestibule, B Antichambre, C 2nd Antichambre, D Salone, E Chambre à coucher, F Cabinet, G Escalier, H Salle du Commun, I Cuisines, J Cour, K Cabinet du Bibliotheque, L Passage, M Remises, N Cour, O Salle à manger, P Garderobe, Q Chambre du jardinier. First Floor Plan (right): A Pallier, B Antichambre, C Chambre, D Cabinet, E Chambre pour domestiques, F Chambre, G Cabinet, H Arrière Cabinet, I Chambre, J Cour, K Corridor.

lation became a factor in planning; for example, light could be introduced through the use of inner courts, observed in the Hôtel de Janvry, and, in other instances, through the use of lanterns. Dining rooms had been indicated on plans in the previous period but they were more frequently identified on plans of this period. The corners of rooms were often rounded; this was related to the decorative intent of the spaces rather than as a response to functional need.

Amenities occasionally included such advances as rotating fireplaces that could warm one room and reverse to warm an adjacent space. Bathrooms sometimes were provided with their own heating units; they began to be placed near bedrooms. Lifts were provided on occasion to serve supper to private parties without the presence of servants.

INTERIOR ARCHITECTURE AND DECORATION

Régence, a transitional period, reflected changes over the period from 1700 to 1730. At the beginning there was a greater relationship to the Louis XIV style, but evolving characteristics showed greater consonance with the Louis XV style. This is not to imply, however, that an exact sequence of change occurred; stylistic features from either end of the spectrum might be found in the early, middle, or late period. Generally, the balance of features in the earlier period was often closer to the Louis XIV style, while in the latter part of the period they were nearer the Louis XV style. The stylistic progression toward the Louis XV style was from formality to informality and a more relaxed character; from symmetry to asymmetry; from Baroque relief, where the emphasis was on high light and shadow, to shallow relief; from rigid outlines to softer configurations; from geometric rigidity to freedom of delineation; from distinct structural lines to blurred compositions. Of these paired contrasts, the latter features, in each case, are characteristic of the Louis XV style.

Instrumental in the formulation of the Régence and the Louis XV styles were trends instigated by designers whose influences were revealed through engravings, commissions, and employment by royalty with subsequent adoption of their innovations. The design leaders discussed in the following were not always confined to their influence in one specific period; rather, their prestige in some instances spanned the periods of Régence and Louis XV. Their major contributions and the design features they promoted can be discerned in the discussion on characteristics of interior architecture and decoration.

Régence. The engravings of Jean Bérain (1640-1711) led the way to alterations in the use of the grotesque ornament and in chimneypiece design. While the grotesque ornament was not new, Bérain's contribution was that he gave greater delicacy to this decoration. He showed chimneypieces that were not only smaller in scale but represented the use of the *garniture de cheminée* (set of chimney ornaments), comprised of symmetrically disposed porcelain on each side of a central clock. Claude Audran III (1657-1734) worked with Bérain, so their design contributions overlap. Audran's engravings, along with those of Bérain, were the source for the dissemination of grotesque and arabesque ornament; both were an influence on the wide spread use of chinoiserie and singeries. Drawings from the hand of Audran show ceiling treatments embellished with arabesques of unusual delicacy. Louis XIV was pleased with his designs, which led to the Rococo. Audran was the first to use singerie at Marly. Pierre Le Pautre (1660-1744) created one of the first rooms to forecast the direction toward the Louis XV style in his design for the Antechambre de l'Oeil de Boeuf at Versailles, around 1707 (Figure 11-3). Features that anticipated the Rococo were: (1) large mirrors, used more frequently (and in the most important interiors) after the establishment of the royal manufactory in the late 17th century; (2) depressed arches for doors and windows; and (3) the use of gold-highlighted cross-hatching (diaperwork) for the coved transition to the ceiling. In this room the cove is very deep and children in sculptured relief frolic in front of the diaperwork. The frieze is divided by consoles into rectangular segments decorated with festoons, ribbon, etc. Pierre Le Pautre's book of engravings entitled *Cheminées à la royalle* was published around 1698.

Robert de Cotte (1656-1735) was one of the foremost architects of the Régence period and one of its originators. He was an assistant in the offices of Jules Hardouin-Mansart.

FIGURE 11-3 Antechambre de l'Oeil Boeuf (c 1707), Versailles, Pierre Le Pautre. Anticipated the direction toward the Louis XV style. Lauros-Giraudon, Paris.

Active in the early 18th century, he had an interest in moving from formality to informality. As one of the initiators of the Rococo style in architectural ornament he was responsible for a number of Parisian hôtels. Gilles-Marie Oppenord (1672-1742), architect and decorator, was instrumental in the flowering of the Régence and early Rococo styles; during the period of the regency he worked for Philippe, duc d'Orléans. Many of his decorative designs were engraved and published. Oppenord had worked in Rome in the late 17th century and was familiar with the work of Borromini; sculptural influence, therefore, was observed in his use of fluted pilasters, large overmantel mirrors, and such motifs as cartouches, trophies, and flying putti. Among his specialties was the creation of wrought-iron work used extensively for the banisters of staircases and balconies.

Louis XV. Jean Aubert spanned the period of the Régence and Louis XV styles and until his death in 1741 was among the most important designers in the Louis XV style. His use of ornament exceeded the bounds of panel frames and at times he extended decoration from the cornice onto the ceiling. Decorations were often highlighted with gold. Genre pittoresque (picturesque style) was important to him. A French carver, sculptor, and decorator, Nicolas Pineau (1684-

FIGURE 11-4 Panel Drawing, 1720-1725, Nicolas Pineau. Pineau provided leadership for more delicate, asymmetrical, vertical characteristics culminating in the Louis XV style. Musée des Arts Décoratifs, Paris. Union Centrale des Arts Décoratifs.

1754) was employed by the Czar of Russia, for whom he carved in Rococo detail the Cabinet of Peter the Great in the Grand Palais at Peterhof; the rococo motifs included cartouches and trophies (arms and armor commemorative of triumphant battles or military leaders). Representations of plants were often used by Pineau; tendrils coiled around moldings and mirrors were surrounded by palm trees or other natural vegetation. Asymmetry, delicacy, low relief, and verticality often characterized his work (Figure 11-4). From his return to France and beginning in 1732 he, with Juste Aurèle Meissonier (1695-1750), assumed leadership for the lighter and more delicate Rococo decoration. While the influence of Meissonier was more evident through his publication, Pineau's prestige came about through his commissions for the hôtels of influential families. Juste Aurèle Meissonier (1695-1750), French goldsmith and decorator, was instrumental in disseminating the Rococo style. Meissonier was a highly innovative designer whose influence was more important in spreading Rococo design than that of any other designer; through the publication of *Livre d'ornements* (book of ornamentation) he recommended patterns for ornamental detail, architecture, and various innovations. His fame was based primarily on his metalwork, with its asymmetrical arrangements, and his extravagant grottoes (cave-like representations that included such design elements as shells, waterfalls, and fountains). The greater three-dimensionality of his work was largely due to his training as a goldsmith. Gabriel-Germain Boffrand (1667-1754), an architect and engineer, spanned the period of the Régence and Louis XV styles. A highly talented designer, he was one of the most influential architects of the Regency. A major commission from 1736 to 1739 was for an oval salon in the Hôtel de Soubise, Paris. Illustrated in this interior is his preference for varied room shapes and complex spaces. The walls feature a series of arches over doors, windows, and mirrors; between these are smaller round-headed panels. Spandrel paintings above the panels are capped with a band of Rococo detail including cartouche shapes that move downward to connect to the larger arched shapes of the doors. Like spokes of a wheel, vertical bands of plasterwork radiate from the horizontal band to connect to the motif in the center of the ceiling.

Materials and Decorative Techniques

Materials often used in interiors of the Régence and Louis XV periods were terracotta, wood, marble (rare except in palaces), carved boiserie, and fresco or relief designs in plaster and gilt—if plaster, shallow relief was typical. The Martin brothers (Guillaume and Etienne-Simon) developed a varnish imitating Chinese lacquer called *vernis martin,* which was a rich green in color. How each of these was used is discussed in the following section.

Interior Architecture and Decorative Elements

Floors

Régence. Marble was used rarely, except in palaces; black and white marble was arranged in squares or lozenges. Limestone was recessed to receive marble tile or laid flush and scored to represent tile. Other materials employed included terra-cotta, in square or hexagonal shapes, and faience, which was tin enameled for small rooms with drains. Oak parquet and wood arranged in blocks was widely used. Carpet was used in a limited way.

Louis XV. Tile flooring widely used in this period included terra-cotta (the most common), limestone, marble (rare except in palaces), and faience (often imported from Holland). Primarily of oak, parquet configurations were commonly arranged in squares or otherwise compartmented. A floor comprised of oak squares, termed *parquet de Versailles,* of around 1735, is laid in the Varengeville room in the Metropolitan Museum of Art, New York. Although carpets were more common in the succeeding period, Savonnerie (a royal property) was an important manufacturer of carpets; the repertoire of designs reflected the Rococo style.

Walls

Régence. Carved boiserie was a major wall treatment in the period of the Régence. Initially, the outlines for the panels were strong and, in some instances, Baroque heaviness prevailed, as did some use of classical elements, which had characterized design in the late

FIGURE 11-5 Régence, Petit Luxembourg (1710), Gabriel-Germain Boffrand. Blurring of structural lines as rounding of corners of rooms, ornament climbs from wall to ceiling. Lauros-Giraudon, Paris

213

French Rococo

17th century. Two engraved examples of the early 18th century illustrate the trend from heaviness to lightness. The first is by Gilles-Marie Oppenord for the Galerie d'Enée in the Palais Royal, the residence of the Duc d'Orléans. The wall is architectural in concept; pedestals in the dado act as visual support for the Corinthian pilasters on the wall above. The whole is crowned with an entablature. The centers of the panels between the pilasters are treated with obelisks carved in the Baroque manner, in which high light and shadow are important design elements. The carved details of the overmantel that emanates from the entablature is also highly baroque but which extend onto the moldings. The carving is composed of winged figures and drapery which cascades and partially frames the mirror. Dividing the frieze into segments by paired consoles, the interstices are decorated by carvings that extend beyond the moldings of the entablature. The second example, lighter and less architectural, is a design by de Cotte and François-Antoine Vassé for the Galerie Dorée in the Hôtel de Toulouse. Pilasters were used here as fictive supports and treated as panels, in the center of which are carved arabesques; the frame, which suggests a panel on the face of the pilaster, is shaped above and below. Anticipating the Louis XV Rococo are the arches and flattened arches, the concave corner bends, cross-hatching, the ornament climbing over moldings, the trend toward the elimination of clear lines, the shallow carving, and the sense of lightheartedness. The contributions of Germain Boffrand in his design for the Petit Luxembourg illustrate further characteristics that led to and were to become typical of Louis XV style (Figure 11-5). Without architectural framework the salon is surrounded by continuous scalloping over doors, windows, and panels. Separation of structural features within a room was blurred; for example, the corners of rooms were rounded and carved stucco ornament above the cornice climbed from the wall to the ceiling. Boffrand's interiors tended to symmetry and control, but he was incredibly original in his approach.

Generally, panels for the wall were divided by a strong dado molding placed low on the wall. Panels above the dado often had some of the following attributes: (1) severely defined but later more active contours and freely used palmettes and C-scrolls; (2) emphasis on verticality, since most elements of the wall extended to the cornice, except for doors; (3) ornamental zones separating from the top and bottom edges; and (4) use of figured medallions in the center of the panel. Mirrors assumed great importance in the decoration of interiors to the extent that entire rooms sometimes were lined with them. Another use was to place mirrors over a console table designed to coincide with the width of the panel

FIGURE 11-6   Louis XV, Boiserie detail, Hôtel de Varengeville (c. 1735), Paris (now installed in the Metropolitan Museum of Art, New York), Nicolas Pineau.

FIGURE 11-7   Louis XV, Mirror Carving Detail, Hôtel de Varengeville (c. 1735), Paris (now installed in the Metropolitan Museum of Art, New York), designed by Nicolas Pineau; commissioned by Duchesse de Villars. Oak, painted white and gilded.

above. The most usual finish for the wood paneling was paint, but especially in rural areas it was sometimes left in its natural state.

Louis XV. Pineau and Meissonier were two designers important in the trend that culminated in the lighthearted compositions of the Louis XV style; with their contemporaries they originated the stylistic trend termed *genre pittoresque.* Pineau, a decorator and carver, was much in demand by architects to execute interior detail. The carved woodwork from the Hôtel de Varengeville (originally in Paris) installed in the Metropolitan Museum of Art, New York, is an example of his work (see Figure C-18). The carved mirror frame and panel details reveal the similarity between his drawings and the extant carving at the Metropolitan (see Figure 11-4 and compare Figures 11-6 and 11-7). While not original to the room, the chimneypiece and flooring are of the same period. The drawing of wall paneling by Pineau illustrates its asymmetry, delicacy, low relief, and verticality.

Many of the characteristics noted in the following are observed in the boiserie of Pineau. Wood paneling (natural, painted, or painted and parcel gilt) was arranged with tall panels placed above a low dado. Varying from narrow to wide and with asymmetrical parts, the panels were not always balanced by the mirror images in contiguous panels, as had often been the case in the previous period. The moldings that bounded panels were often thin and in low relief. Some were highly complex, being comprised of a variety of elements including such motifs as C- and S-scrolls, leafage, shells, vines, ribbons, freehand curves, and so on. Although there might be an underlying rectilinearity defined by moldings, the distinct emphasis was on the Rococo molding details. These carved ornaments typically extended beyond the framework of the panel. If wood was not used, the centers of panels could be decorated with painted canvas, textiles, tapestries, wallpaper, or mirrors; these were held in place with wood moldings. Decorative painters such as François Boucher, Christophe Huet, and Jean-Honoré Fragonard were active in panel decoration, the subjects of which could be landscapes, chinoiserie including woodland scenes, and exotic birds, etc. The overdoor or overmantel panels (termed *trumeaux*), figured prominently in wall composition. The centers of these had decorative treatments such as grisaille paintings, fabrics, tapestries, and mirrors. *Grisaille painting* consisted of one tone in various tints and shades, which gave the impression of sculptural relief; this technique was more prominent in the Louis XVI period. While asymmetry was widespread, balance in the total composition was sometimes adhered to, this meant that elements such as doors required a false door to maintain symmetry. The cornice heading the wall was normally low in projection. Above this, Rococo detailing was often applied to the coved transition to the ceiling; in addition, it partially overlaid the cornice molding.

Windows and Doors

Régence. The heads of both doorways and windows were either round, oval, or depressed arches. These elements were set in deep reveals. Beginning in the period of the Régence and continuing in the Louis XV style were concave corner bends for door frames. The arched shape of the window was introduced by Oppenord. The Antechambre de l'Oeil de Boeuf at Versailles by Pierre Le Pautre incorporated depressed arches for doors and windows, and these were decorated with flower garlands and shells (see Figure 11-3).

Louis XV. Windows and doors were usually set in deep recesses. Square, arc-shaped, round, and flattened arches were shapes drawn upon for headings of windows and doors. Casement windows extended to the floor. When shutters were used, they normally folded into the deep reveals. Trumeaux over doors were ornamented as noted in the discussion of wall composition. Louis XV doors (often double) had four, six, or eight panels. When a curved asymmetrical panel was employed on one leaf it was duplicated on the other in order to attain symmetrical balance (Figure 11-8).

FIGURE 11-8 Louis XV Door. Asymmetrical parts arranged to form symmetrical balance. Drawing by Julie L. Rabun after a Louis XV Door in the Metropolitan Museum of Art.

Chimneypieces

Régence. The fireplace was reduced in size due to the trend toward smaller rooms, but it was still a focal point. It was usual now to incorporate a mantel shelf above which a mirror was mounted. Architectural ornament was given less attention, compared to the Louis XIV period. Used both for mantels and furniture, espagnolettes were incorporated as frames for mantelpieces. The overmantel combined features typical of both Louis XIV and Louis XV: the compass curve of Louis XIV with the delicate linear quality that was to be typical of the Louis XV period. An introduction of S-curves in the firebox surround softened the severity of the bolection molding that had characterized the Louis XIV period. White or colored marble, sometimes combined with ormolu mounts, was a typical material for the mantel; colors included red, black and white, violet, and a multicolored marble with streaks of gray, yellow, red, and violet.

Louis XV. Dimensions for chimneypieces were typically low and often wide (see Figure C-18). Above the mantel shelf mirrors were the most frequent decoration for the

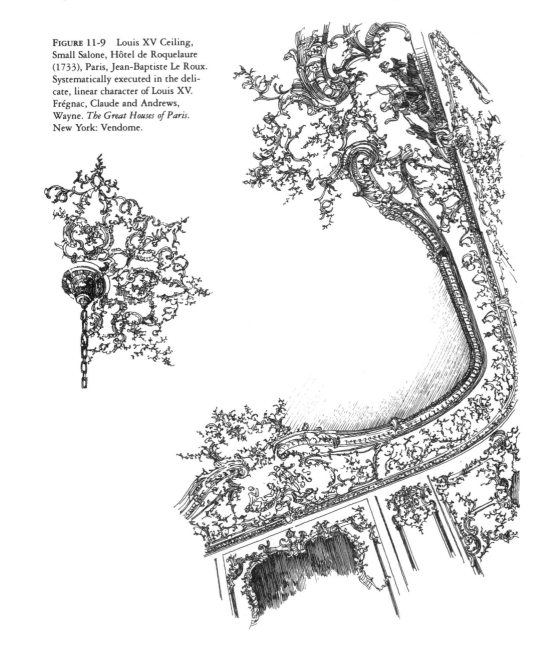

FIGURE 11-9 Louis XV Ceiling, Small Salone, Hôtel de Roquelaure (1733), Paris, Jean-Baptiste Le Roux. Systematically executed in the delicate, linear character of Louis XV. Frégnac, Claude and Andrews, Wayne. *The Great Houses of Paris.* New York: Vendome.

chimneybreast, usually flush with the adjacent wall surfaces; in other words, there tended to be no structural continued chimneypiece. Marble was carved with typical Rococo decorative detailing. Although marble was the common material for the mantel, wood was occasionally used. During summer months the firebox was concealed in some manner by screens such as painted panels, mirrors, etc.

Ceilings

Régence. Panel paintings sometimes replaced the frescoes of former years. However, ceilings were most often relatively flat and plain compared to the elaboration of the wall ornamentation; a center stucco ornament such as a rosette was sometimes used. The Antechambre de l'Oeil de Boeuf at Versailles had a coved ceiling of great depth with diaperwork (cross-hatching), in front of which are children in sculptural relief with highlights of gold. Divisions between walls and ceiling began to be blurred; for example, a cartouche might climb from moldings onto the ceiling. Mirrors were sometimes used on ceilings.

Louis XV. White plaster was common for ceilings. But, particularly as related to the typical coved transition from the wall to the ceiling, low relief ornamental detail was sometimes a significant part of the overall decorative scheme (Figure 11-9). Typical Rococo ornamental motifs were rendered in a delicate and linear manner. For a central rosette, techniques included fresco and relief designs in plaster and gilt; if plaster, shallow relief was typical. At times, blue sky was represented and birds, cherubs, and so on were placed among cloud formations.

Stairways

Rather elaborate wrought-iron banisters for both balconies and stairways became important decorative devices in both the Régence and Louis XV periods. Oppenord was widely known for his designs, which were characterized by imagination and innovation.

Possibly designed by Pineau, this balustrade detail was originally constructed for the staircase to Louis XV's Cabinet des Médailles in the Palais Mazarin (see Figure C-19). Materials are forged iron and bronze (chased and gilt). This rectangular panel alternates with smaller, vertical rectangular panels for the length of the balustrade. Centering the larger unit is the monogram of Louis XV (two intertwined Ls). The design is comprised of sunflowers, cornucopias, scrolls, fruit, and tokens. Each newel is a square fluted column surmounted by a vase of gilt bronze; incumbent griffons are placed before each column.

FURNITURE

The thrust of furniture design was responsiveness to new attitudes of a society where the emphasis was on comfort and pleasure. Furniture became easier to move as a concession to the attention given to the pleasure in conversation; chairs, for example, were more lightly scaled, graceful, and informal. Multifunctional pieces were created that could be adapted to the varied demands of the owners.

Materials and Construction Techniques

Over the periods of the Régence and Louis XV styles the most prevalent materials were wood, lacquer, tortoiseshell, and bronze. The menuisiers and ébénistes used a variety of tools and procedures to fashion them.

Wood was carved, lacquered, veneered, or decorated with marquetry. Beech was the most important wood for seat furniture; other significant woods used in furniture construction were lime and walnut. The ébénistes used less expensive wood for the carcasses of their pieces, since rarer woods were used for veneer and veneer techniques. Regional preferences in France meant that woods native to a particular area tended to figure prominently in the choices of primary and secondary structural features.

The repertoire of woods was expanded at the hands of the ébéniste since he was a specialist in veneer. Many woods were imported in order to attain the color and grain important in surface design. Some of these uncommon woods were purplewood, satinwood, and tulipwood, among many others. Often minute color nuances were consequential. One veneer technique used during the period from 1700 to 1765 involved covering the surface of a carcass with larger sheets of wood with thicknesses of two to three millimeters. These could be arranged in different configurations to capitalize on the direction of the grain. The difficulty faced by the ébéniste lay in the curved surfaces and complex forms on which the pieces of veneer were laid.

On the other hand, the veneer technique of marquetry involved the use of many small pieces of material selected for color; materials included wood (both native and exotic), brass, tortoiseshell, and mother-of-pearl. The designs were representational and complex, as noted in previous discussions about Boulle-work. Designs could be bouquets of flowers, scenes (some chinoiserie and singeries), fruit, birds, etc.

Whether surfaces were veneered or lacquered, bronze mounts were essential to protect the fragile corners; gilt bronze was also highly important as a decorative application to veneered surfaces (see Figure C-17). Bronze was used in other areas such as handles, escutcheons, centers of panels, friezes, the terminals of the legs, and pendants. The bronze mounts were treated by one of three means: (1) mercury gilding, (2) gold leaf gilding, and (3) varnish gilding. The first two processes were very expensive, while varnish gilding was an imitative procedure utilizing alcohol and colored dyes; this had the disadvantage of tarnishing. Mercury gilding (ormolu) was attained through the use of a mixture of gold and mercury; several applications of this amalgamation assured an exceptional gilt finish. Also expensive was the second process, where the bronze was dipped in a solution of mercury, after which gold leaf was applied and heated for a secure application.

While imported panels of oriental lacquer were incorporated in furniture of the 17th century, French artisans in the 18th century attempted to imitate qualities of the Chinese and Japanese lacquers, although they never attained the permanence or brilliance of the original. However, the range of colors that could be attained was large due to the application of coloring agents to the lacquer resin. Many coats of lacquer were applied to the base to a thickness of two or three millimeters. Against this background, one design technique, termed coromandel lacquer, was to render it in relief. The lacquer ground was cut away to the wood, the raised parts outlining the design while the cut-away portion was filled with lacquers of different colors. Shells, flowers, and birds were often represented in these pieces. Contrasted with this technique was one introduced by such craftsmen as the Martin brothers; these lent themselves to delicate painted designs based on artists such as Boucher.

Typical Pieces and Stylistic Features

Seat Furniture

Régence. The Régence style of chair was a transition from the primarily rectilinear forms of Louis XIV to the curvilinear contours of Louis XV. The lighter scale of furniture meant that chairs were easier to move out from the wall to meet new demands for conversation. Compared to Louis XIV, chairs revealed greater delicacy and livelier contours, more delicate and shallow ornament, and less attention to rigid symmetry. However, Régence tended to symmetrical effects and legs were slightly curved. In contrast, Louis XV tended to asymmetry of decorative detail and legs had a more pronounced curve.

It should be noted that the characteristics identified in the following are not all embodied in each chair. Backs, generally lower than Louis XIV chairs, were either fully upholstered or surrounded by a carved and exposed wooden frame; the stiles were straight or curved and the cresting was often serpentine. Rails of the lower back were usually separated from the seat rail. Either squarish seats or those with curved outlines were employed.

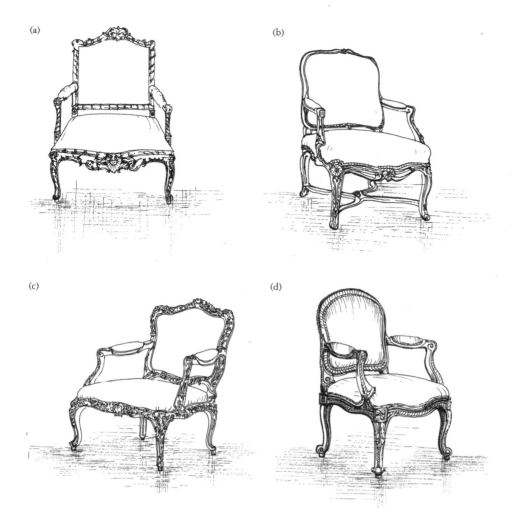

(a)

(b)

(c)

(d)

FIGURE 11-10 Evolution of Fauteuil from Régence through Transitional Louis XV-XVI. A. Régence, B. Régence, C. Louis XV, D. Transitional Louis XV-XVI. By Courtesy of the Board of Trustees of the Victoria and Albert Museum, London. Adapted with permission of Sterling Publishing Co. Inc., NY, NY from *Classical European Furniture Design* by Jose Claret Rubira, published by Gramercy Publishing Company, English translation © 1989 by Sterling Publishing Co., Inc., originally published in Spain as *Meubles de Estilo Frances*, ©1974 by Editorial Gustave Gili, S.A.

New to this period was a method that allowed the upholstery to be changed seasonally. Arm elements began to curve. The arm supports were set back on the side seat rail by approximately one quarter of its length and at times a *manchette* (arm pad) was added to the armrest. The cabriole leg was introduced in late Louis XIV chairs but the curve was slight; this feature was generally retained in the Régence style. On the other hand, Louis XV cabriole legs were more pronounced in curve and typically the curve from the leg into the seat rail was uninterrupted. The seat rail itself was often centered with a shell combined with an acanthus leaf. The terminal ending for legs was either a scroll set on a cylindrical base or a *pied de biche* (doe's hoof). A curved saltire stretcher was often used to connect the cabriole legs, but late in the period the stretcher was often eliminated. Four armchairs illustrate, by comparison, the changes in design beginning with Régence through Transitional Louis XV-XVI (Figure 11-10).

Louis XV. Comfort was the keynote to the design of Louis XV chairs, of which there were several types. Sinuosity of form was thoroughly consistent with the emphasis given to informality, the chair giving no impression of joints. Carved wood was exposed all around the frame; emphasis was given to the asymmetrically carved detail on the cresting of the back, on the center of the seat rail, and on the knee of the cabriole leg. The scroll ending to the cabriole leg rested on a shoe or cylindrical base; the prominent curve of the cabriole flowed smoothly into the seat rail. Stretchers usually did not unite the legs. Seats were upholstered or caned. Curved arm supports were set back on the side seat rail, and the arm-rests of armchairs usually had upholstered manchettes. The finishes included lacquer and parcel-gilt, paint, gilding, and waxed natural wood. Extant painted pieces cannot accu-

FIGURE 11-11   Louis XV Bergère. Carved walnut. Closed armchair, usually a separate cushion. Musée des Arts Décoratifs, Paris Union Centrale des Arts Décoratifs.

rately reflect the variety and brilliance of the colors employed in Louis XV furniture. Two colors were used on one piece—for example, green and white, blue and white, yellow and silver. These colors coordinated with paneling painted in lilac, pale blue, yellow, etc.

Two types of chairs, the fauteuil and the bergère, were common, and each had some characteristics noted in the discussion above. However, the fauteuil was an open armchair. The backs were either cartouche-shaped or *cabriolet,* which describes a back when it is concave. These backs were rarely attached to the seat. The bergère differed from the fauteuil in that the arms were enclosed and the seat cushion was separate (Figure 11-11). The importance attached to the bergère is suggested by a poem by the Marquis de Boufflers entitled "Bergère."

In rich apartments there are
as many as twenty different pieces.
But there is only one which is essential for me.
My little attic is adorned with a simple bergère
rather than a gilded sofa.

In the daytime and at night, without embarrassment,
and full of joy I taste a salutary repose.
I stretch myself in delight!
Oh! what pleasure I feel when I am deep in my
bergère.

I leave it only with regret.
I go to it often.
I should like to rest there my entire life.
I know more than one person in love with it.
But fortunately I alone use my bergère.

The marquise, the seat of which was very wide and deep, is said by some authorities to have been a response to the extreme width of women's dress. Other seating types were important in the Louis XV style. Among these were multiple seating units including the *canapé* (a settee with open or closed arms) and the *sultane* (with two rolled arms), which exemplifies the interest in exotic regions of the world. The concern for comfort and informality was reflected in the *duchesse-brisée* (a two-piece lounging unit for one person) composed of a chair to which a separate foot rest was fitted to the contour of the seat rail of the chair. In addition, there were many stools and benches.

Transitional Louis XV-XVI. This period first showed alterations in the carved detail applied to the organic form of the Louis XV armchair. Such motifs as imbricated scale-work, acanthus leaves, and guilloches (based on antiquity) were controlled elements, compared to the freedom and delicacy of Rococo ornament. At the head of the cabriole leg, at seat rail level, was sometimes a square framed block in the center of which was a carved rosette. Next, structural parts were modified such as cabriole legs, which showed less pronounced curve. Whereas the Louis XV chair was organic in that one part flowed into another, in the transition period sharp distinctions were made between parts of the seat and the leg, for example.

Tables

Régence. In general, stylistic changes of tables showed the same sequential development as chairs; at the beginning some features related to the previous style while new features were introduced relating to the succeeding style. *Console tables* tended to retain some of the heaviness of the Louis XIV style for a time. They were designed to coordinate with the wall panel under which they were placed; the panel was often fitted with a mirror. Mounted on two legs curved toward the wall, the legs themselves were connected with a stretcher in the center of which was a carved ornament in high relief. The whole was often gilded and elaborately carved; marble tops were often used.

Particularly important was the *bureau plat* (or writing table), which often had a surface of tooled leather (Figure 11-12). Ormolu mounts were used to edge such parts as the top, legs, and drawers as well as escutcheons and drawer pulls. Without a stretcher, legs were cabriole, often ending with a *sabot* (a metal protective covering for the feet). The shaped frieze (or apron) of these tables usually contained three drawers. *Espagnolettes* (bronze busts of female figures) were used at the crest of the cabriole leg. Other locations for these figures were on handles, escutcheons, etc.

FIGURE 11-12 Cressent, Charles. *Writing Table (bureau plat),* Widener Collection, © 1996 Board of Trustees, National Gallery of Art, Washington, c. 1735-1745.

FIGURE 11-13   Louis XV, Commode Table. Bernard II van Risen Burgh (before 1730). Oak veneered with Japanese black and gold lacquer; gilt bronze mounts.

Louis XV. Many kinds of tables were introduced at this time; some were multifunctional while others had specific purposes. Mechanical means were sometimes introduced in order to convert a table to more than one function. For example, a writing table could serve as a toilet table by incorporating a mirror on the reverse side of the writing board. Examples of specific-function pieces included gaming tables, work tables, serving tables, and coffee tables. The decorative processes and stylistic features noted previously were typically used for tables as well.

A console table with one drawer served as a dual-function piece (part table and part commode). This piece in the Wrightsman Collection in the Metropolitan Museum of Art, New York, was designed to fit under a wall panel of the same width. The table is japanned and overlaid with asymmetrical ormolu mounts (Figure 11-13).

Storage Pieces

Régence. Although curved outlines were introduced early in the century, storage pieces gave the impression of heaviness. Especially popular in the 18th century, the

FIGURE 11-14   Louis XV Commode A. R. Gaudreau. Drawer front concealed the structural traverse (rail) between the drawers. Double bowed and bombé front. Cupboard at each end. Legs triangular in section Reproduced by permission of the Trustees of the Wallace Collection, London.

Régence commode (chest of drawers) often had three drawers and was mounted on very short legs. Charles Cressent, ébéniste to the Regent, is credited with the form that anticipated the Louis XV commode (see Figure C-20). It had two drawers (a fixed and exposed rail between them), a shaped apron, and tall, slender legs. The shaping of the body was complex; horizontally it was serpentine in outline while vertically the arrangement had a concave top level, convex middle level, and concave lower section. This kind of shaping is termed *bombé*. The type continued in popularity to the period of Louis XVI, when the straight line became prominent. Ormolu mounts were applied to edges, drawer fronts, feet, and so on; ornamental detail was frequently symmetrical.

Techniques were refined during the period of the Régence, especially in terms of bronze mounts, veneer, and marquetry. Forms changed in that designers introduced structural curves; the cabriole leg was prevalent and the apron was often characterized by a downward curve.

Louis XV. Graceful and lightly scaled, the commode was a very fashionable piece of furniture. The preferred form was one in which two drawers were mounted on tall cabriole legs, thought to have been introduced by Cressent during the Régence period; the bombé form, characterized by a complex curved shape, continued to be employed. A curved downward thrust of the center of the apron was characteristic. In some pieces the rail between the drawers continued to be visible, but this traverse began to be concealed by a construction feature that allowed the drawer front to hide it (Figure 11-14). Marble was widely used for the tops. Polychrome lacquer in the Oriental manner was popular; the ground was often dark but at the instigation of the marchands-merciers a white or colored ground was used as a base for typical Rococo painted decoration. Marquetry and bronze applications continued to be favored techniques for ornamenting surfaces. Sèvres porcelain plaques began to be inserted for decorative purposes but they were more popular as ornamental features in Louis XVI furniture. Flowers and leafage were widely used motifs.

Transitional Louis XV-XVI. Pieces usually retained the delicacy of the Louis XV style while introducing the straighter lines and classical detail of the Louis XVI style

FIGURE 11-15 Transitional Louis XV-XVI Commode. Combination of Louis XV and Neoclassical elements. By Courtesy of the Board of Trustees of the Victoria and Albert Museum, London.

FIGURE 11-16   Louis XV, Lit à Turque. Bed parallel with wall, canopy originates from wall, ends of equal height, cushion at each end when not in use. French and European Publications, 610 Fifth Ave., N.Y., N.Y. 10020.

(Figure 11-15). Lines tended to straighten; for example, fronts of commodes tended to have center breakfronts that were more severe than the swelled fronts of those designed in the Louis XV style. The curves of cabriole legs tended to be slight. A frieze might include classical motifs such as the guilloche, Greek key, and acanthus leaves. The frieze might also contain three drawers to coincide with the tripartite division of the frontal planes. Drop handles replace the fixed handles of the Louis XV style.

Beds

In the 18th century the four-post bed became outdated. Beds (*lits,* in French) in vogue during the Louis XV period were of several types. Without posts, the *lit d'ange* had both a head- and footboard, of which the footboard was usually lower; the canopy (or tester), a flat oblong in shape, extended over only a portion of the length of the bed. A *lit à duchesse* was similar except that the canopy covered the entire length of the bed; it, too, had no posts and a low headboard. The *lit à la polonaise,* on the other hand, had head- and footboards of equal height. Iron rods, curved upward and inward, were fastened to each corner of the head- and footboards; from these fabric fell from a centrally positioned dome, the drapery attaching to the rods at each corners of the bed. Giving the impression of a sofa the *lit à turque* had larger dimensions. It had an arched back with end pieces of equal height and was placed parallel with the wall. The canopy for this bed originated from the wall; the draperies were gracefully draped from the canopy over the ends of the bed. When the bed was not in use rolled cushions were placed at each end (Figure 11-16). Each of these forms was popular during both the Louis XV and Louis XVI styles; differences occurred in the style of ornament.

ORNAMENT

Régence. Designers searched for ornamental details that were more imaginative, gay, animated, and entertaining than those of the Louis XIV style. In support of this was a lively interest in foreign cultures, including Chinese, Persian, and Turkish. Figures appeared in compositions dressed in fantastic costume. In support of the interest in Chinese arts designers used such motifs as pagodas, dragons, and peacocks. Bérain's oriental motifs, which he introduced in the late 17th century, are considered to be the initial phase of the Rococo; both chinoiserie and singeries are associated with him. As in Bérain's work the paintings of Claude Audran and Jean-Antoine Watteau depicted monkeys whimsically clothed in stylish Parisian dress. The shell motif was used often. In the early 18th century it was sometimes pierced and a typical treatment was for acanthus leaves to originate from the base of the upright shell; it was often rendered symmetrically. Background treatments included the use of cross-hatching where the center of each lozenge was centered with a small flower. Other motifs included flowers, birds, bows, quivers, arrows, ribbons, exotic birds, patterned medallions, outspread bats' wings, C- and S- scrolls, and espagnolettes.

Louis XV. Some motifs typical of the Régence period continued to be popular in the Louis XV style, but with asymmetrical arrangements of foremost importance. Chinoiserie and singeries persisted and one of their chief proponents was François Boucher, a painter whose work manifested the lightheartedness typical of this era. The shell now included fancy forms, often pierced, and the acanthus leaf was often serrated and elongated. Amidst interlaced foliage were trophies, masks, and enigmatic animals. Other motifs included fountains, stylized flowers (sprays, garlands, bouquets, pendants), plants, fish, leafy scrolls, rosettes, asymmetrical scrolls and curves, palm branches, musical instruments, and symbols of love (arrows, bows).

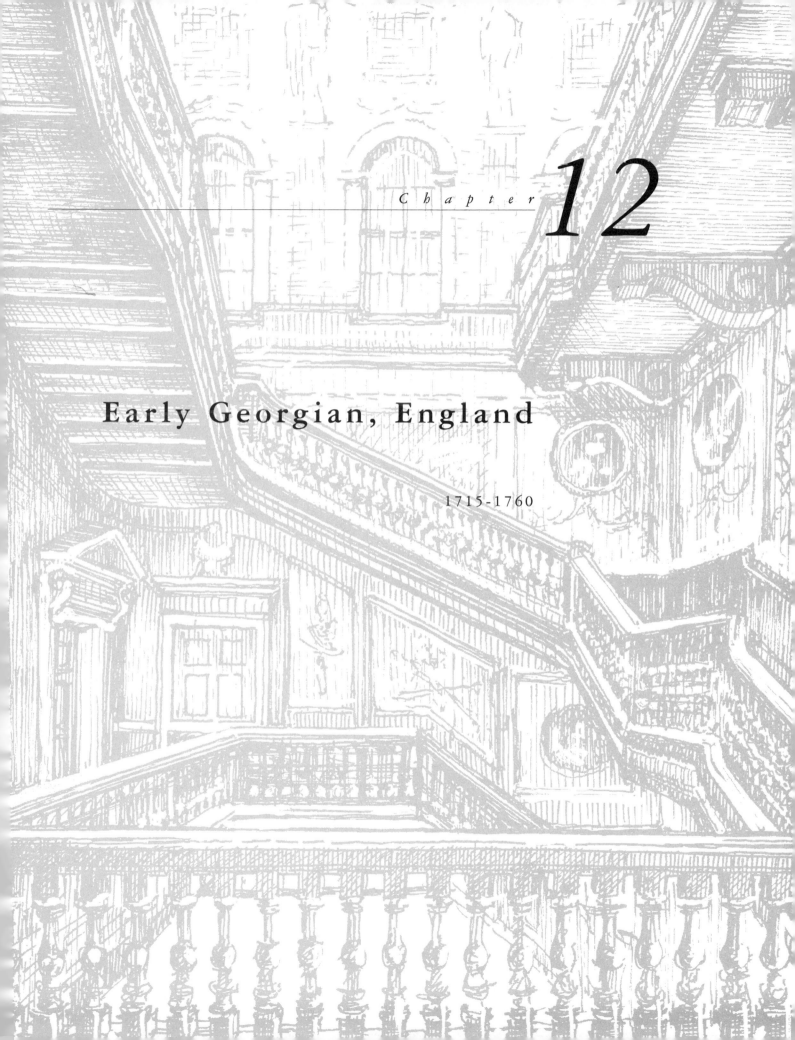

Early Georgian, England

1715-1760

Chapter 12

HISTORICAL SETTING

A number of factors converged to influence the arts in the Early Georgian period: (1) the Act of Settlement of 1701, which prepared the way for the ascension to the throne in 1714 of George I, elector of Hanover; (2) the power of the Whigs, who represented a large proportion of the affluent and educated; (3) the reliance on the study of classical antiquity, both through visits to sites in Italy and publications from ancient, 16th century, and contemporary sources; and (4) the power and prestige of the upper classes based on ownership of land and construction of country houses as evidence of wealth. Each of these major influences is an integral component of the direction taken in the arts of architecture, interior architecture, and design from 1715 to 1760.

The Act of Settlement provided that if there should be no heirs from the union of William III and the future Queen Anne the succession should pass from the Stuart line of monarchs to the Hanovarian line. Thus the first Hanovarian monarch was George I (great-grandson of James I), who was German and who could not speak English. Previous monarchs had often surrounded themselves with artistic advisers and patronage of the arts had been undertaken by the Court; however, George I lacked interest in the arts. Therefore, on his accession, the Whig political party became an influential power in matters of taste.

According to the Whigs there was a moral basis for evaluating the arts. In fact, Lord Shaftesbury had stipulated that, "a man of breeding and politeness is careful to form his judgments of arts and sciences upon the right models of perfection." [1] The models which formed the basis of Whig evaluations lay in: (1) the canons of the classical, (2) the architectural principles of Andrea Palladio (architect and theorist in Vicenza in the 16th century), who had a depth of knowledge about Roman antiquity, and (3) the works of the English architect Inigo Jones, who had been profoundly influenced by Palladio a century earlier. At their disposal in 1715 was the English translation of Palladio's *Four Books of Architecture* (originally published in 1570). Through his study of classical forms Palladio explained the classical concept of a system of harmonic proportion based on mathematics; he claimed this to be the basis for the greatness of Roman architecture. The models the Whigs sought to reintroduce were to be found through archaeological evidence and in Vitruvius, the Roman writer on architecture; these were sources which Palladio also investigated.

In three folio volumes (1715, 1717, 1725), Colen Campbell published *Vitruvius Britannicus,* a survey of English classical architecture of the 17th and early 18th centuries. The reference to Vitruvius in the title reveals his taste for the classical and in his introduction he acclaimed the architectural works of Palladio and Inigo Jones. The designs he included (100 engravings per volume) were to be prototypes for great English houses. Campbell was the pioneer of English Palladianism. The proportionate relationship of the exterior suggested by Palladio was employed by Campbell. Palladio had suggested that a comparative relation should exist between the floors of the houses—basement, piano nobile, and attic. On the exterior, attention was given to the center of the façade where the portico was in a raised position (sometimes as much as 15 feet above ground level); further stress was directed to the portico in that it was crowned by a balustraded parapet. Based upon these characteristics, two features contributed to appreciation of the landscape: (1) the view provided of the surrounding landscape by the raised position and (2) the view through the house by the interior axial arrangement of the hall and salone, as at Hagley, immediately behind the portico.

One model adapted to English conditions was the small, compact classical villa. Palladio's Villa Rotonda (Villa Capra) at Vicenza appears to have been the model for some of the residences designed by Colen Campbell. For example, Mereworth was built between c.1720 and 1723; a section of it appeared in the third volume of *Vitruvius Britannicus.* The domed, cubical form of the residence as it was originally planned arose from a moat, since

---

1. As quoted in Helena Hayward, ed. *World Furniture* (New York: McGraw Hill, 1965), 127.

filled in. On the interior, centering the cube, is the circular salone (35 feet in diameter), which rises 80 feet to the apex of the dome. While the plan follows closely those of Palladio, Campbell eliminated three of the four vestibules. The villa had a number of uses: (1) as a retreat for the nobility, (2) for affluent persons in governmental positions who needed to be near London, and (3) as periodic recreational lodging.[2]

The classical mind-set also extended to a focus on classical education for gentlemen, including the Grand Tour of Europe, where they could view firsthand artifacts from classical antiquity. Gentlemen studied Latin and Greek and the classical philosophers. The major architects saturated themselves with knowledge of the classical through investigations of publications or through the Grand Tour. Giacomo Leoni (c. 1686-1746), although of Italian descent, settled in England c. 1715. He was highly instrumental in the Palladian movement through his translation of Palladio's *Four Books of Architecture* in 1715. The annotated publication of Inigo Jones's copy of Palladio was an inspiration to him. Clandon Park, Surrey, survives as an example of his architecture; the exterior is Palladian in concept but the interior has elements of the Baroque in the ceiling of the hall.

Richard Boyle, third earl of Burlington (1694-1753), made the Grand Tour in 1714-15; he traveled through France, northern Italy, and Rome. While in Rome he became acquainted with William Kent, who was practicing painting. On his second visit to Italy, in 1719, Burlington visited Venice and Vicenza, where he studied firsthand the works of Palladio. He later assumed the leadership role of the Palladian movement. William Kent (1685-1748) first met Lord Burlington in 1714-15 in Italy; in 1719 he was invited by Burlington to return to London with him, where the two promoted the Palladian movement in England. Later he moved away from Roman-inspired design toward more picturesque approaches. Kent's versatility is illustrated by his engagement in several arts including architecture, landscape design, interior decoration, painting, and furniture design. Among his most important works was Holkham Hall, Norfolk, which was based on a fusion of influences including Inigo Jones, Palladio, and Roman models. These architects and others, along with the wealthy landowners who commissioned them, were enthusiastic in their design of country houses.

It behooved these wealthy landowners, as leaders in the community, to richly adorn their country house interiors. Toward this end interiors revealed in chronological sequence Baroque, Palladian, and Rococo influences. Each of these directions in design overlapped to a greater or lesser degree; for example, in the same room during the Baroque period Palladian architectural detailing might be employed. The Baroque, more influential for the interior than for the exterior, represented a combination of the classical combined with the drama and movement associated with the English Baroque of the late 17th century.

James Gibbs (1682-1754) was the major proponent of the Georgian Baroque. After a period in Rome beginning in 1703 to study for the priesthood, he changed his direction to architecture. While in Italy he visited Palladio's buildings. On his return to England in 1709 he became well known for his design of St. Mary-le-Strand, which revealed a combination of Wren-influenced and Baroque features. Although his religion and politics (Catholic and a Tory) presented some difficulties for him, his influence on regional builders was enhanced by the publication, in 1728, of *Book of Architecture* and by *Rules for Drawing the Several Parts of Architecture* (1732). The former illustrated his earlier country houses and was a popular pattern book. Internationally, Gibbs's influence is observed in the design of the White House, Washington, D.C. In the design of the hall at Sudbrooks Park, Petersham (c.1725), he employed the Baroque features of floating pediments, scrolled shoulders, and oeil-de-boeuf windows.

Palladianism began to be introduced during the period of the Georgian Baroque. This classical ideal of the Whigs was perfectly appropriate as a symbol for the power of the landed aristocracy whose residences were central to the country estates. Suited to the palatial residence, Palladianism could also be adapted to smaller interiors.

---

2. Christopher Hussey, *English Country Houses, Early Georgian, 1715-1760* (London: Country Life, 1955; rev. ed., 1965), 22. Page number from the rev. ed.

By the mid-18th century, however, Palladianism had lost impetus. In its place the Rococo stylistic movement was the result of influences from France and from books of engravings; it was a delicate, nonarchitectural approach to decoration, two aspects of which were chinoiserie and Gothic. Although the classical element was considerably on the wane in the latter part of this period, Rococo elements were often set within classical frames.

The basis of power lay in landed property and the country house. Social and political prestige came from the property owners, who constructed or renovated their residences in the current fashion. Country houses were stylistic models of the richer landowners who brought the latest fashions in furniture and new forms in architecture to their country seats. This was visible evidence of their wealth. These fashions were admired and adopted by other visiting country gentlemen and transmitted down the social scale to squires and yeomen and, finally, accepted into the local vernacular.

The upper-class landowner was often influential at both the local and national levels. One way of consolidating his power was through entertainment, since the country house was functionally important for pleasure; these recreational activities also furthered his aspirations for authority within his community. Entertainment in the large country house often meant that the landowner could influence seats of Parliament. The wealthy landowners often fostered the intermingling of aristocracy, gentry, and middle classes; this led to less formal living. The assembly was one means by which the affluent encouraged the mixing of social classes and the plans of their houses evolved to accommodate this activity. As defined in the 18th century, an *assembly* was "a stated and general meeting of the polite persons of both sexes, for the sake of conversation, gallantry, news and play." [3] Assemblies could include such activities as balls, supper, cards, tea drinking, dancing, etc. These events could take place concurrently in different rooms; one result of this was the arrangement of rooms in a circuit around a staircase.

Freedom to build was influenced by the fact that England was peaceful, strong, and secure due to the victories of John Churchill Marlborough; Marlborough was a great general and statesman who triumphed in many battles in Europe in the War of Spanish Succession, 1701-14. In addition, civil conflict had ended. Further impinging on the ability to build lay in the improvement of agricultural methods, with the consequence that there were larger proceeds from the land; however, tenant rents were more important than proceeds from agricultural products.

A complete union of the landscape with the residence was sought. The landscape became even more important than it had been in the Baroque period, during which the landscape was conceived as a continuation of the mansion's classical rule. Lancelot Brown (1716-1783), called Capability Brown because of his practice of telling his patrons that their estates had great capabilities, was a major contributor to this trend. He replaced formal gardens with informal arrangements incorporating serpentine waters and clumps of trees.

SPATIAL RELATIONSHIPS

A new approach to space planning typified the residences of the period from about 1720 to 1770. Versatility in planning to accommodate social events was the motivating force for this change. With the emphasis on social activities the need arose for sequences of communal rooms. This contrasted with the late 17th century planning concept, in which the hall and salone served as the introduction to state apartments with a hierarchial sequence of rooms beyond; a visitor could progress in this sequence to the extent of his perceived importance as deemed appropriate by the owner.

---

3. As quoted in Mark Girouard, *Life in the English Country House* (Harmondsworth, Middlesex, England: Penguin Books, 1980), 191.

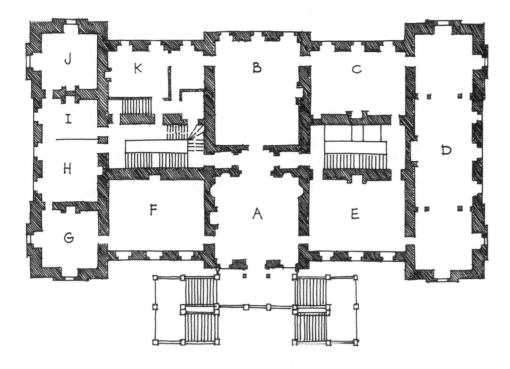

FIGURE 12-1 Principal Floor, Hagley Hall, Worcestershire (1753-1759), Sanderson Miller. A Hall, B Salone, C Drawing Room, D Gallery, E Dining Room, F Library, G Dressing Room, H Bedroom, I Dressing Room, J Bedroom, K Dressing Room. Courtesy of Country Life Picture Library.

Spatial Features of the Floor Plan and Three-Dimensional Spatial Characteristics

The assembly, as noted previously, involved activities (cards, supper, dancing, conversation, etc.) that took place simultaneously in different rooms, thus requiring a circuit of rooms. Hagley Hall can be taken as one plan that incorporates the sequence of rooms suited to the assembly (Figure 12-1).

At Hagley, a three-story house, the principal floor above the basement is approached by a double flight of stairs. Both public and private spaces are provided on this floor. The proportion of space devoted to public activities was altered to give more attention to public activities. On the west are three private apartments, each comprised of a bedroom and dressing room. On the east are public rooms consisting of hall, salone, drawing room, and gallery. Although the position of the hall and salone suggest the proximate relationship of the formal arrangement of the 17th century, these rooms were not the central focus nor the ceremonial center of the residence. The functional use of the salone was for dancing, receiving guests, and, infrequently, for dining; although not the case at Hagley, the dining room was often the best and largest of the public rooms. In the private area the dressing room was used as private sitting room and sometimes as a study where the landowner saw people on business; it was often elaborately decorated.

Hagley was flexibly arranged to accommodate guests of different numbers. A small assembly might utilize the drawing room, the dining room, and the gallery. However, for a larger group the hall and salone could be added. Still larger assemblies might embrace the apartments and library, utilizing the entire principal floor of these activities.

The custom began in the late 17th century for ladies to retire to the drawing room following dinner. This practice led George, first Lord Lyttleton, for whom Hagley was constructed, to write to Sanderson Miller, an architect, to request modifications to the plan in view of concerns from Lady Lyttleton. He stated that he believed:

> that no gentleman architect will have so great a regard to convenience as you or know so well how to give us the rooms we want. We are pretty indifferent about the outside, it is enough if it is nothing offensive to the eye. . . . She wishes for a room

FIGURE 12-2   Entrance Vestibule, Mereworth Castle, Kent (c. 1720-1723), Architect Colin Campbell, Decorators Bagutti, Sleter. Georgian Baroque with figures representing the arts and sciences. Shells surmount the doors. Courtesy of Country Life Picture Library.

FIGURE 12-3   Circular Domed Hall, Mereworth Castle, Kent. Thirty-five feet in diameter and eighty feet to the apex of the dome. Space lighted by round windows in the dome. Duplication of motifs from the vestibule in the circular domed hall. Courtesy of Country Life Picture Library.

of separation between the eating room and the drawing room, to hinder the ladies from the noise and talk of the men when left to their bottle, which must sometimes happen even at Hagley.[4]

Thus at Hagley a sound barrier is provided by the position of the staircase between the drawing room and the dining room.

Spatial relationships and the role played by ornament to define these relationships were exceedingly important. The hall often was a dramatic space an example of which can be seen at Mereworth (Figures 12-2 and 12-3). Here the hall is approached through a narrow, barrel-vaulted entrance vestibule from which one emerges into the towering circular domed hall, 35 feet in diameter and 80 feet to the apex of the dome. Providing access to the bedroom suites at the attic level is a projecting gallery supported by regularly spaced brackets interspersed with decorative plaster motifs. Vertically, spatial relationships and the exploration of space are enhanced in a variety of ways: (1) the repetition of the overdoor scalloped shells centered with busts in the vestibule and at the attic level of the domed hall; (2) the replication of modeled figures fabricated in a Baroque manner surmounting the arched openings on the principal floor and the pediments at the attic level; and (3) the light, although not brilliant, provided by the round windows in the dome. Horizontally,

4. As quoted in Christopher Hussey, *English Country Houses, Early Georgian, 1715-1760* (London: Country Life, 1955; rev. ed., 1965), 198. Page number from the rev. ed.

FIGURE 12-4 Stone Hall, Houghton Hall, Norfolk (cornerstone laid 1722), Colin Campbell's design. Cubical spatial concept of forty feet from the main floor through the attic story. Courtesy of Country Life Picture Library.

the visual experiences the visitor could anticipate in the circuit encouraged exploration of the spaces since it was often the case that: (1) in the circuit, one room was larger and more magnificent than other rooms; (2) sometimes there were different ornamental treatments in the sequence; and (3) occasionally, color schemes varied from room to room in the spatial arrangement.

But the spatial concept at Houghton was one of geometry, wherein the architect dealt with cubical volumes or rectangular spaces (Figure 12-4). The Stone Hall is a cube of forty feet that extends from the main floor through the attic story. The interest created by the focal points provided by the following encourages investigation of the three-dimensional space: (1) the balustraded projecting gallery, (2) the cove ornamented with frolicking boys modeled in the round, and (3) the stucco ceiling modeled in a circular panel in the center of which is the Horace Walpole arms, with the Garter star in the spandrels. Rectilinearity of spaces was ideally suited to the display of the collections of the owners; paintings were often hung between the dado and the cornice. Coupled with this were strong architectur-

FIGURE 12-5 Great Staircase, Houghton Hall, Norfolk (cornerstone laid 1722). Mahogany. Heavy balusters arranged in a continuous string. Mural painting of fictive reliefs on canvas by Kent. Courtesy of Country Life Picture Library.

al features such as doors, windows, and chimneypieces. Both Palladian and Baroque elements are observed at Houghton, Palladian in the library and state drawing room and Baroque in other spaces.

Sometimes the stairs were afforded an inordinate amount of space (Figure 12-5). The replication of stairs, placed in opposite positions, was approved by Palladio; these were advantageous in terms of aesthetics, spaciousness, and function.

INTERIOR ARCHITECTURE AND DECORATION

Three stylistic phases characterize interior architecture and decoration of the Early Georgian period; in chronological sequence, these are Baroque, Palladian, and Rococo. Style characteristics of the Baroque include the use of modeled figures (often in restless or forceful positions) fashioned in high relief. Baroque motifs were often set within the framework of a complete order.

Since Palladio did not write extensively about his interiors, the Palladians used a variety of sources to fill the void. One source was the employment of Italian designers; for example, stuccoists Giovanni and Giuseppi Artari and Giovanni Bagutti were in demand for the decoration of country houses. Documentary sources were available by reference to the drawings of Inigo Jones based on his study of Palladio. In addition, John Webb (1611-1672), drew many of the designs of Inigo Jones, by whom he had been trained. Further, William Kent and Henry Flitcroft (1696-1769) published in 1727 *Designs of Inigo Jones;* for this publication Flitcroft redrew plans and elevations of Jones.

The classical ideal and Palladianism lost momentum beginning in the 1740s. Rococo was a decorative movement devoid of an architectural approach. Introduced from France, the style was characterized by the detailing of delicate linear motifs, asymmetry, undulating lines, and natural forms found in grottoes (as shells and scroll forms); these were often set within a classical frame. Aspects of the Rococo were Chinese and Gothic: The inspiration for the use of Chinese motifs was due to the importance of the East India Company. Gothic found wider acceptance following the publication in 1742 of Batty Langley's *Gothic Architecture Improved.* Plaster and wood were the materials most frequently used for decorative detailing.

Materials and Decorative Techniques

Wallpaper, painting, stucco, and scagliola were materials of primary importance during the Early Georgian period. The country house was richly decorated. This was especially true of the hall, salone, and main staircase.

Wallpaper began to be an important means of decorating walls late in the 17th century and became more widely used in the 18th century. Papers were either hand painted, hand blocked, or machine printed. Wallpaper was often in sheets, three feet by two feet. Patterns varied, but two very interesting ones were embossed by applying particles of wool to the paper with an adhesive. Sometimes simulations of stucco were represented on paper. To apply paper to the wall a three-step process was used: (1) canvas was stretched over a frame of wood, (2) the paper was applied to the canvas, and (3) the frame with canvas and paper was then fastened to the wall.

Painters of decoration rendered a variety of themes that included mythological scenes, scenes of tribute to war heroes, and acclaims to monarchs. Decorative painting was accomplished in several ways. One method was to paint directly on the plaster wall, which required that the painter first prime the wall surface with a thin coat of paint or a size; oil on plaster was the medium appropriate to England, since fresco deteriorated in the dampness of the English climate. Another method of decorative painting was to first paint with oil on canvas or paper of a predetermined size and shape and then apply the panel to the wall or ceiling. Stucco surrounds often enframed these paintings and sculptural motifs were sometimes incorporated, either painted or in relief. Trompe l'oeil was a means used by the painter of the ceiling at Moor Park, Hertfordshire, where a fictive cupola and balustrade were first painted on canvas and then applied to the ceiling; the painting is surrounded by stucco relief (Figure 12-6). It was also the painter who was responsible for marblizing and graining, the first in imitation of marble and the latter simulating wood grain.

Scagliola, as a technique for imitating marble, was perfected by the middle of the 18th century. It was a compound of calcined gypsum mixed with sand, glue, and isinglass solution.

> Pure gypsum was broken into small pieces and calcined; as soon as the largest fragments lost their brilliancy, the fire was withdrawn, the powder passed through a fine sieve and mixed up with sand, a glue and isinglass solution. In this solution the colours required to imitate the marble were diffused and, like *stucco-marmor,* mingled and incorporated in the gypsum surface. This was then polished and finished with various oil mixtures and pure oil.[5]

Isaac Ware, in his book *A Complete Body of Architecture,* published in 1756, suggested that stucco ornament was a material most appropriate for the grandest rooms. Materials for stucco were lime, sand, plaster (gypsum), and some ingredient to retard setting, such as sour milk, alcohol, or wine. The type of armature used as a base for the stucco depended on the depth of the relief; the stucco was applied around such appropriate armatures as wooden forms, nails, etc. Binding materials such as hair or straw were also used. Repetitive work was often press-molded while single figures in higher relief were often fashioned in

---

5. Geoffrey Beard, *Craftsmen and Interior Decoration in England, 1660-1820* (London: Bloomsbury Books, 1986), 36.

FIGURE 12-6   Hall Ceiling, Moor Park, Hertfordshire (c. 1732), Painter, Gaetano Brunetti. Fictive cupola and balustrades surrounded by stucco relief Copyright Anthony Kersting.

situ. In press-molding the design was cut into hardwood and transferred by pressing the mold into the still-moist stucco. The repertoire from which the stuccoist drew his design sources included engravings, decorative stuccowork of Italy, and the Italian stuccatori Giovanni and Giuseppe Artari and Giovanni Bagutti, who worked for the architects commissioned to design many of the country houses.

Plaster wall and ceiling surfaces were the bases for several decorative applications. The ingredients included plaster of Paris (calcined and finely ground gypsum), sand, and water; the addition of animal hair gave tensile strength and acted as a binder. This medium was applied to laths nailed to the joists; successive coats of plaster were needed.

Interior Architecture and Decorative Elements

Although the Early Georgian style can be identified, stylistically there was tremendous variety. The interpretations and combinations of the classical theme were incredibly diverse.

Floors

Materials for floors were primarily wood and stone (especially in the entrance); marble was used only in the grandest houses. If wood, oak was the first choice, after which elm was the most favored; fir and pine were widely used by the mid-18th century. Planks were usually 12 inches wide in the early 18th century; later, nine-inch widths became more prevalent. Wood floors were sometimes painted and canvas floorcloths with painted designs were also employed. Floors were laid in parquet designs; craftsmen often followed pattern

books. Geometric patterns were represented in Batty Langley's *Builder's and Workman's Treasury of Designs* (1739) and John Carwitham's *Kinds of Floor Decorations Represented Both in Plano and Perspective* (1739). When carpets were used a stained edge was applied to the wooden floor.

Walls

Through his writings Isaac Ware was widely influential; he was strictly Palladian in his approach, having been trained by Lord Burlington. For wall treatment, Isaac Ware recommended stucco, wainscot, and wall hangings such as wallpaper, tapestry, and fabrics. He stated that:

> of the three kinds we have named, the grandest is that in stucco; the neatest, that in wainscot; and the most gaudy, that in hangings. For a noble Hall, nothing is as well as stucco; for a parlour, wainscot seems properest; and for the apartments of a lady, hangings.[6]

Full-height paneling was never completely outmoded but it seems to have been more prevalent up to around 1740 (Figure 12-7). Oak (early 18th century) and later pine and fir were the preferred woods; the latter, less expensive woods were often painted and sometimes marblized. Woodwork was often painted in pale colors and carved detail sometimes highlighted with gold. The proportionate wall divisions were related to the classical orders and included a dado, a field, and an entablature; in place of a full entablature a frieze or cornice (sometimes massive) headed the wall.

---

6. Isaac Ware, *A Complete Body of Architecture* (London, 1756), 468; quoted in Nathaniel Lloyd, *A History of the English House from Primitive Times to the Victorian Period* (London: Architectural Press, 1931; reprint, London: Architectural Press, 1975), 138. Page refers to reprint edition.

FIGURE 12-8 Drawing Room or
Tapestry Room, Hagley Hall,
Worcestershire (1753-1759),
Sanderson Miller. Probably Soho
tapestry designed to fit spaces.
Ceiling paintings by James Stuart,
c. 1758; Roman goddess of flowers
in the large center panel with ancil-
lary cupids in the four corners.
Courtesy of Country Life Picture
Library.

The dado might be paneled with some other treatment above. Tapestries, silk bro-
cades, velvets, and wallpapers were materials sometimes installed above the dado; these
were attached to battens. An edging (called *fillet*) for wallpaper or fabric was constructed
of metal, wood, or composition; designs were included in Thomas Chippendale's *The
Gentleman and Cabinet-Maker's Director* (1762). (see Director, 1762, No. CXCIV and No.
CXCV.) Chippendale chose to divide the designs into two groups: (1) specifically appropriate for paper hangings, and (2) suitable for borders of damask or paper hangings. These
represented distinctly Rococo detailing.

Tapestries in the medieval and Tudor periods were intended to be loose hangings, but
beginning in the 17th century a tendency to have them fit more tautly arose. During the
Early Georgian period tapestries were designed to fit exactly between the dado and the cornice. In this manner they became more decorative than pictorial, as had been the motivation for their earlier usage. The Rococo tapestries in the drawing room at Hagley may be
from the English Great Wardrobe Looms in Soho (Figure 12-8). Designs were of flowers,
birds, figures, rococo scrolls, wreaths, the seasons, etc.; compositions were sometimes of
oriental inspiration. The manufacturing source of many tapestries during the Early
Georgian period tended to be French and from the tapestry works of Gobelins and
Beauvais. Some were Brussels tapestries. However, tapestries from the earlier English
Mortlake factory were sometimes reused.

Walls were articulated in various ways. For example, niches (semicircular or semiel-
liptical in plan) punctuated the wall for the display of sculpture. Collectors also displayed
sculptural pieces on brackets mounted on the walls. There were also instances of damask-
covered walls on which mounted paintings alternated with painted plaster and niches.
Sculpture in niches was also accomplished through trompe l'oeil painting, as at Moor Park,
Hertfordshire (see Figure C-21). Francesco Sleter painted chiaroscuro[7] figures in niches in
the hall at the gallery level. These were first painted on canvases and then mounted on the
walls. Equally important in structural features as well as ornamentation of the interior was
the use of stucco.

Stucco became important after the first quarter of the century, although paneling was never entirely outmoded. The impetus for stucco decoration was due to travelers who had gained knowledge (1) from travels in Italy; (2) from the Italian stuccoists employed in England to undertake important commissions and who had firsthand knowledge of stuccowork executed by Pietro da Cortona at the Palazzo Pitti in Florence; and (3) from engravings, although some may have been from an earlier period and, therefore, outdated. Stucco and related materials were used in a variety of ways: relief decoration in such places as moldings and friezes; capitals mounted on scagliola engaged columns; portrait medallions; putti; brackets; figures giving the impression of supporting a wooden armature. Sometimes color was integrally applied to the stucco mixture and at other times the stucco remained white on a colored ground. Another medium that yielded three-dimensional ornament was papier-mâché, sometimes used to simulate wood carving or for the fillets edging the application of textiles to walls.

Whatever the decorative treatment, walls were articulated with door cases, windows, and chimneypieces that were architectural in concept.

Windows and Doors

The trim for doorways and windows varied from very simple to exceedingly complex decorative treatments. Both were set in deep reveals. Generally, the most elaborate doors and windows were reserved for the principal story. Simplicity characterized the houses of the middle class. By the mid-18th century mahogany was the favorite wood for doors; otherwise, painted deal was employed to simulate paneling.

Casement windows continued to be used, but the double-hung window was standard in more stylish houses. Rectangular panes were usually arranged six over six; other arrangements depicted a lattice design illustrating the Chinese taste of the Rococo period. Glazing bars, at first heavy, later became thinner; some were richly carved. Internal shutters were folded flush into the jambs. On the inside, flush panel construction was employed while regular panel construction was revealed when the shutters were folded into the jambs. By the middle of the century panels were usually coordinated with the paneling of the room.

Window openings were most often rectangular but there were other configurations. Some had flattened, arched heads while others were sometimes double lancets, representing the Gothic influence during the Rococo phase of the Early Georgian. There was some use of the Palladian window (also called Venetian or Serlian), characterized by an arrangement of three openings in which the central one was widest and had a round, arched opening springing from the cornices of the side lights; the two outer windows had flat cornices (Figure 12-9). Four pilasters or columns articulated the tripartite arrangement. The Venetian window was often used by Palladian designers.

A massive window doorway in the salone at Houghton Hall, Norfolk, illustrates the architectural influence in the detailing of windows as well as doors (Figure 12-10). The enframement is

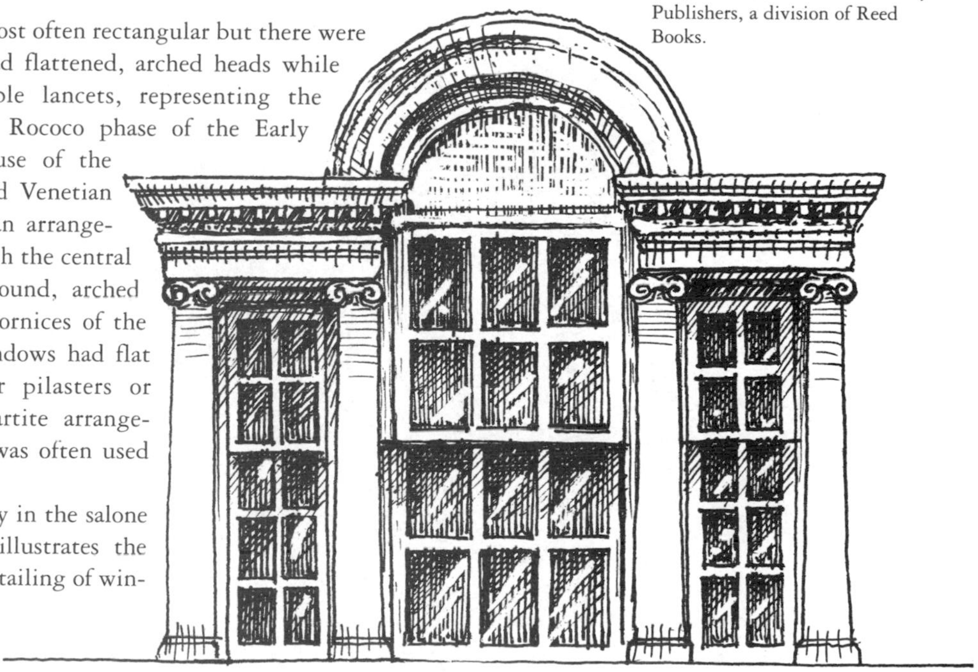

FIGURE 12-9 Palladian Window (also termed Venetian or Serlian). From Calloway, Steven. *The Elements of Style.* © 1991. Michael Beazley Publishers, a division of Reed Books.

---

7. *Chiaroscuro* is a technique whereby subtle gradations of light and dark are used to model figures or forms; this method is more appropriate to oil painting than to tempera, which is a quickly drying medium.

FIGURE 12-10 Window Doorway, Salone, Houghton Hall, Norfolk (cornerstone laid 1722). Architectural detailing for windows. Outside measurement with the columnar enframement measures ten feet, six inches. Paneled shutters in deep reveal. Courtesy of Country Life Picture Library.

composed of columns resting on plinths (rising to dado level), the outside points of which measure ten feet, six inches; the order supports a broken pediment in the center of which is a bust. Carved ornamentation is highlighted with gilt. Egg (two and one-half inches across) and tongue carving edges the deep reveal at the wall level. In the Marble Parlor at Houghton Hall, a simpler frame is used; here, a simple carved molding frames the opening at the wall level and pilasters, originating at dado level and extending to the entablature, are spaced regularly on the walls.

An *architrave-cornice* is one in which the frieze has been eliminated from the entablature. For some windows the architrave (the molded frame surrounding a door or window) had a lateral projection at the lintel; this configuration is referred to as a *crossette* or *shouldered* architrave) (see Figure 12-7).

Both single- and two-leaf doors were used. The number of door panels was often determined by the importance of the floor. For example, a two-paneled door typified upper floors. Panels were sometimes sunken but at other times were framed by a small molding with fielded panels (plain and raised central panel surface). However, on the principal story six-paneled doors were common with an arrangement of both vertical and horizontal panels or vertical and square panels (see Figure 12-7). In some cases skilled craftsmen created decorative treatments including inlay and carved molding set within the panel frame in rich materials, among them rosewood, ivory, ebony, and satinwood. With the overdoor treatment doors sometimes extended to full room height (see Figure 12-8).

The simplest doors had plain cases with architrave moldings, some of which were formed with crossettes; carved enrichment included such motifs as beaded rope patterns, leafage, and egg and dart designs (also called egg and tongue). More elaborate treatments, usually architectural, were used on doors for the principal story. Adjacent to the architrave molding on the outside it was often the practice to use: (1) engaged columns either supporting the entablature of the door or in some instances extending to the entablature of the wall, or (2) pilasters, which were occasionally paneled. With the simple architrave the overdoor treatment may have included one of the following: a horizontal entablature, a pediment (triangular or broken), or overdoor panels with stucco tablets of framed paintings. The latter often coordinated with and extended to the entablature heading the wall. When pilasters, columns, or engaged columns bounded the doors the pediment encompassed the composition; alternatively, decorative brackets were used as supports for the entablature or pediment. Fluting, stop fluting, or reeding enriched columns and pilasters. The decorative treatment for the broken pediment could be a bust, vase, or other object. Especially in the 1720s, Baroque figures were employed on the slope of the shallow pediment. Details of the entablature included at times a pulvinated frieze carved with laurel leaves and crossed ribbanding; a carved tablet enriching the frieze; and dentils as part of the cornice detail.

Chimneypieces

The chimneypiece was the focal point of the Early Georgian interior and considerable attention was lavished on it in terms of the ornamentation of the architectural elements as well as its position in the room. There was a correlation between the degree of elaboration and the social class of the resident as well as the hierarchical significance of the space. Marble and wood were the materials most often used in the construction of the lower part; however, the overmantel was often of stucco, wood, or marble (in the most exceptional examples). Scagliola was also used at times.

In his pattern book of 1756, *A Complete Body of Architecture,* Isaac Ware categorized the chimneypieces as being simple, which meant that it terminated at its cornice (which formed the shelf at times) or at a pediment at shelf level; the continued type indicated a superstructure of wood, stucco, or marble. Said another way, the chimneypiece was either one or two stories in height. The continued chimneypiece was used less frequently as the 18th century progressed. A mantel shelf was not always used.

The firebox was usually rectangular, with an architrave frame. Moldings were often carved with ornament derived from classical sources. Exceptions to this were those of curved outline reflecting Rococo influence and those showing Gothic influence using some form of Gothic arch. In addition to structural outline, carved ornamental detail reflected the foregoing and, in addition, sometimes featured Chinese decoration. The diversity in composition of the first story was almost infinite. The entablature *or* the cornice in combination with a lintel *or* the cornice in concert with the frieze was supported by one of the following: pilasters, engaged columns, consoles, or terms (the bust or upper part of the human body that springs from a pilaster, console, bracket, etc.). A tablet breaking the frieze was often combined with a corresponding break in the cornice; the head of a Roman goddess was sometimes carved on the tablet—for example, Aurora, goddess of dawn. Pulvinated friezes were also employed.

Sir Henry Cheere (1703-1781) seems to have provided chimneypieces in the Rococo manner. A drawing in the Metropolitan Museum of Art illustrates his use of human figures and festoons of flowers on the frieze. Flowers and leafage on the pilasters are surmounted by shells at frieze level (Figure 12-11). In the style of Cheere is a chimneypiece for the dining room originally at Kirtlington, Oxfordshire; this example has carved terms and brackets (consoles) (Figure 12-12).

FIGURE 12-11 Chimneypiece
Drawing, Sir Henry Cheere. Rococo
manner. By Courtesy of the Board
of Trustees of the Victoria and
Albert Museum, London.

FIGURE 12-12 Chimneypiece,
Dining Room (c. 1748),
Kirtlington Park, Oxfordshire.
Wood, plaster, marble. Rococo in
the manner of Sir Henry Cheere.
Carved terms and brackets.
(Reerected in the Metropolitan
Museum of Art, New York). All
rights reserved, The Metropolitan
Museum of Art, Fletcher Fund,
1932 (32.53.1).

The frieze had a great variation of other carved ornamental designs, examples of which are noted in the following enumeration. During the Rococo period of Early Georgian repetitive motifs were used representing Gothic arches, quatrefoils, etc. A mask centering swags of drapery was a favorite decorative detail of William Kent. Treated in a Baroque manner was a symmetrical arrangement of scrolling acanthus leaves and stems emanating from a central basket.

The continued chimneypiece represented an extension of and structural integration with the first story although, occasionally, a separate framed panel was placed above and separate from the mantelpiece. The overmantel was often in a tabernacle arrangement consisting of columns or pilasters supporting an entablature and pediment (see Figure 12-4). The center of the tabernacle frame was often reserved for a painting, mirror, or other decorative treatment. Triangular pediments, broken pediments, and scrolled open pediments were each depicted in the pattern books, such as Gibbs's *Book of Architecture* (1728). Another terminal treatment for the overmantel was the flat entablature. The arrangements and carved details were closely related to the first story of the chimneypiece, doors, and windows.

Ceilings

Plaster was often the material used as the base for decorative treatment for the ceiling, whether for painting or stucco relief renditions. It was rare to have elaborate painted ceilings except in the homes of the wealthiest citizens; however, small painted panels were often combined with other treatments. The subjects of paintings, regardless of size or shape, included trompe l'oeil depiction of an allegorical representation of the arts and sciences and, from mythology, portrayals of gods and goddesses such as Dionysus (god of fertility and wine) and Ceres (goddess of agriculture). The types of arrangements were numerous.

An excellent example of the work of William Kent as a painter is the ceiling of the Painted Parlor at Rousham, Oxfordshire; Kent was also the architect for this renovated residence (see Figure C-22). The major molding which frames the painting is a guilloche formed of cockleshells. Painted around 1740, it is in a grotesque style executed in oil on canvas. A center medallion depicts, from Roman mythology, Bacchus (god of wine), Ceres (goddess of agriculture), and Venus (goddess of vegetation); from the medallion emanate diagonal bands between which are rendered on a white ground landscape scenes with painted frames and arabesques. The Palladian treatment of the walls of this room features wainscot (originally grained paneling) with recessed panels; a dado rail carved with the guilloche; a typical Kent design for the continued chimneypiece, with a Medusa[8] mask carved on the frieze of the mantel below; and an overmantel of carved and gilt wood with crouching eagles on each side. Brackets on the wall support the sculpture collection of General James Dormer, who was responsible for having the Jacobean mansion refurbished between 1738 and 1740.

Pattern books were instrumental in the dissemination of design ideas for ceilings. Some of the most instrumental were Batty Langley's *The City and Country Builder's Treasury* (1745), which included plasterwork designs for ceilings, his *A Sure Guide to Builders* (1729), which illustrated a modillion cornice, and James Gibbs's *Book of Architecture* (1728), which depicted cartouches of plasterwork. The plasterwork cartouche was used on wall panels, on friezes, and as corner pieces for coved ceilings.

Representing the Baroque phase of the Early Georgian style is the ceiling of the hall at Clandon Park, Surrey, probably constructed around 1730 (Figure 12-13). The stucco relief with representations of Hercules and Iole in the central medallion is based on the Carracci, a family of Italian painters; engravings of the Roman ceiling by Carracci were

---

8. Medusa, in Greek mythology, was one of three Gorgon monsters. Having once been beautiful, she so provoked Athena that the goddess made her so hideous that all men who looked on her were turned into stone.

FIGURE 12-13 Ceiling, Hall of Clandon Park, Surrey. Baroque figures deceptively support the molding in the composition; legs extend onto the cornice. Forty-foot cube hall. © National Trust Photographic Library.

published in the third quarter of the 17th century. Both the elements and the organization are typically Baroque; the figures deceptively appear to support the molding at the edges of the composition and their legs extend into the cornice. Wooden armatures would have been required for the parts of these figures that were executed essentially in the round. The craftsmen were probably Artari and Bagutti.

One difference between designs of the Palladian period and the late 17th century Baroque was that the relief tended to be shallower in the hands of the Palladians. Refined moldings with Roman motifs were used frequently. Among the earliest examples of ceilings of Early Georgian Palladianism are to be seen in Mereworth Castle, Kent, in the gallery, installed 1723-1725 (Figure 12-14). The preference of the Palladians was for architectural compartmentalization based on Palladio and introduced to England by Inigo Jones. Here, paintings within the compartments were executed by Francesco Sleter, a painter and decorator. The deep, coved transition has trompe l'oeil painting to represent ornament in relief.

A Rococo ceiling at Hagley Park may be taken as having style characteristics of this decorative approach (see Figure 12-8). A painting in the center of the ceiling was

FIGURE 12-14   Ceiling, Gallery, Mereworth Castle, Kent. Architectural compartmentalization based on Palladio and introduced to England by Inigo Jones. Painted by Francesco Sleter. Courtesy of Country Life Picture Library.

framed by an oval, low-relief stucco border with delicate ornamental detail. Appropriately, the Roman goddess of flowers (with ancillary cupids at the four corners) is depicted in the painting, consistent with the other stucco decoration of trailing leaves and stems. Lord Lyttleton wrote of James Stuart that he "has engaged to paint me a Flora, and four pretty little Zephrys, in my drawing room ceiling, which is ornamented with flowers in stucco, but has spaces left for these pictures. He thinks all my stucco well done."[9]

Stairways

The position of the stairs within the plan was of utmost importance, as this related to the accommodation of the assembly. Guests usually arrived from the entrance level to the floor above (the floor arranged for the circuit of rooms) by the main stairs; this staircase was the most elaborately decorated (see Figure 12-5). Stair treatment became simpler as each of the upper floors was reached, being plainest as one approached the attic level. Configurations for the stairs were straight flights and rectangular landings in ordinary residences; the more elaborate were circular or oval in shape and lighted from a dome above. In addition, there were stairs designed specifically for the use of servants.

Closed string stairs with massive balusters and a flat rail continued to be used in this period. However, the open string staircase became more common during the Early Georgian period and with it the use of decorative tread ends of carved detail; the decorative detail was representative of the period: Baroque, Palladian, or Rococo (Figure 12-15). The number of balusters set into each tread varied from one to three; there are examples of continuous balustrading. Wooden balusters were often fancifully turned in spiral, flute, and column shapes. Three different turnings were sometimes used per tread. Typically, each turned member had blocked sections both above and below the

9. H. Avray Tipping, *English Homes Period V Vol. I, Early Georgian, 1714-1760* (London: The Offices of Country Life, 1921), 328.

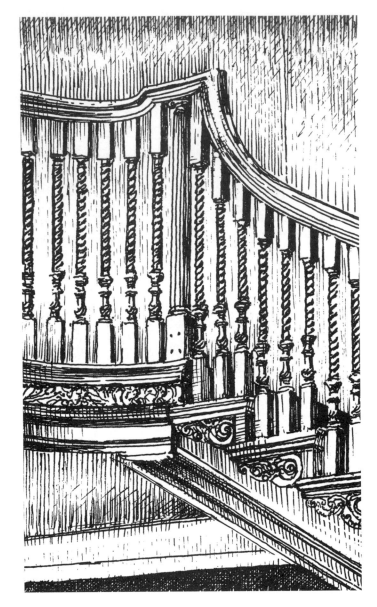

turning. The Palladian manner was to use large balusters and wide handrails.

The newel post, as well as the initial posts at the landings, received special attention. The newel was usually the most elaborate. The design of the newel sometimes represented an order. Among other designs were those of complex double-twist turning and faceted baluster form. Metal balustrade units (not continuous) were also set on each tread. A continuous balustrade of wrought iron, cast iron, or steel with gilt highlighting was sometimes combined with wooden newels. Rococo ornament in metal or Chinese fret in wood were forms used for continuous balustrades.

Handrails were usually of wood or iron and were less wide than those of the 17th century. They often began with a volute at the base of the stairs and followed the outline of the first tread. When stone staircases became common the use of metal for the railings became common likewise.

Treads of wood were usually oil-painted to simulate wood grain or painted in a flat paint. However, in more elaborate treatments mahogany for the treads and risers as well as the landings was inlaid with expensive materials such as ebony, holly, and ivory. Cantilevering of the stairs was not common until the end of the period, but there are a few examples.

FURNITURE

Furniture styles covered in this section are Queen Anne (c. 1700-1720), Georgian (c. 1720-1745), and Chippendale (c. 1745-1770). While these dates do not exactly coincide with those of planning concepts and interior architecture stylistic parallels can be drawn. Dates are significant only in the sense that they represent the period of greatest popularity; stylistic features may have begun in the previous period or extended into the succeeding period. Thus, the style characteristics defined as Queen Anne in this work overlap the period of George I.

Following the Baroque period of the late 17th century the Queen Anne style offered a diametrically opposite approach to furniture design. Early 18th-century Queen Anne furniture can be characterized as exquisite and constrained in contrast to the previous period of overelaboration. It is a style distinguished by exceptional craftsmanship, walnut wood, and a fine sense of proportion.

The Georgian furniture style had two mainthreads. One was based on the form of Queen Anne furniture but was more heavily decorated. The other was architects furniture designed to complement the interiors in which it was placed; this had little influence on general trends in furniture design, since these pieces were for the specific enhancement of residences of the wealthy upper class. William Kent was among those who designed for this select group. Of Kent's wide range of design activities Horace Walpole noted:

> Kent had an excellent taste for ornaments, and gave designs for most of the furniture at Houghton, as he did for several other persons. Yet chaste as these ornaments were, they were often immeasurably ponderous. His chimneypieces, though lighter than those of Inigo, whom he imitated, are frequently heavy, and his constant introduction of pediments and the members of architecture over doors and within rooms, was disproportioned and cumbrous. . . . his oracle was so much consulted by all who affected taste, that nothing was thought complete without his assistance. He was not only consulted for furniture, as frames of pictures, glasses, tables, chairs, etc., but for plate, for a barge, for a cradle. And so impetuous was fashion, that two great ladies prevailed on him to make designs for their birthday gowns. The one he dressed in a petticoat decorated with columns of the five orders; the other like a bronze, in a copper-coloured satin, with ornaments of gold.[10]

Furniture was used by Kent in the same way he conceptualized interior architecture and landscape design; he was interested in vistas and the position of furniture in a space could become a focal point to draw attention to specific parts of the total composition.

The interest in Baroque furniture, defined here as Georgian, began to wane in the fourth decade of the 18th century in favor of an adaptation of the French Louis XV style. This freer approach was opposed to the classical ideals that had held sway during the earlier part of the century. Pattern books published in England during the early 1740s were instrumental in the initiation of the Rococo. Engravings by De La Cour, a Frenchman working in England, illustrated chairs that retained some Baroque qualities; characteristics included chair backs with interlaced bands.

Publications heralded each phase of the Rococo. In 1744 and 1746 respectively, Matthias Lock published *Six Sconces* and *Six Tables,* in which he went a step closer toward the understanding of and advancement toward the Rococo; these books showed greater appreciation for the relationship between ornament and form as well as illustrated the freedom of execution that characterized the style. In 1742 Batty Langley published *Gothic Architecture Improved,* which depicted Gothic chimneypieces; the Gothic was first an influ-

---

10. Horace Walpole, Architects in the Reign of George II, in *Anecdotes of Painting in England* (Strawberry Hill, 1762-71); quoted in Ralph Fastnedge, *English Furniture Styles, 1500-1830* (Middlesex, Harmondsworth, England: Penguin, 1955, reprint, 1964), 125. Page is from the reprint.

ence on interior architectural features, later reflected in furniture design. Both Romantic and Picturesque tendencies were at work. The Romantic approach, first noted in the Gothic, revolved around the need to express feelings and free expression. The Picturesque focused on arrangements in an irregular manner. One manifestation of the Picturesque was in chinoiserie, depicted in Matthias Lock's *A New Book of Ornaments* (1752), in which he illustrated chimneypieces, mirrors, and tables. By the mid-18th century designers generally subscribed to the individuality, originality, and freedom encompassed by the Rococo.

Gothic, Rococo, and Chinese themes were all represented in Thomas Chippendale's *The Gentleman and Cabinet-Maker's Director*, a trade catalog issued in three editions (1754, 1755, 1762). Among researchers there is considerable disagreement about the credit due to Thomas Chippendale for having originated the designs that appear in his pattern book. Undisputed is the fact that nothing of the scale of the *Director* had been produced before. Furniture pattern books that were prevalent after mid-century must have contributed greatly to the activity in this area, although craftsmen were by no means slavish copiers of the designs represented in the publications.

Thomas Chippendale (1718-1779) was the son of a carpenter and grew up in the village of Otley in Yorkshire. Prior to his establishment in St. Martin's Lane in London, Chippendale had shops in Conduit Court and Spur Alley Ward. His premises consisted of a shop, timber yard, and workshops. The extent of his operation was suggested by Cescinsky based on an account in the *Gentleman's Magazine* of April 1755 of a fire

> . . . which broke out in his Workshops, in which the chests of twenty-two workmen were burnt. He must have been in a large way of business at this date, as tool-chests would imply cabinetmakers only, and would take no account of carvers, polishers, finishers, upholsterers, clerks and other people incidental to such a factory.[11]

Edwards and Jourdain have indicated that component parts may have been made in the Chippendale workshop and used in the furniture of minor makers. They substantiate this claim by the pencil inscription "6 pedestals for Mr. Chippendale's" backs appearing on the base beneath the splats of chairs from the Tomes Bequest to the Victoria and Albert Museum; the splat design is identical with that of Plate XII in the 1754 edition of the *Director*.[12]

Materials and Construction Techniques, c. 1702-1770

Beginning in the late 17th century new decorative processes placed emphasis on surface decoration; veneering, japanning, and gesso became significant techniques of ornamentation. In the span of years from 1702 to 1760 walnut and mahogany were the primary woods employed in England. In the Queen Anne period and into the Georgian emphasis was given to the use of walnut veneer, craftsmen capitalized on the exceptional patterning of this wood. The move away from the Baroque was responsible in part since more natural effects resulted and less emphasis was given to the stylistic effervescence of the previous period. Walnut was a wood imported from France and Virginia; richly figured American black walnut was streaked with dark brown. The supply of walnut diminished around 1720 when there was a wood famine in France with a resultant embargo on exportation from the Continent.

This shortage prompted craftsmen to turn to mahogany as their primary wood in the second quarter of the 18th century; it was imported from Cuba, Santo Domingo, and Puerto Rico. Its advantages were that it was close-grained, hard, and heavy. Crisp carving

---

11. Herbert Cescinsky, *English Furniture from Gothic to Sheraton* (Grand Rapids, Michigan: Dean Hicks, 1929), 284.

12. Ralph Edwards and Margaret Jourdain, *Georgian Cabinet-Makers* (London: Country Life, 1946), 1.

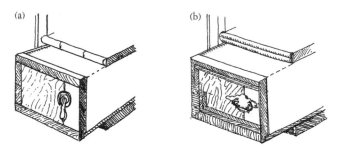

(a)   (b)

FIGURE 12-16 Drawer Front Details. A. Last two decades of 17th century and early 18th century. Angled border. Half round molding on rail between drawers. B. Late 17th century and early 18th century. Crossbanding and/or herringbone with two or three molded strips placed on carcass frame. Courtesy of Country Life Picture Library.

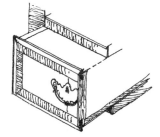

FIGURE 12-17 Drawer Detail, Decorative Veneer Construction. Crossbanding on carcass frame and framing the drawer front. Projecting lip molding surrounds drawer. Courtesy of Country Life Picture Library.

was possible due to these properties. Initially mahogany was used almost exclusively in the solid form; however, by mid-century, when there was great demand for case pieces (such as cabinets and commodes), it was appropriate to return to veneers. This was feasible since mahogany could be attained in larger sheets than had been typical of walnut; red pine was often the base (or carcass) for mahogany veneer.

In contrast to mahogany, walnut was of considerable decorative value since its strong patterning lent itself to such veneer techniques as quartering, crossbanding, and feather edging (herringbone), techniques which began to be used in the late 17th century. The construction detail of drawer fronts prevalent in the last two decades of the 17th century continued into the early years of the 18th century (Figure 12-16a) Drawer fronts were walnut veneered with the grain of the border placed at an angle; however, the half round molding on the carcass frame was solid walnut. Beginning in the last decade of the 17th century and continuing into the early 18th century, more decorative treatments were typical (Figure 12-16b). Here, either crossbanding or herringbone (feathered) veneer borders were used to frame the drawer fronts; two or three contiguous moldings on the carcass frame gave the impression of reeding. Then around 1710 and continuing into the mahogany period, the drawer front bounding was crossbanding with a solid walnut lip molding projecting forward on the edge (Figure 12-17). The rail between the drawers was also crossbanded. Occasionally English craftsmen followed the Dutch practice of veneering only the fronts of case pieces, with the sides displaying the less expensive carcass wood.

Gilding, gesso, and carving were processes that could be used together. English gilders rivaled the French in the quality of their work. In water gilding the surface was first prepared by applying successive layers of white gesso (a paste of size and whiting). This was allowed to dry, after which it was "given a coat of coloured bole—an earth combined with iron oxide—and allowed to dry. At the gilding stage, the bole was wetted with sized water so that the gold leaf could adhere."[13] Authors of a treatise published in 1688 advised, "Lay

13. Geoffrey Beard, *Craftsmen and Interior Decoration in England, 1660-1820* (London: Bloomsbury Books, 1986), 93.

on your gold . . . pressing it gently and close . . . if your work be sufficiently moist, you'll perceive how lovingly the gold will embrace it, hugging and clinging to it, like those inseparable friends, Iron and the Loadstone."[14]

Gilding was a corollary to gesso. A soft wood served as the base for the gesso. A thick liquid mixture of whiting and size was painted onto this base in a predetermined pattern or to a precarved surface. Following surface hardening the design was sharpened with a tool. If particularly strong relief was called for wood was carved and adhered to the surface, after which a thin coat of gesso was applied to it. Finally, the entire surface was gilded. This process was used for mirror frames, side tables, and small panels of chair splats or legs.

There was a resurgence of interest in the technique of japanning in the mid-18th century that was directed at the novice rather than the professional craftsman. In fact, a pattern book containing about 1500 designs was issued entitled *Ladies Amusement, or the Whole Art of Japanning Made Easy.* Contrary to the technique of the late 17th century, however, it was recommended that varnish be applied directly to the ground without first priming the surface with size and whiting.

Typical Pieces and Stylistic Features, Queen Anne, 1702-1720

The Queen Anne style represents a revolutionary change in the form of furniture. Compared to late 17th century furniture, curved lines usurped straight lines; soft outlines superseded angularity and severity; simplicity supplanted overelaboration; low relief and veneering displaced high-relief carving; dignity and comfort in accord preempted dignity alone as the primary consideration for design.

Seat Furniture

The backs of Queen Anne chairs were lower than their counterparts in the previous period, and the curve was introduced (Figure 12-18). The hoop back, in which the uprights and the top rail formed a continuous curve from just above the seat, was typical; a cyma curve sprang from a vertical straight portion that originated at the seat. The uprights, slightly rounded on the front face, occasionally rose straight to the rounded shoulders. The cresting of the back was often characterized by a concave center. The splat in the center of the back was vase- or fiddle-shaped and was normally attached to a shoe piece at seat level; usually it was not pierced. With attention to comfort, the profile of the back was spoon-shaped, designed to conform to the human spine. Occasionally both the back and the seat were fully upholstered.

Seats were of two shapes. One was trapezoidal, with rounded corners; the other was of horseshoe contour. Occasionally the front seat rail was shaped or valanced. Typically a slip seat was fitted within the seat rails, accomplished by reducing the thickness of the upper edge of the seat rail for this purpose. A slip seat could be easily lifted out for reupholstering.

Both open armchairs and side chairs were constructed in the Queen Anne style. The arm supports originated from the side seat rail set a few inches back. Scroll-over arms extended beyond the supports. An aeriel view would reveal the convex curve of the armrest. Later the armrest extended beyond the support and ended in a volute or scroll.

Initially only the front legs were cabriole; these ended in either a *pied-de-biche* (or hoof-shaped) or pad foot (a disk-like ending). As Georgian characteristics became more evident the claw and ball foot was introduced. The back legs were square in section or plain turned between blocked sections above the stretcher; characteristically, the back legs were raked (Figure 12-19). The cabriole form for the back leg was a later feature. At first the legs were joined with three turned stretchers (H-shaped), one joining the front and back legs on each side and one cross member uniting them. Stretchers were then eliminated and were later reintroduced for some chairs in the stylistic period of Chippendale, when they were used with legs of square section.

14. J. Stalker and G. Parker, *Treatise of Japanning and Varnishing* (1688); quoted in Fastnedge, 101.

FIGURE 12-18 Queen Anne Side Chair. Solid vase-shaped splat. Hoop back. Back uprights in a cyma curve. Horseshoe-shaped slip seat. Shell-carved knee with pendant husk on cabriole leg. By Courtesy of the Board of Trustees of the Victoria and Albert Museum, London, W.26-1912.

FIGURE 12-19 Queen Anne Side Chair. Japanned. Legs united by stretchers at two levels (H-shape, turned single placed higher). Rear leg turned between blocked sections. Drawing by Julie L. Rabun after a Queen Anne side chair in The Metropolitan Museum of Art.

Simplicity was the major characteristic of the Queen Anne style. Ornamentation came from the use of figured walnut as a veneer on the splat and the uprights of the back. When leaf carving was used on the edges of the splat it was accomplished by adhering a block of wood to the veneered surfaces and then carved; the connection was so impeccable as to be virtually imperceptible. Occasionally marquetry panels were introduced in the designs of splats. Legs were left plain or a carved shell with pendant husks or acanthus leaves ornamented the knees. These carved decorations were occasionally hipped—that is, the carving extended from the knee of the leg onto the seat rail.

Tables

Specialized table forms were significant; one of the most important was the card table. Gaming tables were designed specifically for such games as backgammon and chess. Tea tables and toilet tables were also popular.

Tables were multifunctional in that when they were open they served one purpose and when they were closed they could be used as side tables. A typical card table had four cabriole legs; two of the legs attached to the hinged and folding frame underneath the table top moved with the frame to allow for the extended, open position. The tabletop had projecting rounded corners (each a segment of a circle); in the open position these were dished to form a surface for candles (Figure 12-20). Crossbanded walnut ornamented the edges of the top. Elliptical depressions on each side of the table top were used for money or counters. Textiles (such as green cloth, velvet, and needlework) were used to cover the surface of the top. Card or tea tables with folding circular tops sometimes had four taper-turned legs that terminated with pad feet; in this case three legs were often stationary and the fourth was a hinged gateleg that supported the top when it was opened.

FIGURE 12-20 Queen Anne Card Table (c. 1730). Beech. Painted in imitation of Chinese lacquer. Rounded corners. Cabriole legs ending in pad feet.

FIGURE 12-21 Queen Anne Chest of Drawers or Tallboy. Top section narrower than lower. Graduated depth of drawers for each section. Bail handles. Bracket feet.

Storage Pieces

Chests of various types were increasingly in demand during the 18th century. The chest-on-chest (synonymously, tallboy or double chest of drawers), chest of drawers, and bachelor chest were typical forms of the Queen Anne style (Figure 12-21). The tallboy was typically designed in two levels, the top section of which was neither as wide nor as deep as the lower section of drawers. The upper segment often had four levels of drawers that graduated in depth, the shallowest at the top (a row divided horizontally into three small drawers) and the deepest just above the molding that divided it from the chest below. In the lower chest there were normally three graduated drawers, the deepest at the base. A slide at the top of the lower section was functionally employed for care of clothing. The bracket feet (often mitered) provided no real support for the tallboy; rather, a block mounted inside the carcass extended slightly below the bracket to provide the strength to support the piece. The corners of the upper chest were frequently canted (or, synonymously, chamfered or splayed) and either treated with fluting or left plain. The surface of the canted edges often ended in a curve termed a *lamb's tongue* in the form of an ogee or cyma molding.

The chest on stand was a chest in two sections mounted on tall cabriole legs, here ending in the claw and ball foot (Figure 12-22). Carved shells ornament the knee of the cabriole while low-relief carving is used on the stiles of the lower portion. The apron is outlined with an arched center bounded by bold cyma curves. Inset fluted quarter columns were sometimes used at the corners of the upper section; here the column is mounted with a Corinthian capital, above which is a simple cornice. Pieces of this type were neither as architectural nor as heavy as was typical of Georgian examples. The drawer fronts are veneered so that the pieces are mounted symmetrically; each drawer front is surrounded by mitered crossbanding and a small molding. Keyhole escutcheons here are identical with the back plates for the bail handle.

Beds

Stylistically, beds of the Queen Anne period were not significantly different than the William and Mary style. Very tall, slender posts supported a boldly shaped tester. Complex draping, often damask, was typical of the early 18th century. The great height of rooms meant that the beds harmonized with the lofty spaces.

Typical Pieces and Stylistic Features, Georgian, 1720-1745

The aristocracy and the landed gentry, rather than the royal court, were the arbiters of taste during the period of Georgian furniture. The advancement of the arts was a primary motivation of this group. Palladianism was an enduring influence due to the significance placed on the Grand Tour for all educated men. For the grandeur of the residences built in the Palladian manner it was appropriate to design furniture of Baroque character consonant with their interiors; pieces were designed for specific positions in specific rooms and often reflected architectural treatments. The opulence of the furniture would have been inappropriate for more modest residences; therefore, simplified forms based on the Queen Anne style were adapted to middle-class homes. Diversification of form and ornament is highly characteristic of the pieces of furniture constructed during this period.

FIGURE 12-22   Queen Anne Chest on Stand (early 18th century). Walnut veneer on oak and deal. Chest in two sections mounted on tall cabriole legs. Shaped apron. Quarter inset columns. Spread eagle brasses with bail handles. By Courtesy of the Board of Trustees of the Victoria and Albert Museum, London.

Seat Furniture

Compared to the typical Queen Anne chair, the following were modifications made to Georgian chairs: backs, lower and wider; splats, wider and more elaborately decorated with carving, or pierced; seats, wider; front seat rails, sometimes depressed in the center and often ornamented with shells; legs, wider as well as greater breadth for the bracket under the seat rail.

Regardless of the type of piece, furniture can be identified by frequently used motifs characteristic of various phases of the Georgian style. These included eagles' heads and claws; lions' masks and paws; satyrs' masks; and cabochons and leaves (Figures 12-23, 12-24, and 12-25).

Tables

The passion for card playing infiltrated all levels of society during the reign of George I. George II and Queen Caroline are said to have played cards every evening for high wagers. The card table was a piece of furniture that would have been used for assembly activities (see Figure 12-24). A folding frame allowed the table to be used flexibly as both a card table and, in its folded position, as a side table. To open and close the table, hinges were used at the points noted in the illustration. Structurally, one way to secure the frame when it was extended (to form a square table) was to move an internal sliding tray to a position that locked the extended frame at the hinge.

In a letter of 1741 the Countess of Hartford, apparently disgruntled by the demands imposed by the assembly, indicated that:

> Assemblies are now so much in fashion that most persons fancy themselves under a necessity of inviting all their acquaintances three or four times to their houses, not in small parties, which would be supportable, but they are all come at once, nor is it enough to engage married people, but the boys and girls sit down as gravely at

FIGURE 12-23   Early Georgian Side Chair (c. 1730-1740). Mahogany. Breadth and ample proportions of the Georgian style. Leg with satyr mask knee, paw feet. Horseshoe-shaped seat. Slip seat. Rear legs with flared ending at floor level. Cabochon centers the back.

FIGURE 12-24 Georgian Card Table (c. 1740). Mahogany. Accordion type. Cabriole legs terminating in paw feet. Acanthus-carved knees hipped at juncture of frame. Richard T. Crane Jr. Memorial, Photograph © 1996, The Art Institute of Chicago. All rights reserved.

FIGURE 12-25 Georgian Breakfront Bookcase (c. 1730). Architectural in concept. Style of William Kent. By Courtesy of the Board of Trustees of the Victoria and Albert Museum, London.

whist tables as fellows of colleges used to formerly; it is actually a ridiculous, though I think a mortifying sight, that play become the business of the nation from the age of fifteen to fourscore.[15]

An important piece used in the dining room was the sideboard table. There was great variation in the design of these pieces. Usually highly decorative, this type of table was frequently influenced by architectural designers such as Kent and Flitcroft and were often based on the Venetian Baroque. Of carved and gilt wood, the apron under the frieze is centered with a double shell from which ornate sculptural swags emanate (see Figure C-23). Bold S-scroll legs in this piece are terminated with eagles' heads; from this point boldly conceived acanthus leaves are directed toward the center shells.

Significant alternate treatments included: friezes carved with classical motifs; marble, scagliola, or mosaic tops; terms or sphinxes as supports. These ornamental pieces were used beneath mirrors and between windows and in a variety of rooms including the drawing room and salon, and in the dining room as a sideboard table.

Storage Pieces

Architecturally treated in the style of William Kent, this bookcase is carved and painted pine with gilt highlights for the ornament; this type of piece was clearly in the domain of the architect (see Figure 12-25). The breakfront was introduced in the first half of the 18th century and became more prevalent in the second half, becoming less architectural in concept as well. Strong classical influence was revealed in the use of the cornice from which the central arch sprang; above this was a broken triangular pediment. The terminal carving on the pilasters represented brackets sculpted with acanthus leaves below in a carved pendant arrangement.

Constructed of carved mahogany and mahogany veneer, the commode typically had four long drawers of graduated depth. Mahogany gradually replaced walnut as the preferred wood. These pieces were often of bombé form and supported on heavy lions' paw feet consistent with the flamboyance of the Baroque. Although a marble top is used on this example, the preferred material for the top came to be mahogany (Figure 12-26).

Beds

In the Georgian period the elaborate draping of the previous period was usually eliminated. Above short cabriole legs with claw and ball feet, the exposed posts at the foot of the bed were carved beginning above mattress level (Figure 12-27). A plinth base often replaced the cabriole around 1750.

Typical Pieces and Stylistic Features, Chippendale, 1745-1770

Some research to date suggests that Chippendale may not have been responsible for the designs that appeared in the *Director;* rather, they may have been drawn by Matthias Lock and Henry Copeland. Although some furniture designs had been included in previous pattern books, no work devoted solely to furniture had been undertaken on a large scale prior to the publication of *The Gentleman and Cabinet-Maker's Director.* The book established the Rococo style that bears the stylistic designation of Chippendale. The *Director* was widely subscribed to by cabinetmakers, upholsterers, aristocrats, and craftsmen. While it was widely distributed and influential, there was by no means slavish copying of its designs. The later work of Chippendale reveals that he was influenced by Robert Adam and constructed furniture in the neoclassical style.

---

15. Countess of Hartford, letter, 1741; quoted in Percy Macquoid, *A History of English Furniture, The Age of Mahogany, 1720-1770* (London: Lawrence & Bullen, 1906; New York: Dover Publications, Inc., 1972), 88. Page refers to reprint edition.

FIGURE 12-26 Georgian Commode (c. 1730). Mahogany and mahogany veneer. Bombé shape. Marble top. Mahogany tops typical by mid-18th century. By Courtesy of the Board of Trustees of the Victoria and Albert Museum, London.

FIGURE 12-27 Georgian Bed, c. 1740. Claw and ball feet ending the short cabriole leg. Posts reeded above mattress level. Paneled headboard. By Courtesy Country Life Picture Library.

The predominant influence on English design of this period was French Rocaille, the antithesis to the classical thrust of the Georgian. Orders were generally eliminated or, if they were utilized, hardly distinguishable. Ornament was unrelated to structural needs. Decoration was characterized by curved lines, rock work *(rocaille),* shells *(coquilles),* flowers, fruit, foliage, fantastic use of birds, animals, human figures, etc. Asymmetry was the preferred arrangement of ornamental detail.

Seat Furniture

The stylistic diversity in the treatment of chair backs clearly reveals the aspects of the Chippendale style: Rococo, Gothic, Chinese. The backs were distinguished by openwork designs that either filled the back or contained within a splat. Splats were joined to a shoe piece at seat level and continued to the cresting of the back; typically the splats were wider at the base, became narrower near the center, and were widest at the top. The ornate splat called a *ribband back,* influenced by the French rocaille, was bounded by two elongated C-scrolls intertwined with carved wavy ribbon; the splat was headed by a bow and tassel (Figure 12-28). The overall shape of the back was narrowest at the seat and widest at the crest. The crest of the back was usually serpentine; the terminal point of the serpentine crest was treated in one of two ways: either the shoulders were rounded into the stiles or the ear pieces were uplifted, giving greater emphasis to the serpentine linear character of the crest. A chair, again of Rococo taste, illustrates the upturned and scrolled ear pieces of the crest (called *Cupid's bow*) (Figure 12-29). Both slip seats and upholstery over seat rails were typical. The front seat rail was often straight but sometimes shaped. Occasionally both the front and rear legs were cabriole; however, frequently the front legs were cabriole ending in either the scroll or claw and ball foot while the back legs were raked with a flared ending at floor level.

When the Marlborough leg (square in section and untapered) was employed, H-shaped stretchers connected the legs, often with one stretcher uniting the rear legs at a

FIGURE 12-28 Chippendale Ribband Back. Carved mahogany. Interlaced ribbons and C-scrolls make up the splat. By Courtesy of the Board of Trustees of the Victoria and Albert Museum, London.

FIGURE 12-29 Chippendale, Rococo Manner (c. 1750). Carved mahogany.

FIGURE 12-30 Chippendale, Chinese Manner (c. 1755-1760). Carved mahogany. Fretwork fills the back. Marlborough legs united by stretcher. By Courtesy of the Board of Trustees of the Victorian and Albert Museum.

higher position (Figure 12-30). When the Chinese taste was employed the openwork fret frequently filled the back. The Chinese influence was also revealed in the application of motifs to the seat rails (cut-card latticework) as well as in the openwork detail of the stretchers.

Gothic taste was often combined with Rococo detail. Interlaced Gothic arches, quatrefoils, and tracery designs represent some of the medieval adaptations (Figure 12-31). Marlborough legs were often used, joined by an H-shaped stretcher.

Tables

Dining tables were not represented in the *Director*. However, a typical arrangement consisted of a center table used in conjunction with separate extension tables. These were normally of either of two configurations: (1) a rectangular drop-leaf variety, and (2) a semicircular drop-leaf type. Either of these extensions could be detached and used in other positions in the room. Other tables often constructed during the Chippendale period included sideboard tables, breakfast tables of the Pembroke type, center tables, gaming tables, toilet tables, and tea tables. Strong parallels can be drawn between the structural and ornamental characteristics of chairs for this period and the stylistic identification of tables.

An outstanding variety of table constructed in mahogany during the Chippendale period was the tea table. This met the social custom of the English of inviting friends for tea. While a variety of tables for

FIGURE 12-31 Chippendale, Gothic Manner (c. 1760-1765). Contours of the Gothic arch form the splat. By Courtesy of the Board of Trustees of the Victoria and Albert Museum, London.

this purpose was introduced, the tripod table with a circular top was predominant (Figure 12-32). These pieces were designed with a central carved shaft from which emanated three supports ending in scroll, claw and ball, or padded snake feet. The tops might be hinged to allow tilting or rotating, or feature a pierced gallery, among other possible variations. Rococo, Chinese, and Gothic structural and decorative detail were applied to these pieces.

Storage Pieces

The commode, based on the French rocaille taste, tended to be a highly decorative piece which was very fashionable in 18th century England. Designed in this taste, these pieces were often used in drawing rooms; in fact, these rooms were not considered appropriately appointed without the inclusion of the commode (Figure 12-33). Characteristic ornamental devices could include some of the following: carving, veneering, ormolu mounts, and lacquering. The commodes were constructed with drawers, a combination of drawers and doors, or drawers enclosed by doors.

FIGURE 12-32   Chippendale Tea Table, Rococo Manner (c. 1760). Carved mahogany. Tripod stand. By Courtesy of the Board of Trustees of the Victoria and Albert Museum.

Beds

Beds of the tester type were no longer heavily draped, as had been typical of the styles of William and Mary and Queen Anne. Emphasis was given to carved posts; around 1750 the cabriole was replaced with a plinth of square section (Figure 12-34). A pagoda-shaped tester was often employed for beds designed in the Chinese manner; consistent with this was the fret arrangement of the headboard. Japanning and gilding as well as carving were decorative techniques. Beds in the Rococo style were also fashionable.

ORNAMENT

Ornamental detail during the Early Georgian period with its diversity of stylistic approaches can often be generalized among interior architecture, decoration, and furniture design. However, at some points there were dichotomous approaches. For example, during the Queen Anne period furniture was simple and ornamented with a limited repertoire of motifs; this style overlapped the Georgian Baroque interior, with its emphasis on movement, high relief, symmetry, and great interest in classicism.

During the Palladian period much of the decorative element was derived from classical sources including carved and gilded friezes of *rinceaux* (scrolled acanthus stems and leaves) in the Roman taste, stems and scrolling leaves of acanthus, mask-centered drapery

FIGURE 12-33 Chippendale English Commode, Style of Thomas Rococo Manner (c. 1755). Veneered with some carving. Philadelphia Museum of Art: Purchased: The McIlhenny Fund.

FIGURE 12-34 Chippendale Tester Bed, Chinese Manner (c. 1750-1755). Japanned. By Courtesy of the Board of Trustees of the Victoria and Albert Museum.

swags and friezes with Vitruvian scrolls. Particularly characteristic of William Kent was the use of such motifs as sphinxes, putti, flowers and fruit in swag form, lion masks, human masks, pendant shells, single or double shells, all accomplished in a heavy Baroque manner. Heavy scroll supports, wave ornaments, scale patterns, and money patterns on stretches and uprights of chair backs were widely used motifs. His architects' furniture for wealthy patrons was fabricated with strong reliance of classical architectural elements and the design of pieces for specific rooms, specific places, and stationary positions. Simpler pieces of furniture were designed for the modest residences for which architects' furniture would have been inappropriate. Georgian furniture tended toward heaviness and prevalent motifs included the cabochon and leaf, ribbon, honeysuckle, shell, acanthus pendant, rosette, husk, lion mask, satyr mask, dolphin (sometimes scaled), eagle's head, lion's paw, and carved grotesque.

An ornamental and nonarchitectural approach characterized the Rococo period for both interiors and furniture design; its repertoire of motifs derived from French rocaille, Chinese, and Oriental tastes. From the Rococo, designs were executed in a delicate linear mode including C- and S-shaped scrolls, fantastic scrolls and curves, floral motifs, cascades of water, masks, birds, and winged dragons. When designs were based on those of Thomas Johnson, Rococo ornamentation was bolder and more spirited compared to the more loosely conceived and relaxed treatment of the earlier Rococo. Based on the influence of the Orient were pagoda shapes, lattices, Oriental birds, Oriental figures, etc. The Gothic influence, based on an interest in the medieval period, was first introduced as an architectural style. However, architectural details were used decoratively both for interior architectural elements and for furniture embellishment such as the lancet arch, ogival arch, overlapping arches, the crocket, pinnacle, quatrefoil, and fret.

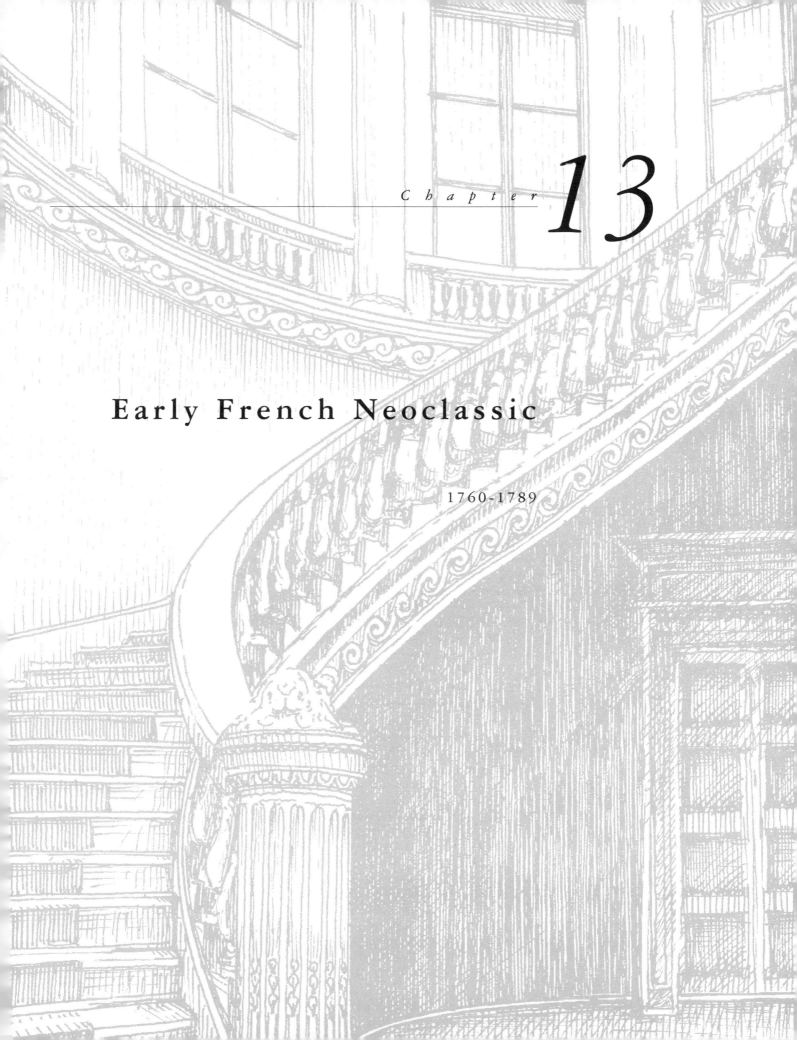

Chapter 13

Early French Neoclassic

1760–1789

HISTORICAL SETTING

A number of factors were responsible for the movement toward the neoclassical style that began during the reign of Louis XV in the 1740s, before the Rococo movement had run its course. The motivation for change grew from opposition to the Rococo, which was criticized for its excesses, asymmetry, and perceived disorderliness. Events, personalities, publications, and theories all led to the focus on classicism: (1) traditionalists (such as Blondel and Gabriel) who looked to the classicism of the 17th century as their source of inspiration; (2) students who studied in Rome, having received the Prix de Rome award from the Academy of Architecture; (3) excavations of the ancient cities of Herculaneum and Pompeii; (4) the interest in classic purism of Madame de Pompadour, who exercised influence both through her personal design decisions and through the power she exerted over political appointments affecting the direction of the arts; (5) architects (such as Soufflot and Piranesi) who looked to the revival of classical antiquity based on archaeological knowledge; (6) a moral basis that permeated the 18th century Age of Enlightenment; (7) publications undergirding the reliance on Roman and Greek antiquity; and (8) Palladianism. In addition, the Seven Years War (1756-1763), with its impact on the economy, determined the amount of building activity and the zenith of neoclassicism of the Louis XVI style in architecture and design.

To begin with, on the one hand, the classical traditionalists looked longingly to the arts of the Grand Siècle (17th century) as their source of inspiration and, on the other hand, the antiquarians sought to rely on the firsthand knowledge of the ancients through the study of archaeological remains. Jacques François Blondel (1705-1774), a traditionalist, was a great admirer of François Mansart (a leader in 17th century French classicism in architecture) and other masters of that century; as a professor he focused students on great designs of the past, especially those of Mansart. He was influential in education through his position as director of the Ecole des Arts; one of his aims was to address the deficiencies of arts education by increasing the number of subjects available to students. He later became a professor at the Academy of Architecture. In four volumes of *Architecture françoise* (1752-1756) Blondel demonstrated an inclination to classicism in his descriptions of the architecture of Paris. However, antique forms based on Greco-Roman and English Palladianism were foreign to him. As a theorist, he placed great emphasis on proportion, the orders, and the principles of convenance and bienséance. To him convenance was the principle that governed the relationship between architecture and social requirements; thus the rank of the owner of a building was to be reflected in its decoration. Due to his influence and that of Gabriel, the architecture of the 1750s and 1760s was based primarily on 17th-century antecedents.

Jacques Ange Gabriel (1698-1782), as a leader in the neoclassical movement, represented the French tradition since he was descended from a long line of architects and received his training under his father. He did not travel to Italy; therefore, he was thoroughly ingrained with the French architectural heritage. As a conservative Gabriel was fully committed to the French classicism of François Mansart; however, by mid-century he had moved away from the major influence of the Mansart school. Gabriel designed the Petit Trianon for Louis XV, who commissioned it as a private residence for his mistress, Madame de Pompadour. Although totally French in composition, it does show some influence of English Palladianism.

Rome became a center for many architects who were interested in the revival of antiquity. The impact of classical antiquity on France originated in the 1740s from the fact that the young Prix de Rome winners from the Academy of Architecture in Paris began to study (on a three-year scholarship) at the Académie de France (French Academy) in Rome. Here these student architects could study firsthand extant remains of Roman antiquity, view monuments of the Renaissance, visit the sites of excavations of the classical cities, and interact with architects from other countries who were profoundly influential in the neoclassical movement of the second half of the 18th century.

A fundamental change to classical purism advocated by Madame de Pompadour, the highly influential mistress of King Louis XV, was significant in the revival of interest in antiquity. First, through her influence, she secured a commitment that her brother, Abel Poisson (1727-1781), would become director general of the Bâtiments du Roi (Minister of Arts). Having ensured this position, Pompadour sent her brother to Italy to study, during which time he toured northern Italy, Rome, and Naples for two years. Thus his years of focus on classical antiquity between 1749 and 1751 were pivotal; he was accompanied by Abbé Leblanc and Jacques Germain Soufflot, whose responsibility it was to advise on the purchases of works of art. Upon Poisson's return in 1751 he was given the post of Minister of Arts and later received the title of Marquis de Marigny in 1754. Later Marigny became an advocate for Greek revival, *goût grec*.[1]

Jacques Germain Soufflot (1714-1780), although he was active during the Rococo movement, was a major exponent of design based on antiquity. He was not bound by the traditional point of view espoused by Blondel and Gabriel. Soufflot studied Roman antiquities on his travels in Italy; his approach was to base his designs on individual investigation of antiquity and, in particular, on recent excavations.

Giovanni Battista Piranesi (1720-1778), an Italian engraver and architect, went to Rome in the 1740s. He was influenced by artists who depicted ancient Roman monuments in imaginary settings and in ruin scenes. There were far-reaching implications of his knowledge of the excavations of Herculaneum, which had begun in 1738. Among the several books of engravings for which he was responsible were *Carceri* (c. 1745) and *Le Antichità Romane* (1756). The purpose of the former was to show the application of archaeology to contemporary design while that of the latter was to show construction features along with plans and sections. It was his belief that archaeological ruins could inspire creativity. As a print dealer by 1745 he resided in Rome across from the French Academy and through his contacts with persons of many nationalities (for example, the English architects Robert Adam and Sir William Chambers) he proved a motivating force in the 18th-century neoclassical movement. Neoclassicism and the reliance on antiquity became an international movement in the 1750s.

Although there had been antique revivals before in the history of design, the moral intent of 18th century neoclassicism emphasized plain living, giving attention to open-air and rural pursuits. The result was simplicity in architectural form, the introduction of rustic objects, and stress on informal gardening. With regard to the latter an important spokesman was Jean Jacques Rousseau (1712-1778), French philosopher and political theorist, who espoused concern for the unspoiled beauty of nature. Emanating from this was the attention given to the irregularity of Chinese art as well as investigations into other cultures. The concept developed that buildings should be designed in terms of their landscape setting; thus, informal arrangements were deemed appropriate for both domestic buildings and their natural setting. France was influenced by England in this picturesque movement, which focused on the aesthetic experience through an intense interest in pictorial effects of both architecture and garden. Architecture, in effect, was thought of in terms of how it could be integrated with its environment. Prompting cognizance of this approach were publications with illustrations showing buildings of historic interest in either natural or landscape settings.

A conflict arose concerning the merits of Roman versus Greek influences on design. Piranesi represented the pro-Roman group. Books of engravings were available to give information on ancient Roman and Greek monuments. Piranesi and the Englishman Robert Wood presented the pro-Roman side with publications in the 1750s.[2] Impetus for the pro-Greek approach was provided in France by David le Roy, in England by James Stuart and Nicholas Revett.[3] Above all was the major influence of Johann Joachim Winckelmann (1717-1768), a German classical archaeologist and historian of ancient art

---

1. Wend von Kalnein, *Architecture in France in the Eighteenth Century,* trans. David Britt (New Haven: Yale University Press, 1995), 131.

2. *Le Antichità Romane* (1756) by Giovanni Battista Piranisi; *The Ruins of Palmyra* (1753) and *The Ruins of Balbec* (1757) by Robert Wood.

3. *Les Ruines des plus beaux monuments de la Grèce* (1758) by David le Roy; *Antiquities of Athens* (1762) by James Stuart and Nicholas Revett.

who settled in Rome in 1755. Winckelman's *History of Ancient Art* (1764) presented an idealized version of Greek art and architecture, for he had never experienced these arts firsthand; rather, he based his judgments on his esteem for artists of the High Renaissance, such as Raphael. For the remainder of his life Winckelmann was involved in research in southern Italy and study at the Vatican Library.

Another stimulus to the archaeological approach was the publication in 1765 of *Oeuvres d'architecture* by Marie-Joséph Peyre, which gave a tremendous boost to the neoclassical movement. Peyre had been a winner of the Prix de Rome and went to the Academy in Rome in 1753; he became one of the most distinguished architects of the second half of the 18th century. On his return to Paris the design innovations he introduced were to become standard residential features. From Roman antiquity he derived the colonnade, the emphasis on symmetry, and circular rooms (borrowed from Roman baths). Earlier in the century it had become customary for the vestibule and staircase to form separate entities, but the contribution of Peyre was to incorporate the two, often with a spatially exciting circular stair lit by a coffered dome.

Building activity was at a virtual standstill during the Seven Years War, a worldwide conflict. France lost its American colonial possessions to Britain and the impact on the economy was devastating. The end of the war coincided with the most consequential thrust by architects and publications for the archaeological approach that launched the neoclassicism phase of the Louis XVI style in 1760s architecture and design.

SPATIAL RELATIONSHIPS

Subject to criticism in the 18th century were not only the decorative excesses of previous styles but also the ritualistic spatial arrangements of the Baroque and Rococo periods in which the appartement de parade was fashionable. Formality had been the focus; it received less emphasis during the height of the Rococo period. Now, however, subtlety and constraint were keynotes.

Although some generalizations can be made about the spatial treatments of the Louis XVI period, there is not one plan type that pervades the period. Rather, the client was the key to interior organization as each worked with the leading architects of the period. Generally, plans were less complicated and the use of circular spaces was increased, reflecting the influence of the Roman baths of antiquity. The relationship of the interior to the landscape or countryside beyond was also emphasized by architects. To show the variety that characterized the period the works of some of its leading architects will be commented on in the following.

The Petit Trianon at Versailles, commissioned by the king, may be taken as an example of this trend (Figure 13-1). The Trianon was to be a residence where the king and Madame de Pompadour could have privacy and enjoy a natural setting and farm life. Designed by Ange-Jacques Gabriel, it was constructed from 1761 to 1764. The residence was designed in three stories and the architect dealt with the different levels in relation to the gardens. From the principal floor on the west, external stairs allowed access to the king's garden. The position of the dining room provided a straightforward view of the garden on the west. Spaces were square or rectangular. The original plans provided unusual conveniences such as a mechanical table that could be set in the basement and elevated to the dining room above; the purpose was to allow greater privacy without interference from servants, but the table was never constructed.

When Louis XVI came to the throne in 1774 his Queen, Marie Antoinette, began to alter the landscape at the Petit Trianon to the style of an English garden with the assistance of Antoine Richard (a gardener) and Richard Mique (an architect). Part of the transformation included the construction of a model village (hamlet or small village) designed by Mique. The implication of this was to stimulate interest in informal landscape based on the inclusion of such features as the rustic farm and dairy, irregular lakes, undulating lawns, and grottoes. The major thrust advocated by Rousseau was exemplified here by the emphasis on simplicity and the return to nature.

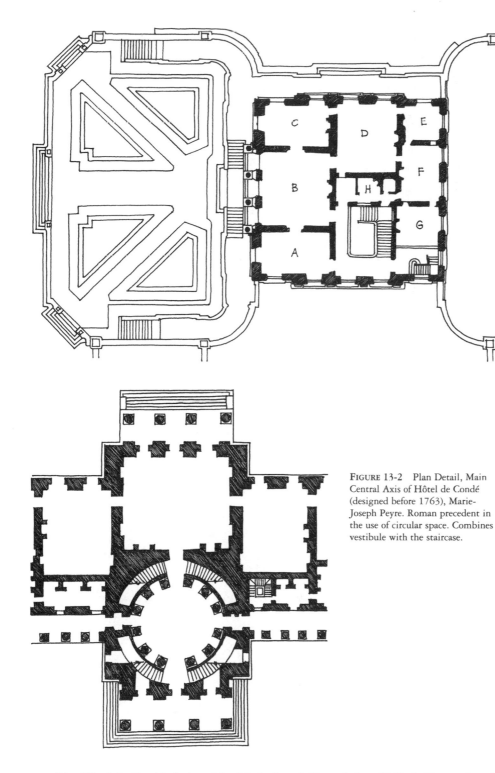

FIGURE 13-1 Petit Trianon (1761-1764),Versailles. Plan, Principal Floor, Ange-Jacques Gabriel. A Ante room, B Dining Room, C Small Salon, D Salon, E Boudoir, F Bedroom, G Dressing Room, H Bathroom.

FIGURE 13-2 Plan Detail, Main Central Axis of Hôtel de Condé (designed before 1763), Marie-Joseph Peyre. Roman precedent in the use of circular space. Combines vestibule with the staircase.

The Hôtel de Condé, designed by Marie-Joseph Peyre before 1763, is illustrative of the influence of a traditional Parisian house type in which the main residential structure surrounded the court on three sides and, as in this case, a columned screen was used to connect the wings and to separate the court from the street. Roman precedent was in the use of the circular space (here in the vestibule) and in the application of a columnar screen. As illustrated on this detail of the main axis of the Hôtel de Condé, Peyre was innovative in uniting the vestibule and staircase, a practice which had not been followed since the early 17th century; to the French the staircase had been a *chef d'oeuvre,* not merely a functional necessity (Figure 13-2). Therefore, the earlier spatial arrangement, which had been devot-

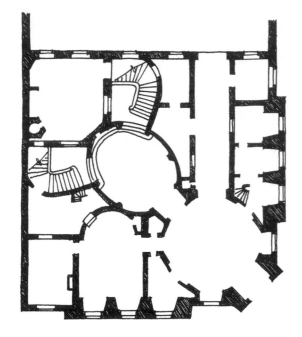

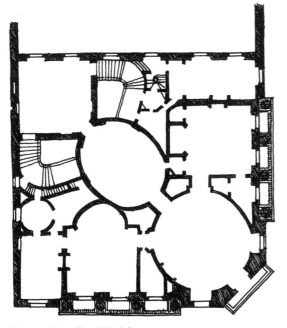

FIGURE 13-3   Plan, Hôtel de Montmorency, Paris (designed 1769), Claude-Nicolas Ledoux. Creative planning in the use of diagonal axial arrangement.

ed to the stairway in a separate room, was important in terms of pretension as well as necessary amenity. The Romans used straight flights of stairs, so there was no classical precedent for the use of a circular grand staircase.

A major contributor to the design of domestic architecture after the mid-18th century was Claude-Nicolas Ledoux (1736-1806). Not only was he innovative in spatial treatment but his plans show great diversity. His knowledge of antiquity and Italian architecture probably came from printed sources, since there is no evidence that he toured Italy. He did, however, visit England, where he became familiar with English Palladianism; drawing from it, he included in his work such elements as plain columns, light-dark contrasts, and limited decorative detail. For the Hôtel de Montmorency, designed in 1769, Ledoux dealt with a corner lot for each side of which he designed identical facades (Figure 13-3). The circular entrance at the corner provided access for the carriage, which could then progress underneath the house by way of a long narrow corridor to the court beyond. The diagonal axial arrangement of interior spaces on the ground level originated with the oval vestibule leading to the space beyond; from here identical staircases rose to the first floor. A reverse diagonal axial sequence began with the antechamber, continued through the oval antechamber, and terminated with the circular salon. The reception rooms were parallel to the street.

Ledoux designed the pavilion for the Château of Louveciennes, which was completed by 1771; his client was Madame du Barry, the new royal mistress (Figure 13-4). The pavilion was constructed for entertainment purposes, not as a residential unit. Characterized by diverse room shapes and density of planning, the visitor entered into the transverse oval dining room *(salle à manger),* beyond which was a square Salon du Roi bounded on the left by a round space and on the right by an apsidal space. The position of the pavilion was designed to emphasize the view from the salon to the countryside beyond the Seine and from the sides to the gardens.

Light-filled three-dimensional spatial treatment often centered around the stairway. For example, the stairchamber sometimes extended to the height of the building and was crowned by a coffered dome from which light penetrated the interior. The stairwell was frequently circular in the 1770s and 1780s; consequently, the staircase itself was often semicircular. For the Palais Royal (1766-1768) architect Pierre Cotant d'Ivry attained an imposing spatial impact by using double flights of oval stairs that converge at the balcony level; the dome above allowed light to penetrate the interior. Further, by using trompe l'oeil painting at the balcony level the spatial extension was magnified (Figure 13-5). Ledoux used the dome to advantage in his spatial treatments for the stairwell at the Château of Bénouville and in addition, at the Hôtel de Montmorency he extended the first floor oval antechamber to two stories in height and topped it with a gallery and dome. Within the plan the staircases were often placed centrally.

INTERIOR ARCHITECTURE AND DECORATION

Materials and Decorative Techniques

Materials and techniques remained essentially the same as those of the Louis XV period. Wood, paint, metal, plaster, marble, and other stones were important in the articulation of

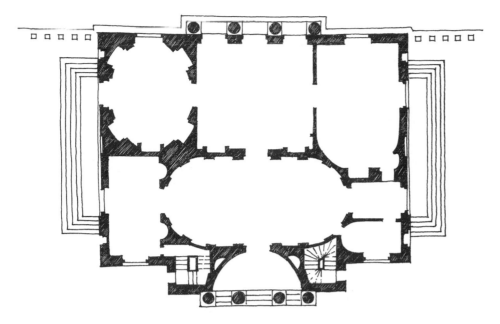

FIGURE 13-4 Plan, Pavilion, Château of Louveciennes (completed by 1771), Claude-Nicolas Ledoux. Variety in room shapes: oval, square, apsed end.

FIGURE 13-5 Staircase, Palais Royal (1766-1768), Paris, Pierre Contant d'Ivry. Spatial extension through double flights of stairs, trompe l'oeil painting at balcony level, dome allowing light-filled space. Based on a photograph. Kalnein, Wend von, *Architecture in France in the Eighteenth Century,* Yale University Press Pelican History of Art: 1995.

the neoclassical interiors of the Louis XVI period. Carved moldings in classical profile were executed in wood or plaster; painted designs were rendered on wood or canvas; metal ornament was applied, for example, to the flutings of columns; the designs of panel fields were sometimes executed in paint or carried out in bas-relief.

Interior Architecture and Decorative Elements, 1755-1775

Generally, the period from 1730 to 1790 can be divided into segments of 20 years. Initially there were only minor introductions of classical detail. In this early period there was reaction to the excesses of the Louis XV style, but it continued to predominate until around 1750. This was followed by the support in court circles for classical antiquity; however, during the period of transition characteristics of both styles were used in combination. For example, in the interior by Contant d'Ivry for the Palais Royal, Paris, Rococo elements were restricted to details such as the chimneypiece, candelabra, and the use of the palm stem to frame mirrors; rectilinearity predominated and the walls were architecturally articulated by the use of pilasters with Corinthian capitals. The tendency on the part of traditionalists, such as Gabriel to look to the period of Louis XIV as their source of inspiration was also transitional. Although the design derivation is evident, the execution was more disciplined. Such features as the ponderous swags and deeply ornamented cornices reappeared. Differences occurred in the more accurate treatment of the orders and the even distribution of emphasis coupled with typical Louis XVI motifs. The triumph of the fully developed Louis XVI style was apparent around 1770.

Floors

Parquet floors of different woods were most common; marble was used in large and formal rooms, primarily in palaces. Other materials included faience, limestone, and terracotta. In addition, large Oriental rugs were utilized as well as those from the French factories of Aubusson and Savonnerie.

Walls

The mature style of Louis XVI was characterized by a return to classical architectural features, where symmetry and rectilinear treatments were emphasized. When circles and ellipses were used they were disposed within a rectangular environment and ornament was usually confined within its geometrically shaped frame. Consistent with the sources of influence, moldings for panels were classical in profile. Rococo characteristics that continued in use included continuous paneling, vertical emphasis, low relief, and delicacy of treatment.

Horizontally, the walls were divided by a low dado above which the main field was treated with overall vertical emphasis; the transition to the ceiling consisted of a classic cornice or entablature. Vertically and within the main field above the dado the wall was articulated in a number of ways: (1) a system of vertical panels of varied width (wide bounded by narrow panels); (2) pilasters arranged singly or in pairs, sometimes separated by panels decorated with arabesques; (3) classical orders framing doors, chimneypieces, and windows; (4) paired engaged columns employed in the same manner as pilasters; (5) niches containing classical sculptural figures.

Panels were of wood or plaster with moldings of wood or plaster in classical profile. The width of panels below the dado duplicated those placed above. A variation in the outline of rectangular panels was used at the corners by a reentrant angle or a concave rounding; the space outside was often filled with a rosette. Rectilinearity predominated; however, panel headings were occasionally arched. The system of vertical rectangular panels was sometimes altered for rooms that were particularly tall (Figure 13-6). In these instances a narrow row of horizontal panels was sometimes inserted, either above the dado or in place of the dado rail. In the system of wide and narrow vertical panels, the narrow horizontal panels were sometimes placed above the wider vertical panel near the ceiling while the narrow vertical panels extended to the ceiling. Moldings were frequently of classical profile, either plain or carved with classical motifs (such as the honeysuckle); they were in low relief and often painted in contrast to the field. Ornamentation for the panel field consisted of painted or relief designs; sculptural decoration tended to replace pictorial representations. Painted designs (such as landscapes and arabesques) were executed on wood or canvas. Decorations in relief were either carved or accomplished in stucco. Other treatments consisted of stretched materials including textiles, paper, and tapestries. Extravagant measures were taken by designers to attain symmetry including the use of concealed and false doors and the duplication of treatments on opposite walls.

Occasional use was made of full height panels uninterrupted by a dado rail. Precedent for this was set by Etienne-Louis Boullée (1728-1799) and Claude-Nicolas Ledoux, two neoclassical architects known for their inventiveness, originality, and imaginativeness. At the Hôtel de Monville (1764) Boullée focused his attention on architectural embellishment in which exquisite intricately carved pilasters bounded full-height decorative panels; these were surmounted by a deep classic entablature. In a contrasting manner Ledoux used a different design syntax for the full-height panels of the salon in the Hôtel d'Uzès (1764-1767) (see Figure C-25). Ornamental detail of these are reminiscent of the Rococo of the early 18th century, but with greater discipline in execution. The composition featured a succession of trees that appeared to be implanted in the floor; trophies of war were depicted on the limbs. The design was set within a rectangular frame in a total arrangement of other panels typical of the Louis XVI period.

Windows and Doors

Casement windows that extended to the dado or to the floor were common. Headings were either arched or rectangular. If rounded, they were typically disposed within a rectangular frame; the same disposition was typical of arched panels and mirrors (see Figure 13-6). Window trim was low in projection. They were sometimes bounded by pilasters. Usually set in deep recesses, the shutters often matched the paneling of the room when they were folded within this embrasure. Panes of glass were made larger as the 18th century progressed.

FIGURE 13-6   Salon, Hôtel d'Uzès (1764-1767), Designed by Charles-Nicolas Ledoux and sculpted by Joseph Métivier. Salon in the Musée Carnavalet, Paris. Full-height panels featuring a succession of trees with trophies of war. Musée Carnavalet. © Photothèque des Musées de la Ville de Paris, Giraudon, Paris.

Door openings had either rectangular or arched heads. Plain architrave moldings framed the door openings; otherwise, the moldings were carved with motifs of classical origin such as pearls and rais de coeur. As with windows, doors were sometimes framed by pilasters or engaged columns. Overdoor treatments included the use of a bracketed cornice, a plain or carved frieze, or an entablature. Above this a panel was usually incorporated in the total door composition; the panel ornamentation was left plain or could include such treatments as grisaille painting, carved detail, tapestry, and medallions sometimes supported with figures and set within a rectangular frame. Door paneling was usually consistent with the wall paneling (see Figures C-24 and C-25).

Chimneypieces

Materials for the fireplace included wood, limestone, and marble in a variety of colors. Characteristically low and small, mantel shelves were typically comprised of an entablature for which a variety of supports were employed: caryatids, terms, engaged columns, pilasters, scrolled consoles, brackets, etc. Bronze ornamental detail was often used to decorate the frieze under the mantel shelf. The chimneybreast sometimes projected, but it was also constructed at the same level of the wall paneling. Mirrors were commonly used in the overmantel with frames that coordinated with the tops of other mirrors and overdoor treatments in the room (see Figure 13-6). Arched headings for the mirror were invariably set within a rectangular frame; spandrel decoration was typical. Rectangular headings were also employed. Like windows and doors, the chimneypiece was at times emphasized by the use of classical orders on each side.

Ceilings

Forming the boundary between the wall and ceiling was an unbroken horizontal line comprised of a cornice or entablature. The most elaborate entablature could include a decorated frieze with a dentiled or bracketed cornice; rooms with taller ceilings were more likely to have this degree of elaboration. On the other hand, plain entablatures were also used (see Figure 13-6). A cornice alone might be treated very simply or dentiled. While a coved transition was occasionally used, this was not as common as in previous periods. Plain, flat ceilings were common; painted ceilings sometimes simulated sky and clouds. Occasionally the ceiling was treated with a central medallion. Domed ceilings were used to surmount stairwells and sometimes other spaces as well.

Stairways

Beginning in the 1770s circular spaces for stairways were frequently employed, with the consequent shaping of the staircase to conform to the shape of the stairchamber. However, rectilinearity and straight flights of stairs continued to be used. Often combined with the vestibule instead of being placed in a separate room, the stairs were often set on the central axis. Balustrade design related to the orientation of the architect and the time period of its construction. For example, in the oval stairwell of the Palais Royal, the wrought-iron balustrade contained elements of the rococo in the use of some free curve but also elements typical of the neoclassical in the regularity of the repetitive circular units as the major decorative unit (see Figure 13-5). In other installations architecturally shaped vase forms in wrought iron were also employed. For example, at the Hôtel de Gallifet the circular flight of stairs is boldly conceived in an architectural manner (Figure 13-7). The newel post is the emphatic introduction to the stairs; this column-like newel is stop fluted and headed by a band carved with the classic egg and dart motif, the whole being surmounted by acanthus leaves. The use of the baluster as an architectural element originated in the Renaissance; the Romans did not use the baluster. Composed of a single bulb, the balustrade the architect used here is in a massive form and closely spaced; a wide handrail unites the balusters. The classic Vitruvian scroll is carved on the closed string staircase and on the frieze.

FIGURE 13-7
Staircase, Hôtel de
Gallifet, Paris
(designed c. 1775),
Etienne-François
Legrand. Typical of the
1770s and 1780s in the
use of the semicircular
staircases.

FURNITURE

Materials and Construction Techniques

Among the woods employed in furniture of the Louis XVI style were mahogany, king-wood, ebony, satinwood, purplewood, and tulipwood. For the polychrome effects of mar-quetry other exotic woods and materials were significant. Mahogany received new atten-tion because it could be used in large sheets of veneer. These often capitalized on the mot-tled patterns attained from cutting the veneer from parts of the tree where the branches or roots joined the trunk. In addition, solid mahogany was used for the first time. Mahogany used as both veneer and solid wood had the result of blurring the distinction between ébénistes and menuisiers.

Ornamental techniques that relied on polychrome results were veneer processes, inserts of porcelain plaques, japanned tin inlays, verre églomisé, Vernis Martin, and pietra dure. Veneer using both parquetry (geometric designs) and marquetry (representational designs with an emphasis on floral motifs) relied on woods of an infinite variety of differ-ent colors. Natural colors could also be altered by staining, scorching, etc. Japanned tin was usually decorated with flowers and inset into the tops of tables. Sèvres porcelain plaques decorated with such motifs as bouquets, symbols of rustic life, and garlands of flowers were popular for furniture panels; these were sometimes curved to conform to the friezes of round tables. The *verre églomisé* technique involved painting on the reverse side of glass and then applying gold or silver as a backing. Invented by the Martin brothers in the period of Louis XV, Vernis Martin was a lacquer technique using various colors; green was especial-ly prominent. Furniture featuring this technique was coordinated with the paneling against which it was placed. Polychrome effects were occasionally attained by the use of

Coromandel lacquer screens, which were sometimes mounted on doors; in the 17th century and later this lacquer technique was characterized by designs incised into the surface. The introduction of an Italian 17th-century technique, *pietra dure,* involved a mosaic of stones laminated to the surface of furniture.

Highly significant in the decorative processes was the use of metal: steel, brass, wrought iron, and bronze. Structurally, wrought iron was sometimes used for table legs, which reflected the archaeological finds from the excavations of Herculaneum and Pompeii. Otherwise, metal was used for decorative enrichment. Examples include strips of metal outlining panels, pierced galleries surrounding or partially surrounding the tops of desks and shelves, escutcheon plates, rectangular or ring drop handles, and inlays in flutes of legs. The friezes of pieces were often ornamented with metal; both Greek and Roman antiquity was the source of inspiration for the decorative motifs. An innovation introduced by the ciseleur Pierre Gouthière was the combination of a matte and lustrous finish for metal mounts.

Typical Pieces and Stylistic Features

Seat Furniture

Contrary to the fluidity of form associated with the style of Louis XV furniture, the Louis XVI style is characterized by well-defined joints. Typically the wood frame, carved in low-relief classical patterns, was exposed all around the upholstered sections, the seat as well as the back (Figure 13-8). Finishes included natural, gilt, and painted and parcel-gilt. Backs did not usually attach to the seat rail and the contours were often cabriolet. A variety of shapes for the backs was employed including medallion, trapezoid, rectangle, and rectangle with a flattened arched cresting; finials were sometimes used (Figures 13-9, 13-10, and 13-11). Late in the period chair backs were sometimes supported by columns, as the medallion back. Square, circle, and trapezoid were common shapes for seats; the front seat rail was frequently bowed, ending with the flat, framed rosette. Armrests were usually in one of two configurations: (1) horizontal in position, or (2) joining the back with a down-sweeping curve, becoming level, and extending approximately two thirds the length of the side seat rail. Customarily, upholstered manchettes were utilized (see Figure 13-11). The terminus of the armrest was frequently a whorl that extended slightly beyond the arm

FIGURE 13-8 Fauteuil Detail (early 1780s), Jean-Baptiste Sené. Spirally fluted quiver leg, foliated scroll supporting the shield back, guilloche carved on curved side rail, framed rosette heading the legs, arm support originating above the leg and sweeping back in a curve.

FIGURE 13-9 Fauteuil. Medallion backs. Left: carved birch, guilloche carved serpentine seat rail, cresting with carved ribbons bow with floral sprays, Beauvais tapestry upholstery. Right: by J. B. Lelarge (1743-1802), beech with simple carved molding, carved foliage for the supports for the back, yellow satin upholstery (embroidered), stop fluted legs. Reproduced by permission of the Trustees of the Wallace Collection, London.

FIGURE 13-10 Fauteuil en Cabriolet. Trapezoid. By Courtesy of the Board of Trustees of the Victoria and Albert Museum, London.

FIGURE 13-11 Armchair (Fauteuil) Designed by Georges Jacob. Gilded wood. Square back. The Metropolitan Museum of Art, Gift of J. Pierpont Morgan, 1906 (07.225.107).

support. Usually the arm support (typically rectangular in cross section) originated above the leg and swept back in a curve to join the armrest. Alternatively, a vase-shaped support originated from the side seat rail and occasionally a terminal figure positioned above the leg arose vertically above the seat rail. Seat frames, just above the legs, normally contained a square frame in the center of which was a rosette (observed from the front, back, and side). Tapered legs were either round or square in section; these were often enhanced with straight or spiral flutings (sometimes referred to as quiver legs) (see Figure 13-8). Late in the period the back leg was often of sabre form. Types of seat furniture included the fauteuil (armchair), bergère (upholstery-enclosed sides with a loose cushion on an upholstered base), canapé (sofa), chauffeuse (low chair), and marquise (small sofa or large armchair).

Tables

Innumerable variations of tables were available to meet a range of functional needs. Legs of tables were usually round or square in section and tapered; fluting was often employed. Caryatids began to be used toward the end of the period. Pierced metal galleries were often used to partially or completely surround the tops (see work table in Figure C-24). The friezes were often decorated with metal ornaments. Some types of tables were work tables (tricoteuses), for which the pierced gallery served the purpose of holding balls of wool or silk; small tripod tables (athéniennes), sometimes used as a basin stand; tables with one or two shelves to give privacy at meals without the use of servants (tables servantes); candlestands (guéridons), with a round top mounted on a pedestal base; and ladies writing tables (bonheur-du-jour), with a superstructure of shelves or enclosed storage at the back of the writing surface. Many varieties of gaming tables were available.

The bureau plat (writing table) continued to be fashionable in the Louis XVI period. The Wallace Collection example has the following characteristics: lacquered in green and gilt Vernis Martin; spirally fluted legs surmounted by double-tailed siren caryatids; chased and gilt bronzes; top of green morocco leather; and three drawers in the apron, each ornamented with foliated scrolls (Figure 13-12). Sometimes a writing slide was incorporated on the longer side of the table. Tops for small writing tables included leather, velvet, veneered wood, and marquetry.

The fall front desk (secrétaire à abattant) was a particularly important piece in the Louis XVI period and was often architectural in concept. The top normally contained a long drawer in the frieze (Figure 13-13). The central panels of both levels have reentrant angles or scooped corners outside of which rosettes are placed. This feature was also used on wall panels. When a cabinet base was used, doors oftentimes enclosed shelves or drawers. Some fall front desks were mounted on tall legs without benefit of any lower storage (Figure 13-14). This piece has a bow front, the drop front of which is mounted with a large circular

FIGURE 13-12 Bureau Plat by R. Dubois (1737-1799). Vernis Martin lacquer. Top inlaid with tooled and gilt green leather. Chased and gilt mounts of bronze. Spirally turned legs surmounted with double-tailed siren caryatids. Reproduced by permission of the Trustees of the Wallace Collection, London.

FIGURE 13-13 Fall Front Desk (Secrétaire à Abattant). Jean Henri Riesener (1735-1806); Mounts by Pierre Gouthière (1732-1813). Lacquered black and gold panels. Canted corners ornamented with floral pendant arrangement. Trapezoidal panel. Short legs shod with acanthus leaves of gilt bronze. All rights reserved, The Metropolitan Museum of Art, Bequest of William K. Vanderbilt, 1920 (20.155.11).

FIGURE 13-14 Secrétaire à abattant. Possibly by Martin Carlin. Bow front with Sèvres plaques. Pierced gallery of gilt bronze partially surrounds top of Carrara marble. Reproduced by permission of the Trustees of the Wallace Collection, London.

Sèvres porcelain plaque with spandrels of porcelain. Sèvres plaques are also used below, on the drawer. Bronze mounts (chased and gilt) fashioned as swags of drapery are used on the frieze drawer. Pilasters are ornamented with elaborate floral pendants; a lion's head surmounts the pendants at the frieze level. Certain desks were designed to be used while standing *(secrétaires debout)* while others were provided with a mechanical device to raise the writing surface for use while standing *(à la tronchin)*.

Storage Pieces

Commodes were very common in the Louis XVI style and came in many shapes and sizes; in fact, some were as much as nine feet, ten inches. Both two and three levels of principal drawers were fabricated; shallow drawers were incorporated in the frieze, one or three drawers in a row. Rails between the drawers were either exposed or nonexposed. Sometimes drawers were concealed by two doors, three doors, or by sliding doors. The fashion for the breakfront, in which the center section projected forward, was outmoded by around 1780. Legs were short, round in section, and tapering; these resembled a top, often with bronze feet *(sabots)*. The corners were straight, canted, or column-like, with fluting often added; on occasion the corners were treated with caryatids. Structural lines were often ornamented with gilded bronze mounts such as scrolling friezes, bouquets, flower garlands, and pendant arrangements using various motifs (Figure 13-15). A new type was the *demilune commode,* which was semicircular in shape and featured two drawers in the front and a curved door on each side. Corner commodes *(encoignures)* were correlated with the commode.

Beds

The types of beds constructed in the Louis XV style continued to be fashioned in the Louis XVI style. Legs and general contour were those characteristic of the Louis XVI seat furniture (Figure 13-16). Ornament was derived from the repertoire of motifs typical of the period. The most common bed was the *lit à colonnes* (four-poster bed). Headboards were placed against the wall and the contour of the canopies followed that of the particular type

FIGURE 13-16 Bed (Lit), Louis XVI. Attributed to George Jacob, French (1739-1814). Carved and gilded wood, L213.4 cm. Arrows encased in a quiver. Crest of ends in form typical of some chairs. © The Cleveland Museum of Art, 1996, John L Severance, 1954.151.

FIGURE 13-17 Bed (Lit à l'Anglaise). Carved gilt wood. Quiver uprights. Ornament includes guilloche, ribbons, torches, flowers, leaves. Designed to fit in an alcove. By Courtesy of the Board of Trustees of the Victoria and Albert Museum, London.

of bed. Another type of bed was designed to fit in a niche or alcove; typically it had two or three enclosed sides (Figure 13-17).

ORNAMENT

In the transitional phase for the interior, Rococo motifs were often set within rectangular frames; characteristically treated in a light and graceful manner shells, floral motifs, and C-scrolls were often used. These were incorporated with classical elements such as modillioned cornices, medallions, palmette friezes, and urns. When Louis XIV inspiration was desired designers employed such motifs as the female mask as a cresting for mirrors, large-scale trophies, and oval medallions surrounded by garlands.

In the 1760s ornament became subordinate to its architectural surround. Symmetry in arrangement received greater attention and some emphasis was given to vegetable forms. The motifs of Le Brun of the 17th century were also used where panels were decorated with flowers and tendrils.

During the period of dominance of the antique revival the work of Peyre's *Oeuvres d'architecture* was of paramount significance. The following emanated from this source: the introduction of columns on the inside of the building; classical orders to articulate the walls; pilasters in pairs separated by arabesques; modillioned and dentiled cornices; relief panels; sculptural decoration replacing pictorial; and niches containing classical statuary. In 1768 a leading source of influence was the book of engravings by Charles Delafosse (1734-1791), *Nouvelle Iconologie historique.*

Among the repertoire of popular decorative motifs the following were important: flowers, trophies, key patterns, pearl beading, trellis designs, lozenge designs, trailing leaves, acanthus leaves, wreaths, caryatids, imbricated scale-work, tassels, fringes, Vitruvian scrolls (wave patterns), palmettes, laurel wreaths, landscapes, human figures, lion masks and paws, egg and dart, simulated draperies, ribbon streamers, musical instruments, and bundles of arrows bound with ribbons.

FIGURE C-1 Wall Painting, Style I, Tablinum, House of Sallust, Pompeii. Solid walls. Stucco and paint to simulate stone and marble. Pilaster of stucco. Gemeinnützige Stiftlung, Leonard von Mott.

FIGURE C-2 Wall Painting, Style II, Cubiculum, Villa of Mysteries, Pompeii. Three-dimensionality attained through painted perspective rendering. Architectonic representations deny the plane of the wall. Gemeinnützige Stiftung, Leonard von Mott.

FIGURE C-3 Wall Painting, Style III, Red Cubiculum, Boscotrecase, Pompeii. Ornament received precedence over realism in architectural renderings. Emphasis to flat plane of the wall. Illusionistic landscapes in aedicular arrangements. Wall divisions into three zones. Gemeinnützige Stiftung, Leonard von Mott.

FIGURE C-4 Wall Painting, Style IV, Pompeii, A.D. 70. Fictive architecture resumed (space, back lighting, airy renditions). Units of architectural representations relate to Roman theater. Stucco relief and illusionistic painting combined. Gemeinnützige Stiftung, Leonard von Mott.

FIGURE C-5 Villa Barbaro at Maser (1528-1588); Architect, Andrea Palladio; Painter, Paolo Veronese. Trompe l'oeil fresco (1560-1562) representing fictive architectural elements. Stucco cornice. Photo by Signor Paolo Marton, Treviso, Italy.

FIGURE C-6 Francis I Gallery, Château de Fontainebleau. Wainscot on lower wall with heavy molding marking dado level; panels vary in shape and size. High-relief cartouche above. Parquet wood floor in herringbone pattern. © Réunion des Musées Nationaux, Lagiewski.

FIGURE C-7 Buffet (Armoire), c.1580. Attributed to Hughes Sambin. Carved pinewood. Polychrome and gilt panels in lower section. Terms support capitals. Musée du Louvre, Paris. © Réunion des Musées Nationaux.

FIGURE C-9   Great Staircase, Knole, Kent (1605-1608). Open
well (with flights at right angles to each other) emerged in the
first years of the 17th century; balustrade painted in trompe
l'oeil on the outer wall includes newel and leopard symbol of the
family. © National Trust Photographic Library, London.

FIGURE C-10 Great Staircase, Knole, Kent (1605-1608). Seven ages of man and the virtues depicted in grisaille by Paul Isacson. © National Trust Photographic Library/Andreas von Einsiedel.

FIGURE C-11 Jacobean Wainscot Chair (c. 1600). Oak, carved, and inlaid. Crest of back extends beyond stiles with hackets below. Armrests drop in the front. Perimeter stretcher. By Courtesy of the Board of Trustees of the Victoria & Albert Museum, London.

FIGURE C-12 Hôtel Colbert de Villacerf (Mid-17th century). Polychrome grotesques in rectangular panels. Musée Carnavalet. © Lifermann, Photothèque du Musée de la Ville de Paris.

FIGURE C-13 Hall of Mirrors,
Versailles (1678-1686) by Louis Le Vau
and Jules Hardouin Mansart.
Introduction of the use of paired con-
soles in the frieze.
© Réunion des Musées Nationaux.

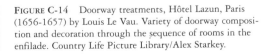

FIGURE C-14 Doorway treatments, Hôtel Lazun, Paris
(1656-1657) by Louis Le Vau. Variety of doorway composition and decoration through the sequence of rooms in the
enfilade. Country Life Picture Library/Alex Starkey.

FIGURE C-15 Queen's Closet, Ham House, London. Original textile hangings. Parquet floor. © National Trust Photographic Library/John Bethell.

FIGURE C-16 Japanned cabinet on stand, Carolean. Carved stand. Chinoiserie applied to background. By Courtesy of the Board of Trustees of the Victoria & Albert Museum, London.

FIGURE C-17 Louis XV commode. Detail of gilt bronze application on splayed side panel (1739). A.R. Gaudreau and J. Caffiéri. Rococo detail: scroll, floral splays, trellis background. Reproduced by permission of the Trustees of the Wallace Collection, London.

FIGURE C-18 Louis XV, Hôtel de Varengeville (c. 1735), Paris (now installed in The Metropolitan Museum of Art, New York). Original paneling commissioned from Nicolas Pineau by Duchess de Villars. Carved, painted and gilded oak.

FIGURE C-19 Louis XV, Balustrade Detail (c. 1725). Originally a staircase leading to the Cabinet des Médailles, Hôtel Mazarin. Forged iron and bronze, chased and gilt. Reproduced by permission of the Trustees of the Wallace Collection, London.

FIGURE C-20 Régence Commode (c. 1730), attributed to Charles Cressent. Bois satiné and amaranth. Symmetrical metal mounts with trellis background. Bombé. Musée du Louvre, Paris. © Réunion des Musées Nationaux/Jean Schon Schormans.

FIGURE C-21 Upper Hall, Moor Park, Hertfordshire, painting probably by F. Sleter. Two-story forty foot cube. Trompe l'oeil sculpture represented in niches. Copyright Anthony Kersting.

FIGURE C-22 Painted parlor, ceiling by William Kent (c. 1740), Rousham, Oxfordshire. Grotesque style. Oil on canvas. Ceiling painting framed by a guilloche of cockle shells. Copyright Anthony Kersting.

FIGURE C-23 Geogian table. (1730). Scagliola slab for tabletop, Florence, 1726; bears the arms of the second Earl of Lichfield. Carved and glit wood. S-scroll legs with head of the eagle. Elaborately carved shell in pendant position of apron. By courtesy of the Board of Trustees of the Victoria & Albert Museum, London.

FIGURE C-24 Grand Salon, Musée Nissim de Camondo. Carved paneling in white and gilt. Insertion of small horizontal panels often used in unusually tall rooms. Savonnerie carpet. Service Photographique, Union Centrale des Arts Décoratifs.

FIGURE C-25
Grand Salon, Hôtel d'Uzès (1764-1767), Charles-Nicolas Ledoux and sculpted by Joseph Métivier. Full height panels featuring a succession of trees with trophies of war. Musée Carnavalet. © Photothèque du Musée de la Ville de Paris.

FIGURE C-26 Anteroom, Syon House, Middlesex, Robert Adam (1761-1765). Early Adam characteristics in the Neoclassical style. Copyright, Anthony Kersting.

FIGURE C-27 Long Gallery, Syon House, Middlesex. Midperiod characteristics of the work of Robert Adam. Decorative and non-architectural in concept. Plasterwork and painting in complex geometric arrangement. Copyright, Anthony Kersting.

FIGURE C-28 'Etruscan' Dressing Room, Osterly House, Middlesex. Late characteristics of Robert Adam illustrating the integration of decorative and architectural elements within a room. Two-dimensional and linear. By courtesy of the Board of Trustees of the Victoria & Albert Museum, London.

FIGURE C-29 Integration of Pier Glass Mirror with Table, Robert Adam (1777), Breakfast Room, Osterly Park House. Table with alabaster top; square section tapering legs; short flutings on apron with paterae carved above each leg. Pier glass mirror with terminal figures dividing the mirror in three parts; vase finials. By Courtesy of the Board of Trustees of the Victoria & Albert Museum, London.

FIGURE C-30　Sideboard table with pedestals, Arrangement Influenced by Robert Adam. Eating Room, Osterly Park House. Sideboard table with Greek fret carved on the frieze with paterae regularly spaced along the surface; rams' heads in the frieze head each of the four legs. Doric sideboard pedestals symmetrically arranged with the table. By Courtesy of the Board of Trustees of the Victoria & Albert Museum, London.

FIGURE C-31　Commode, Osterly Park, Middlesex. Robert Adam (c.1775). Correlation of architectural and decorative elements within the space — commode with door frame and chimneypiece. By Courtesy of the Board of Trustees of the Victoria & Albert Museum, London.

FIGURE C-32   Breakfast Parlor (1812), Sir John Soane.
Innovative lighting through the dome, lantern lights,
and reflections through the use of mirrors. By courtesy of
the Trustees of Sir John Soane Museum, No. 13 Lincoln's
Inn Fields.

FIGURE C-33   Second Empire Hôtel de Païva (1850s). Avenue des
Champs Elysées, Paris. Architect Charles Garnier. Renaissance, Baroque,
and Rococo influences. Giraudon, Paris.

FIGURE C-34
Second Empire
Carved Cabinet
by Henri
Fourdinais. Prize
winner at the
1867 Universal
Exhibition.
Renaissance influ-
ence. Bethnal
Green Museum,
London.

FIGURE C-35 Drawing Room, Carlton Towers, Yorkshire (1873-1877). Plaster simulation of stamped leather highlighted with gold. Copyright Anthony Kersting.

FIGURE C-36 Papier mâché panels in japanned metal. Painted floral decoration and gilt brass mounts. By Courtesy of the Board of Trustees of the Victoria & Albert Museum, London.

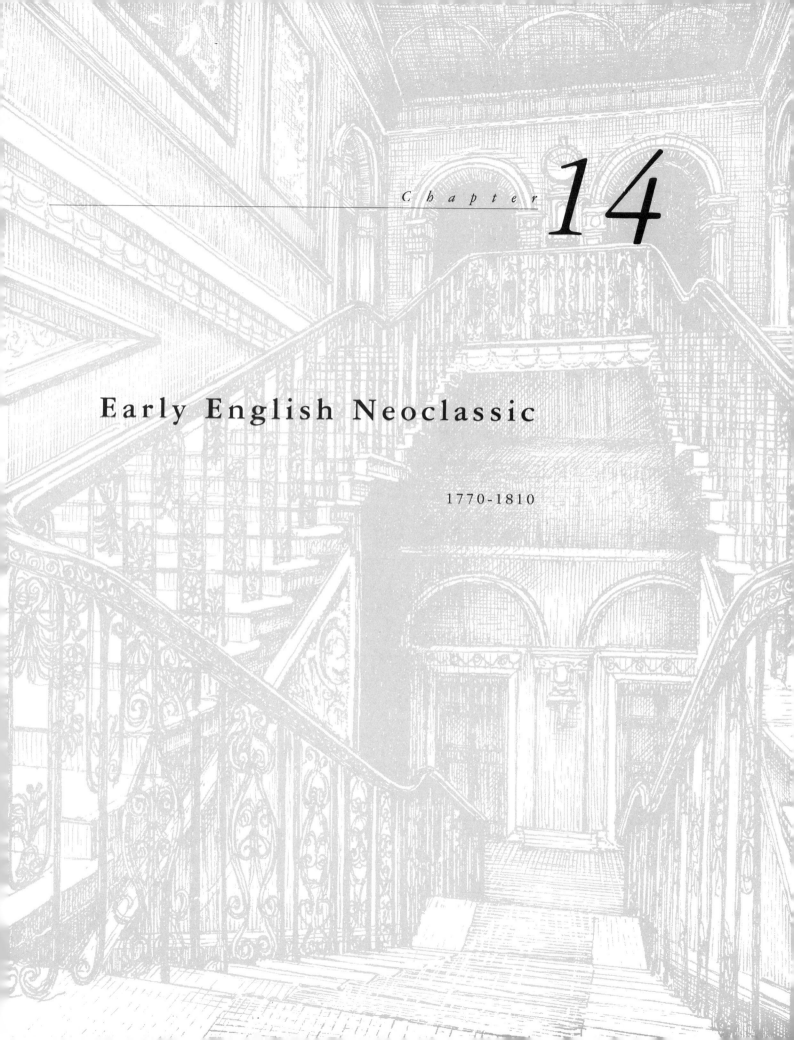

Chapter **14**

Early English Neoclassic

1770-1810

HISTORICAL SETTING

The English neoclassical movement began as a reaction to the excesses of the Baroque and Rococo. Generally, there was the felt need for ordered arrangements, simplicity, and quiet distinction; there came to be a predilection for the linear, the symmetrical, and low relief as opposed to the plasticity typical of the Baroque. The direction and characteristics of the neoclassical movement in England were the result of a number of influences: (1) the Italian Renaissance; (2) the travel and study of persons in Europe who were to be influential architects and designers in England; (3) the study of archaeological excavations; (4) publications; and (5) the beginnings of the industrial revolution and the advent of new materials.

Central to the neoclassical movement in England was Robert Adam (1728-1792), an architect who exhibited his exceptional talent as an imaginative designer. When Adam returned to London from Italy in 1758 conditions were ripe for a change in direction in architecture and design. Design derived from Roman antiquity was not new to the English, who had been introduced to Palladianism through the works of Inigo Jones in the early 17th century. Inigo Jones had studied in Italy with Palladio, the most influential of the Italian Renaissance architects who relied on Roman symmetrical planning and harmonic proportions. Then, in the early 18th century, Colen Campbell, William Kent, and Lord Burlington led the English Palladian revival, which was confined to domestic buildings. Adam's father was a leading Scottish architect whose style was based on the Palladians. With this background Adam was not strongly opposed to the established mode; for example, he sometimes combined neo-Gothic exteriors with classically rendered interiors—a picturesque approach. Contrasted to the previous period, however, his mature style was light, opulent, and elegant.

While Adam was in Rome from 1754 to 1758 he was affiliated with the French Academy at the Villa Medici. He had the opportunity to study the works of Italian Renaissance masters and to travel. For example, he visited the ruins of the combined palace-fortress of the Roman emperor Diocletian. With an architect and two draftsmen he recorded enough information to reconstruct the building; he then published, in 1765, *The Ruins of the Palace of Diocletian at Spalatro.*

One purpose of Adam's sojourn to Rome was to sharpen his drawing skills. Toward this end the French architect and neoclassical draftsman Charles Louis Clérisseau was highly instrumental through his instruction. Among the hundreds of drawings extant from the offices of Adam are examples of antique architecture and decorative detail based on Roman antiquity.

Due to changed perceptions of theorists about antique Roman architecture greater freedom to plan and design was afforded the neoclassical architects. For example, in the Frenchman Abbé Laugier's *Essai sur L'Architecture,* published in England in 1755, not only did the author endorse the use of geometric shapes but also promoted the idea of an innate sense of proportion instead of a set of rules regarding harmonic proportions. The ancients had developed the concept of relating the proportionate system of architecture to music; they correlated musical chords and the proportions thereof to ratios of rooms and entire buildings, the measurements of which would be 1:2, 2:3, or 3:4. The Renaissance architects adopted the idea of these proportions as being the means by which Roman architects achieved their superb architectural successes.

Both Robert and his brother James Adam were obligated to Giovanni Battista Piranesi (1720-1778) for the discriminating analysis he proposed regarding the foundations of classical architecture. Piranesi, a Venetian who settled in Rome around 1745, also endorsed greater freedom and inventiveness in the use of Roman prototypes in evolving of a new architectural style; he was an architect, engineer, engraver, and architectural theorist. As an engraver he produced highly imaginative views of Roman ruins and through these as well as through his *Parere sull'architettura,* published in 1765, he exercised an intense influence on the direction of neoclassical architecture. Piranesi favored Roman over Greek architecture.

Fortified with picturesque drawings and new attitudes about antiquity, designers were not hampered by rules. Adam used the technique of picturesque drawing to replace the 17th and early 18th century practice of providing wooden models of proposed design ideas and solutions to the client; in fact, his commission for Kedleston was secured based on his Roman drawings. While Adam's work can be classed as neoclassical he was eclectic in that he had the capacity to freely combine stylistic elements. The buildings he represented in wash and watercolor, pen, pencil, etc., were set in landscapes that were often more important than the architecture depicted; the mood of the drawing was of greatest significance. Ideas from these imaginative depictions were later utilized in detailed plans for real architecture.

The thrust of prominent publications influenced the direction and style characteristics of the neoclassical movement. The authors of these included Comte de Caylus, illustrations of Herculaneum frescoes in publications from 1752 to 1767; Sir William Hamilton, representations of Greek and Etruscan vases, 1766-67; Robert and James Adam, *The Works in Architecture of Robert and James Adam,* the first volume in 1773, endorsement of movement and spatial modeling; and Sir William Chambers, *Treatise of Civil Architecture* (1759), later entitled *A Treatise on the Decorative Part of Civil Architecture* (1791), illustrations of interior architectural elements such as fireplaces, windows, doors, and ceilings.

Sir William Chambers (1723-1796) was among a group of prestigious competitors of Robert Adam, although his works were not as stylish. His work illustrates another source of influence on the English neoclassical movement. Born in Sweden of Scottish parents, Chambers received his architectural training in Paris under the tutelage of Jacques-François Blondel, who had his own school of architecture. Blondel was a traditionalist who was instrumental in preparing the ground for neoclassicism in France.

Chambers received further training in Italy from 1750 to 1755, after which he began his practice in London. Influential in the direction his architecture took was English Palladianism tempered by the impact of contemporary neoclassical architects with whom he had associated in Paris, including Soufflot. Chambers was critical of Adam's designs, indicating that his interpretations were "toy work."

Both Adam and Chambers were responsible for the alteration of country residences, the decoration of interiors, the restoration of existing buildings, and complete architectural design. The family resources to undertake the work for the country estates in this period were due in some measure to the wealth accrued from the beginnings of the industrial revolution. Prefabricated parts based on machine processes impacted interior design and included such materials as cast iron, cast artificial stone and marble (coade stone), stucco duro, ormolu, papier-mâché, carpets, and wallpaper.[1]

Improvements in agricultural methods in the latter part of the 18th century also increased income, which enabled the construction, updating, and renovation of country estates for the landed classes. The owners took more responsibility in the administration of their farmland, including enclosure, planting, and, in general, supervision of tenants; these practices increased production and income.

SPATIAL RELATIONSHIPS

Spatial characteristics of the early neoclassical period were impacted first by reliance on Roman antiquity and second by contemporary precepts that allowed greater freedom in planning and design. In the first instance, Imperial Roman baths were the basis for the contrasting of room shapes within one residence that characterized plans of the late 18th century. In the latter instance, the theory of harmonic proportions as the key to beauty began to be questioned; it had been developed by the ancients, adopted by Italian Renaissance architects, and expanded by Palladio. Piranesi was among the contemporaries of Adam who questioned the rules that had been espoused; he and others advocated greater latitude and creativeness in the use of Roman antecedents. In addition, in Volume I of *The Works in Architecture of Robert and James Adam* the Adam brothers introduced the concept of movement.

---

1. See prefabricated materials in Christopher Hussey, *English Country Houses, Mid Georgian, 1760-1800* (London: Country Life, 1956), 26-28.

Movement is meant to express, the rise and fall, the advance and recess, with other diversity of form, in different parts of a building, so as to add greatly to the picturesque of the composition. For rising and falling, advancing and receding, with the convexity and concavity, and other forms of the great parts, have the same effect in architecture, that hill and dale, fore-ground and distance, swelling and sinking have in landscape: That is, they serve to produce an agreeable and diversified contour, that groups and contrasts like a picture, and creates a variety of light and shade, which gives spirit, beauty and effect to the composition.[2]

In the architectural works of Adam the qualities of "movement . . . rise and fall . . . advance and recess," were significantly enhanced by the utilization of columnar screens set in front of apses or columns set in front of walls.

Spatial Features of the Floor Plan and Three-Dimensional Spatial Characteristics

Three country houses, each with a neoclassical interior, are discussed in this section to illustrate various aspects of space planning of this period in England. Kedleston, under construction from 1758 to 1768, represents the work of three architects: Matthew Brettingham, James Paine, and Robert Adam; Adam was brought into the project in 1761 and was able to make some alterations on the exterior and in interior space planning. The reconstruction of Syon was undertaken by Adam, who was charged by the Duke of Northumberland to maintain the exterior walls but to execute the interior in the neoclassical style. Beyond the exterior, a stark medieval structure, was a transformed interior, created by Adam using the classically inspired repertoire of design. His phases of design were represented in the interior spaces which ranged from bolder architectural features to more delicate, decorative, and non-architectural characteristics. Doddington, by the architect Samuel Wyatt, was constructed from 1776 to1798; however, it represents the beginning stages of space planning concepts that were to become more prevalent in the early years of the 19th century.

The plan for Kedleston was composed of a square central block flanked by four pavilions joined by quadrant corridors (Figure 14-1). The overall relationship of the pavilions with the central mass was the contribution of Brettingham; only two were finally constructed. Paine adopted the northeast and northwest wings proposed by Brettingham that represent, in exterior style, Burlington's Palladian classicism. And Paine was largely responsible for the plan for the central block. Adam, however, altered the space uses for the rooms on the east, in which the sequence of rooms was devoted to the arts—music, painting, and literature. He also rearranged the rooms of the apartment on the west designated for the most important guests; these rooms included an anteroom, dressing room, state bedroom, and wardrobe. Further, changes by Adam included the alteration of the original round drawing room which projected from the south facade; this was modified by retaining a circular room as a saloon but setting it within the south façade.

The northeast pavilion was constructed as family quarters while the northwest pavilion was devoted to the kitchen. The relationship of the kitchen pavilion to the dining room was functionally effective. The layout of the floorboards in each of the quadrant corridors was related to the status of the occupant in each wing; for example, leading to the family wing the boards conformed to the curve of the passageway while to the kitchen wing they were laid perpendicular to the corridor walls.

As one enters the central block into the hall from the exterior flight of stairs it becomes evident that the axial relationship of this space to the saloon is akin to Roman spatial concepts; in his book *Ruins of Spalatro,* Adam noted the theme of the atrium. The atri-

---

2. Robert Oresko, ed., *The Works in Architecture of Robert and James Adam* (London: Academy Editions, 1975), 46.

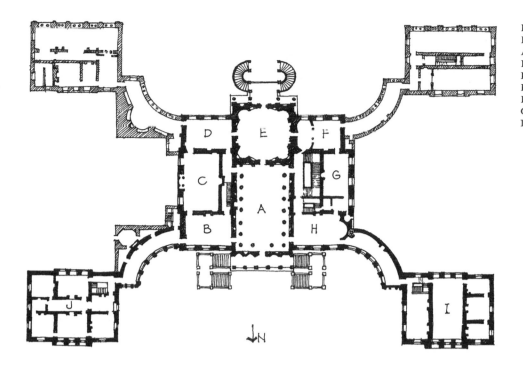

um of the Roman house was characterized by the limited light that came from the compluvium, an opening in the roof that allowed rainwater to enter the impluvium (a basin in the floor to collect it). By analogy, the hall at Kedleston is characterized by low light levels provided in a limited manner by three contiguous oval skylights. Vertical extension of space is enhanced by the fact that these are the source of exterior light.

The monumental rectangular hall is lined with 16 freestanding columns set out from the walls on the east, west, and north; on the south wall were four engaged columns. Depth of spatial treatment and a sense of mystery was attained by the juxtaposition behind the columns of niches containing classical figures, two chimneypieces, and grisaille panels.

The design of the Corinthian capitals was based on columns still standing in the Roman forum. These giant fluted columns of green-veined alabaster were used to articulate space; their repetition directs the movement of the viewer toward the saloon. It is a dramatically charged spatial experience to walk from the hall, with a height of 40 feet, into the salone, with a height of 60 feet. This lofty circular room was achieved through the placement of niches in the corners of a square room, which had been a Pompeian device. The ceiling of this room is a coffered dome in white and gold. Apparently craftsmen in an earlier century had been given a hard time by an earlier baronet, since workmen repainting the ceiling in the 20th century found an inscription above the cornice that read "Lord Scarsdale is a booger."[3] When examining the Pantheon in Rome Adam sketched elements later used at Kedleston such as oculi, coffering, and niches.

Syon, a reconstruction undertaken by Robert Adam, cannot be exceeded in terms of spatial variety (Figure 14-2). In the sequence of state rooms (1) the hall is a basilica type with apsidal ends (one oval and one rectangular) that utilize the Doric order; (2) the anteroom is a rectangle reduced to a square by the arrangement of the columns; (3) the dining room is a triple cube (66 feet long x 21 feet wide x 21 feet high) with apsidal ends, its proportions manipulated through the use of columns and recessions; (4) the drawing room is of simple rectangular shape; and, finally, (5) in the long gallery (136 feet long, 14 feet wide, 14 feet high) the proportions challenged Adam to compositionally divide the wall spaces into repetitive units through the use of closely spaced pilasters centered by such

---

3. Comments of Lord Scarsdale to students of the Attingham School on a tour through Kedleston, Summer, 1983.

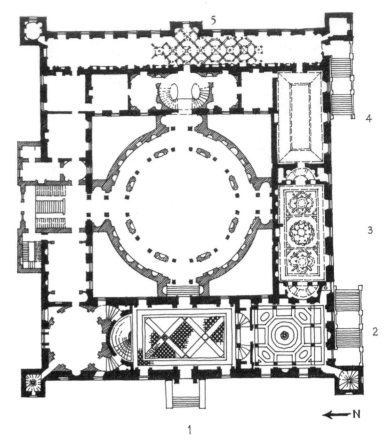

FIGURE 14-2
Quadrangular Plan,
Syon House,
Middlesex. Robert
Adam 1761-c. 1770.
1 Entrance Hall, 2
Anteroom, 3 Dining
Room, 4 Drawing
Room, 5 Long
Gallery. Courtesy of
Country Life Picture
Library.

architectural elements as chimneypieces and doors. This last example demonstrates Adam's ability to integrate a traditional Jacobean space with neoclassicism. Planned but unexecuted, presumably because of prohibitive cost, was the rotunda designed to fill the courtyard of this quadrangular structure. The geometric forms employed in interior architectural planning frequently had their origin in classical prototypes.

Characteristically, Adam related his spatial surfaces through linear relationships as in, for example, the repetition of closely related compositions on the floor and the ceiling. In this manner he created a sense of spatial drama, often with selected archaeological themes. He was intent on utilizing the Roman system of decoration.

Doddington, in Cheshire, represents features of space planning that became more characteristic of the early 19th century (Figure 14-3). Samuel Wyatt (1737-1807) adopted the stylistic feature of using a circular bow with a low dome; here the space is found in the saloon. Typically, variety in the shapes of rooms was a feature of neoclassical interior planning; in this plan apse-ended, circular, oval, and square spaces provided variety.

The trend during the latter part of the 18th century was a response to lifestyle changes. Gradual alterations in planning reflected more informal entertaining. Houses were designed for house parties, with the consequent need to have easier access from the main floor to the landscape around the house. Little by little the basement began to be dug deeper, necessitating the use of areaways to allow light to penetrate the space. This was still disadvantageous in terms of opening the house to the landscape; ultimately the basement was fully underground. This allowed the attainment of the ultimate goals: (1) to have the main rooms at ground level, thereby opening the house to the garden with the frequent use of French windows, and (2) to incorporate a servants' wing at ground level, often as an asymmetrical addition. Intermediate steps in this direction at Doddington are seen in the partially underground basement and the addition a servants' wing.

Doddington represents an intermediate step in the general trend of the late 18th century. Here the main floor is still situated above a rustic basement. Initially the basement

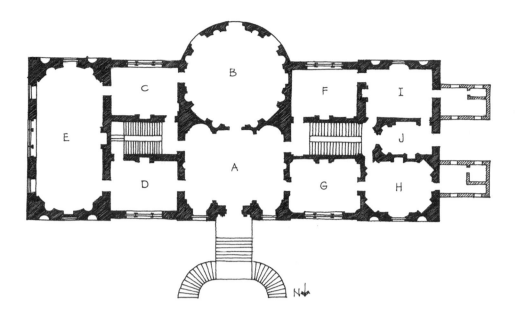

FIGURE 14-3 Main Floor, Doddington Hall, Cheshire. Samuel Wyatt (1776-1798). A Hall, B Salone, C Drawing Room, D Ante-Room, E Dining Room, F Dressing Room, G Library, H Dressing Room, I Bedroom, J Wardrobe. Service wing southwest of the main residence. Courtesy of Country Life Picture Library.

was used for servants' bedrooms since the plan did not call for a servants' wing (added later). Extending in a curve from the west wing of the house, the servants were at the greatest distance from the dining room. Therefore, to facilitate service, a track and trolley were installed in the underground passage from the servants' quarters to the basement of the main residence.

INTERIOR ARCHITECTURE AND DECORATION

The major influences on Adam's interior architecture and decoration were (1) archaeological studies, (2) French decorative tradition, and (3) Renaissance masters. First, it was his aim, based on archaeological studies, to capture the essence of Roman decorative detail and to adapt it to contemporary needs. For example, during his tenure in Italy he visited the ruins of Diocletian's palace at Spalatro (Diocletian [245-313] was emperor of Rome from 284 to 305). There he attained through his study enough information to reconstruct the building, which he illustrated in his 1764 book *The Ruins of the Palace of Diocletian at Spalatro.* Adam was also influenced in his studies by the works of Robert Wood on notable Roman buildings located in Palmyra (a city in in Syria, politically important following Roman control) and Baalbek (an ancient city in Lebanon). The adaptation of ceiling designs from Palmyra are particularly reflected in Adam's compositions of the 1760s. Greek influence is noted in his use of the Ionic order, based on the recounting by J. D. Le Roy[4] of the Erechtheum (a 5th-century B.C. temple of the Aeropolis at Athens). Second, although not of paramount significance, some French influence related to decorative tradition that is observed in his work could have been inspired by his association of Charles Louis Clérisseau. Some early furniture designs were of Rococo form with classical carved detail; iron balustrades also reflected French influence. Third, in the ornamental detail of Renaissance artists, Adam specifically referred to such past masters as Michelangelo, Giulio Romano, and Raphael. He assumed that these masters had based their compositions of grotesques by studying the originals, many of which were not extant in the 18th century.[5] Found in Roman buildings, the term grotesque (from the Italian *grotto*) described an imaginative combination of animal, human, and floral motifs.

---

4. J. D. Le Roy was the author of *Les ruines des plus beaux monuments de la Grèce* in 1758. This publication was responsible for Adam's use of a Greek model, the Erechtheum.

5. John Summerson, *Architecture in Britain, 1530 to 1830* (Harmondsworth, Middlesex, Great Britain: Penguin, 1970), 426.

Materials and Decorative Techniques

During the early neoclassical period a gradual change in technology revealed new materials and the slow change from hand to machine processes. Materials of great significance to neoclassical designers were plaster and stucco, scagliola, paintings, ormolu, papier-mâché, textile and wallpaper coverings, and carpets.

Although plaster and stucco were not new to the English, they were highly important in the execution of the decorative work of Robert Adam. Plaster walls were very common, even in middle-class homes. Plaster was comprised of lime, sand, water, and a binder such as animal hair. It was usually applied in three coats with the top layer finer than either of the previous layers. Paintings could be applied directly to the plaster surface; paintings were also executed on paper or canvas and applied to ceilings and walls. Stucco ornament, usually of classically derived decorative detail, was often applied to friezes, cornices, ceilings, frames for paintings, and so on. For particularly fragile linear designs the ornament was sometimes reinforced with thin wire. The trophies in high relief set within panels in the anteroom at Syon were executed by the craftsman most often commissioned to execute decorative plasterwork for Adam, Joseph Rose.

Known in ancient times and popular in the 17th and 18th centuries, the technique of making scagliola was perfected by the middle of the latter century. The material was often formed to imitate marble, which was expensive. Scagliola was used in such areas as columns, floors, tabletops, and pedestals. The material was composed of calcined gypsum, sand, glue, and isinglass solution. Pigment was applied to this mixture for appropriate color and pattern, after which it was polished with oils.

Paintings were of considerable significance in decorative schemes and especially important for ceilings. Adam particularly favored the outstanding Swiss painter Angelica Kaufmann, who worked in London from 1766 to 1781; in addition, he often commissioned the Italian Antonio Zucchi. The subjects of paintings included classical mythology, landscape, and portraiture. The paintings were often set within stucco frames.

Ormolu, made of gilded bronze, was used as an application to furniture but also in the decoration of interior elements. For example, it was used to ornament chimneypieces, doors, and doorcases. At Syon it was inset into the marble ground of doorcase pilasters.

Papier-mâché was a material fashioned primarily of paper made into a pulp with the addition of glue. In its semifirm state it was placed in molds and as it dried it became hard and durable. It was sometimes used as a substitute for stucco ornament in relief applications in ceilings. Moldings were also made of papier-mâché.

Techniques for the ornamentation of wallpaper included machine printing, hand painting, and hand blocking. One popular variation was embossing, whereby wool was ground to a powder and affixed to paper by sticky oils. Simulations of stucco for wallpaper design were used in the neoclassical period. The manner of attaching wallpaper and textiles to walls is explained in the section on Early Georgian style. One space in the residence that was normally devoid of textiles was the dining room since designers considered the absorption of odors offensive.

Carpet factories in operation during the latter part of the 18th century were Wilton, Kidderminster, and Moorfields. Adam often designed carpets to coordinate with or echo the ceiling design.

Interior Architecture and Decorative Elements

Robert Adam was proficient as an architect, but his main contribution to the early neoclassical movement in England was as an interior architect (examples of his space planning were noted in the previous section) and as a decorator. Contrasting the character of Adam's early decorative detail in the decade beginning in 1760 and that in the decades following shows his style changing from large scale to small scale and from strong relief to low relief; it became elegant, attenuated, and linear. He coordinated the design of interior architectural elements with minor decorative elements such as candlesticks, doorknobs, escutcheons, and fire grates. His later work was the subject of criticism from some of the leading figures of the day, who bitingly referred to his decorative work as childlike, as characterized by superfluous ornament, and even as bits of needlework.

Floors

Wood, brick, and stones of various types were the materials most frequently used. Probably the most widely used material was unvarnished fir or pine; for more imposing residences polished oak was sometimes utilized. Parquet floors, when employed, were laid in simple or complex designs.

The designs for floors significantly echoed the patterns of the ceilings in order to attain harmony and unity among the surfaces of the interior. For example, at Syon the black and white marble floor of the entrance hall is not identical to the ceiling but the diagonals reflect those of the compartmented ceiling (see Figure 14-2). Another purpose served here is to provide axial direction to the sequence of state rooms, the next room in succession was the anteroom. Scagliola in strong colors of yellow, red, green, blue, and brown was used for the floor of the anteroom; the design again echoes that of the ceiling but is not identical. Carpets, increasingly common in the latter part of the century, were also designed to coordinate with the ceiling composition.

A design for floors throughout the 18th century was termed *carreaux d'octagones*. As can be seen at Woodhall Park, Hertfordshire, the floor is comprised of black diamonds positioned at the junctures of larger intersecting squares.

Walls

The typical wall composition was divided by dado, main field, and entablature. Increasingly, wood paneling was replaced by plaster for the dado. Above the dado the field was treated with wallpaper, textiles, plain plaster, or plaster with relief designs in stucco; designs were based on a repertoire of classically derived ornament. Whether or not there was paneling in the dado, a dado rail of wood was usual. Treatment of the dado rail varied; it could include moldings with such decorative details as egg and dart and fluting. Occasionally, however, the dado rail was eliminated and the plaster wall extended to the baseboard.

Textile application between the dado rail and the cornice included damasks, velvets, and tapestries. Fibers included wool, silk, and cotton. The Tapestry Room at Newby Hall, Yorkshire, featured one of six sets of tapestries designed by Boucher and the Scotsman Nielson and produced by the Gobelins factory for English residences. Adam was responsible for the installation of four of these. The tapestries were designed to fit exactly into the wall space reserved for them and the design coordinated with similar design units in the ceiling.

Articulation of wall spaces varied widely from simple to complex. The classical design vocabulary was the common thread among these compositions; ornament was often based on freely adapted Roman prototypes and sometimes on Renaissance interpretations of antiquity. Arrangements of enframed ornamental detail consisted of vertical rectangles, horizontal rectangles, and sometimes medallions. These were used singly or grouped in varied shapes, proportions, and direction. Within these enframed panels one or a combination of the following provided the decorative detail: bas-relief stucco (as arabesques, grotesques, trophies, etc.) and painting (grisaille, figurative, landscape, etc.).

Three rooms illustrate the stylistic changes that took place in the work of Adam from the early monumental interior decor (represented by the Syon anteroom) through the intermediate stage in the direction toward delicate linearity (portrayed in the Syon gallery), and, finally, to the extreme delicacy, attenuation, and thin linear character of his late work (depicted in the Etruscan dressing room at Osterly).

The anteroom at Syon (1761-1765) is approached through the rectangular apsed end of the entrance hall, screened by Doric orders. The difference in floor level from the origi-

FIGURE 14-5   Entablature with Pulvinated Frieze. Based on an engraving in Charles Cameron's *The Baths of the Romans.* With permission of Academy Group Ltd.

FIGURE 14-4   Ionic Capital. Based on drawings of the Erectheum of J. D. Le Roy (1758). With permission of Academy Group Ltd.

FIGURE 14-6   Robert Adam's adaptation of classical decorative elements for the Ionic capital and frieze in the Anteroom, Syon House, Middlesex.

nal structure necessitated the use of a short flight of curved stairs beyond the columns. The focus of the anteroom centers largely on the rather heavy architectural elements typical of Adam's early interiors (see Figure C-26). The green marble columns were found on the Tiber River in Italy and shipped to England; each has gilt Ionic capitals with white and gilt bases. Columns are important to the manner in which (1) space is articulated, (2) proportions are visually altered, and (3) spatial drama is attained through the forward and backward movement through the positioning of architectural elements and decorative detail.

Regularly spaced around the wall are 12 pilasters with a freestanding column in front of each. In this manner prominence is systematically given to the forward placement of the column and secondarily to the architectural or decorative element in the intercolumnar spaces—door, window, niche, trophy panel, chimneypiece. But the most compelling attention is given to the full heavy entablature with its decorative frieze. The entablature changes direction as it is supported by the forward position of the columns. In this manner a surface was created to support each of twelve gilt statues.

Visually, the rectangular space of the anteroom is altered by the position of the columns on the south wall (see Figure 14-2). Here they are placed eight feet from the wall, whereas on the other three walls the columns are closely spaced in relation to the pilasters.

The Ionic capitals and the design of the frieze in the Syon anteroom illustrate that it was never Adam's aim to exactly reproduce ancient ornament but to use classical prototypes as inspiration; Piranesi had helped to give credence to this idea. Engraved sources, of which there were many, provided a source for his designs—for example, the volute and necking of the Ionic capital from the Erechtheum (421-405 B.C.) (Figure 14-4)[6] and the entablature from a Roman bath[7] are examples of Adam's adaptation of Greek and Roman sources (Figure 14-5). Based on the Erechtheum capital Adam duplicated the shape but chose to use decorative relief; further, he used the anthemion motif from the necking of the capital as the repetitive unit for the frieze (Figure 14-6). From the Roman entablature the ornament from the pulvinated frieze is used as the decoration on the necking of the capital at Syon.[8]

Decorative panels played an important role in wall composition in the Adam interior. In the Syon anteroom panels were isolated with no attempt at grouping, each of independent interest. The large rectangular trophy panels on the north wall are executed in high relief and represent classical weapons and military paraphernalia. The design of these is again based on engravings by Piranesi of the Trophies of Marius and Octavianus.[9] Other decorative panels in the anteroom that figure conspicuously in wall composition and direct attention to the intercolumnar spaces are those placed above the attic; gilt arabesques in relief are conspicuously displayed against a green background, as are the trophy panels.

In the design of the long gallery at Syon (1763-1768) Adam was presented with an unusual challenge due to the proportions of the space (136 feet long, 14 feet wide, and 14 feet high). In all, 62 thin, delicately painted arabesque pilasters are used to articulate the wall spaces in the gallery (see Figure C-27). On the outside wall they are used to frame each window and the interceding wall space; however, on the long inside wall Adam chose to use groups of four closely spaced pilasters to flank wider intervening spaces centered on chimneypieces, with painted landscape scenes above and tabernacle framed doorways grouped with bookcases on each side. The pedestals of the pilasters are an integral part of the design of the dado and their forward projection aids in modulating the length of the gallery. Interspersed with plain dado paneling are segments enhanced with S-fluting. A theme of roundels and circular recesses is used throughout, some with ancestral paintings, terra-cotta pots in the recesses, and stucco reliefs of classical derivation.

The overall impression the gallery gives is one of delicacy, two-dimensional surface decoration, and a sense of unity in the total composition that is decorative and nonarchitectural in concept. By contrast the earlier anteroom is characterized by boldness, high relief, and three-dimensionality. The separate elements of design based on antiquity each draw attention to themselves (trophies, capitals, entablatures, statues); the overall impression is strongly architectural.

Adam worked at Osterly for 20 years beginning in 1761. Here, the complete range of changes in his approaches to design may be viewed. His later work focused on a central idea and integrated all elements of the interior. Essentially in its original state, the Etruscan dressing room (c. 1775-1776) is a superior example of a totally unified composition (see Figure C-28). The design of this room was based on Greek red- and black-figure vases, which were then considered to be of Etruscan origin.

All surfaces within the room are very closely related—ceiling, doors, walls, chimneyboard, chimneypiece, carpet, ceiling. While Adam retained from his earlier work such elements as pilasters, entablature, and compartmented ceilings, they assume a different role here since they are more decorative and executed with extreme delicacy; in short, his approach was nonarchitectural. Designs are two-dimensional, slight, and linear.

The sparsely decorated ornament for the walls was executed on canvas in colors of terra-cotta and black on a blue background. The wall composition is based on a series of

---

6. Reasonably accurate engravings of the buildings on the Acropolis from J. D. Le Roy, *Les ruines des plus beaux monuments de la Grèce* (1758).

7. The engraving of an entablature illustrating pulvinated frieze in Charles Cameron, *The Baths of the Romans,* 1772.

8. Damie Stillman, *The Decorative Work of Robert Adam* (London: Alec Tiranti, 1966), 32.

9. Engravings by G. B. Piranesi in *Trofei Di Ottaviano Augusto* (1753).

fragile arabesque arches that enframe tablets of nymphs and children commemorating the rites of love at the Feast of Venus; medallions of painted animated female figures; and, centered within the arch just above the dado, female figures dancing around tripods. In addition, other classically derived motifs are utilized, such as sphinxes and urns. Above the chimneypiece is a trompe l'oeil painting of a shallow vase on a pedestal integrated with two female figures.

Windows and Doors

In the town house, bay windows began to be used around the mid-18th century; they were either semihexagonal or curved. The most common form of window was the double-hung. The number of panes varied. As the century progressed the glazing bars became finer. Venetian windows were also employed along with classical details in the frieze, such as festoons. On the exterior of town houses the hierarchy of the floor could be discerned by the disposition of windows in the façade. The piano nobile was most dominant; for example, either the windows of the drawing room extended to the floor or the sill was very low, in which case the French door was utilized. Rectangular frames were common but round headed windows were also used, in which case the panes within would follow the arch and rectangular panes would be used in the lower section. Windows were at times heavily draped; the example at Harewood illustrates a trompe l'oeil treatment in carved wood to represent graceful folds heading the window (Figure 14-7).

Six-panel doors were most common. Painted fir or pine was used in modest interiors, while mahogany was utilized in the best. Panels were often enhanced with frames of neo-classical details such as flutings, beaded moldings, and guilloches. Some panels were painted with Etruscan detail, as at Osterly, other techniques of embellishment were carving and inlay (See Figure C-28). The single-leaf door was most prevalent, but some double doors were used in the most important rooms and in the grandest houses. Since round or circular rooms were often incorporated in plans, doors were curved to follow their contour

FIGURE 14-7
Trompe l'oeil Drapery in Carved Wood. Gallery, Harewood House, Yorkshire. Designed by Robert Adam. Crafted by Chippendale. Drapery simulated in dark blue. Courtesy of Country Life Picture Library.

(Figure 14-8). A variety of door surrounds included simple molded architraves, pilasters with a decorative entablature, and brackets to support the cornice placed outside the architrave surround.

Chimneypieces

Marble, wood, and stone were the major materials employed in chimneypiece design, for which the techniques of enrichment included carving, inlay, and painting. The most common vertical supports for the entablature were pilasters, engaged columns, panels, and stiles, treated very simply. The frieze was usually the most highly adorned part of the entablature (see Figures 10-9 and 10-10). At frieze level, just above the vertical support, was often a rectangular or square decorative block. Most chimneypiece friezes were treated with a continuous pattern related to room and door friezes. It was sometimes interrupted with a central tablet, often pictorial and correlated with wall and ceiling panels, but the decorative detail of the central tablet could also be related to the use of the room as, for example, a figure symbolic of Music. The cornice became the mantel shelf, which was composed of simple moldings or a complex series of moldings; sometimes it was dentiled. The stile or pilaster had a supporting base or block. Occasionally a continued chimneypiece was employed.

Early in the period chimneypieces were architectural in concept, reflecting the Burlington influence of the Early Georgian style; both structural elements and decorative detail were large scale. Caryatids were employed, as were heavy consoles to support the

FIGURE 14-9 Continued chimney-piece crowned by a triangular pediment. Typical frieze detailing in the manner of Adam. Courtesy of Country Life Picture Library.

FIGURE 14-10 Chimneypiece characterized by wide uprights, sometimes painted. From Calloway, Steven. *The Elements of Style.* © 1991. Michael Beazley Publishers, a division of Reed Books.

FIGURE 14-11 Overmantel mirror, carved and gilt wood using classic detail—griffins, urn, anthemion. c. 1774. By Courtesy of the Board of Trustees of the Victoria and Albert Museum.

295

Early English Neoclassic

entablature. While the continued chimneypiece was occasionally used, by the 1770s the mantel shelf became wide enough for ornaments to be placed in front of a mirror.

A repertoire of classical motifs was the basis for most of the decorative detail. These included medallions, urns, painted scenes with classical figures, the sun god Helios in his chariot, palmettes, anthemion, Greek keys, floral festoons, flutings, heads of gods, lyres, patera, sphinxes, and rams' heads. Repetitive ornament was sometimes accomplished through applications to wood using modeled gesso or by casting soft metals, such as pewter, after which the ornament was painted.

By the mid-1760s delicacy, linearity, and bas-relief ornament was characteristic. Painted decoration was used on slender stiles, but wide uprights were characteristic also (see Figure 14-10). Mirrors with classical detail were used instead of the continued chimneypiece (Figure 14-11). As another form of decoration above the mantelpiece, stucco panels filled with ornament in relief, with representations of classic figures, were employed.

Ceilings

Around 1754 the ceiling of the Red Drawing Room at Hopetoun House, West Lothian, Scotland, was designed by John and Robert Adam. In the ceiling plasterwork they introduced dainty Rococo details composed of foliage, shells, and scrolls in an asymmetrical arrangement; some classical detail is also observed in the use of, for example, the modillion brackets of the cornice (Figure 14-12). The same combination of classical and Rococo elements is observed in Adam's transitional designs for furniture.

FIGURE 14-12 Ceiling Detail, Red Drawing Room (c.1754), Hopetoun House, West Lothian, Scotland. Robert Adam's early use of Rococo detailing for plasterwork coupled with some classic motifs.

FIGURE 14-13 Ceiling, Tapestry Room (1763), Croome Court, Worcestershire. Robert Adam. Plasterwork.

Throughout the period, most ceilings were flat, with the occasional use of a coved transition from the wall to the ceiling. In the halls and stairwells of the residences of the most affluent, some ceilings were barrel vaulted. Plain plaster ceilings with simple cornices were common for houses of owners of moderate means.

The trend for ceiling ornamentation was from simple, high relief (often boldly sculpted) and heavy compartmentalization to highly complex, low-relief, linear, delicate, intricate designs; the change to greater delicacy began to be observed in the mid-1760s (Figure 14-13; see also C-27). Usually ornamentation was accomplished in plasterwork, but sometimes carved wood was applied to the ceiling. Coupled with stucco frames was the use of panel paintings. Decorative paintings were executed on paper or canvas and applied within stucco frames in the form of circles, squares, rectangles, hexagons, and ovals.

While there was considerable variation in ceiling design, one frequent composition was the arrangement of subordinate panels around a central, more dominant unit of design; the latter replaced large decorative ceiling paintings. Another popular enrichment was the

FIGURE 14 14
Grand Staircase,
Harewood House,
Yorkshire (1765).
Robert Adam. Plan of
single lower flight
divides at landing to
become two, a result
of restricted space.
Lighting is from an
adjacent court.

coffered ceiling with geometric compartments, with moldings in slight relief; small paintings were utilized in this configuration also. Classical motifs were common.

Stairways

Wood was the primary material used for almost all stairways; stone, however, was utilized in grand houses. Most stairs were open string and stair end configurations which were simple and elegant. Combinations of materials were not uncommon—for example, a wrought-iron balustrade and mahogany handrail combined with a stone staircase. Balustrades of metal could appear to be more intricately conceived than wood; these often incorporated classical motifs, such as the anthemion. If wood, balusters were either turned or square in section and often placed two per tread. The newel was comprised of a single turned member or a post surrounded by balusters. Handrails (flatter in this period) usually encircled the newel either in a tight or loose coil.

The plan of the staircase depended on the amount of space available. In tight spaces semicircular or curved sweeps could economize space. In one configuration the stairs began in one central flight to a landing and then divided in two (Figure 14-14). The stair rail is wrought metal with anthemion motifs and an intricately decorated handrail with the Vitruvian scroll.

FURNITURE

In his desire for the complete harmony of interiors Adam designed furniture for the residences for which he had commissions, such as Osterly, Kedleston, and Syon. Not only did he create new forms of furniture but he ultimately brought to these a new classicism. His style was later widely adopted by other designers. It should be remembered that Adam did not design for the general public, only for specific patrons, and that his pieces were fabricated by furniture makers who were his contemporaries—for example, Chippendale, and Hepplewhite and Sheraton.

Materials and Construction Techniques

Although mahogany was suited to the flat carving typical of early Adam furniture, later in the century satinwood and harewood became more prevalent. Satinwood was particularly useful as a veneer but was also utilized as solid wood.

Marquetry was revived as a technique of decoration. The ornamental design of Adam's furniture frequently correlated with the stucco arabesques of his walls and ceilings. Woods of different colors produced an elegant corollary to support the theme of the interior. Marquetry and painting were used on the same pieces.

Painting was an alternative technique used by Adam to color-coordinate furniture with plasterwork schemes; it became fashionable around 1770. Figural paintings were often set within oval or circular medallions and were in colors coordinating the decorative scheme or executed *en grisaille*. Sometimes painting was applied directly to the surface; at other times it was rendered on copper sheets and inset into the surfaces of the pieces.

Ormolu mounts were utilized for enrichment in a variety of ways. Neoclassical ornaments (such as the ram's head, anthemion, acanthus, vase, and foliated scrolls) appeared as edgings for shelves, capitals, decorative swags, and friezes.

Gilding was used on furniture for many rooms but was especially important for drawing room pieces. Both oil and water gilding techniques were used. In polishing, both matte and high gloss finishes were produced, sometimes on the same piece.

Composition material of whiting, resin, and size replaced carving as a medium for relief designs; it was molded and adhered to furniture with glue or pins. The use of festoons as ornamentation necessitated wire reinforcement. Areas where festoons were prominent were for mirrors, both on and under friezes of tables, etc.

FURNITURE: ADAM

Initially, Adam's designs for furniture reflected earlier 18th-century influences. For example, he was influenced by an interest in the Gothic as reflected in Kent's revival of the style earlier in the century. Adam's first venture into the use of the Gothic style for furniture was a chair that was not fabricated until the late 1770s; the design is documented by dated drawings (c. 1761) in the Soane Museum. This chair was for the chapel (since demolished) at Alnwick Castle (Figure 14-15). Gothic detail is noted in such features as verticality, spire-like finials with protrusions suggesting crockets, quatrefoils, the series of cusped arches underneath the seat rail, etc.

When Adam began to introduce classical detail he used a Rococo form, but the motifs carved on the seat rail represent the neoclassic repertoire he was to draw on frequently in his later designs: sphinxes, anthemions, foliated scrolls, etc. (Figure 14-16). Still further in the classical direction is a chair design, probably by Adam, constructed c. 1765 (Figure 14-17). Thin tapering fluted legs and an anthemion splat (a motif used often by Adam) anticipate some of his steps in the direction of neoclassicism.

Adam was probably influenced by the Louis XVI style for a medallion-back chair, the drawing for which is dated April 24, 1777. The back is supported by winged sphinxes; this same motif is used as acroteria on the cornice of a state bed at Osterly and on the crest of a pier glass mirror, also at Osterly; on a pediment an acroterion is an ornament used at the apex and at the lower angle. A major difference between this chair design and Louis XVI is the splay of rear legs, typically English.

Typical Pieces and Stylistic Features

Adam's contributions to design trends for furniture were adopted by lesser designers for commodes, side tables, pier tables, dining room sideboards, and mirrors, but not often chairs.

FIGURE 14-15 Gothic chair, Design by Robert Adam. First designed c. 1761.

FIGURE 14-16 Rococo form with classic detail on seat rail by Robert Adam.

FIGURE 14-17 Robert Adam designs move toward more classical influence. Anthemion splat.

FIGURE 14-18 Carved and gilt oval back armchair to a design by Robert Adam, 1777, for the state bedroom

Tables

The number of tables from the designs of Adam abound. These tables reflected his desire to coordinate ornamental schemes. Their intent was usually decorative. In Adam's mature style tables were lightly scaled and rectangular, but sometimes semioval, in plan. Table legs were usually straight and tapering, either round or square sectioned; a plinth base was common for those of square section. Marquetry and painted designs were preferred as techniques of ornamentation. Stringing was used to outline structural members, with a thin wood veneer of contrasting color for decorative effect. An Osterly table with an alabaster surface embodies the foregoing characteristics. The short flutings, here employed on the apron, were often used in the late 18th century (Figure C-29).

The practice of flanking the sideboard table with accompanying pedestals probably was due to Adam's influence. The drawing for the eating room at Osterly is dated 1767. The gilt table at Osterly has features that typify Adam's work: slender baluster legs with very narrow incut necks and lotus capitals above; a frieze ornamented with the Greek key, rams' heads, and paterae; pendant ornament is used underneath the frieze. The flanking Doric pedestals crowned with urns are painted white with gold highlights (Figure C-30).

Storage Pieces

An Osterly commode (c. 1770) for the drawing room from an Adam design is credited to the furniture making firm of William Ince and John Mayhew; other craftsmen were responsible for the marquetry medallions (see Figure C-31). It is semicircular in plan, hollow inside, decorated with marquetry of harewood and satinwood and with bacchantes, figures of Venus and Cupid in the medallions; ormolu mounts were used for moldings. Adam's desire for the harmonious relationship of all aspects of a room is well demonstrated by comparing the decorative detail of the commode with the architectural ornament in the same room (as on the door, ceiling, and mantel): the duplication of the frieze featuring griffins supporting a medallion, foliated scrolls of like arrangement, the guilloche band for the wainscot and on the commode. Further relationships can be observed in the use of the octagonal frame for the coffered ceiling and in the octagonal frame for the medallion of the commode (see Figure C-31).

Mirrors

Mirrors figured prominently in Adam interiors. Of the types most popular in later design two were most notable. The oval mirror was frequently surrounded by complex compositions of such motifs as festoons, urns, and sphinxes. The innovative tripartite mirror developed by Adam featured a large, tall center glass flanked by lower, narrow vertical glasses. This arrangement was somewhat akin to the Palladian or Venetian window in the differences in height in the tripartite unit (see Figure C-29). This example has attenuated terminal figures dividing the three segments and festoons carried from side to side; the cresting is composed of vase and anthemion finials along with cupids and foliated scrolls.

FURNITURE: HEPPLEWHITE

Documentary evidence about the life of George Hepplewhite is sparse. He was a furniture designer and cabinetmaker who had established himself in London by 1760. Appearing in three editions (1788, 1789, 1794), *The Cabinet-Makers & Upholsterer's Guide* was first published by A. Hepplewhite and Co. two years after the death of George Hepplewhite; his wife, Alice, to whom the cabinetmaking business passed, was responsible for its publication. On June 27, 1785 the value of his estate was "less than £600" which does not suggest that his business was highly successful.[10] Although the style was not original, the trade catalog was an effective tool for cabinetmakers. The style name of Hepplewhite, therefore, is derived from the association of his name with his publication.

The stylistic manner of Robert Adam can be discerned in the designs that appear in the *Guide.* Adam's influence is observed in splats fashioned as urns or vases as well as in the use of such motifs as rosettes, wheatears, and festoons of husks or drapery. Legs, square or round in section, taper with carved leaf ornament.

---

10. Joseph Aronson, introduction to *The Cabinet-Maker & Upholsterer's Guide,* by George Hepplewhite, third edition of 1794 (New York: Dover Publications, 1969), v.

FIGURE 14-19   Hepplewhite Shield Back (c. 1788). Mahogany. Carving and inlay decorative detail. By Courtesy of the Board of Trustees of the Victoria and Albert Museum.

FIGURE 14-20   Hepplewhite Heart-shaped Back (c. 1780). Mahogany. Spade feet terminate front legs. All rights reserved, The Metropolitan Museum of Art, Fletcher Fund, 1929 (29.118.2-3).

Typical Pieces and Stylistic Features

Seat Furniture

Chair back shapes associated with Hepplewhite are shield, oval, and heart. The innovation of the shield back is often attributed, incorrectly, to the Hepplewhite firm. A variety of motifs was used for the splat enclosed by the shield: festoons of drapery, classical urns, wheatears, rosettes, pendant husks, Prince of Wales feathers. The splat detail within the shield often originated from a semicircular shoe piece at the base of the shield. Usually the shield was not attached to the seat rail; rather, it was placed a few inches above it. Most frequently legs were straight and either round or square in section; front legs of square section usually terminated in a spade foot (tapered square section enlargement terminating the leg) (Figure 14-19). Stretchers were usually omitted. Carving (such as pendant husks), painting, and fluting were means by which legs were ornamented. The proportions of the trapezoid seat meant that rear legs were placed unusually close together; these sometimes had outward-turning feet. Serpentine, bowed, and straight shapes were used for the front seat rail.

Oval chair backs were often filled with radiating geometric designs. Sometimes Prince of Wales feathers radiated from a base within the oval. Heart-shaped backs were formed of three interlaced ovals arising from a pointed base (Figure 14-20). One popular means of ornamenting the center of the heart was to unite the structural frame with carved drapery swags. Regardless of the type of chair back chairs were lightly scaled, stretchers were usually omitted, upholstery over the seat rail was common, and arm supports originated above the legs and curves back to meet the armrests.

Tables

Dining room furniture common in the latter part of the 18th century included the sideboard table without drawers and flanked by pedestals introduced by Adam and a sideboard that combined the separate units into one piece with drawers and storage. In plan

view there was considerable variation. A more complex arrangement can be described based on a design appearing in the third edition of the *Guide*. The center section, with one long drawer, is serpentine, with canted inner legs; the concave end compartments are composed of two deeper drawers each. The deep side drawers are divided to provide a rack for bottles, a lead-lined receptacle for water to rinse glasses, and space for plate; the long center drawer was for table linen. While this piece has six legs, smaller varieties of the sideboard were frequently supported by four legs.

In his designs for side tables, console tables, and pier tables Hepplewhite owed a great deal to those of Adam. These were often highly ornamental and based on a classical repertoire of motifs, with inlay and painting as predominant techniques.

Storage Pieces

In the third edition of the *Guide* a simple chest of drawers was illustrated with a serpentine front. Some, however, were designed with straight or bowed fronts. These pieces usually had graduated drawers. Some had a top drawer compartmented for toilet articles; when open, a hinged mirror could be tilted for use. The brasses varied in style; a common one was an oval backplate (sometimes stamped with classic detail) with bail handles of brass; bail handles also originated from two small backplates. The shaped apron often curved into the outward splayed feet (also called French bracket feet) (Figure 14-21). Ornamentation for these was in the form of stringing, banding, and so on.

Beds

There are few extant beds in the Hepplewhite style, but the four-poster bed was illustrated in the *Guide*. The posts were normally fluted above a vase-shaped lower section; legs were tapered and square in section, with spade feet. Illustrated in the Hepplewhite trade catalog were straight cornices as well as decorative pediments.

FURNITURE: SHERATON

Sheraton (1751-1806) had practical experience as a journeyman cabinetmaker. Based on this training and on his superior ability as a draftsman he was in a position to furnish designs to other cabinetmakers. His *Cabinet-Maker and Upholsterer's Drawing Book,* published between 1791 and 1794 in four parts, gives a good indication of the trends of the last decade of the 18th century. Subsequently he published the *Cabinet-Maker's Dictionary* (1803) and the *Encyclopedia* (1805). According to a report by Adam Black, future publisher of the *Encyclopaedia Britannica,* Sheraton was in dire financial straits in 1804.

> He [Sheraton] lived in an an obscure street, his house half shop, half dwelling-house, and looked himself like a worn-out Methodist minister, with threadbare black coat. I took tea with them one afternoon. There were a cup and saucer for the host, and another for his wife, and a little porringer for their daughter. The wife's cup and saucer were given to me, and she had to put up with another little porringer. My host seemed a good man, with some talent. He had been a cabinetmaker, was now author and publisher, teacher of drawing, and I believe, occasional preacher. I was with him about a week, engaged in most wretched work, writing a few articles, and trying to put his shop in order, working among dirt and bugs, for which I was remunerated with half a guinea. Miserable as the pay was, I was half ashamed to take it from the poor man.[11]

Sheraton died in 1806.

Typical Pieces and Stylistic Features

Seat Furniture

Chairs were lightly scaled and the straight line was prevalent in Sheraton designs. While Sheraton illustrated the shield back in the *Drawing Book,* he preferred the rectilinear form (Figure 14-22). A central splat was formed by the position of the back uprights coupled with such motifs as the urn, festoons of drapery, and lyres. A raised center section of the back was sometimes accomplished by the extension of the framing members of the splat above the cresting rail; frequently this was rectangular but sometimes an arched form

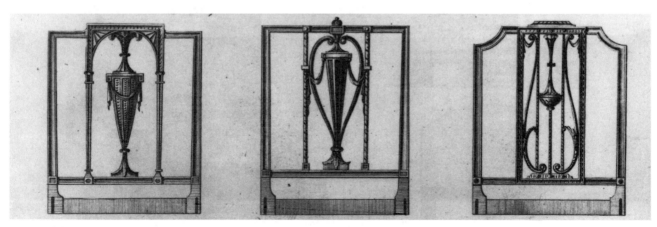

FIGURE 14-22   Sheraton Chair Backs from the *Drawing Book,* Part III, Plate 36. By Courtesy of the Board of Trustees of the Victoria and Albert Museum, London.

---

11. Alexander Nicolson, ed., *Memoirs of Adam Black,* (1885), 32; quoted in Ralph Fastnedge, *English Furniture Styles from 1500 to 1830* (Baltimore, Maryland: Penguin Books, 1964), 223.

was employed. Occasionally columns were the framing members of the central splat. Sometimes attenuated curved lines were used in the central splat, which relieved the severity of the straight lines. The splat emanated from the rail, placed several inches above seat level (Figure 14-23). Sheraton favored the tapered, round-sectioned leg but also utilized the tapered, square-sectioned leg; stretchers were not a usual feature. Vertical reeding with a ring collar was often used for round legs. Armrests sometimes curved downward, originating almost from the cresting of the back; others were straight and rested on incurved arm supports. Some arm supports were reeded vase shapes. Arm supports originated above the legs or from the side seat rail. Seats were usually trapezoid in shape but sometimes round. Upholstery was often over the seat rail or, alternatively, a decorative seat rail was used below a partially upholstered rail.

Mahogany was often used for chairs but softer woods were also utilized, in which case painting was used to coordinate with the color scheme of rooms. Some pieces were japanned in black and ornamented with colorful flowers while others were painted white with gilding.

Tables

Many types of tables were designed by Sheraton, including Pembroke tables, dining tables, pier tables, sideboards and sideboard tables, worktables, and sofa tables. The Pembroke table was among the most utilitarian pieces, often used for serving meals. It was constructed of two drop leaves and a drawer set in the apron under the fixed table surface. Sheraton devised a harlequin Pembroke in which concealed compartments, drawers, and pigeonholes were used for the accessories needed for writing, sewing, etc.; this section could be raised or lowered by a ratchet mechanism. Square-sectioned, tapered legs were usually fitted with brass caps and casters.

Dining tables were sectional with round-sectioned tapered leg, usually reeded. Drop leaves were common for the end sections. Tops normally had rounded corners with the edges reeded. A late development was in the use of pedestals on a base. Paw feet were brass and casters were standard.

Pier tables were extremely delicate and for these Sheraton recommended the use of stretchers; in the *Drawing Book* he illustrated concave stretchers. Satinwood veneer was

Figure 14-24
Sheraton Worktable (c.
1790). Satinwood with
mahogany stringing.
By Courtesy of the
Board of Trustees of
the Victoria and
Albert Museum,
London.

used for the tabletop surface and polychrome decoration was widely used. Figurative paintings, realistically represented floral arrangements, and classical vases were some of the decorative treatments. Border designs as well as paintings within medallions were utilized.

In the *Drawing Book* Sheraton gave special attention to the worktable. These pieces sometimes served more than one utilitarian purpose; for example, in the same piece ladies' sewing supplies and writing surfaces were provided (Figure 14-24). The example from the Victoria and Albert Museum incorporates a pouch mounted on a frame that slid like a drawer and a surface, hinged in the front, that could be raised for use as as a slanted writing surface.

Storage Pieces

Bookcases and secretary bookcases were normally tall pieces and designed in two tiers. The upper stage had two glazed doors; the lower tiers varied according to the functional intent of the piece. Sheraton illustrated a piece that incorporated a tambour closure for a writing surface that would glide into position; below, doors enclosed shelves. One secretary bookcase was crested with a domed outline formed by delicately conceived foliage. In the design for the configuration for the glazing bars Sheraton, compared to Hepplewhite, preferred thinner bars and greater elongation for their curved lines. Also characteristic of Sheraton was the use of elongated ovals, portions of ovals, and overlapping ovals. Ionic capitals sometimes surmounted the pilasters of the bookcase section.

Beds

Beds depicted in the *Drawing Book* were of unusual design compared to the type that wealthier clients usually desired. Recommendations for draperies were complex, with attention given to festooned valances and extravagant ornament. The four-poster bed was the most popular form in the late 18th century. It was characteristized by cylindrical posts, most often reeded, which tapered upward from a vase-turned section; the posts rested on plain bases of square section. Posts rose to a height of eight or nine feet.

ORNAMENT

A great deal of attention was given to ornament derived from the Italian Renaissance and classical motifs of antiquity. Adam was the major figure and leader in decorative detail; lesser designers followed his lead. Among the prevalent motifs were paterae, urns, swags or festoons (of husks, for example), husks, wheat sheaves, acanthus leaves, fluting (for legs, pilasters, and friezes), radial fans, classical figures, mythological scenes related to other decorative surfaces in the room, wreaths, anthemia, masks, lunettes combined with a radiating design, medallions, arabesques, drapery swags, interlaced branches of vines, imaginary animals (sphinxes, griffins), animal motifs (lions, birds), guilloches, egg and dart motifs, ribbons, rams' heads, masks and heads of gods, and lyre. Sheraton made less use than Hepplewhite did of ornamental detail such as grotesques, husks, paterae, and festoons. Painted figural subjects and naturalistic floral ornament were used more extensively by Sheraton than Hepplewhite; however, Hepplewhite also illustrated these.

Chapter **15**

Late French Neoclassic

1789-1820

HISTORICAL SETTING

The direction of architecture and design was impacted by the events that transpired between 1789 and 1815. Political, social, and economic instability led to the French Revolution in 1789; general European wars were sparked in turn and extended from 1792 to 1802.

Problems began to emerge in France before the end of the reign of Louis XV. State finances were steadily breaking down. Obstacles to economic reform were imposed by parliamentary bodies. Further, there was an escalating demand for governmental reform based on the more liberal English system. While Louis XVI was aware that reform was essential, both economic and political, new courses of action were denied him because of subversion within the nobility and the 1787 refusal of the parliamentary body to adopt new measures. The ultimate result of the failure to enact changes was state bankruptcy and destruction of the monarchical system. Historians are not in total agreement about the causes of the enormous public debt that resulted in national bankruptcy; however, it may have originated in some combination of factors including waste, two centuries of wars, an ineffective tax system, and French intervention in the American Revolution. This instability culminated in the demise of Louis XVI, who was convicted of treason and guillotined in January 1793.

Two design styles are embodied in the series of political changes which occurred between 1789 and 1815: Directoire (1789–1804) and Empire (1804–1815). Three governments were operative during the Directoire stylistic period—Revolutionary (1789–1795), Directory (1795–1799), and Consulate (1799–1804)—each of which influenced the repertoire of decorative motifs. The direction of the arts during the Empire style was influenced by Napoleon Bonaparte. Napoleon declared himself emperor of France in 1804; abdicated in 1814 and was exiled to Elba; returned to France to rule for one hundred days; abdicated the second time in 1815; and spent the rest of his life in exile on St. Helena.

A number of these factors related directly to trends in the arts in the late 18th and early 19th centuries. Fundamental to the effect on architecture and design and overlapping in their influence were financial stringency, political changes (change in governments, uncertainty due to these changes, curtailment of crown support), and administrative reforms by the Convention in 1793 that abolished the Academy of Architecture.

Financial stringency influenced the decorative arts in the selection of materials and the processes employed. As a result less expensive woods and simplified decorative processes were utilized. This meant that (1) beech often replaced mahogany, which was used for more expensive furniture; (2) there was less use of veneer in favor of solid wood; and (3) time-consuming decorative processes such as marquetry were minimized. With the prevalent use of solid wood the role of the ébénistes was virtually nonexistent; instead, the menuisiers sometimes veneered furniture, although their role had traditionally been to work in solid wood.

The furniture craftsmen reacted to the uncertainty of the last decade of the 18th century in a variety of ways. Those interested only in lucrative returns tended to design in the latest fashion without passion for new creations while others, who had worked for the crown, continued to work in the same mode. Then there were the true innovators who had not worked for the crown and who looked enthusiastically to archaeological discoveries; Georges Jacob is representative of this group. The stylistic variety evident during this period is a reflection of these different approaches. During his term as emperor Napoleon was instrumental in stimulating the cabinetmaking industry through his patronage.

During the last decade of the 18th century the dissolution of the monarchy influenced the quality of furniture, since there was no longer royal patronage. Unsettled conditions were not conducive to innovation. The new patrons did not demand the same quality in design and craftsmanship; consequently, standards were lower. Quality was sacrificed also by the fact that guilds were eliminated; before this craftsmen were required to place an identifying stamp on their products.

Standards of quality were also compromised due to events which transpired following the dissolution of the Academy of Architecture. The Academy had brought international attention to French architecture, which had been firmly established by Jean–Baptiste

Colbert in his capacity as Vice-Protector in 1661 during the reign of Louis XIV. Official standards of taste were prescribed by the Academy, which felt that all aspects of art, including its practice and appreciation, could be reduced to prescripts subject to instruction. The Academy had direction and control of royal buildings; further, it made decisions regarding competitions. The validity of this approach was questioned by the National Assembly and in 1791 the Academy was stripped of its function of overseeing royal buildings. Many objected to the special privileges enjoyed by members of the Academy. In an administrative reform decision by the Revolutionary Convention in 1793 the Academy of Architecture was abolished altogether. The consequence of this action was a lowering of architectural standards. There were no established criteria for judging the qualifications of architects. Therefore, any person, regardless of background or familiarity with the profession, could declare himself an architect—even engineers and building contractors. Times were extremely difficult for architects; royal architects not in agreement with the revolutionary movement were without work; some were even executed. Little building activity was undertaken during this period. With the establishment of the Directory in 1795 an Institute was organized into five Academies, one of which was an Academy of Fine Arts. Following experimentation with various organizational structures the Académie des Beaux-Arts was formed in 1816.

Political changes were reflected in changes in decorative motifs. Examples include the use during the Republic of bundles of fasces and lictors' axes. After Napoleon's expeditions into Egypt came the use of scarabs, lotus capitals, etc. The *N* for Napoleon and the stylized bee for Bonaparte replaced the intertwined Ls of the previous monarchial periods.

Through his appointments of Charles Percier (1764–1838) and Pierre François Léonard Fontaine (1762–1853) as official architects in 1801, Napoleon strongly influenced the direction of the arts. However, these two architects were known more for their decoration and furniture design. Their prestige extended throughout Europe through publications as well as the reputation of their decorative work at Malmaisson and at the Tuileries, each a primary residence for Napoleon. Publications included *Palais, maisons, etc., à Rome* in 1798 and, in 1801, *Recueil de décorations intérieures.*

In 1810 Napoleon appointed a commission to study the status of the arts. Among the recommendations was the repudiation by the architect Mathurin Crucy of the school of Blondel (operated his own school from 1743 to 1762), a traditionalist as represented in the works of Mansart. On the other hand, the commission praised the works of those who duplicated elements from ancient examples, as the architect Claude Etienne Beaumont; he had borrowed features from the Roman Pantheon and from temples.

SPATIAL RELATIONSHIPS

Architectural innovations were rare during the Revolution. Building activity, teaching, and practice were all disrupted. However, some architects instituted changes in the late 18th century that gradually came to be accepted in later stages of the Directoire and in the Empire. During the period of turmoil when architects could not undertake commissions, the time of many was used to publish. The contents of their publications included (1) drawings, (2) accomplishments of the 18th century relevant to the early 19th century, (3) theory, and (4) practical aspects of building. Greater emphasis was placed on use and purpose, geometric form, and economy. Since neoclassical features continued to be a factor in the Napoleonic era, many buildings represented a continuation of 18th-century antecedents.

Spatial Features of the Floor Plan and Three-Dimensional Spatial Characteristics

Among the younger group of architects was François-Joseph Bélanger (1744–1818); he and others made innovations that continued into the early 19th century. Changes in the plan and in the decorative style of the years just before the Revolution included giving the plan greater depth and providing for a more centralized ground plan. In view of the density of planning it became essential to use top lighting to funnel light to the innermost rooms. The dramatic effects achieved by this worked well for those interior architects who wished to capitalize on strong light–dark contrasts, where shadow played a role in the articulation of interior space. The lighting was channeled through a central domed space lit by a lantern above. There are also instances in which the dome was encompassed on the inside with a balustrade, behind which were windows.

Principal architects of the Revolutionary period were Etienne–Louis Boullée (1728–1799) and Claude–Nicolas Ledoux (1736–1806). Boullée was highly creative but often impractical in the solutions he recommended; he was interested in geometric architecture and in symbolism. To achieve a sense of the vastness of space he contrasted the repetition of small columns with the larger dimensions of a room. Ledoux as well as others promoted architecture based on geometric forms for their aesthetic and symbolic properties—sphere, cube, cylinder, pyramid. To him the sphere symbolically stood for infinity and perpetuity, since all points on the surface were an equal distance from the center. Both Boullée and Ledoux were interested in shadow as a means to animate and give emphasis to planes.

The plan by Louis Le Masson for Abbots Palace at Royaumont, constructed from 1785 to 1789, represents changes in the plan that became prevalent just before the Revolution (Figure 15-1). Circular rooms were often used, as revealed here for the dining room and library, each of which extends to form a projecting bow on the exterior; in other houses rooms of circular shape might include the salon, the stair hall, and hall. The irregular spaces around these were utilized in a variety of ways; incorporated in the Abbot's Palace are spaces for secondary stairs, liquor cabinets, and so on. In many residences it became the practice to place the staircase in the center of the plan as a expedient for economy, especially for smaller houses. The custom of placing the staircase in the central vestibule began in the 1760s and became very common in the 1770s and 1780s (Figure 15-2).

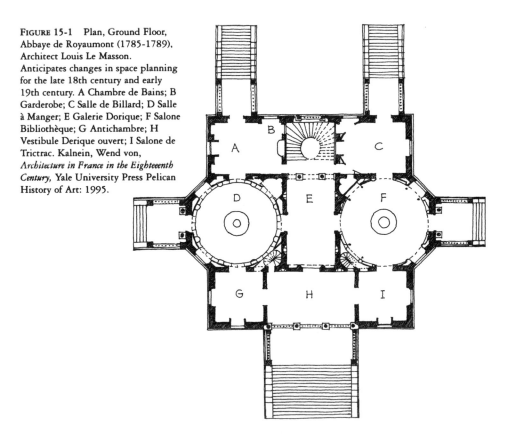

FIGURE 15-1 Plan, Ground Floor, Abbaye de Royaumont (1785-1789), Architect Louis Le Masson. Anticipates changes in space planning for the late 18th century and early 19th century. A Chambre de Bains; B Garderobe; C Salle de Billard; D Salle à Manger; E Galerie Dorique; F Salone Bibliothèque; G Antichambre; H Vestibule Derique ouvert; I Salone de Trictrac. Kalnein, Wend von, *Architecture in France in the Eighteeenth Century,* Yale University Press Pelican History of Art: 1995.

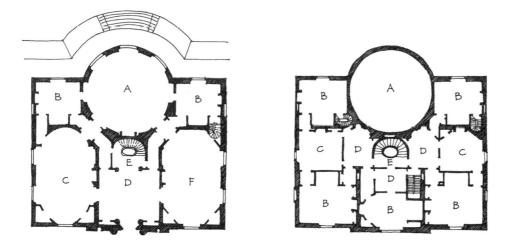

FIGURE 15-2 Plan, Château of Bagatelle, Bois de Boulogne, Paris Central stair and vestibule; emphasis on diversity of room shapes. Left, ground floor: A Salone; B Boudoir; C Salle à Manger; D Vestibule; E Escalier; F Salle de Billard. Right, first floor: A Salone montant; B Chambre à Coucher; C Cabinet; D Antichambre; E Escalier.

Although the circular room was typical, in 1788 an investigation into a total circular plan (replacing the rectangular plan) was undertaken by Henry (given name uncertain). However, within the circumference of the total space room shapes were diverse: triangular, oval, rectangular, square, oval, octagonal, etc.

The house designed by Paul–Guillaume Lemoine and built in 1790 for the playwright Beaumarchais anticipates the emphasis on the apartment house in the 19th century. The house faced the garden, while the large block of apartments and shops faced the street. The residential portion of the building partially encircled the round forecourt. The interior planning included round and oval room shapes as well as rectangular spaces. But for both the interior and exterior the major emphasis was placed on circularity.

The English garden was of major interest to the French; many studied in England and brought back ideas to France. For this residence the extensive garden layout was designed by Bélanger.

INTERIOR ARCHITECTURE AND DECORATION

Materials and Decorative Techniques

The materials and decorative techniques were not significantly different from those of the previous period. Wallpapers, textiles, stucco relief, marble and stone, wood for floors, painting, and bronze mounts were materials extensively use in the period from 1789 to 1815.

Interior Architecture and Decorative Elements: Directoire and Empire

During the Empire period (late neoclassical) there was a tendency to more accurately revive classical models, whereas in the early neoclassical period of Louis XVI designers consciously, freely adapted and interpreted designs based on antique sources of influence. The Louis XVI style can be characterized as elegant, graceful, refined, feminine, delicate, utilizing light colors, and unarchitectural; at the other end of the continuum the Empire style can be described as stiff, rigid, grandiose, pretentious, and emphasizing strong value contrasts. The Directoire style, a transition between Louis XVI and Empire, retains some of the features of Louis XVI while at the same time assumes some of the attributes of the Empire—neither as delicate as the preceding nor as rigid as the succeeding style. Decorative elements from the style of Louis XVI were used in the Directoire period while motifs introduced in the Directoire were retained in the Empire period; in addition, new motifs originated with the Empire style.

Some characteristics of works commissioned during the reign of Louis XVI were used later in the Empire style. For example, in 1777 Bélanger designed a tent bedroom for the Château of Bagatelle in Paris, a residence of the Comte d'Artois. The extensive use of real textiles or fictive drapery in this interior was later the model for many others—for example, the sumptuous tent bedroom of the Empress Josephine at Malmaison. One progression of influence led through Percier, who had worked for Bélanger and Pierre–Adrien Pâris before the Revolution; Percier and Fontaine were then employed by Empress Josephine in 1799 to renovate Malmaison, a job undertaken between 1800 and 1802.

It was largely through the efforts of Percier and Fontaine that the Empire style was created. Together they wrote *Recueil de décorations intérieuers* (1801). Through the painter Jacques Louis David (1748–1825) they met Napoleon Bonaparte, after which they became his architects initially in his position as First Consul and later when he was Emperor. Their style was pure classicism and they were the major arbiters of taste. Not only were they architects but they designed in many media of the decorative arts: furniture, wallpaper, glass, bronzes, and so on. In fact, they were more involved in decoration and furniture design than in architecture. Typically their decorative details were treated as separate units, as had been characteristic of the late 18th century when grotesque embellishment was reintroduced. Their designs were linear and colorful.

Floors

Floors for both the Directoire and Empire styles were treated in a similar manner. Wood was employed using parquet or plain planks. Marble was used for more important rooms. The designs of rugs sometimes echoed the ceiling treatment.

Walls

Directoire. Wall treatments of the Directoire period often had features both looking back to the Louis XVI style and looking forward to the Empire style. Usually the interiors of this period were more delicately conceived than those of the Empire. Walls were plain, painted, or sometimes more elaborately treated with panel arrangements and stucco embellishments. Simulated panels were accomplished in a variety of ways: (1) painted panels rendered on a plaster surface; (2) fabric stretched that represented panels; and (3) paper applied that represented panels. In panel arrangements narrow panels often alternated with broad divisions. Plain walls were sometimes fully covered with paper printed with small design motifs. While the dado was sometimes omitted it continued to be used in many instances.

The interiors of the Hôtel de Bourrienne, Paris, represent the transitional nature of the Directoire period (Figure 15-3). Examples of two characteristics illustrate the relationship to the preceding style and to the succeeding style. In the main salon stiffer and more rigid arrangements anticipate the Empire. Here, the overdoor treatment displays the disposition of the lunette within a rectangular frame, which was typical of the Louis XVI style. The general impression is one of classicism based on archaeological evidence through the use of such motifs as the candelabrum, palmette, and female figures in classic attire; the grandiose character of the Empire is not yet evident. Tall, narrow panels flank the wider unit of the mantel and overmantel mirror. Carved architectural frames enclose painted ornament as well as relief decoration. Within the narrow panels cameo–like representations (light against a darker ground) are depicted in medallions and in the lozenge; these are united by stiffly conceived units. The cornice of the entablature is supported by scrolled modillions with an acanthus carved on the lower surface of each; lozenges framing different decorative motifs alternate with the modillions. The mantel, plain and without ornamentation, was often used in the Empire style.

The dining room of the Hôtel de Bourrienne is separated from the adjacent space by a colonnade of Corinthian columns which visually sets it apart, yet allows visual extension. In addition, Corinthian columns in the round are repeated and set in front of but very close

FIGURE 15-3 Main Salon, Hôtel de Bourrienne, Paris. Directoire style. Decorated by François-Joseph Bélanger. Frégnac, Claude and Andrews, Wayne. *The Great Houses of Paris*. New York: Vendome

FIGURE 15-4 Wall Elevation (c.1790). Home of Architect François-Joseph Bélanger. Pairs of columns articulate wall surface. Kalnein, Wend von, *Architecture in France in the Eigteenth Century*, Yale University Press Pelican History of Art: 1995.

to the wall. The panel arrangement is typical in the use of wider panels flanked by tall narrow panels that originate above the dado. The wider panel is comprised of a mirror with an arched crest, the whole set within a rectangular frame; the narrow panels on each side are ornamented with arabesque stucco bas-reliefs of Pompeian derivation. The relief figures of women depicted in flowing dress are repeated between each arch of the arcaded facade. Bélanger, designer of this interior, introduced some of these elements prior to the Revolutionary period. The whole is more delicately conceived than the Empire style.

Bélanger, in his own home of around 1790, illustrated the use of the column in the articulation of the wall surfaces (Figure 15-4). Here he used pairs of slender columns between which he placed sofas under panels of large mirrors or other framed sections. Roundels with figural motifs were placed between the arches in the very deep arcaded frieze.

The grotesque style, based on antiquity, was used by designers including Bélanger. Introduced in the early 1770s for a bath house of the Hôtel de Brancas, it became very fashionable in the latter part of the century. Wallpapers were also printed with designs based on the grotesque.

Empire. The Empire style is represented in the Salon of the Seasons of the Hôtel de Beauharnais, Paris (Figure 15-5). Built in 1713, the house passed into the hands of Eugène de Beauharnais, stepson of Napoleon, who began the renovation in 1803. Beauharnais was reprimanded by Napoleon, who received a bill for one and a half million francs. The grandiose interior exhibits the characteristics of the Empire style in its grand scale, severity, formality, and heaviness. Walls are articulated by a series of pilasters that flank large paintings (in the manner of Pierre–Paul Prud'hon), doors, mantel, and mirrors. The pilasters, originating at dado level, are capped with elaborate gilt capitals while the base of each is ornamented with an arabesque headed with an eagle. The eagle (symbolic of autocratic power) was a frequently used motif during the Empire period. In the salone the very deep frieze is enhanced by regularly spaced eagles with spread wings united by festoons.

Other than the characteristics noted in the foregoing description alternative treatments of the Empire style included the use of plain walls, fresco, stretched fabrics, painting, and wallpaper. Draped textiles were highly significant; a superb example is the bedroom of the Empress Josephine in the Château de la Malmaisson near Paris; it is in the form of a tent with textiles draped between regularly spaced, slender, gilded columns. Wallpaper was sometimes printed to simulate drapery. Architectural features continued to include semidetached columns. The dado persisted, although it gradually dropped from fashion.

Windows and Doors

There was an inclination toward simplicity of treatment for doors and windows. Part of the simplification were the tendencies (1) to omit architectural features such as architraves, columns, and pilasters; (2) to delete the base for columns and pilasters; (3) to make door panels shallower; and (4) to construct moldings with flatter outlines.

When arched headings were employed for windows there was a preference for the diagonal disposition of dividing bars within the circular head. Beginning with the Directoire period fewer and larger panes were used for windows. The pediment without a horizontal base and a very low pitch was introduced; this element was also introduced for furniture.

Doors had single or double leaves. The number and size of panels varied: three for a single door, six to eight for double doors. Larger rectangular panels that varied in proportion were vertically disposed, while small rectangular panels were placed in horizontal positions. Square panels were coordinated with the rectangular panels. Panels tended to be shallow and at times were framed with carved moldings, although some were treated very simply with a plain architrave frame. Ornamental detail within the panel varied.

The double–leafed doors in the main salon of Hôtel de Bourrienne have six panels (three for each leaf) (See Figure 15-3). A small, horizontally positioned rectangular panel separates the vertically positioned rectangular panels above and below; this is unlike the Louis XVI arrangement whereby the smaller horizontal rectangular panels were aligned with panels of like position in the adjacent panel system. Ornamentation of the panels consists of a candelabrum in the taller upper panels while lower panels are centered with lozenge forms from which the anthemion emanates. Brackets are used to support the rather strong projecting cornice. The anthemion, a popular classical motif, is carved on the frieze. In the overdoor treatment a rectangular frame embraces an arch, the spandrels ornamented with the anthemion and dependent foliage.

Of the Empire period, the Salon of Seasons in the Hôtel Beauharnais has double–leafed doors with a total of eight panels (four for each leaf) (see Figure 15-5). Again, a small, horizontally positioned rectangular panel separates the upper panels from the lower ones. Sometimes, as observed here, painted designs were rendered in the panels. Door heads were straight; the deep frieze above the door head was decorated with a gilt relief design. Between the cornice of the door and the entablature heading the wall a painted design was prominent.

Chimneypieces

In the Directoire period materials most commonly employed were marble, stone, and wood. Chimneypieces were usually low and severe in form. A mantel shelf was supported in a number of ways: elongated scroll brackets, caryatids, or round columns. Gilt bronze

FIGURE 15-6
Chimneypiece Based on
Napoleon's Study at the
Palace of Compiègne.
Rectangular firebox,
low mantel shelf, rigid
decorative detail.
Courtesy of Hacker
Books, Inc. New York.

was sometimes used for columns and pilasters. Overmantel treatments were often mirrors or large paintings.

Of the Directoire period, the main salon in the Hôtel de Bourrienne has a very simple mantelpiece that is void of any decoration (see Figure 15-3). Columns in the round that support the mantel shelf rest on a plinth base. The overmantel mirror and the mantel are flanked by tall narrow panels.

In the Empire period mantels were low and without extended overmantel treatment. A straight lintel often headed the firebox opening. While the mantels were often plain, there was applied decoration at times; the mantels were often of black marble (see Figure 15-5). Supports for the mantel shelf were often of plain, freestanding columns, caryatid figures, or pilasters, as at Beauharnais; the frieze is ornamented with gilded festoons where the eagle with spread wings is used in the interstices. The space between the mantel shelf and ceiling was usually occupied by a mirror of the same breadth.

The chimneypiece of Napoleon's study at the Palace Compiègne represents Empire characteristics (Figure 15-6). The framing pilasters are decorated with stiffly conceived decorative elements, as is the frieze above. A mirror is placed between the low mantel shelf and the frieze, as was typical.

Ceilings

Ceilings of the Directoire period were flat, concaved to a flattened arc, or barrel vaulted. A restrained cornice divided the ceiling from the wall. The edges carried geometric or classical decoration; the latter type of treatment also decorated the center of the ceiling at times (see Figure 15-3). Fresco ornamentation was sometimes used for concave and barrel–vaulted ceilings. In addition, plasterwork designs in geometric shapes—circles, squares, hexagons, and octagons—that enclosed classical figures were sometimes used for flat ceilings. By 1790 Bélanger was using medallions (either painted or in relief plaster) in coffered ceilings; in addition, figural representations incorporated with arabesques were predicated on classical examples. Scenes of antique ruins within medallions were also used on walls.

The tall ceilings of the Empire period were often flat or barrel vaulted. Tent shapes were probably influenced by way of Napoleon's military conquests as well as the late 18th-century use of textiles by Bélanger. Sometimes the ceiling was geometrically arranged using a large variety of motifs from the classical repertoire (see Figure 15-5). A drawing by Percier and Fontaine for the King of Spain and a room they designed in the Palace of Arranjuez illustrate their use of barrel–vaulted ceilings.

Stairways

The location of the staircase was often the center of the plan. The central vestibule in which it was placed was often circular. Thus, a semicircular configuration for the stairway was common. Top lighting was important; often a dome served this function.

FURNITURE: DIRECTOIRE AND EMPIRE

Financial austerity meant changes in furniture. This implied less frequent use of veneer, marquetry, and bronze mounts, and a consequent emphasis on the use of solid wood. Mahogany was used only for more expensive furniture; beech was often a replacement. During the late Neoclassical period there was a tendency to more accurately revive classical models, whereas in the Louis XVI period designers freely adapted and interpreted designs based on antique sources of influence. As a transition, the Directoire style had features which related it to the immediate past style of Louis XVI and to the succeeding style of the Empire. Based on more stringent simulation of classical models, forms of the Empire style were severe. The architects Percier and Fontaine supplied designs for interior architectural elements as well as for furniture. In the desire to attain uniformity individual and creative approaches were suppressed in favor of one particular concept of design. Napoleon wished to convey through large–scale pieces of furniture that which was magisterial, luxurious, and opulent.

During the Empire period monumentality, rather than furniture designed to human scale, was the objective of designers. This aim was achieved in a number of ways: (1) the grand scale; (2) placing pieces on a plinth base (as beds, case pieces, etc.); and (3) strength and stateliness as suggested by an emphasis on rectilinear form. These pieces were designed to fit within pretentious settings.

Changes in trade in the late 18th century meant that guilds were eliminated. Thus, the stamp of the craftsman that had been a guarantee of quality was not required. Ebénistes were virtually eliminated since there was limited emphasis on veneering and marquetry. Stylistic changes between 1789 and 1797 were primarily related to decorative motifs, although a few structural alterations can be observed. After this phase, social and economic changes meant that more structural changes could occur. The numbers of different types of pieces became more limited in the Directoire and Empire periods compared to the Louis XVI period. While the foregoing was true for Paris in rural areas furniture continued to be made in the style of Louis XVI.

Materials and Construction Techniques

Mahogany was used primarily as a solid wood. Emphasis was given to strong patterning for decorative and ornamental effects; this was attained through the use of cutting to yield the strongest striations, mottling, etc. Other woods employed included elm, yew, beech, and ash.

FIGURE 15-7   Directoire Fauteuil (late 18th century). Carved and painted. Musée des Arts Décoratifs, Paris. Union Centrale des Arts Décoratifs.

FIGURE 15-8   Directoire Gondola Chair (c. 1803). Carved, painted, gilt, swan arm support. All rights reserved, The Metropolitan Museum of Art, Gift of Captain and Mrs. Fitch, 1910, in memory of Clyde Fitch (10.152.12).

Carving was sometimes employed, although as a decorative process it was time-consuming and expensive. Veneering and inlay were more expensive processes also, but they were important for the more expensive pieces. Inlay capitalized on the play of light inlays against darker mahogany or dark inlays against lighter woods. The inlay motifs were those typical of the period; stringing of contrasting value was an important outlining technique, often to emphasize structure. Materials for inlaid decorative details were brass, steel, and ivory, but these were usually reserved for furniture of the highest quality.

In previous periods bronze mounts were used to protect marquetry or to emphasize structure. However, in the Empire period stress was given to the continuity of the wood surface; thus, the function of bronze mounts was strictly embellishment. Gilt bronze mounts were chased with a matte finish. The motifs used were those typical of the period such as bees, palmettes, mythological scenes, and female figures.

Some pieces based on the klismos capitalized on painting for decoration. In these instances painted paper strips were glued to the traverse.

Typical Pieces and Stylistic Features: Directoire

Seat Furniture

Because of the diversity that characterized the period of the Directoire, the range of features will be noted. Back types consisted of those which were fully upholstered, some with a backward scroll of the crest of the back; others that were pierced used various center treatments, many derived from classical decorative motifs. The gondola form (introduced in this period) was shaped as though to envelop the sitter. Terminus forms for armrests often had animal heads such as lions, rams, and eagles, although more simple endings were also used. Arm supports included the frequently used baluster or colonnette. In addition, important support forms were the sphinx, swan, and griffin. Seats were upholstered and the seat rails were usually revealed. Legs were either round or

FIGURE 15-9 Directoire Commode (late 18th century). Brass inlay. Molding provides visual separation of upper drawer level from lower two drawers Musée des Arts Décoratifs, Paris. Union Centrale des Arts Décoratifs.

FIGURE 15-10 Directoire Bed (Lit) (late 18th century). Mahogany. Terminal figures; low pitch pediment for head- and footboards. Musée des Arts Décoratifs, Paris. Union Centrale des Arts Décoratifs.

square in section and tapered, sometimes fluted or reeded; rear legs were usually sabre. Sometimes a square framed block headed the legs at seat rail level; a carved rosette, either framed or unframed, was often used in this position. Curule support forms were also employed.

Two chairs illustrate some of these characteristics. The first shows the retention of features common to the Louis XVI style: fluted, round–sectioned, tapered legs headed with a framed block containing the rosette at seat rail level; bowed front seat rail; vase–shaped arm support that continues from the leg; the use of an arm pad which softly flows into the armrest. Differences are in the use of the sabre rear leg and in the backward scroll of the cresting of the back (Figure 15-7). The gondola chair was a new form that still includes features that relate it to the previous style: the square–sectioned and tapered front leg decorated with fluting; the unframed rosette at seat rail level; the bowed front seat rail (Figure 15-8). Characteristics new in the Directoire style include the gondola form, the use of the rear sabre leg, and the use of the swan for the arm.

Tables

Directoire tables represented a continuation of Louis XVI types but they were usually treated more severely. Legs were of square or round section and tapered; casters were often employed. Round or oval dining tables were usual. Other types included such functional pieces as the *guéridon,* a small circular table that served as a stand for a candlestick; the *tricoteuse,* a worktable, usually with a gallery around the top and often two shelves below the top; the *jardinière,* a stand used as a container for plants; the *desserte,* a small serving table with an undershelf; and bedside tables.

Storage Pieces

Commodes were quite varied in the Louis XVI style but in the Directoire style there was essentially one model, which was characterized by short legs, some with paw feet. The general effect was more severe than that of the Louis XVI style. The standard commode had three drawers with rectangular drawer pulls; sometimes a molding separated the top drawer from the lower two. Both fluted and nonfluted pilasters were employed, sometimes in a splayed position. In the place of pilasters, columns or terminals were sometimes used. The top sometimes had outset rounded corners on the front edge. A gallery around the top was often used, the pierced design of which was frequently lozenge (Figure 15-9).

Beds

The Directoire bed that is illustrated has typical features, but there was diversity in the design of these (Figure 15-10). One type had dossiers (headboards and footboards) of equal height with low-pitch triangular pediments; the uprights used here are terminal figures. Rolled-over dossiers of equal height were introduced late in the period; other uprights included turned balusters.

FIGURE 15-11   Fauteuil, Jacob Desmalter (c. 1803). Mahogany. Winged terminal figures end in paw feet. Square back. Gilded bronze mounts. Musée des Arts Décoratifs, Paris. Union Centrale des Arts Décoratifs.

Figure 15-12   French, Armchair. Empire Fauteuil (c. 1800). Honduran mahogany, beech, ormolu silk velvet, gold thread. Courtesy Philadelphia Museum of Art: SmithKline Beecham Corporation Fund for the Arts Medica Collection.

Figure 15-13 Empire Console Mahogany, chased and gilt bronze. Winged female terminal figures on plinth base. Bust and feet of bronze. Mirror backing. Fontainebleau. Photographs courtesy of Réunion des Musés Nationaux.

Typical Pieces and Stylistic Features: Empire

Although mahogany was a preferred wood for the Empire period, other woods included oak, walnut, elm root, maple, ebony, and purplewood. A general characterization of the Empire style can include the following: heavy, large-scale, severe, sharp corners, imposing grandeur, moldings almost eliminated, smooth columns both engaged and disengaged, uninterrupted flat surfaces, heavy bases for cabinet pieces, and symmetry.

Seat Furniture

The combination of features for the Empire style was so diverse that the gamut of attributes will be noted in the following. Generally chairs were large-scale pieces intended to be placed against the wall. Compared to the Directoire, backs were often vertical with straight line emphasis, square or rectangle giving a sense of greater rigidity (Figure 15-11). The S–profile for uprights was utilized at times. The gondola form was widely used. Some backs were pierced with centers of lyre, lattice, etc., but many backs were upholstered. The crest of the back sometimes had a backward rolled scroll; pedimented crests were also utilized, usually with a low pitch. Armrests were essentially parallel with the floor and when a manchette was incorporated it was stiffly conceived. For the arms various elements were used, such as mythological figures (swans, griffins, sphinxes); human forms (caryatids, terms); architectural elements (columns); and cornucopias. Arm supports were often a continuation of the front legs uninterrupted at the seat rail; their form could be lion monopodia, caryatids, swans, eagles, terminal figures, etc. (Figure

Figure 15-14 Bonheur du jour (1805-10) Charles-Joseph Lemarchand. Acajou, bronze mounts. Musée des Arts Décoratifs, Paris. Union Centrale des Arts Décoratifs.

FIGURE 15-15 Empire Athénienne. Design Attributed to Charles Percier (1764-1838); Ormolu Mounts by Martin Guillaume Biennais (1764-1843). Chased and gilt bronze, amboyna wood. A triangular base and one shelf with incurved sides. B Detail, athénienne. Swan supports for round top; classical wave motif decorates the rim of top. The Metropolitan Museum of Art, Bequest of James Alexander Scrymser, 1926 (26.256.1).

15-12). The sabre leg was often used for the rear legs. Some legs were turned and tapering; cylindrical fluted legs legs resumed popularity.

Tables

The console was among the most common pieces of Empire furniture; it was rectangular with a narrow frieze. Supporting the top, possibilities for legs included columns, caryatids, winged figures, or other fantastic figures. the legs originated from the plinth, where a lower shelf united them. A mirror placed at the back created an impression of greater size because of the reflection (Figure 15-13).

Table forms produced during the Empire period were, in many instances, the same as those developed in the Louis XVI and Directoire periods. Differences related to the manner in which the decorative ornament was rendered—very formal and stiff in the Empire period. Larger tables tended to be round; the tops of these were simple wooden pieces sometimes decorated with inlay. Alternative materials to wood for tabletop surfaces were marble, porphyry, glass, and so on. Among other types of tables the following were constructed: guéridon (in various shapes), worktable, dining table, athénienne.

The *guéridon* was more informal than other tables produced in the Empire period. Geometric shapes included those used in decorative enhancement, such as the square and the hexagon. These pieces tended to deviate from the archaeological accuracy of other pieces.

The *bonheur du jour* was a small ladies' writing table with drawers. Sometimes provisions were incorporated for cosmetics and a mirror. In the example illustrated terminal figures are used on two levels. Also typical of the Empire period were severe silhouettes, the general elimination of moldings, and heavy plinth bases (Figure 15-14).

While the *athénienne* was not a new form it had a specialized function in the Empire style. It held a water basin and jug. Typically the basin had tripod supports resting on a plinth base of triangular form with incurved sides. This table has legs ending in paw feet; heading each leg is a swan that supports the basin (Figure 15-15).

Legs varied considerably in the Empire period. These included some with: a single central support, mythical monsters based on antique elements, lyres, terminal figures, and monopodia.

Storage Pieces

Essentially two types of commodes typified the Empire. One type consisted of three drawers placed on short feet; some were mounted on plinth bases. One extant piece has

FIGURE 15-16 Empire Commode. Mahogany. Chased and gilt bronze mounts. Strong projection of top drawer level supported by Egyptian-influenced terminal figures originating at plinth base. Musée des Arts Décoratifs, Paris. Union Centrale des Arts Décoratifs.

FIGURE 15-17 Empire Lit en Bâteau. Mahogany. Gilt bronze mounts. Winged sphinx at base of equal height head and foot boards. Musée des Arts Décoratifs, Paris. Union Centrale des Arts Décoratifs.

pilasters with capitals of bronze; the pilasters terminate with animal paw feet. The other type had two doors that concealed either drawers or shelves. In one Empire example terminal figures with Egyptian heads bound the piece; gilt bronze mounts are used on the drawer fronts with dancing figures in flowing dress. The whole is mounted on a plinth base (Figure 15-16).

Beds

Of the four sides of the bed, only one was given significant decorative treatment, since the long dimension was customarily placed parallel with the wall. Beds were designated by constructional features: *à la* turque (ends of equal height); *à l'antique* (single headboard); *en bâteau* (boat–shaped); *couchette* (a small bed). Bed hangings were highly significant in the final treatment. If beds had uprights in somewhat the same manner as Louis XVI the delicate colonettes were replaced by such structural features as heavily scaled pilasters, columns, and terminal figures. Another type of bed of major importance was the *lit bâteau*. The ends were of equal height, inclined, and scrolled over; a variation was the use of one tall end treated as above. Beds were sometimes treated in a very reserved manner; at other times the array of motifs representing the Empire repertoire of ornament was extensively utilized (Figure 15-17).

ORNAMENT: DIRECTOIRE AND EMPIRE

In the period from 1789 to 1815 motifs were often significant in terms of the immediate political situation. While specific motifs were introduced to reinforce one government or another between 1789 to 1804, the same motifs, in some instances, continued to be important in the Empire style.

Three different governments were operative during the period designated as the Directoire style: Revolutionary, Directory, and Consulate. Revolutionary symbols included the fasces, which was based on a Roman symbol of power and composed of a bundle of rods enclosing an ax; clasped hands symbolizing fraternity; and the Phrygian bonnet. During the governmental period of the Directory significant motifs included the lozenge, palmette, and lyre. The lozenge had not been used in the Louis XVI period as a motif but in the Directoire style it was an important one. The lozenge was sometimes inlaid to frame another motif. The palmette was used as a repeated motif for bands of decoration, applied decoration, and to embellish friezes. In the Consulate period the following motifs assumed prominence: swans, chimeras (mythical dragon–like animals), dolphins, caryatids, eagles, sphinxes, lotus, papyrus, lilies, date palms, and scarabs.

The distinction of certain motifs was often directly related to events of great significance, such as political events or military campaigns. For example, after the storming of the Bastille, which marked the beginning of the French Revolution, the motif of clasped hands became a symbol of fraternity. Napoleon's Egyptian campaigns prompted the use of such motifs as the male sphinx, lotus flowers, and scarabs.

Classical and other motifs that had been introduced in the Directoire period continued to be used in the Empire period. The motifs were disposed in a very systematic, orderly, and stiff manner. Elements used decoratively were geometric forms (lozenges, octagons, circles, etc.) important in and of themselves or used as frames for other motifs; classical figures in flowing gowns; motifs from the animal world (some based on mythology), including swans, eagles (symbolic of autocratic power), griffins, winged horses, chimeras, and sphinxes; floral and plant forms based on the ivy, olive, oak, laurel, acanthus, palm leaves, etc., in such arrangements as wreaths or festoons; lyres used both structurally and decoratively; and symbols of war, including quivers, arrows, and shields. Other symbols included the bee, the star, and the letter N, each of which was associated with Napoleon.

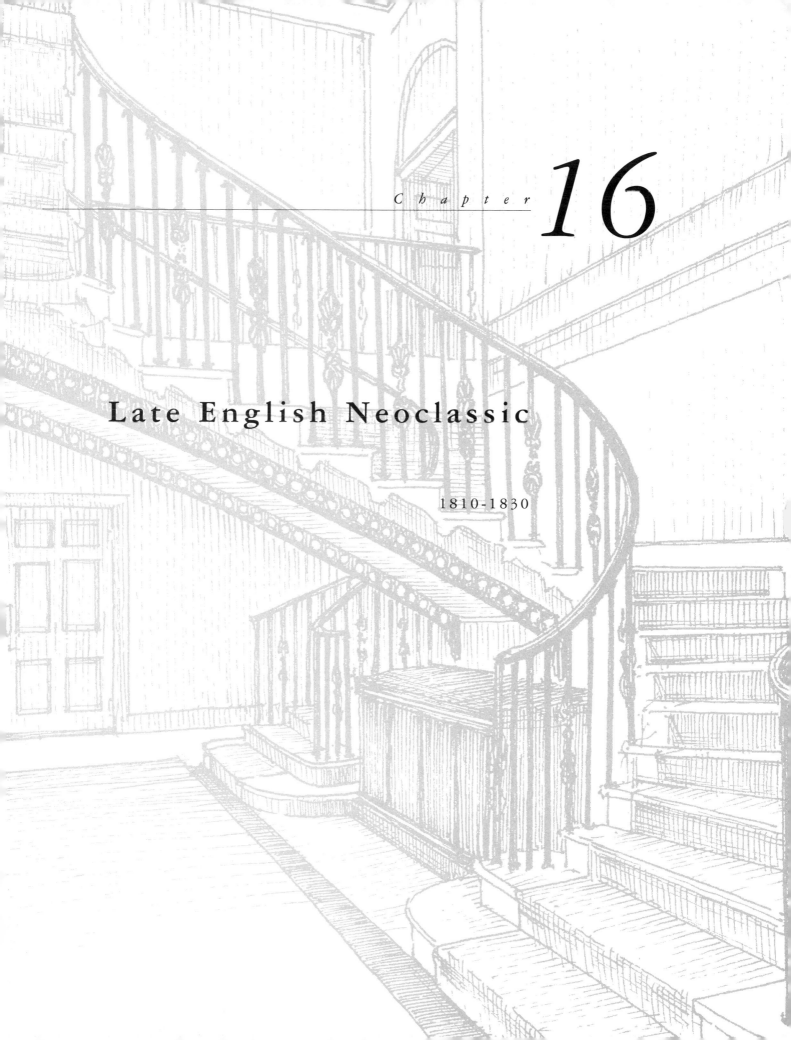

Chapter 16

Late English Neoclassic

1810-1830

HISTORICAL SETTING

Although stylistic trends began to occur in the late 18th century, Regency characteristics, in terms of interior architecture and design, essentially continued for the first four decades of the 19th century. Historically the term *Regency* does not coincide with the regency of George, Prince of Wales, who ruled beginning in 1811 in the stead of his father, George III (who was insane), until his accession as George IV (1820–1830), followed by his brother, who became William IV (1830–1837). In an art historical sense there are common stylistic features that are encompassed under the umbrella term of Regency.

Relatively few country houses were constructed during this period, but many were renovated. Building was depressed in part because of the French Wars, beginning in 1792, and the Napoleonic wars, which continued until the Battle of Waterloo in 1815. Consequently, there was a depreciation of currency value coupled with increased costs for materials and labor.

English designers were personally associated with leading French architects and designers, including Percier and Fontaine, and they were influenced by the upheavals in France. The military sequence of events led to certain stylistic features in furniture design such as the use of the sabre leg; the eagle, associated with Napoleon and French militarism; fasces (an axe in a bundle of rods), symbolic of the office of the Roman consul and adopted by Napoleon; and Egyptian motifs, due to the military campaigns of Napoleon.

Based on aesthetic and visual principles, the Picturesque movement influenced architecture, interior design, and relationship to the landscape setting. The theorists looked to 17th-century Italian and French landscape painters (Salvator Rosa, Gaspar Poussin, and Claude Lorraine) who had depicted architectural elements in informal landscape environments with attention to a mixture of styles.[1] The formulation of a more exact definition of the Picturesque began to be formulated in the latter part of the 18th century with the publication of three books in 1794 and 1795.[2] According to the Picturesque, landscape gardens were characterized by untamed features including streams, clusters of trees, and so on. Since the movement relied on visual values, the emphasis in architecture led to an emphasis on: (1) irregularity, (2) asymmetry, and (3) appreciation of historic architecture of all periods but not in terms of imitation. A plethora of previous styles and cultures were drawn upon; this was not an attempt to accurately revive a style but to convey an atmosphere, aura, mood, or feeling of the past style. Functionally, interior arrangements reflected the influence of the Picturesque movement in informal distribution of rooms, in the inclusion of a conservatory, and in the emphasis on a view from the interior to the landscape beyond. The architects sometimes used different sources of inspiration for exterior and interior, for example, an irregular castellated building with a classic interior or a combination of both Gothic and Chinese on the interior. John Nash and John Soane were leading architects of the Picturesque movement.[3]

John Soane (1753–1837) was a highly original architect responsible for both exterior and interior architecture. His spatial solutions were complex and unanticipated, the results of which were between classical and picturesque. After 1800 the Picturesque quality of his work became more evident through the use of such features as: (1) inventive top lighting, sometimes by means of a shallow dome to replace windows, (2) complex floor levels, and

---

1. Gaspard Poussin (1615–1675), French landscape painter; Claude Lorraine (1600–1682), French landscape painter giving impetus to 18th-century natural scenery in landscape gardens; Salvator Rosa (1615–1673), Italian landscape painter whose works are characterized by untamed and barbaric scenes.
2. Richard Payne Knight, *The Landscape, a Didactive Poem,* a criticism of the landscaping approach of Capability Brown; Uvedale Price, *Essay on the Picturesque, as Compared with the Sublime and the Beautiful,* painting out the desirability of adding aesthetic value as a criterion for evaluation; Humphrey Repton, *Sketches and Hints on Landscape Gardening,* stating that each landscape has the potential for greater enhancement.
3. Christopher Hussey, *English Country Houses, Late Georgian, 1800–1840* (London: Country Life, 1958), 17–26.

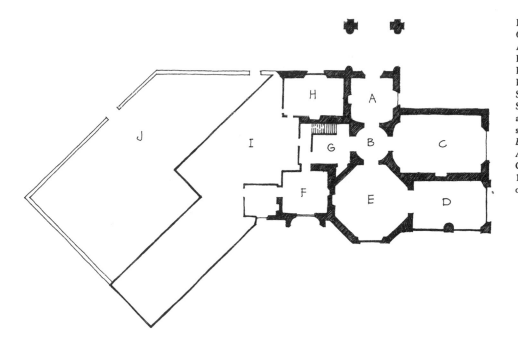

FIGURE 16-1 Plan, Luscombe Castle, Devonshire (1799-1804). Architect John Nash. Rooms: A Entrance Hall; B Vestibule; C Dining Room; D Conservatory; E Drawing Room; F Library; G Stairway Hall; H Servant's Hall; I Servants' Wing; J Kitchen Court and Drying Yard. Function of spaces changed over time. *Life in the English Country House, A Social and Architectural History,* by Mark Girouard, Yale University Press: 1978. By courtesy of Curtis Brown on behalf of Mark Girouard.

(3) mirrors—sometimes dozens—which had the effect of receding planes and of disguising divisions (See Figure C-32).

John Nash (1752–1835) was the greatest architect of the Picturesque movement, representing all aspects in his works. He designed in many styles—Italian farmhouse, classical, castellated Gothic, Indian—each of which was characterized by asymmetrical exterior silhouettes. A distinguishing feature of the Regency period was the acceptable practice of combining discordant styles. A case in point is the small residence of Luscombe Castle, Devonshire, with an asymmetrical castellated medieval exterior combined with a classical interior decor. It was orientated to take advantage of the surrounding landscape in a picturesque manner (Figure 16-1).

Individualism permeated design trends during the Regency. Styles of influence were selected on the basis of individual merits often backed by archaeological evidence. The eclecticism that characterized the period permitted influence from a diversity of styles as well as the liberty to combine elements from a plethora of styles—Greek, Roman, Gothic, Egyptian, Tudor, etc.

Henry Holland (1746–1806) was a primary leader of the early phase of the Regency period. He was instrumental in the transitional phase when, in the late 18th century, there was intense interest in Greek art and architecture characterized by severity of form, restricted ornament, simple lines, and symmetry. In working for the Prince Regent he combined motifs from Louis XVI and Directoire styles.

Thomas Sheraton, in his later publications, sensed the changes that were to take place and, in essence, predicted the Regency style; these are illustrated in the *Cabinet Dictionary* (1803) and in *Cabinet–maker, Upholsterer and General Artists' Encyclopedia* (1804–1806). In the *Dictionary* he illustrated, for the first time in England, couches of Greek inspiration.

Impetus for each ancient stylistic influence was associated with publications as well as current events. For example, the fashion for Egyptian was influenced by Dominique Vivant Denon, Director General of the Museums of France under the First Empire, who wrote an account of Egypt in 1802 entitled *Voyage dans la Basse et la Haute Egypte*. Furniture design in both France and England was influenced by this classic work. Forms and motifs of antiquity appeared (such as sphinxes, lotus, lions' paws, winged discs) as arm supports for armchairs, as terminal figures for chimneypieces, and as decorative enhancement in the use of ormolu mounts. Archaeological accuracy was applied by the Englishman Thomas Hope (1769–1831) and by the Frenchmen Charles Percier and Pierre François Fontaine, creators of the Empire style. English publications were also instrumental in promoting Egyptian taste—for example, Sheraton's *Cabinet Encyclopaedia* (1804–1806) and *Household Furniture* (1807), by Thomas Hope. Imagination was fueled by Nelson, the English naval hero, and his victory at the Nile, as well as by the Egyptian campaigns by Napoleon.

Parallel with the interest in Gothic and Picturesque approaches was the Greek basis for designs that would eliminate the more decorative Roman. Impetus was given by the purchase in 1816 of sculptures from the Parthenon in Athens. Further attention was focused by the Greek revolt against the Turks in 1821; Lord Byron, the English romantic poet, died in 1824 while working for the cause of Greek independence. Some implications for design were in the emphasis on broad and flat surfaces; also, a pediment of Greek derivation was employed in which an *akroter* (often a stylized palmette leaf) was used to ornament the top angle of the pediment. It was also used at the corners on such pieces as wardrobes, bookcases, and bureaus.

Publications focused on more than one ancient culture. Hope, in his concern for the trends of the time, desired to provide authoritarian information on architecture and furniture. As a young man he had spent eight years drawing architectural remains in such countries as Greece, Egypt, Turkey, Syria, and Spain. As a collector and an archaeologist, Hope's first residence was one in which he planned rooms as appropriate settings for individual collections. From this, Hope published *Household Furniture and Decoration* in 1807, which served as the fundamental authority on Greek, Roman, and Egyptian style. His interior architecture was characterized by large scale, simple forms, surface plainness, and minimal use of ornament. As a friend of Percier he derived forms from the French Empire. In addition, he was influenced by his knowledge of archaeological evidence.

Cabinetmaker George Smith published a pattern book in 1808 entitled *A Collection of Designs for Household Furniture and Interior Decoration;* it featured 150 colored plates, including illustrations of furniture within the context of interior decoration. His training as a cabinetmaker is revealed in the practical bent of his designs, although they often tended toward excessive ornament. His furniture showed Gothic, Chinese, Egyptian, Roman, and Greek influences. While his publication was issued one year after Hope's, his designs were dated from 1804 to 1807 and they show a heavy indebtedness to Hope, whose house was open periodically to the public; through Smith the ideas of Thomas Hope were more widely publicized.

The Regency was a period of fast change; seen in (1) practical planning with attention to amenities, comfort, and enjoyment; (2) informality of arrangement and the desirability of furniture that could be moved easily; (3) larger areas for fenestration; and (4) indoor plants that diminished the barriers between the indoor and outdoors. There were divergent tendencies over the span of the Regency—some simple, others more elaborate, some graceful, others heavy and robust.

SPATIAL RELATIONSHIPS

Compared to the formal apartment system utilized in previous periods, during the Regency emphasis was given to more informal and functional arrangements in order to facilitate communication between parts of the residence as well as to improve indoor–outdoor integration. Diversity in spatial relationships was typical and greater attention was paid to compactness and convenience. There were new designations for spaces such as parlor, study, morning room, and conservatory. The latter was, in part, a response to the fashion of growing plants indoors and led to the introduction of the *jardinière* (plant container).

Spatial Features of the Floor Plan and Three–Dimensional Spatial Characteristics

A new attitude regarding the position of the main rooms began in the late 18th century, as shown in the design for Doddington, Cheshire, by Samuel Wyatt (discussed in Chapter 14); this house was a harbinger of space planning concepts that were to be pervasive in the

Regency period. More informal planning began with a change in lifestyle in which houses were arranged for house parties. Consequently, main rooms were at ground level to encourage closer relationships between the interior and the exterior. Residents could easily walk from the interior to the landscape beyond through French windows. In addition, servants' wings were provided in asymmetrical attachments to main residences instead of rooms being placed in the basement. The conservatory often had the function of camouflaging the servant's wing.

Luscombe Castle is an example of planning to take advantage of the increasing attention to informality and to the role of indoor arrangements in connecting with the surrounding landscape (see Figure 16-1). It was designed by John Nash and constructed between 1800 and 1804. Nash used the Gothic Revival style with irregular silhouette and asymmetry, which suited this approach. Windows from the dining room, conservatory, drawing room, and study (or library) were in direct line for a view of the park; the windows come to the floor so that outdoor areas were easily accessible.

On the interior, public rooms were located at ground level and varied in shape. Some state and family apartments continued to be incorporated at ground level in some of the larger residences. Bedrooms, however, in most houses were planned for upper levels. But the social rooms were of prime importance in view of the informality of the period and of their importance to facilitating the house party. For the country residences these activities usually coincided with some event such as hunting, political discussions, or races.

Masculinity was associated with the dining room, femininity with the drawing room. It was common for ladies to retire to the drawing room following dinner. Daytime activities were often varied and, according to paintings of the period, the drawing room was utilized for informal daytime use such as music and other recreational activities. Informal activities also took place in the library but these were usually of a quieter nature. In common rooms, such as living rooms, furniture was often left in position for conversation, lounging, etc. In larger houses billiard rooms were sometimes incorporated.

At Sezincote, Gloucestershire, light is used to give a sense of drama on entering the stairway. From the hall one finds light filtering mysteriously through lunette windows beneath the dome. The manner in which the short flights of double stairs originate from the shorter dimension of the rectangular space is unusual. These two short flights of stairs are aligned with doors from the entrance hall (Figure 16-2). From this landing a single middle flight crosses the space and from a second landing the stair divides again to

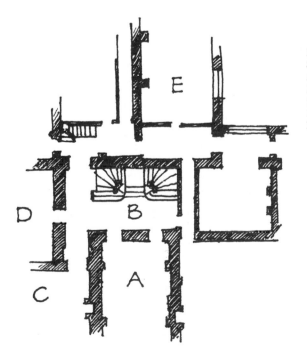

FIGURE 16-2 Plan, Staircase Hall, Sezincote, Gloucestershire (c. 1805). Architect Samuel Pepys Cockerell. A Entrance Hall; B Staircase Hall; C Billiard Room; D Library; E Servants' Hall. Courtesy of Country Life Picture Library.

FIGURE 16-3 Staircase, Sezincote, Gloucestershire (c. 1805). Architect Samuel Pepys Cockerell. Courtesy of Country Life Picture Library.

approach the upper level, one right and one left. In an early use of cast iron for structural purposes the single flight is supported by a segmented girder ornamented with a pierced guilloche pattern (Figure 16-3).

The highly inventive Sir John Soane, in his treatment of his residence at No. 13 Lincoln's Inn Fields, used several means to generate exceptional spatial interest (see Figure C-32). Summerson explains his Picturesque approach:

> The Picturesque element expresses itself in the treatment of the principal rooms, courts, and corridors. In the library (ground-floor front) there are hanging arches, Gothic inspired, which 'detach' the ceiling from the walls; tall bookcases, inset with strips of mirror, stand beneath and beyond the arches, while above the bookcases, and remoter still, is a deep mirror-frieze which, reflecting the whole ceiling, hints at yet further receding planes. It is impossible to say on which plane the actual wall exists; for all aesthetic purposes it is not there. Similarly, in the adjoining dining-room, an ample window looks out into the Monument Court, furnished with fragments to be seen in relation to the vases and pots ranged on the broad cill inside the room, blurring the division between room and court. Recession was always the aim, its effect intensified, very often, by ingenious top-lighting, which . . . became . . . an invaluable instrument of effect. Thus in the little domed breakfast room at the Museum, concealed lantern-lights

on two sides allow sunshine to slip in between the dome and wall, so that the wall is brighter than the centre of the room, where, however, its brightness is reflected in tiny convex, circular mirrors.[4]

INTERIOR ARCHITECTURE AND DECORATION

Disparate influences, roughly synthesized, characterized interior solutions of the Regency period. The constituent elements of the style were derived from: (1) concurrent French styles of the Directoire and Empire styles; (2) an interest in past styles based on archaeological evidence as well as current publications focusing on cultures of antiquity; and (3) a focus on the Picturesque movement, for which refinement of definition was being undertaken.

Materials and Decorative Techniques

Techniques and materials were not significantly different from the preceding period. For relief ornament both plaster and papier–mâché were used. Other materials of importance were scagliola, marble (sometimes inlaid with strips of brass), wallpaper, and cast and wrought iron. In addition, simulations were employed to imitate more expensive woods and marble.

Interior Architecture and Decorative Elements

Divergent stylistic influences were evident in the Regency period. These included Roman, Greek, Egyptian, Chinese, and Gothic. The late phase was severely Greek in derivation. There was stylistic diversity as well as other divergent tendencies—from subtle, refined, and elegant to strong, ponderous, and sturdy.

Floors

Residences of the wealthiest relied on parquetry or inlay work similar to French styles. In more modest interiors, however, fir or deal boards were utilized, painted or stained. Stone was sometimes used in entrance halls and, occasionally, mosaic installations were introduced. Scagliola was utilized to imitate marble. An example of extreme contrast in value is observed in the hall at Dodington Park, Gloucestershire, by James Wyatt, where black, red, and white marble was laid in a geometric pattern set in strips of brass. The use of carpets increased. They were installed wall to wall; in so doing strips of carpet were sewn together for the perfect fit to the room.

Walls

The standard division for walls was typical: dado, field, and cornice. Painted simulations (marble, stone blocks, or the grain of expensive wood) were sometimes used for the wood dado although plain colors were also employed. The baseboard, capped with a molding, was about eight inches in height. The field of the wall was often of plaster above the dado rail. When the dado was eliminated various materials were utilized between the baseboard and the entablature.

Many other treatments were incorporated in the interiors by trendsetting architects; they incorporated stylistic elements from the variety of sources that pervaded the period— Tudor, Chinese, French Directoire and Empire, Gothic, Egyptian, Hellenic, Pompeiian, Etruscan. Some of the diversity in wall composition is noted in the following discussion.

---

4. John Summerson, *Architecture in Britain, 1530 to 1830* (Frome, Somerset: Penguin; first paperback edition, based on fifth hardback edition, 1970), 491.

At Dodington Park (1797–1817), architect James Wyatt articulated the walls of the dining room by using full-height yellow scagliola pilasters that rise from the floor through the dado and extend to the entablature. Strong value contrast with the wall below is achieved by the marbled porphyry entablature. Niches and wall recesses for specific pieces of furniture were used in the same room; these originate at floor level.

Henry Holland reconstructed Southill, Bedfordshire, from 1797 to 1817. His compositions were often severe and precise and later work was distinguished by stiffer enrichment than his earlier work. In the dining room at Southill walls were painted green with white stucco. Above the dado, moldings framed wide rectangular panels alternating with tall narrow panels; the latter were porphyry–colored and provided strong value contrast. The panel width above was repeated below the dado rail. In the drawing room crimson silk hung above the dado.

Designs for some wallpaper revealed that Chinese paper continued to be prized in the 19th century. In some instances the wallpaper was set within individual rectangular frames between the dado and the entablature, as at Tregothan, Cornwall. In other methods of application wallpaper covered the wall between the baseboard and the cornice; for example, at Mamhead, Devonshire, the designer used flocked stone–colored wallpaper with motifs of Gothic derivation, quatrefoils with darker grey crosslets.

Windows and Doors

The Picturesque movement, which stressed views and accessibility from the residence to the landscape impacted window design (Figure 16-4). Facilitating this was the use of full–length glazed windows, either sash or casement (also termed *French windows*); bow

FIGURE 16-4 Windows, Luscombe Castle, Devonshire, (1799-1804). Architect John Nash. Interior-exterior relationships emphasized by the picturesque movement. Courtesy of Country Life Picture Library.

FIGURE 16-5   Window with colored band of lights surrounding clear glass panes. Shutters fold into shutter boxes.

FIGURE 16-6   Double Door. Mahogany with inlay of contrasting woods. Two handles. Entablature in the manner of Architect James Wyatt. Courtesy of Country Life Picture Library.

windows were also employed to extend and enhance the view. Regardless of length, the shapes of panes were primarily square or rectangular; however, more complex configurations such as Gothic detailing and the pointed arch altered the contour. A band of narrow lights sometimes marked the outermost bounds of the window; these were often red or blue, but other colors were used (Figure 16-5). Glazing bars tended to be thin and complex in contour.

Windows were round-or square-headed. An example of the use of some of the foregoing features is illustrated in the plan for the round-headed staircase window at Sheringham, Norfolk. The lower sash was to have been painted with classical design in order to camouflage the yard below; the outermost bound of the upper window was to have been a border of colored glass etched with arabesques.

Shutters continued to be used during the Regency period (See Figures 16-4 and 16-5). Some storage arrangements for shutters included folding them into shutter boxes in splayed reveals, folding them at right angles to the window within the reveal, and storing them in shallow splayed frames. Shutters became rare after mid–century.

Doors were usually of four or six panels and single– or double–leafed; if double–leafed, there were usually two handles but in rare instances a single handle was used. Some doors were paneled (sunken or fielded) while in other examples the doors were flush, suggesting panels by the use of contrasting bands of darker wood; inlay occasionally ornamented the panels (Figure 16-6). For more important doors mahogany was used. Some doors were painted while wood graining was used for others to simulate more expensive woods such

FIGURE 16-7 Chimneypiece.
Classical influence in the use of the
fret on the stiles originating from
the floor. Courtesy of Country Life
Picture Library.

as mahogany or rosewood. Surrounds varied; some were plain and narrow, others wide and flat. Examples of decorative treatment for the surround included such detailing as reeding, simple molding patterns, and running patterns of imbricated scalework. If corner blocks were employed they were sometimes plain, while others were ornamented with such motifs as roundels or lion masks.

Simpler doorways utilized only the door architrave as the finish. Overdoor treatments were diverse. Examples include the shallow pediment, sometimes utilizing acroteria; the entablature, sometimes with decorative enrichment; and the cornice, supported with brackets. Doors were also capped with panels of plaster casts of animals as the combined use of lion and vase, a Hellenistic motif and influenced by the Louis XVI feature of an arched head placed within a rectangular frame, but with detailing of the Regency period.

Chimneypieces

A rectangular firebox opening was typical; exceptions were related to such stylistic influences as the Tudor arch, which sometimes formed the upper bounds of the firebox opening. Simplicity characterized the firebox surround. The stiles arose either directly from the floor or from a plinth base (Figure 16-7). The most typical surround was one in which the jambs were capped with corner blocks at frieze level and decorated with roundels; the central tablet at frieze level continued to be used for the first part of the Regency period. Reeding was widely used to give surface enrichment to the jambs; otherwise, occasional use was made of Greek motifs as well as Egyptian, Gothic, and others. Wider jambs resembling pilasters capped with boldly rendered leaf forms began to be employed in the third decade of the century. Materials most widely used were wood or marble; wood was painted to simulate either other woods or marble. Ornamentation was sometimes rendered in a type of papier-mâché, molded and applied to the surfaces. The mantel shelf was deeper and wider than those of the English Early Neoclassical period.

Mirrors were used as overmantel treatment in more important rooms. The decorative detail of the mirror surround was coordinated with that of the mantel below.

FIGURE 16-8   Central ceiling medallion, terra-cotta.

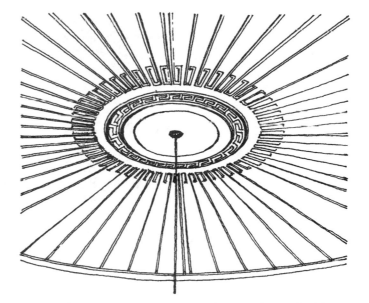

FIGURE 16-9   Shallow dome with radiating fret design from the breakfast room in the Soane Museum. Courtesy of Country Life Picture Library.

Ceilings

Compared to the ceilings of the Early English Neoclassical period, Regency ceilings were generally more severe. Overall ceiling treatments in many instances reinforced the stylistic influence, as a pargework ceiling recalling the Jacobean period. Coffering was sometimes used in which terra–cotta medallions ornamented the center of the lacunar. The major emphasis was toward simplicity; the central medallion was a focus (Figure 16-8). In addition, moldings at the edge of the ceiling plane were often arranged to reflect the room shape. Ornamentally the greatest attention centered on the entablature, or parts of it. Decoration for the frieze might incorporate one or a combination of such motifs as the guilloche, anthemion, fret, and festoons. The cornice was often composed of classically correct Greek moldings; these were available commercially. Bolder and stiffer designs were favored.

Many ceilings were flat but shallow domes and segmental vaulting were also utilized. The shallow dome of the breakfast room at the Soane Museum makes decorative use of the Greek fret to frame the opening. Radiating adaptations of it unite with the outermost frame of the circle (Figure 16-9). For the segmental vaulted ceiling of the White Drawing Room at Broughton Hall, Yorkshire, the architect used the Greek fret to define rectangular compartments spaced regularly over the surface.

Stairways

The stairway was indicative of the wealth of the family. Stairs ascended in straight flights or arose in configurations of graceful curves. More expensive materials were combinations of stone, mahogany, and cast-iron balusters. If stone was used for the main flight of stairs it was often cantilevered; the treads had strongly articulated nosing that continued to the tread ends. Most stairs were of open string construction but occasionally a closed string was employed. Wrought iron continued to be used for balusters but cast iron came to be preferred; these materials allowed more complex outlines for the balusters. The design as well as the number of balusters per tread varied. Pattern books illustrated classical elements, Gothic detail, etc., in arrangements that were two per tread, one per tread, two different designs of baluster per step, and so on.

In the staircase at Sezincote, Gloucestershire, the balusters are of bronze ornamented with the anthemion. Because of the shaping of the treads the number per tread varies between one, two, three, and five balusters per tread (see Figure 16-3).

For more moderate homes and for stairways on upper levels of more grand residences wood was the primary material; painted wood in drab colors or wood grain simulations were employed for the treads. Frequently there were two balusters per tread; these were often of square cross section. Ornamentation, which was not emphasized, was largely confined to the newel.

FURNITURE

Thomas Sheraton had introduced designs of classical derivation as well as Egyptian in the *Dictionary* and *Encyclopedia* between 1803 and 1806. The influence of ancient cultures was intensified by the attention focused on Egypt because of the defeat by Viscount Horatio Nelson (the English naval hero) of the French fleet led by Napoleon I in 1798, called the Battle of the Nile. While the ornamental detail illustrated in the later Sheraton publications was significant, a more academic approach was provided by Thomas Hope because of his intense interest in archaeology.

Hope was influenced by the French through his friendship with Percier, an architect and designer, and also by his architectural studies in Egypt, Turkey, Syria, and Greece. These influences were reflected in his 1807 publication *Household Furniture and Decoration;* he incorporated such design elements from ancient civilizations as the lyre, the lion monopodia, the winged sphinx, the Egyptian head, the palm leaf, and the Greek fret. Hope's designs were more archaeologically accurate than those of other designers and were widely influential.

Hope's designs were popularized through the publication by George Smith in 1808 of *A Collection of Designs for Household Furniture and Interior Decoration.* Hope himself resented the fact that his designs were widely copied. Smith's designs differed from Hope's in that he also showed those of Chinese and Gothic derivation. Some of the commonalities between the two were the use of the animal monopodia, the Roman curule form, the arm supports in the form of the sphinx, the lotus motif dividing a column, etc.

At the beginning of the 19th century furniture forms were lightly scaled. Before the end of the first decade forms became heavier, with some emphasis of bronze applications. Among features illustrated in Sheraton's *Drawing Book* retained in the Regency period were the use of reeding for legs and edges of tabletops, kidney–shaped tabletops, and splayed paw feet.

Materials and Construction Techniques

Although there were some advances in machine tools for woodworking, momentum for industrial production did not begin until the mid-19th century. Machines began to be operated by steam but this did not impact design to a significant extent. Important techniques precluded the need for new mechanical processes at this point in time. First of all, there was a preference for plain surfaces, and when ornamentation was employed it was largely in the form of cast–metal decoration; to a significant degree the latter replaced carving. When carving was used it was accomplished by hand and was usually for pieces for the very wealthy.

Techniques of importance in the Regency period were veneering with its associated applications of stringing and banding, cast metal, carving, painting, églomisé, and lacquer. Regency designers placed great emphasis on prominent figure and color of veneers. Rosewood, figured mahogany, and zebrawood were popular because of the grain and color; amboyna, satinwood, and maple were also employed. Solid wood was largely replaced by veneered pieces, except for chairs and those pieces which were painted or lacquered. Inlays providing textural or value contrast were often in brass, holly, yew, or ebony. Inlay motifs varied with the stylistic influence; for example, classical ornaments might include such motifs as the fret, honeysuckle, or palmette. From the French Directoire, English designers used the lozenge as an inlay motif in such places as around keyholes, on doors, and around drawer pulls. Brass inlay was used for single isolated motifs as well as for continu-

x

ous patterns on such surfaces as pilasters, friezes, tabletops, and fronts of drawers. Stringing figured prominently as a means to outline design units or to emphasize edges of pieces.

Cast brass was prominently used for ornamentation while bronze was rarely used. Metal was used for such parts as doorknobs, plates for doorknobs, galleries, strips of bead molding, and colonnettes. Although ormolu (gilded metal) was used there was also great use of lacquered brass; sometimes these two were used on the same piece.

Carving was largely replaced due to the strong emphasis on veneering for decorative purposes. However, some parts of furniture required carving, as the lion monopodia and dolphin supports. Carved ornamentation was used on both wood and papier-mâché; the same degree of deep relief was possible with each material.

Painting was used for large groups of furniture pieces. It was utilized for furniture made of cheaper woods, those of high quality, often with the addition of gilt highlights, and for enhancing a decorative scheme. The vogue for naturalistically painted floral arrangements became important later in the Regency period. Sometimes floral arrangements and classical ornament were painted on an ebonized background for the same piece.

The art form termed *églomisé,* in its strictest sense, was accomplished through the application of gold leaf to the reverse side of glass, after which decoration was attained by engraving. This process was used for mirrors and sometimes for cabinets. Painting on the reverse side of the glass was also undertaken but it is not considered églomisé. Gold and black renditions as well as colorful landscapes were undertaken in both of these processes.

The fashion for chinoiserie in the Regency period led to a fascination with oriental lacquer. In this period it was frequently the case that panels were purchased from foreign trading centers and incorporated by English craftsmen into cabinets. Human figures were widely used in Chinese lacquer and materials inset in the surface included jade and ivory. In Japanese lacquer, however, human figures were rare; scenic panels were typical. The lacquer surface was built up of from ten to as many as twenty or more coats. A paste of clay was built up for areas of intended relief and painted.

Typical Pieces and Stylistic Features

Seat Furniture

At the beginning of the 18th furniture was lightly scaled. Among the chairs exhibiting this more fragile and elegant quality was the Trafalgar chair (Figure 16-10). Its name

FIGURE 16-10   Trafalgar Chair. Sabre legs, curved knee of the leg, caning, spiral turning (stiles and crest of the back), lightly scaled.

FIGURE 16-11 Sidechair Based on the Greek Klismos. Decoration in black and red, as observed on ancient vase paintings. By Courtesy of the Board of Trustees of the Victoria and Albert Museum, London.

FIGURE 16-12 Armchair in the Egyptian taste (c. 1806). Lion monopodia leg and arm support. Ebonized carved wood highlighted with gilding. Based on a design in George Smith's *Collection of Designs for Household Furniture.* By Courtesy of the Board of Trustees of the Victoria and Albert Museum, London.

is most likely derived from the naval hero Nelson's 1805 defeat of the French and Spanish fleets at Cape Trafalgar on the southwestern coast of Spain; near this date the chair had attained its height of development. It remained popular until the 1820s. The chair is distinguished by sabre legs that are rectangular in cross section with the narrow edge to the front. The knee of the leg at the juncture with the side rails of the seat forms an unbroken curve; the side seat rail forms a continuous curve as it meets the stile of the back. A slight backward scroll of the stile at the crest of the back is typical. Sections of spiral turning (also called rope molding) usually ornament the stiles at the level of the horizontal crosspiece of the back; the turning also centered the crest rail of the back. Caning was common for the seat surface. Frequently made of beech, these chairs were often painted black and were commonly used in the dining parlor.

Chair designs were quite diverse. Particularly in the latter part of the period innovation was emphasized, resulting in the production of rather   pretentious designs. Frequently there was a backward scroll of the side pieces of the back at the cresting, sometimes undecorated, as was the case with the Trafalgar chair, but occasionally terminating in a mask. Horizontality was accentuated in the detail of the back and backs were often low. Especially for designs based on Greek models a concave back crest was characteristic; typically it was curved as though to envelop the sitter and was flat, broad, and deep (Figure 16-11). This type usually had sabre legs. Egyptian influence is also noted in chair design (Figure 16-12). In the Egyptian taste, this chair is of carved wood, ebonized, and gilded. Here the lion monopodia is used for the front legs and continues to form the arm support. George Smith depicted a similar design in his *Collection of Designs for Household Furniture.*

Typical of most chairs in the Regency style was that armrests were set high on the uprights of the back. In some instances the armrest continued in a strong, uninterrupted curve and rested on the side rail; in other examples, the armrest extended in a scroll beyond

FIGURE 16-13 Armchair (c. 1820). Carved mahogany. Heavier and later Regency style with classical influence. By Courtesy of the Board of Trustees of the Victoria and Albert Museum, London.

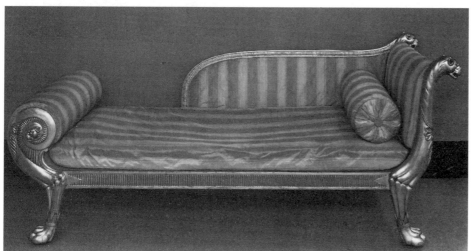

FIGURE 16-14 Sofa in gilded wood with lion monopodia supports. By Courtesy of the Board of Trustees of the Victoria and Albert Museum, London.

the arm support. Other than the sabre, legs were straight and rectangular or round in section; reeding was often use as decorative enhancement.

Later in date, this example displays slight classical influence in the use of such features as the ram's head resting on the side seat rail at the juncture of the back uprights, the sabre rear leg, and the concave cresting rail (Figure 16-13). Although carving was not a significant decorative technique in the Regency period, this chair is made of carved mahogany.

The sofa was a fashionable form in the Regency style and often based on Greek prototypes. Usually the sofas were characterized by outward curving ends and strongly incurved legs. In this example, an animal head centers the scrolled lower end while the lion monopodia supports are used for the taller end (Figure 16-14). These pieces were used for reclining; bolsters were common.

Tables

Sofa tables were widely used in the first years of the 19th century, especially for the library, parlor, and drawing room. They were intended to stand in front of the sofa for the use of such ladies' activities as writing, and reading. Larger than Pembroke tables, they also differed in that the drop leaves were attached on the short sides. Supports were sometimes lyre in shape or turned and often connected by a stretcher, or the support was sometimes a central pedestal with four incurved legs. In size, they could be as big as five feet by two feet.

Round tables were popular in the Regency period, frequently mounted on triangular pedestals. The triangular base has incurved sides with paw feet at the points of the triangle (Figure 16-15). These pieces were used as breakfast tables or as game tables, sometimes called loo tables. Thomas Hope designed this piece for his own home and it was published in *Household Furniture and Interior Decoration* (1807).

FIGURE 16-17 Bookcase Based on Sheraton's *Cabinet Encyclopedia* (1806). Painted stucco busts for the terminal figures. Classical influence in the use of pediment and acroteria in the form of the anthemion. By Courtesy of the Board of Trustees of the Victoria and Albert Museum, London.

The dressing table was usually larger than those of the late 18th century and followed Smith's recommendation that there should be no handles; the design is similar to those illustrated in George Smith's publication *Household Furniture* (Figure 16-16). Of mahogany with an inlay of ebony, this piece has shaped trestle supports roughly derived from Roman examples. The emphasis given flat surfaces was a characteristic shared with the French Empire style.

Storage Pieces

Sheraton's *Dictionary* and *Encyclopedia* continued to be influential in the formation of the Regency style; both motifs and forms were derived from these sources. This combination bookcase and cabinet in the Regency style is an example whereby the design is closely allied with one appearing in Sheraton's *Cabinet Encyclopedia* of 1806 (Figure 16-17). Classical relationships are noted in the use of the pediment enhanced with acroteria at the apex and at the terminal points of each side; the anthemion figures prominently in the design of the acroteria and on the frieze as an ebony inlay. Term supports of the upper section incorporate painted stucco busts of two late 18th and early 19th political figures, Charles James Fox (Whig party leader) and William Pitt (Prime Minister under George III). Terminal figures are also used below for the cabinet section. Supports are paw feet in the front and turned in the rear.

Beds

Like other furniture pieces, beds showed great diversity in form. As with French examples, some were designed to be placed parallel with the wall. These were of two types, one with outward scrolled ends, the other in the manner of Louis XVI. Both were often draped from a shaped crown near the ceiling, with drapery placed over the ends of the bed. Other types of beds were four-poster and canopy; these were also draped with valances and curtains.

ORNAMENT

Ornamental detail characterizing the English Regency period can be largely related to the ancient cultures whose influence was advocated by leading designers, many of whom showed archaeological accuracy through their own studies. The techniques and materials for decorative detail were accomplished through inlays of brass and ebony, ormolu mounts, carving, and painting. Forms were influenced in the same manner.

While motifs were derived from ancient cultures, designers sometimes took liberties in their application. For example, the Egyptian sphinx was depicted as male and without wings, but designers sometimes represented it as female and with wings. Other decorative detail drawn from the repertoire of Egyptian motifs included Egyptian heads as terminal headings for pilasters, legs, etc.; lion masks; winged sun disks; and lotus flowers.

Chinese influence is noted in the utilization of japanning and lacquer work. Motifs included the use of Oriental figures and dragons. Another indication of Chinese influence is in the carving of chair frames in imitation of bamboo; occasionally bamboo was represented in painting. The form of pieces sometimes incorporated the pagoda roof motif.

Classical Greek and Rome were major influences in the early 19th century; this was reflected in structural outline as well as in decorative detail. Significant ornamental detail included such motifs as swans, lyres, stars, paterae, anthemia, rosettes, palm leaves, figural classical scenes, wreaths, acanthus leaves, and laurel leaves. Examples of structural elements included the use of sabre legs, caryatids, and scrolled ends to such pieces as sofas.

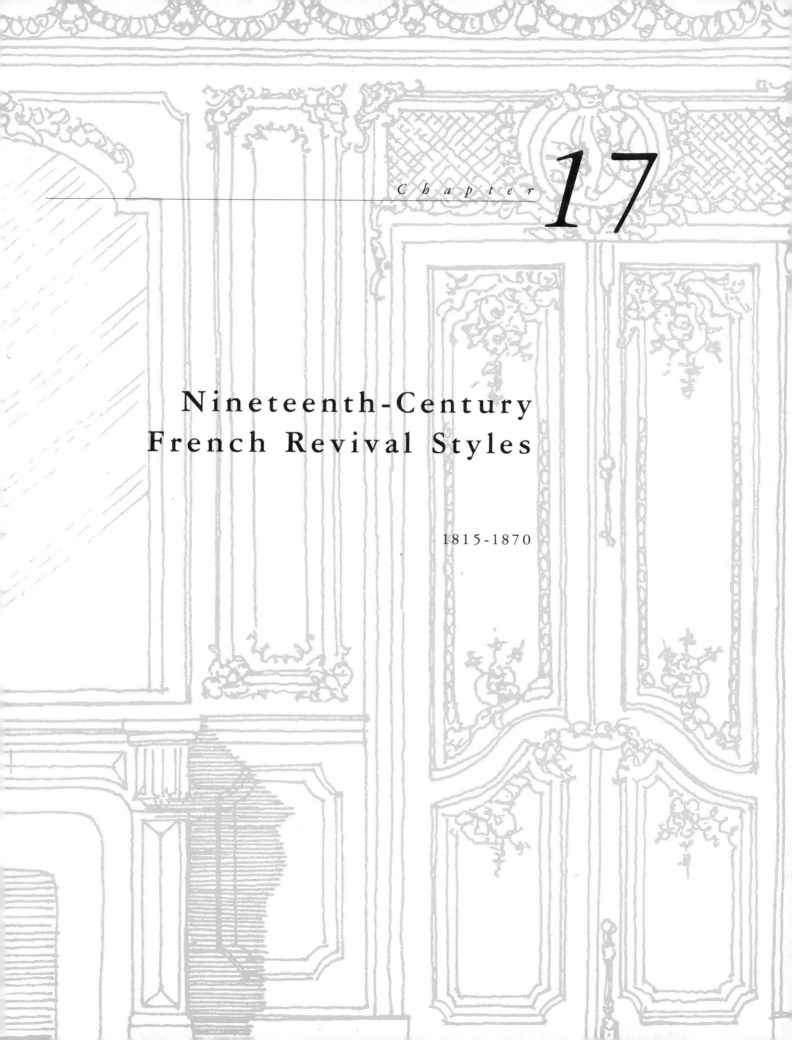

Chapter 17

Nineteenth-Century French Revival Styles

1815-1870

HISTORICAL SETTING

While changes in design were not directly related to changes of dynasty, the general trend of the period was influenced by the social, technological, and economic policies of the leaders and did impact design of interiors and furniture. Napoleon I abdicated in April 1814, after which he was exiled to Elba, a sovereign principality given him by allies. With his followers he returned to France in March 1815. He ruled for 100 days, was defeated at Waterloo, abdicated a second time, and spent the remainder of his days on the island of St. Helena, a British crown colony. Napoleonic influence on the arts continued to about 1830. There was only slight interest on the part of the ébéniste to experiment and there was no ascendant or uniform style that developed in the first 15 years of the Restoration. The habit of looking to past styles and of copying them began around 1830. Styles of influence extended from Gothic to Louis XVI. But the intensity of unmitigated reliance on past styles reached its height in the Second Empire.

The Bourbon Restoration covers the period from 1815 to 1830. Louis XVIII (1755–1824), brother of King Louis XVI, was proclaimed King by émigrés in 1795. However, he fled France in that year, 1795; was hunted by Napoleon, assumed the throne in 1814, fled during the 100 days of Napoleon's rule, and ruled as king from 1815 to 1824. Ruling from 1824 to 1830, Charles X (1757–1836) was the brother of Louis XVIII. The two-day July Revolution of 1830 resulted in the abdication of Charles, who died in exile. Precipitating the revolution was the opposition of the propertied middle class to the conservative and repressive policies of the king and his minister. Thus the foundation was laid for the influence of the bourgeois, reflected in the direction of design through their purchasing power; bourgeois influence intensified in the period of the Second Empire.

With an inherited claim to the throne, the younger branch of the Bourbon-Orléans line assumed power in the person of Louis Philippe (1773–1850), king of France from 1830 to 1848. During his tenure the bourgeois gained in power, business opportunities increased, industrialization gained momentum, and colonial expansion was undertaken. It was a period of peace and prosperity; however, people who did not own property still could not vote.

These kings had neither the resources nor the authoritarian power to play a significant role in matters of design. During the period from 1815 to 1848 residential building activity was minimal and architectural design did not develop along specific stylistic lines. This was due to the lack of leadership, an aristocracy lacking in financial resources, and cyclical periods of depression.

However, beginning around 1840 three factors contributed to the need to construct apartment buildings as an alternative method to meeting residential shortages: (1) urban growth, (2) growth of the middle class, and (3) high land values. The apartment complexes during the Restoration were small, simple, and practical. Known for small residences and apartment complexes, one of the most influential architects of the early 19th century was Jean-Nicolas-Louis Durand (1760–1834). He equated a functionalist approach with agreeable results. The use of historical and symmetrical ornament was characteristic of his work. Since suburbs were being developed, modest hôtels could be built outside the inner city, which allowed a substitute for apartment building; in this way citizens could escape the high land values of the inner city. Some changes instigated in the period of the Restoration gained strength during the Second Empire, 1848–1870.

Napoleon III was the emperor during the Second Empire. Following the revolution of 1848 Louis Napoleon Bonaparte (Napoleon III) was elected president of the French Republic and by coup d'état assumed dictatorial power as emperor of France from 1852 to 1870. He appointed Georges-Eugène Haussmann (1809–1891) to oversee an urban renewal project, the policies of which impacted apartment construction. Coupled with the priority given to meeting the housing shortage of the middle classes was the desire to protect the health of citizens. Building ordinances regulated the height of buildings (and the number of floors) by relating it to the width of the street; the intent was to allow sunlight to penetrate in the interest of health.

Industrialization gained momentum during the Second Empire and influenced apartment building. The emphasis was on component parts and construction rather than on beauty and planning. Simplicity characterized the apartment complex and creative approaches were not key to designing. The appeal to many tastes was perhaps one of the reasons for the simplicity of the apartment complex.

Even with the emphasis on the building of apartment complexes the construction of new hôtels continued to meet other residential needs. Those built by the nouveaux riches were usually ornate and composed of a mixture of stylistic elements; favored styles were Renaissance and Baroque. This was symbolic of their financial riches and their desire to be recognized socially.

Napoleon III was not personally interested in the arts but he did wish to promote industrial advances that affected both social and economic stability; he desired to display the magnificence of his court and through his surroundings to promote the preeminence of the French court. Conditions were not favorable for inventiveness or creativity since designers looked to the past for their sources of design. In pattern books were facsimiles of styles of the past; these were published earlier as *Mélanges d'Ornaments Divers* by Leconte in 1838 and *Repertoire de l'Ornemaniste,* issued in 1841 by Blaisot.

Napoleon III was interested in the impact on society of decisions on art matters. For example, rather than make assessments on matters of artistic merit he made decisions based on technical merit; his conclusions were premised on how products could be made available to all levels of society and how that decision would impact employment. Empress Eugénie did have some ability in artistic matters; she was eclectic in her approach as revealed through the mixing of different styles of furniture (First Empire, 18th century, and contemporary pieces). In this approach it is assumed that she followed contemporary fashion rather than initiating the movement. The Empress had an intense interest in Marie Antoinette and the Louis XVI style to the extent that she commissioned the French designer Perron to design a pavilion in the Louis XVI style for the 1867 Exhibition; this influenced interiors worldwide. While the imitation of past styles began in the period of Louis Philippe, greater interest in antiques began to assert itself during the Second Empire; this approach gave the bourgeois a sense of self-confidence by providing them a bridge to tradition. Pieces of furniture based on past styles were not always facsimiles. Designers felt they had something to offer and could enhance earlier styles. For example, technically they felt that their methods were better because greater precision was possible with machines for such delicate processes as marquetry.[1]

SPATIAL RELATIONSHIPS

Beginning in the latter part of the reign of Louis Philippe apartment building began to be important as a means of meeting the housing needs of the growing middle classes. Apartment buildings were built around either three or four sides of a courtyard. The exteriors were simple, with the façade being interrupted by the introduction of a balcony at the level of the piano nobile. Contributing also to the simplicity was the fact that windows were spaced regularly regardless of the disposition of rooms on the interior and they progressively decreased in height from lower to upper floors. Rooms in these earlier apartment complexes were small and ceiling heights were lower at the the upper stories of the building. Typically, shops were at ground level.

In the Second Empire the ground floor of the apartment complex continued to be devoted to commercial space; the *entresol,* which gradually became a full story, separated the ground floor from the piano nobile above. Two balconies were often used on the façade, one at the piano nobile level and another at the attic level, which meant that in a six-story building there were three stories between balconies and in a five-story building, two sto-

---

1. Jean-Marie Moulin, "The Art of the Second Empire," originally published in *The Magazine Antiques*, Brant Publications, Inc., 114, no. 4 (October 1978): 780–781.

ries. The mansard roof contained one or two floor levels; rooms at this level were lighted by inset windows; some were top lit instead.[2]

The scale of building increased during the Second Empire; interiors also were more spacious. While simplicity continued to be characteristic of the facades, interiors were more decorative. The primary floor was the piano nobile, which usually had the highest ceilings; building regulations stipulated eight feet.

INTERIOR ARCHITECTURE AND DECORATION

Materials and Decorative Techniques

The industrial revolution impacted the design of furniture and interior elements. Processes that were previously attainable only by the wealthy were now economically accessible for the middle classes. These included such mass-produced materials as papier-mâché and plaster simulating gilded bronze. Interior elements as well as furniture details were reproduced in historical styles regardless of stylistic accuracy; however, a historic designation was all-important to the consumers of this period.

Interior Architecture and Decorative Elements

From the First Empire to the reign of Louis Philippe, 1815–1830, there were not widespread changes in design, rather Napoleon I period was paramount. During the reign of Louis Philippe, 1830 to 1848, one impetus for change came as a result of interest in the writings of Sir Walter Scott, British novelist and poet. His novel, *Waverly* (1814) began his series of prose romances referred to as the *Waverly Novels.* In France this prompted an interest in Scotland which was aided by the enthusiasm of the Duchesse de Berry earlier in the 1820s. The continuously horizontal wallpaper designs of Jean Zuber depicted scenes roughly based on Scott's novels. Other scenic backgrounds were grounded in current events in Spain or Italy; coordinated with these was a wainscot paper for the dado based on medieval precedent. The assumption by designers was that Abbotsford, Scott's residence in Scotland, was Gothic. Interiors reflected styles of the past from Gothic to Louis XVI. In fact, designers often combined styles within one space, such as Gothic and French Renaissance. Victor Hugo's novel of 1831, *Notre-Dame de Paris,* prompted designers to use the medievalism as a basis for historical design.

Wealthier classes observed deficiencies in the often coarse combinations of styles of the past. This sometimes prompted families to purchase the finest historical interior components to install in their residences; or, alternatively, to acquire and install entire rooms of earlier centuries in their houses. The internationally famous Rothschild family of bankers is one example.[3] They bought authentic interiors from early residences to install in England at Waddeson Manor, Buckinghamshire, and in France at Ferrières. To families who could afford this approach it was symbolic of their ancestry. These early original settings provided a backdrop for antique furnishings—furniture, paintings, tapestries, sculpture, and other works of art.

---

[2]Anthony Sutcliffe, *Paris: An Architectural History* (New Haven and London: Yale University Press, 1995), 91–92.

3. The basis of the family fortune was laid by Mayer Amschel Rothschild in Germany. Two of his five sons established banking centers in London and Paris. Nathan Meyer Rothschild (1777–1836) of London was instrumental in aiding in the defeat of Napoleon. He and his son, Baron Lionel Nathan de Rothschild (1808–1879), were extremely influential in international banking, as they provided loans to governments of various countries. They were great patrons of the arts and celebrated philanthropists.

FIGURE 17-1 Second Empire. A variety of influences from past styles. Louis XV stylistic influence. Sometimes referred to as the Louis XIV style. Sutcliffe, Anthony. *Paris, An Architectural History.* New Haven and London. Yale University Press, 1993.

For interiors created during the Second Empire any style of the past was fair game for inclusion. Among the successful designers was Charles Gamier, the architect for the Hôtel de Païva (see Figure C–33). He appreciated each style of the past, admiring each for its inherent beauty; further, he felt that a designer had to be eclectic to value eclecticism. Thus, in the salon of the Hôtel de Païva he combined stylistic influences of the Baroque, Renaissance, and Rococo; the residence exuded a luxurious mixture of rich materials such as onyx and other marbles, textiles, mirrors, rich woods, and bronzes.

The Louis XVI style was an exceedingly prominent stylistic influence during the Second Empire. At the 1867 Exhibition a pavilion in the Louis XVI style was featured. Following this the Louis XVI style influenced interiors around the world.

As observed in a painting by Gustave Clarence Rodolphe (1824–1888) entitled *The Flute Player* and dated 1861, the Pompeian style was also employed.

> The emperor's first cousin Prince Napoleon (1822–1891) built the Maison Pompéienne in the Avenue Montaigne in Paris in 1860. The play being rehearsed is an improvisation based on a painting in the House of the Tragic Poet in Pompeii, and the players are friends of the artist and of the prince: the critic Théophile Gautier (1811–1872), the dramatist Emile Augier (1820–1889); and, from the Comédie Française, the actor François Got and actresses Madeleine Brohan and Marie Favart. The prince himself also takes part in the play. Boulanger copied this and similar painting directly onto a wall of the Maison Pompéienne. The painting is an interesting commentary on the life of the aristocracy in the Second Empire, when intellectuals, artists, actors, and courtiers mingled, and it indicates the serious interest in the classical world during the 1860s.[4]

The Gothic Revival style and the Louis XV style (at the time referred to as Louis XIV) were also of significance during the Second Empire (Figure 17-1). While designers imitated past styles they also made a conscious attempt to develop a new fashion.

Communication between Séchan and his son-in-law (both theatrical designers) about a design for the Sultan in Constantinople is revealing in terms of how a design problem was approached. Séchan gave the following directions to his son-in-law:

> [A] small very luxurious room in a resounding Louis XIV style similar, but smaller and more delicate, to the king's bedchamber at Versailles or the Tuileries with a

---

4. Moulin, "The Art of the Second Empire," 777.

pretty cornice of decorative brackets as the Galerie d'Apollon, and the doors and chimneypieces should have two pretty frames crowned by a circular ornament in the style of the Tuileries, the Louvre or Versailles with a chimneypiece also in the Louis XIV style like those of Le Pautre or Daniel Marot. This woodwork should be painted and gilded rather like an altar tabernacle. At the Louvre the unrestored Henry II rooms will give you an idea of what I have in mind . . . I think that, in view of the absence of walls, between the cornice and the wainscot what resembles a wall should be covered in hangings of velvet and red silk (the Sultan's favourite colour) with a pelmet above in the style of Daniel Marot. . . . The bed should be in the same manner as in a design by Le Pautre.[5]

FURNITURE

Prior to the Restoration furniture was significantly influenced by the ruling monarch and his director of the arts. However, both the aristocracy and the middle class influenced design trends during this period. First of all, when the aristocracy returned from exile it was natural for them to patronize the craftsmen they had previously known; for this group, therefore, traditions of the past were influential. They often looked to the immediate past but made some changes: forms were softer; excessive reliance of bronze mounts on mahogany was rejected, decorative detail was daintier, carving was used to soften the straight lines of furniture, native woods were employed instead of exotic woods, and Napoleonic austerity was avoided. The middle class, although uneducated in matters of taste, played an increasingly important role in setting design trends. Since their residences were often apartments they valued small, comfortable, and functional pieces of furniture.

Disparate influences were at work during the Restoration. The industrial revolution gained momentum, machine processes began to replace craftsmen, and there were new directions in terms of aesthetic theories. To meet the needs of the middle classes machine processes were essential, because traditional methods relying on craftsman techniques were expensive. However, some finishing continued to be done by the craftsman even though the machine was used for such processes as cutting veneers. Replication of historical models was not typical of the period of Louis Philippe or of the first years of the Second Empire; rather, historic examples were used as sources of inspiration.

Contemporaries during the Second Empire were critical of the furniture manufactured at that time. Criticism leveled against it included the assessment that the designers and the pieces produced lacked focus and creativity, were unimaginative and relied on a melange of styles, and added nothing in the copying. Revivalism was rampant; accurate details were borrowed from styles from the 16th through 18th centuries, but the authenticity of the total piece was not an overriding concern.

For royal residences a central unit, *Mobilier de la Couronne,* was responsible for inventory of all furnishings, allocation of furniture to other royal residences, and storing out-of-date furnishings as needed by these households. In furnishing the palaces most frequented by the Emperor and Empress, this department had the authority to reallocate stored furnishings as need arose. Documentary evidence based on the records of the Mobilier de la Couronne revealed that the emperor lived at the Palace of Compiègne with furnishings that had been there for almost 50 years without alteration. Fashion had changed and new furnishings were needed to entertain guests. Evidence from these administrative archives illustrates exactly in what manner the alterations were fashioned. Eclecticism was revealed by the way in which pieces representing different stylistic periods were combined within one room—Empire, 18th century, and contemporary furnishings.[6] Some traditional pieces

---

5. Colombe Samoyault-Verlet, "Furniture in France Under the Second Empire," *The Connoisseur* 199 (December 1978): 269–270.

were updated to meet contemporary standards of comfort by adding to the earlier form lush tufted upholstery.

Exhibitions played a considerable role in motivating competition and in stimulating improvement in skills of the craftsmen; because furniture was based on historical precedent the study by craftsmen of models of the past was also instrumental in improving their skills. Technical skill was a major criterion for selection of exhibition pieces; Henri Fourdinois received a prize for his Renaissance–style cabinet in 1867 in Paris (see Figure C-34). Major Universal Exhibitions were held in London (1851 and 1862) and in Paris (1855 and 1867). Beginning in 1863 the Union Centrale des Beaux–Arts systematically held exhibitions aimed at improving the quality of industrial products; the name of this group was changed in 1877 to Union Centrale des Arts Décoratifs. Its stated purpose was to promote interaction between the designer and the industrial artist and it eventually led to standards promoted by those who initiated the modern movement.

Cabinetmakers and architects were employed by families to make decisions about furnishings and the approach of each was different. Cabinetmakers, who were usually upholsterers also, specified furniture and textile products for their clients; some even supplied their own designs, as Fourdinois (a craftsman who produced work of the highest quality in terms of craftsmanship). The architects, on the other hand, were responsible for the entire scheme of the interior.[7]

Materials and Construction Techniques

Restoration. Wood was a major material used during the Restoration. Because of the cost of importation designers relied on native woods and capitalized on a range of colors through techniques of surface decoration. Among the woods of importance were ash, elm, satinwood, olive, sycamore, maple, and purplewood.

Many of the woodworking techniques prominent in the 18th century were eliminated during the First Empire. Moldings, for example, had been used in a limited manner and carving, when it was employed, was often misused because it altered basic structural form for such parts as legs of tables and chairs.

Veneering, marquetry, and inlay received new life due to the creative use of native woods, new color combinations, and new motifs. In veneering, craftsmen capitalized on patterning that could be attained through the innovative use of the natural decorative figure, burrs, roots, and so on. From around 1790 to the Restoration marquetry was largely abandoned as a technique of decoration because of economic hardships; it was a time-consuming decorative procedure. Restoration craftsmen reintroduced marquetry, relying on indigenous woods and fresh color combinations. Inlay became a prominent decorative technique of great technical superiority; the ornamental effect often revealed strong value contrasts between the motifs and the base wood.

The distinction between the craftsmen who worked primarily in solid wood (menuisiers) and those who specialized in veneer techniques (ébénistes) became blurred during the Restoration. Craftsmen worked in both of the techniques.

Second Empire. A distinction was made between the type of wood utilized for high-style furniture and more moderate pieces. Purplewood and ebony were used a great deal for high style pieces. In addition, the best pieces were very well constructed. A number of materials were employed for inlay, which continued to be an important technique for ornamenting furniture—tortoiseshell, costly woods, silver, porcelain, ivory, and so on.

---

6. Jean-Marie Moulin, "The Furnishing of the Palace of Compiègne During the Second Empire," *The Connoisseur* 199 (December 1978): 247–255. The author, through the records of the Mobilier de la Couronne, traces how furnishings remained in situ in specific locations for periods of time as well as how and when they were removed to new locations among the Royal residences.
7. Samoyoult-Verlet, "Furniture in France Under the Second Empire," 269.

Pearwood and beech were common for moderate pieces; these woods were sometimes dyed black to simulate ebony. Certain woods were believed to be appropriate for specific historically derived pieces, as oak for neo-Renaissance, since carving played a highly significant role for these pieces.

Designers relied heavily on historical styles. It was a period of imitation based on traditional French styles. Certain styles were considered appropriate for specific rooms, as Henry II for dining rooms or, for drawing rooms, Louis XIV, XV, or XVI. Tufted pieces and those with drapery were often relegated to bedrooms. On the other hand, more severe pieces of ebony or rosewood, considered masculine, were deemed appropriate for smoking rooms and libraries.

The wide disparity of styles precludes a single definition of style characteristics of pieces produced during the Second Empire. Craftsmen derived accurate details from a diversity of French historic periods from the 16th century through the 18th centuries. However, accuracy was not always of paramount concern. In summary, it was a period of revivalism and a period during which the upholsterer was preeminent; a period when there were pieces of amazing originality contrasted with lack of creativeness; a period during which exceedingly high-quality products were produced contrasted with commonplace furniture of low quality from industry.

Typical Pieces and Stylistic Features: Restoration

Initially Restoration furniture of all types was strongly influenced by the Napoleonic Empire and its furniture of characteristic heaviness; however, gradually it became more lightly scaled and less rectilinear. An imitation of earlier styles became ascendant. Artistic merit was subordinate to matters of technique; but industrial processes were essential to provide for the increased numbers in the middle classes and their requirements for simple, comfortable, and lightly scaled furniture for apartment living.

FIGURE 17-2 Restoration chair, Alphonse Jacob-Desmalter, (1825). Egyptian and classic influences. Musée des Arts Décoratifs, Paris. Union Centrale des Arts Décoratifs.

Seat Furniture

The following characteristics illustrate the variety observed in Restoration chairs. The diversity in the treatment of backs is noted by the following descriptors: upholstered, straight, backward scroll, rounded top, openwork centered with cross bars, arcaded revealing Gothic influence with crocketed finials, and gondola, in which the back curved to envelop the sitter and the contour sloped downward to near the seat. Arm supports were sometimes in the form of chimeras; for the gondola a simple S-form was employed or else a curved support integral with the forward ending. Legs were sometimes turned and columnar. The sabre leg was widely used. The back sabre legs tended to be more splayed than those of the Empire. When the sabre type was utilized for front legs they were square in section with an inward curve; alternatively, but still square in section, the top of the leg (just under the seat rail) was characterized by a strong outward curve while the lower part tapered in a typical treatment based on classical precedent (Figure 17-2). Stretchers were sometimes employed (perimeter or arranged in a U configuration), but in many instances they were omitted entirely. Casters began to be used more frequently during this period. Favored in the period of Napoleonic dominance the *méridienne* was widely used (Figure 17-3). This piece was a short sofa or daybed with one arm higher than the other so that the sitter could recline in a half-seated position. A fascination with the Middle Ages prompted an interest in furniture designs based on Gothic architecture in the so-called cathedral style. This was reflected in a variety of features such as tracery, finials of spire-like form with crockets, and ogee arches (Figure 17-4).

FIGURE 17-3 Restoration Méridienne (1835). Mahogany. Simplified forms influenced by the middle class. Musée des Arts Décoratifs, Paris. Union Centrale des Arts Décoratifs.

FIGURE 17-4 Restoration Gothic. Cathedral style based on the interest in the Middle Ages. Crocketed finials, tracery, ogee arches. Musée des Arts Décoratifs, Paris. Union Centrale des Arts Décoratifs.

Tables

Unlike many pieces of the Restoration the bureau plats became heavier and more complicated, especially in the Louis Philippe period; the tops often had many shelves for organizing papers or books. Dining tables were also large in scale; supports for tables var-

FIGURE 17-5   Restoration
Sideboard (or Desserte), Period of
Louis-Philippe (c. 1840-1845).
Mahogany. Mirror back extends the
view of decorative objects placed on
shelves. Openwork side panels.
Musée des Arts Décoratifs, Paris.
Union Centrale des Arts Décoratifs.

FIGURE 17-6   Restoration
Commode, Fisher (c. 1827).
Mahogany. Technological advance
allowed for very fine veneer. Doors
conceal drawers. Gilt bronze
mounts. Musée des Arts Décoratifs,
Paris. Union Centrale des Arts
Décoratifs.

ied and designers used such figures as lyres, winged figures, cornucopia, and lions' paws.
Many types of tables were produced, including guéridons with monopodia supports or
tripods, worktables, and many specific-use tables. The pedestal table with a single support
was common. The pedestal support was often reeded with a bulbous swelling; it rested on
a shaped base of rectangular or triangular form from which heavy lions' paws emanated.
The triangular base often had incurved sides. Although seemingly contradictory to the
foregoing, multi-functional pieces became consequential because of the demands of smaller living spaces.

The sideboard table *(desserte)* illustrated is of eclectic derivation. These pieces were used for the display of decorative objects; a mirror backing extended the display. Naturalism is evident in the carved side panels set apart by the turned supports (Figure 17-5).

Storage Pieces

Commodes with three drawers continued to be constructed without change until c. 1825, after which they became more lightly scaled. Drawers were sometimes concealed behind doors (Figure 17-6). Pilasters and columns tended to be eliminated. Bronze mounts became thinner; in general, compared to the Empire style, use of decorative detail was moderate. Light woods, sometimes with dark inlay, were typical. Around 1840 darker woods superseded lighter tones.

Beds

Restoration beds were boat-shaped or rectangular with columnar uprights or pilasters. Upholstery was extensively used and canopies of heavy drapery were common.

Typical Pieces and Stylistic Features: Second Empire

Seat Furniture

The upholsterer and the cabinetmaker were of equal importance in the Second Empire; in fact, cabinetmakers also advertised themselves as upholsterers. There was a remarkable and lavish display of upholstery for seat furniture. Multiple-seat units were produced by such names as *indiscret* (upholstered settee) and *canapés de l'amitié* (settee for two or three people) (Figure 17-7). Tufting was widely used and attention to comfort was paramount.

While stylistic features were utilized from several centuries a popular inspiration came from the Rococo style of Louis XV (Figure 17-8). Since industrialization gained momentum the consequences were that moldings were simpler and ornamental detail more limited; however, the inclination to extravagant decorative detail led craftsmen to carve addi-

FIGURE 17-7 Second Empire Canapé (or Settee). Louis XV influence. Carved and gilt wood. Widely used by the wealthy bourgeoise. Musée des Arts Décoratifs, Paris. Union Centrale des Arts Décoratifs.

FIGURE 17-8 Second Empire Chaise (c. 1860). Palisander. Louis XV influence. Emphasis on comfort through the use of tufting. Musée des Arts Décoratifs, Paris. Union Centrale des Arts Décoratifs.

tional motifs for application to the frames of chairs. Materials were wood, cast iron, wrought iron, and papier-mâché. Late in the Second Empire Louis XVI stylistic derivations were widely used partially because of the interest of the Empress Eugénie in Marie Antoinette.

Tables

Great diversity was seen in table design, in terms of both stylistic derivation and size. Supports were turned in various configurations or carved in the form of colonnettes, chimeras, sphinxes, lions', human figures, and so on. Tops were round, oval, octagonal, square, or rectangular. Techniques of decoration included marquetry, églomisé (whereby the reverse side of glass was painted with gold decorative detail), glass overlaying dried flowers, and mosaic. Especially in the Louis XVI style decorative application featured floral painting directly on wood and inlay of porcelain plaques from the Sèvres factory; the Louis XV and Louis XVI styles were often used for small tables. New forms included hat stands and umbrella stands. Particularly significant in this period were pieces painted white with gold highlights. Toilet tables were widely used but in extremely varied form.

Storage Pieces

Modification of forms based on historical precedent was typical; there was normally some deviation (Figure 17-9). Alteration might be in structural form, in the materials employed, or in decorative detail. For example, Louis XIV and Louis XVI were styles drawn upon by Second Empire designers. The 19th-century designer might, for instance, use spirally turned feet on an otherwise Boulle cabinet. Floral sprays executed on panels in the 18th-century style of Louis XVI would have employed colorful woods in veneers, but in the 19th-century the designer might substitute inlay of marble and other stones. Further, decorative detail could be selected that had no precedent in the historical style.[8]

FIGURE 17-9 Second Empire Bas d'Armoire (1852-1870). Palisander veneer with inlay of citronnier. Musée des Arts Décoratifs, Paris. Union Centrale des Arts Décoratifs.

Beds

Beds were based on either one historical style or a combination of features integrating decorative and structural elements of more than one derivation. A Louis XV-style bed was designed by Monbro the elder, a French designer, for the Englishman John Bowes; Monbro received commissions from clients both in France and England. The bed frame, fully exposed, was heavily carved with asymmetrical decorative detail. Both the headboard and footboard were upholstered; a canopy was richly detailed with shirring, fringe, and tassels under which full length draperies cascaded onto the floor at the headboard. French Renaissance and Louis XVI styles were also used.

ORNAMENT

Restoration. Some motifs of the Empire style continued to be used during the Restoration. Decorative detail, however, tended to be smaller; those ornaments that had been accomplished in bronze mounts during the Empire were now realized through the technique of inlay in a variety of materials such as pewter, painted porcelain, and ebony. While motifs such as griffins, dolphins, chimeras, and palmettes were derived from the Empire period, they tended to be smaller and did not play as prominent a role as previously.

A movement influencing not only the visual arts but literature and music, Romanticism was responsible for the tendency to rely on naturalistic elements. Colorful sprays of flowers were sometimes painted on the black backgrounds of japanned pieces.

Archaeological interest in the Middle Ages contributed to the use of Gothic detailing. For example, backs of chairs were tall with an overall Gothic arched outline, the cen-

---

8. Jacqueline Viaux, *French Furniture,* trans. Hazel Paget (New York: G. P. Putnam's Sons, 1964), 181.

ter executed in tracery detail and crocketed finials portraying elements from medieval architecture.

Other motifs of significance were cherubs, lyres, swans, dolphins, and cornucopias; the latter three were sometimes used for arm supports. Geometrical motifs were important in and of themselves—squares, circles, rectangles, ellipses, lozenges. Based on classical precedent were such ornamental details as the egg and dart and pearl beading.

Second Empire. Most decorative detail of the Second Empire was derived from antique models. The style of derivation and the motifs employed were often correlated. In the Louis XIV style Boulle marquetry was easily copied and highly prized by craftsmen of the Second Empire; however, simulations of materials or substitute materials were replaced in Boullework—pearwood dyed black for the ebony of the original technique, simulated tortoiseshell, or the use of steel to replace brass and pewter.

Among the most prevalent historical styles of influence was Louis XV. Both structure and decorative details were adapted, although structural forms are easily recognized. Pieces in this style were sometimes laden with carved detail including shells, floral detail, and volutes.

When the Louis XVI style was emphasized it was sometimes produced with extreme accuracy, although discordant effects were produced when tufting, fringe, flashy metal mounts, or tassels were used with these basically accurate forms.

Chapter 18

Nineteenth-Century English Revival Styles

1830-1901

HISTORICAL SETTING

The situation for English gentlemen in the 1830s was comfortable: they were wealthy, some had profited from the Industrial Revolution, and some benefited from the discovery of minerals on their property. They were protected by the Corn Laws, which regulated the import and export of grains; imports were restricted unless prices were high. The landed estates profited from these laws, which protected their economic interests.

Material prosperity attained by the middle classes was due in large measure to industrial expansion; this allowed them to acquire the wealth needed to establish themselves as landed gentry. Markets were opened both nationally and internationally by the expansion of the railway system and shipping interests. Market expansion was beneficial to such products as wool, cotton, and iron. This brought about factories, banking houses, and so on, which, were further indications of the affluence of the Victorian era.

At the same time established landed families became wealthier also. While traditionally, political power had been vested in them as landed aristocracy, now they shared the power with the middle classes, who had been critical of the way in which their parliamentary policies affected the country. The Reform Bill of 1832 liberalized the manner of choosing representatives to the House of Commons; the reallocation in the process of selecting members of Parliament was advantageous to larger communities and new towns. Further, middle-class men were given franchise in the selection process. A shift toward the greater need of the urban population was aided by the repeal of the Corn Laws in 1846.

At first as the nouveaux riches moved into communities and became part of the landed gentry they desired to be accepted by the established families. They did not have independent aesthetic standards; this meant that when new country houses were constructed the new owners emulated their neighbors. Later in the1860s and 1870s, as this group gained in self-assurance, they began to show greater independence; many relied on the French Renaissance style for exteriors.

Throughout the period from 1830 to 1901 there were two conflicting strains of development: one of traditionalism, the other based on the felt need for reform and innovation. The progressive designers of the 19th century introduced tenets that led to 20th century developments and the design precepts espoused by the Bauhaus in its educational program. However, the prevailing stylistic trends lay with the majority, who were uninstructed in matters of taste and who purchased commercially produced furniture, much of which was of inferior quality. Greater emphasis on factory production began around 1835 and the majority of the furniture produced from these processes was based on past styles—Gothic, classical with primary reliance on Greek, Louis XIV merging with Rococo, and Elizabethan which combined elements of the late 16th and 17th centuries, including late 17th-century Baroque.

But the dependence on past styles was not confined to furniture design. New residences were being constructed, renovations were being undertaken, and houses were being enlarged during the Victorian period and among the most fashionable styles were Gothic and Elizabethan. The image the owners wished to maintain was related to the style selected for their residences. Those with a preference for Gothic viewed themselves as first and foremost Christians while those with a preference for Elizabethan considered themselves English country gentlemen; the latter were singularly English.

A. W. N. Pugin (1812–1852) led the cause for the Gothic revival. He received both decorative and architectural commissions. While many of his ideas are forward looking (progressive), some looked solidly to the past; even in one piece one can discern both archaeological accuracy and patterns free of any period influence. His early furniture designs were in the Regency Gothic style. His conversion to Catholicism in 1834 significantly impacted his philosophy, for he looked to the Middle Ages as a period of exemplary social structure to serve as a model for his day. In his book of 1841, *The True Principles of Pointed or Christian Architecture,* he showed the significance of the Gothic in terms of honestly revealed structure and the function of each part; in his discussion he seems to advocate functionalism, a major tenet in early 20th century design. Pugin believed that the exterior elevation was subordinate to the plan for which convenience was of highest significance.

The Crystal Palace Exhibition of 1851 was organized by the Society of Arts with significant input from the Prince Consort. This exposition showed the exceptional affluence of the English but it also revealed a deficiency in design quality. Criticism of standards of quality in the industrial arts pointed, in part, to the lack of education and lack of ability to evaluate design of an uneducated middle class. There was an attempt on the part of the exhibitors to outshine their competitors; thus, attention was given to ostentatious display of decorative detail. After 1851 many pieces were produced on an even grander scale. Exhibition furniture does not give an accurate picture of the major production of the time. These pieces were constructed primarily to show innovations and to demonstrate novelty. The misconception that all early Victorian furniture was overelaborate is based on the exhibitions; leading manufacturers, to gain recognition, employed sculptors instead of architects to design pieces. Some exhibition pieces after 1851 were characterized by vast scale; this feature was noted also in furniture made for residential use.

SPATIAL RELATIONSHIPS

In that residential arrangement was highly prescriptive, a "machine for living:" would be an appropriate description for the Victorian house. The stratification of the interior was highly complex; spaces were designated for women, men, children, servants. Rooms were designed for specialized activities within each area. In the servant's wing, rooms were designated for lamps, pastry, etc., and in the wing devoted to communal purposes, rooms were specified as galleries, music rooms, and so on.

Spatial Features of the Floor Plan and Three-Dimensional Spatial Characteristics

Plans of two large Victorian country residences are illustrated to show relevant spatial features: Thoresby Hall, Nottinghamshire, and Merevale Hall, Warwickshire (Figures 18-1 and 18-2). Other houses will be cited to illustrate specific features of the plan as well as three-dimensional characteristics.

A major feature of the residence was the diversity of specialized entrances into the house. At Merevale there were six exterior entries; private, main, and servant were three of these (see Figure 18-2). For other houses there were those specified for garden, business, men, luggage, and kitchen. Likewise, some stairs were expressly used as main staircases while others were expressly used for men, bachelors, women, or young women. As well, corridors were explicitly for specified groups (butlers, men, etc.). Servants were kept invisible and this meant long corridors and back stairs designed to avoid encounters with family members.

The stratification of the residence is well delineated in Thoresby Hall, where one block is devoted to servants' activities, a central block to communal activities, and a third section to the family wing (see Figure 18-1). Children were housed near their parents, either adjacent to or immediately above on the next floor. Here, rooms for the governess, a schoolroom, nurseries, and a bathroom are located on the first floor above the parents' suite. Private stairs for the parents provided easy access to the children.

The ground floor plan for Merevale illustrates the degree of specialization both for the communal spaces and for the servants' block (see Figure 18–2). In the servant's wing are spaces specifically for baking, scullery, game larder, larder, pastry, lamps, cleaning room, still room, housekeeper's room, butler's room, and so on. In addition to those spaces normally included in the communal block, a billiards room is introduced. In some residences smoking rooms began to appear in the mid-19th century; men usually retired to this room following the withdrawal of women from the group.

The hall was used for a variety of activities: dancing, dinners, balls, gathering before dinner, and so on. Further, it was used by people of more than one social level-servants, gentry, nongentry. It became an all-purpose living room. So important was this space that it was sometimes added to existing structures; in new structures it normally had a central location.

FIGURE 18-1 Plan, Thoresby Hall, Nottinghamshire (1864-1875). Architect Anthony Salvin. Right: Ground plan (A-D, servant's wing; E-J, communal spaces; K-M, family wing. Left: First floor plan O-Q, children's facilities. Function of individual spaces: A Upper part of kitchen; B Male servants; C Pantry; D Serving room; E Dining room; F Breakfast room; G Library; H Hall; I Drawing room; J Billiard room; K Boudoir; L Dressing room; M Bathroom; N Bedroom; O Governess; P Nursery. *Life in the English Country House, A Social and Architectural History,* by Mark Girouard, Yale University Press: 1978. By courtesy of Curtis Brown on behalf of Mark Girouard.

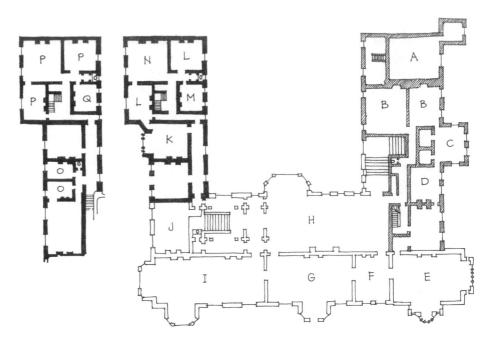

FIGURE 18-2 Plan, Ground Floor, Merevale Hall, Warwickshire, (1838-1844). Architect Edward Blore. A Entrance hall; B Staircase; C Dining room; D Library; E Saloon; F Billiard room; G Drawing room; H Morning room; I-J Spaces for the owner; K Servants' hall; L Butler; M Housekeeper; N Still room; O Cleaning room; P Lamps; Q Pantry; R Children's dining room; S Cook's room; T Larder; U Pastry; V Kitchen; W Baking; X Scullery; Y Brewing; Z Laundry. 1 Main entrance; 2 Private entrance; 3 Servants' entrance. **By courtesy of Curtis Brown on behalf of Mark Girouard.** *Copyright as printed in the original volume.*

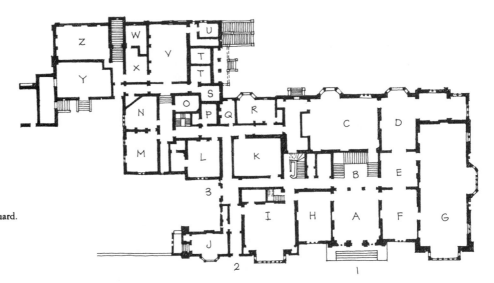

The dining room, drawing room, and library had about the same relationship adjacency as had been the case in earlier houses. The dining room was considered a masculine space while the drawing room: was regarded as feminine. A variety of activities took place in the drawing room morning calls from visitors who arrived by carriage for conversation; assembly before and after dinner; balls, and afternoon tea. Both dining and drawing rooms often opened to the conservatory.

As one moves from room to room in both Thoresby Hall and Merevale Hall, the series of rooms in the communal block reveals constant contrasts in size, proportion, and shape; some of these differences lie in the varied manner in which the bays are articulated. The character of lighting was a highly significant factor in the distinctive manner in which space was perceived; at Merevale large sheets of glass replaced smaller leaded lights for windows.

Merevale Hall has several spatial features typical of this period. Ground floor rooms were fashionably tall during this period. The dining room ceiling is 19 feet tall while other rooms at ground level are 17 feet 3 inches. Wall alcoves were sometimes incorporated for

pieces of furniture and in this residence the recess containing the sideboard is lined with velvet; a massive mirror is placed over the sideboard. Whether placed in a recess or not, grandiose case pieces were appropriate for rooms of this proportion.

Spatial excitement was frequently generated in and around the staircase hall, where lighting played a key role. Sometimes, however, it was the decorative treatment that from the ground level to upper levels, encouraged the exploration of vertical spaces. Repetition of the arched form gives a sense of unification at Merevale, where the arches on the ground floor are duplicated on the first floor through the incorporation of arcaded corridors and the use of arched windows overlooking an internal courtyard (Figure 18-3).

Among the most melodramatic staircase halls of the 1840s is the one at Harlaxton Manor, Lincolnshire, which, in its exuberance, exceeds the ostentatious detailing of most interiors of the time (Figure 18-4). In a melding of stylistic features including Elizabethan, Jacobean, and Baroque the observer is encouraged to view the vertical space in a series of theatrical units that culminate in a trompe l'oeil sky. At one level a balcony is supported by immense scrolls combined with brawny Atlas figures; from Greek mythology, the figures of Atlas are symbolic since, after the defeat of the Titans, Atlas was condemned to hold up the sky on his head and hands. Adding drama at this level is the use of complex plaster curtains ensconced with cherubs, the whole being attached to the baroque scrolls by real cords. At a higher level another balcony is supported by enormous shells and marine creatures with male heads; each creature has two tails. At this level is an arcade, the arches of which are framed by baroque scrolls; and from these feigned plaster drapery is used. Completing this highly complex composition are six colossal pendants arranged around the trompe l'oeil sky.

Modulation of space was sometimes articulated in the use of columns to visually separate spaces without completely segregating either of the areas. At Kelham Hall,

FIGURE 18-4 Staircase Hall, Harlaxton Manor, Lincolnshire, (1831-1838). William Burn. Stylistically influenced by Elizabethan, Jacobean, and Baroque elements. Enhanced verticality through a series of theatrical units. Copyright Anthony Kersting.

FIGURE 18-5 Drawing Room, Kelham Hall, Nottinghamshire, (1858-1861). Architect Sir George Gilbert Scott. Combination of medieval structural vaulting with classical decorative detail. Courtesy of Country Life Picture Library.

Nottinghamshire, the separation of the two-story music hall from the corridor is accomplished by an arcade of Gothic arches. Within the music hall vertical extension of space is encouraged through the use of a triforium gallery on one side and an enormous chimneypiece on the other; each leads to the vaulted ceiling. The naturalism that characterized interiors as well as some furniture of the period is evident here in the design of the capitals; flowers, foliage, and figures from the animal world are represented with accuracy. In the drawing room at Kelham Hall a single medieval cluster column centers the space; from this emanates the vaulted ceiling. The spandrels are decorated with arabesques. The combination of different styles was typical of the Victorian era (Figure 18-5).

The ground floor central corridor at Kelham originates at the music hall and extends through the length of the house. Along the corridor measured emphasis is attained through the use of a series of vaulted spaces, each separated by spanning pointed Gothic arches given emphasis by virtue of the value contrast. Corridors on the upper levels are also broad and spacious but treated more simply; top lighting is used for the topmost corridor.

INTERIOR ARCHITECTURE AND DECORATION

Materials and Decorative Techniques

The large rooms that typified country residences required the use of materials or materials in combination that were high in compressive and tensile strength. Cast iron is low in tensile strength while wrought iron is high in both qualities. During the Victorian period iron was used in a variety of ways: as exposed wrought-iron girders; as girders completely covered with plaster; as wooden beams; combined with glass for conservatories, etc.

Around the mid-19th century a number of factors combined to make it feasible to install larger panes of window glass: manufacturing processes, excise duty, and window tax. First, the use of blown glass, prior to the Victorian period, precluded production of glass in large panes. Manufacturing processes in the 1830s enabled the fabrication of large sheets and plate glass. The excise duty was eliminated in 1845 and this cut the price of glass significantly. Then, in 1851, the window tax was repealed. It had been based on weight and, compared to windows of blown glass, plate glass (3/4 inch thick) was heavier, thus adding considerably to the expense of the purchaser. With these changes it became technically and economically feasible to install large panes of glass in the late 1850s. Large panes were used in both casement and sash windows; however, the weight of the glass tended to be excessive for casement frames and more appropriate for sash windows.

A combination of canvas and plaster was a versatile material, a process patented in 1856. The melding of fiber reinforcement with plaster permitted a variety of forms to be cast including precast panels, cornices, and central medallions for ceilings.

Textural interest for walls and ceilings was accomplished through the use of lyncrusta and anaglypta. *Lyncrusta* was originally used to simulate leather wall coverings; in bas-relief, it was often applied to the dado. *Anaglypta* was a type of lightweight, molded wallpaper that, again, provided textural variation for both ceilings and walls.

Interior Architecture and Decorative Elements

The people who built country houses in the Victorian period were country gentlemen and those of the middle class who had attained wealth and chose to establish themselves as landed gentry. While classical interiors waned two major styles were fashionable, Gothic and Elizabethan. The style chosen by the nouveaux riches was, in many instances, one of emulation, for many wished to be accepted as equals by the landed aristocracy. However, when they asserted their independence they often chose the revived French Renaissance style; there was also an important influence from luxuriant 18th century French interiors. These newly rich sometimes recreated earlier French boiseries and sometimes imported authentic boiseries of the 16th or 18th centuries.

Floors

Plain wood, parquet, carpet, and floorcloth were the primary treatments for floors in the Victorian period. Modest homes featured plain pine floors. Central area rugs were bordered by floorboard, stained and polished. Parquet was also a method of decoration for the area around the rug; this was accomplished by either real parquet or by stencil designs of simulated parquetry. Floorcloths (printed canvas) afforded an alternative by simulating rug patterns, parquet, or tile. Linoleum was introduced in the second half of the 19th century.

Walls

The Victorians tended to divide the wall into three areas: floor to dado rail, dado rail to architrave, and architrave to ceiling level; however, sometimes the dado rail was eliminated and wallpaper covered the wall from the baseboard to the cornice. Wallpaper (now produced in rolls), wood paneling, textiles, painting to simulate marble, patterned tiles, and stenciled and painted decoration were all means of treating the wall surfaces. Marbling and stenciling were used by all levels of society. Patterned tiles were especially prevalent in hallways and corridors. Sometimes fragments from earlier centuries were combined in the Victorian period, as in the music room at Highclere Castle, Hampshire. Emphasis was frequently given to a deep frieze through its decorative treatment. Frieze papers and occasionally glazed tile were used; in one instance such tile was ornamented with medieval mythological scenes.

The diversity with which walls were treated is typical of the Victorian period and most often related to the sources of stylistic influence. At Carlton Towers, Yorkshire (1873–1877), the vast Venetian drawing room is said to have been inspired by Venetian vases (see Figure C-35). The black paneled dado, taller than usual, has painted panels spaced periodically in the composition; some represent characters in Shakespeare's *Merchant of Venice*. Above the dado the wall is plastered with a stamped design simulating leather; the design is highlighted with gold against a light gray ground.

Belvoir Castle, Leicestershire (complete by 1825), is an early example of the style that became typical later in the Victorian period: a mixture of Gothic, Baroque and Rococo, Norman, and classical. The Gothic style of Belvoir's exterior is repeated in the stairway, guardroom, and corridors. Punctuating the upper walls of the guardroom are arches of early English inspiration through which a commanding view opens onto the grand staircase. Located in the central round tower is the Elizabeth Salone (named for the fifth duchess of Rutland) with features of 18th century rococo. This is apparently the initial introduction of the French rococo decoration in the 19th century; it became very fashionable later (Figure 18-6). Above the paneled dado are tall narrow panels in groups of three, the tops of which are united by arched rococo frames. These are separated by single panels which, above the dado, have a separate rectangular base followed by a shortened but still tall panel, again headed with rococo detail. The single panels are also used to bound the overmantel mirrors as well as the floor-length mirror on the adjoining wall.

Figure 18-6 The Elizabeth Salon, Belvoir Castle, Leicestershire (completed 1825). Decorated by Matthew Cotes Wyatt. Anticipates later Victorian use of Rococo stylistic influence. Copyright Anthony Kersting.

FIGURE 18-7   Music Room, Harlaxton Manor, Lincolnshire (c. 1850). William Burn. Baroque and Rococo decorative influence. Anthony Kersting. Detail: Music room chimneypiece. Courtesy of Country Life Picture Library.

Heading the wall is a highly decorative coved frieze uniting the entire scheme, including the bay. The colors are crimson and gold.

At Harlaxton Manor, Lincolnshire (1831–1838), the music room gives the full impact of Baroque and Rococo elements; the Victorians sometimes referred to this under the stylistic designation of Louis XIV (Figure 18-7). Above the dado the wall is articulated with a series of rectangular panels of varying widths. Panels of mirrors headed with depressed arches are topped with panels to reconstruct the ensemble into overall rectilinearity. A highly complex plaster relief above the overmantel mirror extends into the coved transition to the ceiling. Within the coved transition are paired baroque bracket scrolls that extend over the molding below uniting the planes. Diaperwork ornaments the spaces between the brackets.

A style used by the nouveaux riches for exteriors was French Renaissance, an example of which is Waddeson Manor, Buckinghamshire (1874–1889), built for Baron Ferdinand de Rothschild. The exterior draws on elements of several historic châteaux. On the interior French Rococo influence is also observed (Figure 18-8). Practices of the time included either a re-creation of a historical style or, as at Waddeson, using actual 18th century boiseries; many pieces (furniture, carpet, etc.) had been in the princely palaces of France.

FIGURE 18-8
Morning Room,
Waddeson Manor,
Buckinghamshire.
Constructed for Baron
Ferdinand de
Rothschild.
Assemblage of origi-
nal 18th-century
pieces from European
palaces. Courtesy of
Country Life Picture
Library.

Windows and Doors

By the late 1850s large sheets of plate glass became feasible because of the removal of the excise duty and the window tax. Both casement and sash windows were employed, but the heaviness of the glass made it more appropriate for sash windows.

Headings for windows often related to the stylistic influence. Types included lances, round, square, and depressed arch. Door headings were treated in essentially the same manner.

Important doorways could have cornices and pediments above them. Also, overdoor treatments, like windows, often related to the stylistic influence; for example, in rococo interiors the trumeau or a rococo relief immediately above the doorway surround could be used (see Figure 18-6).

The number of panels in doors and the arrangement varied widely; some were fielded. If glazing was used in the doors it was not uncommon for a stained glass border to be employed.

Chimneypieces

Slate, wood, and marble were the materials used most frequently for the surround. Wood, the least expensive, was the most common material for modest homes and for less important rooms in the houses of the wealthy. Panels of patterned and colored tiles were frequently splayed within the firebox surround; a purchaser had the option of choosing the glazed tile or not. Tiled register grates could be purchased separately from the surrounds (Figure 18-9).

FIGURE 18-9 Chimneypiece. Characteristic use of splayed panels of decorative tile within the firebox recess. From Calloway, Steven. *The Elements of Style.* © 1991. Michael Beazley Publishers, a division of Reed Books.

Cast iron was a material of more frequent use in the Victorian period. It was used for grates but also for the chimneypiece. It was sometimes painted to simulate wood.

The stylistic character of the chimneypiece reflected the period styles important at the time: Gothic, Elizabethan, Adam, Georgian Revival, Rococo, etc. (see Figures 18-7 and C-35). Mirrors for the overmantel were fashionable. Late in the Victorian period a very complicated overmantel was introduced, usually consisting of columns, a central mirror, and shelves and niches for displaying decorative objects.

Ceilings

The variation in ceiling design was extraordinary, yet many were treated very simply. In form they could be flat, of continuous tunnel vaulting of semicircular or pointed section, or lierne vaulted. Examples of decorative enhancement for the ceiling include pargework in the Elizabethan manner, a series of exposed timbers, coffering, painting, and patterned ceiling papers. Plasterers were important in producing relief designs sometimes used for such surfaces as the frieze in rendering motifs appropriate to the stylistic influence (festoons, flowers, etc.).

Exceedingly important were the central rosettes or medallions; these units were made of plaster, papier-mâché, or fibrous plaster. In the best rooms gasoliers often hung from the rosettes. Families of moderate means limited themselves to a simple cornice and a central rosette.

Examples of ceiling treatments will illustrate some to the diversity (see Figures C-35, 18-3, 18-5, and 18-6). Representing an influence of the Renaissance based on ancient Romans decorations is the painted coved ceiling at Prestwold Hall (1842–1844), Leicestershire (Figure 18-10). Here the designer was influenced by the grotesques Raphael had painted for the Vatican. In the spandrels leading to the major central grotesque are rectangular framed landscapes depicting Prestwold in its various stages of development. The Victorians rejoiced in ornate decoration resulting from overall patterning that played on light-dark effects, of which this is a prime example.

FIGURE 18-10   Hall Ceiling, Prestwold Hall, Leicestershire. William Burn. Renaissance influence based on the work of Raphael and his designs for the Vatican. Courtesy of Country Life Picture Library.

The medieval ruins of Castell Coch, Glamorganshire (now Cardiff Castle), were restored and adapted between 1868 and 1885 to serve in the summers as an occasional country residence. The vaulted ceiling of the drawing room is its outstanding feature (Figure 18-11). Highlighted in gold, the spines of ribs are enhanced with butterflies in relief; these are regularly spaced. Between the ribs stars and flying birds are painted against a deep blue ground that represents the sky.

Another example of a ceiling of outstanding merit is in the morning room at Waddeson Manor; it is flat and bordered with relief design of combined Rococo and Baroque detailing (see Figure 18-8). At Harlaxton Manor the dining room ceiling is formed of highly complex, exuberantly modeled Elizabethan pargework with periodic pendant drops.

Stairways

Because of the diversity of treatments it is difficult to generalize about specific details. However, both open well and dogleg configurations and both closed and open string stairs were utilized. In more modest residences, if space and economy were considerations, a dogleg arrangement was often employed. These usually were constructed of soft wood.

Turned balusters, simple at the beginning of the period, became increasingly more complex as the use of steam power made it economically feasible. The variation in stylistic influence reflected the eclecticism of the Victorian era. The square section balustrades of the Regency period continued to be used at the beginning of the Victorian era.

In homes of wealthier citizens the drama of lighting (sometimes top lighting) was very important, especially for the staircase hall (see Figure 18-3). The following features were

FIGURE 18-11   Drawing Room Ceiling, Cardiff Castle, Glamorganshire (1868-1885). Vaulted ceiling with butterflies in relief on the spines of the ribs. Painted blue background represents star studded sky with birds flying in the foreground. Courtesy of Country Life Picture Library.

often observed: open well, stone or marble, cantilevering, cast-iron balustrades, simple balusters, complex turned members, and handrails of polished mahogany or oak. One advantage of the cast-iron balustrade was that it could be personalized, for example, with the monogram of the owner; this was, however, an expensive substitute for wood.

Steps were often covered with a carpet runner secured with stair rods which fitted into metal eyes at each end; the rods were positioned at the juncture of the tread and riser. Service stairs were sometimes covered with floorcloth or with linoleum; a metal nosing for the edge of the tread was sometimes used with linoleum.

FURNITURE

Eclecticism is descriptive of the Victorian era, during which designers borrowed and integrated elements from a variety of past styles; in other words, the resulting forms were an amalgam of features from other styles adapted to contemporary use. The dividing line between styles was often obscure to the designers of Victorian furniture. Because the stylistic features were merged into one piece it is sometimes difficult to assign a precise stylistic derivation. A practice sometimes used was to put together fragments of earlier pieces, advocated on the basis of economy. Victorian designers were influenced by industrialization and the mechanical processes, which gained momentum through the 19th century.

As noted earlier, there were conflicting trends during the period—one traditionalist, the other progressive. This section will focus on the styles of the past reflected in the furniture produced during the long reign of Queen Victoria. Under the umbrella of Victorian the period can be divided into trends typical of early (to c. 1855), middle (to c. 1870), and late (to 1901). The early period was predisposed to Classical (Grecian), Louis XIV (combining features of Baroque and Rococo), Elizabethan (reflecting both Tudor and Stuart elements), and Gothic styles. While the latter had been a factor during the Regency period there was a revival of interest in the 1830s and 1840s.

At the beginning of the Victorian period classically derived forms continued to be produced based on Regency furniture; the primary emphasis was on Greek influence. Both form and detail tended toward coarseness compared to the previous period. By around 1835 Greek had fallen from favor while Louis XIV and Elizabethan were generally accepted.

The introduction of the Louis XIV revival style became evident in the late 1820s. Reflected in details, it meant the replacement of the anthemion with scrolls and shells as decorative motifs. Termed *Louis XIV,* the revival began as a more accurate reflection of the *ancien régime;* then designers began to add Louis XV excesses. This style was thought of as appropriate to more feminine rooms, such as drawing rooms and boudoirs. While the revival was derived primarily from the French, in some instances mid-18th century Georgian Rococo is incorporated. Because of its more decorative and exuberant qualities this style was not favored by architects; it was, however, embraced by the trade.

As part of the national heritage, the Elizabethan revival received its impetus from the1835 Parliamentary Select Committee, who commended Gothic or Elizabethan as the preferred style for the Palace of Westminster. The popularity of these styles was also related to the novels of Sir Walter Scott *(Kenilworth);* his own home was renovated after 1819 in a picturesque style reflecting the Tudor and Stuart periods. Based on these incentives, designers believed that the style represented sixteenth century Tudor design but, stylistically, it included late 17th century Charles II characteristics. Pattern books illustrated the style: Henry Shaw, *Specimens of Ancient Furniture* (1836); Robert Bridgens, *Furniture with Candelabra and Interior Decoration* (1838), which included designs in Grecian, Gothic, and Elizabethan, the major style illustrated; T. F. Hunt, *Exemplars of Tudor Architecture and Furniture* (1829–30). Pattern books published between 1835 and 1850 reveal that the designation of a style name was very important. This revival, unlike the Louis XIV revival, was sanctioned by architects and, of course, it was very important not only for exteriors but for interior design also.

A. W. N. Pugin was one of the main advocates of the Gothic revival. He was very critical of his contemporaries for not understanding the Gothic principles. Pugin made

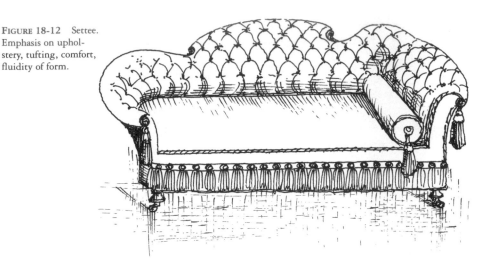

FIGURE 18-12 Settee. Emphasis on upholstery, tufting, comfort, fluidity of form.

scathing attacks about the furniture then being produced which, he concluded, made inappropriate use of architectural features for furniture design. He felt it incongruous to use miniature flying buttresses, crockets, turrets, and excesses in ornamentation. He observed that a person would be lucky, on departure from a Gothic interior, to avoid injury from the overabundance of decorative detail. The pattern book he published in 1835, *Gothic Furniture in the Style of the Fifteenth Century,* along with his other efforts, did not have a significant impact on commercial furniture production.

Some pieces produced during the early Victorian period had no definite recognizable stylistic influence and defy categorization. Many forms produced in the 1840s and 1850s were determined by attention to bodily comfort; these pieces were commercially produced. Melding of parts of furniture into one another was also typical. For example, arms and backs of seat furniture flowed into one another; sharp distinctions between pedestal support and the base tended to be eliminated. Seat furniture was characterized by fluidity of form, full upholstery, little exposure of wood, and bulkiness (Figure 18-12). Plasticity was also a feature of case pieces.

The early period was followed with less plastic furniture. Curves continued to be employed, but they were concise and more exacting; for example, the ends of cabinets could be quarter circles. Other features that set this period apart include flat patterns for inlay, influenced by A. W. N. Pugin; wide glazed doors; the replacement of the pedestal with colonnettes; and simulations of one material with another.

Trends just after the mid-19th century deemphasized curves, with consequent interest in straighter lines, and upholstery, in favor of greater exposure of wooden parts. By the late 1860s there was the introduction of Louis XVI stylistic influence. Further, there was a resurgence of interest in marquetry, porcelain plaque inserts, and ormolu.

Great diversity and novelty were typical of commercially produced furniture in the late Victorian period. Almost any style was subject to reproduction—Chippendale, Hepplewhite, Sheraton, Empire, Renaissance, etc. Some styles were adapted but some were identical to the original. Such pieces as cabinets, chimneypieces, and wardrobes categorized as Renaissance were architectural in concept; these featured an array of niches, shelves, and columns among their characteristics. Inlay and carving were important decorative techniques. This style was adopted by architects around 1880.

Materials and Construction Techniques

Cast iron was a popular material for chairs, tables, and benches intended for garden or conservatory use; it was sometimes used to imitate upholstery and fringe, to simulate tree trunks and roots, etc. Hollow iron tubes were employed for beds and rocking chairs. At times cast iron was needed as a reinforcing material for papier-mâché furniture, but this depended on the size of the finished product.

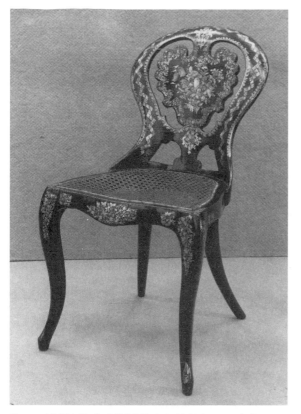

FIGURE 18-13 Papier-Mâché Chair (mid-19th century). Rococo influence. By Courtesy of the Board of Trustees of the Victoria and Albert Museum.

FIGURE 18-14 Elizabethan Side Chair (c. 1845). Late 17th-century influence. By Courtesy of the Board of Trustees of the Victoria and Albert Museum.

Papier-mâché consisted of pulped paper that was sized, placed in molds, and baked. Not only was it used for decorative accessories but also for chairs, bedsteads, etc. It was usual to have these pieces lacquered black and then painted with brightly colored ornament; mother-of-pearl inlay was often used.

The predominant kinds of wood varied with the period. In the early Victorian period mahogany, oak, walnut, and rosewood were prominent. In the late Victorian period satinwood and tulipwood were favored.

A material used for molded ornament and for whole objects was *gutta-percha,* made from the hardened sap of the tree *Dichopsis gutta.* Pieces of furniture of gutta-percha were displayed at the 1851 exhibition.

Typical Pieces and Stylistic Features

Seat Furniture

Representing two revivals are a chair with Louis XV influence and one of Elizabethan revival. Rococo curves characterize the former, which was most commonly used for dining and drawing rooms (Figure 18-13). Major features were the balloon back and cabriole leg. The balloon back was an important invention before midcentury; the concave curve of the back begins just at the seat level, above which it swells an a strong convex curve. Made of papier-mâché, it is painted black with polychrome decoration.

The Elizabethan revival side chair has a number of features which relate it to the late 17th century (Figure 18-14). Charles II stylistic attributes are evident in the use of spiral turning and the openwork arched cresting of the back contained between the uprights; further, the divisions of the back, although not identical to, are reminiscent of late 17th-cen-

tury style. Other chairs in the Elizabethan revival style incorporated features of the Restoration style such as caning and the upright front stretcher.

Tables

The carved walnut table (mid-19th century) illustrates the Victorian love of ostentation, sinuous forms, and plasticity (Figure 18-15). It combines baroque curves with realistically carved motifs. A polychrome porcelain plaque is inset into the tabletop surface. The design for the neo-Gothic walnut loo table is based on a design by A. W. N. Pugin who was both traditionalist and reformer (Figure 18-16). In the use of the ogival arch as the support for the table Pugin demonstrates his interest in archaeology, while the tabletop is inlaid in a flat pattern and akin to his interest in reform. It was constructed in 1847.

FIGURE 18-17 Sideboard Table (1857). Designed and Carved by Gerrard Robinson. Oak. Carved with a scene from Robinson Crusoe. Irregular outline. Naturalistic detail. By Courtesy of the Board of Trustees of the Victoria and Albert Museum, London.

The illustrated sideboard table was designed and carved by Gerrard Robinson in 1857. This curious piece represents the many impractical pieces constructed during the Victorian era. Composed of naturalistic detail, the carving represents a scene from Robinson Crusoe, a character created in the early 18th century by Daniel Defoe (Figure 18-17).

Storage Pieces

There was a diversity of stylistic features produced from the 1840s to the late 19th century. These included designs based on 18th-century English styles including Adam, Chippendale, Sheraton, and Hepplewhite. In addition, Gothic, English Regency, Italian Renaissance, and 18th-century French styles were influential in the variety which characterized Victorian design.

Almost any historical style was subject to adaptation or reproduction by the commercial producers; the Renaissance style was among the most elaborate. Some sideboards were crested by a broken segmental pediment and, in an architectural concept, incorporated caryatids, niches, brackets, and shelves. Elaborate carving was utilized; mirrors were often incorporated in these pieces, particularly in the second half of the 19th century. Some of these lofty cabinets of broken outline were as much as fourteen feet tall.

The English cabinet illustrated was the design of a French artisan; manufacturing processes were undertaken by the firm of Jackson and Graham. Because of the number of techniques essential to execute the piece, it required at least forty craftsmen to complete the cabinet (Figure 18-18).[1]

---

1. Helena Hayward, ea., *World Furniture* (New York: McGraw Hill, 1965), 212.

FIGURE 18-18 Cabinet (1855). French Designer. Made by firm of Jackson and Graham for Paris Exhibition of 1855. Approximately 14 feet tall. Manufacturing processes: carving, inlay, gilding, casting. Inset porcelain plaques. By Courtesy of the Board of Trustees of the Victoria and Albert Museum, London.

FIGURE 18-19 Cabinet. Made for the 1867 Paris Exhibition. Adam stylistic influence. Early use of design based on 18th-entury models. By Courtesy of the Board of Trustees of the Victoria and Albert Museum, London.

The Adamesque satinwood cabinet reflects the late Victorian designer's interest in the revival of 18th-century antecedents. This cabinet was displayed at the Paris Exhibition of 1867. The surface decoration is polychrome marquetry with Wedgwood inserts (Figure 18-19).

Beds

Brass and iron beds became very popular in the second half of the 19th century. The first patent was issued in 1848. Many were partially concealed by drapery and the half-tester became popular again. This baldachin bed has a canopy that partially extends over the bed (see Figure C-36). Constructed around 1850, it is made of japanned metal with panels of papier-mâché richly painted with floral ornament.

ORNAMENT

Ornamental detail was as diverse as the historical styles on which furniture and interiors were based. Embellishment was derived from the English repertoire (medieval through the

18th century); from the French (Renaissance through the Empire); and from the Classical (Greek and Roman, or these influences as filtered through the Italian Renaissance). The Victorians sometimes imitated nature in minute detail and sometimes allegoric or symbolic meaning was attached to ornament.

The following are examples of motifs related to specific substyles of the Victorian style. Scrolls, volutes, and shells were used with the Rococo influence. Gothic is represented by such motifs as ogee arches, lancet arches, crockets, and quatrefoils. The naturalistic tendencies meant that nature was imitated in minute detail—trees, flowers of all description (sunflowers, hollyhocks) sometimes arranged in festoons. Representing the animal world were squirrels, foxes, monkeys, and others.

Selected Bibliography

Amery, Colin, ed. *Period Houses and Their Details.* London: The Architectural Press, 1978.

Badawy, Alexander. *A History of Egyptian Architecture: The Empire (the New Kingdom) from the Eighteenth to the End of the Twentieth Dynasty, 1580–1085 B.C.* Berkeley: University of California Press, 1968.

_____. *A History of Egyptian Architecture: The First Intermediate Period, the Middle Kingdom, and the Second Intermediate Period.* Berkeley: University of California Press, 1966.

Baker, Hollis S. *Furniture in the Ancient World: Origins and Evolution, 3100–475 B.C.* New York: Macmillan, Giniger, 1965.

Beard, Geoffrey. *Craftsmen and Interior Decoration in England, 1660–1820.* London: Bloomsbury Books, 1981.

_____. *The Work of Robert Adam.* New York: ARCO Publishing, 1978.

Blomfield, Sir Reginald. *A History of French Architecture from the Death of Mazarin till the Death of Louis XV, 1661–1774.* Vol 2. London: G. Bell and Sons, 1921.

Blunt, Anthony, ed. *Baroque and Rococo Architecture and Decoration.* New York: Harper & Row, 1978.

Boardman, John, et al. *Greek Art and Architecture.* New York: Harry N. Abrams, n. d.

Braham, Allan. *The Architecture of the French Enlightenment.* London: Thames and Hudson, 1980.

Braun, Hugh. *An Introduction to English Mediaeval Architecture.* New York: Frederick A. Praeger, 1967.

Brilliant, Richard. *Roman Art from the Republic to Constantine.* New York: Praeger Publishers, 1974.

Brion, Marcel. *Pompeii and Herculaneum: The Glory and the Grief.* New York: Crown Publishers, 1962.

Cantacuzino, Sherban. *European Domestic Architecture: Its Development from Early Times.* Great Britain: Dutton, Studio Vista, 1969.

Clarke, John R. *The Houses of Roman Italy, 100 B.C.–A.D. 250.* Berkeley: University of California Press,1991.

Cook, Olive. *The English Country House: An Art and a Way of Life.* New York: G. P. Putnam's Sons, 1974.

Cook, R. M. *Greek Art: Its Development, Character, and Influence.* New York: Farrar, Strauss, Giroux, 1972.

Costantino, Ruth T. *How to Know French Antiques.* New York: Clarkson N. Potter, 1961.

Dinsmoor, William Bell. *The Architecture of Ancient Greece: An Account of its Historic Development.* Rev. and enl. based on the first part of *The Architecture of Greece and Rome,* by William J. Anderson and R. Phené Spiers, 1902. New York: Biblo and Tannen, 1973.

Eberlein, Harold Donaldson. *Villas of Florence and Tuscany.* New York: The Architectural Record Company, 1922.

Edwards, Ralph. *The Shorter Dictionary of English Furniture.* London: Country Life, 1964.

Edwards, Ralph and Margaret Jourdain. *Georgian Cabinet-Makers* London: Country Life, 1946.

Edwards, Ralph and L. G. G. Ramsey, eds. *The Connoisseur's Complete Period Guides.* New York: Bonanza Books, 1968.

Fastnedge, Ralph. *English Furniture Styles from 1500 to 1830.* Baltimore, Maryland: Penguin Books, 1964.

Fletcher, Sir Banister. *A History of Architecture on the Comparative Method.* New York: Charles Scribner's Sons, 1956.

Frégnac, Claude and Wayne Andrews. *The Great Houses of Paris.* Translated by James Emmons. New York: Vendome Press, 1979; distributed in U. S. by Viking Press.

Frégnac, Claude, ed. *French Cabinetmakers of the Eighteenth Century.* Paris: Hachette, 1963; New York: French and European Publications, 1965.

Girouard, Mark. *Life in the English Country House: A Social and Architectural History.* Harmondsworth, Middlesex, England: Penguin Books, 1980.

_____. *The Victorian Country House.* New Haven and London: Yale University Press, 1985.

_____. *Hardwick Hall: A History and a Guide.* London: The National Trust, 1976.

Hackenbroch, Yvonne. *English Furniture with Some Furniture of other Countries in the Irwin Untermyer Collection.* Cambridge: Harvard University Press, 1958.

Harris, Richard. *Discovering Timber-framed Buildings.* 2nd ed. Aylesbury, Bucks, U. K.: Shire Publications, 1979.

Hayward, Helena, ed. *World Furniture.* New York: McGraw-Hill, 1965.

Hills, Nicholas. *The English Fireplace: Its Architecture and the Working Fire.* London: Quiller Press, 1983.

Hodge, Peter. *Aspects of Roman Life: The Roman House.* Rev. ed. Harlow, Essex, England: Longman Group, 1975.

Husscy, Christopher. *English Country Houses: Early Georgian, 1715–1760.* Rev. London: Country Life, 1965.

_____. *English Country Houses: Late Georgian 1800–1840.* London: Country Life, 1958.

_____. *English Country Houses: Mid-Georgian.1760–1800.* London: Country Life, 1956.

Jackson-Stops, Gervase and James Pipkin. *The English Country House: A Grand Tour.* New York: New York Graphic Society, 1985.

Jourdain, Margaret. *English Decorative Plasterwork of the Renaissance.* New York: Charles Scribner's Sons, 1966.

_____. *English Interior Decoration, 1500–1830.* London: Batsford, 1950.

_____. *Regency Furniture, 1795–1830.* Rev. and ed. by Ralph Fastnedge. London: Country Life, 1965.

Kalnein, Wend von. *Architecture in France in the Eighteenth Century.* Translated by David Britt. New Haven and London: Yale University Press, 1995.

Killen, Geoffrey. *Ancient Egyptian Furniture.* Vol. 1, Warminster, Wilts, England: Aris & Phillips, 1980.

Kirk, John T. *American Furniture and the British Tradition to 1830.* New York: Alfred A. Knopf, 1982.

Kraus, Theodor. *Pompeii and Herculaneum: The Living Cities of the Dead.* Translated by Robert Erich Wolf. New York: Harry N. Abrams, 1975.

Lavedan, Pierre. *French Architecture.* Harmondsworth: Penguin, 1956.

Lawrence, A. W. *Greek Architecture.* 4th Rev. ed. by R. A. Tomlinson. New Haven: Yale University Press, 1983.

Lloyd, Nathaniel. *A History of the English House, from Primitive Times to the Victorian Period.* 1931. Reprint, London: The Architectural Press; New York: Architectural Book Publishing, 1975.

Masson, Georgina. *Italian Villas and Palaces.* New York: Harry N. Abrams, 1959.

Mazzotti, Giuseppe. *Venetain Villas.* Rome: Carlo Besetetti–Edizioni d'Arte, 1957.

Meeks, Caroll. *Italian Architecture, 1715–1914.* New Haven: Yale University Press, 1965.

Millon, Henry A. *Baroque and Rococo Architecture.* New York: Braziller, 1961.

Moulin, Jean-Marie. "The Art of the Second Empire." *The Magazine Antiques* 114 no. 4 (October 1978): 776–783.

Musgrave, Clifford. *Adam and Hepplewhite and Other Neoclassical Furniture.* New York: Taplinger, 1966.

_____. *Regency Furniture, 1800 to 1830.* Rev. ed. London: Faber and Faber, 1970.

Odom, William M. *A History of Italian Furniture from the Fourteenth to the Early Nineteenth Centuries,* 2 vols. Garden City, New York: Doubleday, Page & Co., 1918/1919.

Pevsner, Nikolaus, John Fleming, and Hugh Honour. *A Dictionary of Architecture.* Rev. and enl. Woodstock, New York: The Overlook Press, 1966.

Pevsner, Nikolaus. *An Outline of European Architecture.* Baltimore: Penguin, 1960.

Pradère, Alexandre. *French Furniture Makers: The Art of the Ebéniste from Louis XIV to the Revolution.* Translation by Perran Wood. Malibu, California: The J. Paul Getty Museum, 1989.

Richter, G. M. A. *The Furniture of the Greeks, Etruscans, and Romans.* London: Phaidon Press, 1966.

Richter, Gisela M. *A Handbook of Greek Art.* 6th ed. London: Phaidon Press, 1969.

Rogers, John C. *English Furniture.* 3rd ed., rev. and enl. by Margaret Jourdain. London: Country Life, 1959.

Samoyault-Verlet, Colombe. "Furniture in France Under the Second Empire." *The Connoisseur* 199 (December 1978): 264-271.

Saylor, Henry. *Dictionary of Architecture.* New York: John Wiley & Sons, 1952.

Schottmüller, Frida. *Furniture and Interior Decoration of the Italian Renaissance.* New York: B. Westermann, 1928.

Smith, Earl Baldwin. *Egyptian Architecture as Cultural Expression.* Rev. ed. by Alan Gowans. American Life Foundation, 1968; distributed by Century House, Watkins Glen, N. Y.

Stillman, Damie. *The Decorative Work of Robert Adam.* London: Alec Tiranti, 1966.

Summerson, John. *Architecture in Britain, 1530–1830.* 5th ed., rev. and enl. Harmondsworth, Middlesex: Penguin Books, 1969.

Sutcliffe, Anthony. *Paris: An Architectural History.* New Haven and London: Yale University Press, 1993.

Thornton, Peter. *The Italian Renaissance Interior, 1400–1600.* New York: Harry N. Abrams, 1991.

_____. *Seventeenth Century Interior Decoration in England, France, and Holland.* New Haven: Yale University Press, 1978.

Tipping, H. Avray. *English Homes, Period V* Vol. 1, *Early Georgian, 1714–1760.* London: Country Life, 1921.

Verlet, Pierre. *French Furniture of the Eighteenth Century.* Translated by Penelope Hunter-Stiebel. Charlottesville and London: University Press of Virginia, 1991.

_____. *French Royal Furniture.* New York: Towse, 1963.

Viaux, Jacqueline. *French Furniture.* Translated by Hazel Paget. New York: G. P. Putnam's Sons, 1964.

Ward, W. H. *The Architecture of the Renaissance in France.* 2nd. ed., rev. and enl. New York: Hacker Art Books, 1976.

Watkin, David. *A History of Western Architecture.* New York: Thames and Hudson, 1986.

Watson, F. J. B. *Wallace Collection Catalogues: Furniture.* London: Clowes, 1956.

Watson, F. J. B. and Carl Christian Dauterman. *The Wrightsman Collection.* New York: The Metropolitan Museum of Art, 1970; distributed by the New York Graphic Society, Greenwich, Ct.

Wilson, Michael I. *The English Country House and its Furnishings.* New York: Architectural Book Publishing, 1978.

Wittkower, Rudolf. *Art and Architecture in Italy, 1600 to 1750.* Baltimore, Md.: Penguin Books, 1969.

Index

A

Abacus, 12, 26
Abbots Palace, 310
Académie de France, 264
Académie des Beaux-Arts, 309
Academy of Architecture (France), 157, 264, 282, 308–309
Academy of Fine Arts, 309
Act of Settlement, 228
Adam, James, 282
Adam, John, 295
Adam, Robert, vii, 178, 256, 265, 282–283, 284, 291, 295, 297, 306
Adam furniture, 298–300
Aedicular arrangements, 49
Aeolians, 24
Age of Enlightenment, 264
Age of Walnut, 193
Aisle construction, Medieval, 65
Akroter, 328
Alae, 42
Alberti, Leon Battista, 82, 120
Alexander the Great, 25
Alexander Visiting Roxana (Sodoma), 101
Allegory of Divine Providence and Barberini Power (da Cortona), 140–141
Alnwick Castle, 298
Altars, Greek, 29

American Revolution, 308
Anaglypta, 363
Anne of Austria, 156
Annulets, 26
Antechamber, 85
Antechambre de l'Oeil de Boeuf (Versailles), 210, 211, 215, 217
Apartment buildings
    Louis Philippe, 345
    Restoration, 344, 345
Apartment concept, introduction of, 84–85
Apollo Drawing Room (Versailles), 166
Appartement de commodité, 209
Appartement de parade, 209
Arabesque, 90, 110, 111
Arcaded cortile, 86
Arcade posts, 65
Arcading, 125–126
Arched doors, 71
Arched-frame windows, 70
Archer, Thomas, 184
Architectura, 119
Architectural standards, 309
Architectural style, 49
Architectural treatises, Renaissance, 82–83
Architecture. *See also* Interior architecture
    Egyptian, 4–8
    Greek, 25–30
    interior, vii

Neoclassic, 265
relationship to furniture design, 75
Renaissance, 82
Architecture (de Vriese), 122
Architecture françoise (Blondel), 264
Architrave-cornice, 240
Architrave moldings, 241
Architraves, 26, 188
Arcuated construction, 41
Armchairs. *See also* Seat furniture
Baroque, 151–152
Renaissance, 112
Armoire à deux corps, 171
Armoires, 79
Baroque, 153, 154
Louis XIII, 171, 172
Arrises, 26
Artari, Giovanni, 234, 236
Artari, Giuseppe, 234, 236
Artisans, patronage for, 156
Arts
Baroque manifestations in, 177
centralization of, 156
moral evaluation of, 228
Assemblies, 230, 231
Athéniennes, 276, 322
Atrium, Roman, 42, 43
Attics, 32
Aubert, Jean, 211
Audran, Claude, 210, 225
Aumbry, 79
Axial planning, 42, 43, 142, 143

B

Back stairs, 181
Bagutti, Giovanni, 234, 236
Baldachin bed, 374
Balloon-back chairs, 371
Balusters, 170, 272
early Georgian, 245
turned, 368
Balustrades, 129
Baroque, 150
iron, 193
Banquet, 121
Banqueting House, 119
Barbet, Jean, 165, 189
Barham's Manor House, 125
Baroque style, 140
characteristics of, 234
Barrel vault ceilings, 93, 160
Bar tracery, 70–71
Bauhaus, 358
Beam ceilings
Egyptian, 12–13
Beamed ceilings
Baroque, 165–166
Egyptian, 12-13
Renaissance, 93, 109, 122
Beams
exposed, 73
Medieval, 65
Beard, Geoffrey, 190
Beauharnais, Eugène de, 314–315
Beaumont, Claude Etienne, 309
Beauty, Renaissance theory of, 84
Beauvais tapestry works, 238
Bedchambers, Renaissance, 85
Bed frame, Renaissance, 138
Beds
Chippendale, 260
Directoire, 319, 320

Early French Neoclassic, 278–279
Early Georgian English, 253, 256
Egyptian, 20–21
Empire, 323–324
English Renaissance, 136–138
English Revival, 374
French Baroque, 173
French Renaissance, 115
French Rococo, 224
Georgian, 256, 257
Greek, 37
Hepplewhite, 302
Italian Baroque, 154
Italian Renaissance, 100–101
Late English Neoclassic, 342
Louis XVI, 278–279
Medieval, 79–80
Queen Anne, 253
Restoration, 353
Roman, 57
Second Empire, 355
Sheraton, 306
Victorian, 374
William and Mary, 203–204
Beeswax, use of, 9
Bélanger, François-Joseph, 309, 312, 314, 317
Belton, 190
Belvoir Castle, 364
Benches, Medieval, 77
Beningbrough Hall, 179, 180, 182, 186, 190
Bérain, Jean, 189, 206, 210, 225
Bergère, 220, 276
Bernini, Gianlorenzo, 141
Berry, Duchesse de, 346
Bienséance, 208
Bishop's Palace, 62
Black, Adam, 303
Blenheim Palace, 179, 191
Blicking Hall, 128
Blind tracery, 75
Blondel, Jacques François, 177, 208, 264
Boffrand, Gabriel-Germain, 212, 213
Boiserie, 162, 212
Louis XV, 214
Bolection moldings, 190, 216
Bombé shaping, 223
Bonaparte, Napoleon, 308, 309, 344
Bonheur du jour, 276, 321, 322
Bookcases
Regency, 341
Sheraton, 305
Book of Architecture (Gibbs), 229, 243
Border design, Roman, 48
Borromini, Francesco, 141, 147, 211
Boucher, François, 214
Boufflers, Marquis de, 220
Boulle, André Charles, 168, 173
Boullée, Etienne-Louis, 271, 310
Boulle marquetry, 356
Boulle-work, 168, 170
Bourbon Restoration, 344
Boyle, Richard, 229
Bradbury, Robert, 184, 190
Brass beds, 374
Breakfront bookcase, Georgian, 255
Brettingham, Matthew, 284
Brick
sun-dried mud, 31
terra-cotta, 41
Bridgens, Robert, 369
Bronze
as a furniture material, 33

for stools, 54
studding of, 33
Bronze Age, 24, 28
Bronze furniture, Roman, 52
Bronze tables, 55–56
Brosse, Salomon de, 157, 158
Broughton Hall, 335
Brown, Lancelot (Capability), 230
Buffet, Medieval, 79
Builder's and Workman's Treasury of Designs (Langley), 237
Building
during the Baroque period, 140, 176
early Georgian, 230
Building guides, 120
Building materials, Egyptian, 2. *See also* Materials
Bulbous legs, 134
Bureau plat, 170, 221, 276
Burghley, 182, 191–192
Burlington, Lord, 229, 282
Buttery, Medieval, 65

C

Cabinet aux Miroirs, 164
Cabinet des Médailles, 217
Cabinet Dictionary (Sheraton), 327
Cabinet Doré (Versailles), 162, 163
Cabinet Encyclopedia (Sheraton), 328, 341
Cabinet-Maker, Upholsterer and General Artists' Encyclopedia (Sheraton), 327
Cabinet-Maker and Upholsterer's Drawing Book (Sheraton), 303, 305, 306, 336
Cabinet-Maker's Dictionary (Sheraton), 303
Cabinet-Maker's & Upholsterer's Guide, The (Hepplewhite), 300
Cabinets, Victorian, 373–374
Cabriole leg, 219
Cabriolet, 220
Caffiéri, J., 207
Camera, 85
Cameron, Charles, 290
Campbell, Colen, 184, 228, 282
Canapé, 221
Canapés de l'amitié, 353
Candelabra, 90, 91
Cane chairs, 199, 338
Baroque, 194, 198
Canopy beds
Medieval, 80
Renaissance, 136
Cantilevered stairs, 246
Caquetoire, 112, 113
Carceri (Piranesi), 265
Cardiff Castle, 368
Card tables, 251, 252
Georgian, 254, 255
Carlton Towers, 364
Carolean furniture, 193–199
Carpaccio, Vittore, 92, 100
Carpet factories, Neoclassic, 288
Carpets, Rococo, 212
Carracci, Annibale, 144
Carracci family, 243–244
Carreaux d'octagones, 289
Cartouche, 107, 165
Carved furniture. *See also* Carving
Baroque, 150
Medieval, 75
Carved paneling, 72, 162
Carving
Baroque, 204

on beds, 115
Elizabethan, 130
French, 78
Medieval, 67
mirror, 214
Neoclassic, 292, 318, 337
on panels, 68
Renaissance, 95, 138
Rococo, 211–212
Carwitham, John, 237
Caryatids, 115
Casa del Tramezzo di Legno, 51
Cassapanca, 98, 99
Cassone, 98, 99, 153
Cast iron, 367, 370
Castle plan, 62
Castles
French, 105–106
Medieval, 60
Cathedra, 53
Cathedrals, Medieval, 61
Catholic Church, reforms in, 140
Cavetto molding, 11
Caylus, Comte de, 207, 283
Ceiling painting, 73, 296
Ceilings
Early English Neoclassic, 295–297
Early French Neoclassic, 272
Early Georgian English, 243–245
Egyptian, 12–13
English Baroque, 190–192
English Renaissance, 128
English Revival, 367–368
French Baroque, 165–166
French Renaissance, 109
French Rococo, 217
Greek, 33
Italian Baroque, 148–149
Italian Renaissance, 93–94
Late English Neoclassic, 335
Late French Neoclassic, 316–317
Medieval, 73
Roman, 51–52
Cellini, Benvenuto, 104
Central hall, Egyptian, 7
Certosina, 95
Chair finials, 17
Chair of Hetepheres, 16
Chair jointing, Egyptian, 14, 15. *See also* Joints
Chairs. *See* Seat furniture
Chair-tables, 131
Chaise, 169
Chambers, Sir William, 265, 283
Chambre de parade, 209
Chapels
Medieval, 64
Renaissance, 86, 122
Charles II, King, 176, 177
Charles II furniture, 193
Charles VIII, King, 104
Château Chambord, 106
Château de Maisons, 157, 164
Château de Malmaison, 312, 315
Château of Ancy-le-Franc, 106
Château of Bagatelle, 311, 312
Château of Bénouville, 268
Château of Blois, 108, 157, 161, 167
Château of Louveciennes, 268, 269
Château Vaux le Vicomte, 157–158, 159
Châteaux, 61, 105–106
floor plans of, 158–161
Chatsworth, 187, 188, 189, 190, 191, 192, 193
Cheere, Sir Henry, 241

Cheminées à l'Italienne (Le Pautre), 165
Cheminées à la moderne (Le Pautre), 165
Cheminées à la royalle (Le Pautre), 210
Cheminées et Lambris à la mode (Le Pautre), 190
Chest-on-chest, 253
Chest on stand, 202–203
Chests. *See also* Storage pieces
Baroque, 199
Medieval, 75, 76, 79
Renaissance, 135–136
tall-leg, 19–20
Chiaroscuro, 239
Chief Groundes of Architecture (Shute), 123
Chimney ornaments, 210
Chimneypieces
Early English Neoclassic, 293–295
Early French Neoclassic, 272
Early Georgian English, 241–243
English Baroque, 189–190
English Renaissance, 127
English Revival, 366–367
French Baroque, 164–165
French Renaissance, 108–109
French Rococo, 216–217
Greek, 33
Italian Baroque, 148
Italian Renaissance, 92–93
Late English Neoclassic, 334
Late French Neoclassic, 315–316
Medieval, 72–73
Chinese lacquer, 342
Chinoiserie, 206, 225, 230, 337
Chip carving, 95
Chippendale, Thomas, 238, 248
Chippendale furniture, 247, 256–260
Cinquefoil lights, 70
Circular stairways, 73, 74
Ciseleur-doreur, 207
City and Country Builder's Treasury, The (Langley), 243
Civic architecture, Greek, 30
Civic ritual, Greek, 25
Clandon Park, 229, 243, 244
Clapboard wall construction, 68
Classical motifs, 324, 342
Classical orders, 26
Classical styles, interest in, 83, 207, 264
Clay models, Egyptian, 4
Clay plaster, in mural painting, 8–9
Clerestory windows, 6
Clérisseau, Charles Louis, 282, 287
Closet, 179
Medieval, 64
Renaissance, 122
Cochin, Nicholas, 207
Coffered ceilings, 51, 94, 297, 335
Coffered false domes, 181
Coffering, 33, 109
Colbert, Jean-Baptiste, 157, 308–309
Collar beams, 65
Collection of Designs for Household Furniture and Interior Decoration, A (Smith), 328, 336, 338, 341
Collonnade, 26
Columns
in antis, 28
Egyptian, 2, 11, 12, 13
Greek, 26–28
marble, 31
Roman, 41, 43–45, 50–51
Columns in the round, 110
Commode
Chippendale, 260, 261

Directoire, 319, 320
Empire, 322–323
Georgian, 257
Louis XIV, 172, 173
Louis XV, 207, 223
Louis XVI, 278
Osterly, 300
Restoration, 352
Rococo, 222
Transitional Louis XV–XVI, 223
Commode dressing table, Hepplewhite, 302
Commode table, 222
Commodité, 208
Commonwealth period, 131, 132
Communal living
Medieval, 60, 62
Renaissance, 120
Complete Body of Architecture, A (Ware), 235, 241
Compluvium, 29, 42
Composite order, 45–46
Concrete
discovery of, 41
Roman use of, 46
Consoles, 162
Empire, 321, 322
Console tables, 221
Construction techniques
Early English Neoclassic, 298
Early Georgian English, 248–250
Egyptian, 14–15
English Renaissance, 130–131
English Revival, 370–371
French Baroque, 167–168
French Renaissance, 110
French Revival, 349–350
French Rococo, 217–218
Greek, 33–35
Italian Baroque, 150–151
Italian Renaissance, 95
Late English Neoclassic, 336–337
Late French Neoclassic, 317–318
Medieval, 75–76
Roman, 52
Continental chairs, 198
Corbel, 72
Corinthian columns, 27–28
Cornice, 26
Cornice molding, stucco, 52
Corn Laws, 358
Coromandel lacquer, 218, 274
Corridors, Baroque, 182
Cortile, 83
Cortona, Pietro da, 140–141, 143, 145, 148–149, 239
Cotant d'Ivry, Pierre, 268, 270
Cotelle, Jean, 166
Cotte, Robert de, 165, 210–211, 213
Couches. *See also* Beds
Greek, 37
Roman, 57
Couchette, 324
Council of Trent, 140
Country residences
alteration of, 283
British, 178–183
decoration of, 235
Egyptian, 5, 7
Georgian, 230
Court, peristyle, 28
Court cupboard, 130, 136
Courtonne, Jean, 208–209
Coved ceilings, 93–94
Covenance, 208

Crafts. *See also* Guilds
  Medieval, 75
  specialization of, 207
Craftsmanship
  decline of, 118
  perfection in, 207
Craftsmen, migration of, 119
Crédence, Medieval, 78, 79
Credenza, 98, 99
Cressent, Charles, 223
Cromwell, Oliver, 118
Cromwellian chair, 132–133
Cromwellian period, 130
Cromwellian style, 138
Crossbanding, 194–195, 202, 249
Crossette, 148
Crossette architrave, 240
Cross-hatching, 217
Crown plate, 65
Crown-post construction, 65–66
Cruck construction, 66, 67
Crucy, Mathurin, 309
Crusades, artistic ideas from, 61
Crystal Palace Exhibition, 359
C-scrolls, 35, 37, 193, 214
Cubiculum, 42
Cuisine, 209
Cup and cover legs, 134, 136
Cupboards
  Louis XIII, 171
  Medieval, 79
  Renaissance, 98–100, 136
  Roman, 56–57
Cupid's bow, 258
Curule chairs, 77, 96
Curule-form stool, 54
Cycladic cultures, 24

D

Dado, 10, 32
  bands of, 50
Dado molding, 213
Dais, Medieval, 62
da Maiano, Giovanni, 118
Dante chairs, 95, 96
Dark Ages, 24
David, Jacques Louis, 312
da Vinci, Leonardo, 82, 104
da Vries, Johannes, 119
Daybeds, 198
De architectura (Vitruvius), 25
Death of Henri II woodcut, 115
Decoration
  Early English Neoclassic, 287–297
  Early French Neoclassic, 268–272
  Egyptian, 8–13
  English Baroque, 184–193
  English Early Georgian, 234–246
  English Renaissance, 122–129
  English Revival, 363–369
  French Baroque, 162–167
  French Renaissance, 106–109
  French Revival, 346–348
  French Rococo, 210–217
  Greek, 30–33
  Italian Baroque, 144–150
  Italian Renaissance, 87–95
  Late English Neoclassic, 331–336
  Late French Neoclassic, 311–317
  Medieval, 67–74
  Roman, 45–52
Decorative materials. *See* Materials

Decorative painting
  Baroque, 185
  early Georgian, 235
  Egyptian, 14–15
Dei Grande, Antonio, 144
Deir el Medina, Craftsman's Residence at, 4, 6
Delafosse, Charles, 280
Delftware, 189–190
della Robbia, Luca, 82
del Nunziata, Toto, 118
Demilune commode, 278
Denon, Dominique Vivant, 327
Design, continuum of, viii
Designs of Inigo Jones (Kent and Flitcroft), 234
Desks, Louis XVI, 276–278
Desserte, 320, 353
de Vriese, Vredeman, 122
Diamond-shaped glass panes, 127
Diaperwork, 210, 217
di Giorgio, Francesco, 82, 85
Dining room furniture, Hepplewhite,
  301–302. *See also* Dining tables
Dining tables
  Chippendale, 259
  Medieval, 78
  Neoclassic, 304
  Renaissance, 100, 134
Diocletian palace, 287
Diphros seat form, 35–36
Directoire furniture, 317–320
Directoire style, 308, 311
  ornamental detail in, 324
Directoire walls, 312–314
Doddington, 284, 286–287, 328
Dodington Park, 331, 332
Dogleg stairways, 129
Dome ceilings, 160
Domestic architecture, Egyptian, 3
Domus, 41
  orientation of, 43
Door leaves, Medieval, 71
Doors
  Early English Neoclassic, 292–293
  Early French Neoclassic, 271–272
  Early Georgian English, 239–241
  Egyptian, 12
  English Baroque, 188–189
  English Renaissance, 127
  English Revival, 366
  French Baroque, 164
  French Renaissance, 108
  French Rococo, 215
  Greek, 32–33
  Italian Baroque, 147–148
  Italian Renaissance, 90–92
  Late English Neoclassic, 332–334
  Late French Neoclassic, 315
  Medieval, 69–72
  Roman, 51
  simulated, 188
Dorians, 24
Doric columns, 26
Dossier, 77, 80, 320
Double-hung windows, 188, 239, 292
Dovetail joints, 95
Dowel joints, 15, 34
Draped beds, 80, 154, 173, 204
Drapery, *trompe l'oeil*, 292
Drawer pulls, 203
Draw tables, 113, 135
Dream of Saint Ursula, The (Carpaccio), 92,
  100–101
Dressing tables, 202, 203, 340

Dressoir, 78, 114
Dripstone, 69, 70
du Barry, Madame, 207, 268
Ducal Palace, Mantua, 90
Duchesse-brisée, 221
Durand, Jean-Nicolas-Louis, 344
Dutch influence, 177
Dyrham Park, 187, 188

E

Earpiece, 148
East India Company, 197, 235
Ébéniste, 167, 207
Ecclesiastical architecture, 73
Echinus, 26
Edict of Nantes, 104, 156, 157, 177
Education, classical, 229
Églomisé, 337, 354
Egyptian design, 1–21
  in furniture, 13–21
  historical setting of, 2–3
  interior architecture and decoration in, 8–13
  ornamental detail in, 21
  spatial relationships in, 4–8
Egyptian influence, 327, 336, 338
Egyptian motifs, 342
Egyptian society, 3
Electrum, 10
Elements of Architecture (Wotton), 120
Elizabeth I, Queen, 119
Elizabethan period, 119
Elizabethan revival, 369
Elizabethan style, 358
El-Luhan Urban Mansion, 5, 8
Emblema, 48
Empire furniture, 321–324
Empire style, 308, 312
  ornamental detail in, 324
Empire walls, 314–315
Enclosure system, 176
Encoignures, 278
Enfilade, 209
Enfilade arrangement, 84, 159, 160, 178, 183
English architecture, influences on, 61
English Baroque design, 176–204
  in furniture, 193–204
  historical setting of, 176–178
  interior architecture and decoration in,
    184–193
  ornamental detail in, 204
  spatial relationships in, 178–183
English Civil War, 118
English Early Georgian design, 227–262
  in furniture, 247–260
  historical setting of, 228–230
  interior architecture and decoration in,
    234–246
  ornamental design in, 260–262
  spatial relationships in, 230–234
English Neoclassic design, early, 282–306
  in furniture, 297–306
  historical setting of, 282–283
  interior architecture and decoration in,
    287–297
  ornamental design in, 306
  spatial relationships in, 283–287
English Neoclassic design, late, 326–342
  in furniture, 336–342
  historical setting of, 326–328
  interior architecture and decoration in,
    331–336
  ornamental design in, 342

spatial relationships in, 328–331
English Renaissance design, 118–138
  in furniture, 130–138
  historical setting of, 118–119
  interior architecture and decoration in, 122–129
  ornamental detail in, 138
  spatial relationships in, 120–122
English Revival design, 358–375
  in furniture, 369–374
  historical setting of, 358–359
  interior architecture and decoration in, 363–369
  ornamental design in, 374–375
  spatial relationships in, 359–363
Engraved chimneypieces, 164–165
Engraved designs, publication of, 207
Engravings
  French, 177
  Régence, 210
En grisaille execution, 298
Entabulature, 110, 114, 127, 138, 241
  concave curve, 148
Entasis, 26
E-shaped plan, 120
Espagnolettes, 221
Essai sur l'Architecture (Laugier), 282
Etruscan civilization, 40
Etruscan dressing room, 291
Eugénie, Empress, 345
Evelyn, John, 154, 190, 193
Exedra, 42
Exemplars of Tudor Architecture and Furniture (Hunt), 369
Exeter, 126
Exhibitions, role of, 349, 359

F

Faience, 12
Faience tile, 10
Farthingale chair, 132
Fauces, 42
Fauteuil, 169, 219–220, 274, 275, 318, 320
Fenestration. See Windows
Feudal system, 60
Figural painting
  Renaissance, 89
  Roman, 50
Figurative tapestries, 69
Figures
  Egyptian, 10–11
  Roman, 49
Filarete, 82
Fillet, 238
Finials
  Greek, 35
  Renaissance, 96
  stairway, 129
Fireplaces, corner, 189–190. See Chimneypieces; Hearth
First Book of Architecture made by Sebastian Serly, translated out of Italian into Dutch and out of Dutch into English, 119
Flemish art, 156
Flemish ornamentation, 138
Flemish pattern books, 130
Flemish tapestries, 124
Flitcroft, Henry, 234
Floorcloths, 364
Floor matting, 123
Floor plans
  Early English Neoclassic, 284–287

Early Georgian English, 231–234
  Egyptian, 4–8
  English Baroque, 178–183
  English Renaissance, 120–122
  English Revival, 359–363
  French Baroque, 158–161
  French Renaissance, 105–106
  French Rococo, 207–210
  Greek, 28–30
  Italian Renaissance, 84–87
  Late English Neoclassic, 328–331
  Late French Neoclassic, 309–311
  Medieval, 62–66
  Roman, 42–45
Floors
  Early English Neoclassic, 289
  Early French Neoclassic, 270
  Early Georgian English, 236–237
  Egyptian, 10
  English Baroque, 185
  English Renaissance, 123
  English Revival, 364
  French Baroque, 162
  French Renaissance, 107
  French Rococo, 212
  Greek, 31–32
  Italian Baroque, 146
  Italian Renaissance, 88
  Late English Neoclassic, 331
  Late French Neoclassic, 312
  Medieval, 68
  Roman, 48
Floral marquetry, 195, 197, 199
Florence, mosaics from, 150
Fondeur-ciseleur, 207
Fontaine, Pierre François Léonard, 309, 312, 317, 327
Fontainebleau, 106–107, 166
Formal house, 178
Fouquet, Nicolas, 159
Four Books of Architecture (Palladio), 228, 229
Fourdinois, Henri, 349
Four-poster beds, 115, 173
  Hepplewhite, 302
  Louis XVI, 278
  Sheraton, 306
Fragonard, Jean-Honoré, 214
Frame, defined, 78
France, adoption of the classical in, 104
Francis I, King, 104
Francis I Gallery (Fontainebleau), 106, 107
Francis I style, 110
  in ornamental detail, 115
  for seat furniture, 111
  in storage pieces, 113–114
  in tables, 112–113
French Academy. See Academy of Architecture (France)
French architecture, influences on, 61
French artistic ideals, 177
French Baroque design, 156–174
  in furniture, 167–173
  historical setting of, 156–157
  interior architecture and decoration in, 162–167
  ornamental detail in, 173–174
  spatial relationships in, 157–161
French Neoclassic design, early, 264–280
  in furniture, 273–279
  historical setting of, 264–266
  interior architecture and decoration in, 268–272
  ornamental design in, 279–280

spatial relationships in, 266–268
French Neoclassic design, late, 308–324
  in furniture, 317–324
  historical setting of, 308–309
  interior architecture and decoration in, 311–317
  ornamental design in, 324
  spatial relationships in, 309–311
French Renaissance design, 104–115
  in furniture, 110–115
  historical setting of, 104
  interior architecture and decoration in, 106–109
  ornamental detail in, 115
  spatial relationships in, 104–106
French Renaissance style, 365
French Revival design, 344–356
  in furniture, 348–355
  historical setting of, 344–345
  interior architecture and decoration in, 346–348
  ornamental design in, 355–356
  spatial relationships in, 345–346
French Revolution, 308
French Rocaille influence, 258
French Rococo design, 206–225
  in furniture, 217–224
  historical setting of, 206–207
  interior architecture and decoration in, 210–217
  ornamental design in, 225
  spatial relationships in, 207–210
French windows, 164, 332
Fresco decoration, Baroque, 148–149
Fresco painting
  Baroque, 144
  Renaissance, 87
  Roman, 46–47
Fresco secco, 87
Fresco technique, 9, 146
Friezes, 26
  Medieval, 68
Fringed furniture, 201
Fronde outbreaks, 156
Fulcra, 37, 52
Functionalism, 358
Furniture
  Adam, 298–300
  animal legs for, 16, 17, 21
  Carolean, 193–199
  Chippendale, 247, 256–260
  Directoire, 317–320
  Early English Neoclassic, 297–306
  Early French Neoclassic, 273–279
  Egyptian, 13–21
  Empire, 321–324
  English Baroque, 193–204
  English Early Georgian, 247–260
  English Renaissance, 130–138
  English Revival, 369–374
  French Baroque, 167–173
  French Renaissance, 110–115
  French Revival, 348–355
  French Rococo, 217–224
  Georgian, 247, 253–256
  Greek, 33–37
  Hepplewhite, 300–302
  industrial production of, 336
  Italian Baroque, 150–154
  Italian Renaissance, 95–101
  Late English Neoclassic, 336–342
  Late French Neoclassic, 317–324
  Louis XIII, 168–169, 170, 171, 173–174

Louis XIV, 169, 170, 173, 174
Louis XV, 219–223
Louis XVI, 274–279
in Medieval design, 74–80
papier-mâché, 371
portable, 74
Queen Anne, 247, 250–253
Régence, 218–224, 337–342
Restoration, 349, 350, 350–353
Roman, 52–57
Second Empire, 349–350, 353–355
Sheraton, 303–306
Transitional Louis XV–XVI, 221, 223–224
turning of, 95
Victorian, 369–374
William and Mary, 199–204
Furniture craftsmen, Rococo, 206–207
Furniture design, viii
Furniture finishing, 130
Furniture hangings, 137
Furniture joints, Egyptian, 15. *See also* Joints
Furniture pattern books, 248. *See also* Pattern
books
Furniture with Candelabra and Interior Decoration
(Bridgens), 369

G

Gabriel, Jacques Ange, 264, 266
Galerie d'Apollon (Louvre), 141
Galerie d'Enée (Palais Royal), 213
Galerie Dorée (Hôtel de Toulouse), 213
Galleria, 85
Gamier, Charles, 347
Gaming tables, 251
Georgian, 254, 255
Garderobes, 64, 179
Garniture de cheminée, 210
Gateleg tables, 134–135, 199
Gaudreau, A. R., 207
Genius, 43
Genre pittoresque, 211, 214
Gentleman and Cabinet-Maker's Director, The
(Chippendale), 238, 248, 256
Geometric floor arrangements, 48
George I, King, 228
George III, King, 326
Georgian Baroque style, 229
Georgian design, early. *See* English Early
Georgian design
Georgian furniture, 247, 253–256, 253–256
Georgian period, early, 228
Gesso, 14, 95
Ghiberti, Lorenzo, 82
Gibbons, Grinling, 177, 185, 204
Gibbs, James, 229, 243
Gilding, 14
early Georgian, 249–250
furniture, 218
Neoclassic, 298
Gilt leather, 188
Girouard, Mark, 178
Glass
manufacturing of, 164, 363
use in windows, 127
Glazed windows, 70, 92
Glorification of Urban VIII's Reign (da Cortona),
145
Glorious Revolution, 176
Gobelins tapestryworks, 156, 157, 238, 289
Gold inlay, 12
Gold leaf gilding, 218
Gold work, Rococo, 212
Gondola chair, 318, 319

Gothic architecture, 119
Gothic Architecture Improved (Langley), 235, 247
Gothic art, 60
Gothic detailing, 355–356
*Gothic Furniture in the Style of the Fifteenth
Century* (Pugin), 370
Gothic motifs, 79
Gothic Revival style, 329, 347, 358
Gothic style, 82, 104, 247–248, 358
Goudge, Edward, 184, 190
Gouthière, Pierre, 274
Graining technique, 164, 186
Grand Palais (Peterhof), 211
Grand Tour of Europe, 229
Great Bed of Ware, 137
Great dining room, 178
Great Fire of London, 176
Great Staircase of the Ambassadors (Versailles),
167
Great Wardrobe Looms, 238
Greek culture, Roman assimilation of, 40
Greek design, 23–37, 328
in furniture, 33–37
historical setting of, 24–25
interior architecture and decoration in,
30–33
ornamental detail in, 37
spatial relationships in, 25–30
Greek revival, 265
Grisaille painting, 214–215
Grotesque, 90
defined, 287
Grotesque design, engraved, 91
Guardaroba, 86
Guéridons, 276, 320, 322
Guilds
importance of, 206–207
Medieval, 75
Gutta-percha, 371
Gwynne, Nell, 188
Gypsum concrete, 10
Gypsum plaster, 9

H

Hackets, 132
Haddon Hall, 63, 64, 69, 73
Hagley Hall, 231, 238
Hagley Park, 244–245
Hall
Medieval, 62, 73, 105–106
Renaissance, 120–121
Hall furniture, Medieval, 78
Hall screen, Medieval, 62, 63
Ham House, 185, 187
Hamilton, Sir William, 283
Hammer beam construction, 66, 67
Hampton Court, 122, 191
Hanovarian monarchs, 228
Hardouin-Mansart, Jules, 158, 210
Hardwick Hall, 120–121, 124, 125, 129
Harewood House, 297
Harlaxton Manor, 361, 362, 365, 368
Harlequin Pembroke table, 304
Harrington, Sir John, 133
Hatton Garden, 237
Hausmann, Georges-Eugène, 344
Hawksmoor, Nicholas, 184
Hearth, open stone, 62. *See also* Chimneypieces
Helladic cultures, 24
Hellenic period, 24
Hellenistic period, 24, 32
Henrietta Maria, 185
Henry II, King, 61, 104

Henry II style, 110
in beds, 115
in ornamental detail, 115
for seat furniture, 111–112
in storage pieces, 114–115
in tables, 113
Henry IV, King, 104, 156
Henry VII, King, 118
Henry VIII, King, 61, 118
Hepplewhite, George, 300
Hepplewhite furniture, 300–302
Heraldic devices, 68, 69
Heraldic motifs, 73
in glass, 127
Herculaneum, 42, 51
excavation of, 207, 265
H-form palaces, 142
Hieroglyphs, as decorations, 19, 20
Highclere Castle, 364
Hinges, strap, 70, 71
History of Ancient Art (Winckelmann), 266
Holkham Hall, 229
Holland, Henry, 327, 332
Holland House, 126
Hooded chimneypieces, 72, 92
Hood-mold, 69, 70, 71
Hope, Thomas, 327, 328, 336, 340
Hopetoun House, 295
Hôtel Colbert de Villacerf, 162
Hôtel de Beauharnais, 314–315
Hôtel de Bourrienne, 312–313, 315, 316
Hôtel de Brancas, 314
Hôtel de Condé, 267
Hôtel d'Ecoville, 105
Hôtel de Gallifet, 272, 273
Hôtel de Janvry, 209–210
Hôtel de Lionne, 160
Hôtel de Matignon, 208
Hôtel de Montmorency, 268
Hôtel de Monville, 271
Hôtel de Païva, 347
Hôtel de Roquelaure, 216
Hôtel de Soubise, 212
Hôtel de Toulouse, 213
Hôtel de Varengeville, 214
Hôtel du Jars, 157
Hôtel d'Uzès, 271
Hôtel Lambert, 157, 161
Hôtel Lazun, 164
Hôtels, 61, 105
Houghton Hall, 233, 234, 239, 240
House façades, Renaissance, 120
Household Furniture and Decoration (Hope), 328,
336
House of Faun, Pompeii, 42
House of the Bicentenary, 51
House of the Wooden Partition, 51
H-shaped plan, 120
Huet, Christophe, 214
Hugo, Victor, 346
Huguenot artists, impact of, 104, 177
Human figures
Egyptian, 10–11
Roman, 49, 57
Humanism, Renaissance, 84
Hundred Years War, 61
Hunt, T. F., 369
Hypostyle, 3

I

Illusionism, 88, 89
Baroque, 141, 144–146, 148, 162, 166, 192
Roman, 43, 47, 48, 49

Illusionistic paintings, 88, 89
Impluvium, 42
In antis columns, 28
Ince, William, 300
Incised carving, 95
Incrustation, 32, 49
Indian textiles, 151
Indiscret, 353
Individualistic design, 327
Industrial production, 336
Industrial Revolution, 346, 348, 358
Inlay work
  Egyptian, 14
  Greek, 34
  Neoclassic, 318, 336
  Renaissance, 87, 95, 110, 130
  Revival, 349
  Roman, 52
Innocent X, Pope, 140
Intarsia, 87, 92, 95
Interior architecture
  Early English Neoclassic, 287–297
  Early French Neoclassic, 268–272
  Egyptian, 8–13
  English Baroque, 184–193
  English Early Georgian, 234–246
  English Renaissance, 122–129
  English Revival, 363–369
  French Baroque, 162–167
  French Renaissance, 106–109
  French Revival, 346–348
  French Rococo, 210–217
  Greek, 30–33
  Italian Baroque, 144–150
  Italian Renaissance, 87–95
  Late English Neoclassic, 331–336
  Late French Neoclassic, 311–317
  Medieval, 67–74
  Roman, 45–52
Intricate style, 49–50
Ionians, 24
Ionic columns, 26–27
Iron beds, 374
Italian Baroque design, 140–154
  in furniture, 150–154
  historical setting of, 140–141
  interior architecture and decoration in, 144–150
  ornamental detail in, 154
  spatial relationships in, 141–144
Italian Renaissance design, 82–101
  in furniture, 95–101
  historical setting of, 82–84
  interior architecture and decoration in, 87–95
  ornamental detail in, 101
  spatial relationships in, 84–87
  spread of, 118
Italy, as the springboard for the Renaissance, 82
Ivory couch, 56
Ivory furniture legs, Egyptian, 14

J

Jacob, Georges, 308
Jacobean period, 125–126, 128, 130, 134, 138
Jacopo, Giambattista di, 107
James II, King, 176
Japanese lacquer, 337
Japanning, 196–197, 250, 273, 342
Jardinière, 320, 328
Jesuits, influence of, 150
Joggled lintel, 72
Johnson, Thomas, 262

Joiner's guild, 130
Joints
  dovetail, 95
  dowel, 15, 34
  mitered, 110
  mortise and tenon, 14, 15, 95
  scarf, 14
  tenon, 34
Jones, Inigo, 83, 118, 119, 184, 229, 234, 244, 282

K

Kaufmann, Angelica, 288
Kedleston, 284–285
Kelham Hall, 361–363
Kenilworth (Scott), 369
Kent, William, 229, 234, 243, 247, 262, 282
Kinds of Floor Decorations Represented Both in Plano and Perspective (Carwitham), 237
Kirtlington Park, 241, 242
Kline, 37, 42
Klismos and Diphros vase painting, 34
Klismos Chair, 34
Klismos seat form, 35
Knole, 129

L

Lacquered furniture, 150–151, 168, 196–197, 218
Lacunae, 51
Ladies Amusement, or the Whole Art of Japanning Made Easy, 250
Lafosse, Charles de, 166
Laguerre, Louis, 177, 181, 182, 185, 191, 192
Lamb's tongue, 253
Lancet windows, 70
Landscapes, distance, 86
Langley, Batty, 235, 237, 243, 247
Lapis specularis, 51
Lares, 43
Lathe
  introduction of, 35
  Roman use of, 52
Lattice stool, 15
Laugier, Abbé, 282
Lavatories, Renaissance, 86
Le Antichità Romani (Piranesi), 265
Leather, use on walls, 188
Leather embossing, 164
Leblanc, Abbé, 265
Le Blond, Jean-Baptiste Alexandre, 209
Le Brun, Charles, 141, 157, 159, 162, 166, 167, 174, 177, 185
Ledoux, Claude-Nicolas, 268, 271, 310
Lemoine, Paul-Guillaume, 311
Le Nôtre, André, 159
Leoni, Giacomo, 229
Le Pautre, Jean, 165, 166, 177
Le Pautre, Pierre, 189, 190, 210, 215
le Roy, David, 265
Le Roy, J. D., 287, 290
Letto, 100
Le Vau, Louis, 157, 159, 160
Lighting
  in Greek residences, 32
  on stairways, 181
  Victorian, 368
Lime plaster, 9, 46
Linenfold embellishment, 123–124
Lit à colonnes, 173, 278
Lit à duchesse, 224
Lit à la polonaise, 224

Lit à turque, 224
Lit bâteau, 323, 324
Lit d'ange, 224
Little Wenham Hall, 69
Livre d'architecture (Barbet), 165
Livre d'ornements (Meissonier), 212
Lock, Matthias, 247, 248
Lodging rooms, Medieval, 64
Loggia, 6, 7, 84
Lorraine, Claude, 326
Louis Philippe, 344, 345, 346
Louis XIII furniture, 168–169, 170, 171, 173–174
Louis XIII style, 156
Louis XIV, King, 156, 157, 206
Louis XIV furniture, 167, 169, 170, 173, 174
Louis XIV revival style, 369
Louis XIV style, 156, 157, 210
Louis XV, King, 206, 207, 264
Louis XV furniture, 219–223
Louis XV style, 206, 210, 212, 214–215, 216–217, 225
Louis XVI, King, 308
Louis XVI furniture, 274–279
Louis XVI period, 266
Louis XVI style, 270, 311, 345, 347
Louis XVIII, King, 344
Louvre workshops, 156
Low Countries, craftsmen from, 119, 122
Lozenge motif, 324
Luscombe Castle, 327, 329, 332
Luxembourg Palace, 157, 158, 159, 162
Lyncrusta, 363
Lyttleton, Lord, 231, 245

M

Maderno, Carlo, 141
Maison de la Collene, 29, 30
Maisons, 105
Majolica tiles, 88, 107
Manchettes, 219
  upholstered, 274
Manor houses, 104–105, 120
  Medieval, 60
Mansart, François, 160, 164, 167, 264, 157, 159
Mantelpieces, Baroque, 148
Manufacture Royale des Meubles de la Couronne, 157
Manuscripts, illuminated, 76
Marble work
  Baroque, 146, 162, 185
  Greek, 25
  Renaissance, 88
  Rococo, 212, 217
Marbleizing technique, 164, 186
Marchand-merciers, 207
Marie Antoinette, Queen, 266
Marlborough, John Churchill, 230
Marlborough legs, 258, 259
Marot, Daniel, 173, 176, 177, 185, 189
Marquetry, 14, 87, 95, 110, 162, 168, 195, 201, 218, 298, 349
Marquetry floor, 163
Marquise, 221
Martin, Etienne-Simon, 212
Martin, Guillaume, 212
Martock Manor House, 70
Mary II, Queen, 176
Masson, Louis Le, 310
Materials
  Early English Neoclassic, 288, 298
  Early French Neoclassic, 268–270, 273–274

Early Georgian English, 235–236, 248–250
Egyptian, 8–9, 14–15
English Baroque, 184–185, 193–197
English Renaissance, 122, 130–131
English Revival, 363, 370–371
French Baroque, 162, 167–168
French Renaissance, 107, 110
French Revival, 346, 349–350
French Rococo, 212, 217–218
Greek, 30–31, 33–35
Italian Baroque, 144–146, 150–151
Italian Renaissance, 87–88, 95
Late English Neoclassic, 331, 336–337
Late French Neoclassic, 311, 317–318
mass-produced, 346
Medieval, 67–68, 75–76
Roman, 46–47, 52
Mau, August, 48
May, Hugh, 176, 177
Mayhew, John, 300
Mazarin, Cardinal, influence of, 156
Medallions, 107, 115
ceiling, 335
Medici, Marie de, 156, 157, 162, 185
Medici family, 83
Medieval design, 60–80
in furniture, 74–80
historical setting of, 60–61
interior architecture and decoration in,
67–74
ornamental detail in, 80
spatial relationships in, 61–66
Megaron structures, 28
Meissonier, Juste Aurèle, 212, 214
Mélanges d'Ornaments Divers (Leconte), 345
Melon legs, 134
Menuisier, 167, 207
Mercury gilding, 218
Merevale Hall, 359, 360–361
Mereworth Castle, 228, 232, 244, 245
Méridienne, 350, 351
Metal furniture, Roman, 52
Metalwork
Neoclassic, 274, 337
Rococo, 212
Metopes, 26
Middle Ages. See Medieval design
Middle class, prosperity of, 358
Miller, Sanderson, 231
Minoan cultures, 24
Mique, Richard, 266
Mirrored walls, 188
Mirrors, 164
Adam, 300
in Rococo decoration, 213–214
Mitered joints, 110
Mobilier de la Couronne, 348
Modillion, introduction of, 45
Molding
carved, 110
classical, 27
decorated, 188
fireplace, 190
Medieval, 66, 69
papyrus, 21
Renaissance, 92
stucco, 49, 50
Monasteries, 75
dissolution of, 118
Medieval, 60–61
parlors in, 64
Monbro the Elder, 355
Monumental architecture, Egyptian, 2, 3

Moore Park, 235, 238
Moquettes, 168
Mortise and tenon joints, 14, 15, 95, 110
Mortlake tapestries, 187–188
Mosaics
Baroque, 150
Roman, 47, 48, 50
Mosaic floors, 31
Movement, concept of, 284
Mud, as a building material, 2
Mule chest, 136
Murals
Baroque, 163
Egyptian, 9
Medieval, 68–69
Mycenaean plan, 28

N

Naos, 3
Napoleonic Wars, 326
Napoleon III, 344, 345
Nash, John, 326, 327, 329
Necessari, 86
Nelson, Viscount Horatio, 328, 336
Neoclassicism, 265. See also English Neoclassic
design; French Neoclassic design
English, 282–283
promotion of, 207, 208
New Book of Drawings, A (Tijou), 193
New Book of Ornaments, A (Lock), 248
Newby Hall, 289
Newel, 129
Newel post, 246
Newel staircases, 73–74
Nile River Valley, 2
Nonesuch chest, 135
Nonesuch palace, 118
Notre-Dame de Paris (Hugo), 346
Nouveaux riches, 358, 363
Nouvelle Iconologie historique (Delafosse), 280
Nudes, Renaissance, 110

O

Oak plank floors, Medieval, 68
Oeuvres d'architecture (Peyre), 266, 280
Oil painting, Renaissance, 89
Oppenord, Gilles-Marie, 206, 211, 213, 217
Optical illusions, Renaissance, 86. See also
Trompe l'oeil painting; Illusionism
Opus musivum technique, 47
Opus sectile technique, 31, 32, 48
Opus signinum, 48
Oratory, 64
Oriental lacquer, 168, 196–197
Oriental porcelain, 189–190
Ormolu, 288
Ornamental design
Early English Neoclassic, 306
Early French Neoclassic, 279–280
English Early Georgian, 260–262
English Revival, 374–375
French Revival, 355–356
French Rococo, 225
Late English Neoclassic, 342
Late French Neoclassic, 324
Ornamental detail
Egyptian, 21
English Baroque, 204
English Renaissance, 138
French Baroque, 173–174
French Renaissance, 115

Greek, 37
Italian Baroque, 154
Italian Renaissance, 101
Louis XV, 225
in Medieval design, 80
Restoration, 355–356
Régence, 225
Roman, 57
Second Empire, 356
Ornamentalists, master, 167
Ornate style, 49
Osterly, 291–292, 298, 300
Oval stairway, 142
Overdoor treatments, 188–189
Overmantel, 127, 214, 216
early Georgian, 243
Overmantel mirrors, 295, 333, 367
Oysterwork, 196

P

Paine, James, 284
Painted furniture, 337
Painted Parlor, 243
Painting. See also Decorative painting
Egyptian, 10
illusionistic, 32
Medieval, 67–68
on plaster, 125
Palace Compiègne, 316
Palaces
Baroque, 140, 141–144
English, 178–183
Palais Mazarin, 217
Palais Royal, 206, 213, 268, 269, 272
Palazzo, plan of, 84
Palazzo Barberini, 140–141, 142, 145
Palazzo Colonna, 144
Palazzo de Giustizia, 149
Palazzo Doria, 87
Palazzo Farnese, 144
Palazzo Mattei di Giove, 141
Palazzo Pitti, 141, 146, 148–149, 239
Palazzo Strozzi, 85
Palermo Stone, 2
Palladian ceilings, 244
Palladianism, 229–230, 253, 264, 268, 282
Palladian period, ornamental detail in, 260
Palladian revivals, 184
Palladian walls, 243
Palladian window, 239
Palladio, Andrea, 82, 83, 119, 184, 228
Palmette motif, 324
Palmyra, 287
Panchetto, 98
Panel back chair, 111
Panel drawing, Rococo, 211
Paneled chests, 130, 135–136
Paneled doors, 188
Paneling
Baroque, 185–187
in beds, 137–138
carved, 72
English, 75
linenfold, 123–124
Neoclassic, 270–271
Renaissance, 89–90, 107–108
Rococo, 213–214
Roman, 50
wood, 68
Pantry, Medieval, 65
Papal aristocracy, influence of, 150
Papier-mâché, 239, 288

Papier-mâché furniture, 371
Parchemin, 124
Parere sull'architettura (Piranesi), 282
Pargework, 122, 128, 367
Paris, European culture and, 177
Parker, George, 197
Parlors
    Medieval, 64, 69
    Renaissance, 121–122
Parquet de Versailles, 212
Parquet floors, 107, 289
    Baroque, 162, 185
Parquetry, 14, 196
Partitions, Roman, 51
Pastas house, 29
Pastiglia, 95
Patronage system, 83, 156, 308
Pattern books, 119, 122, 207, 212, 243, 247, 369
Pavillion de Louveciennes, 207
Pax Romana, 40
Peake, Robert, 119
Pebble mosaics, 31
Pedestal leg, 199
Pedestal tables, 113, 352
Pedimented doorways, 127
Peloponnesian War, 25
Pembroke tables, 304
Penates, 43
Pepys, Samuel, 176
Percier, Charles, 309, 312, 317, 327, 336
Pericles, 24
Peristyle, Roman, 42
Petit Luxembourg, 213
Petit Trianon, 264, 266, 267
Pettifer, James, 184, 190
Peyre, Marie-Joséph, 266, 267, 280
Philip of Macedonia, 25
Piano mobile, 84, 141, 292
Picturesque movement, 248, 326, 330, 332
Pied de biche, 170, 219, 250
Pierced panel staircase, 193
Pierced tracery, 75
Pierced-work furniture, 194
Pier tables, 304
Pietra dura, 150, 152, 274
Pilasters, 32, 49, 110, 111, 126
Pilgrim's Hall, 73
Pineau, Nicolas, 211–212, 214
Piranesi, Giovanni Battista, 265, 282, 283, 291
Pittoresque style, 211, 214
Plaster molds, 184
Plaster of Paris, 236
Plasterwork, 8–9, 123
    Baroque, 146, 184, 190
    early Georgian, 243
    Neoclassic, 288, 317
    Renaissance, 124, 135
    Rococo, 217
    Roman, 46
Plating, Roman, 52
Plywood woodworking, Egyptian, 15
Poggio Torselli, 143, 147, 149
Poisson, Abel, 265
Pompadour, Madame de, 207, 264, 266
Pompeiian style, 347
Pompeii, 41, 42
    excavation of, 207
Pompeiian house, 44
Porcelain, Oriental, 189–190
Porphyry, 50
Portico, 6

Post-and-beam (lintel) construction, 2, 40
Post beds, 101. *See also* Four-poster beds
Poundisford Park, 62
Poussin, Gaspar, 326
Pratt, Roger, 176
Prefabricated parts, 283
Press cupboard, 136
Press-molded stucco, 235–236
Prestwold Hall, 367, 368
Priene, residence at, 28, 29
"Priest's holes," 119
Primaticcio, Francesco, 104, 107, 162, 166
Princess Sitamun chair, 18, 19
Printing techniques, 83
Private space, progression toward, 84, 85
Privy chambers, Medieval, 64
Prodigy houses, 119
Proportion, in Greek architecture, 28
Protestant architects, persecution of, 104
Pugin, A. W. N., 358, 369–370, 372
Punic Wars, 40
Puritans, 118, 132, 193
Purlins, 65
Pyramidal chimney hood, 72

Q

Quadratura frescoes, 148
Quadratura painting, 144, 145
Quartering, 194
Queen Anne furniture, 247, 250–253
Queen's Closet (Ham House), 185, 187
Queen's House, 119
Querouaille, Louise, 188

R

Rails, 68
Rambouillet, Madame de, 164
Ram's horn, 199, 200
Rebuilding Act of 1667, 176
Reception rooms, Egyptian, 7
Rectangular table tops, 36
Recueil de décorations intérieures (Percier and Fontaine), 312
Red Drawing Room (Hopetoun House), 295, 296
Refectory table, 100
Régence furniture, 218–224, 337–342
Régence style, 206, 210–211, 212–214, 215, 216, 217, 225, 326, 327, 328
Regency period, 331, 333
Reigate Priory, 182, 193
Relief, stucco, 46
Relief patterns, plaster, 10
Religious themes, Egyptian, 13, 14
Renaissance, 82–84
Renaissance architecture, 119
Renaissance design. *See* English Renaissance design; French Renaissance design; Italian Renaissance design
Renaissance refectory table, 55
Repertoire de l'Ornemaniste (Blaizot), 345
Residences
    Baroque, 141–142
    French Renaissance, 104–105
    Roman, 41
    storied, 30
Restoration furniture, 193, 349, 350–353
Revett, Nicholas, 265
Rhodian peristyle, 28–29
Ribband back, 258
Richard, Antoine, 266

Richelieu, Cardinal, influence of, 156
Ridgepole, 65
Rinceaux, 260
Robinson, Gerrard, 373
Rococo period, ornamental detail in, 262
Rococo style, 206
    characteristics of, 234–235
Roman design, 39–57
    in furniture, 52–57
    historical setting of, 40–41
    interior architecture and decoration in, 45–52
    ornamental detail in, 57
    spatial relationships in, 41–45
Romanesque art, 60
Romanticism, 248, 355
Romayne work, 77, 80, 123
Room proportions, Baroque, 143
Rooms, specialization of, 120
Room sequence, 120, 121
Rooms of state, Baroque, 184
Rosa, Salvator, 326
Rose, Joseph, 288
Rothschild family, 346
Round-topped tables, 36–37
Rousseau, Jean Jacques, 265
Royal households, Medieval, 64
Rubens, Peter Paul, 162
Rucellai family, 83
Ruelles, 159
Rugs, Egyptian, 10
Ruins of the Palace of Diocletian at Spalatro, The (Adam), 282, 284, 287
Rules for Drawing the Several Parts of Architecture (Gibbs), 229
Rush floors, 68

S

S. Carlo alle Quattro Fontane, 141
Sabre leg, 322, 350
Sacchi, Andrea, 146
Sala, 85
Sala di Apollo (Palazzo Pitti), 149
Saletta, 85
Salle à manger, 209
Salle du dais, 209
Salones, 159, 178
Saltire, 169, 200
Samnite House, 44, 45
Sarcophagi, Roman, 56
Sash windows, 188
Savonarola chairs, 54, 95, 96, 97
Savonnerie carpet manufacturers, 156, 212
Savot, Louis, 177
Scaenae frons, 49
Scagliola, 150, 190, 235, 241, 288, 289, 331
Scamozzi, Vincenzo, 92
Scarf joint, 14
Scarsdale, Lord, 285
School of Fontainebleau, 107
Scott, Sir Walter, 346, 369
Screens, Medieval, 62, 63
Screen walls, 50
Scrittoio, 86
Seat furniture
    Adam, 298–299
    Carolean, 197–199
    Chippendale, 258–259
    Directoire, 318–319
    Early French Neoclassic, 274–276
    Early Georgian English, 250–251, 254
    Egyptian, 15–19

Empire, 321–322
English Renaissance, 131–134
English Revival, 371–372
French Baroque, 168–170
French Renaissance, 111–112
French Rococo, 218–221
Georgian, 254
Greek, 35–36
Hepplewhite, 301
Italian Baroque, 151–152
Italian Renaissance, 96–98
Late English Neoclassic, 337–339
Louis XV, 219–221
Louis XVI, 274–276
Medieval, 77
Queen Anne, 250–251
Restoration, 350–353
Régence, 218–219
Roman, 53
Second Empire, 353–354
Sheraton, 303–304
Victorian, 371–372
William and Mary, 199–201
Seaweed marquetry, 195, 196, 201
Second Empire, 344–345, 347, 348
Second Empire furniture, 349–350, 353–355
Secrétaire à abattant, 276–277
Secrétaires debout, 278
Secretary bookcases, Sheraton, 305
Sedia, 97
Sella curulis, 54
Sensusert II, Pharaoh, 8
Serlian window, 239
Serlio, Sebastiano, 82, 92, 104, 119
Service rooms
  Baroque, 160
  Medieval, 64–65
Settee, 199
  Victorian, 370
Seven Years War, 264, 266
Seymour, Edward, 118
Sezincote, 329–330, 335
Sgabello, 98
Shaw, Henry, 369
Shelf mirrors, 216
Sheraton, Thomas, 327, 336, 341
Sheraton furniture, 303–306
Shouldered architrave, 240
Shute, John, 123
Shutters, 188
  internal, 239
  Medieval, 70
Sicily, development of, 40
Sideboard table
  Georgian, 256
  Restoration, 352, 353
  Victorian, 373
Side chairs
  Baroque, 152
  Elizabethan, 371
  Georgian, 254
  Neoclassic, 338
  Queen Anne, 251
Side tables, 134–135, 201
Singeries, 206, 225
Six Sconces (Lock), 247
Six Tables (Lock), 247
Sleeping chayres, 198
Sleter, Francesco, 238
Smith, George, 328, 336, 338, 341
Soane, John, 326–327, 330
Sofa
  Regency, 339
  Renaissance, 134

Sofa tables, 340
Soffit, invention of, 28
Solar, 64
Somerset House, 118, 185
Sotto in su, 146, 148, 166
Soufflot, Jacques Germain, 265
Soul houses, 4
Southill, 332
Space planning, vii. *See also* Spatial relation-
  ships; Three-dimensional spatial charac-
  teristics
Spada Palaces, 141
Spanish influence, 150, 153
Spatial relationships
  Early English Neoclassic, 283–287
  Early French Neoclassic, 266–268
  in Egyptian design, 4–8
  English Baroque, 178–183
  English Early Georgian, 230–234
  English Renaissance, 120–122
  English Revival, 359–363
  French Baroque, 157–161
  French Renaissance, 104–106
  French Revival, 345–346
  French Rococo, 207–210
  in Greek design, 25–30
  Italian Baroque, 141–144
  Italian Renaissance, 84–87
  Late English Neoclassic, 328–331
  Late French Neoclassic, 309–311
  in Medieval design, 61–66
  in Roman design, 41–45
Specimens of Ancient Furniture (Shaw), 369
Spere, 62
Sphinx, use in chair design, 35
Spiral staircases, 109, 128–129
  Renaissance, 94–95
Spiral turning, 194, 198
Split spindles, 125, 130
S-scrolls, 193, 214
Stairways
  Early English Neoclassic, 297
  Early French Neoclassic, 272
  Early Georgian English, 245–246
  English Baroque, 193
  English Renaissance, 128–129
  English Revival, 368–369
  French Baroque, 167
  French Renaissance, 109
  French Rococo, 217
  Italian Baroque, 149–150
  Italian Renaissance, 94–95
  Late English Neoclassic, 335–336
  Late French Neoclassic, 317
  Medieval, 73–74
  as ornamental features, 122
Stalker, John, 197
Stamped leather, 188
State apartments, 178
Stiles, 68
St. Mary-le-Strand, 229
Stone slab flooring, 68
Stone wall revetments, 50
Stonework
  Egyptian, 9
  Renaissance, 88, 123
Stools
  Baroque, 197, 199, 201
  Egyptian, 15–17
  Medieval, 77
  Renaissance, 98
  Roman, 54, 54
Storage pieces
  Adam, 300

Carolean, 199
Chippendale, 260
Directoire, 320
Early French Neoclassic, 278
Early Georgian English, 253, 256
Egyptian, 19–20
Empire, 322–323
English Renaissance, 135–136
English Revival, 373–374
French Baroque, 171–173
French Renaissance, 113–115
French Rococo, 222–224
Georgian, 256
Greek, 37
Hepplewhite, 302
Italian Baroque, 153–154
Italian Renaissance, 98–100
Late English Neoclassic, 341
Louis XV, 223
Louis XVI, 278
Medieval, 78–79
Queen Anne, 253
Régence, 222–223
Restoration, 353
Roman, 56–57
Second Empire, 354
Sheraton, 305
Transitional Louis XV–XVI, 223–224
Victorian, 373–374
William and Mary, 201–203
Strap hinges, 70, 71
Strapwork, 107, 128, 129, 138
String staircases, 245, 246
Strozzi family, 83
Stuart, James, 265
Stuart monarchs, 118
Stuccatore, 149
Stucco moldings, 49, 50
Stucco relief, ceiling, 33, 52
Stuccowork
  Baroque, 146, 147
  early Georgian, 235–236, 239
  Neoclassic, 288
  Renaissance, 89, 107
  Roman, 46
Stylistic periods, viii
Sudbrooks Park, 229
Sudbury, 180, 181, 190–191, 193
Sultane, 221
Summerson, Sir John, 119
Sure Guide to Builders, A (Langley), 243
Suspended ceilings, 122
Syon House, 284, 285–286, 288, 289–291

T

Tables
  Adam, 299–300
  Carolean, 199
  Chippendale, 259–260
  Directoire, 320
  Early French Neoclassic, 276–278
  Early Georgian English, 251–252, 254–256
  Egyptian, 19
  Empire, 322
  English Renaissance, 134–135
  English Revival, 372–373
  French Baroque, 170
  French Renaissance, 112–113
  French Rococo, 221–222
  Georgian, 254–256
  Greek, 36–37
  Hepplewhite, 301–302
  Italian Baroque, 152–153

Italian Renaissance, 100
Late English Neoclassic, 340–341
Louis XV, 222
Louis XVI, 276–278
Medieval, 78
Queen Anne, 251–252
Régence, 221
Restoration, 351–353
Roman, 54–56
Second Empire, 354
Sheraton, 304–305
Victorian, 372–373
William and Mary, 201
Tables servantes, 276
Table tops, inlaid, 152
Table turnings, Baroque, 152
Tablinum, 42, 43
Tabourets, 169
Tabula, 78
Tallboy, Queen Anne, 252, 253
Talman, William, 184
Tapestries
    Baroque, 146, 187–188
    early Georgian, 238
    Medieval, 61, 69
    Neoclassic, 289
    Renaissance, 89, 107, 124
    Rococo, 238
    wall treatments with, 164
Tapestry Room (Newby Hall), 289
Tea tables, 201, 251
    Chippendale, 259–260
Tel el-Amarna country villa, 5
Tempera, Roman use of, 47
Temple architecture, Egyptian, 3
Temple of Vesta, 41
Tenements, Pompeiian, 41
Tenon joints, 34
Terms, 115
Terra-cotta chest, Greek, 37
Terra-cotta flooring, 31
    Rococo, 212
    Roman, 48
Terra-cotta tile, 88
Terrazzo floors, 146
Tesselatum, 47
Tessellated mosaic, 31–32
Tesserae, 47, 48
    glass, 50
Tester, 80, 136
Tester bed, 203–204
    Chippendale, 261
Textile hangings
    Medieval, 69
    Renaissance, 137
Textiles
    application to furniture, 75, 76, 77
    Baroque, 146
    in bed treatments, 80, 101, 173
    Indian, 151
    Neoclassic, 315
Thoresby Hall, 359, 360
Thoroughfare rooms, Medieval, 64
Three-dimensional spatial characteristics
    Early English Neoclassic, 284–287
    Early Georgian English, 231–234
    Egyptian, 4–8
    English Baroque, 178–183
    English Renaissance, 120–122
    English Revival, 359–363
    French Baroque, 158–161
    French Renaissance, 105–106
    French Rococo, 207–210
    Greek, 28–30

Italian Renaissance, 84–87
Late English Neoclassic, 328–331
Late French Neoclassic, 309–311
Medieval, 62–66
Roman, 42–45
Throne chair, 111
Thrones
    Greek, 35
    Roman, 53
Tie beam, 65
Tijou, Jean, 193
Tile flooring, Rococo, 212
Tiles
    earthenware, 68
    Egyptian, 2
    glazed, 10
Tiryns Palace, 28
Tomb paintings, Egyptian, 4
Tombs, Egyptian, 8, 14
Toro, Jean-Bernard, 206
Torrigiano, Pietro, 118, 122
Town houses, 292
    French, 61, 105
    French Baroque, 160
Trabeated construction, 30, 41
Traceried windows, 83
Tracery, carved, 79
Trade, influence on art, 61
Trafalgar chair, 337–338
Transitional Louis XV–XVI furniture, 221, 223–224
Transitional Louis XV–XVI style, 206
Trapezai, 36
Treatise of Civil Architecture (Chambers), 283
Treatise of Japanning and Varnishing, A (Stalker and Parker), 197
Treatise on the Decorative Part of Civil Architecture, A (Chambers), 283
Trefoil motif, 79
Trestle supports, 100
Trestle tables, 54–55, 112, 134
Triclinia, 42
Tricoteuses, 276, 320
Triglyphs, 26
Tripartite plan, 6, 7
Tripod table, 55
Tripod tea table, 260
Trompe l'oeil architecture, 49
Trompe l'oeil painting, 45, 86, 235. *See also* Illusionism
    Greek, 32
    for staircases, 129
True Principles of Pointed or Christian Architecture, The (Pugin), 358
Trumeaux, 214, 215
Truss, 65
Tudor monarchs, 118
Tudor period, 130
Tunnel vault, 93
Turnings
    Baroque, 194
    for furniture, 130, 133
    Renaissance, 138
    stairway, 129
Tuscan order, 46
Tutankhamen, tomb of, 15, 17
Tympanum, 26

U

Unifying principle, defined, 185
Union Centrale des Beaux-Arts, 349
Upholstery, 77, 132, 133
    Baroque, 198, 200

for beds, 154, 173, 204
    Elizabethan, 130
    Indian textile, 151
    Neoclassic, 318
    Renaissance, 96
    Second Empire, 353
    wool, 168
Urban VIII, Pope, 140
Utilitarian facilities, Roman, 41

V

Vanbrugh, Sir John, 184
Varnish, green, 212
Varnish gilding, 218
Vassé, François-Antoine, 213
Vaulted ceilings, 109
Veneer
    Baroque, 167–168, 194–195
    early Georgian, 248, 249
    Egyptian, 15
    Neoclassic, 273, 318, 336
    Rococo, 217–218
    Roman, 52
    walnut, 202
Veneered surfaces, decoration of, 218
Venetian ceiling design, 94
Venetian glass, 92, 164
Venetian windows, 239, 292
Venice, architectural character of, 83
Vernis Martin, 212, 273, 276
Vernon, George, 191, 192
Verre églomisé, 192
Verrio, Antonio, 177, 182, 185, 191, 192
Versailles, 192
    expansion of, 157
Vestibules, Baroque, 144
Vestibulum, 42
Victorian furniture, 369–374
Victorian residences, 359–363
Villa Barbero, 89
Villa Boscoreale, 51
Villa Rotunda (Capra), 228
Villas
    Baroque, 143–144
    country, 140
Villa Sacchetti del Pigneto, 144
Villa Sassetti, 148
Vitruvius, Pollio Marcus, 25, 33, 46, 82
Vitruvius Britannicus (Campbell), 184, 228
Vouet, Simon, 166
Voyage dans le Basse et la Haute Egypte (Denon), 327

W

Waddeson Manor, 365, 366, 368
Wainscot chair, 131–132
Wainscotting
    Medieval, 68
    Renaissance, 90, 107
Wall hangings
    Renaissance, 88, 89
    seasonal, 188
Wall painting
    Pompeiian, 45
    Roman, 47, 48
Wallpaper, 235
    Neoclassic, 332
    ornamentation of, 288
    Victorian, 364
Wall plate, 65
Walls
    articulated, 238

Early English Neoclassic, 289–292
Early French Neoclassic, 270–271
Early Georgian English, 237–239
Egyptian, 10–11
English Baroque, 185–188
English Renaissance, 123–127
English Revival, 364–365
French Baroque, 162–164
French Renaissance, 107–108
French Rococo, 212–215
Greek, 32
Italian Baroque, 146
Italian Renaissance, 88–90
Late English Neoclassic, 331–332
Late French Neoclassic, 312–315
Medieval, 68–69
Roman, 48–51
Walpole, Horace, 233, 247
Ware, Isaac, 235, 237, 241
Water gilding, 249, 298
Watteau, Jean-Antoine, 206, 225
Waverly Novels (Scott), 346
Webb, John, 234
White House, The, 229
Whitewash, 9, 10, 68, 89
William III, King, 176
William and Mary furniture, 193, 194, 199–204
Winckelmann, Johann Joachim, 265–266
Winde, William, 190
Windows
    Early English Neoclassic, 292–293
    Early French Neoclassic, 271–272

Early Georgian English, 239–241
Egyptian, 12
English Baroque, 188–189
English Renaissance, 127
English Revival, 366
French Baroque, 164
French Renaissance, 108
French Rococo, 215
glazed, 70
Greek, 32–33
Italian Baroque, 147–148
Italian Renaissance, 90–92
Late English Neoclassic, 332–334
Late French Neoclassic, 315
Medieval, 69–72
Roman, 51
Window seats, Medieval, 69
Windsor Castle, 182, 191
Wing chair, upholstered, 198
Withdrawing room, 121
Women's rights, in Rome, 41
Wood, Robert, 265, 287
Wood bending, Egyptian, 15
Wood carving, Baroque, 184–185. *See also* Carving
Wood decorating, Renaissance, 94
Wood furniture, Greek, 33
Woodhall Park, 289
Wood joinery, Greek, 34. *See also* Joints
Wood painting, 164
Wood paneling, 68. *See also* Paneling
    Renaissance, 125–127
Woodwork, painted, 237

Woodworking, Renaissance, 87
Works in Architecture of Robert and James Adam, The (Adam), 283
Work tables
    Neoclassic, 276
    Sheraton, 305
Wotton, Sir Henry, 120
Wren, Sir Christopher, 176, 177–178, 184
Writing tables, 221
    Baroque, 170
    Louis XVI, 276
Wrought iron, 193, 217
    Neoclassic, 274
    Victorian, 363
Wrought iron balustrades, 246
Wyatt, James, 331, 332
Wyatt, Samuel, 284, 286, 328

X

X-form curve, 54

Y

Yorkshire-Derbyshire chair, 133

Z

Zuber, Jean, 346
Zucchi, Antonio, 288